# DIPLOMAT IN BERLIN

## 1933-1939

Ambassador Lipski after presenting his credentials to Hitler, November, 1934

Papers and Memoirs of
Józef Lipski, Ambassador of Poland

# DIPLOMAT

# IN BERLIN

# 1933 - 1939

Edited by Wacław Jędrzejewicz

*Columbia University Press* 1968 *New York and London*

Wacław Jędrzejewicz, former Polish army officer, diplomat, and
cabinet member, is now Professor Emeritus
of Wellesley and Ripon colleges.

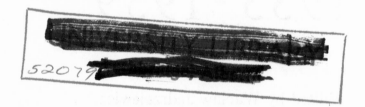

# Preface

AMBASSADOR Józef Lipski's archives are on file in New York at the Józef Piłsudski Institute of America for Research in the Modern History of Poland. They consist of his reports (and also those of other Polish ambassadors); instructions received from Warsaw; various kinds of documents; notes; press clippings; texts of his articles, lectures, and speeches; correspondence; and a few photos.

Judging from the arrangement of these archives, as well as from remarks made to his family and closest friends, it is obvious that Lipski intended one day to publish these materials, possibly in the form of memoirs. His untimely death in Washington on November 1, 1958, forestalled this plan.

Mrs. Anna Maria Lipski, the Ambassador's widow, and I have undertaken to carry out the Ambassador's intentions. Through an orderly arrangement of his documents, we have presented the historical sequence of events between Poland and Germany during the years 1933–39 leading up to the outbreak of World War II.

This book is by no means intended to be a history of Polish-German relations. However, to those engaged in research in this period, it might well serve as another source for a definitive scholarly work. Lipski's reports, reminiscences, notes, and articles, as well as the instructions received by him, give the historian a rich reservoir of facts pertaining to Polish-German relations during the six years prior to the war, at the same time drawing a realistic picture of the man to whom the Polish government entrusted the responsible post of ambassador to Germany.

In our opinion, one of the major contributions of this publication is that it presents the day-to-day work and activities of a Polish diplomat at a key post. Lipski's archives thus represent a valuable contribution to the general history of diplomacy. They give his thoughts, intentions, and actions, and his communications with his government. These are all the more interesting since they were written, not *post factum* when events might easily be accommodated to fit final results, but rather in the *statu nascendi* of political moves often pregnant with fateful consequences. From his reports we can learn at firsthand what was known to the Polish Ambassador in Berlin, how he acted, what his intentions were, what conclusions he drew from the situation, and how he informed his government. In this respect, the material accumulated here might well serve a scholarly purpose for both present and future diplomats.

This book contains 163 selected documents. In addition, there are numerous handwritten notes, such as a detailed account of Lipski's conversation with Piłsudski on November 5, 1933. These notes are invaluable for a historian, since they illustrate the political climate connected with the events. There are also articles published in Polish in London during the years 1947–51. Unknown to many because of the language barrier, they are presented here for the first time in English translation. It seemed important to include these articles because in them the author repeatedly refers to his reminiscences, opinions, and comments on the trend of events, in which he often played a leading role. Some small stylistic alterations have been introduced; and when the author gave a résumé of his reports or of instructions received, this has been replaced by the full texts of the documents referred to, thus increasing the historical value of the articles.

In preparing the papers for publication, special care was taken to supply them with commentaries, indicating the special circumstances within which a particular event took place. It was assumed that the reader has some acquaintance with Polish-German relations. Thus, the commentaries are as concise as possible, containing the minimum of what must be known to understand the text of a particular document. The editor's commentaries are given in reduced type, to distinguish them from Ambassador Lipski's texts and from other documents.

In the selected bibliography, only basic works are cited, some of which were published after the author's death.

Lipski was an eminent diplomat of the Polish Foreign Service. He was very well educated, with a splendid command of foreign languages. With years of service in Polish legations in London and Paris, and with long service in the Ministry of Foreign Affairs in Warsaw as chief of the Western Department, he was especially well prepared and well qualified for the position of envoy and, later, ambassador in Berlin. With the easing of Polish-German relations in the middle of 1933, he envisaged for Poland a long-range policy of neighborliness with Germany, based on the nonaggression declaration of January 26, 1934, of which he was the main author and architect. He was deeply convinced that this declaration was the basis for continuing friendly Polish-German relations, mutually advantageous to both countries. He firmly supported the policy of the Polish government at that time: to side with neither the Germans against Soviet Russia within the framework of the Anti-Comintern Pact, nor with Russia against Germany. After the Munich Agreement in the autumn of 1938, when Ribbentrop pushed forward territorial claims against Poland, Lipski decided that his mission of maintaining good relations with Germany had failed and he presented his resignation to Foreign Minister Beck. It was refused. He tried again in the spring of 1939, and again it was refused. Thus, he remained at his post to the bitter end: September 1, 1939.

Lipski was a man of peace; he believed in peace and could see no profit for Germany in a war. However, to him as to nearly all of his contemporary statesmen, the character of the man with whom he had to negotiate—Adolf Hitler—remained a dark enigma until the spring of 1939.

Along with all other Western diplomats, Lipski believed that *pacta sunt servanda*. He believed that agreements concluded in good faith should be respected and that they should be altered only by the common consent of the states concerned. Hitler did not see things in this way, although this became fully apparent only on March 15, 1939, after the occupation of Prague. Correct evaluations of Hitler, unfortunately, began to appear only after the outbreak of the war.

Here are Hitler's words, as quoted by Hermann Rauschning:

"I am ready to underwrite and undersign anything. I will do whatever can render my politics easier. I am ready to guarantee all frontiers and to conclude—with whomever and whenever—nonaggression pacts and pacts of friendship. . . . Why should I not settle agreements today in good faith and break them tomorrow in cold blood—if the future of the German people is at stake."

Possibly the best characterization of Hitler was given by Sir Nevile Henderson, ambassador of Great Britain in Berlin, writing later during the war:

"In the midst of one of his tirades against the Poles in August, 1939, I interrupted Hitler to observe that he seemed to forget how useful the agreement with Piłsudski had been to him in 1934. Hitler's answer was that it had never been of any use whatsoever, and that it had merely made him unpopular with his own people. He had a phenomenal capacity for self-deception, and was able to forget everything which he had ever said or done in the past, if it no longer suited his present or future purpose to remember it. . . . Verbal or written engagements had absolutely no meaning for him once they ceased to contribute to the greater glory of Adolf Hitler and of Germany. They were merely provisional documents to be torn up whenever it suited him: whereupon he would then offer another agreement in exchange."

This was the man with whom Lipski had to deal—a man whose actions were often unpredictable and irrational. So, after six years of trying to maintain peace, when the first German bombs fell on Poland there was only one course of action left for the Polish Ambassador: to put on a soldier's uniform and join the ranks of the Polish forces.

And that is what Józef Lipski did.

*Wacław Jędrzejewicz*

# Acknowledgments

THIS BOOK was intended to be written by my late husband, Ambassador Józef Lipski. Many diplomats and politicians had rendered controversial opinions concerning his mission in Berlin in the fateful years 1933–39, and he was preparing to give them an answer, utilizing the extensive material in his papers. Premature death frustrated this intention to write his memoirs. The urgent need for the publication of such a book, however, survived him. That book now finally appears thanks to the selflessly devoted and highly conscientious efforts of its editor, Professor Wacław Jędrzejewicz, who knew so well the two major figures of this book, Ambassador Józef Lipski and Foreign Minister Józef Beck.

The biographical sketch of Józef Lipski by Alexander Janta attempts to place in its true historical perspective the diplomatic career and professional skill of Poland's ambassador to the key diplomatic post of Berlin in the trying and fateful years preceding and up to the eve of World War II. Janta's biographical effort has been facilitated by recollections of three persons close to Józef Lipski at different stages of his life: Andrzej Lipski, Paweł Starzeński, and Henryk de Malhomme.

I am indebted to Andrew W. Cordier, dean of the School of International Affairs at Columbia University, for a grant to complete the translation and preparation of the manuscript. I also extend thanks to Professor Henry L. Roberts for his earlier encouragement. My gratitude goes to Professor Philip E. Mosely, of the European Institute at Columbia University, for his words of high esteem, reckoning Ambassador Józef Lipski as "truly one of the outstanding minds of the interwar period." Thanks are extended to Professor Zbigniew Brzezinski, director of the Research Institute on Communist Affairs at Columbia University, for his assistance, advice, and support in promoting this project, which in his opinion "will be a major and significant contribution to our understanding of the antecedents of World War II." Professor Joseph Rothschild, of the Department of Public Law and Government at Columbia University, is thanked for his advice and continuous assistance.

The Józef Piłsudski Institute of America for Research in the Modern History of Poland generously gave access to its archives and made a financial contribution.

To Bernard Gronert and William F. Bernhardt, of Columbia University Press, I express my appreciation for their efforts in the preparation of the manuscript for the printer. Thanks also are extended to Miss Pauline C. Ramsey, librarian and bibliographer, for her guidance and technical assistance and for compiling the bibliography; to Mrs. Maria de Görgey for rewriting the English translation of the manuscript, technically adjusting and copying; and to Mr. Henry Archacki, who has diligently and artistically prepared the photographs.

*Mrs. Józef Lipski*

# Józef Lipski, a Biographical Note

WORLD WAR II exploded in his hands. This is no mere figure of speech in the case of Józef Lipski, the Polish ambassador to Hitler's Germany in the years preceding 1939, and through the days immediately before the German assault on that fateful September 1.

Yet the work of the man, whose difficult mission in Berlin ended in catastrophe, was sincerely and thoroughly dedicated to the preservation of peace.

In World War I he had escaped military obligation thanks to the fortunate, though skillfully engineered, coincidence of being then a student in neutral Switzerland. For young Poles from the Poznanian area, the overwhelming majority of whom wished victory for the Entente, the opportunity to avoid conscription, which German citizenship imposed on them, was a welcome one.

When World War I was over and Germany defeated, Lipski immediately joined the newly organized Polish Foreign Service, eventually to rise, thanks to his linguistic talents, his skill as negotiator, his personal affability, and a particularly keen knowledge of German problems, to one of the crucial positions of Polish diplomatic relations, that of ambassador in Berlin.

Now, on the eve of World War II, with the failure of Lipski's mission already certain, Göring, with whom the Polish Ambassador succeeded in developing a closer personal relationship than with the other associates of the German dictator, in a parting interview expressed regret at having to lead his Luftwaffe against Poland. This statement Lipski countered by saying that in such case he would join the Polish Army to shoot at the invading planes. In the light of the Polish Ambassador's known prowess in gunning flying birds, with which Göring, being more than once his host at official shooting parties, was well acquainted, the retort appears in its proper meaning.

In a small but significant way, Lipski's prediction was realized.

After a perilous journey through bombed and burning Poland, to give a last report to his government, he eventually made his way to France. Though forty-five years old and in a physical condition which would have gotten him easy exemption from military service, the now former Ambassador nevertheless enlisted as a volunteer, started his cadet schooling as a private, endured harsh training and highly uncomfortable quarters in the winter barracks of a Brittany boot camp, and at the earliest opportunity confronted the Germans, as promised a gun in hand. The machine-gun unit he commanded is credited with shooting down a German plane.

This phase was short-lived and ended in a new defeat that took place on the front line of the Polish Grenadier Division fighting a rear-guard action against overwhelming German forces in Lorraine and in the Vosges mountains. The time was June, 1940.

The rapid French collapse forced the Poles to disband their forces, or what remained of them, after fighting to the bitter end. Many, the author of this biographical note among them, fell into German hands. Sergeant Lipski, showing considerable stamina and good tactical judgment, managed to slip through German lines at the head of a group of three fellow soldiers, disguised as French civilians. He would have made a prize prisoner in German hands, and better than anybody he was aware of the asset his capture would have represented for the Goebbels propaganda circus.

He was therefore all the more strongly determined to deny the enemy so manifest an advantage. The supreme test came in Besançon, where he walked boldly into the office of the commanding German officer at the railway station and talked him into giving the group of fugitives Lipski headed a permit for free passage despite the restrictions of movement imposed by the German curfew.

In view of the fact that his face was often photographed in Germany over the previous years as Polish Ambassador in Berlin, hence presumably familiar, the achievement assumes its rightful place. Lipski himself would describe it later as possibly the most successful negotiation he ever conducted with the Germans, one that really worked.

It worked so well that shortly he was able to reach London, where a promotion to first lieutenant, the Cross of Valor with three clusters, and the Croix de Guerre from the Free French awaited him, together with an assignment as political counselor to the then Polish commander in chief and prime minister, General Sikorski.

Here again his German experience was of prime usefulness, and not only to the Poles.

In the growing literature of memoirs of foreign diplomats and observers of the Nazi power-play which led to World War II, the memoirs of Lipski, which should stand next to those of Sir Nevile Henderson, André François-Poncet, or Robert Coulondre, are alas missing. What remains, however, are his papers, a primary source to illuminate a tragic period of European history. They contain, by implication, the portrait of a man who carried the gruesome burden of what now seems to have been a hopeless mission in a Europe divided against itself and falling victim piecemeal to German cunning and German aggression.

The memoirs of another ambassador in Berlin at the outset of the Nazi period, André François-Poncet, show us Lipski as a man who was "silent, restrained, and aloof." Meetings of some foreign representatives, which the French Ambassador called "information clearings," used to take place in an elegant Berlin restaurant, Horcher, well known among the gourmets of the German capital. Lipski, on the verge of signing the nonaggression declaration with Hitler, refused to discuss this forthcoming development. Such were his instructions, and in addition he was well aware that Horcher was an easy and professionally manned listening post for the German secret service. Any indiscretion on his part would have immediately been known by the Germans, thus reducing the chances of success for the difficult arrangement in the making.

Conditions of a totalitarian system made the necessity of avoiding such type of diplomatic gatherings and contacts painfully clear.

Lipski preferred to remain aloof and, according to the nature of his assignment, though not of the nature of his outgoing, convivial disposition, to seek instead a way of coming close to the men responsible for Germany's future course. They in turn subjected his life, his mind, and his educational and professional preparation for the task he was given to perform to a very searching test. He had, indeed, a background made as if by order for the role that he was called to play in Berlin. He was born on June 5, 1894, in Breslau (the Polish, much older, name being Wrocław), the capital of Lower Silesia, a city of German pride and prosperity but still permeated with historically Polish roots. Young Lipski was the heir to a name and a family tradition of strong Polish resistance to the attempts at Germanization. In the nineteenth century this pressure for Germanization had assumed both cultural and economic forms against the Polish majority in German-annexed territories. Józef Lipski's great-grandfather, for instance, was a leader in the national and democratic people's uprising of 1848 and subsequently was for a time held prisoner in Berlin's Moabit. The father, in turn, a successful manager of the family estate in the province of Poznania, stood in the forefront of Polish resistance to the Kulturkampf initiated by Bismarck which aimed at undermining not only the cultural foundation of Polish life in the provinces taken by Prussia as a result of the eighteenth-century partitions but, principally, the roots of Polish economic strength. Stubborn resistance against the so-called colonization policy, which aimed at depriving Poles of the estates and farms they had cultivated for generations, was not only part of the Lipski family tradition but was also a hard school of political and economic practicality: survival, both individual and national, being at stake.

Portraits of distinguished forebears adorned the walls of the old manor at Lewków, which was the future ambassador's family place. Among them were Andrzej Lipski, bishop of Cracow and crown chancellor during the reign of Sigismund III in the early seventeenth century, and another historical personality, Cardinal Jan Alexander Lipski, who one hundred years later was Polish Primate in the time of the Saxon kings.

The high school which the boy attended had been founded by his great-grandfather to counteract German encroachments; by now, however, the teaching was all in German. In consequence, Polish language, literature, and history had to be not only taught, but lived, at home. The mother, from another Lipski family, prominent in the eastern borderlands of Poland, was as deeply religious as she was cultivated; as kind as demanding; speaking seven languages and managing the large household with a firm grip. She exercised a strong influence in the development of the two boys she raised—Józef and an elder brother Jan—tending with equal care the 400 beehives for which the family estate was famous.

The product of this system of education was multilingual, possessing equal fluency in Polish and in German, a solid foundation of Greek and Latin, an excellent command of French, and the beginnings of an initiation into the language of Shakespeare. But most important was to be his intimate knowledge of the two national worlds, that of Poland and that of Germany, historically intertwined, geographically overlapping, and yet, except for a few periods of enlightened liberalism, such as the first part of the nineteenth century, juxtaposed in perennial and at times cruel conflict.

One of the possibilities of countering German pressure lay in the cultivation by the Polish gentry and intelligentsia of a lively Franko-philic tradition, which dated from the seventeenth century when a Polish princess became queen of France while French princesses more than once were queens of Poland. Later and more particularly through the experience of the nineteenth-century emigration, centered in Paris, which provided visionary leadership to the subjugated nation, every educated Pole came to speak French and to hope to go "Ouest," eventually. This penchant also characterized Józef Lipski still in his teens.

The threat of an imminent war in which Poles living on all sides of the hostile camps could be forcibly involved prompted the decision to send the boy away for his higher education. In consequence, during the years of World War I, Lipski completed his studies of law and econom-ics at the University of Lausanne in Switzerland. He graduated in social sciences and gained a broad international outlook on the problems and the place of his people in the now ravaged and rapidly changing Europe.

A new Poland emerged from the carnage thanks to the defeat of all three partitioning powers.

The Lausanne student, whose interest in political matters grew keen, was now ready to assume service in the foreign affairs of the newly founded state. In December, 1918, he was named secretary to the Lon-don mission of the Polish National Committee, whose headquarters dur-ing World War I had been in Paris. At the very outset of his diplomatic career Lipski was instrumental in preparing Paderewski's historical jour-ney to Poland on board a British cruiser. The arrival of this man, who was a living legend among his people, became the spark provoking an uprising in the western German-held territories of Poland to bring about their joyous reunion with the rest of the newly liberated country.

After serving in London and Paris, with a brief interlude in the Polish Legation of Berlin, Józef Lipski at thirty-two became the head of the Western Department of the Foreign Office in Warsaw. This position kept him intimately acquainted with all aspects of European politics and brought him close to many leading personalities of the period.

When Mrs. Woodrow Wilson and Bernard Baruch came to Poland in 1928 for the unveiling of President Wilson's monument in Poznań, Józef Lipski accompanied them as official representative of the Polish government during their entire visit.

Already prior to his appointment in Warsaw, and later, in his capacity as the head of the Western Department, he played a conspicuous role in a number of international conferences, representing Poland at Locarno in 1925, The Hague in 1929 and 1930, and Lausanne in 1932. Signs of danger in the political development in Germany which he observed were the source of more than one alarm, especially in view of the lack of Western determination and solidarity to resist Hitler's campaign to undo the Versailles settlement. It was the recognition of this bitter reality which led to Poland's nonaggression declaration with Germany, signed on January 26, 1934. Lipski's role in negotiating this declaration brought about his selection by Marshal Piłsudski on November 1, 1934, to be in the future the first Polish ambassador in Berlin, and hence to be the man to deal directly with Hitler.

At the outset of his mission, Lipski's goal was a policy of long-range improvement in traditionally strained neighborly relations. He did his best to serve this interest, with the understanding that such was to the advantage of both partners.

This ultimately abortive mission must be viewed against the accumulating evidence, painfully clear to those responsible for Poland's foreign policy, that it was not possible to count on Western solidarity in case of German aggression. The Western alliance was not a reliable foundation on which Poland could base its security. Poland was left alone with two dynamic and potentially aggressive neighbors, and in case of a showdown, declarations to the contrary notwithstanding, it would have to face the brunt of German military power.

The moment that the chances for success of his essentially peaceful mission were shattered by the collision course on which Hitler had embarked, Lipski asked to be relieved of his Berlin post. Three times Warsaw rejected his resignation. Not that further illusions were harbored, but because even now in the gallop toward a European catastrophe, Poland saw no better man to represent its peaceful determination—but at the same time its firmness to resist—than Lipski.

It was an irony that in the year of the outbreak of war Lipski became dean of the Berlin diplomatic corps. He had endured longer than any of his foreign colleagues the unthankful, nerve-racking, and—toward the end—heartbreaking task of representing his country in the Nazi capital. Exposed more often than any foreign diplomat to direct personal contacts with Hitler, he found himself at the decisive moment in a situation in which the latter, already determined on war, deliberately avoided another confrontation with the Polish Ambassador.

Once the war erupted, Lipski continued to serve, as already shown, first as a soldier, later as political adviser to the Polish government-in-exile. In this capacity he accompanied General Sikorski, the prime minister and commander in chief, on his visit to the United States in 1942, renewing many contacts with prominent Americans whom he knew from his days of Warsaw and Berlin.

After the war, with the city of his birth back within the borders of Poland and his family estate nationalized by the Stalin-imposed government that received the recognition of the Western allies after Yalta, Lipski became the unofficial representative of Poles-in-exile at Washington, D.C. He established himself in the minds of a number of American political personalities, whom he contacted or who contacted him to discuss postwar developments in Europe, as a man of restrained wisdom and carefully measured judgment.

The former Polish Ambassador in Berlin passed away in Washington, D.C., on November 1, 1958. He was buried at the capital's Mount Olivet cemetery, the only inscription on the stone that marks his grave being, in addition to his name: Wrocław 1894 Washington 1958—a life span encompassing one of the most tragic periods of human history.

There is no finer tribute paid him than a passage in the book of Carl J. Burckhardt, a Swiss professor and diplomat, who as a former high commissioner of the League of Nations in the free city of Danzig was singularly well placed to observe and judge the behavior of those who were directly involved in the mounting drama of Hitler's attempt at conquering the world. In his book *Ma Mission à Danzig,* Burckhardt said:

"In the years preceding the war few men occupied a post more thorny than the ambassador of Poland in Berlin, Józef Lipski. In the framework of his instructions he acted with an admirable dignity and firmness; he was, without question, since 1933 the man of the German-Polish *détente,* one of the artisans of the agreement of January 26, 1934, an efficient negotiator in all the later attempts at a rapprochement between the two countries. . . . German he knew as well as his own language. He was certainly, as I have said before, one of the best-informed ambassadors in the Berlin of the epoch, nobody knowing as well as he did the always changing constellations of personalities directing the Third Reich.

"He went far in his concessions and his offers, he took account of the instability and the susceptibilities of the Führer, he flattered his immense pride, always restless, always seeking applause. . . . but when the sovereign rights of Poland and the honor of his country were at stake, he showed himself as firm as a rock, and at the end of his mission destined to failure, he acted in terms of one sovereign power toward another power, with an always measured and controlled rigor, as few knew how to do."

For those who knew Józef Lipski, no truer words have been spoken.

*Alexander Janta*

# Contents

The Eastern Pact   May–December, 1934    143
  Documents 28–32

Introduction of Conscription in Germany   January–May, 1935    163
  Documents 33–42

The Death of Marshal Piłsudski. The Currency Conflict with
  Danzig   May–July, 1935    200
  Documents 43–47

German Refunds for Transit across Polish Pomerania
  July, 1935–March, 1936    218
  Documents 48–56

Remilitarization of the Rhineland (March, 1936) and Blomberg's
  Directive (June, 1937)    251

The Battleship *Leipzig* in Danzig and Danzig Problems
  Summer, 1936    257
  Documents 57–63

Beck's Conversation with Neurath   January, 1937    279
  Document 64

Declaration about National Minorities   June–November, 1937    288
  Documents 65–74

Hitler Discloses His Designs   November, 1937    309

Attempts to Draw Poland into the Anti-Comintern Pact
  November, 1937    313

Weighty Decisions of the Third Reich   November, 1937–
  February, 1938    318

Beck in Berlin   January, 1938    321
  Documents 75–77

Changes in the Reich's Top Rulers. Conversations with Göring in
  Warsaw. The Anschluss   February–March, 1938    339
  Documents 78–81

Resumption of Polish-Lithuanian Relations   Spring, 1938    352
  Documents 82–86

*Illustrations follow p. 354*

# Analytical Table of Documents

# DIPLOMAT IN BERLIN

## 1933–1939

# Abbreviations

| | |
|---|---|
| A.A. | Auswärtiges Amt |
| *British Blue Book* | Great Britain. Foreign Office. *Documents Concerning German-Polish Relations and the Outbreak of Hostilities between Great Britain and Germany on Sept. 3, 1939* |
| *DGFP* | Germany. Auswärtiges Amt. *Documents on German Foreign Policy, 1918–1945.* Series C: 1933–37. Series D: 1937–45 |
| *Diariusz* | Szembek, *Diariusz i teki Jana Szembeka, 1935–1945.* Vol. I (1935), Vol. II (1936) |
| *German White Book* | Germany. Auswärtiges Amt. *Zweites Weisbuch der deutschen Regierung: Dokumente über die Entwickelung der deutsch-polnischen Beziehungen und die Ereignisse von 1933 bis zur Gegenwart* |
| *Journal* | Szembek, *Journal, 1933–1939* |
| *Livre jaune* | France. Ministère des Affaires Étrangères. *Documents diplomatiques, 1938–1939* |
| *Polish White Book* | Poland. Ministerstwo Spraw Zagranicznych. *Official Documents Concerning Polish-German and Polish-Soviet Relations, 1933–1939* |

# Shadow over the Polish-French Alliance[1]
## 1929

---

FOR CENTURIES, Poland and France were linked by a spontaneous and genuine friendship, deeply rooted in both countries. These mutual bonds of sentiment persisted, notwithstanding various (more or less successful) fluctuations of the political alliance. In its inaugural period, during Poincaré's premiership in France (1922–24), the alliance developed as a useful instrument for both partners, but difficulties set in with the initiation of the subsequent Franco-German rapprochement. Thus, Locarno[2] loosened the impact (that is, the automatic applicability) of the alliance; the Thoiry policy[3] smoothed the path for the Young Plan[4] and hence for the premature evacuation of the Rhineland,[5] which was decided upon during the First Hague Conference in August, 1929. Acting on the sidelines of this conference, the Polish government spared no efforts to restore the automatic applicability of the Franco-Polish alliance and avoid appellatory recourse to the League of Nations. From the time of the Locarno agreements, contradictory opinions had formed the basis for optional interpretations in this latter respect.

Despite increasing hostility toward Poland in Germany after the summer of 1930, and an upsurge of revisionist propaganda against the Polish frontiers, the West indulged in further concessions to Germany. German war indemnities were canceled at the Lausanne Conference in

---

[1] Published in *Bellona* (London), 1957, Nos. 1–2.

[2] The Locarno agreements were signed October 16, 1925.

[3] A conference between Briand and Stresemann was held at Thoiry, September 17, 1926, regarding the settlement of disagreements between France and Germany. Briand demanded an increase in war indemnities; Stresemann, the withdrawal of the Rhineland occupation and an earlier solution of the Saar question, where a plebiscite was to be held in 1935.

[4] The Young Plan was established at a conference of experts, held February 9–June 7, 1929, under the leadership of Owen D. Young. The Young Plan reduced reparations obligations of Germany, as compared with the Dawes Plan. It was approved at the First Hague Conference.

[5] In June, 1930, the Rhineland was finally evacuated by the French Army.

July, 1932, and in December of the same year the Great Powers conceded equality of armaments to Germany.

Poland was absent from all these conferences and meetings of the
Western Great Powers, during which crucial decisions vital to its very
existence were taken, and could but indirectly influence the trend of
events.

After the signing of the Rhineland Pact,[6] with France constrained by
the British guarantee, Paris became ever more closely bound to London,
yielding to its influence and often to manifest pressure. For Great Britain, Europe's safety (alternatively Great Britain's safety) ended at the
Rhine as far as Britain's direct engagements were concerned.

In the political constellation of that time, the Polish alliance was
shifted to the background of French foreign policy and its role as an instrument of common action toward German problems became restricted.

For France this alliance still retained its value as a reinsurance factor
in case of armed conflict with the Reich. A weakening of France's
internal situation contributed to its gradual dependence on London's
decisions. But public opinion in Poland, where the alliance with its
Western confederate was firmly relied upon, was still ignorant of this
fact. However, Polish diplomats were better informed and strove to cope
with this new turn in the situation. From the moment Hitler came to
power and the threat to Poland's interests began to grow, Piłsudski took
more energetic steps (the case of the *Wicher*[7] and Westerplatte[8]) in

[6] The Rhineland guarantee pact was the main pact of the Locarno agreements,
involving Germany, France, Great Britain, Italy, and Belgium.

[7] Poland had an agreement of *port d'attache* with Danzig which was to expire
in 1932, since the Senate of Danzig refused Poland's demands for its extension.
According to this agreement, a foreign navy entering the port of Danzig was to
be greeted by one of the Polish Navy's warships. In June, 1932, a squadron of
British warships was to visit Danzig. Owing to irregularities of the *port d'attache*
question, the Polish government called the British government's attention to the
untimely date of the visit, but the visit took place nevertheless. Under these circumstances, Marshal Piłsudski ordered the Polish destroyer *Wicher* to enter
the Danzig harbor, salute the commander of the British squadron, and depart
after an exchange of courtesy visits. The commander of the *Wicher* received an
additional order: in case the Polish flag was insulted by Danzig, he was to open
fire and bombard targets in the port of Danzig.

The *Wicher* executed the first part of the order and exchanged courtesy visits
with the British squadron, thus stressing Polish rights in Danzig. The Danzig
Senate lodged a protest, but no demonstration was staged. The *Wicher* case was
widely commented upon in Europe and at the then current session of the League
of Nations

[8] For Westerplatte, see pp. 53–59.

order to incite the West to common action with Poland. He also wanted to stress his determined attitude to Berlin.

The Polish-French alliance had been concluded during the journey to France of Józef Piłsudski, head of the Polish state, in February, 1921. He was accompanied by General Kazimierz Sosnkowski, minister of war, and Eustachy Sapieha, minister of foreign affairs. This visit took place in a friendly atmosphere of appreciation on the part of the French population and their leaders for the Polish armed victory that had so successfully stopped the Bolshevik invasion of Europe. In the eyes of the French people, Poland was a factor in the security of East Central Europe and a buffer state between Soviet Russia and Germany.

The help extended by France to Poland at the hour of danger contributed to an upsurge of friendship and confidence on the banks of the Vistula. Political motives were also favorable for the establishment of a firm basis of collaboration between the two nations.

The political treaty signed on February 19, 1921, by Sapieha and Briand was supplemented two days later (with reference to Article 3 of the agreement) by a secret military convention.[9] This article stated that, in case of unprovoked aggression against one of the signatory nations, the governments of both countries would be in touch in order to defend their territory and to protect their legitimate interests within the limits defined in the introduction to the agreement. This related to the maintenance of peace in Europe, to security and the defense of the territories of both countries, and to their mutual political and economic interests, through recognition of treaties mutually agreed to, as well as of treaties which might be recognized by both countries in the future.

Other clauses of the political agreement referred to conferences on foreign affairs in the spirit of the treaties and in accordance with the League of Nations Covenant, to mutual economic collaboration, and to consultations prior to entering into new agreements in Central and Eastern Europe.

The validity of the entire agreement, together with the military convention and a 4-million-franc French credit to purchase war material for Poland, was made dependent (according to final Article 5) on the signing of economic treaties, that is, a trade and oil agreement, as well as the

---

[9] For the text of the political agreement, see *Livre jaune*, p. 351. For the military convention, see Wandycz, pp. 394–95.

so-called bilateral agreement (*droits, biens, et intérêts*). The latter
agreement was essential for the French concession companies in Poland
established before 1914.

The coupling of political and economic matters, when the interests of
private French enterprises were also involved, was by its nature hardly
conducive to good relations, and often resulted in unnecessary friction.

Obligations under the military convention were far more explicit than
under the political treaty. According to its text, if the situation in Germany became a menace—creating a danger of war against one of the
countries, and especially in the event of German mobilization or the
necessity for common action in order to fulfill the Versailles Treaty—
both governments were to "reinforce their war preparedness to the extent of being in the position to give each other rapid assistance and act
jointly." In case of German aggression, "both countries pledged to assist
each other in accordance with the mutual understanding."

The military convention also contained resolutions in case Poland
were threatened or invaded by Soviet Russia. French obligations in that
event would be to check the Germans and secure for Poland a supply of
war matériel by land and sea. It should be remembered that, at the time
of the signing of the treaty, Polish-Soviet war entanglements seemed far
more probable than aggression by a Germany defeated by the Allies.

Criticizing the too far-reaching obligations of France toward Poland,
Ambassador Noël contended that originally Marshal Foch himself had
been against making a military agreement with a country which, in his
opinion, still had "ni frontières, ni gouvernement, ni armée." On the
basis of clarifications obtained from General Weygand, Noël described
the circumstances in which the decision on the alliance was made. This
supposedly happened at a reception given at the Elysée Palace by President Millerand for Piłsudski and his entourage. After dinner the French
President invited the Polish guests into his study. He was accompanied
by Premier Briand and War Minister Barthou, but Marshal Foch and
other high French military men were not invited to join in the negotiations at which the bases of the alliance were established.[10] In my opinion this version, taken from Noël's memoirs, calls for deeper scrutiny.

An alliance with a powerful France was of great importance for Poland, strengthening its international position and its position with regard
to Germany and Soviet Russia.

[10] Noël, p. 100.

The year 1921 was a year of important achievements for Poland: the alliance with France, a peace treaty with Soviet Russia, and the restoration of a part of Upper Silesia.

However, already in April, 1922, the first clouds gathered on the horizon—forerunners of future dangers. In an atmosphere of total surprise to the participants of the Genoa Conference (April 16, 1922), Walter Rathenau and Chicherin signed the Russo-German friendship treaty at Rapallo.

Owing to difficulties encountered by the negotiation of the economic agreements, the settlement of the alliance with France dragged on for the whole year 1921. A more favorable turn came after the fall of Briand's cabinet—when Poincaré assumed the leadership of the government in January, 1922.

Since I was at that time transferred to our legation in Paris, after three years in London, I had an opportunity, to a certain extent, to observe French affairs at firsthand. I remember how, in his first conversation with Polish Envoy Count Maurycy Zamoyski, the new Prime Minister of France declared that he desired the negotiations to be terminated promptly and that he would give orders to this effect to his subordinates.

Zamoyski, the chief advocate of the Polish-French rapprochement ever since the time of the National Committee,[11] of which he was a member and representative to the French government, left the Quai d'Orsay in an optimistic mood on this occasion, feeling that things were at last moving. And indeed economic agreements were concluded soon afterward, and the alliance thus achieved binding power.

Poincaré was one of the last French statesmen who—following the path of inherited tradition—strove to carry on an independent policy on the continent. The period of his administration was marked by sharp friction with Germany over war indemnities, while London generally took a negative position toward French demands. But Germany was not the sole cause for Poincaré's disagreement with Great Britain; he also opposed Lloyd George's idea of drawing Soviet Russia into European collaboration, with the camouflaged concept of German participation in the economic restoration of the Soviet Union (Genoa Conference). In

11 The Polish National Committee, formed in Paris in August, 1917, under the leadership of Roman Dmowski, was acknowledged by the Allied countries as representing Poland. In 1919 it represented Poland at the Versailles Peace Conference.

his political designs at that time, Poincaré realized the importance of Poland as an element of peace based upon the support of a powerful France. At the time when French troops occupied the Ruhr coal basin, Polish-French collaboration was developing successfully. During this period Warsaw rejected the secret suggestions of Soviet agents to let the Red Army pass through to Germany in case a revolution broke out in that country, in exchange for a free hand for Poland in East Prussia.

French elections in May, 1924, brought a total defeat of the national bloc in which Poincaré found his support. This closed one of the chapters in the history of independent French policy.

Poincaré, who was at the peak of his power in the international arena after the breakdown of passive resistance in Germany, was taken completely by surprise by the results of the elections. It was generally said that Poincaré was so deeply absorbed in foreign affairs that serious changes which occurred inside France escaped his attention. He was blamed for not having made essential changes in the posts of prefects— *faire valser les prefets,* as the French say—prior to the elections.

Shortly before the elections Poincaré paid a visit to the Polish Legation at 12 Rue Marignan to take part in the ceremony of decorating General Weygand with the Polish order of *Virtuti Militari.* In his conversation with the newly appointed envoy, Alfred Chłapowski, who replaced Maurycy Zamoyski, he seemed to be quite sure of the outcome of the voting. As an aside to this matter, I would like to note that I accompanied Chłapowski to Nancy on May 3, the Polish national holiday. Nancy was considered a fortress of "Poincarism." In his speech, the Polish Envoy referred to Poincaré as a great son of Lorraine. In the evening of the same day, when the Envoy went to a gala performance at the opera with the prefect of Nancy, the vice-prefect took me over to a local café, where by chance I quite unexpectedly became a witness to backstage election intrigues. Several friends and acquaintances of the vice-prefect came to our table asking him for information and guidance. In amazement, I listened to the then current election slogans of the *cartel des gauches,* such as the necessity of collaborating with the Soviets by entering into diplomatic relations with them. When I made a slightly puzzled remark, my host declared with a broad sweep of his arm: "If the boss wins—everything is all right; if he loses, I am covered from the other side." This was the first alarm bell.

The fall of Poincaré had its repercussions on Polish-French relations, which were wrongly accused of being right-wing. The defeat of the national bloc was used in propaganda hostile to Poland. Also, the overthrow of President Millerand by the newly elected parliament was connected with his pro-Polish attitude in 1921. Shortly afterward a manifesto appeared, signed by a number of French politicians of the left wing, against the so-called white terror in Poland—that is, persecutions of the minorities. It was later discovered that these politicians had been misled by "fellow travelers" very active at the time.

In March, 1924, soon after the change of government in France, General Stanisław Haller, chief of the Polish General Staff, came to Paris. During his stay there, Mr. Duca, the foreign minister of Rumania, was also in Paris holding conversations with the French government about the security pact. The chief of his cabinet, Mr. Constantinesco, informed me one day that Duca was receiving alarming news from Bucharest about the movements of Soviet troops on the Rumanian border, and inquired whether we had confirmation of these rumors. In the absence of the envoy, who was in Poland at the time, I arranged a meeting between General Haller and Minister Duca. Upon verification by Warsaw, these rumors proved to be exaggerated and caused by nervous tension on the frontier line. On this occasion I had a long talk with General Haller about his conversations with the [French] Army. He stated at that time that he felt the French military authorities were negatively disposed toward the obligations of the military convention with Poland in regard to the Soviets, and in his opinion no substantial aid could be expected in the event of trouble. The validity of the alliance was therefore limited to Germany only.

A new period in German foreign policy started from the time Stresemann took over the government and strove for closer understanding with the Western Powers. The British government, then represented in Berlin by Lord D'Abernon, a zealous supporter of an understanding with the Reich, played an intermediary role between Berlin and Paris. Financial problems were pushed to the foreground. The German economy, supported by American capital upon the introduction of the Dawes Plan, was making rapid progress. War indemnity payments in favor of France were carried out in accordance with the plan. From the financial field, conversations were shifted to political problems. Negotiations begun in February, 1925, reached the quite substantial form of the

Locarno treaties in October. Polish-French relations suffered a serious
setback during these months. Difficulties with which Polish diplomacy
had to contend were caused on the one side by the obstinate refusal of
the Reich to abandon the idea of territorial revisions in the east, and on
the other by the negative attitude of the British government to the
extension of its guarantees beyond the Rhine line. The Rhineland
Pact—a threat to the Polish-French alliance system—could easily jeopardize the security of Europe.

Count Aleksander Skrzyński, Poland's foreign minister, was at that
time very skillfully active on the international chessboard. With remarkable energy and ability he defended the interests of Poland by remaining
in constant touch with Paris, and also by dealing directly with London.
Through his journey to the United States and his discussion with
Chicherin when the latter passed through Warsaw (September 27,
1925), he tried to inject some vigor into Polish foreign policy.

War Minister General Władysław Sikorski, in his concern over the
military convention with France, traveled to Paris to put pressure on
French military and political authorities (April, 1925). In a letter addressed to the prime minister, Władysław Grabski, dated June 25, 1925,
General Sikorski stated his conditions as follows:

1) Maintenance of a demilitarized zone in the Rhineland.

2) Readjustment of the military convention of 1921 to the new situation so as not to affect the *casus foederis.*

3) The conclusion of the Polish-German arbitration agreement
simultaneously with the Rhineland Pact, taking territorial matters out of
its jurisdiction and obtaining a French guarantee identical with the British guarantee in the West. The Polish-German conflict should therefore
be taken to the League of Nations, in case of a breach of the treaty by
Germany without armed action. If, however, the Reich should launch an
attack, even in the form of an attack perpetrated by a civilian organization, sanctions should follow immediately.

4) Securing for Poland a place on the Council of the League of
Nations.

Direct relations between Poland and Germany showed no sign of
improvement during the period of talks between the Great Powers in the
West. A short-term temporary economic agreement between Poland and
Germany, concluded in January, 1925, expired in June of the same
year, on the date of the expiration of the negotiated resolution to admit

Polish coal from Upper Silesia to the German market. Efforts made by the Polish government to extend the term of the temporary agreement were unsuccessful, and the import of coal was stopped. Thus a Polish-German tariff war began which was to last until March, 1934. The outflow of German capital from Polish banks was another blow to the financial situation of Poland, which at that time manifested ever more threatening signs of an approaching currency crisis.

The tariff war broke out at a time most undesirable for Poland's foreign policy, when the bulk of her efforts was concentrated on negotiations with the West.

The death of President Friedrich Ebert, in February, 1925, and the struggle for his succession absorbed the attention of the world for some time, focusing it on the internal situation of Germany.

I was in Berlin at the time and had an opportunity to observe from the windows of the British Embassy on the Wilhelmstrasse the funeral procession of the Socialist President of the Weimar Republic. There was no trace in that cortege of the prewar-style German drill-parades. The display was very modest. The late President was fondly remembered by members of the diplomatic corps.

Proffering Hindenburg's candidacy was a rather provocative step as far as the West was concerned. Skrzyński received incredulously my report with regard to the chances of a former commander of the Great World War to win the elections. After the plebiscite of April 26, 1925, international opinion quickly returned to normal and negotiations between Germany and the Great Powers went ahead.

In August, 1925, Skrzyński obtained affirmation from Briand and Austen Chamberlain that Poland would be admitted to the [Locarno] conference. Beneš, who at that time was not encumbered by quarrels with Germany, had an easy task, and he profited automatically from the achievements of his Polish colleague.

As head of the German section at the Polish Ministry of Foreign Affairs, I was present at the Locarno Conference, which led to the conclusion of several interconnected agreements, though the German government formally ignored guarantee pacts signed by France, Poland, and Czechoslovakia. The basis for the understanding was the Rhineland Pact.

Article 2, wherein exemptions from the prohibition of aggression and the launching of war were fixed between Germany, France, and Belgium, was of essential value for the working of the Polish-French alliance. Namely, power could be used

1) in case of defense of one's territory or of a flagrant breach of the provisions concerning the demilitarization of the Rhineland,

2) in the execution of Article 16 of the League of Nations Covenant,

3) in case of freedom of action for members of the League (provided by Article 15, par. 7, of the League of Nations Covenant) if the Council did not pass a unanimous decision (parties engaged in the disagreement being excluded) should armed conflict take place.[12]

Points 2 and 3 above were adjusted to the resolutions of the Covenant of the League of Nations, which in theory foresaw only these two cases of war.

In accordance with the Locarno resolutions, action under the Polish-French alliance was based on these very articles, which were adapted to the guarantee treaties signed by France, Poland, and Czechoslovakia.

Accordingly, allied assistance could immediately be applied in the Polish-French agreement in execution of Article 16 or by Article 15,

[12] Article 15, par. 7, of the Covenant of the League of Nations: "If the Council fails to reach a report which is unanimously agreed to by the members thereof, other than the Representatives of one or more of the parties to the dispute, the Members of the League reserve to themselves the right to take such action as they shall consider necessary for the maintenance of right and justice."

Article 16: "Should any Member of the League resort to war in disregard of its covenants under Articles 12, 13 or 15, it shall *ipso facto* be deemed to have committed an act of war against all other Members of the League, which hereby undertake immediately to subject it to the severance of all trade or financial relations, the prohibition of all intercourse between their nationals and the nationals of the Covenant-breaking State, and the prevention of all financial, commercial or personal intercourse between the nationals of the Covenant-breaking States and the nationals of any other State, whether a Member of the League or not.

"It shall be the duty of the Council in such case to recommend to the several Governments concerned what effective military, naval or air force the Members of the League shall severally contribute to the armed forces to be used to protect the covenants of the League.

"The Members of the League agree, further, that they will mutually support one another in the financial and economic measures which are taken under this Article, in order to minimize the loss and inconvenience resulting from the above measures, and that they will mutually support one another in resisting any special measures aimed at one of their number by the Covenant-breaking State, and that they will take the necessary steps to afford passage through their territory to the forces of any one of the Members of the League which are co-operating to protect the covenants of the League.

"Any Member of the League which has violated any covenant of the League may be declared to be no longer a Member of the League by a vote of the Council concurred in by the Representatives of all the other Members of the League represented thereon."

par. 7, in case of a breach by Germany of the Rhineland Pact's resolutions toward France and the arbitration treaty toward Poland, and in case of unprovoked German aggression against one of these countries.

This intricate legal system, as compared with the previous state of affairs, caused an obvious deterioration in the Polish situation.

In spite of the reference to previously concluded agreements, in the introduction to the Polish-French guarantee treaty, this was not sufficient to safeguard free operation of the military convention. French lawyers might in the future raise the question whether this convention was compatible with the [French] constitution and with the Covenant of the League. At any rate, the operation of the convention was restricted by the fact that the whole Locarno system was based on the Covenant of the League. From the moment Locarno was signed, there were doubts whether the act of assistance was to be dependent on a prior decision by the Council of the League.

In contrast to this dependence on the League, mutual British-French assistance (in accordance with Article 4 of the Rhineland Pact) was to be automatic in case of so-called *agression flagrante,* that is, unprovoked aggression such as crossing the frontier, starting war operations, or marching troops into the demilitarized zone.

Although, during the conference itself, discussion by Germany of territorial problems was avoided and Poland was able to maintain a common front with the West, the difference introduced at Locarno between the western and eastern frontiers of Germany threatened to become the heaviest burden for Poland in the future.

Upon his return to Warsaw, Skrzyński tried to interpret the Locarno agreements in a light most favorable for Poland. He made reference to his close collaboration with Briand and Chamberlain, as well as to the general spirit of understanding prevailing at the negotiations ("the spirit of Locarno").

However, the agreements met with criticism in the Polish Sejm, especially from the right-wing party, which tried to establish with documents that the Rhineland Pact weakened the alliance with France. For propaganda reasons Germany set the acceptance of the *status quo* in the west against the possibilities it envisaged in the east. Skrzyński therefore had to be on the defensive at home and abroad, and he sometimes went too far, creating the illusion that he was not sufficiently aware of the shortcomings of the treaties. It should be said, however, that Skrzyński—at a

time so precarious for Poland—succeeded in skillfully adapting himself
to the new situation in Western Europe. He moved closer to Great
Britain, contributed to a large extent to the abolition of prejudice against
Poland still rampant amidst leftists in France, and prepared the ground
in Geneva for future attempts by Poland for a permanent place on the
Council of the League.

In 1927 the French ambassador in Poland, Jules Laroche, approached the Ministry of Foreign Affairs with a proposition for the
readjustment of the alliance agreements of 1921 (political and military)
with the Locarno treaties. This project, presented by the French Ambassador in writing, was handed over to me, since I was at that time acting
head of the Western Department. He stressed the principle that all
agreements, and therefore also the military convention, had to be binding within the limits of the Covenant of the League of Nations, and that
therefore the application of *casus foederis* was restricted to cases as
foreseen by Article 16 and Article 15, par. 7, of the pact. The French
Ambassador questioned the validity of the military convention, which,
in his opinion, was not in accordance with the requirements of the
French constitution and with the obligations of the League. I remember
that Marshal Piłsudski decided that discussions on these subjects should
not be undertaken with the French side.

Former French Minister of Foreign Affairs Bonnet wrote about this
intervention of Laroche as follows:

"In 1927, on the initiative of our General Staff and under the pretext
of bringing certain dispositions of our military convention up to date
that had been overridden by events, an attempt was made to proceed
toward its revision, with a double aim—to include it within the frame of
the Locarno agreements, and to cancel the guarantee given by us to
Poland vis-à-vis Russia. On Poland's side the negotiations showed no
result." [13]

The mission of Marshal Franchet d'Esperey to Poland in November,
1927, which was connected with this proposition by Laroche, was also
aimed at introducing changes in the military convention. In this case too
the attitude of Piłsudski was unyielding.

General Kutrzeba [14] told me in London about the circumstances

[13] Bonnet, *Fin d'une Europe,* pp. 134–35.
[14] Gen. Tadeusz Kutrzeba (1886–1947), deputy chief of the General Staff,
1922–27. After 1928 he was commander of the War Academy. In the September
campaign of 1939 he was commander of the army "Poznań."

under which he was sent by Marshal Piłsudski to Paris in the summer of 1928. Piłsudski instructed him to investigate the attitude of French military authorities toward the military convention with Poland. In his conversation with General Debeney, the chief of the French General Staff, General Kutrzeba declared in the name of the Marshal that, in case of German aggression against France, Poland would mobilize immediately and take military action. Further, General Kutrzeba asked what France would do in case of an attack on Poland. General Debeney replied evasively that in such circumstances the decision would fall to the political authorities. But he did add most significantly that the decision of the French government would depend in the first place on the attitude of London.

Attempts to tighten the alliance with France were undertaken by Poland during the discussions of the Western Powers with regard to the premature evacuation of the Rhineland. This problem arose in the fall of 1928 during the session of the League of Nations in Geneva. In conversations with the Great Powers, the German government obstinately insisted that, on the basis of the Dawes Plan and the Locarno resolutions, the Allied armies should leave German territory, in accordance with Article 431 of the Treaty of Versailles. The French government's point of view was that an early evacuation of the Rhineland could take place only by way of a special agreement in exchange for concessions in the field of indemnities and security measures. Belgium supported France, while British and Italian opinion was generally in accordance with the German point of view.

On September 16, 1928, a communiqué was issued at Geneva, signed by France, Germany, Great Britain, Italy, Belgium, and Japan, announcing the opening of official conversations on the evacuation of the Rhineland, as well as on the summoning of a commission of experts for the final settlement of war indemnities. Both of these problems were later the object of consultations at the Hague Conference in August, 1929. In Warsaw they were discussed from the Polish point of view. Since a premature evacuation could become a threat to Poland's security, the minister of foreign affairs, August Zaleski, tried to find adequate measures to balance the situation on the French sector. Discussions were held in government circles on a 2-billion-franc loan for Poland's armaments.

Simultaneously, various projects were considered in the Ministry of Foreign Affairs in Warsaw with the aim of safeguarding the alliance with France, over which some shadows were cast owing to the progressing German-French rapprochement. The concept of an agreement between Poland, France, and Germany was discussed. The result of these discussions was the selection of the so-called Pattern D of the Treaty of Mutual Assistance, elaborated on by the Committee of Arbitration and Security at Geneva and confirmed by the Assembly of the League of Nations. This type of agreement included three vital elements: nonaggression, peaceful settlement of disputes, and mutual assistance. If it were expanded to cover Poland, France, and Germany, it would in a certain way serve as an extension of the Rhineland Pact in the east, although it would be without the British guarantee and without the clause on the maintenance of the territorial *status quo*. Pattern D did not include such a clause, since it was felt that the resolutions of the League on this matter would be guarantee enough.

Personally, I had serious objections to this concept, since I feared a further watering-down of the Polish-French alliance. Besides, introducing Germany as a third partner into relations between Poland and France could seriously jeopardize the balance to Poland's disadvantage.

In my opinion the best course to follow would have been to strengthen Polish-French relations through a bilateral understanding. I was anxious to restore the automatic action of the alliance on the basis of an agreement containing a formula of *agression flagrante* styled on Article 4, par. 3, of the Rhineland Pact. The recently signed Kellogg Pact,[15] which condemned war and excluded it from international relations, went further than the Covenant of the League, thus creating a basis for a new treaty of alliance between Poland and France.

In the course of the Hague Conference, we worked out with Jan Mrozowski, president of the Supreme Court in Warsaw, and Włodzimierz Adamkiewicz, legal counselor of the Western Department in the Ministry of Foreign Affairs, a text on these principles which was approved by Mr. Zaleski and became the basis for negotiations with the French partners.

Prior to the opening of the Hague Conference, the Polish Embassy in

[15] The Kellogg-Briand Pact renouncing war was signed in Paris on August 28, 1928.

Paris presented an *aide-mémoire* to the Quai d'Orsay promoting several Polish motions aimed at strengthening the alliance with France. Referring to possible consequences of premature evacuation, the note expressed concern that this fact might contribute to the growth of a nationalistic atmosphere in the Reich.

At the First Hague Conference, which lasted from August 6 to August 31, 1929, Poland was represented by August Zaleski, minister of foreign affairs, and Jan Mrozowski as delegates of Poland, and by a group of political and economic experts. I took part in this conference in the capacity of secretary-general of the delegation. At the head of the secretariat of the conference was Lord Hankey, and secretaries of other delegations formed a team which remained in close mutual contact.

The work of the conference took place in two commissions: political and financial. Participation in the first was limited to the six inviting countries: France, Great Britain, Belgium, Italy, Germany, and Japan. The political commission worked on the early evacuation of the Rhineland. The Polish delegation had no access to it and could not even obtain minutes of its respective sessions.

On the margin of the conference, Polish-French talks were conducted and recorded by our secretariat. I am quoting the full text of this report, since it properly illustrates the course of the negotiations.

"1) During the first discussion, which took place at The Hague between Minister Zaleski and Prime Minister Briand, both ministers agreed that measures should be taken to strengthen Polish-French relations. Briand made a proposition that matters referred to in the *aide-mémoire* of the Embassy should definitely be settled in Paris in the interval of time between the end of the conference and the opening of the Assembly of the League. Briand considered commendable the suggestion of Minister Zaleski to profit by the presence of competent officials at The Hague and start talks on these matters without further delay, adding that Berthelot [16] would be at our disposal.

"2) Adam Tarnowski, head of the Eastern Department, had an informative talk with Massigli [17] based on previous exchanges of opinion between the Embassy in Paris and the Quai d'Orsay on the subject of

[16] Philippe Berthelot, secretary-general of the French Foreign Ministry, 1920–22, and 1925–32.
[17] René Massigli, political director of the French Foreign Ministry.

Pattern D of the pact between Poland, Germany, and France. M. Massigli declared that the Quai d'Orsay would not oppose such an agreement, although he doubted that the German side would agree to it.

"3) In his talk with Berthelot, Minister Zaleski, making reference to his and M. Briand's common desire to strengthen Polish-French relations, expressed the thought of introducing the formula of *agression flagrante* to the political agreement between France and Poland, as was done with the Rhineland Pact. Berthelot in general agreed with this concept, but with the reservation that it was necessary to investigate it from the legal point of view. At the same time he appointed M. Massigli to continue conversations on this subject with the Polish delegation.

"4) Two days later M. Massigli, upon meeting Mr. Zaleski at a session of the financial commission, mentioned that the *agression flagrante* formula met with legal difficulties owing to the text of Article 2 of the Rhineland Pact.

"5) Detailed talks with M. Massigli were started by the head of the Western Department, Mr. Lipski, who handed him an outline of the Polish-French agreement. At the same time he stated as follows: The Polish-French agreement of 1921 was already adapted to this general understanding in 1925, when the Locarno treaties were concluded. At present a new event had occurred in the field of security, namely, the conclusion of the Kellogg Pact, which was endowed with even deeper moral value by the fact that the United States belonged to it. This pact had already been tested in practice in the Chinese-Soviet conflict. A country which transgressed its clauses, resorting to war, would incur the unfavorable opinion of nearly the entire world.

"For the above general reasons we based the construction of our new Polish-French agreement on the Kellogg Pact.

"Besides, from the legal point of view, the Polish-French Locarno Pact provided for two alternatives in bringing armed assistance to the two nations, namely, in case of aggression under Article 16 of the Covenant of the League or in case of a legal war under Article 15, par. 7, of the same pact. The Kellogg Pact covered both of these eventualities by Article 1, excluding all war.

"Here it was pointed out to M. Massigli that the *agression flagrante* formula was mentioned in the *note introductive* of the works of the Committee of Arbitration and Security, presented to the IXth Assembly of the League of Nations as one possibly to be applied in the proposed regional treaties of mutual assistance.

"M. Massigli, who considered the idea of linking the new agreement with the Kellogg Pact interesting, stressed that he had to study the text. He had some doubts whether it could be reconciled with the Rhineland Pact. As to the question what our real intentions were, and if we were most interested in having a free hand—unhampered by the League—in case of aggression by Germany, M. Massigli received a positive answer, with the explanation that we were interested in having our *accords techniques* [18] develop freely. Questioned casually about the mobilization, M. Massigli declared firmly that we were free to mobilize. Further, M. Massigli asked whether we were abandoning Pattern D and whether we would not like to try to approach Germany on this matter. He received an evasive reply.

"6) At the next interview M. Massigli announced that, when the plan was presented to jurists (headed by Fromageot),[19] they declared that it could be interpreted as inconsistent with Article 2 of the Rhineland Pact.

"When questioned as to detailed legal objections, he explained that Article 2 of the Rhineland Pact foresaw the possibility of French troops marching across the zone under three circumstances:

"a) transgression by the Germans of declarations concerning the zone;

"b) a decision of the Council under Article 16 of the Covenant;

"c) in case of a legal war under Article 15, par. 7, of the Covenant.

"In his opinion two cases of war might occur in practice. Either it would be started by Germany as surprise aggression, in which case even France would have to mobilize prior to coming to our aid, and in the meantime a decision of the League would be taken, or the war would be preceded by a period of tension in diplomatic relations. In the latter case there would be no delay in coming to our aid. Therefore, from the practical point of view, M. Massigli did not consider the *agression flagrante* very meaningful, especially since the introduction of this provision could undermine the Rhineland Pact, which France considered very important.

[18] In respect to the military convention of 1921.
[19] Henri Fromageot was legal adviser of the French Foreign Ministry.

"Mr. Lipski remarked that our interpretation of Article 16 of the Covenant of the League made no reference to the *vote du conseil* that determined who the aggressor was. The aggressor reveals himself— 'l'agresseur se désigne lui-meme.' Therefore, paragraph 1 of Article 16 stated that a member of the League who undertook war steps would be considered *ipso facto* in a state of war with all the members of the League. As, under Article 2 of the Rhineland Pact, France could start war action against Germany in compliance with Article 16 of the Covenant of the League, the formula of *agression flagrante* could be applied.

"M. Massigli replied that such an interpretation could indeed give us a freedom of movement and could if necessary be utilized. However, it was contested. Therefore, treaty definitions to this effect could be regarded as incompatible with the Rhineland Pact. Questioned about the possible formula defining the matter of starting mobilization, M. Massigli replied that he would have to have it in writing, so that there would be time to think it over.

"He said that he would discuss this with M. Berthelot.

"7) In a conversation with Minister Zaleski on August 24, 1929, during the crisis of the conference, M. Briand stressed that he definitely wanted to begin talks with us without delay on the tightening of the alliance and that he would instruct M. Berthelot accordingly. He also remarked that M. Massigli had prepared certain formulas with regard to mobilization.

"8) On August 26 conversations took place between M. Berthelot, Minister Zaleski, and Mr. Lipski. When asked about the formulas prepared by M. Massigli on the instructions of M. Briand, M. Berthelot replied that M. Fromageot did not accept them, since he had doubts as to their compatibility with the Covenant. As to Pattern D, M. Berthelot volunteered the opinion that it would be difficult to apply to Germany and that there would be reason to fear that Germany would try to insert resolutions which could be awkward for French-Polish relations. Minister Zaleski asked M. Berthelot explicitly—since it was impossible for him to present the mobilization formula for fear that it might also not be in accordance with the Covenant—what would happen in case of German aggression. M. Berthelot replied that we had a military convention which would then be applied. Minister Zaleski then declared that Ambassador Laroche, when he brought up the plan to change this convention, had questioned its legal value. M. Berthelot tried to argue that

Laroche probably presented the matter in a false light, and that the convention was still valid.

"Coming back to the question of the formula introducing the *obligo* of mobilization, Lipski remarked that after his talks with Massigli he tried to work out a text with Polish jurists which would dispel all French doubts. He said that this text had evidently not yet won the approval of Polish military authorities, especially of Marshal Piłsudski. As M. Berthelot insisted that he would like to study this text, it was given to him for unofficial study. Mr. Lipski added some explanatory remarks to the text. M. Berthelot said that M. Massigli did not have any objections to a formula of this sort, but he could not make any statement without the jurists' opinion."

In this report it was not mentioned that in the course of his second talk with me M. Massigli said that in case of a conflict with Germany a consultation would take place between Paris and London and that in his opinion much would then depend on the attitude of Great Britain.

Upon my return to Warsaw I had a long talk with Ambassador Laroche on the subjects under discussion at The Hague. M. Laroche, who was a director at the Quai d'Orsay during the Locarno negotiations, argued that the French delegation was wrong when it contended that the operation of the guarantee pact between Poland and France required the decision of the League. Here he referred to the terms of the agreement which mentioned explicitly *immediate* assistance. He reported to his government in this vein, thus concluding the matter.

At The Hague Minister Zaleski conferred with the French delegation on the problem of loans. This matter was also discussed by treasury representatives of both countries present at the conference. They did not, however, go beyond a general exchange of opinions. At the close of the conference a Polish-French communiqué was issued, announcing collaboration of both countries in the field of financial operations. Out of these conversations came further negotiations in Paris that resulted in a loan for Poland to build a railway to transport coal from Silesia to Gdynia.

# Early German Plans to Annex the Polish Seacoast[1]
## *1930*

IN MARCH, 1930, there came to an end a period in Polish-German relations marked by endeavors of the Polish government to establish, by means of direct negotiations, some sort of normal coexistence between the two countries. This period had begun with a conversation between Foreign Minister Zaleski and Stresemann that took place at Geneva on March 7, 1927, during a session of the Council of the League of Nations. In February of that year the German government unexpectedly broke off trade negotiations with Poland that had been going on for two years in Berlin, giving as a reason the dismissal of four German directors from Polish Upper Silesia.[2] The meeting of the two ministers had as its aim the finding of a solution to a situation awkward for both parties. In the course of this exchange of opinion it was decided to seek an understanding through diplomatic channels, beginning with the most drastic question—the rights of physical and legal persons in the future Polish-German commercial treaty.

After several talks with the German minister in Warsaw, Ulrich Rauscher, that were carefully prepared by our lawyers under the expert leadership of Counselor Adamkiewicz, I set the text of a report on resettlement on July 21, 1927. This seemingly modest achievement, however, had deeper meaning for the future. It cleared the way for trade

---

[1] Published in *Sprawy Międzynarodowe* (London), 1947, Nos. 2–3.

[2] In January, 1927, four German citizens of the Schlesisch-Dabrowaer-Bahn-Exploitationsgesellschaft operating in Upper Silesia were, in accordance with the Polish law, deported from Poland. They received a notice of removal a year in advance, and their endeavors to obtain an extension of stay were refused by the Polish authorities owing to the unemployment among white-collar workers prevailing at that time. The Polish government's judgment under these circumstances was that foreign citizens should leave Poland in order to provide priority of employment to Polish citizens. This disposition was vehemently protested by the German government. See Krasuski, *Stosunki polsko-niemieckie, 1926–1932*, p. 85.

negotiations on a purely economic level. It also encouraged both negoti-ating parties to seek further solutions and overcome obstacles with re-gard to problems where there was a chance to reconcile Polish-German interests.

With considerable cooperation on the part of Minister Rauscher, who was not a professional diplomat and was therefore free from the anti-Polish complex so characteristic of Prussian bureaucrats, several agree-ments were concluded during the period from July, 1927, to March, 1930, in spite of the bitter opposition of German nationalistic circles, where the slightest tendency to normalize relations with Poland was furiously rejected.

At that time we signed a lumber agreement, which was financially profitable for Poland, an emigration agreement, which settled the diffi-cult problem of agricultural workers who resided in Germany for a long time, an agreement on the nitrate fertilizer factory at Chorzów, an agreement dealing with deeds, and several others.

The most important was the liquidation agreement of October 31, 1929, signed after the First Hague Conference in execution of the pro-visions of the Young Plan. Connected with agreements signed by Poland during the Second Hague Conference in January, 1930, this treaty freed Poland from any German financial claims under the Peace Treaty. These claims were pending before international courts, namely, the Mixed Polish-German Arbitration Tribunal in Paris and the Permanent Court of International Justice at The Hague.

Negotiations on the trade treaty, which was to end the tariff war that had been dragging on between the two nations since June, 1925, were due to be concluded in the first days of March, 1930. The terms for the signing of the agreement were already fixed when news reached Warsaw that, upon acceptance of the Hague agreements by the Reichstag on March 12, the Reichspräsident excluded from ratification the liquidation agreement with Poland. The Polish government countered by witholding its signature from the trade agreement. This step was effective. After a few days, the German Envoy disclosed to the Polish Ministry of Foreign Affairs the text of a strictly confidential telegram from his government, informing him that the doubts which Hindenburg had with regard to the ratification of the liquidation agreement were clarified and that the Reichspräsident would soon sign the ratification document. It was later disclosed that Hindenburg had yielded to the pressure of German agrarians, who bargained with him in connection with the liquidation agreement on financial subsidies for their landed estates in East Prussia.

The trade treaty was signed in Warsaw on March 17, 1930. However, it remained a dead-letter pact. The Müller cabinet collapsed on March 27, before it could present the trade agreement with Poland to the Parliament for ratification.

From the moment the Western Powers decided to proceed with the premature evacuation of the Rhineland for the sake of relaxing the tension present in their relations with Germany, German nationalism reared its head. During the weak rule of Brüning, a struggle for power broke out in Germany. Anti-Polish feelings spread like wildfire. The question of revision of frontiers with Poland became the watchword. In August, 1930, public opinion in Poland was aroused by a speech delivered by Treviranus, a member of the Reich government, who, during a demonstration in front of the Reichstag in Berlin on the occasion of the evacuation of the Rhineland by the Allies, called for a drive eastward to recover territories lost to Poland.

From British diplomatic documents [3] it is obvious that at the same time—on July 3, 1930—Curtius, the Reich foreign minister, made it quite clear in his talk with the British ambassador that the Polish-German frontier must be changed, and declared that in response to Briand's memorandum on European federation the government of the Reich would unequivocally state its stand on this matter.

The tide of German revisionist propaganda grew faster and stronger in the following years, finding an outlet in the daily press, in all kinds of publications, in speeches of political party leaders, in various public demonstrations, in excursions to the "bleeding eastern frontier of the Reich." The Polish Corridor was the main target for attack. The most insignificant frontier incidents gave rise to diplomatic protests in Warsaw, supported by outbursts in the nationalistic German press. This propaganda was not destined solely for the home-market. Its chief aim was to persuade public opinion abroad that the territorial situation in the east could under no circumstances be maintained. German propaganda for revision of the Corridor problem gained considerable ground in America, in England, and also in France. The Corridor problem was becoming more and more of a handicap for Poland's international position.

[3] *Documents on British Foreign Policy, 1919–1939*, Series 2, Vol. I, No. 311.

What was behind this revisionist campaign undertaken at such an expenditure of energy and means?

So far as the real attempts of the Germans are concerned, some light was shed by one of the few documents pertaining to this period disclosed at the Nuremberg trials. It is a memorandum worked out by the staff of the German Navy that provided the historical background for the German war organization and its mobilization plan.[4]

The memorandum explained that, owing to the prohibition of mobilization preparations imposed by the Treaty of Versailles, the German General Staff was compelled to draw only a very restricted team of workers into these activities, and that work was done primarily only from the theoretical point of view. Beginning in 1930—"owing to the ever-growing tension in Polish-German relations"—the Reichswehr changed from theoretical planning to the elaboration of the mobilization plan *Verstaerkerungsplan*. This plan was to be adopted in case of a *local* conflict with Poland, that is, without the participation of other countries on the side of Poland. The plan was based on the strategic principle of a "blitz-annexation" of the Polish naval base at Gdynia. The period needed for carrying out the mobilization was fixed at 72 hours. It was also taken into consideration that the occupation of Gdynia might not be the final step in war operations.

This document, which does not fully explain the German plan, still throws some light on the leading idea of competent German Army circles, and at the same time also on the political leadership of Germany. It should be stressed that a practical mobilization plan existed only with regard to Poland, while German preparations against other countries remained theoretical. The operation was planned as a local confrontation with Poland based upon the problem of the Corridor, and it was founded on the premise that the West would not come to Poland's aid.

Germany probably expected that as a result of its propaganda activities it would obtain the agreement of the Western Powers to revise the Corridor problem at an internationally favorable moment. This concept was, to some extent, a prologue to the Munich agreements.

[4] *Trial of the Major War Criminals,* Vol. XXXIV, Document C-135.

# From the Nomination of Wysocki as Envoy
## Up to Westerplatte
### *January, 1931—March, 1933*

DR. ALFRED WYSOCKI, undersecretary of state at the Ministry of Foreign Affairs, was nominated envoy to Berlin on January 10, 1931. Roman Knoll had been his precedessor at this post since July 1, 1928.

The years 1931 and 1932 marked a crucial period of discord in Polish-German relations. The tariff war, started in 1925, was still dragging on. Although negotiations led to the signing of the trade agreement (March 17, 1930) and its ratification by the Polish Sejm (March 11, 1931), the German Parliament postponed ratification indefinitely.

Chancellor Brüning's government was determined in its anti-Polish policy, pushing openly to the forefront the problem of revision of the Polish-German frontier. Foreign Minister Curtius made no bones about the matter; in his conversation with Great Britain's ambassador, Horace Rumbold, on July 3, 1930, he declared plainly that Germany could not be reconciled to its present frontier in the east.[1]

Soon afterward, on August 10, Reich Minister-without-portfolio Gottfried Treviranus delivered a speech in front of the Reichstag building in Berlin, in the course of which he said:

"In the depth of our souls we remember the torn land on the Vistula, the bleeding wound on the eastern border, this crippled split in the Reich's lungs. We think of what brutal pressure forced Wilson to an abnormal separation of East Prussia, to what equivocal fate Danzig was sentenced. The future of the Polish neighbor who, to a certain degree, owes his country to sacrifices of German blood can only be safe if Germany and Poland are not constantly in a state of alarm caused by an unjustly drawn frontier line. . . . Frontiers of injustice will not withstand the right of the nation and the national will to live." [2]

To a vehement protest by August Zaleski, Polish minister of foreign affairs, the German Legation in Warsaw responded that "the speech of the Reich Minister neither alters the bases of Polish-German relations nor is irreconcilable with the binding treaties. It is unthinkable that Minister

[1] *Documents on British Foreign Policy, 1919–1939*, Series 2, Vol. I, No. 311.
[2] Quoted from Krasuski, *Stosunki polsko-niemieckie, 1926–1932*, p. 297.

Treviranus would intend to evoke by his speech the impression that Germany plans to change the Polish-German frontier by force. Indeed, it is obvious that German foreign policy tends to revise the Polish-German frontier by peaceful methods; this point of view has been shared by all German governments, and has been clearly stated by them all." [3]

In March, 1931, Chancellor Brüning himself, in a speech delivered at Bytom, attacked Poland's frontiers.

Simultaneously, the German government was busy in the forum of the League of Nations, where it accused the Polish government of violating the rights of German minorities in Poland. In 1931 debates in the League on this matter lasted from January to September.

Józef Lipski was head of the Western Department at the Polish Ministry of Foreign Affairs during these years. In his office and under his direction, political instructions were prepared and forwarded to Mr. Wysocki in Berlin.

DOCUMENT 1     Lipski to Wysocki

Warsaw, February 23, 1931
*Strictly Confidential*

Thank you very much for the letters of February 16 and 21. In view of the considerable accumulation of problems to be discussed by the Ministry and the Legation which are not yet quite ready for basic instructions, I am taking the liberty of making a brief outline of certain problems of mutual interest in the range of Polish-German relations, and informing you on the subject of a number of current matters. I utilize, in doing so, the authorization contained in your letter, and I assume that information supplied in this way will save time and will facilitate the exchange of opinions between the Department and the Legation.

*1. Development of Internal Relations in the German Reich*

We are intensely absorbed in this problem, which, in my opinion, is becoming a sort of pivot in the development of international relations for the near future.

It is worth noting that the deprivation by Germany of its strongest political postwar personality—Stresemann—the rapid reaction of German nationalistic opinion to the accomplished evacuation of the Rhineland, and, finally, the outcome of the last elections to the Reichstag have

[3] *Ibid.*, p. 298.

all resulted in a temporary sobering effect in the West which is undoubtedly favorable to us. The impossibility of normal parliamentary governments in the Reich, Hitlerite subversive action, the upsurge of Communist votes, all these must have naturally caused a slowdown in the
tempo of collaboration with the Germans. Thus, in the eyes of well-
informed international observers, the importance of Poland as a peace-
contributing factor must have grown, situated as it is between a Germany in a state of political chaos and Bolshevik Russia.

In view of the above reasons, we are laying great stress upon the
necessity of observing closely a certain development of deeper significance which has been in the making for several months on the territory
of the Reich, an activity conducted by Chancellor Brüning (as far as we
can judge from here) with great consistency, and until now with some
degree of success, aimed at appeasing the German mentality: that of
forming a government which would inspire confidence beyond the frontiers of the Reich (as a matter of fact, a return of the Stresemann
system), considering of course the present altered position of Germany
and the changes in the international situation which have since occurred.
Evidently, such an attempt to restore a normal system of government in
the Reich must provide the Chancellor with far-reaching possibilities to
claim material and moral assistance from the West, bearing in mind the
tremendous interests of the Western Powers in Germany. We have to
consider this fact most seriously, since it results from the whole international constellation of our times. I should just like to mention the almost
panicky apprehension of French opinion to any kind of political or
financial convulsion. English opinion considers the normalization of relations with Germany as a factor of utmost importance to European
peace and a guarantee against too close contacts of the German right
wing with the Soviets. The role undertaken by the Chancellor is very
risky and difficult under the present circumstances, since he has to fight
on all fronts with Hitlerites, Communists, and even certain groups of the
center. Brüning's personal assets in this decisive contest are of the greatest importance for determining the probability of the final results of his
action. On many occasions, in my conversations with foreign representatives on the shortage of outstanding personalities in Germany, I was told
that Brüning is the man of vision. Already in the spring of last year
some well-informed American diplomats called my attention to Brüning.
I report here for your information several characteristic opinions about

him that I have recently noted. Mr. Poliakoff states that a final breach of
the center by the Hitlerites will push Brüning on the track of a more
peaceful policy, which might have an undesirable effect on Poland's
interests in England.

From Stockholm I have the opinion of an eminent editor of Swedish
journals with a thorough knowledge of the German situation who is
personally acquainted with Chancellor Brüning. In his opinion, Brüning
is the man who will accomplish a basic change in German policy. He is
apparently far better educated than Stresemann and has plenty of arguments to support his thesis: "He has the appearance of a very refined
and sophisticated Catholic Monsignor." This editor's thought is that Brüning will try to launch the idea of a rapprochement with France and has
already recruited quite a number of adherents in Germany. In military
circles which oppose this concept, Brüning is nevertheless respected as
an officer with a distinguished record gained during the Great War.

Summing up the above information, the question arises what course
Brüning will take in his foreign policy. Even before Geneva, especially
when the Chancellor was touring the eastern provinces, the moderate
tone of his speeches—devoid of provocative revisionistic allusions—was
very significant. I should even say that the Chancellor's pronouncements
were to a certain degree dissimilar in tone from the aggressive accent
Curtius was obviously proffering to the right wing. Rumors have persistently circulated in Geneva about misunderstandings between Brüning
and Curtius and the alleged secret intention of the Chancellor to take
over the portfolio of the Minister of Foreign Affairs. Brüning—in my
opinion—is striving in the first place to create an atmosphere of confidence for his government in the international field, and he is therefore
avoiding too drastic anti-Polish or other stances. However, the success
of his mission depends on the restoration of the unbalanced financial
situation of the Reich by reinforced credit abroad. Hitlerism is, to a
large extent, a product of the economic crisis. A mitigation of the crisis
means appeasement of radical right- and left-wing elements.

I suppose that a further stage of the Chancellor's plans will be a
revision of the Young Plan, which is closely connected with the attempts
to revive Germany economically. In this respect, Hindenburg's statement on the reparations burdens, made on the occasion of the presentation of your letters of credence, seemed very characteristic, along with
the well-known resolution of the Reichstag. It appears that the revision

of the Young Plan has already become quite a pertinent question in the program of the German government for the near future.

I have taken the liberty of expanding more fully on the above problem, as we are presently quite absorbed in it here. Of course, it is difficult to have a complete grasp of these complicated matters from Warsaw and I would therefore very much appreciate your *mise au point* with regard to my suppositions, which might not be in accord with the actual situation.

### 2. Ratification of the Liquidation and Trade Agreements

The delay in the ratification of the liquidation agreement occurred when matters pertaining to foreign policy came up during a discussion at the Commission for Foreign Affairs and it consequently became necessary to await the return of Minister Zaleski from Geneva. Besides, there was a change of officials in charge of the agreement; Professor Krzyżanowski was replaced by Deputy Jeszke from Poznań. This fact was also a cause for the delay in ratification. As the matter stands now, the trade agreement with Germany will be discussed by the Commission for Foreign Affairs on Wednesday, February 25, and then both agreements will be presented simultaneously to the plenum. On this occasion Mr. Zaleski will deliver a speech dealing with the two agreements. At the Senate Mr. Wielowieyski was appointed to be in charge of the liquidation and trade agreements, and he has already prepared his report. Therefore it is to be expected that approximately within a fortnight the agreements will be ratified. . . .

### 4. Zechlin Case

For some time the German Legation in Warsaw has been circulating rumors that Herr Zechlin, at present German consul general at Petrograd, will replace Director Trautmann at the Auswärtiges Amt. The German Legation is, of course, trying to serve this bit of news in the most digestible form for the Ministry of Foreign Affairs, and ostensibly praises Herr Zechlin's accomplishments in the field of Polish-German collaboration. It was suggested that, in his capacity as the greatest expert on Polish-German relations, Herr Zechlin prepared the agreements to which Rauscher only put the final touches.

As a matter of fact, the truth about Herr Zechlin—who has a perfect knowledge of the situation in Poland, who worked in Poznań for a long time before the war, and who speaks fluent Polish—is that he has been one of the most rabid opponents of any sort of understanding with Poland. Mr. Schimitzek [4] is in a position to inform you fully on this. Only in 1927, upon direct negotiations with Stresemann, was the change of the official in charge of the Polish Desk at the A.A. effected, and Herr Zechlin was transferred to Russia.

His return to replace Trautmann, besides being a big promotion for him, could in my opinion be interpreted as a tendency of the A.A. to follow the line of continual disputes in its relations with Poland on the question of minorities. From the point of view of the general German policy, this is not impossible. The Germans are well aware that at the present time their claims for a revision of our frontiers have no practical chances for realization. Their ideas on this problem anticipate a number of stages, such as financial reinforcement (revision of the Young Plan), growth of military power (possible fiasco of the disarmament conference), and the revision of frontiers only at the third stage.

Nevertheless, especially since they are counting on such a long procedure, they try to keep the problem of Polish-German relations in a state of agitation, even if only for the benefit of their domestic and international public opinion. Reaction in Germany against the political aspects of our treaties was so strong because for international opinion this meant a stabilization of the *status quo*.

But to return to Zechlin.

It is obvious for us here that a reaction of the Legation in Berlin against this nomination is out of the question, since this could jeopardize the whole contact for the future. On the occasion of a talk I had with Geisenheimer, who knows Zechlin only too well (since Zechlin spoiled his chances of concluding the trade agreement, so important for coal interests in Silesia), I brought up the subject. Geisenheimer told me that there are two nominations under discussion for the post of Trautmann: Zechlin or von Grünau, former consul general at Katowice. Herr G. will at any rate try to give the word to Bülow. . . .

## 7. German Pacifists

German pacifists (in the person of Professor Foerster) have approached us for more substantial financial aid, finally claiming very considerable sums. The matter is under discussion at the Ministry of Foreign Affairs.

[4] Stanisław Schimitzek, counselor of the Polish Legation in Berlin since February, 1931.

The pacifists declare that, under the present conditions in Germany, their activities should be strongly backed. They stress that, in the general campaign of lies pervading the whole German press, their press organs alone are in a position to inject some portion of truth into German opinion with regard to the real situation in Poland and its attitude toward Germany.

Your confidential opinion as to the effectiveness of more substantial aid from us in support of this movement would be of great assistance to us.

### 8. Concrete Works in Polish-German Relations for the Future

In the field of Polish-German negotiations we have a series of projects in preparation. The next two weeks are to be devoted to pushing the liquidation and trade agreements through the chambers. You have probably already been informed that on February 16 the ratification documents of the valorization agreement were exchanged, together with annexes.

Future negotiations will deal with the liquidation of still pending incidents of the Graebe-Naumann [5] claim, cancellation of the Arbitration Tribunal in Paris, a complex of insurance problems which are of great importance and urgency, and, finally, a number of secondary matters of a legal-settlement nature (Prądzyński's negotiations).

We discussed with Schimitzek before his departure that it might be useful if some negotiations of a more general character, and with good prospects for finalization, were entrusted to the care of the Legation in Berlin in order to create an important contact with German offices on concrete matters. If you agree with this suggestion, please let me know, since I must set up a plan for these negotiations in the near future.

### 9. General Considerations

I am now turning to our general tactics toward Germany. It seems to me that they must develop basically as follows: We should make a further outward display of our good will. Putting agreements up for ratification has undoubtedly had a salutary effect abroad.

Even in Germany this achievement was favorably commented on by the leftist and the democratic press.

[5] Kurt Graebe and Eugene Naumann, of the German minority in Poland, lodged a claim with the League of Nations against the Polish government, accusing it of applying the land reform to the detriment of Polish citizens of German origin.

Here I pass to another point. We should endeavor to emphasize the principle of collaboration with elements in Germany which sincerely strive for the peaceful development of international coexistence. This principle, which the Germans themselves could hardly oppose, would give us a certain freedom of action; for example, in the field of economic relations in connection with the possibility of putting the trade agreement into practice. Additionally, this [principle] puts us on the same level as France and England. Referring further to my previous remarks about Brüning's policy, it is my opinion that French and English politicians will undoubtedly look for support to the so-called *elements raisonables* in Germany. An attempt to find bases for contact with these elements, although exceedingly difficult, is—in my view—the only possible direction for our action within the Reich.

The practical application of these principles in the fields where they would meet with the response of German public opinion (such as the question of our relations with German minorities in Silesia, the application of land reform, and many others) would, in my opinion, require more extensive investigation and coordination of the exact line of action.

We are conducting studies here on this.

*Józef Lipski*

DOCUMENT 2    Lipski to Wysocki

**Warsaw, May 20, 1931**

I would like to inform you, in strict confidence, about our intended policy toward Germany, which has been approved by Marshal Piłsudski in the course of his recent consultations with Minister Zaleski and Vice-Minister Beck.[6]

In view of the development of the international situation in connection with the recently created Austro-German union,[7] the Marshal feels

---

[6] Józef Beck had been undersecretary of state at the Ministry of Foreign Affairs since December 2, 1930; he became minister of foreign affairs on November 2, 1932, and held this post until 1939.

[7] A customs union between Austria and Germany was concluded on March 21, 1931. However, the Council of the League of Nations decided to submit to the Permanent Court of International Justice the question as to whether such a customs union could be established. On September 5, 1931, the Court decided

that the Polish government should at present avoid anything which might in the future restrict its freedom of action.

Bearing this in mind, the Marshal does not consider it advisable for us to enforce the trade agreement with the Reich for the time being.

In the light of these basic directions, I asked Minister Beck, when I discussed Polish-German relations with him, how we should deal with a number of concrete problems still pending between Poland and Germany which should now be finalized, such as: negotiations on insurance problems, Graebe-Naumann, cancellation of the Mixed Polish-German Arbitration Tribunal, etc. I drew Minister Beck's attention to a certain relaxation in secondary matters in Polish-German relations, which is confirmed by your reports. Consequently, this might be the right moment to try to finalize these concrete matters, taking advantage of the tension in which the Reich finds itself on the western and southern sectors.

Minister Beck fully agreed with my point of view, and felt that all matters of this kind should be concluded in the favorable moment of a better atmosphere. The Marshal is only concerned with the question of the trade agreement, which is of basic importance, and is to a certain extent binding.

I take the liberty of informing you of these matters confidentially in order to keep you abreast of these momentous events.

Obviously I am not disclosing to the Germans any change of tactics with regard to the trade agreement; I avoid conversations on this subject. At any rate, I abstain from taking any steps through interested parties, which would otherwise act to speed up the enforcement of the agreement by the German side.

I succeeded in delegating Lechnicki [8] to Geneva; he will provide information both to the Western Department and to the Legation in Berlin about the backstage rumors of Geneva. He is confidentially instructed on how to remain reserved toward the German delegation with regard to

that this union conflicted with the protocol signed with Austria on October 4, 1922, by England, France, Italy, and Czechoslovakia, and later by Belgium and Spain, calling upon them to "abstain from any negotiations or from any economic or financial engagement calculated directly or indirectly to compromise this independence" (see *DGFP*, Series D, I, 552).

[8] Tadeusz Lechnicki, deputy head of the Western Department at the Ministry of Foreign Affairs.

this basic economic problem, in case the Germans launch some tentative initiative in our direction.

I would like to take this opportunity to inform you that, according to news obtained from French circles, Ambassador Margerie is due to retire in the near future. Also, the fate of Ambassador Fleriau in London and of Count Clausel in Vienna is sealed. It will be a matter of some interest to see whom the French will send to Berlin. I think such a decision will not be taken before June 13, that is, the date when Laval's cabinet is due to resign. Besides, the question whether Briand will stay or retire from office, even if only for a time, is of utmost importance for us. For the moment, in case Briand resigns, I think Herriot will have the best chance, especially since he is labeled as a pacifist minister abroad. At the same time he does not appear to be a red scarecrow to the right wing, owing to his recent very firm public statements proclaiming respect for treaties and the security problem.

In the whole question of the last French elections, I am concerned by the fact that the leftists in France, who suffered an obvious defeat at the presidential election, will strive by all means possible to take revenge in the year 1932.

*Józef Lipski*

DOCUMENT 3     Wysocki to Lipski

Berlin, May 23, 1931

I am much obliged for the information contained in your letter of May 19,[9] all the more valuable since I was not aware of the subject of consultations recently held at the Belveder.[10] For my part I would like to add that for a long time now I have never mentioned the trade agreement in my conversations with official persons in Germany. Whenever I am asked for an opinion, I always refer to the changed situation due to the customs policy of Minister Schiele, which is depriving us of any benefit the agreement might otherwise bring us. Personally, I do not believe that the ratification of the agreement will be possible before the

[9] The exact date is May 20, 1931.
[10] The palace where Piłsudski lived.

Reichstag session in the fall if the government does not alter its attitude toward the right wing and the agrarian party.

In my last conversation with M. Margerie I tried to sound his chances of remaining in Berlin.

He was very depressed by Briand's possible resignation, evidently considering him as his protector. He was visibly upset because of plotting which in the last moment prevented his election. He declared that complete chaos prevails at present at the Quai d'Orsay, since nobody knows whether Briand will remain or retire and who will be his successor. They apparently plan to recall to active service an undersecretary of state, which—in Margerie's opinion—would be detrimental for the course of affairs.

If Margerie should leave Berlin, I would be one of those sincerely regretting his loss, as ours was a relation of true friendship, facilitating the arduous task of obtaining information.

In accordance with the Ministry's request I had two conversations with the Yugoslav envoy, Balugdzic. I shall report separately on the results.

Looking forward to the continuation of our correspondence, which is always of value and very useful to me, I remain . . .

*Alfred Wysocki*

DOCUMENT 4    Lipski to Wysocki

June 9, 1931

General attention is increasingly focused on two basic problems in the international arena, namely, the question of war indemnities and the future disarmament conference.

The conference at Chequers, about the results of which, outside of fragments of information from our Embassy, I do not yet possess full details, has undoubtedly made topical to a great extent the possibility of a revision of the Young Plan. The attitude taken by the United States will be a decisive factor, since the whole question of German payments is closely connected with the complex of inter-Allied debts. Stimson's and Mellon's trips to Europe should be given our closest attention, and we have today instructed the posts concerned accordingly. Filipowicz [11] informs us today of the possibility of certain American concessions in the financial field, provided their rearmament demands are properly satisfied.

In connection with these problems, it is essential for us to acquire the most complete analysis possible of the internal political and economic situation of the Reich. Germany outwardly plays the Stresemann card, pointing out that, if it does not obtain satisfaction with regard to reparations, a political upheaval will take place which Brüning will be unable to master, and then a Hitlerite government will come into power, proclaiming the abolition of obligations under the treaty. It is to be expected that the ghost of chaos in Germany has a somewhat haunting effect on the minds of the potentates of international finance. According to what Skirmunt [12] says, even Henderson thinks the situation in Germany is extremely tense. Consequently, it is important to understand what is to be considered tactics in the behavior of the responsible German elements and what is reality. In my opinion, from our point of view we should observe the situation in Germany from two angles: political and economic. Undoubtedly, some financial burdens in the Reich may politically serve as a brake to the active policy of aggression against Poland; on the other hand, a breakdown of the German market economically would result in deteriorating repercussions on the whole complex of Eastern Europe's economy, by which we would also suffer. So, in my opinion, the best situation from our point of view would be the state of a certain dependence of the German economy on the West through reparations payments, with the avoidance, however, of too strong shake-ups and disturbances on the international financial market with respect to economic development in this part of Europe.

I have taken the liberty of drafting these few loose thoughts for your information, making the observation that we here are preparing a very close consultation with regard to problems connected with the possible revision of the Young Plan. Therefore, any information pertaining to this question, and particularly with regard to the internal situation of the Reich, will be of utmost interest to us.

*Józef Lipski*

[11] Tytus Filipowicz, Polish minister in Washington.
[12] Konstanty Skirmunt, Polish ambassador in London.

DOCUMENT 5    Wysocki to Zaleski

NO. 2823/T                                        Berlin, July 9, 1931
                                                  *Confidential*
                                                  [Addressed *ad personam*]

German foreign policy has entered a phase of official visits. With Chequers already over, the next step will be Paris and then Rome. The governments of the above powers did not propose these visits; the initiative came from Germany. Italy alone, through its ambassador here, asked not to be overlooked at a moment when Germany is seeking personal contacts with other states. Also on his own initiative, but as a direct result of a skillful propaganda campaign, the American secretary of state, Stimson, will visit Berlin.

   However, most significant of all these trips will be the departure of the Chancellor and the Minister of Foreign Affairs to Paris.

   On the occasion of the realization of the Hoover Plan,[13] the Germans have become convinced once again how powerful France is financially, and in consequence also politically.

   I had the opportunity of discussing this matter with several prominent Berlin bankers, who were unanimous in declaring that an understanding with France is an urgent necessity: "Our stock exchange will not calm down so long as the hostile attitude toward us prevails in Paris." Even financial potentates of the United States make the further flow of their capital dependent on the relaxation of tension in French public opinion and of French mistrust of Germany. Berlin is also well aware that the initial difficulties in Paris over the immediate approval of the Hoover Plan stem almost exclusively from the French opinion that this project is the first step of an action initiated by the Germans to abolish the Young Plan and free themselves from any burden of war obligations. It is now therefore very important that this mistrust be dispersed and disbelief turned into confidence.

   German banking circles are behind this initiative and heavy industry is following in their footsteps. The German government, whose indulgence toward belligerent nationalism is rather alarming, agrees in principle with this necessity; Brüning's broadcast speech confirms this.

-----

[13] The Hoover Plan (1931) instituted a moratorium on war indemnities to relieve the Germans in their financial situation.

However, he is concerned about the forthcoming political discussion in Paris and about the obligations which perhaps will have to be accepted in order to appease France and regain its confidence. These obligations, if pushed too far, might topple him in the country, since the government of the Reich will then be obliged to suppress those German politicians whose activity is the very source of disturbances that make Europe resent Germany.

At any rate, the moment is near when something could be gained from Germany. Under threat of a repeated run on banks for foreign currency, and the withdrawal in panic of their own and foreign capital, the Germans are ready for a good many sacrifices. Would it not be advisable to take advantage of this moment?

After looking through informational material and reports of the Legation for the last several months, I have come to the conclusion that Germany's attitude toward Poland has not improved in the least.

In my conversations with German officials, primarily with President Hindenburg, they stressed the necessity of relaxing and improving our relations. These, however, were just empty words. The attitude of the government toward the trade agreement, which could easily be ratified by the Parliament when the Nationalists and the Hitlerites retire from it; the behavior of Luther, the president of the Reichsbank, who most vigorously vetoed our election to the council of the Basel Bank; the failure to extend the wheat agreement; the declaration that Germany will abstain from any agreement for export of grain if Poland takes part in it (my conversation with Soviet Ambassador Khinchuk); and, finally, the attempt to seduce Rumania, Hungary, and Yugoslavia with favorable terms for trade agreements with the goal of totally isolating Poland— here is the harvest of the last months. If we add to this the Stahlhelm demonstrations in Wrocław, the recent vindictive publications by eminent university professors, the speeches of high-ranking officials, and the tone of the press campaign, we shall then understand the irrefutable truth that, when the question of Poland arises, there is no difference between the opinion of the Reich government and that of General-Oberst von Seeckt, who says in his *Wege der deutschen Aussenpolitik* that "in all questions of German foreign policy *Poland should be treated as a basic enemy.*"

What is to be done? Should it not be ascertained if this is, indeed, the actual state of affairs? Should we not strive precisely now, during this period of constant visits and discussions, to draw Polish-German relations into the orbit of international interests, to strive for some personal direct exchange of opinion between the heads of the two countries and their ministers of foreign affairs?

I am taking the liberty of asking you to give some thought to this question and to inform me accordingly of your decision, so that I can if necessary undertake, first, preliminary, strictly confidential, and private investigations, and later discuss the question of a possible Polish-German meeting, not only with Minister Curtius, but particularly with Chancellor Brüning.

In view of the atmosphere prevailing here, I exclude *a priori* the possibility of an official visit in Warsaw or Berlin, but consider that a meeting on neutral ground could probably be arranged.

Awaiting your reply, on which will depend my inaugural talks and my endeavors to obtain an audience with Chancellor, which, in view of this constant traveling and heavy work-load, will not be an easy task, I remain . . .

*Alfred Wysocki*

DOCUMENT 6   Wysocki to Beck

Berlin, July 19, 1931

English and American visits are postponed either until the end of this month or until the beginning of August. In case you are not inclined to consider my suggestion to prepare the ground here for a direct understanding between the governments of Poland and Germany along the lines accepted by England and France, I would like to have your answer whether it would be possible for me to start, about August 1, a cure as prescribed by my doctor. . . .

Coming back to my idea, I am taking the liberty of drawing your attention to the fact that I see no reason why Poland should not discuss touchy matters with Germany, even the question of the revision of the frontiers and German political claims. The present state of silent subterranean strife in the economic, financial, and propaganda fields cannot last much longer. Particularly since Germany is determined, as soon as order is restored in its own finances, to settle the Young Plan and, after the disarmament conference, "the Polish question." Now, if we take up this problem, which is a main source of concern and lack of confidence toward Germany, as well as toward Poland, we will gain the support of a part of world opinion, and we will have the backing of a powerful France to face a weakened and isolated Germany. We have no guarantee that the present situation will not change for the worse. Even here in Berlin I can see how the questions of the revision of frontiers and of the Corridor are becoming more and more timely. There is an increasing number of foreign politicians and journalists who are of the opinion that Poland will inevitably have to give in under the pressure of public opinion. I am convinced of this from what I hear from Americans and Englishmen, who are genuinely surprised to hear my stereotyped arguments that I refuse so much as to discuss these matters for the simple reason that they just do not exist for me.

A frank, even slightly brutal, but basic exchange of opinions between the prime ministers of both countries and their foreign ministers would lead not only to the conclusion of the trade agreement but also to a considerable relaxation in the field of propaganda and in the policy of economically isolating Poland. In a few months Germany will again stand firmly on its feet, ready for further action, and again radical nationalistic elements will take over here. Would it then be worth while to argue with this kind of Germany?

Please let me have at least your opinion on this question.

Awaiting your reply, I remain . . .

*Alfred Wysocki*


DOCUMENT 7    Wysocki to Lipski

NO. 2994/T                                      Berlin, July 20, 1931

Yesterday was cold and dreary, and it was raining. So I went to the movies, since I was awaiting news from Paris at any moment and decided not to leave town. I must confess that, absorbed as I was in my thoughts about what was happening in Paris just then at the Brüning and Curtius conferences, I hardly paid attention to what was shown on the screen. Suddenly I was aroused out of my meditations by shouts: "Heil, Heil," and by sounds of a melody well known from the time of the war. On the screen, detachments of the Reichswehr were cavalcading on superb horses and in perfect war drill, followed by *Totenkopf* hussars, Bavarian uhlans, dragoons, etc. Finally, the picture changed, showing the General Staff reviewing the parade. In the forefront, clad in his characteristic black hussar uniform covered with decorations, stood Marshal Mackensen, next to him General von Einem, a general in active service of the Reichswehr, and Commander von Stülpnagel of the IVth Wehrkreis. Mackensen's entourage consisted of nearly one hundred military dignitaries of all branches, in smartly tailored prewar uniforms obviously just fresh from the tailor shops. Since this was a sound film, we were treated to some speeches as well. The old mayor of Dresden, Socialist Dr. Külz, talked as if he had never had anything in common with a party which often, when necessary, came out against militarism. He recalled the old saying of Derfflinger, "Aufgesessen und angetrabt" ["They mounted and rode on"], and repeated it twice with obvious delight.

The audience rose time after time with applause and shouts to salute the Army.

And all this was happening on July 19, 1931, on the second day of the Paris conference. . . .

N.B. There is something else I have on my mind. Germany constantly threatens that, if it is not granted a loan or this or that political concession, it will become a stage for Communist disturbances and a Bolshevik country. This argument can be heard here at every step. However, it is difficult to believe. Now, when the banks were closed the Communists had a unique opportunity to start disturbances. The population was stupefied, deprived of cash, and whipped into a panic by the press, which, by order of the Presseleitung, painted as black a picture of the situation as possible. And what did the Communists do? They issued a rather mild proclamation and avoided clashes with the police anywhere in Berlin; in the provinces, in two or three localities of the western industrial basins, they did shoot at the police, and the police shot back at the Communists, but it was all done so delicately that not a single man was killed or even injured. Does this not appear as a sort of insurance of the German rear by Bolshevik organizations, with the silent blessing of Moscow?

*Alfred Wysocki*

DOCUMENT 8    Lipski to Wysocki

NO. P·II. 5307/31                              Warsaw, October 20, 1931
                                               *Confidential*

Thank you very much for your letter of October 15, No. 4201/T. I can assure you that, together with Lechnicki and Fiedler, we are working very hard to establish a principal line of action toward Germany in connection with the possibility of discussions for a mutual relaxation of tensions. Presently we are still handicapped by the illness of Mr. Zaleski, who is bedridden and does not accept political reports, which is causing a delay in obtaining final decisions on these matters. However, I expect to secure them in a couple of days, and I am even considering a visit to Berlin by Lechnicki or myself in order to discuss these matters personally with you.

In the meantime I would like to share some conclusions with you, established here in our Department upon investigation of news signaled by our Berlin Legation with regard to indications that the Germans desire some sort of rapprochement with Poland.

Undoubtedly, in the minds of responsible German leaders there is a gradual recognition that, in view of Brüning's policy toward France and the approaching international settlements of great importance for Germany (reparations, disarmament), it has become a matter of urgency to clarify the Polish-German problems to the extent that they should not jeopardize German foreign policy.

It is also possible that the very nature of German internal affairs, owing to the acute economic crisis which threatens to become more serious with the oncoming winter season, combined with certain political disorders, is forcing the government of Chancellor Brüning, who as a representative of the center is in constant fear of Communism, to seek better relations with the immediate eastern neighbor of Germany.

From our point of view, however, it is most important to determine to what extent this German attempt at rapprochement is just a matter of strategy designed to evoke a desirable effect in the West, and to what extent we can count on some genuine effort to normalize relations with Poland. And also we should determine how far Germany is prepared to go in seeking an understanding with Poland.

We understand that it will be possible to answer this question only in the course of preliminary talks with our German partners, discussions for which we must have absolutely precise instructions.

I would like to call your attention to the fact that the first attempt at a Polish-German understanding on a larger scale was achieved during the period of the realization of the Young Plan. Then, as you recall, Germany found itself in a similar forced situation in relation to Poland and, realizing that it would be impossible for it to pass through the Hague Conference without an agreement with Poland, decided to conclude the liquidation agreement with us, completed later on by means of an economic understanding.

During these attempts at a rapprochement, we acted quite openly, using the apparatus of the press, winning over particular spheres of interest inside the Reich, and finally opening a broad discussion in the parliamentary forum. It then became obvious that German public opinion was not quite ripe for a rapprochement with Poland. The usefulness of the liquidation agreement was not canceled, since it had a completely realistic side, especially in the financial field. However, its political value, as a direct factor in Polish-German relations, decreased nearly to zero.

These past experiences compel us to use especially careful tactics if talks with Germany are to be undertaken once more.

As far as the formalities are concerned, in our opinion, this time such conversations should not be given press coverage for internal use. We have to bear in mind the difficulties with which Chancellor Brüning has to cope on the home front, which might greatly increase once he decides to take up the Polish question in earnest. As to the attitude we should adopt in face of the advances now made by the German side, which indicate an inclination on their part to begin talks, we think that too much zeal on our part would not help the cause.

For the time being, we should define our position as that of a state which in the last months has taken a number of steps that indicate our far-reaching good will toward our western neighbor.

And just to illustrate our efforts: the trade agreement was ratified, an objective stand was maintained in the face of the Austro-German union, a moderate reaction was displayed toward the Stahlhelm incident at Wrocław, the Young Plan was favorably received, the Polish press acknowledged with satisfaction the peaceful endeavors of the Reich Chancellor.

What was the German government's attitude at that time? The trade agreement was not ratified, the lumber and wheat agreements were not extended, aggressive action was taken against us on the territory of the Reich, our candidacy for the International Bank was opposed, etc.

*Lipski*

Years later Mr. Wysocki wrote about the 1931–32 period of his diplomatic service as follows:

In the long span of my service I have never lived days and months so personally enervating and disagreeable as those during the years 1931 and 1932. The atmosphere was becoming oppressive. At the Auswärtiges Amt I was received with haughty indifference as a representative of an illusory state, *ein Saisonstaat*. The prominent historian Professor Hoesch, president of the East European Institute, gave his students the following thesis to work on at a seminar on modern history: "Owing to what political and economic reasons can the Polish state not exist?" The daily press published accusation after accusation, putting the blame on Poland for instigating a war against the Reich and for persecuting German minorities, and circulated with relish any bit of news unfavorable to Poland. Journalists of Jewish origin played quite an important role in this campaign, clad in the long robes of defenders of "threatened Germania"; by attacking Poland they tried to safeguard their own position in the face of ever-growing nationalistic feelings. Not far from our Legation vulgar demonstrations took place regularly that illustrated the tragic fate of German victims of the brutal Polish soldiery. Also, we were boycotted socially, and we received invitations only for strictly official receptions at the Auswärtiges Amt. The tariff war ruined our economic balance, and each payment of German reparations was intentionally postponed indefinitely.

This situation can best be illustrated by a conversation I had in the summer of 1932 with an elderly lady whose garden adjoined that of the Legation. As we were both fond of flowers and plants, we often tended them with my wife. One day the lady approached the iron fence and expressed her surprise that we put so much work and expense into this garden. When I asked her why she was so surprised, she declared that after all we would soon be compelled to leave it all. It was my turn to express my astonishment, and I was informed that we would have to leave Berlin very soon, as the war with Poland would start at any moment. She added that her son said so, and he was in the Stahlhelm, where this was common talk.

Shortly afterward I received instructions [to which Mr. Lipski referred] that I should "investigate the attitude of the main political parties toward Poland."

I did not approach politicians of the stature of Hugenberg, at that time omnipotent leader of the nationalists, owner of several newspapers and a press agency, or Seldte, the chief of the Stahlhelm, or Treviranus, who just recently had said: "Give us back our territories and I will be the first to go to Warsaw and toast your health and peace between Poland and Germany." I confess, however, that I was counting to some extent on the cooperation of the Catholic Center Party, whose leader, Brüning, was the head of the government. I therefore called on Msgr. Kaas, director of the foreign department of the Center, and on von Papen, a very generous benefactor of this party, and a favorite of old President Hindenburg. However, they were both rather evasive and considered the settlement of the Corridor problem a condition *sine qua non* of normal Polish-German relations.

Hagemann was a man of confidence of the Center. He was the editor of the foreign department of *Germania*. In my interview with him he said that he considered that Germany's most urgent and essential demands were: total equality, settlement of the revision of the frontiers, and the annexation of Austria.

To my question as to what should be understood as the revision of frontiers, he replied that it meant recovery of all territories basically German and the removal of the anomaly, namely, the Corridor—a wedge thrust into the living body of the Reich. Hagemann further informed me, with a certain naïveté, that the Center was striving to achieve its demands not by war but by exclusively peaceful methods.

I then realized that the program of the Catholic Center in no way differed from that of the nationalists, retaliators, and Prussian Junkers; that the Center people only pretended that they wanted to reach these goals by peaceful methods, while the others openly called for war.

Only the Socialist Löbe, at that time president of the Reichstag, avoided aggressive accents in his speeches. He stressed the advantage of discontinuing mutual accusations and press attacks; he thought it advisable to appease public opinion and improve commercial relations, but he called the Corridor an anomaly difficult to accept, and declared that the Socialists disagreed with the ideology of the regime in Poland.[14]

[14] Alfred Wysocki, "Początek dramatu," *Tygodnik Powszechny* (Cracow), Feb. 15, 1959, No. 7 (525).

# Westerplatte[1]
## March, 1933

---

AFTER HITLER'S COMING TO POWER amidst general agitation, when unfettered Nazi forces, for long years fed on ultranationalistic catchwords, were exhilarating in the atmosphere of victory and their propaganda penetrated to the incendiary centers on the borders of the Reich, provoking ferment and many incidents, a dispute between Poland and Danzig occurred in connection with the problem of the harbor police in the Free City. This matter had serious consequences.

Polish-Danzig disputes had a long story behind them, reaching back to the resolutions of the Versailles Treaty, which were later developed and completed by the Paris Convention [2] and the Warsaw Agreement.[3] On these fundamental international acts were based later resolutions of the high commissioners of the League; decisions of the Council of the League of Nations; sometimes, in more intricate cases, even sentences of the International Tribunal at The Hague; and, finally, agreements and conciliatory understandings between parties.

The intricacy of Danzig law suits, as well as their complicated procedure, often obscured the very purport of the disputes, creating a false picture of the real intentions of the Danzig Senate, whose action was inspired by Berlin. The Free City of Danzig was an ideal springboard for German revisionism, which constituted the main goal of Germany's foreign policy toward Poland.

Through disputes and everlasting differences, which were shifted from

[1] Printed in *Bellona* (London), 1951, Nos. 1–2.
[2] The Paris Convention, concluded on January 9, 1920, dealt with the settlement of archives ceded by Germany to Poland in accordance with the Treaty of Versailles, repayments to families of soldiers mobilized by Germany, pensions and annuities for residents of territories ceded to Poland, the settlement of guarantee matters for the issuance of Polish marks during the occupation of the Polish Kingdom, and the obligation by Germany to conclude an agreement on financial matters according to Article 238 of the Versailles Treaty.
[3] A trade agreement signed in Warsaw on March 17, 1930.

Danzig to the international forum at Geneva, Germany attempted to mold international opinion, explaining that the situation on the Polish-German frontier created by the Treaty of Versailles was untenable.

The problem of the harbor police in Danzig began in the year 1921, when the Council of the Harbor and Water Communications, composed of delegates of Poland and the Free City, as well as a neutral representative, decided to have a security service of its own to control the vast territory of the harbor and its establishments, including the custom-free zone.

The High Commissioner of the League, by a resolution of June 6, 1923, agreed that the Harbor Council should be given police personnel by the Danzig authorities as requested. This decision at first met with a protest from both the Senate and the Polish government. The Free City did not want to have an independent police force at the harbor, while Poland—in order to safeguard its trade interests—wanted the harbor police, subject to the Council, to be composed of Polish functionaries.

In September, 1923, an agreement between Poland and Danzig was reached, both parties accepting as a basis for the understanding the above-mentioned resolution of the High Commissioner. This agreement was binding for two years, when each of the parties was entitled to "revise its standpoint." In the year 1925 the League of Nations based its decision on the Polish-Danzig agreement of September, 1923, confirming the rights of the Harbor Council to control the police and issue orders to them. This situation lasted until 1933. The Senate was ill-disposed toward these rights of the Council, and when, owing to several incidents at the time that Polish vessels docked in Danzig in the beginning of the year 1933, the Polish delegate at the Harbor Council demanded that directives for the security service be explicitly stated, his motions met with a protest of the Free City representative. This was not a good omen for the future.

By a note of February 15, 1933, addressed to the [Polish] commissioner-general, Kazimierz Papée, the Senate unexpectedly and without previous talks with the Polish government canceled the agreement of September, 1923, giving notice at the same time about instructions issued for the withdrawal of the security service controlled by the Harbor Council and introducing their own police instead. By such action the Senate created a *fait accompli* in a territory where the main interests of Poland's foreign trade were concentrated.

This action of the Senate gave Warsaw food for thought. The Ministry of Foreign Affairs was investigating this matter not only because of the threat to Polish interests in Danzig but, in the first place, in the light of Polish-German relations. These relations were in a state of crucial tension, caused by incidents with Polish minorities, mass offenses and acts of violence against Jewish citizens of Poland and their property, and chiefly by constant revisionist agitation on the Polish frontier. An interview with Hitler by the *Sunday Express* of February 12, 1933, complicated the drastic situation still further, in spite of later commentaries from Berlin that free alterations were made in the text of the Chancellor's declarations. Speaking of the Corridor, Hitler stressed that it was a great injustice for the German nation. A few days later the Polish Minister of Foreign Affairs, in his speech before the Commission for Foreign Affairs at the Diet, replied significantly that the Polish government would adopt the same attitude toward Germany and German problems as was taken by the Reich toward Poland.

After long deliberation the Polish government gave an answer to the Danzig action. On February 20, 1933, the Commissioner-General of Poland handed one note to the Senate of the Free City and another to the Council of the Harbor and Water Communications.

The first of these notes confirmed that the Senate had broken the agreement with Poland unilaterally and that it had withdrawn the police force controlled by the Harbor Council without a previous understanding. The note stressed that the Polish-Danzig agreement did not foresee any change of the existing status either *de jure* or *de facto* by way of one-sided action. This argument was presented in the claim of *action-directe* against the Free City presented by the Polish government to the High Commissioner of the League on March 7 (that is, the day after the reinforcement of the Westerplatte garrison).

In the meantime, Warsaw wanted to settle the matter locally, avoiding entanglement in League procedures, the effectiveness of which seemed rather doubtful. Standing by its objections to the illegal action of the Senate the Polish government nevertheless expressed its consent to the cancellation of the 1923 agreement, which, as the note stated, created a totally unsatisfactory situation as far as security at the harbor was concerned, since the police ceded by the Senate to the Harbor Council were unable to handle incidents that had repeatedly occurred on previous occasions when Polish vessels touched at the harbor. This evoked the concern of Polish public opinion, especially in economic circles. At the end of the note, the Polish government reserved the right to undertake necessary steps to safeguard the interests of its citizens in case the Council of the Harbor and Water Communications was not in a position to maintain order in the harbor territories, especially in the free zone included in its administration. These obligations imposed on the Council resulted from the Paris Agreement.

The note to the Council of the Harbor and Water Communications, more precise in its contents, explained the aims of the Polish government. It suggested that the Harbor Council, in accordance with its rights, should without further delay organize its own security service. This force could be subordinate to the commander of harbor pilots, since the tasks of the pilots and the police were closely connected. Since the pilot personnel was recruited exclusively from Danzig citizens, the Polish government was ready to place at the disposal of the Harbor Council an adequate number of trained policemen. Confirming that the situation resulting from the Danzig arrangements was illegal, the note requested the immediate withdrawal of the Free City police and stressed the extreme urgency of the matter.

In spite of urgent requests by the Polish government, this matter dragged on for nearly three weeks and the "exlex" situation persisted.

Meanwhile, serious events were taking place inside the Reich. Immediately upon coming to power Hitler disbanded the Reichstag and fixed the date of elections for March 5, 1933.

A brutal campaign with no holds barred was launched to destroy the opposition. In Hitler's government at that time, only two 100 percent Nazis were seated: Göring and Frick. Both, however, held key positions —Frick as minister of the interior of the Reich, Göring as minister president in Prussia. Both acted through the police apparatus supported by S.A. storm-detachments. Police methods, however, proved to be insufficient to destroy all opponents and to obtain a majority in the new parliament on such short notice.

So the new masters of Germany conceived a plot to capture the imagination of the German masses and direct their energy against "enemies of the nation and the state": to induce the old and ailing President Hindenburg to sign the decree suspending constitutional freedom in the name of the struggle against Communism.

The glare that swept the night's darkness over the Reichstag on February 27–28, 1933, was to accomplish this task. Nazi propaganda branded this act as "a crime of the Communist Van der Lübbe," a half-demented cretin.

I still recall the sensation this news provoked in Warsaw. It was the winter carnival season. That very evening the annual ball took place at the residence of Count and Countess Tyszkiewicz, at 5 Matejko Street, to which, as usual, several ambassadors and ministers were invited. At a certain moment, news was circulated by an employee of the Ministry of Foreign Affairs that the Polish Telegraph Agency had dispatched a message from Berlin about the Reichstag fire. Evidently this news was a sensation for the assembled guests. All eyes turned to Minister von Moltke, who quietly left the ball and hastened to his legation in order to put through a telephone call to Berlin. Since he was a self-possessed diplomat, he returned to the ball after some time, confirming the news by making scant comment. We were lost in conjecture, unable for the moment to grasp what was happening, while subconsciously we assumed that the burning Reichstag was a sort of symbolic torch kindled on the ruins of the abolished edifice of a Germany erected in the aftermath of Versailles.

Marshal Piłsudski keenly observed events inside Germany. Basic instructions with regard to Polish-German relations, as well as on more important foreign policy problems, were inspired by him or required his confirmation.

In the years 1931–32, in connection with increasing tension in the anti-Polish atmosphere in the Reich, Piłsudski recommended that Minister Wysocki probe the attitude of the main political parties toward Poland and orient himself as to the possibility of improving relations between the two countries. Wysocki executed this task by engaging in conversations with a number of leading German politicians, from Social Democrats down to German Nationals. In these talks certain differences could be noted. However, all parties inserted into their programs the revision of frontiers with Poland, if only by different methods. The most drastic approach was taken by the German Nationals. Their representative bluntly declared that he felt that any collaboration with Poland should depend upon the previous settlement of the problem of the Corridor and Upper Silesia in accordance with German demands.

Demagogic catchwords were of such importance at that time of chaos and struggle for power in Germany that none of the political parties could possibly afford to take a more conciliatory stand toward Poland. Consequently, Wysocki's talks hit a dead-end.

A memorandum of Wysocki from these times, dealing with one of his conversations with Piłsudski, has been preserved.[4]

This talk took place at a rather critical moment when, after the downfall of Brüning's cabinet, Hindenburg commissioned von Papen to form a new government. The Marshal wanted to be informed about the internal situation of Germany. One of the basic questions asked of Wysocki was: "Is the present political situation in Germany a cause for concern, and will its further development become a danger to us?" A detailed analysis presented by Wysocki led the Marshal to assume "that it is not to be expected that internal difficulties will decrease, but rather that they will increase, which will obviously weaken the aggressive impetus of that nation externally."

In the course of this conversation the problem of Hitler's coming to power was discussed, since this was the subject of the Marshal's direct question. Mr. Wysocki was of the opinion that "Hitler is neither a military genius nor an extraordinary personality" and that his success was to a great extent due to the fact that he managed to stir the German masses by purely demagogic catchwords, devoid of deeper meaning, while stirring their senses. Questioned by the Marshal, Mr. Wysocki gave the cautious reply that "everything seems to indicate that sooner or later Hitler will be faced with the necessity of taking over the government of the Reich," adding at the same time a comment most characteristic of the opinion of foreign observers in Berlin at that time: "Hitler will follow waiting tactics, since he is actually afraid of power, which would force him to fulfill all the promises he showered so profusely for so many years, and which in fact are impossible to realize. His coming to power may at the same time mark the beginning of his party's decay."

To the Marshal's question: "What is your opinion of the paramilitary organizations in Germany?" Wysocki replied: "There exists beyond any doubt a direct connection between them and the Ministry of the Reichswehr. They are an *ersatz* army, at least morally if not in fact. In the course of many centuries the Hohenzollern rulers implanted into the Germans a passion for militarism. As long as a German organization enables them to wear a uniform it will be very popular in Germany, until

[4] The text is in Józef Lipski's papers in the Piłsudski Historical Institute in New York (File 1).

compulsory conscription is again introduced in case of war. Anyhow, such assault-units of National Socialists who wear uniforms, take military pay, live in barracks, and drill often very strenuously and in purely military style may render invaluable service to the Army in time of emergency."

The Marshal did not concur in this opinion, saying: "It seems to me that you overestimate the importance of these organizations. There are a lot of appearances which are misleading, but they have not the real values of a true soldier. Leaders of such organizations and their officers often complain about the inadequate human material. The soldier who returned from the Great War ceased to be a good soldier. The postwar generation is often physically weak and unwilling to submit to the rigor of military discipline. Observers of the exercises and organization of these units repeatedly stated that, beyond *paraden marches,* roll-calls, and speeches, not much is happening there. And there is no question of comparing the value of such organizations with regular soldiers."

At the end of the conversation the Marshal asked about the chances for a monarchy in Germany, to which Wysocki replied that under the present circumstances this was out of the question.

When Jan Szembek, former minister of Poland to Bucharest, became undersecretary of state [November 5, 1932], Piłsudski sent him on a courtesy and information mission to Paris and London, instructing him to stop in Berlin on his way back. His visit in Berlin was chiefly designed for propaganda display. Following the Marshal's instructions, Szembek refrained from calling attention to the tension in Polish-German relations in his conversations at the Wilhelmstrasse, but expressed his conviction that, unless a reasonable *modus vivendi* were found, unforeseen consequences might follow.

Writing about this journey during the war, Szembek stated that the Marshal's guiding idea was to prod France into a more active policy toward its Polish ally. Strained Polish-German relations became an ever-increasing burden for Poland in the west. That is why Piłsudski took these measures, in order to maintain a certain balance on the political chessboard.[5]

In the late afternoon of March 5, 1933, I was unexpectedly summoned for a consultation to the Raczyński Palace, where the Foreign

[5] Letter of Szembek to Lipski from Lisbon dated August 31, 1942 (in Lipski's papers, File 3).

Minister resided at that time. I found several senior employees of the Ministry of Foreign Affairs already there, among them the head of the Danzig Desk. Directly on his return from the Belveder, Beck announced to us that Marshal Piłsudski had issued an order to reinforce the garrison which kept watch over the munitions stores at Westerplatte. A detachment of 120 armed soldiers was to board the cargo ship *Wilia,* which was to land the next day at dawn. Beck justified Piłsudski's decision by the threat to Polish interests in Danzig harbor and by circulated rumors of an intended assault of Hitlerite gangs on Westerplatte. He further explained to us that in deciding on this step the Marshal wanted first of all to test Germany's actual state of readiness; therefore the Minister asked me, as the head of the Western Department of the Ministry, to observe closely all possible reactions in Berlin. On the other hand, a determined attitude by Poland should be properly appreciated in Paris and London, rousing these countries to more energetic action in the face of the growing threat of Hitlerism.

To fill in the complete background of the situation, it is necessary to add that the whole West European press, alarmed by the drastic changes in the Reich, was at that time filled with sensational rumors about Hitler's schemes. In international circles and in the powerful Jewish organizations, anti-German feelings were growing fast. The same also occurred in America.

The Ministry of Foreign Affairs proclaimed a state of emergency and round-the-clock shifts were instituted at the Minister's cabinet, at the Danzig Desk, and at the Western Department. I therefore spent the night at the telephone, constantly receiving information from Berlin about the election results. Radio stations controlled by the National Socialists broadcast triumphant communiqués about Hitlerite victories at the polls for hours on end. From 196 mandates obtained in November, 1932, the National Socialists rose in strength to 288, thus receiving 43 percent of all the votes. In coalition with the German National Party, they were assured of a majority in the future parliament.

I realized that the news which would be reported from Danzig the next day would cause a serious shock at the chancellery of the Reich!

In the early morning hours of March 6 I was at the Ministry when news reached us that our detachment had landed at Westerplatte without incident. During the whole day reports streamed in from Danzig.

While Berlin was silent, protests were received, first from the High

Commissioner of the League of Nations in Danzig, followed by protests and warnings from representatives of France and Great Britain.

The Polish press published the following official communiqué:

"The Polish government has recently been informed that diversive elements in Danzig plan an assault on the peninsula of Westerplatte, where Polish stores of munitions and war matériel are located, guarded by a small detachment of Polish forces. In consequence, on March 6, a temporary reinforcement of this detachment was ordered. The Commissioner-General of the Polish Republic in Danzig informed the High Commissioner of the League of Nations about this order."

The *de facto* and *de jure* situation, as far as the Polish garrison at Westerplatte was concerned, was as follows:

The Poland-Danzig agreement of June 23, 1921, authorized Poland to keep a garrison on the peninsula to safeguard the munitions stores. On the basis of this agreement, the High Commissioner of the League of Nations was to be kept informed by the Polish side of the strength of the garrison. He was also entitled—upon agreement with the Polish government—to establish the number of the guarding detachment. The munitions stores were completed in the beginning of 1925 and the Polish government wrote a letter to High Commissioner McDonnell on April 18, 1925, for permission to send a detachment of two officers, 20 noncommissioned officers, and 60 soldiers. The League of Nations, by its decision of December 19, 1925, confirmed the Polish motion.

On the morning of March 6, 1933, the Commissioner-General of Poland informed High Commissioner Rosting about the reinforcement of the garrison. He explained that this step was precipitated by police measures taken by the Danzig Senate, as well as by the threat by ultra-nationalistic elements in Danzig to attack Polish munitions stores. The Commissioner-General of Poland was explicit in his assurances that the reinforcement of the garrison was only temporary and that, in accordance with the resolution of the League of Nations of December 19, 1925, the detachment would confine its functions strictly to guarding Westerplatte.

The High Commissioner of the League of Nations, who was unofficially advised by the Polish side on the previous day, could have availed himself of his rights to confirm the temporary reinforcement of the Polish garrison until the problem of the harbor police was settled and a calm atmosphere restored in Danzig. Mr. Rosting, formerly employed by the League's secretariat, by nature a man easily intimidated, took a purely formal stand; he expressed his protest and demanded the withdrawal of the detachment.

Only a few hours after this conversation, the Danzig Senate intervened at the office of the High Commissioner of the League. The intervention took the form of a letter which advised that from the ship *Wilia,* whose arrival at the harbor had been announced a few days before, a Polish crew of more than 100 men had landed armed with machine guns and other weapons. Aboard this ship were 40 cases of explosives weighing 1,720 kilograms.

The Senate inquired whether the reinforcement of the guard at Westerplatte had the consent of the High Commissioner, and if so, for what reasons?

The High Commissioner declared that it had occurred without his consent, thus compromising his stand in the conflict.

A rapid exchange of notes followed. The Senate demanded—according to Article 39 of the Paris Convention—the issuance of a declaration by the High Commissioner of the League imposing on Poland the obligation to return to the previous force of the garrison. It also lodged a claim of *action-directe,* that is, of a breach of the binding rules by one-sided action. The High Commisioner transferred the problem to the League of Nations. For its part, the Polish government accused the Senate of *action-directe* in introducing its own police force into the harbor.

In accordance with the rules of procedure, the High Commissioner, in his letter of March 7 addressed to the Commissioner-General of Poland, fixed a term of 48 hours for a reply by the Polish government, and 24 hours for a retort.

The Commissioner-General of Poland refused to give an answer until the deletion from the Danzig claim of a paragraph offensive to the Polish government. A dispute by letter was opened on this subject, which lasted until March 9. On this day Beck left for Geneva to attend the extraordinary session of the Council of the League. Before leaving Warsaw, he had no illusions about the attitude of Paris and London. The greater the tension in the West in connection with Hitler's behavior, the more cautious became the Great Powers' diplomacy (not to mention that of the smaller countries).

The Polish government's action was the cause of consternation at the

Wilhelmstrasse. This was obviously connected with apprehension that the Great Powers might interfere against Hitler. The step taken by Poland could therefore be regarded as a prelude to common action. Confirmation of these forebodings may to some extent be found in the conversation of the Chancellor with Mr. Wysocki on May 2, 1933.[6]

A report of the German Minister in Warsaw dated March 11, 1933, in the form of his account of conversations with representatives of the Great Powers at the Council of the League,[7] throws some interesting light on this matter.

According to von Moltke,[8] the majority of foreign diplomats in Warsaw defined the reinforcement of the Westerplatte garrison as "a violent reaction in the style of Beck." It resembled the *Wicher* case, with the difference that this time action was carried through with Marshal Piłsudski's consent (here Moltke was wrong; as is known, the *Wicher* case was personally directed by Piłsudski).[9] "I did not find among the diplomats here a single one who in more or less strong words would not criticize or negatively judge the Polish action," wrote Moltke. He added, however, that his collocutors called attention to the inopportune notice given by the Free City concerning the agreement on the harbor police. This step of the Senate was criticized, especially by the ambassador of Great Britain [Sir William Erskine], about whom Moltke complained that he usually showed bias in Polish-Danzig and Polish-German matters.

Reflecting on the motives that induced the Polish government to take such a step, von Moltke considered that the argument of threat alone was not convincing from the diplomatic point of view. Other secondary reasons probably existed as well. The step was possibly an answer to the elections in Germany. In all probability it was to serve as a warning to those who represented the idea of the revision of frontiers in Europe.

In his conclusions, von Moltke was obviously not far from the truth.

[6] Hitler then said: "The Germans will not acknowledge . . . any rights of Poland to Danzig which would overstep the frame of the existing treaties. They would also consider the occupation of Westerplatte by reinforced Polish garrisons illegal, and would have reason—Germany, not Poland—to get alarmed."

[7] *DGFP*, Series C, Vol. I, No. 74.

[8] After the death (on December 18, 1930) of Ulrich Rauscher, German envoy to Poland, his post was filled, on February 27, 1931, by Hans Adolf von Moltke, former director of the Eastern Division of the Auswärtiges Amt.

[9] "Zajazd O.R.P. 'Wicher' na Gdańsk", *Wiadomości* (London), No. 108, April 25, 1948, and T. Morgenstern, "Wejście O.R.P. "Wicher' do Gdańska w 1932 r.," *Bellona* (London), 1953, No. 1.

The epilogue of the Westerplatte incident took place at Geneva. The League of Nations avoided making a public display of quarrels and contentions as a matter of principle. Resolutions were agreed to between the parties involved even prior to their being placed on the agenda of the Council of the League. Thus, an apparent atmosphere of harmony and understanding was created among the delegates. Touchy issues were settled in backstage conversations or at secret sessions of the Council.

During the sessions at Geneva, the secretariat of the League played the role of chief stage manager. Its influence was far-reaching and deeply rooted. It had at its disposal an apparatus technically of the highest order; it was thoroughly acquainted with the background and arcana of every case; it knew perfectly the standpoint of particular delegations, paying most attention to the attitude taken by representatives of the Great Powers, thus adjusting its tactics to the prevailing international situation. Seeking solutions of compromise was the key problem of the secretariat. It also excelled in composing skillful formulas which often contributed to smoothing out difficulties.

Outsiders were lost in the labyrinth of Geneva proceedings. There were no secrets hidden from old-timers who had a master key to intricate resolutions and speeches of the delegates, in which the essence of their proposals was camouflaged by the sheer phraseology of the League.

In both Danzig matters turned over to the League of Nations (Westerplatte and the harbor police), the procedure did not deviate from the normal course.

The role of *rapporteur* was filled by Sir John Simon, the stiff and aloof spokesman of the British government.

In international matters Paris acted in full agreement with London, since the foreign policy of France was influenced by England. When the case of the Westerplatte garrison appeared in the forum of the League in the form of a claim against the Polish government concerning an *action-directe,* it became obvious that the French government was not inclined to collaborate more actively with Poland in view of the new situation in Germany and the growing danger of Nazism.

From the behavior of Germany in the face of the incident in Danzig, it was evident that Hitler did not yet have real strength at his disposal, and that his violent outbursts were to a great extent just sheer bluff. This, however, did not convince the Great Powers. The spontaneous reaction of the Polish government in Danzig was inconvenient for them in practice and highly disturbing, since these powers were also ready to apply a policy of appeasement toward Hitler.

Under these circumstances, the Polish delegation met with general criticism and strong pressure, backed up by threats of the *rapporteur* to place before the Council a report unfavorable to Poland. Therefore, the necessity for a compromise arose. It was reached on the eve of the session of the Council of the League, that is, on March 13, 1933. The compromise consisted in the restoration of the *de facto* situation in the case of the harbor police as it had existed on February 15, 1933, and in the obligation of the Polish government to reduce the garrison to its previous numbers.

At the session of the Council everything went in accordance with the set plan.

Sir John Simon informed those present that, in view of the announced declaration of the Polish Minister of Foreign Affairs, he would refrain from presenting his report.

Beck directed his opening question to the president of the Danzig Senate, asking whether the authorities of the Free City could guarantee that the rights of Poland on the Westerplatte peninsula would not be violated. President Ziehm replied affirmatively.

The delegate of Poland then declared that his government would withdraw the additional detachment at Westerplatte without delay, adding at the same time that the Polish move was of a temporary character and was not intended to create a precedent for the future.

Sir John Simon urged that the decision of the Polish government be put into life without delay, whereupon the Polish delegate expressed his readiness to fix immediately a precise date and hour for an understanding with the High Commissioner of the League. The *rapporteur* confirmed that the matter was settled, and, going over the contents of the agreement, he admonished both parties (Poland and Danzig) that neither of them had the right "to take the law into its own hands."

On behalf of the Free City, Ziehm stated that the agreement would remove the state of confusion which had prevailed in Danzig during the preceding few days.

The delegate of Germany, Herr von Keller, said, in part, that the attention of the whole world was focused on the Danzig incident and that the German nation followed the development of this problem with great anxiety and some concern.

The delegate of France—the "golden-tongued" Paul-Boncour—succeeded in sweetening the pill for the delegate of Poland by a well-rounded sentence. He praised the conciliatory stand taken by the Polish government to settle the dispute, and explained that the step taken by Poland in Danzig was dictated by the necessity of a prompt decision in view of the general tension in relations.

The delegate of Ireland, Lester, who later succeeded Rosting in Danzig and incurred the Nazis' disfavor by his protest against the *gleichschaltung* of the Free City, described the incident as unfortunate. He added, however, that the incident had had a happy ending, thanks to the sage behavior of the Polish government, which deserved appreciation. At the same session the report about the case of the harbor police was accepted, together with motions.

The Westerplatte case vanished from the agenda of the Geneva debates afterward. Its deeper meaning would only be appreciated many years later. The former ambassador of France in Berlin, André François-Poncet, referred to this incident in his memoirs, rightly stressing its weight and importance for the later decisions of the Polish government.[10]

R. Wendelin Keyserling [11] described his meeting with the Polish Foreign Minister in London in the spring of 1939, at the moment of tension in Polish-German relations. In the course of this conversation Beck allegedly referred to the Westerplatte case, explaining that its conclusion convinced Marshal Piłsudski about the necessity of entering into direct talks with Hitler.

[10] François-Poncet, p. 165.
[11] Keyserling, pp. 296–97.

# The Four-Power Pact and Revisionism[1]
## March, 1933

WHILE THE Westerplatte case was under discussion in Geneva, we received important news at Wierzbowa[2] about Italian-German relations from the Polish ambassador in London, Konstanty Skirmunt, usually well informed and a man who carefully weighed each word of his reports.

DOCUMENT 9    Skirmunt to Beck

Polish Embassy in London                    March 9, 1933
NO. 18/conf./33                              *Strictly Confidential*

In the course of the last weeks I received very confidential information about Italian politics from a most reliable source.

Since Hitler came to power in Germany, Ambassador Grandi,[3] in his conversations with friends (not in the Foreign Office), expressed concern about Mussolini's special support granted to the German government for all its activities, extending even to the field of the disarmament conference. Grandi was especially troubled, it seemed, by the news that, in order to ease internal difficulties for Hitler's government, Mussolini was prepared not only to agree to the *Anschluss* but to place this problem before the international forum on Italy's initiative. Under these circumstances, with the meeting of the Great Fascist Council close at hand, Grandi decided to leave for Rome to—as he said—fight it out with Mussolini.

Arriving in Rome on March 3, Grandi remained there for only one day and did not attend the Great Council, which was finally postponed.

[1] Printed in *Bellona* (London), 1951, No. 3.
[2] The Ministry of Foreign Affairs was located at Wierzbowa Street in Warsaw.
[3] Dino Grandi, former minister of foreign affairs (1929–32), at this time Italian ambassador in London.

He considers the result of this journey to be a fiasco. The sole advantage he succeeded in achieving was a promise that Mussolini, while supporting possible German plans for the *Anschluss* when they are presented, will not push the problem on his own. Besides this, Grandi failed to convince Mussolini on any other issue. Mussolini, in his opinion, is more than ever isolated from contact with the world and totally under the influence and orientation of the surrounding group of his closest collaborators and of General Balbo. Mussolini—as Grandi puts it—considers himself not only the chief of the Italian government but the pope of Fascism, and is primarily interested in the Hitlerite movement and its impact on Italian politics. As for Mussolini's possible trip to Geneva for a meeting with MacDonald and Daladier, for which MacDonald was pressing for real and prestige reasons, Grandi was convinced that under no circumstances would his chief go to Geneva and that he is putting pressure on Hitler to prevent him also from going to Geneva. Mussolini's goal seems to be to frustrate the chances of any way out of the impasse at the disarmament conference and to put up to ridicule any statesmen who would undertake this ungrateful task. Such a point of view is a source of deep concern for Grandi, who considers the present international situation to be genuinely dangerous and who is obviously most anxious to maintain very close relations with Great Britain. He adds that the expedition to Rome was connected with a certain risk for his personal position, and that in his opinion it really is endangered.

From another source I was informed that during the recent visit to Rome of Avenol, the secretary-general of the League of Nations, Mussolini stressed in his conversation with him the necessity of territorial concessions for Germany in the east and of a "partition of Czechoslovakia." The subject of this conversation was disclosed to the Czechs.

The information given above is known to the French government through its embassy here and possibly, if not to the full extent, also to the Foreign Office. When, on March 3, Undersecretary of State Vansittart summoned me to inform me about the planned trip of MacDonald and Simon to Geneva, we conversed at length about German and Italian politics. Vansittart stated clearly that the British government is concerned about the development of events in Germany, and he agreed with me when I called his attention to the constant support extended by Italy to Hitler's policy.

I gathered that Vansittart is definitely convinced about the possibility of Italy's promoting the *Anschluss* idea. On the other hand, he disagreed with my opinion as to a possible Fascist *coup d'état* in Vienna. However, the London press has openly been discussing this possibility for the past two days. News about the probability of the *Anschluss* also reached me from other sources and coincided with the possible planned visit of Hitler to Rome at the end of March. According to information in my possession, Mussolini and Hitler communicate with each other, completely bypassing diplomatic channels—at any rate, absolutely eliminating the Wilhelmstrasse. The Soviet ambassador here told me that he knows that Mussolini talks with Hitler by telephone every day. . . .

At the last moment I learned that the day before yesterday [March 8] a political gathering took place at Lady Londonderry's, at the so-called Arch Club, with the participation of MacDonald, Baldwin, Ambassador von Hoesch, and the Austrian and Swedish envoys. I heard from the last-named that at this gathering there was an unofficial discussion about the *Anschluss,* and the opinion was expressed that this was an immediate and unavoidable danger; the majority of those present thought that it might bring about a war. Polish-German matters were not discussed.

Grandi called on Simon just before the latter's departure. Rumors about this visit, which reached me indirectly from the Foreign Office, seem to point to the fact that Grandi was very open in his talk with Simon when he spoke about the error of his chief, even at the risk of his personal position, and that he impressed upon Simon the necessity of arranging a meeting for MacDonald with Mussolini as the only solution to influence the latter's policies. Simon, who is jealous of his personal influence—as I was told by the Foreign Office—let Grandi unburden himself of his feelings, and showed no reaction whatever in exchange.

*K. Skirmunt*


The news of Mussolini's alleged *volte-face* on the subject of the *Anschluss* was quite a surprise. The general opinion was that the Italian government was against any attempt at uniting Austria with Germany, for fear that Germany's expansion southward might become a threat to Italy's interests in the southern Tyrol.

Energetic objections by Rome concerning the initiative for the German-Austrian customs union at the time of Brüning and Curtius had confirmed us in our convictions. However, Skirmunt's information did not exclude the hypothesis that, in view of the planned visit of Mac-Donald and Simon to Rome, Grandi purposely gave an alarming report of Mussolini's readiness to offer all possible concessions to Hitler, in order to press the British statesmen to a more conciliatory attitude in their talks with the Italian side.

Such alternative probabilities notwithstanding, the very fact that competent London circles deliberated over the *Anschluss* question—moreover, with a certain undertone of resignation—was a characteristic sign of the then currently prevailing feeling toward German activities. The fact that the Hitlerite movement had originated in southern Germany and that Hitler, an Austrian by birth, had mastered the Reich focused all eyes on the Austrian problem, especially since, upon seizing power, the National Socialists started an energetic propaganda campaign both on the border and inside the territory of that country.

Mussolini's talk with the secretary-general of the League of Nations, Avenol, disclosed that the revisionist idea had made alarming progress in the mind of the chief of the Italian government against the background of ideological kinship with the Hitlerite Reich and that it might be expressed by the desire to shift German expansion eastward, in the direction least threatening for Italy. Mussolini's statement on the partition of Czechoslovakia was symptomatic of his hostile attitude toward the policies of the Little Entente and of his personal animosity toward Beneš.

At that time I had long conversations on these matters with Undersecretary of State Szembek, who asked for detailed information on the development of the German situation, owing to Marshal Piłsudski's very intense interest and his demands for a precise analysis of the situation. In the course of these conversations the idea was conceived for me to make a short trip to Germany in order to orient myself on the spot. I wrote to this effect to Mr. Wysocki, Polish minister in Berlin, on March 14, 1933, communicating for his information the contents of Skirmunt's report and announcing my arrival in Berlin after the return of Minister Beck from Geneva. This plan, however, was not realized. Shortly afterward news came streaming in about the Four-Power Pact, propagated by Mussolini during the visit of MacDonald and Simon in Rome [March

18]. The Italian plan would have created a sort of Power directorate for establishing common policy lines on all European problems and also on matters reaching beyond Europe's limits, as well as on colonial questions. In its original text, the document pressed openly for the revision of peace treaties in cases threatening to provoke conflict between countries, transferring the decision in matters of prime import for the disarmament conference from the League of Nations to direct understandings within the framework of the four powers. From confidential sources obtained by the Ministry of Foreign Affairs, it was evident that in his Rome talks Mussolini pointed bluntly to the Pomeranian Corridor as a problem requiring settlement within the framework of the planned political pact. . . .

News about the planned agreement evoked a serious commotion in Warsaw. An impulsive reaction showing the Polish government's dissatisfaction was the sudden recall of the newly appointed ambassador to the Quirinal, Jerzy Potocki,[4] the former aide-de-camp of Marshal Piłsudski. Potocki was to replace Stefan Przeździecki, who died when on leave in Warsaw. Ambassador Przeździecki held a high social position in Rome and enjoyed the personal confidence of high-ranking Italian elements.

The negative attitude of the Polish government toward the Four-Power Pact was not based solely upon purely prestige reasons, as was often erroneously remarked by the foreign press. The causes were far more important. According to the words of Mussolini—spoken on June 7, 1933, in Rome on the day when the Four-Power Pact was being prepared for initialing—this understanding was to become a further development and application of the Locarno agreements. Contrary to the democratic principle of equality for all states contained in the League of Nations Covenant, here a system based upon the hegemony of the Great Powers of Europe was being formed. In this system of powers, France could under certain circumstances be isolated, and its vote would not be sufficient to safeguard the vital interests of its eastern allies in the face of compromise solutions adopted by the Great Powers at their expense. In the very concept of the Four-Power Pact a serious danger was involved for the region of East Central Europe. The independence of smaller countries situated between Germany and Russia was threatened by the Hitlerite doctrine of *Lebensraum* and in the east by the still

[4] Potocki resigned on March 24, 1933, before even going to Rome.

lurking power of the Soviets, ever ready for further expansion in favorable circumstances.

In this situation, Warsaw's reaction was quite justified and correct. Already presaged were the haunting specters of Munich, Teheran, and Yalta.

Notwithstanding the changes introduced in the Italian text and French-British endeavors to conciliate the resolutions of the agreement with the principles and procedure of the League of Nations, the Polish government stood firm in its objections both to the text of the pact and, primarily, to the very principles on which it was based.

In an interview with the delegate of the Polish Telegraph Agency on June 8, 1933, that is, the day after the pact was initialed in Rome, the Polish Minister of Foreign Affairs thus defined the attitude of the Polish government toward the contracted agreement:

"First of all, it should be made clear that any resolutions whatsoever passed on the basis of this pact which would directly or indirectly concern the interests of the Polish state would in any event have no binding power for the Polish government. The Polish government did not accept any obligations concerning any kind of collaboration with the bloc of the four states as an international organ. The stand of the Polish government on this matter was clearly stated at the time."

As for the relation of the Four-Power Pact to the League of Nations, the Minister declared:

"Decisions and resolutions of the Council of the League and its organs can have binding power only if a strict observance of the letter and spirit of the Covenant of the League is respected. In case of any anomaly in the functions of the Council of the League, the Polish government would be forced to reserve to itself an absolutely free hand."

The Little Entente was also against the pact, considering itself, like Poland, threatened by it. However, the representatives of the Little Entente finally agreed with the principle of the pact when a number of alterations were introduced in the text of particular articles and a guarantee from the French government was obtained. In this respect, Poland's stand differed essentially from that of this group of three countries.

When news of the Italian plan of the Four-Power Pact was circulated, a journey by Beck to Paris, Prague, and Belgrade was planned in order to establish a common line of action with these governments. There was a moment of great tension at Wierzbowa as weighty decisions were taken at Belveder. Beck had some hopes then that a closer contact might be established between Warsaw and Prague in the face of a common threat; such contact would contribute to a broader consolidation of relations in East Central Europe based on good will and proper understanding of the situation of all countries concerned. This was an exceptionally favorable moment to demonstrate the solidarity of the smaller nations threatened by both totalitarian systems. Though Polish diplomatic posts were properly instructed in anticipation, and the visits were already announced, the journey did not take place. What was the cause of this change of decision?

In Beck's memoirs [5] we find some explanation of the circumstances which precluded the planned visit to Prague. Beck writes that, in connection with the Four-Power Pact, he envisaged the first opportunity in a long time to enter into a serious understanding with Czechoslovakia; abandoning the previous reserve toward that country, he proposed to the Czechoslovak government a friendly exchange of opinions. A meeting in Prague with Masaryk and Prime Minister Beneš was fixed for a common discussion of policies. However, even before the Polish Minister could reach the capital of Czechoslovakia, Prague was—as Beck writes— "already bowing before the Pact of the Four Powers and as could be expected in advance shunned any more pronounced attitude."

Describing this incident in more detail, Beck blames some of the smaller Central European countries for their ultrasubmissiveness to the Great Powers, which was an obstacle in forming a solid front.

Neither did the visit to Belgrade take place. On his way to Belgrade Beck also planned to stop in Budapest to demonstrate friendly Polish-Hungarian relations, in accordance with his policy. Owing to the inflamed state of Yugoslav-Hungarian relations at that time, the plan to visit the capital of Hungary brought a protest from the Yugoslav government, causing tension and finally resulting in a cancellation of the visit.

In our debates at the Ministry of Foreign Affairs on revisionist tactics practiced by the German authorities—even in the Weimar era—we came to the conclusion that, although revisionist action was carried out to exert immediate pressure on Poland and to weaken its international position, the Reich was pursuing a far-reaching goal in this policy.

[5] Beck, *Final Report*, pp. 38–39.

In my letter of February 23, 1931, to Mr. Wysocki in Berlin, I defined the role of Brüning as a successor to Stresemann.[6]

Such systematic revisionist action had far-reaching consequences, not only creating an impact on direct relations between Warsaw and Berlin but causing a serious setback for Poland in the international forum in the political and financial fields. Polish diplomatic representatives reported the progress of German propaganda for revision of the Corridor in the United States, in Great Britain, and in neutral countries. Alarming rumors also came out of France with regard to pacifist feelings spreading all over the country.

On January 29, 1933, that is, on the eve of Hitler's coming to power, the Polish Embassy in Paris reported rumors which had stubbornly circulated for some time about Poland's secret negotiations with Germany on the subject of Pomerania. The report stressed that, "while in right-wing circles news about secret Polish-German negotiations is causing some anxiety, the left wing accepts it with satisfaction as a possible prelude to Polish territorial concessions in favor of Germany without the necessity of any exterior pressure."

Almost simultaneously (January 15, 1933), Mr. Wysocki reported from Berlin that "revisionist tendencies are growing from day to day. The East Prussian Exhibition is in itself not a provocation, but it has become the arena for daily demonstrations, lectures, and speeches attended by schools, universities, and other institutions. This whole tide is streaming from the Auswärtiges Amt and the Reichpressestelle."

Sympathies enjoyed by the Germans in international circles suffered a serious setback when the Hitlerite government began to impose its undemocratic regime by violence. However, the growing distrust of the West toward the new German regime was accompanied by uneasiness and fear about the possibility of a conflict, which had to be avoided at any price. The chronic inflammable condition of Polish-German relations created the impression that the Corridor problem could be the very cause of the explosion.

A report of the former counselor of the Ministry of Foreign Affairs, Tomasz Bielski, sent to Mr. Babiński, the Polish minister at The Hague, and dated March 19, 1933, gives an interesting explanation of the atmosphere prevailing at that time. Mr. Bielski, who was married to a Dutch woman with important social connections, had access to high society

---

[6] See Document 1, p. 25.

and especially to financial circles. Since prior to his transfer to The Hague he had worked for several years in the Western Department of the Ministry of Foreign Affairs and was well acquainted with political questions, he often shared his observations with headquarters.

Holland was at that time a center on the crossroads of various currents, and the market of this neutral rich country was of great importance. I am quoting below some remarks by the author of the letter:

"Hitler's coming to power, the result of the last elections in Germany, the speech delivered by the Chancellor at Königsberg, and, finally, the Westerplatte incident brought the problem of the so-called Corridor to the forefront and it became one of the topics under discussion here. Although the local press did not give too much space to this problem, and in spite of the fact that a number of articles were obviously friendly to us, this matter is becoming a source of concern for public opinion, which is growing more and more skeptical as far as the *status quo* is concerned. This was very clear in my conversations here with representatives of financial and intellectual circles.

"Pro-German, pro-French, or pro-Polish sympathies notwithstanding, everyone is more or less agreed that the present state of tension in Danzig and in Pomerania is impossible to maintain in the long run, and that some change must be made if there is to be any relaxation in European relations.

"Pro-German arguments are the least complicated. These are statements similar to those that may be heard in Berlin and Rome, London, or even Paris. The Germans are considered to be absolutely right; Polish arguments are unknown, treated lightly, or accused of exaggerations. Polish policy is regarded as a sign of 'imperialistic' tendencies in Paris that have driven Europe into ruin. The only remedy would be to give satisfaction to 'justified' claims of the Germans. Then, as if by magic, Europe would become a land flowing with milk and honey.

"Among the adherents of such concepts should be counted a considerable part—if not the majority—of the representatives of finance and trade in Rotterdam and, to a lesser degree, in Amsterdam. These circles, although recently disappointed and embittered by Germany's behavior (customs duties, frozen credits, currency restrictions, etc.), are all more inclined to accept the National Socialist movement in Germany than Communism, assuming that Hitler as Chancellor will undoubtedly be more moderate than Hitler the chief of the opposition, and that the

'Fascist order' installed in Germany offers a better chance of retrieving frozen credits than a possible Communist chaos. This standpoint is openly confirmed by quotations from the Amsterdam exchange.

"Since Hitler's earlier aggressive declarations against Poland are still remembered, and since the Chancellor's last speech at Königsberg— considered by many here as a declaration *sui generis* of war on Poland —has confirmed public opinion about the intentions of German policy in the east, Hitler's coming to power is synonymous with the increase of the possibility of disturbances on the eastern frontier of the Reich. The conclusion is simple. An unknown and faraway Poland should at last give in to Germany for the sake of European peace, instead of prolonging the atmosphere of tension.

"Pro-French arguments are different. They consider that, faced with a Hitlerite Germany, France was swept by genuine panic and helplessness instead of by a sound reaction, so that one can expect even further opportunism and pacifism from it, even to the point of defeatism. Under such conditions, a joint French-Polish action seems to be problematical, and the opinion prevails that in case of any armed conflict we should not count on France. No one here believes in a general European war caused by the Corridor problem. The possible conflict—according to these assumptions—would be localized and Poland would be forced to succumb to the overwhelming power of Germany in short order.

"It is difficult to judge at a distance what the real feelings in France are. According to news reaching me here from financial circles, it may be concluded that the atmosphere is really alarming, as far as the Paris exchange is concerned. Allegedly, in these circles the revision of the Corridor is considered a must, and it seems already a foregone conclusion. This information might be biased, and circulated on purpose by specific sources; however, it seems to be worthy of careful study. Also, I met with such opinions locally. For instance, Professor Siegfried, who visited here in the autumn, did not conceal his skeptical remarks as to the possibility of maintaining the Corridor. The former French minister here, M. Camere, told all the Dutchmen he came across that France does not attach much importance to its alliance with Poland, and that it would not risk any adventure with the Germans concerning the Corridor. I encountered similar more or less skeptical opinions among many Frenchmen residing here or traveling through Holland. It will also be worth noting that special thanks were extended to the director of the

Franco-Polish Bank in Paris at a shareholders' meeting for not engaging his bank during the current year in further financial operations in Poland."

Two weeks later, on April 5, Bielski, in a letter to the director of the Minister's cabinet, Mr. R. Dębicki, wrote:

"Anxieties about the Corridor in financial circles are increasing, and this psychological feeling might add to my difficulties in obtaining credits for Polish industrial undertakings. These fears have gone so far that bills of exchange endorsed by the Bank of Poland are not to be discounted."

The capital market was always most sensitive to all possible political entanglements in East Central Europe. In the years 1926–27, and during the following years when the Polish government was negotiating for the American stabilization loan and when attempts in general were made to attract foreign credits to Poland, I was often questioned in detail by American representatives in Warsaw about the development of Polish-German relations. I often discussed this subject with Mr. Charles Dewey, the American adviser of the Bank of Poland, who made all possible efforts to strengthen Polish credit in America.

# The Wysocki–Hitler Conversation [1]
## April—May, 1933

---

PIŁSUDSKI'S DECISION to establish contact with Hitler was probably made during the first days of April, when the Great Powers were negotiating the Four-Power Pact. This is confirmed by the fact that an instruction, signed by Beck, was dispatched to Polish Envoy Wysocki in Berlin on April 4, 1933.

This instruction was kept in strict secrecy even from senior officials of the Polish Ministry of Foreign Affairs. The various political sections of the Ministry had no knowledge of it, nor of the preparations leading to the meeting of the Polish Envoy with the German Chancellor.

The Marshal's intention at first was to send to Berlin Undersecretary of State Szembek, who, as stated in the above-mentioned instruction, was to undertake with Hitler, and "only with him in person, a conversation of the utmost importance" and to raise subjects of "primary concern." The condition that the meeting had to be with Hitler personally was due to the mistrust prevailing in Warsaw toward the Auswärtiges Amt, traditionally hostile to Poland.

German diplomacy had been bred on the cult of Bismarck. The Iron Chancellor, creator of a Germany united under the Prussian dynasty of the Hohenzollerns, had become for future generations of the German Foreign Service the ideal master-statesman. Thanks to his farsighted and skillful policy, and supported by military power, he had attained for his fatherland through numerous victorious campaigns the standing of a great power, and he had successfully consolidated its conquests. Bismarck's approach to the Polish problem was well known. He considered the creation of a Polish state a threat to Prussia, a vanguard of France on the Vistula. The downfall of the Hohenzollern monarchy after World War I and the introduction of a republican regime had produced no

[1] Published in *Bellona* (London), 1951, No. 3.

basic changes in the Wilhelmstrasse. The spirit of Prussia continued to permeate that office.

Although successive foreign ministers of the Weimar period belonged to various political parties, the caste of clerks remained within the same old framework. Only a few nonprofessional diplomats were admitted into their tight group; they were mainly recruited from those who, at the outbreak of the November Revolution of 1918, had joined the ranks of social democracy (the November Socialists).

Ulrich Rauscher was one of these November Socialists. He was the press chief of the Reich during the Kapp Putsch (March, 1920) and he was famous for publishing, after the departure of the president and the government to Dresden, under their signature but without their knowledge, an appeal to the German working classes calling for a general strike. This appeal had so decisive an impact that it led to a breakdown of the Kapp revolt.[2]

Later, as envoy in Warsaw, Rauscher participated in economic negotiations between the two governments (1927–30) and he made a positive contribution to the normalization of Polish-German relations.[3]

There were periods during which German governments found it expedient, for the sake of high-level government interests, to conclude agreements with Poland. This was especially true of the negotiations leading to the liquidation agreement of October, 1929, in connection with the Young Plan. At such times it was usually the old-guard bureaucracy that offered the most resistance and put the greatest difficulties in the way of settlement. Among the top officials of the Auswärtiges Amt there were also persons of greater vision, of course, who did not suffer from an anti-Polish complex and who understood the necessity of seeking solutions to intricate Polish-German problems. But they were not in a position to set policy.

Wysocki replied on April 6, after conducting a confidential investigation, that permission for a private conversation with Hitler had to be obtained from the German Foreign Office, and he asked for authorization to take this up with Neurath. He emphasized that Hitler might be embarrassed by such a meeting, from the point of view of internal politics, and that a refusal could be expected. He amplified on this in his

[2] Meissner, p. 87.

[3] Rauscher, named envoy to Poland on May 30, 1922, died December 18, 1930.

telegram of April 8, explaining that "Hitler, busy with the reconstruction of Germany, intent on filling all offices, and beset with struggles within the ranks of his own party and the government, might not be ready to make any declaration with regard to Poland, since this might put a weapon in the hands of right-wing elements and compromise him in the court of public opinion."

As can be seen from a letter written by Wysocki on April 9, he was doubtful whether, under these circumstances, the conversation would even be advisable. He thought Hitler was still too weak to "risk anything that might lower him in the estimation of Hugenberg and the Prussian nationalists, to whom even the slightest attempt to iron out Polish-German controversies is in itself a crime and treason of the state."

The Envoy feared that the Germans might use the meeting for propaganda purposes detrimental to Poland and he advised limiting the talks to a specific subject, namely, a declaration on the Danzig problem.

Nothing much happened until April 18, 1933, when Beck sent Wysocki the following instruction.

DOCUMENT 10    Beck to Wysocki

Warsaw, April 18, 1933

Pursuant to the instruction issued to you by letter of the 4th inst. and the information forwarded to me by telegrams 1, 2, and 3, and your letter dated April 9, this is to inform you that in view of the delay in Undersecretary Szembek's departure for a conversation with Chancellor Hitler I have decided completely to give up the idea of sending Mr. Szembek and to choose a more natural and appropriate form of communication with the Chancellor. I would like you to talk to the Chancellor and to limit your conversation to a single topic, namely, Danzig.

Please, therefore, take up with Chancellor Hitler the following:

Referring to your government's instructions, please tell the Chancellor that, in the opinion of some, he is held responsible, either as Chancellor of the Reich, or as chief of his party, for attempts to intervene in the internal affairs of Danzig, contrary to other rights and legal interests of Poland. We do not see the Chancellor personally making such attempts. However, we would like to inquire whether he would not consider it advisable publicly to denounce such action, thus putting an end to Polish suspicions. Continuation of the situation as it now exists would, in our opinion, unnecessarily create difficulties that would force us to draw dire conclusions.

As a minimum act of *démarche* I would consider the publication of a communiqué in the German and Polish press, stating therein that the Chancellor is against any action directed against Polish rights and legal interests in the Free City of Danzig.

A good way to resolve this problem would be a public declaration by Hitler, with no mention at all of your conversation with him.

The Marshal considers this conversation extremely important, in view of the necessity of establishing our policy on Danzig, which to a great extent would depend on the result of this exchange of ideas. I know, of course, that the outcome of this talk may be negative, or that the Germans may be purposely vague. The worst that could happen, in my opinion, would be an evasive reply, with no public declaration by Hitler.

I add that we are interested in a concrete solution for the present and for the near future, and not in a general discussion of principles on the Danzig problem.

*Beck*

Obviously the Marshal considered the moment a very critical one, for he simultaneously prepared a decree for issuance in case of war with Germany, a decree complete with the President's signature.[4] While striving to get an understanding with Hitler and a public declaration from him regarding Poland's rights in Danzig, the Marshal was also making preparations in case the talks failed at reaching a satisfactory conclusion.

It is difficult to determine exactly all the elements of Piłsudski's strategy at that time. Taking advantage of the chill in Soviet-German relations, he strengthened Poland's security in the east. In July, 1932, Poland signed a nonaggression pact with Moscow, bringing about a

[4] Maj. Mieczysław Lepecki's report in *Wiadomosci* (London), No. 26, June 26, 1949, states that on the same day, April 18, 1933, the Marshal had him type the original draft of the decree, calling into being, in case of war with Germany, a government of national defense and national unity and establishing new organs of military and civilian authorities. Below on the left-hand side was the notation: "I agree—I. Mościcki."

*détente* and a rapprochement with the Soviets. And in July, 1933, the Polish government, along with other neighbors of Soviet Russia, signed a convention clearly defining the term "aggression." This convention had first been proposed by Litvinov in the spring of 1933 during a session of the disarmament conference at Geneva.

To resist the Hitlerite threat Piłsudski's main hope lay in the possibility of French-Polish collaboration. He took steps to establish this through military channels rather than through normal diplomatic exchange; he had more confidence in the discretion of the military.

At that time tension in Belveder circles was such that a possible war of prevention was seriously under discussion. Rumors of this reached the Germans. Meissner, at that time undersecretary of state under Hindenburg, wrote that in the spring of 1933 Hitler learned from reports of the German Legation in Warsaw that the Polish government had proposed to France the taking of preventive action against Germany, and that the Chancellor feared such a suggestion might meet with favor in French right-wing circles.[5] At the same time former Chancellor Brüning was warned by the Reichswehr and the German Secretary of State that Piłsudski was investigating in Paris to see if France would be willing to join Poland in bringing military pressure to bear on Germany. Pressed by military and diplomatic circles, Brüning called Hitler's attention to the gravity of the situation.

Hitler was shocked to find out about the unfavorable reaction shown by the West toward the government he had formed. He deluded himself that, with time playing in his favor, international public opinion would accept events as they developed inside Germany. However, with Nazi ideology being violently crammed into everyday life, with war being proclaimed not only against Communists but also against democratic parties, professional unions, and above all against the Jewish population, the foreign press was aroused to sharp criticism and protests. Hitler was disturbed by all this, and when a clerk showed him such reports in the press he said that soon Paris, Warsaw, and Prague would write in a similarly contemptuous way about Germany and its government, but that when the German nation achieved power its neighbors would show more respect.

[5] Meissner, p. 335. See also W. Jedrzejewicz, "The Polish Plan for a 'Preventive War' against Germany in 1933," *The Polish Review* (New York), XI, No. 1 (1966), 62–91.

Hitler reiterated this at a cabinet meeting on March 15, 1933, persuading his ministers that Germany's reputation abroad had not deteriorated in the least.[6] This was also probably his answer to telegrams and reports sent in by chiefs of German diplomatic posts abroad, who were feeling the first impact of a cooling toward the Reich.

Right-wing nationalists were represented in the government and they were seriously concerned about the internal situation in Germany. Vice-Chancellor von Papen worked hard for a *modus vivendi* with the churches, and through personal contacts he tried to counteract anti-German propaganda in the United States (declaration of March 27, 1933, to the German-American Chamber of Commerce in New York). The Reichswehr and the Auswärtiges Amt recommended moderation in foreign policy, for fear of possible complications abroad.

Hitler was well aware that symptoms of distaste evoked by Nazi methods, as expressed by critical press commentators and public opinion abroad, did not of themselves constitute a serious threat to the Reich. His real worry was over those who wanted to take direct action. He felt that Piłsudski was one of these and that as a protective measure he had reinforced the Westerplatte garrison.

Thus, that which in the Marshal's tactics irritated the Western Powers and was labeled as rash impulsiveness in Polish policy was better interpreted and understood by perceptive government officials in Germany. Berlin closely followed every move made by the Belveder.

In spite of Warsaw's pressure for the earliest possible meeting (the Ministry of Foreign Affairs at first urged that it should take place as early as April 19), and in spite of personal intervention at the Wilhelmstrasse by the Polish Envoy, a decision on the date of the meeting was delayed for a number of days. Finally, on April 25, Director of Protocol Count Bassewitz informed Wysocki that the meeting was fixed for April 28. However, on the very next day he rescinded this by letter, regretfully advising that the Chancellor was obliged to postpone the meeting until May 2 at 12 o'clock noon, owing to unexpected changes in his official schedule. This change, one can guess, was due to the fact that on April 28 Hitler was to receive the Soviet ambassador. Four days earlier (on April 24) a serious incident had occurred in German-Soviet relations,

[6] *Trial of the Major War Criminals,* Vol. XXXI, Document PS-2962.

namely, the German police had raided the Soviet trade offices of DEROP (Deutsche Vertriebsgesellschaft für Russische Ölprodukte A.G., an organization for marketing Russian petroleum products). Breaking into the archives, they appropriated a number of documents.

In the early period of his regime, in spite of the struggle against Communism inside Germany, Hitler was reluctant to allow ideological conflict to influence relations between the two nations. He still felt too weak to take a positive stand against Soviet Russia. He placed great value on the continuation of economic relations with that country, and he stressed this point when he reported to President of the Reich Hindenburg.[7]

As for the Soviets, despite the blow they suffered when the German Communist Party was smashed, they had no desire to sever relations with Hitler's Reich. Their rapprochement with the Western Powers and the strengthening of ties with their smaller neighbors in Eastern Europe were aimed both at tightening their security and at obtaining trump cards to be used in negotiating with Berlin. Moscow was also worried about the Four-Power Pact.

Both parties therefore were seeking a *modus vivendi,* even though the atmosphere was one of mutual distrust.

As a result of Hiter's conversation with the Soviet ambassador there was an exchange of ratification documents on May 5 putting into effect the long-delayed conciliatory agreement of January 25, 1929, as well as the protocol of June 24, 1931, extending the Berlin Treaty. Thus, the understanding achieved sometime previously at Rapallo was further continued in force.

Foreign Minister of the Reich von Neurath was also present at the Wysocki-Hitler conference, which took place at noon on May 2, 1933, and lasted for forty minutes. However, the discourse was exclusively between the Polish Envoy and the Chancellor, and only at the end, when the matter of a communiqué was raised, did von Neurath speak out. In his report to Beck on May 2, 1933, Wysocki included instructions received from Warsaw, as well as additional information received orally from the chief of the Danzig Section of the Polish Ministry of Foreign Affairs who had made a special trip to Berlin.

[7] Meissner, pp. 341–42.

## DOCUMENT 11    Wysocki to Beck

NO. N/49/6                    Berlin, May 2, 1933
*Strictly Confidential*

The main part of Envoy Wysocki's report of his conversation with Chancellor Hitler is published in *Polish White Book*, No. 1, p. 11. In that text, a statement made by Hitler, in the paragraph beginning with the words "The Chancellor is a pacifist . . . ," is omitted:

"The Treaty of Versailles was to bring happiness to Europe, but it actually brought misfortune. We would certainly talk in quite a different manner with a representative of Poland, the Chancellor said, turning directly to me, had the peace treaty assigned to Poland access to the sea further eastward from Danzig, instead of tearing up German territory. If not for that malicious and senseless act, Polish-German relations would undoubtedly adjust to the realities of the situation, and we would iron out as peaceful neighbors our political and economic problems. Continual concern and anxiety for the political morrow, etc. . . ." [8]

After the last sentence of Wysocki's report as printed in the *Polish White Book*, p. 13, the text of his report continues as given below; this material was omitted in the *Polish White Book:*

When I took leave of the Chancellor I was escorted to the door by Baron von Neurath, who asked me to wait for him in order to discuss the matter of the communiqué. I then gave him the previously prepared main paragraph of the draft of the communiqué, which I intended to draw up as follows:

". . . reckoning with the situation created by the negotiations, the Reich Chancellor is against such activity, which would be directed against the rights and just interests of Poland in the Free City of Danzig."

After a ten-minute wait in the Chancellor's drawing room, Minister von Neurath handed me the communiqué that he and the Chancellor had drafted, with the words: "The Chancellor is offering you much more than you requested."

Looking at the text of the Minister's draft, I realized that it reached beyond any instructions I had received, and that consequently I would have to telephone you for further instructions.

The draft read as follows:

[8] For Baron von Neurath's memorandum on this conversation, see *DGFP*, Series C, Vol. 1, No. 201.

"The Polish envoy, Mr. Wysocki, today paid a visit to the German Reich Chancellor. The conference dealt with current political questions regarding Germany's relations with Poland. The Reich Chancellor stressed the firm intention of the German government to keep its assumptions and proceedings strictly within the frame of the existing agreement. The Reich Chancellor expressed his wish that the two countries should dispassionately examine and handle their mutual interests bilaterally."

After a discussion with Secretary of State Bülow concerning the persecution of Polish citizens of the Mosaic faith living in Germany, I suggested to Minister von Neurath that a confirmation of the Chancellor's peaceful intentions toward Poland be printed in orders issued by him as chief of the National Socialist Party and sent to all units and organizations of that party.

Minister von Neurath not only promised to consider this but assured me in advance of compliance with my suggestion, for which, as he said, he found the ground well prepared and toward which the Chancellor was well disposed. However, quite unexpectedly he returned to the communiqué he had drafted at noon, declaring that he had serious misgivings about whether it could be published in the form of an official German communiqué. It would, in his opinion, give the impression of acknowledging some uncommitted wrongs, and this he could not go along with. He then proposed another text, which I forthwith turned down since it contained nothing but a series of empty statements.

Finally, after a lengthy discussion, the Minister stated that he would not object to the publication in the Polish press of the communiqué in its original wording, provided that the Minister of Foreign Affairs in Warsaw summoned the German envoy, who would then publish in the German press an identical communiqué with the sole difference that it would refer to the Polish Minister of Foreign Affairs and the Polish government.

This communiqué, according to von Neurath, would read as follows:

"After the German Reich Chancellor had received yesterday the Polish envoy, Dr. Alfred Wysocki, the Polish Minister of Foreign Affairs in Warsaw also invited the German envoy, von Moltke. The conference dealt with current political questions regarding Poland's relations with Germany. The Polish Minister of Foreign Affairs stressed the firm intention of the Polish government to keep its assumptions and proceedings strictly within the frame of the existing agreement. The Polish Minister of Foreign Affairs expressed his desire that both countries should dispassionately examine and handle their mutual interests bilaterally."

On reading this I made no effort to conceal my dissatisfaction. I declared that I was accepting this new proposition *ad referendum,* and I immediately began to talk about those Germans who, to further their careers, were trying to win favor with the National Socialist Party, or who, to save themselves because they had Jewish blood in their veins, were now in the vanguard of those strongly attacking Poland and who were against any attempts to bring about peaceful relations with it. I had in mind, of course, those clerks of the Auswärtiges Amt who had prevailed upon Minister von Neurath within the brief span of a few hours to change his mind about the communiqué he had previously drafted.

*Dr. Alfred Wysocki*

Minister Beck immediately informed Marshal Piłsudski of the contents of Wysocki's telegrams and the reports of his conversation with Hitler. On May 3, in the early hours of the morning, I was summoned by the Minister to discuss the communiqué, whereupon the following instruction was drawn up for Envoy Wysocki.

DOCUMENT 12    Beck to Wysocki

Telephone message to the Polish Legation in Berlin sent from the Minister's Office on May 3, 1933, at 2:10 A.M.

Please request a meeting with von Neurath and in accordance with your government's instructions inform him as follows:

The Chancellor's declaration handed to you and confirmed by the Chancellor in a communiqué was received by the Polish government with satisfaction and is duly appreciated. You must express firm exception to the changes which the Auswärtiges Amt has tried to make in the communiqué. Von Neurath's proposed changes have totally altered the desire expressed by the Chancellor for a *détente* in mutual relations. We must therefore stubbornly insist that the Chancellor's decision to have the Wolff Agency issue the communiqué in its original wording be carried out. Whereupon we are ready to receive Moltke and, after consultation with him, have the Polish Telegraph Agency issue a communiqué reading more or less as follows:

"Bearing in mind the contents of the conversation held on May 2 between the Chancellor of the Reich and the Envoy of the Polish Republic in Berlin, as published by the Wolff Agency, which conversation introduces a spirit of *détente* in Polish-German relations, Minister Beck received the German Envoy and emphasized that the Polish government, for its part, was firmly intent on keeping its posture and activities strictly within the framework of existing treaties. He further expressed his wish that both countries study their mutual interests and deal with them dispassionately."

If you encounter resistance, please make it known that we will be forced to report on the development of this whole problem to higher quarters.

DOCUMENT 13   Wysocki to Beck

Telephone Message from Envoy Wysocki in Berlin on May 3, 1933, at 18:50 [6:50 P.M.]

Envoy Wysocki communicates that he has executed the telephone instruction of this day. Von Neurath agreed that the Wolff Agency would publish a communiqué, the contents of which would conform strictly with that approved by the Chancellor, with the additional information that von Neurath had been present at the conversation. It was also agreed that after Minister Beck's conversation with Envoy von Moltke a communiqué would be issued by us to the Polish Telegraph Agency, in accordance with this same text.[9]

International public opinion was taken aback by the contents of the Wysocki-Hitler conversation. That Hitler would agree on a *détente* with Poland was most unexpected, and political circles kept speculating about the reasons for such action. Rumors were circulated at that time, thoroughly without foundation, that the Polish government, in exchange for this declaration, had agreed to close its eyes to the *Anschluss*. This

[9] *Ibid.,* No. 206.

same story was repeated again later, when the nonaggression declaration with Germany was concluded. Even during my wartime stay in London I had to deny these rumors.

On May 4 the Ministry of Foreign Affairs sent to its diplomatic posts abroad a statement explaining Poland's posture toward Germany. The statement made it clear that, because of the tension in Polish-German relations caused by German atrocities against Polish citizens and Polish minorities, and because of Hitlerite excesses in Danzig threatening Poland's rights and interests in the Free City, the Polish government had deemed it imperative to consult with high-level authorities of the Reich. The Polish government could not establish a policy toward Germany based on rumors and diversionary acts. After briefly reporting on the results of the Wysocki-Hitler meeting, the instruction pointed out that "the understanding reached as a result of our *démarche* in Berlin wipes out all rumors which the Germans have been circulating about our supposed intentions of waging a preventive war."

It was damaging to Poland to stand accused by peace-minded Western countries of inciting to war. Now was the time to silence such rumors.

On May 4 the Minister of Foreign Affairs informed the Ambassador of France about these recent developments. He then stated that, without any prejudice as to the real value of the Chancellor's declaration, he considered it a positive fact that "Hitler was backing away from an unpleasant confrontation with Poland." He also reminded M. Laroche that the same press which yesterday had printed rumors of a possible Polish-German war might today just as easily go to the opposite extreme and write about an alliance. He asked the Ambassador to use his influence with the French press and ask them to report only the known facts.[10]

The Ministry of Foreign Affairs asked the various embassies and legations to report foreign reaction to Hitler's declaration. Among others, the chargé d'affaires assigned to the Italian government, Mr. T. Romer, wrote:

"I can report that the *détente* brought about by our *démarche* in Polish-German relations came as a great surprise here and was received with genuine satisfaction. Some persons expressed the hope that this would contribute toward an easing of the Polish-Italian tensions engendered by the Four-Power Pact. Considerable propaganda advantage will

[10] Laroche, pp. 127–28.

be gained locally since this will dispel German-inspired rumors that we are intent on waging a preventive war with Germany because of its territorial claims. These rumors have been circulating rather subtly in Rome for some time now."

The Polish envoy in Budapest, Mr. S. Łepkowski, reported on May 10, 1933:

"The minister of foreign affairs, Mr. Kanya, expressed his satisfaction at the *détente* in Polish-German relations. However, I had the distinct impression, as far as he himself was concerned, that this satisfaction was neither enthusiastic nor heartfelt. Very pointedly he immediately began to talk about the *Anschluss,* and he seemed visibly disturbed by the conciliatory attitude of Hitler toward Poland, as well as toward Russia, and how this might fit in with Germany's designs on its neighbors to the southeast."

The envoy in Belgrade, Mr. Schwarzburg-Gunther, reported Yugoslav reaction as follows on May 10:

"With regard to reflections on the conversations of Minister Wysocki with Chancellor Hitler, public opinion here, as well as official opinion within the Ministry of Foreign Affairs, seems to be of two minds. On the one hand, there is genuine satisfaction, basically friendly toward Poland, that Poland's relations with its western neighbor have taken a turn for the better; though this turn might be only temporary, it is still a great advantage for Poland. On the other hand, there is a sort of anxiety that Poland's success on this most important front could put it into a position of such great advantage that it might become estranged from the Little Entente and might feel it no longer needed support from allies and friends."

The English press took a noncommittal attitude toward the Wolff Agency communiqué. The big newspapers, such as *The Times,* the *Daily Telegraph,* and the *Manchester Guardian,* printed the facts in just a few lines. Only the *Daily Express* published a short commentary by its Berlin correspondent, Delmar, adding that the meeting between the Envoy and the Chancellor would contribute to an easing of the serious tension between Germany and Poland. The Polish Telegraph Agency's correspondent in London attributed the comparative silence of the English press to a growing hostility toward Hitler.

On May 16 Ambassador Skirmunt telegraphed:

"Today, awaiting an interview with Simon, whom I shall see at the end of the week, I called on Undersecretary of State Vansittart, informing him about the recent developments in Polish-German relations. Vansittart showed some skepticism. He acknowledged that British opinion showed an extraordinary unanimity of negative feelings toward Hitler's government. He said that, in his opinion, Hitler's speech tomorrow, even if moderate and peaceful, should be looked upon with suspicion and should not have any influence on public opinion; the Germans had already done a lot of talking, and behavioristically the German mentality was such that it would now insist on direct action. He assured me that, for their part, the British had done everything possible to establish and develop an understanding with France and the United States. Generally speaking, I was confronted with a total about-face in the Foreign Office's attitude toward Germany."

This change was not, as a matter of fact, due exclusively to unfavorable British reaction to Hitlerite methods. First of all, it was not in line with Britain's interests that, at this very moment when the West was negotiating with Germany on difficult problems pertaining to the Four-Power Pact, the Reich should ease tension in the east by a sort of compromise with Poland and a sort of conciliation with the Soviets. It must be remembered that the Foreign Office in general, and Vansittart in particular, were far less favorably disposed toward the Hitler regime than most British political and government circles. Differences of opinion became drastically obvious in ensuing years, when Neville Chamberlain, as prime minister, tried for an understanding with Hitler, acting completely on his own and without Foreign Office approval.

Initial reaction of the French press was limited to a mere printing of the communiqué, making no effort to play it up as a news story. But French diplomacy, on the other hand, was aroused by this about-face shown by Berlin and Warsaw.

On May 6 M. Laroche called at the Western Department to get full information on German matters. We had a long, informative discussion with him.[11] M. Laroche evaluated the meeting of the Polish Envoy with Hitler as a step in the right direction toward introducing an element of calm into relations between the two countries. He was not quite sure, however, how long this conciliation would last, or what the practical results would be. Referring to economic ramifications, M. Laroche brought up the problem of the boycott of German goods in Poland.

[11] The full text of this conversation is available in Lipski's papers at the Piłsudski Institute in New York, File 3.

Even Moltke was complaining to him about this, stating that *Gazeta Polska* had taken an unfriendly stand toward Germany on this subject. I explained that this boycott had come about because of the persecution of Jews in Germany, and that the whole problem had a much wider scope, reaching beyond relations between just Warsaw and Berlin. Reactions to the boycott had come from numerous countries, most recently from Turkey and the Balkans. Governments had no influence in this area. Jewish merchants followed the advice of their international unions. As far as easing of tension was concerned, I pointed to a number of treaties agreed on two years ago and still not ratified by Berlin, to the necessity for prompt and efficient settlement of border incidents, thereby pacifying the people residing near the borders, and, finally, to the need for a strict observance of the Polish-German radio agreement.

When we talked about the internal situation in Germany, the Ambassador expressed the idea that the time might come when Hitler would have to take some drastic action in order to appease the masses. We talked about differences within the government itself, between Hitlerites and right-wing nationals. The Ambassador wondered about von Papen's chances of taking over the portfolio from von Neurath, in case some changes were made in that quarter. I told him that I was convinced that neither Hindenburg nor the Herrenclub should thank von Papen for bringing Hitler into the government, and that in this case the Vice-Chancellor's action had been ill-advised and was anything but a stroke of genius.

Since the removal from influence of conservative Prussian elements, the Wilhelmstrasse existed in a kind of dream world of political isolation. As proof of this I told him about our recent protestations of anti-Jewish atrocities; the Auswärtiges Amt offered us words of sympathy, but no action was forthcoming. This office could not even reply to our notes, lest it lay itself open to criticism by party officials.

Our deepest concern was Austria. M. Laroche expressed his fear that, if Hitler felt the need for a victory abroad, he could turn against Austria as a weak country that would offer no military opposition. Italy would not move to help Austria, neither would France, "at least, I presume not," Laroche added. So everything would end with a sharp diplomatic protest. When asked by the Ambassador about our point of view I replied that Dollfuss' trip to Rome was motivated by a fear that the Reich's ministers would gain Mussolini's support for the *Anchluss*. I said that a direct move by Germany should not be expected, but that, nevertheless, things were happening inside Austria. The entrance of large numbers of the Heimwehr into the Hitlerite S.A. was significant. In official agencies too the Nazi element was increasing. The provinces were ahead of Vienna in this respect, since in Vienna socialists abounded and there were strong international influences. Chancellor Dollfuss was defending himself against reactions throughout the country by applying the old law from the time of the world war, which enabled the government not to convoke parliament.

In agreement with our point of view that the danger consisted in the developing internal situation, the Ambassador mentioned in passing that some people said that Hitler's declaration was the result of Poland's conciliatory attitude toward the Reich's annexation of Austria. I branded this as one more rumor based upon sheer fantasy. When asked by the Ambassador about Poland's stand with regard to the *Anschluss* I stated that the *Anschluss* would certainly be a great catastrophe and would threaten our economic interests. When the government of Poland concluded a Treaty of Preference with Austria, we also had in mind the idea of obtaining some sort of security in the area of economic exchanges with that country.

M. Laroche informed me of his purely personal pessimistic conviction that the *Anschluss* was only a matter of time. He pondered on what would be the repercussion on German-Italian relations. He said that two contradictory opinions existed. While some people thought that the *Anschluss* would estrange Italy from Germany, others were of the opinion that a complete rapprochement would take place between the two nations, owing to the untenable situation in which Italy would then find itself. I thought at that time the *Anschluss* would be something of a burden for Italy in its relations with Germany.

In the course of this long conversation the Ambassador informed me that he had seen Ovsieyenko—the Soviet ambassador—who had expressed great satisfaction over his talk with Marshal Piłsudski. Ovsieyenko's attitude toward Hitler's Germany was supposed to be very unfavorable. He thought that Germany was beginning to feel isolated from the West. On the other hand, the Soviet Ambassador considered anti-German reaction in England to be minimal and feared the possibility of an anti-Soviet understanding between the Hitlerites and certain British circles. Speaking of this to Laroche, Ovsieyenko probably had in mind the announced visit of Rosenberg to London. According to Ambassador Skirmunt's report (May 4, 1933), the *Evening Standard,* in announcing the visit of the chief ideologist of the Hitlerite party, recommended him highly. In connection with the almost simultaneous removal of Easterman, the editor of the *Daily Express* (who went over to the *Daily Herald*), rumors spread in the world of journalism in London as to possible contacts and collaboration between Beaverbrook and Rosenberg.

A few days after the publication of the communiqués Envoy von Moltke left for Berlin to report to his government.

In the Western Department we were busy establishing the line of our further tactics toward Germany.

I made a full report thereof, first to Minister Szembek and later to Minister Beck, who issued detailed instructions, following closely the line fixed by Marshal Piłsudski.

In a detailed letter to Envoy Wysocki, dated May 16, 1933, I stressed the basic points of the instruction to serve as informative material for the Legation in Berlin.

### DOCUMENT 14   Lipski to Wysocki

P.II. N.49/50/33.                                    May 16, 1933
                                                *Strictly Confidential*

Sir: As a result of your conversation with Hitler on May 2, 1933, and the ensuing publication of communiqués in Berlin and Warsaw, we are faced with the problem of what of practical value should be drawn from this political fact and what our future tactics toward Germany should be.

Deliberating on this problem in the Department I decided that, first of all, we should define what your aim was when you approached Hitler. Was our idea primarily to investigate the real intentions toward Poland of the decisive factor in the Reich, without drawing far-reaching practical consequences from this step of ours, or do we intend, upon receiving a positive reply from the Chancellor, to undertake further action to normalize Polish-German relations?

I discussed this, in my opinion, rather basic question with the Vice-Minister and the Minister of Foreign Affairs.

Guidelines were established, directing the future activity of the Department, and I take the liberty to communicate them to you to serve as orientation material.

Addressing a question to the government of Hitler as to its intentions toward Poland, as you did to the Chancellor, was unavoidable in view of the growing conviction in public opinion of an ever-increasing tension in Polish-German relations, and of rumors about Poland's alleged intention to wage a war of prevention. Besides, this step was aimed to emphasize Poland's independence in her foreign policy on the international scene.

This action of ours resulted in a clarification of the situation, introducing a certain *détente* in Polish-German relations, and (on this point the Minister placed special emphasis) stressing Poland's importance as a factor to be respectfully considered by the dictator of Germany in formulating his policy.

On the international scene this step of ours did not hurt us in the least; on the contrary, it enhanced our prestige.

So your *démarche* has fulfilled its intentions. But, as to drawing other conclusions about a more lasting *détente* in Polish-German relations, utmost precaution must be observed.

I concede that this caution is due to the undetermined internal situation in Germany, to the ever-increasing hostile attitude of the West to the Hitler regime, and, finally, to the desire of keeping a free hand in the face of such international entanglements.

I now pass to specific Polish-German problems which require special handling as a result of the conversations of May 2 and 4, 1933.

I. The last Polish-German conversations, which evoked a strong repercussion in the press of both countries, undoubtedly brought about some clearance of the atmosphere. Both the government press and the national-democratic press in Poland welcomed the Berlin talks with satisfaction and a full realization of the reality of the situation. We cannot be held responsible for articles in the *Ilustrowany Kurier Codzienny* [*IKC,* a tabloid], banned from Germany and leading a furious campaign against the Hitler government, although the Ministry did everything in its power to soften the *IKC*'s tone. The Vice-Minister even had a personal talk with Deputy Dąbrowski to this effect. We also stopped some anti-Chancellor demonstrations, for example, on the stage, in window displays, etc., with one exception—when hostile anti-Hitler demonstrations came from or were performed by Jewish circles.

Similarly, if the German government were to launch a protest about the boycott of goods we would answer that, as long as the Reich's hostile attitude toward the Jews prevails, the Polish government can do practically nothing.

II. On the subject of the Jews, we have issued, as I have already advised you, instructions to our embassies and legations to act with considerable discretion in their propaganda action, not restraining it, however, in view of its importance in helping certain countries to ascertain and assume an attitude toward Germany.

We are also supporting fully, with due precaution, any claims made by the Jews to the League dealing with the persecution of Jews in Germany.

We do not plan to publish a White Book at this time, although we are continuing work on one.

In this connection the Minister considers it most important that the Polish Legation in Berlin and the consulates under its supervision continue to give assistance to Polish citizens of Jewish nationality living in the Reich, and that they should intervene, as they have been doing, at the central offices and with local authorities.

On the other hand, we do not consider it advisable to give special publicity to this assistance. We possess proof that our efforts to defend Jews in Germany meet with favor for the Polish government in international Jewish circles. This is communicated, among others, from Vienna, America, and England.

The Ministry of Foreign Affairs should certainly be informed without delay about all such steps taken by the Legation in Berlin and the consulates in Germany, in order to make them known to Jewish organizations.

III. The Minister has no restrictions as to the practical settlement of other basic Polish-German matters, namely:

a) ratification by Germany of conventions still pending
b) conclusion of an understanding in border incidents
c) strict observance of the radio agreement of March 31, 1931

In the last field an exchange of letters has already taken place between the Polish and German radio groups, and the German side has stated that it intends to comply with the provisions of the agreement. Copies of the letters will be forwarded to the Legation.

As to another problem, the Minister has some misgivings about whether it is advisable at present to bind ourselves with regard to the press, and he therefore asks you to postpone your discourse with Goebbels. In general, as far as eventual talks with other leaders of the National Socialist Party are concerned, the Minister has not yet committed himself.

Von Moltke returned from Berlin a few days ago. I thought he would discuss the *détente* in Polish-German relations, since I had inferred he would from information received indirectly. However, up until now he has not done so. I am dining with him on the 18th.

General Schindler [12] has made it known that he is very pleased with the way the Marshal received him; Piłsudski made a tremendous impression on him. Schindler, at this first encounter, appears to be a very skilled agent; he stresses his Bavarian origin and his Catholicism. Furthermore, he treats Polish-German differences lightly, even the territorial ones.

*J. Lipski*

I sent this instruction to Berlin on the eve of Hitler's speech in the Reichstag (May 17, 1933).

In his speech the Chancellor struck a conciliatory tone. He expressed his peaceful intentions and tried to reassure Poland and France that the Reich would respect their national feelings and the treaties in force. [13]

Here ends the article written by Jósef Lipski.

Thus, after a long period of difficulties in Polish-German relations, thanks to the initiative of Marshal Piłsudski many problems were now settled in the attempt to secure normal relations between the two neighboring states. Envoy Wysocki's mission in Berlin had been accomplished. In June, 1933, Marshal Piłsudski decided to recall Wysocki from Berlin and name him ambassador to Rome. To the Berlin post he appointed Lipski on July 3, 1933.

On July 13 Hitler received Envoy Wysocki at a farewell audience. In Wysocki's report to Beck on his conversation with Hitler (see *Polish White Book*, No. 4) were the following sentences which were omitted from the *White Book* (after the second paragraph):

"Hitler then repeated a sentence already familiar from his first talk with me on May 2 [1933]: 'If the so-called Corridor had been pushed further eastward, we would sit together today facing each other in peace and mutual understanding of our own interests! It happened otherwise, and now both nations carry the burden of that unreasonable solution.' "

[12] Gen. Max Joseph Schindler, military attaché to the German Legation in Warsaw. For the report by Schindler of his visit with Marshal Piłsudski, see *DGFP*, Series C, Vol. I, No. 221.
[13] *Polish White Book*, No. 3.

# Order of the Reichswehr in Connection with the Withdrawal of Germany from the League of Nations[1]

## October, 1933

WHEN HITLER came to power he fixed a period of five years in which to build up German military forces, that is, until April 1, 1938.

Starting from this date, the Reich's military power was to become a chief trump card in its international gamble. From 1933 basic changes were introduced by the Reichswehr into its previously existing foundations of strategy. In accordance with Hitler's orders, the auxiliary plan, formerly directed exclusively against Poland, was to be shifted, as of April 1, 1934, to a more extensive plan providing for a possible war on two fronts.

Work on the reorganization of the German Army could hardly keep pace with the dynamic policy of the dictator of the Third Reich. Hitler took risky decisions in his international policy, incommensurable with the state of the Reich's defenses. Warnings of the generals were not taken into consideration. Hitler's first risky step was walking out of the disarmament conference and withdrawing Germany from the League on October 14, 1933. Tactics applied by Hitler to the Western Powers, especially to France, with the concealed motive of breaking with the Geneva institution that restricted his actions in the field of armaments, were intended as a security measure for Germany against possible sanctions by the Western Powers. During this period Hitler displayed a far-reaching desire for an understanding when, on June 7, 1933, he concluded the Four-Power Pact; when, on May 5, 1933, he extended the Berlin Treaty of 1926 with Soviet Russia; and when, on July 20, 1933, he signed a concordat with the Vatican. In a series of talks carried on at that time with the French Ambassador, Hitler repeatedly expressed his

[1] Published in *Sprawy Międzynarodowe* (London), 1947, Nos. 2–3.

desire to reach an understanding with France, and made light of all revisionist intentions with regard to Alsace. Germany's top brain-trust was very much concerned with the idea of a preventive war.

François-Poncet, at that time French ambassador in Berlin, wrote about Hitler's attitude as follows:

"To straighten out external politics enough to regain independence, but not far enough to expose himself to a premature war, this is the program he has at present in mind and which he will force himself to follow. Are the Allied Powers able to understand to what extent his mind is obsessed by the fear of isolation and the dread of a preventive war in the first period of his domination? Even if they were fully conscious of it, the democratic nature of their institutions, the pacifism they are imbued with, the repugnance inspired in them and their people by the very idea of war, would prevent them from using the menace of which Hitler is most terrified. From episode to episode their passivity will enhance the audacity of the gambler, and when they wish to react it will be too late; the roles will be reversed, since Hitler will then menace them." [2]

The concept of a preventive war, conceived in the mind of Piłsudski during this time, did not meet with a warm reception in the capitals of the Western Powers. The reinforcement of the Westerplatte garrison on March 6, 1933, a striking symbol of Poland's decision to counteract Hitlerite aggressive attempts, met with firm opposition from French and British diplomacy. However, looking back retrospectively, there existed at that time all the means necessary to arrest Hitler's march and save Europe from so many disasters.

General Blomberg's order [3] issued on October 25, 1933, over a week after Hitler declared that Germany had withdrawn from the League of Nations, confirms to what extent Germany was unprepared to repel a joint French-Polish attack at that time.

A political analysis of this military order is reducible to the statement that the further development of the international situation brought about by Germany's withdrawal from the League of Nations and its walking out of the disarmament conference could lead to the application of sanctions against Germany. Blomberg stressed that, until a decision was made by the Council of the League, the possibility of France's admin-

[2] François-Poncet, p. 140.
[3] *Trial of the Major War Criminals*, XXXIV, 488.

istering sanctions and drawing Poland, Belgium, and Czechoslovakia into this action should be considered. Enumerating various possible moves of the enemy, the order stated that the government of the Reich was prepared to wage local military resistance, regardless of chances of military success. This last sentence is of particular significance.

The line of defense was to run westward along the rivers Roer and Rhine to the Black Forest; in the east from the river Hötzenplotz-Nischlitz and the river Oder, and along the river Ober, in conjunction with the defense of German Pomerania. Against Czechoslovakia defense was anticipated alongside the frontier. Against France and Poland resistance was to be maintained as long as possible, while to Czechoslovakia territory was to be ceded, but "inch by inch."

As compared with military directives of more recent years, the order of October 25, 1933, borders upon improvisation. This was due to a lack of proper military preparedness, as well as to the fact that the German command was taken by surprise by the possible international entanglements resulting from Germany's withdrawal from the League of Nations.

For an appraisal of Piłsudski's move toward Hitler on November 15, 1933, the above order is not without significance. Piłsudski was right in his estimation of the military potential of Germany when he directed me to use the argument of force in my interview with Hitler. Hitler understood: he proposed a nonaggression pact to Piłsudski. With this offer in hand, Piłsudski once more turned to France. He broke off further talks and left for Wilno. And once more Paris responded with no will to act.

On January 26, 1934, the Polish-German declaration of nonaggression was signed.

# Declaration of Nonaggression

## Autumn, 1933—January, 1934

---

THE UNDERSTANDING between Wysocki and Hitler led to a rapid relaxation of tension in Polish-German relations. After the elections in Danzig (May 28), when the Hitlerites came to power in the city (gaining 38 out of 72 mandates), Dr. Hermann Rauschning, president of the city, and Albert Forster, chief of the Nazi Party in Danzig, paid an official visit to Warsaw on July 3, 1933. The Polish-Danzig Agreement was concluded on August 5, liquidating many conflicts,[1] and on September 18 an implementing protocol was signed of which Poland tried to take advantage on the international scene.

On September 25 and 26 Minister Beck met in Geneva with Ministers von Neurath and Goebbels. They had a friendly conversation.[2]

Józef Lipski, the newly appointed Polish envoy in Germany, arrived in Berlin on October 2. On October 17 he had a talk with Minister von Neurath, and on October 18 he presented his credentials to President Hindenburg. In his speech Lipski emphasized that he would perform his mission along the lines of principles agreed to in the conversation of Envoy Wysocki with Chancellor Hitler on May 2, that is, the observance of treaties in force and a dispassionate investigation of mutual interests. Hindenburg stressed the need for a just and fair adjustment of mutual problems. Lipski observed that during the audience not a single Nazi was present in Hindenburg's entourage.

The following handwritten memorandum was found among the papers of Ambassador Lipski:

In the first days of November, 1933, I was summoned to Warsaw. At the Foreign Affairs Ministry I was told that Marshal Piłsudski wanted to see me. Before my departure for Berlin, I had been received by the President of the Polish Republic, but at that time Beck told me that the Marshal would probably be willing to receive me only at a later date.

On November 5 at 6 P.M. the Marshal received me at the Belveder, with Minister Beck also present. Piłsudski was sitting at a little round table in one of the smaller drawing rooms at the rear, on the right-hand

[1] *German White Book*, No. 179.
[2] *Polish White Book*, No. 5; *DGFP*, Series C, Vol. I, Nos. 449 and 451.

side of the entrance. Beck introduced me. Piłsudski stood up and extended his hand, which was small and narrow and impressed me as being very aristocratic. There was a moment of silence. I sat opposite Piłsudski, with Beck on his left.

Piłsudski began the conversation with a question: "You arrive, Mr. Envoy, from a very interesting country; how do you size up Hitler with regard to his regime's stability?"

I replied with a detailed analysis of the situation. First of all I stated that National Socialism was spreading like wildfire over all fields of German life.

However, I called attention to the fact that National Socialism, while a growing *dynamic* movement, showed no *static* features. Hence the difficulty to ascertain whether Hitlerism had constructive elements for durability.

This definition visibly arrested Piłsudski's attention. He remarked casually, "Obviously, it is easier to rule with a whip."

From my analysis of the situation in Germany I concluded that I saw no other person who could compete with Hitler. When I pointed to certain difficulties evident among German leftists (Communists), the Marshal asked what the attitude of the Prussian Junkers was. He remarked that people with such a long tradition for ruling would probably not be easily reconciled to the idea that power was slipping from their grasp. At this point I illustrated with numerous data and comments, pointing to the fact that so-called Prussian elements did not accept the fact that the reins were in Hitler's hands.

Piłsudski, turning to Beck and confirming what great weight he attached to this Prussian influence, said literally, "You see, this you underestimate."

When I finished the political analysis, Piłsudski inquired whether Hitler was not threatened from the economic side.

I gave an extensive factual explanation to the effect that, in spite of economic difficulties, I did not expect any convulsion from this side such as might turn the scale against the regime.

It was rather characteristic that, while Piłsudski followed my political review with great interest, asked questions, and discussed particular points of my statements, he listened rather passively to what I said about the economic situation.

When I finished, he simply said that he acknowledged my conclusions.

Then, addressing himself to Beck, Piłsudski said: "Well, then, *let us try.*"

Issuing detailed instructions for my conversation with Hitler, he was very precise, laid special stress on certain phrases, and repeated the instructions twice:

You will say to the Chancellor that you were summoned to Warsaw to report to Marshal Piłsudski. The Marshal received you in the presence of Minister of Foreign Affairs Beck and, upon listening to your report, recommended that you present to Chancellor Hitler the following trend of ideas on his behalf:

The coming to power in Germany of the National Socialist government caused a considerable uproar among international opinion at large. This event was linked with the possibility of serious military conflicts. Under these circumstances, it was expedient in Poland to consider measures necessary to safeguard national security. The Marshal, far from being impressed by the press and propaganda campaigns, had confidence in the Chancellor and his policies. He did not order any defense measures. The Marshal confirms with satisfaction that Polish-German relations have improved, owing to the Chancellor's personality, and so his expectations have been verified. Reflecting upon the present situation, the Marshal declares that Poland's security is based on two elements— namely, upon direct relations of Poland with other states (in this instance, on Polish-German relations), and upon the collaboration of states within the frame of the League of Nations. The Marshal describes this second element as a sort of reinsurance, ensuing from the fact that the states, as members of the League of Nations, are bound by obligations under the pact of the League of Nations, especially in case of conflict, etc.

Therefore the last decision of the Reich government, resulting in Germany's withdrawal from the League of Nations, deprived Poland of this second element of security. This decision of the Reich provoked a strong stir among international opinion and an agitation of minds.

All this compels the Marshal, as a person responsible for the security of the state, to review the situation.

He would not like to strain the atmosphere between the two states by reinforcing Poland's defense measures.

Prior to taking such a step, the Marshal desires to ask, quite loyally, a question of Chancellor Hitler: whether he is willing to compensate for this loss of a security factor in Polish-German relations.

"Upon your arrival in Berlin, you should immediately ask for an audience with Chancellor Hitler." Pilsudski laid special stress on the sentence about "the necessity of his taking steps to reinforce security," remarking: *"This you must tell him."*

Further, Piłsudski directed me to add on his behalf that security could not be guaranteed for the present only, "für die Gegenwart," as this would have just the opposite effect.

To my question—how to react if Hitler offered a nonaggression pact —Piłsudski replied that this should be seriously taken into consideration.

When I mentioned that I heard from the French side that at the Auswärtiges Amt they were allegedly thinking about a nonaggression pact with Poland, Piłsudski (rather incomprehensibly to me) replied in French: "C'est plutot une intrigue Tchèque."

From the Marshal's general statements I recall a sentence he said casually to Beck, talking about Poland's relations with Germany and Russia: *"Radek went the furthest, for he even wanted to give me the command of the two armies."* [3]

The Marshal also mentioned a certain statement which could be made in Berlin if the occasion arose, but then, looking at Beck, he said that to him (that is, to me) he would not say that, but that Beck would know himself how to do it.

When I asked Beck afterward what the Marshal had in mind, Beck

[3] The nonaggression pact between Poland and the USSR was signed on July 25, 1932. When Hitler seized power on January 30, 1933, Piłsudski tried to improve the rather cool atmosphere prevailing in Polish-Soviet relations by persuading Moscow of Poland's willingness to maintain the contracted pact and to establish friendly contacts as good neighbors. At the end of April, 1933, Mr. Bogusław Miedziński, the general editor of *Gazeta Polska*, a press organ which usually reflected the views of the Polish government, was sent on a special mission to Moscow. There he engaged in preliminary conversations with Karol Radek, editor of *Izvestiia*. He declared to him, on behalf of Piłsudski, that, contrary to what was thought in Russia, Poland was not a sally port to the invasion of Russia and that it would never, under any circumstances, join Germany against Russia (see Miedziński "Droga do Moskwy," *Kultura* [Paris], 1963, No. 188, p. 85).

Radek paid a return visit to Miedziński in Warsaw on July 6–22, 1933. During a number of conversations with Miedziński, he debated the possibilities of a further rapprochement between Poland and the USSR in the cultural, economic, and political fields (USSR *désintéressement* with regard to Lithuania). He also mentioned the possibility of armed conflict between Poland and Germany and Russia's readiness to come to Poland's rescue by supplying war matériel, munitions, and gasoline. He also suggested a possibility of contact between the general staffs of the two states (Miedziński, "Pakty Wilanowskie," *ibid.*, No. 189–90, p. 119).

The above words of Piłsudski probably refer to these conversations of Miedziński with Radek.

explained that Piłsudski had an idea for a certain revision of the Versailles Treaty with regard to the resolution depriving Germany of equality. According to his concept, signatories of the treaty should enter into a single agreement with Germany, revising some treaty clauses, instead of letting the Germans bargain concession after concession from them. All further German claims, as for instance under the territorial clause, would then be considered *casus belli*.

This concept, however, never saw the light of day.

At the end of the conversation, when I had already gotten up to take my leave, Piłsudski, with a gesture of his hand denoting some hesitation, said, looking at me: "If you succeed, well and good; if you fail, I shall not blame you for it."

*N.B.* The Marshal also mentioned during the conversation that, if I should succeed, then Beck would have a headache, but if my conversation with the Chancellor were a failure, then he [the Marshal] would be in trouble (as commander in chief).

The conversation lasted for an hour. Piłsudski was all the time in a very serious mood, and it was obvious that he had a weighty decision on his mind.

At Beck's request, he gave an order for a press communiqué to be published announcing that I had been received at the Belveder.

From the Belveder I left with Minister Beck for the Raczyński Palace, where we wrote down the Marshal's instructions.

On the same evening I left for Berlin.

The communiqué published in Warsaw on the evening of November 5 was telegraphed abroad.

At the station, when I was leaving Warsaw, Konrad Wrzos, a spry journalist smelling big news, was present. He even had a photographer with him, but I arrived at the last moment and the picture was not taken.

Immediately upon my arrival in Berlin, I took the necessary steps at the Auswärtiges Amt to obtain an audience with the Chancellor. I approached the director of protocol, Count von Bassewitz, on this matter.

However, a few days later Count Bassewitz advised me that Chancellor Hitler was busy with the election campaign, touring various cities, and would not be able to grant me an audience prior to the peoples referendum. In the meantime I was received by von Neurath. However I had strict orders from Warsaw that the Marshal's instructions were destined for Hitler only and were to be kept secret. I also had a visit from von Moltke at the Legation. He too was very anxious to learn something about the Marshal's message for Hitler. Von Moltke later told me that, being *au courant* of the situation, he was not mistaken in his suppositions as to what I was to present to the Chancellor.

Secrecy on our part was very appropriate, since the clerks of the Auswärtiges Amt still clung to their negative attitude toward Poland, and any indiscreet hint from me prior to my conversation with Hitler in person could easily be exploited by them to our disadvantage.

The conversation with Hitler took place on November 15 in the presence of Minister von Neurath, and Lipski informed Beck accordingly on the same day.

The text of Lipski's report is included in the *Polish White Book* (No. 6, p. 16). There are, however, two omissions. Lipski's opening words were:

"When the National Socialist government came to power in Germany, this evoked considerable commotion in international opinion, including even the possibility of poltical conflicts. Under these circumstances the necessity arose in Poland to administer measures to reinforce national security. The Marshal, far from being influenced by the atmosphere created by the press and propaganda, trusts the Chancellor and his policies. He has not taken any measures of a defensive character. The Marshal is satisfied to observe that Polish-German relations have improved since this time, owing to the Chancellor's personality, and that his expectations were realized."

At the end of the fifth paragraph, the following sentence of Hitler was omitted:

"Perhaps sometime in the future certain problems can be settled with Poland in a friendly atmosphere, for example, by compensation." (The Chancellor spoke of this as something very distant, never uttering the words "frontier" or "corridor.")

On the same day, November 15, the Wolff Agency issued a communiqué on Lipski's visit with Hitler; according to this communiqué, it was agreed that the Polish and German governments would "deal with the questions affecting both countries by way of direct negotiations, and further renounce all application of force in their mutual relations, with a view to strengthening European peace." [4]

After Lipski's visit with Hitler, a conference was held at the Belveder on November 20 among Piłsudski, Minister Beck, and Undersecretary of State Szembek. The German plan for a nonaggression declaration was not yet known to the Polish side.

Beck reported on the first international press comments about the Berlin visit, stressing that the Russian press took a very correct stand—more favorable than the French.

[4] *Polish White Book,* No. 7; *DGFP,* Series C, Vol. II, Nos. 69 and 70.

A note drawn up by Szembek immediately after the conference reads as follows:

"The Marshal is availing himself of this report. He thinks that the success achieved by us is not a 100 percent success. As a matter of fact, it does not give much. There is positive meaning not in what was done but in the moment when it was done, that is, after Germany left the League of Nations. What will follow next is not known. The Marshal is now interested in two problems: Russia and France. It is easier to come to an understanding with France; with Russia it is much more difficult. You have to be consistent and patient there, otherwise errors might occur which not we, but the Soviets, will profit by. . . . The Marshal says that he intends to summon the French military attaché, receive him in a military manner, and talk to him as one soldier to another. He will tell him *l'historique* of Lipski's conversation, from an angle not very favorable for the Germans, and he will tell him that we want to know what France really wants. *Further talks with the Germans will depend on the answer.* [Emphasis in the original.] The Marshal considers a 'plus' the sending of a chief of the French Second Bureau. This conversation will reach Daladier, probably through General Gamelin. It is rather doubtful whether via Laroche. The Marshal will tell him that this is strictly confidential, and 'si Monsieur Daladier est homme d'honneur' it will end there (these last words referred to keeping it secret from the press)." [5]

After the Lipski-Hitler conversation the Auswärtiges Amt promptly prepared a plan of the declaration, and on November 24 Envoy von Moltke received instructions in Warsaw to obtain an audience with Piłsudski to present him with the draft-declaration.[6]

On November 27 Lipski was summoned by von Neurath. The conversation and his critical remarks are described by Lipski in his report to Beck dated November 30, 1933.

DOCUMENT 15    Lipski to Beck

Berlin, November 30, 1933
*Strictly Confidential*

On November 27 I was unexpectedly summoned by Foreign Affairs Minister von Neurath, who stated to me as follows:

Minister von Moltke has been instructed to ask for an audience with Marshal Piłsudski. The audience was fixed for this afternoon. In this conversation, Moltke was to convey to the Marshal the greetings of

[5] The note is quoted in Szembek's letter to Raczyński of August 31, 1942 (Lipski's papers, File 3).
[6] *DGFP*, Series C, Vol. II, No. 84. See also Nos. 77, 79, and 81.

Chancellor Hitler and at the same time hand him the German draft of the declaration.

Neurath handed me a copy of the plan, stressing that he was doing this as a gesture of courtesy, *à titre d'information*. I noticed at the time that the plan bears the heading *Erklärung,* since nowadays the use of the word "pact" is too commonplace.

At Neurath's request I read the document in his presence but, for obvious reasons, I abstained from making any comment.

Minister von Neurath finally told me that he is awaiting a communiqué about the audience in Warsaw and asked for my assistance in case of any technical difficulties with the publication of the communiqué.

Following your instructions, forwarded to me by Mr. Dębicki, I kept the whole matter strictly secret. However, as I have on occasion for Warsaw, I am taking the liberty of sending you the following observations:

In his talk with me on November 15, Hitler assumed that the possibility of war would be excluded from Polish-German relations. He is ready to have this principle take the form of a treaty. I also stress that after this conversation, as I have already informed you, the Chancellor publicly declared that "there are no questions between the German Reich and Poland which might justify bloodshed" (interview for *Matin*).[7]

The Chancellor further developed the idea that an atmosphere of confidence should be created between the countries by means of relaxation in various fields. The problem of frontiers was not touched on by the Chancellor specifically in the conversation; he only hinted that these matters should be left for the future, in the hope that under favorable circumstances a solution might be found to satisfy both parties.

Let us now take into consideration the known plan;[8] even upon a perfunctory analysis we can discover therein the following points:

[7] In the part of the interview for *Matin* referring to the opinion that no contestable problem existed in Europe which would justify the outbreak of war, the Chancellor stressed: "Everything can be settled between national governments if they are conscious of honor and responsibility. There exist a patriotic Poland and a Germany devoted to their traditions. Between them there are contentions and frictions caused by a bad treaty, but there is nothing else which would be worthy of bloodshed, especially since on a battlefield the best usually perish. Therefore a good-neighborly understanding between Germany and Poland is fully possible." And polemizing on the statement that the present German government had aggressive intentions, the Chancellor expressed himself thus: "I have not the slightest intention of attacking my neighbors. Poland understands this. Situated further east than France, Poland knows us better."

[8] *DGFP,* Series C, Vol. II, No. 81.

The authors of the plan tried not to call the document a pact, limiting themselves to giving it the heading *Erklärung*. Neurath's explanation that this was done in order to avoid the commonplace term, that is, "pact," is not logical. It rather seems that a general definition was used instead of "pact excluding war" or else "pact" with some other adjective —for example, nonaggression—since this would not correspond with the real text of the plan. It was probably not the authors' intention to use a term conforming with the actual meaning of the word "plan."

The first paragraph, purely political in character, tries to shift Polish-German relations from the platform of the Treaty of Versailles to the ground of direct understanding. Hitherto, in German opinion, Poland existed only as a creation of the Treaty of Versailles.

In the second paragraph, attention is drawn to the assertion that maintaining and assuring a "just peace" between the two nations is an indispensable condition for a general peace in Europe. The idea of a just peace, however, might provoke different interpretations, and therefore should be accepted with reserve, especially since the word "justly" takes on a special meaning as it is used in further paragraphs.

The third paragraph ties in the planned declaration with the Polish-German arbitration agreement signed at Locarno and with the Kellogg Pact, and states that obligations ensuing from these agreements should be defined.

This definition follows immediately in the next [fourth] paragraph, when parties bind themselves to seek solutions for *all* contentions that arise between them in a conciliatory way or by arbitration. Such a broad concept of the matter reserves for the Germans the possibility of introducing on the platform of bilateral talks, and later submitting to arbitration, such problems as minorities and even territorial problems. The declaration of abstention from force, in conformity with the principles of the Kellogg Pact in this respect, makes no difference whatsoever here.

The fifth paragraph would in general correspond to the Chancellor's concept that "important problems" which divide the two countries because of a "bad" treaty should be left to a better atmosphere in the future. This semirestriction to settle these problems in the future might also be necessary to the Chancellor, bearing in mind the attitude of the Prussian elements definitely hostile to Hitler's policies toward Poland. However, attention is drawn here to the fact that the expression "schwebende Probleme" was used, which, if accepted, would consist of a mutual ascertainment that in these matters there is contention between the two states about "serious problems" demanding settlement. With the simultaneous acceptance of the principle of obligatory arbitration for all matters under dispute, this entails grave danger of the possibility for one party to raise any problem, even a territorial one, at a favorable moment, without any responsibility of guilt for provoking the conflict. This is of the utmost importance, as far as the *casus foederis* of Poland with its allies is concerned.

If we now compare the plan handed to us, which was probably technically elaborated on by the Auswärtiges Amt, with the contents of my conversation with Hitler on November 15, we can observe that this plan, though drawn along Hitler's lines, nevertheless at many points goes beyond and even changes this line, as it was presented to me by Hitler, to our disadvantage.

In comparison with the declaration of November 15, wherein the willingness of both governments not to resort to force in mutual relations was expressed, the plan imposes on both governments the obligation not to apply force, with the simultaneous formal commitment to submit to conciliation and arbitration all problems deriving from mutual relations, thus impairing guarantees resulting from Poland's membership in the League of Nations as well as from our direct defensive alliances.

When deliberating over this document, two suppositions come to mind which are difficult to confirm; nevertheless, I am taking the liberty of revealing them to you:

Chancellor Hitler, if this step is taken directly by him, wants to find out how far Poland would go to achieve a direct understanding with Germany, its relations with the League of Nations and the Western Powers notwithstanding.

As far as the Auswärtiges Amt is concerned, it is not impossible that this office, composed of persons utterly hostile toward any kind of understanding with Poland, could try, by sufficient editing of the plan, to render difficult the settlement of relations between the new masters of Germany and Poland. For it is quite possible that the Chancellor limited himself simply to tracing general directions, and the Office of Foreign Affairs elaborated on the text, introducing adequate encumbrances.

*Józef Lipski*

Moltke was received by Beck on November 25 [9] and by Marshal Piłsudski in Beck's presence on the 27th, when he handed over the German draft-declaration.[10]

Soon after the conversation with Moltke, Piłsudski received the French military attaché, General d'Arbonneau, with whom he discussed the problem of Polish-German relations, as one soldier to another.[11] Then Piłsudski left for Wilno, taking Moltke's plan with him and issuing no further decisions. He requested an explanation of several points. The long delay in Piłsudski's answer caused considerable trouble for Moltke.

Meanwhile the feelings of German circles toward the Polish Legation in Berlin underwent a radical change as compared with the period referred to by Envoy Wysocki in the article quoted above (see pp. 43–45). This is clear from the letter Lipski wrote to Roman Dębicki, director of Beck's cabinet.

DOCUMENT 16    Lipski to Dębicki

Berlin, December 3, 1933
*Strictly Confidential*

Events and moods develop so rapidly in this dynamic territory of ours that, although I was only in Warsaw on November 4, I already feel the necessity for contact with the Ministry.

As I have to continue my visits to other members of the cabinet, following the rule of protocol, good orientation is very advisable.

On Monday I shall call on Vice-Chancellor von Papen. I am still delaying the visit to Goebbels, since a discussion with him might be highly political in character. However, further delay is becoming embarrassing, and I am afraid of offending Goebbels, who is well disposed toward us.

Owing to my experience with Darré,[12] you will understand that I must take all precautions, since I am practically empty-handed. Ministers of the new regime are very fond of pursuing, so to say, their own

[9] For Moltke's report, see *ibid.*, No. 87.
[10] Moltke's report, *ibid.*, No. 90.
[11] Laroche, p. 141.
[12] Walter Darré became minister of food and agriculture after the resignation of Hugenberg in June, 1933. On November 25, the Polish-German rye agreement was signed; afterward Minister Lipski paid a visit to Minister Darré. As a result of this visit, the Ministry prepared a communiqué for the press quoting opinions of the Polish Envoy on internal German regulations concerning agriculture. Lipski, to whom the text of the communiqué was forwarded for confirmation, had to make a number of corrections.

policy, and at the present moment, seeing as their particular task the leading of Germany away from isolation, they try to be most active in international problems. As if by orders from the top, a change of front toward us is taking place all along the line. In Hitlerite spheres they talk about the new Polish-German friendship. Every activity of mine, even the most insignificant, such as the exchange of ratification documents with regard to the small frontier traffic, serves as an excuse for political enunciations by the press about the rapprochement. Everyone wants to be in contact with us. At a reception for our military attaché, the full brass of the Reichswehr appeared, including General Hammerstein, General Schaumburg, and Colonel von Reichenau, a thing which had never happened before. You can imagine the surprise of other military attachés, the French, etc. Yesterday, at the reception for the football team, the Brown Shirts and representatives of the Reichswehr created a most cordial atmosphere. Rumors are circulated that the Führer himself is interested in this match, and might possibly appear personally in the stands.

My initial response to these demonstrations was to instruct all our professional offices in the territory of the Reich, above all the consuls, to avail themselves of this disposition in order to settle matters hitherto impossible to arrange, and to establish contacts with the authorities to settle whatever is possible and what is definitely to our advantage.

However, as far as my diplomatic tactics are concerned, things are far more complicated, bearing in mind what I have mentioned before—that every step of the Legation is discounted on the outside, and that I do not know what our Ministry's directive is and whether a strong action in Berlin would not cause embarrassment in other territories. I therefore am maintaining a sort of reserve, at the same time being careful not to estrange people of the new regime and to keep them well disposed toward us.

Now if I am to speak of politics, I had the first echo of Moltke's conversation with the Marshal from Secretary of State Meissner, privy adviser of Hindenburg. Meissner told me that he read the report of Moltke, who sounds very enthusiastic about the reception the Marshal accorded him. This was also confirmed by the chief of the Eastern Department of the A.A., who told me that Moltke, who arrived here on Friday, was very much impressed by this conversation and by the Marshal's profound appraisal of Polish-German problems. Director Meyer stressed the fact that Moltke was so promptly received, and that the audience lasted nearly one hour and a half. He touched on the matter of the document, mentioning that he had not drawn it up himself. Stressing that he was only doing his best to accommodate us, he tried discreetly to sound out my point of view, but I kept aloof. Moltke, who called on me today before his departure, also asked about my opinion, but he received no reply. He emphasized that the document reflects ideas of the Chancellor, who practically dictated it. He added that he hopes there will not be too many cancellations on our side.

I think that you will agree with my tactics of absolute silence, which seems to me the only possible way of acting and perhaps to a certain degree also a useful one.

Moltke complained to me about the difficulties he encounters in Warsaw in trade negotiations. He stressed that I have here such a friendly relationship with the authorities, while he sometimes waits in vain for the promised answers of the Ministry of Industry on economic matters. He added that, in response to my request, the A.A. agreed to abolish the *junctim* between the rye agreement and other trade negotiations.

The situation here remains most intricate and it is exceedingly difficult to guess the real intentions of the government. No progress has hitherto been achieved on the French sector. The conversation of François-Poncet with the Chancellor, which has leaked to the press, was exaggeratedly blown up by the local press and presented as an overture for concrete talks. However, the Ambassador told me, and it was confirmed from other sources, that his conversation was only a vague exchange of opinions without any tangible results. The only concrete thing was the Chancellor's firm declaration that the Germans would in any case not return to a League of Nations based on the present principles. In the French Embassy I was told that the conversation of François-Poncet with Hitler is so distorted by both the German and the French press that it is always necessary to revert to the protocol of the conversation to avoid misinterpretations.

At the A.A. I had a talk on French-German relations with the acknowledged friend of Ambassador Wysocki, Köpke. Herr Köpke says that it will be a long time before French opinion changes basically on the subject of Germany. The flow of events in Germany is so dynamic that—in the words of Köpke—French opinion, composed of little people whose very logical minds react very slowly in the face of new international manifestations, simply cannot keep pace. This is causing confusion and consequently a critical approach to all happenings in Germany.

Herr Köpke gave me to understand that the A.A. counted on the fact that a *détente* with Poland would also appease France. However, the turn in Polish-German relations was possibly too rapid, and France had reacted unfavorably. Herr Köpke seems to persist in the assumption that an improvement in relations with Poland is necessary for a *détente* with France.

However, it should not be taken for granted that this opinion prevails here, for the present German foreign policy is far from being uniform, especially where tactics are concerned. A pronounced tendency can also be detected here to separate Poland from France, thus abolishing the so-called French hegemony in Europe. Finally, with regard to German-French relations, I must call your attention to the fact that from rather important official German personages who have certain contacts in Paris I heard quite anxious comments on possible serious conflicts with France resulting from the growth of right-wing forces in France and certain tendencies of the General Staff. On this occasion, statements were quoted even of such persons as Caillaux [13] to the effect that the situation is becoming intolerable. I am noting these loose comments here only to point out how the opinions circulated among the local community differ. Official spheres, however, seem to evaluate the French situation as fluid.

Some German diplomatic action may again be noted on the Italian sector. Mussolini's endeavors to reorganize the League of Nations are discussed, as well as his efforts to force the Four-Power Pact, or perhaps a Five-Power Pact, into the frame of the League. I have no more detailed information at present on this, but I presume that Ambassador Wysocki has probably already reported on this subject.

In conclusion, I would like to draw your attention to the report of the Legation concerning the latest internal German moves with regard to drawing Hess and Röhm into the cabinet. This step, taken at a moment of such international tension, regardless of reasons of a purely internal nature, deserves to be taken into consideration. It means, at any rate, a very important grouping of forces, and at this time of staggering tempo in the policy of the Chancellor it ought to be closely observed.

I am continually watching one point which is, so to say, crystal-clear

[13] Joseph Caillaux, French senator, former prime minister and finance minister.

in the foreign policy of Hitlerite Germany, namely, Austria. Concepts with regard to other international problems are still subject to rather serious fluctuations.

*Józef Lipski*

The Ministry of Foreign Affairs and the Legation in Berlin worked to clarify problems that appeared doubtful to Marshal Piłsudski, so that on December 16 Lipski was in a position to discuss them with Minister von Neurath.

DOCUMENT 17    Lipski to Beck

Berlin, December 16, 1933
*Strictly Confidential*

Following your instructions, I referred today during my conversation with the minister of foreign affairs, Baron von Neurath, to the question of the Oder Navigation Act and to the proposed declaration presented by Herr Moltke to Marshal Piłsudski on November 27.

When I told Herr Neurath that I would like to discuss the Oder question with him in a friendly way, he immediately answered that he was not sufficiently acquainted with this matter and would first have to consult his professional staff. I gave Herr Neurath the following explanation:

The Navigation Act for the river Oder was composed by the International Commission at Dresden on July 29, 1932. However, the Reich government neither signed nor acceded to it. All signatory states of the act have been notified by the government of the Reich as to the reason for its abstention; the Polish government received a note from the German government dated January 13, 1933. Owing to this stand taken by the German government, it was decided within the frame of the International Commission to transfer the dispute to the Hague Tribunal by way of compromise. As far as we are informed, some governments represented at the International Commission have already forwarded their propositions to the German government. The Polish government—in quite a friendly way and wishing to avoid any difficulties—would like, prior to taking any measures in connection with the note of the German government dated January 13, 1933, to be informed about the German government's opinion on this matter, especially since recently the Reich government has taken a special position toward the Hague Tribunal.

Herr von Neurath apparently fully understood our intention and thanked me very much for our friendly attitude. He stressed, however, that he would have to confer with experts on his staff before giving me an answer.

I then took up the question of the proposed document.

I declared that I had been to Warsaw recently and that the document presented to Marshal Piłsudski by Herr Moltke and brought to my attention thanks to Herr von Neurath's courtesy is the subject of careful investigations on the part of our Ministry of Foreign Affairs. As for the principle of abstaining from violence in mutual relations between the two countries, there is conformity of opinion on this point. As far as the external form of the document is concerned, I stated that no objections were raised, although it is rather novel.

Herr Neurath began to elaborate in more detail about the form of the document. He said that his lawyers were at first very reluctant, since they wanted to adorn everything with paragraphs. However, he declared that this form is more appropriate and better serves the purpose of the declaration.

Discussing the form of the document, I said that the Marshal also mentioned to Herr Moltke that such a document without paragraphs is more agreeable to him.

I further stated to Herr Neurath that before the conclusion of our investigations of the document we were anxious to receive some preliminary explanations (*Vorfragen*) as to certain points of the declaration. I pointed out that the first such preliminary question is the problem of the Polish-German arbitration agreement signed at Locarno, which is referred to in the document. I confirmed that this agreement contains a reference in some vital points to the Council of the League of Nations, that is, in Part II, Article 18, wherein it is stated that "if during a month upon conclusion of works of the permanent conciliatory commission both parties will not reach an understanding, the case, on request of one of the parties, will be brought before the Council of the League of Nations, which will rule in accordance with Article 15 of the Pact of the League."

I added that the Locarno agreements were in general negotiated with a view to Germany's entry into the League of Nations. I therefore asked whether there is not a difficulty arising from Germany's withdrawal from the League.

Herr von Neurath agreed that this point really seems to require some explanation. He is not so well acquainted with the juridical side of the problem and is therefore obliged to confer with Gaus.[14] He thinks, however, that the Locarno agreement was referred to because it is a negotiated arbitration agreement between Poland and Germany which could be applied in this case. If this agreement were to be refuted, in all probability a new arbitration and conciliation agreement would have to be negotiated between Poland and Germany. However, Neurath insisted that he was speaking of this matter without authority, owing to his lack of strict juridical information.

I stressed here that in my opinion a reference to the Kellogg Pact would be more in line with the intentions of both governments, and Herr von Neurath agreed. I also added casually, stressing that this was my personal opinion, that Locarno as a whole did not evoke special enthusiasm on our part.

I then passed on to paragraph four of the declaration, saying that we understand the affirmation that "both governments, in case it is impossible to settle controversial matters by direct negotiations, will seek a solution by other peaceful means, and especially by arbitration and conciliation" to mean that in such controversial matters both governments will seek adequate conciliatory proceedings or arbitration by way of a mutual understanding.

Herr Neurath said that he understands it in the same way.

Finally I asked Herr von Neurath what it meant that the agreement should be concluded for *at least* ten years, adding that we have no special objection to the length of time; however, bearing in mind that the text must possess a juridical value and be ratified, it is important to realize the meaning of the words "at least."

Herr von Neurath replied that this paragraph means that the agreement will be binding for at least ten years, and that only after this time may the possible notification of more precise dates of withdrawal take place.

I replied that I was satisfied with this explanation.

[14] Friedrich Gaus, director of the Legal Department of the A.A.

Referring to the whole complex of my questions, Herr Neurath said that it would be best if I would discuss the whole problem with Gaus, and expressed his desire that I should immediately get in touch with Gaus. However, I said that today I was rather busy and would contact Gaus next week, who in the meantime will be briefed by Herr Neurath on the matter. Herr Neurath expressed the opinion that in general it will be necessary for our lawyers to meet to discuss this text.

I put off the conversation with Gaus until next week, supposing that this would meet with your approval. Here I would like to add that, as I was informed by Herr von Bülow, who came to lunch at the Legation, the high government officials are leaving for a holiday period until January 9.

From my conversation with Neurath I drew the conclusion, first of all, that I was right in supposing that the text was elaborated on by the lawyers of the Auswärtiges Amt and not by the Chancellor's pen. I also wish to add that von Neurath told me that the Chancellor questioned him a few days ago about our point of view and that he replied that such matters always require more time for investigation.

In this respect I would like to call your attention to notices published yesterday and the day before in the *Völkischer Beobachter* from Warsaw, stating that the Polish government is taking a wait-and-see attitude in connection with the whole international situation. These notes, rather friendly to us in tone, make a comparison between the nervous tactics of Beneš and the calm reserve of the government in Warsaw.

Taking leave of Herr Neurath, I paid him a few compliments on the occasion of the Polish-German football match, stressing particularly the very friendly role toward us of the Sportsführer for the Reich, Herr von Tschammer und Osten. Herr Tschammer und Osten asked me yesterday, if possible, to lay stress in my conversation with the Foreign Minister of the Reich on the importance of such sport shows for mutual Polish-German relations.

On Monday, at 1 o'clock, I will have an audience with the minister of propaganda, Goebbels, and in the evening I will dine at Herr Neurath's. I advise you of this because I might have an opportunity to convey some of your wishes to Minister Goebbels or Neurath.[15]

*Józef Lipski*

[15] For the German version of this conversation, see *DGFP*, Series C, Vol. II, No. 131.

DOCUMENT 18   Lipski to Beck

Berlin, December 18, 1933
*Strictly Confidential*

I was received today by Minister Goebbels at the Ministry of Propaganda. I began by explaining to Goebbels the cause for the delay of my visit, which was due to my departure for Warsaw, where I stayed a little longer than expected. I conveyed your greetings to Herr Goebbels. Expressing his thanks, Goebbels said that he remembers with pleasure the conversation with you in Geneva.

After these opening remarks, Goebbels declared that he would like in the first place to have a basic talk with me about Polish-German relations. He added that he is a close collaborator of the Chancellor and that he knows him very thoroughly. He knows that if the Chancellor takes a certain line in politics, or if he promises something, he then holds to it closely regardless of difficulties. Goebbels knows that the Chancellor chose the line of understanding with Poland. Herr Goebbels called it a *modus vivendi*. In spite of certain resistance, the Chancellor is undoubtedly acting and will continue to act along this line. In Goebbels' opinion, the Chancellor would like to conclude a nonaggression pact with Poland. The understanding with Poland undoubtedly—Goebbels did not conceal it—will meet with certain obstacles; however, the Chancellor is determined to overcome them. Goebbels was quite frank in referring explicitly to the old Prussian caste of Junkers who, as he put it, led politics for four hundred years and are encumbered by certain formulas. The men of today who have come to power in Germany are new men, young, not compromised, originating from masses of Germans with nationalistic ideas, but who have nothing in common with the *alldeutsch* type striving for expansion at the expense of other nations. The *modus vivendi* with Poland will cause the Germans to suffer considerable sacrifices. But they are aware of more imminent dangers today and the necessity to subordinate secondary interests to them. Such a danger—in Goebbels' opinion—is Communism. The Western states have not grasped the threat of this danger. The condition in Germany was such that, as the Führer said, power could have been seized in the street. A bunch of irresponsible persons could have become masters of the Reich. This very danger of Communism compels Germany to seek an understanding with Poland, and from this angle Polish-German relations are of very basic importance.

Herr Goebbels embarked on a lengthy tirade, stressing that he was talking not as a diplomat but as a sincerely feeling German who belonged to the National Socialist Party. Goebbels wondered if any of the old-regime diplomats would dare to speak so openly with the Polish Envoy. Herr Goebbels was pleased to observe that on the Polish side he sees young people in responsible posts also. He mentioned how pleased he was with the conversation he had with you at Geneva. Would it be at all possible to talk in this manner with a representative of a state which would have to look back to its parliament? When the Chancellor says something, whether for the moment it is popular or not, public opinion accepts it. Everyone believes him, and everyone obeys him. Goebbels gave me to understand that it is they who are aware of the feelings of the masses, and that there is no estrangement between the leaders of the National Socialist camp and the masses.

Going on to matters concerning the press, in Goebbels' opinion it is essential that the press should not bait. He declared himself against an irresponsible press which starts conflicts, taking no responsibility for them.

In answer to this long flow of words, I said more or less this:

In Poland there has always prevailed a certain interest and understanding for the National Socialist idea, and that is why even in spite of very strong international agitation by propagandists, the press in Poland and opinion in general took an objective stand toward the German revolution. Goebbels confirmed this in full. I further stated that, in the period of fifteen years in the aftermath of the war, Polish-German relations had been poisoned by a campaign of hatred. Only since the Chancellor's coming to power and his first words spoken to my predecessor had a change occurred in these relations. My last conversation with the Chancellor was, especially in view of the international situation, a very important event. If under such circumstances we came to ask what should be done in the field of Polish-German relations in order to reinforce security jeopardized by Germany's withdrawal from the League of Nations, this was very proof of the Polish government's wish for, and a resulting tendency toward, good relations with Germany. The communiqué published on November 15 spoke out against resorting to power in mutual relations. The declaration of such a principle by statesmen of both states, fully responsible for their governments, was—I dared say—a clear confirmation of this tendency.

Herr Goebbels added that the communiqué means much more than a treaty signed, for example, with a state which has to refer to its parliament, in the face of which the government is absolutely powerless.

As to the question discussed much longer by Herr Goebbels than I have reported above, namely, Polish-German collaboration with regard to a not clearly defined danger of Communism, I replied more or less along these lines:

I stated that, looking at Poland, one should also bear in mind its history. I reminded him that Poland, as was also mentioned by the Chancellor during our conversation, was often the guardian of the West. I pointed to Vienna and the battle of Warsaw in 1920.[16] I said that, since I was in London at that time, I had had the opportunity to observe how deeply the Labor Party was undermined by subversive Communistic tendencies. We were eyewitnesses to it, since the Polish Legation was formally besieged for several weeks by communized elements. However, I added, the very territory of Poland is not adaptable to subversive experiments. This is a result, on the one hand, of the social structure, owing to the majority of agricultural elements, and, on the other hand, of the patriotic attitude of the population, which, under cover of subversive propaganda, hears the old aggressive tune of the former occupant.

Herr Goebbels agreed that this analysis was interesting but that Germany finds itself in a different situation, owing to a different social structure, and has no defense, like Poland, in a certain natural repulsion against outside infiltration. However, he thought that it makes no difference what elements of resistance are present in the struggle with subversive ideas. Of prime importance for international relations is the fact that a particular state refuses to be enslaved by these ideas. Goebbels also said that he would like me to look thoroughly into their principle of thinking, enter into the closest possible contact with persons in the

---

[16] In the battle of Vienna (September, 1683) the Polish king, Jan Sobieski, defeated the Turkish Army. In the battle of Warsaw (August, 1920), Józef Piłsudski, chief of state and commander in chief of the Polish Army, defeated the Soviet Army and stopped their march to the West. Both battles are recognized as decisive battles in European history. See W. Jędrzejewicz, "Dziewietnaście decydujących bitew świata" [Nineteen Decisive Battles of the World], *Bellona* (London), 1963, Nos. 3–4, pp. 216–23.

Chancellor's camp, and in this way act for the establishment of good relations between the two states. "If that succeeds," Goebbels said, "I feel that both you and I will have great credit in the eyes of history."

Afterward, passing to the question of a press *détente* in propaganda— and this is interesting—Goebbels suggested that at first some resistance had been detected against a rapprochement with Poland, which he, by order of the Chancellor, was energetically suppressing. It was obvious that the resistance came from the old Prussian caste. . . .

*Józef Lipski*

Discussion by Lipski of specific points of the declaration took place on December 20 during a conference with the legal counselor of the Auswärtiges Amt, Gaus. Then came an interval due to the holiday season and a delay in Marshal Piłsudski's final decision.

## DOCUMENT 19  Lipski to Beck

Berlin, December 20, 1933

Following my letter of December 16, I am now reporting on the result of the conversation I had today with Director Gaus to discuss the document in question.

Referring to my conversation with Minister Neurath of December 16, I stressed that, in its study of the plan of the Polish-German declaration, our Department came across a few items requiring additional preliminary clarification. I then posed the first question, namely, whether in view of Germany's withdrawal from the League of Nations further reference to the Polish-German Locarno arbitration agreement would still be valid.

Herr Gaus replied that this question was quite justified because, in connection with Germany's withdrawal from the League of Nations, a problem arises as to the consequences of this fact on the basic Locarno agreement, that is, to the Rhineland Pact automatically connected with the League's structure. On the other hand, Article 22, par. 1, of the Polish-German Arbitration Treaty, signed at Locarno, states as follows:

"The present treaty will be ratified. Ratification documents will be deposited with the League of Nations at Geneva, simultaneously with documents of ratification of the treaty concluded on this date between Germany, Belgium, France, Great Britain, and Italy.

"It will be enforced and binding under the same terms as the treaty mentioned above."

The Rhineland Pact problem connected with Germany's withdrawal from the League of Nations pertains to the field of general policy. Herr Gaus points to the recent debates on this subject in the parliaments of England and France. I am taking the liberty of mentioning here what was omitted in my previous report—that von Neurath confirmed to me on December 16 that the Locarno treaties are still binding. Germany is still a member of the League *de jure,* and therefore nothing formally is changed. Only after two years will Germany legally cease to be a member of the League. Herr Gaus, as a lawyer, is not in theory excluding the necessity of introducing adequate modifications into the Locarno agreements in this case. The Polish-German arbitration agreement might then also be subject to certain alterations. Herr Gaus understands our doubts with regard to Article 22, while he does not expect any difficulties with reference to the League of Nations as far as Articles 18 and 19 are concerned.

Herr Gaus further ascertained that, just because of these certain doubtful points, paragraph three of the declaration includes a provision "to exclude possible ambiguity," etc., and that the following paragraph states that both governments will seek solutions on controversial matters in arbitration and conciliation. The whole text, in his opinion, should be taken more from the political angle than as a purely formal juridical document.

I asked Herr Gaus whether my idea is correct about the obligation to seek a way of settlement by arbitration or conciliation in matters in which diplomatic proceedings fail.

In connection with this question Herr Gaus gave the following explanation:

The obligation to seek a solution of disputes by way of arbitration or conciliation could in practice be carried out (1) by application of the Polish-German Locarno arbitration agreement; (2) by application of a new Polish-German arbitration agreement, which, in case of withdrawal from the Locarno agreement, would have to be negotiated by the two governments; (3) by seeking in each separate case arbitration or conciliation procedures.

Herr Gaus envisages these three alternatives. He personally sees no objection to keeping the Locarno arbitration in binding force for both states, or perhaps replacing it with another agreement. However, he understands the doubts entertained by the Polish side.

He was anxious to explain that the Locarno agreement should not be considered a trap. Just two agreements were referred to—Locarno and Kellogg—since these are two political acts following the Versailles Treaty binding for both states.

I had the impression that Herr Gaus would be inclined to omit reference to the Locarno agreement completely, keeping only the reference to the Kellogg Pact.

He stresses that the text is simply a draft and gives me to understand that he is waiting for Polish counterpropositions on these points.

As to the term "at least for ten years," Gaus gave a reply analogous to Herr Neurath's.

Expressing thanks for the explanations, I stated that I would forward them for the information of the Ministry of Foreign Affairs in Warsaw.

*Józef Lipski*

Only on January 9, 1934, when Piłsudski arrived at the conclusion that France would not stand up to Hitler, was Lipski in a position to present to Neurath the Polish counterpropositions in connection with the declaration of nonaggression, expressing readiness for immediate signing.[17]

In the course of these difficult proceedings Lipski displayed his great talent as a negotiator and his profound knowledge of international juridical problems. Results of further conversations with Gaus are contained in two reports of Minister Lipski dated January 16.[18]

DOCUMENT 20   Lipski to Beck

Berlin, January 16, 1934
*Strictly Confidential*

On January 12 I had a call in the late evening hours from the office of the Minister of Foreign Affairs, informing me that Herr von Neurath

[17] For the notice by von Neurath and the Polish text of the proposition, see *DGFP*, Series C, Vol. II, No. 168.
[18] For the German version of the Lipski-Gaus conversation, see *ibid.*, No. 186.

requested that I call in the next few days on Director Gaus in connection with my previous conversations with Herr Neurath about the Polish-German declaration.

During your stop in Berlin on January 13, I was instructed to conduct conversations with Gaus in accordance with principles set out in Warsaw, and to take *ad referendum* doubtful questions that might arise in the course of the talks. You instructed me to keep in contact with you by wire at Geneva, and with Mr. Szembek, the undersecretary in Warsaw.

On January 16, I was received at 11 A.M. by Director Gaus. Referring to our conversation on these matters on December 20, 1933, Herr Gaus stated that Minister von Neurath, upon acknowledging the alterations introduced by us in the German text, directed him as a specialist to express his opinion on these alterations. Herr Gaus explained to Herr von Neurath the nature of the Polish alterations, although he wished to discuss them with me in order to be fully cognizant of their meaning.

Herr Gaus then stated that the German side—here he made reference to the Chancellor—attaches considerable importance to this document, and therefore it is not possible to deal with it superficially. Here I replied that we also take this declaration very seriously and that is why our Departments had to consider all details and why the work had to last a certain length of time.

Next Gaus mentioned that our conversations are just preparatory proceedings to the principal exchange of opinion between me and von Neurath with regard to the declaration.

Passing on to the text, Gaus stated that three principal points require clarification, while our other amendments are rather of an editorial character. From his statement it developed that he did not think that the omission of the words "just peace" from the second paragraph had any significance; neither did editing changes in paragraph five. With regard to certain definitions introduced by us in connection with the notification for nonextension of the declaration, he said they are rather in agreement with his ideas.

The three basic points referred to by Gaus are the following:

1) *Affirmation that the declaration cannot limit or change obligations for each of the contracting parties under the agreements concluded by them.*

This Polish amendment struck Neurath and particularly affected Hitler. Gaus explained to Neurath that the restriction deals with Poland's obligations under the Covenant of the League, agreements with France of 1921 and 1925, and agreements with Rumania.

Speaking of Hitler's reaction, Gaus stressed that the Chancellor wanted to bestow on the document a political character and free it from any juridical preciseness. Hitler—in Gaus's opinion—obviously cannot appreciate the meaning of our reserve from the technical point of view. Gaus suggested, stressing that he was speaking quite frankly and confidentially, that in the Chancellor's mind this restriction could evoke the impression of a desire to obtain from Germany the acceptance of these treaties, a certain affirmation of their inviolability, and a sort of fear that this formula might serve as a cover for some obligations of Poland unknown to Germany and directed against it.

With regard to this point, I made it clear that explanations given by Gaus and Neurath concerning Polish obligations covered by this formula are fully in accordance with the actual state of affairs. It is absolutely out of the question that the restriction ensuing from Polish obligations could serve as a cover for the intention to compel Germany to recognize the treaties. Besides, I confirmed that our treaties are registered at the League of Nations.

The conclusion that the declaration does not infringe on existing international obligations included in pacts concluded by Poland is indispensable to avoid a collision with the Covenant of the League.

Gaus tried to persuade me that this formula is unnecessary. The declaration merely says that neither state will resort to force in mutual relations in matters which may arise between them.

Stipulating that he was only quoting an example, Gaus touched on the possibility of a German-French military conflict, arising not out of Polish-German problems. In that case, in his opinion, the proposed Polish-German declaration would not create any obstacle for the obligations of Poland under the Polish-French alliance and the Covenant of the League (Article 16).

When I pointed out that the declaration is unthinkable with the omission of the affirmation about international obligations with regard to states like Germany, which are withdrawing from the League, and when I drew attention to a similar restriction included in our pact with Russia, Gaus quoted paragraph four of the preamble to the Polish-Russian pact, which reads as follows:

"Declaring that none of the obligations hitherto assumed by either of the Parties stands in the way of the peaceful development of their mutual relations or is incompatible with the present Pact."

He added that this phrasing is at any rate more digestible than our proposition. He, of course, made the reservation that his statement was just an opinion. In general, Gaus laid emphasis on the form which will cover this restriction, still keeping to his point of view that the restriction is superfluous and requesting that this point be reconsidered.

2) *The declaration cannot concern matters reserved under international law for exclusive competence of the states.*

As far as this reservation is concerned, Gaus agrees that it is inserted in various international texts, as, for example, in the Covenant of the League of Nations and in the General Act established by the League. He only asks why this restriction is necessary, since it is self-explanatory. He has often discussed this subject in the international field with Scialoja and other jurists, who were also against this formula, but still for the sake of tradition introduced it into texts. He would like to be informed whether our lawyers are taking this formula into consideration in practice. In case facultative arbitration were maintained in the declaration by consent of the parties from case to case, the formula would become even more superfluous.

For tactical reasons I accepted this point of view *ad referendum.*

3) *With regard to paragraph five, providing that controversial problems will be settled by peaceful means and in particular by conciliation and arbitration based upon an understanding between the contracting parties in each separate case.*

In view of our insertion of "in each separate case," Gaus asked whether we intend to recognize the Polish-German Arbitration Treaty signed in Locarno as nonexistent, since this treaty provides for obligatory arbitration more extensive than the suggested formula. Cancellation of this treaty is a question of principle, especially in connection with the whole set of these agreements. A broader concept of obligatory arbitration would be replaced by us with a more narrow agreement, which would mean a step backwards.

This is why Gaus insists on an absolutely basic reply on this point.

I answered that I would communicate with Warsaw on this matter.

*Józef Lipski*

DOCUMENT 21   Lipski to Szembek

Berlin, January 16, 1934
*Strictly Confidential*

My conversation today with Gaus, which lasted an hour and a half, concerned matters so entangled that it would be difficult to squeeze into a telegram the very substance of the problems. I therefore had to limit myself to telegraphing only points referred to by Gaus, while I took the liberty of sending a special courier to Warsaw who will deliver the enclosed report to you.

Minister Beck instructed me to forward to him copies of telegrams directed on this subject to Warsaw. Unfortunately, I cannot send him a copy of the report, and I am compelled to supply only an abbreviated telegram, which undoubtedly will not be sufficient basis for taking a decision.

Coming back to the conversation with Gaus, I must first of all say that neither my two conversations with Neurath nor my discussion with Gaus today give me the impression that the matter can be settled promptly. I also suppose that the German side, for deeper reasons, would tend to delay a decision for a certain time. In any case, if I would press for a more urgent finalization, this would prejudice my standing as a negotiator.

Of points referred to by Gaus, it seems to me that the most difficult to agree with is arbitration. In their original text the Germans went far beyond the Polish-German Locarno Arbitration Treaty, while we, on our part, have limited the Locarno agreement. For the German side it is difficult to step backward beyond 1925, and that is why Gaus in his statement points to the consequences of our withdrawal from the Locarno Treaty. This is of course a matter of argument. Nevertheless, Gaus is right when he declares that, if we state in the new agreement that arbitration and conciliation in Polish-German relations might only be applied upon agreement between the parties in each separate case, we are thus canceling the rules of the Polish-German Arbitration Treaty signed at Locarno, ruling for obligatory arbitration. The Locarno Treaty, despite its unsavory political aftertaste owing to its links with the Rhineland Pact, gives the advantage of excluding the possibility of arbitration in matters rooted in the past, and in general contains security clauses which give us good protection. This is best proved by the fact that since 1925 not a single case was brought to Locarno by Germany.

I may stress here that Gaus is not really insisting that reference be made to the Locarno agreement, since he is aware that this might be awkward for us politically. What he definitely does not want is a tightening of arbitration by the declaration.

For lack of time I was unable to disclose the whole of my argumentation in this report. Indeed, I did not fail to stress, in my reply to Gaus's evasive statement that our editing cancels the Locarno arbitration agreement, that this is by no means so.

Finally, I would like to add that I am thinking over the possibility of finding a way out of these particular points and shall not fail to send you by next courier my suggestions in this matter.

*Józef Lipski*

At that time Beck was in Geneva. In a telegram of January 17 to the Ministry of Foreign Affairs he expressed his view of the political situation.

DOCUMENT 22    Beck to the Ministry of Foreign Affairs

*Code Telegram*
Geneva, January 17, 1934
Received: January 17, 9 A.M.

From Lipski's verbal relation it develops that Hitlerite spheres are resolutely striving for a favorable conclusion to our negotiations. In appraising the German situation, the following points are striking: (1) anxiety about isolation, (2) considerable preoccupation with internal problems. Conflict between the Hitlerites and the German Nationals seems to be taking on a sharper aspect. The Chancellor's efforts lean toward an internal reform on a huge scale, a new administrative division of Germany, the completion of unification, and, in practice, the liquidation of the former states of Germany. March is mentioned as a date when the reform will be put into life.

According to the unanimous opinion from various sources in Geneva, the disarmament question will still be a subject for an exchange of opinion between Germany and France before it reaches the conference forum. A crisis in this problem is also foreseen for March. At the Council of the League I am conducting the agreed-to tactic of reserve, so far without objections. Please report on the contents of the telegram to the Marshal.

*Beck*

On January 19 Lipski was received by Marshal Piłsudski in Warsaw and acquired from him the final decisions.[19] The next day he had a conversation with Gaus,[20] and on January 25 he was received by Hitler.

DOCUMENT 23    Lipski to the Ministry of Foreign Affairs

Code No. 14                          Berlin, January 20, 1934

After a long discussion, first of all I composed with Gaus the plan of a formula on international obligations in accordance with paragraph 4 of the Polish-Soviet pact, with the addition that these obligations are not infringed on by the declaration. Secondly, I composed a formula on matters concerning the exculsive competence of the states, in such a way that the declaration does not cover matters which under international law are considered as exclusively internal matters of one of the two states. Gaus will present both these formulas to Neurath and to the Chancellor with our explanations. With regard to the paragraph about arbitration and conciliation, I established—following your instructions —that we consider the agreements binding, including the Polish-German arbitration agreement, and that the words "in each separate case" were introduced by us because of a confusing clause of the said agreement in connection with Germany's withdrawal from the League of Nations. Gaus explained that this whole paragraph in the original German composition lays no new obligations on the parties and speaks only about seeking a solution of disputes by peaceful means, citing arbitration and conciliation as examples. This paragraph sidesteps the question whether the agreement of 1925, binding for both states, may in the future require certain amendments. However, according to Gaus, the words "in each separate case" would be in contradiction with Article 16 of the 1925 agreement.

19 See Namier, *Europe in Decay,* pp. 282–83 (footnote).
20 For Gaus's version, see *DGFP,* Series C, Vol. II, No. 203.

I reserved further conversation over this point for Monday morning in the presence of Makowski.[21] Gaus told me that the German side is pressing for prompt finalization of the agreement.

DOCUMENT 24    Lipski to Beck

NO. 49/8/34                                                  January 25, 1934
                                                              *Strictly Confidential*

I was received today at 11 A.M. by Chancellor Hitler with the minister of foreign affairs of the Reich, von Neurath, also present. Chancellor Hitler first of all expressed his satisfaction that as a result of his conversations with my predecessor and with me an understanding had been reached which will take the form of a Polish-German declaration. This declaration should ensure an appropriate relaxation in Polish-German relations. The Chancellor availed himself of this occasion to pay a courteous compliment to Ambassador Wysocki and to my activity in Berlin.

For my part I stressed that I would like to extend to the Chancellor my thanks for the confidence shown in me and I confirmed that the Polish-German declaration will undoubtedly contribute to a relaxation of the atmosphere. I added that the Polish government duly appreciates the importance of the declaration, and I suggested that this was proved by the fact that last week I was summoned by Marshal Piłsudski, who requested a full report on the negotiations.

In a long declaration the Chancellor of the Reich pointed to the importance of an improvement in Polish-German relations. He underlined Poland's responsible role in the east. Talking about Russia, he said that in contrast with others he is not an optimist as far as Russia is concerned. Namely, he fears that in the future this giant, whose position in armaments is very threatening, could become a danger for Europe. He stressed that, in the field of tractors, for example, Russia is four times stronger than Germany. Discussing the Russian-Japanese conflict, he expressed the opinion that, in the face of such a dynamic trend in Japan, Russia will be compelled to abandon its position in the Far East. It could then direct the full impact of its pressure westward. A very serious danger might then occur for the civilization of the West, espe-

[21] Prof. Julian Makowski was chief of the Treaty Department at the Polish Ministry of Foreign Affairs.

cially since Russia is firmly entrenched in its Communistic doctrine. From this angle the Chancellor considers the role of Poland as very momentous. He said: Poland is the last barricade of civilization in the east. Besides, Poland has already played a similar role. (The Chancellor was making an allusion to the battle of Vienna.)

I stressed that Poland, in the course of its history, often played historic roles as a shield for Western culture, and I mentioned three famous battles: Legnica [Liegnitz, 1241], Vienna [1683], and Warsaw [1920].

Coming back to the Polish-German declaration, the Chancellor stated that it should not only give good results in Polish-German relations but should contribute to a *détente* in the whole of Europe.

Referring to a possibility of war, the Chancellor declared that any war would end in disaster for civilization. For instance, a war between Germany and France would bring about Bolshevism in Germany. Bolshevism in Germany would undoubtedly turn into Bolshevism in the whole of Europe. Because Germany is situated in the center and has so many inhabitants, the radiation would spread to other countries. No one would reap any advantages from the war. A possible shifting of frontiers, in the Chancellor's words, is quite secondary, a trifle as compared with the danger ensuing from the results of a war.

As far as Polish-German relations are concerned, the Chancellor's main concern is that the conviction that Germans and Poles are always *Erbfeinde* should be abandoned. This idea should be weeded out. Were not Polish-Danzig relations very entangled also, and at present were not these relations being arranged on the basis of mutual interests? For the Chancellor had declared to his men at the outset that the Polish nation must be considered *a reality. It is impossible to exterminate the Polish nation.* Both nations have to live side by side. If this principle is accepted, then in the future some solution might be found for both states to overcome difficulties. One thing is weighing on the Chancellor's heart, namely, that on both sides equally the rights of the Polish minorities in Germany and the German minorities in Poland must be respected, for in this field much can be done for a mutual *détente* and many frictions can be removed.

The Chancellor stressed that there were periods in history when we were fighting each other, but at other times we lived in friendship and collaboration.

*Józef Lipski*

The declaration of nonaggression between Poland and Germany was signed in Berlin on January 26, 1934, by Minister von Neurath and Envoy Lipski.[22] Ratification took place in Warsaw on February 24.

The German government informed its posts abroad on January 24 [23] that an understanding had been reached with regard to the declaration, and the Polish government did likewise on January 26.[24] Moltke was received by Beck on January 27, and Beck expressed his satisfaction over the signing of the declaration.[25] On January 30 Hitler stressed the positive aspect of the understanding concluded with Poland in his speech in the Reichstag.[26] Beck replied by his speech delivered at the Commission for Foreign Affairs of the Polish Senate on February 5.[27]

Finally, general remarks with regard to the signing of the declaration were formulated by Lipski in his report of February 5.

DOCUMENT 25    Lipski to Beck

NO. N/49/17/34    Berlin, February 5, 1934
*Confidential*

Public opinion in Germany and governmental spheres which were not kept abreast of the negotiations under way were in general taken aback by the signing of the Polish-German declaration on January 26. The secrecy of the negotiations was very strictly maintained, so that even representatives of the press with the closest links to the A.A. were kept in the dark in connection with the forthcoming understanding. The press, following instructions issued by top authorities, maintained a reasonable reserve, making no restrictions and drawing no conclusions which, in contradiction to the actual state of affairs, could evoke critical comments on the Polish side. This positive attitude of the press toward the Polish-German declaration could only be achieved owing to the fact that the whole press is at present under the control of the government. Nevertheless, German opinion—fed during fifteen years by anti-Polish propaganda—cannot change its attitude toward us from one day to the

[22] For the text of the declaration, see *DGFP*, Series C, Vol. II, No. 219, and *Polish White Book*, No. 10.

[23] For the telegram to Rome and Moscow, see *DGFP*, Series C, Vol. II, No. 211.

[24] For Beck to posts abroad, see *Polish White Book*, No. 11.

[25] For Moltke's telegram, see *DGFP*, Series C, Vol. II, No. 226.

[26] *Polish White Book*, No. 12.

[27] Beck, *Przemówienia, deklaracje, wywiady, 1931–1937*, p. 98; also *DGFP*, Series C, Vol. II, Nos. 230 and 244.

next, and therefore an atmosphere of deep-seated criticism, particularly among people linked with the former *Deutschnationale* camp and elements originating from the east, might be detected, checked by fear of the authority of the Chancellor, who took on himself the responsibility for the agreement with Poland. The Chancellor wanted to express this clearly to public opinion; that is why on the eve of the signing he received me and gave an order to the press to publish a communiqué about the audience with the Polish Envoy. In a lengthy speech before the Reichstag, the Chancellor also substantiated his policy toward Poland, in order to establish a direct impact on the masses of his adherents and prod them to change their hitherto negative stand toward Poland. It is very characteristic that all reference to Poland in speeches delivered by the Chancellor last year, and especially since May, 1933, always laid stress on our valor as a state, this point of view being in striking contradiction to pronouncements by his predecessors. It was obvious that the Chamber could not accept enthusiastically this passage of the Chancellor's speech. Being present in the Reichstag, I could observe the deep silence that at first prevailed when the Chancellor spoke about the understanding reached with Poland. Only gradually a slow reaction came from individual members of the Chamber and calls such as "sehr richtig" could be heard. When the Chancellor finished stating the necessity of balancing Polish-German economic relations, the applause came. It was evident that Hitler was exerting himself in order to impose his will on the audience when he referred to the rapprochement with Poland.

Rumors reach me from the Chancellor's entourage that he was personally very satisfied with the understanding with us. I was also told that the Chancellor is sympathetic toward the Polish nation, appreciating its deep patriotic feelings. The Chancellor's trump card when substantiating his policy toward Poland, and his chief argument, is that the danger threatening from the east might in the future become a reality. He envisages this danger in the Asiatic-Bolshevik penetration, as he calls it, and declares that Poland, true to its historic role, could shield Western, and also German, civilization against this pressure. In this connection the Chancellor always stresses that all matters dividing Poland and Germany, including the frontier problem, which is indeed painful for him as a German, are not to be compared with sacrifices which Germany would have to sustain in case of a war with Poland. He says that territorial gains would be incommensurable with losses, and the war would result in a disaster for European civilization. He wants to force public opinion to respect the Polish nation and accept the fact of the necessity for coexistence, even with prevailing difficulties, assuming that in the future, which he sees as a very long span of time, differences dividing the two nations may fade away.

When I observe this situation in the light of a certain evolution now under way in the Reich, I must agree that this ideology of the Chancellor is a great *positivum* for us, provided that it penetrates more profoundly into the masses of the German nation and reaches young elements, to whom the future belongs. Nevertheless, I must point out again that this whole atmosphere is emanating from the Chancellor himself, and that the people who surround him may only gradually become attracted to his ideas.

However, when discussing the Chancellor's ideology, I do not forget about possible advantages he might reap from the understanding with us, especially in the international field. Nevertheless, I am keeping this problem strictly within the frame of Polish-German relations. If we would accept as a positive factor the present trend in the Chancellor's policy toward us, then it seems to me that it would be highly desirable if in the near future the development of Polish-German relations would follow the line of the Chancellor's ideas. For as soon as elements hostile to us, which are still swarming within the bosom of the administration, slowly recover from the blow of the agreement of January 26, they will do their utmost to compromise—in the eyes of the Chancellor and his confidential ministers—any possibility of collaboration with Poland.

Fully realizing that the development of our relations with Germany does not depend exclusively on problems on the Warsaw-Berlin line, I am nevertheless taking the liberty of enumerating a few principal problems which influence the relations of the two states.

1) If in the near future the Polish-German tariff war is terminated, local opinion will note it as a positive result of the declaration of January 26.

2) Likewise, the attitude of our press with regard to German problems could be exploited to our advantage locally, especially since the present German regime is excessively sensitive to all kinds of international reaction.

In this field our advantages will be great, since the German press, in comparison with ours, has a world-wide scope.

3) A sensitive point for local opinion is the minority problem. The

Chancellor, in his last talk with me, asked that this matter be considered from the point of view of avoiding friction. At the same time he expressed his intention to ensure just treatment for Polish minorities in Germany.

4) In Germany anti-Polish activities are primarily concentrated within organizations created *ad hoc,* such as the Ostbund.

It is characteristic for the German nature that it needs an organization to keep it in a constant state of political tension. A German will lose his belligerent nationalistic attitude for lack of this element of tension.

If we strive to realize in practice the principles contained in the declaration of January 26, we will then be obliged to pay special attention to the eastern provinces of Germany, and to organizations which are still breeding hatred against Poland. Indeed, it would be desirable that our similar organizations, such as the Union for Defense of the Western Frontier [Związek Obrony Kresów Zachodnich], comply with the Reich government's action to curb the anti-Polish activities of the German organizations.

Finally, I would like to bring to your attention some of my observations with regard to the Baltic question, which, after the last revelations of the *Daily Herald,* evoked a big commotion in political circles here. It came to my knowledge that the opinion was fostered in the A.A. here that the plan of the Polish-Soviet declaration pertaining to the independence of the Baltic states was used by Poland to put pressure on Berlin to finalize the declaration of January 26. It is considered that this maneuver was quite successful in forcing the opposition in the A.A. to agree to a prompt finalization of the declaration.

I am citing this detail because in my opinion it is very characteristic. In general, fears are still prevalent here as to our common policy with Russia on the Baltic, and undoubtedly they saw in this a threat against Germany.

*Józef Lipski*

DOCUMENT 26    Lipski to Dębicki

February 8, 1934

Referring to my letter of the 7th inst., No. N/49/23/34, I would like to inform you that yesterday at the reception of President Hindenburg for heads of the diplomatic missions I had the opportunity to converse with Foreign Affairs Minister von Neurath.

Herr von Neurath was very well satisfied with what Mr. Beck said at the Commission for Foreign Affairs of the Senate with regard to Polish-German relations. I took this opportunity to advise Herr Neurath quite informally about Minister Beck's trip to Moscow planned for the near future. I mentioned as well that this trip will be in return for the visit of Chicherin to Warsaw in 1925 and the unofficial visit of Mr. Litvinov to Warsaw. The Soviet government has for a long time been looking forward to a return visit of the Polish Minister of Foreign Affairs.

Herr von Neurath, confirming that he had already been informed about this, characterized Mr. Beck's visit to Moscow as quite a natural thing. I further informed Herr von Neurath in confidence that the idea of a declaration on Baltic problems is no longer timely. Obviously satisfied, Herr von Neurath answered that he never saw any possible interest for Poland in tying itself up with Russia on Baltic problems. He added that this was his deep, purely objective, conviction.

Discussing Minister Beck's visit to Moscow, Herr von Neurath also added that he is not anxious to see Litvinov in Berlin, especially after his last speech, which made an unpleasant impression here.

Hitler also attended the Reichspräsident's dinner party. I approached the Chancellor and stressed that public opinion in Poland received with great satisfaction (*Genugtuung*) his words uttered at the last session of the Reichstag in connection with Polish-German relations.

In reply, the Chancellor expressed his warm appreciation for Minister Beck's speech at the Foreign Affairs Commission of the Senate. He manifested his keen pleasure in view of the rapprochement of the two nations, and stressed that we should now strive to establish collaboration in the economic field.

I also exchanged a few conventional words with President Hindenburg on the subject of Polish-German relations. The President also expressed his satisfaction with the agreement reached, adding that he hopes things will remain as they are.

*Józef Lipski*

# Soviet Russia and the Baltic States
## *January—April, 1934*

---

IN THE FIRST DAYS of January, 1934, news appeared in the European press with regard to the forthcoming Polish-Soviet agreement to guarantee the independence of the Baltic states.

### DOCUMENT 27     Lipski to Beck

NO. N/128/1/34                      Berlin, January 11, 1934
*Strictly Confidential*

News published by the London *Daily Herald* and the Finnish press on the alleged plan of a Soviet-Polish pact to guarantee the independence of the Baltic states reached Berlin the evening of January 4. The usually uniform, summit-disciplined press showed certain diverse tendencies, probably owing to the fact that this news came as quite a surprise to German official circles. Moreover, it was the holiday period when government officials were absent from Berlin. Neither Neurath nor Secretary of State von Bülow was at the Ministry of Foreign Affairs.

The newly formed official German News Agency, created by the merger of the Wolff Agency with the Telegraphen-Union, and headed by persons ideologically akin to the Hugenberg group, on the same day issued an official communiqué categorically denying rumors that Germany proposed a nonaggression pact with Poland in return for acquiescence to Germany's eastward expansion into non-Polish territories. However, the communiqué also stated that competent Soviet and Polish circles apparently harbored anti-German schemes with respect to the territory of the Baltic states. I took the liberty of calling your special attention to this paragraph by telegram.

Characteristically, the National Socialist press in the capital did not publish this communiqué, and tried to present the *Daily Herald*'s revelations as the usual anti-German assault by the Socialist press.

The remainder of the German press presented the proposed pact as a Soviet action and directed its attacks against Moscow.

Lithuania suffered the brunt of the criticism for its alleged friendly attitude toward the Soviet plans. Estonia and Latvia, on the other hand, demonstrated certain reservations with regard to the plans, while Finland took an utterly negative stand. Poland was generally spared by the press, and no critical comments were printed during the first few days. Only on January 10 did the *Völkischer Beobachter* publish correspondence from Warsaw blaming Poland for abandoning the trend it had followed up to that time, and returning—as the paper put it—to the old romantic period. The Warsaw correspondents of the *Berliner Börsenzeitung* and the *Vossische Zeitung* also pointed to Poland as a participant in the Baltic plans.

Considering that no government instruction could as yet be detected in the German press with regard to Poland's stand, it is possible that the German correspondents in Poland were somewhat disoriented as a result of the lack of unanimity in the Polish press.

Although at first they could base their conclusions on the clearly defined position taken by *Gazeta Polska,* later, as the result of a different interpretation provided by the *Agence Telegraphique d'Est* and *Ilustrowany Kurier Codzienny,* they became confused and reported to their German readers that conflicting reactions had appeared in Poland.

Following your telegraphic instructions received on January 5, and confirmed to me verbally in Warsaw on January 7, I made reference to the recent Baltic events during my conversation with Reich Foreign Affairs Minister von Neurath on January 9. I telegraphed my report of this conversation on January 9.

I began by stating that we again found ourselves in a period when many false rumors are being spread by the international press. I pointed to the *Daily Herald*'s version which stated that Germany allegedly offered Poland a nonaggression pact in return for a free hand in non-Polish territories in the east. I declared that *Gazeta Polska* denied this garbled news, and Neurath replied that he had already been informed about this.

Furthermore, I drew his attention to the fact that rumors are being deliberately spread about anti-German activities in the Baltic states, and that Poland is allegedly involved in these activities. I declared that the rumors were groundless. I stated that Poland's policy with respect to the independence of the Baltic states was always quite clear and open. Herr Neurath agreed with this point. For a great many years there was a divergence in this area between Polish and Russian policies. I mentioned the Communist putsch in Estonia and our efforts to draw the Baltic states into the pacts. I stated that, owing to a general improvement of political conditions in Eastern Europe, divergences between Polish and Russian policies had been reduced. Conversation on these subjects between Moscow and Warsaw could only be concerned with a rapprochement on these problems. However, these talks cannot be interpreted as Poland's participation in a Baltic pact directed—as the press mendaciously commented—against Germany. I added that, if the question of a Baltic pact were raised at all, the Polish government would undoubtedly approach Germany also, in accordance with its principle that all states concerned should participate in such a pact.

Herr Neurath replied that he was not taking all this so tragically. Rumors about the supposed intentions of German expansion in the Baltic zone should simply be ignored, since they were sheer nonsense. The latest plans concerning the maintenance of the Baltic states' independence are—in Neurath's opinion—symptoms of Mr. Litvinov's nervousness. Neurath had an opportunity to observe this when the Commissar for Foreign Affairs last passed through Berlin.

Litvinov's nervousness—according to Neurath—is due to the decline of Communism not only in Germany but in other countries as well; to the complicated situation in the Far East; to certain ideas of Rosenberg; and, finally, to the currently emerging rapprochement between Poland and Germany. Neurath says that Litvinov told him that this rapprochement is worrying him.

So far as Moscow's general attitude toward the Baltic states is concerned, Neurath commented that, as soon as Russia's imperialism gathers momentum in its natural drive toward the sea, it will undoubtedly push in the direction of these countries. Keeping them independent as long as possible is in accordance with German interests. However, from Neurath's words it was obvious that he considers the existence of the Baltic states dubious in the long run. He spoke with a certain irony about the Soviet guarantee for Finland, comparing it with assurances given by a wolf to a lamb.

Finally, Herr Neurath said that he doubts whether a guarantee for the

Baltic states, made together with Russia, would be a good policy for Poland, adding that this could expose us in the future to serious complications with Russia.

Herr Neurath thanked me for clarifying these matters. Bearing in mind the whole situation, I felt that it would be pointless to continue the conversation with Neurath on Polish-German problems without first giving him a reassuring explanation of the recent action on the Baltic, which must have greatly disturbed the local official—and especially Hitlerite—circles. Even if von Neurath were *au fond* somewhat skeptical about our declarations, the very fact that he was kept informed by us—as described above—should, in my opinion, make a rather good impression.

This was particularly advisable since in this way Chancellor Hitler, who is particularly interested in Russian affairs, will receive a certain *mise au point* from our side. For I must stress that, in all the conversations I have had in the course of the last months, either with Chancellor Hitler or with other members of the government, that is, with Goebbels, Darré, or Göring, they constantly brought up the problem of Bolshevism and Russia.[1]

*Józef Lipski*

The problem of a possible Polish-Soviet declaration guaranteeing the independence of the Baltic states became the subject of conversations between the German ambassador in Moscow, Rudolf Nadolny, and Commissar Litvinov, and was the subject of the Ambassador's correspondence with the Auswärtiges Amt.[2]

On March 28, 1934, Litvinov handed Nadolny a draft of a German-Soviet pact guaranteeing the independence of the Baltic states. This matter evoked lengthy conversations and correspondence, until Germany finally rejected the Soviet proposition on April 14.[3]

[1] For the German version of the Lipski-Neurath conversation, see *DGFP*, Series C, Vol. II, No. 169.
[2] *Ibid.*, Nos. 187, 240, and 251.
[3] *Ibid.*, Nos. 362, 364, 375, 376, 382, 390, 401, 415, 416, 417, 418, 421, and 423.

# The Ukrainians in Germany and the Assassination of Minister Pieracki
## *June, 1934*

THERE WAS a strong movement championing the cause of Ukrainian independence by Ukrainian nationalists active on Polish territory. This movement encompassed many factions, some of which cooperated with the Polish government and played an important role in the Warsaw Sejm. There were other factions striving clandestinely to achieve their goal by a revolutionary struggle against the Polish state. They were supported either by the Soviet Union (Ukrainian Communists) or by Germany and Czechoslovakia. Minority troubles in Poland coincided with the interests of these countries.

In 1929 a clandestine organization of Ukrainian nationalists was formed from the ranks of the former Ukrainian Military Organization (UON).

Its leaders, headed by Colonel Eugene Konowalec, resided predominantly in Germany and enjoyed the support of the German government. In Germany they also had their operational school to prepare future terrorists. In the territory of Eastern Galicia the UON undertook a series of attempts on Polish offices and outstanding politicians, as, for instance, the assassination of Tadeusz Hołówko, chief of the Eastern Department of the Ministry of Foreign Affairs (August, 1931). The same group assassinated Minister of the Interior Bronisław Pieracki on June 15, 1934, in Warsaw.

It is characteristic that in the Polish government both Hołówko and Pieracki represented a trend favoring far-reaching collaboration with the Ukrainians.

In Ambassador Lipski's papers there is the following note dealing with the assassination of Bronisław Pieracki:

On the initiative of Reich Foreign Affairs Minister von Neurath, Minister Beck stopped in Berlin on his way back to Warsaw from Geneva on June 7, 1934, and had a conversation with Herr von Neurath at his villa on Herman Göring Strasse.

I was present at this interview.

A few days before this meeting, Military Attaché Colonel Szymański informed me that he had been warned confidentially by the chief of the

Reich's Second Bureau that Ukrainian terrorists were preparing attempts on the lives of high-ranking persons in Poland. The German side
stressed the fact that until the Polish-German understanding of January
26, 1934, the Reichswehr had been in close contact with terrorist
Ukrainian elements and therefore wanted to warn Poland about the
attempts in preparation. This was done to avoid their possibly being
held responsible for anything that happened. The Military Attaché telegraphed this information to the Polish General Staff.

Considering this information to be of utmost importance, I instructed
Colonel Szymański to report it personally to Minister Beck. Colonel
Szymański did so, reporting at the Legation in my presence after Minis-
ter Beck returned from his conversation with von Neurath.

We were at that time living through a very turbulent period inside
Germany. Within the ranks of the National Socialist Party serious frictions were occurring between the movement represented by Hitler and
the adherents of Röhm. Röhm blamed Hitler for having deserted the
ideals of National Socialism by following too moderate a line, negotiating with financial circles, and collaborating with the conservative
Reichswehr. Röhm was striving to keep the S.A. the sole power ruling
the National Socialist state. As head of these storm troops, he created a
giant apparatus. During one of his speeches delivered at a meeting organized by Rosenberg at the Hotel Adlon, he quoted an S.A. membership figure of two million.

Beginning in March, 1934, our consul general in Munich, Mr. Lisiewicz, sent information to the Legation in Berlin from the Bavarian
region about friction between Hitler and Röhm over the importance of
the S.A. Röhm persistently refused to reduce the strength of the S.A.,
which Hitler obviously was considering doing under pressure from the
Army. As a result of these tensions within the ranks of the Party, some
people, such as General von Schleicher, started a series of intrigues in an
attempt to dominate the situation. Violent changes in the Reich government would undoubtedly have an effect on Polish-German relations. For
we have to bear in mind that the policy of a rapprochement with Poland,
inaugurated with the agreement of January, 1934, was highly unpopular
with German public opinion. Not only Prussian circles, but also the
National Socialist Party, especially in the eastern provinces of the Reich,
accepted the change of course toward Poland with utmost reluctance.
Polish diplomacy in the Reich had to take various circumstances into

account. Frictions within the ranks of the government itself had to be considered, as well as tense relations between the Auswärtiges Amt, recruited from former officials, and Party leaders. The Reichswehr was then not yet "gleichgeschalted." Some of the generals, for example Blomberg, were openly for Hitler. Others, for example Reichenau, were considered pronounced adherents of the regime and proclaimed their sentiments openly. Others still, in keeping with the old Prussian traditions, eyed the new regime warily. Finally, there were those who, like von Schleicher and von Bredow, plotted secretly and dreamt of seizing power. Under these circumstances, the atmosphere was tense with electricity.

The trip of Propaganda Minister Goebbels to Poland took place on June 12–15, 1934. I was following it with serious misgivings for fear that some anti-German manifestations might take place in connection with the trip. I assigned Mr. S. Dembiński, director of the Polish Telegraph Agency in Berlin, to the team of Herr Goebbels' staff. The Polish minister of the interior, Bronisław Pieracki, was to greet Goebbels at the airport in Warsaw upon instructions from the government, and was to bid him farewell at his departure for Cracow by air on June 16. The visit was not of an official character, since Goebbels came to Poland at the invitation of cultural circles to deliver a lecture on the ideology of National Socialism.

Two unpleasant incidents occurred during Goebbels' visit in Warsaw. During a reception at the German Legation, a rock was thrown from the street to the drawing room, breaking a windowpane. This was only a minor incident, but on the evening of the same day some of the press agencies reported from Warsaw that Marshal Piłsudski had fallen ill, and that the audience fixed for the next day would not take place. I was unable to investigate the source of this rumor fully, or to find out whether it was true that at the last moment there was some hesitation as to whether Goebbels should be received by the Marshal. This information was released by the Iskra agency, at that time directed by Colonel Scieżyński. The Marshal's failure to receive Goebbels would provoke a serious note of discord in Polish-German relations, spoiling the whole effect of the journey, particularly since Goebbels was known to be highly sensitive to any incidents of this sort.

I called the attention of the Minister of the Interior to this situation and in the early morning hours of the next day received a reply that the audience with the Marshal was definitely on. The anxiety on the German side that Goebbels be received by the Marshal may be demonstrated by the fact that, on the afternoon of June 14, at a reception of Reichspräsident Göring, von Ribbentrop—who was said to be already closely associated with the Chancellor—asked with obvious concern whether there was any truth in the rumors spread to the effect that the Marshal would not receive the Reich Propaganda Minister. I was able to reassure him on this point. Parenthetically, the conversation itself did nothing to improve Polish-German relations.

On June 15, Goebbels flew from Warsaw to Cracow, where he stayed for a few hours to visit the monuments of that city. In the afternoon I received information by telephone from Dembiński from Cracow that Goebbels had flown from Cracow via Wrocław (Breslau) to Berlin, where he was to land at Tempelhof at 4:30 P.M. At the same time I received information by telephone from American press sources that an attempt had been made in Warsaw on the life of Minister Pieracki. The Polish Ministry of Foreign Affairs confirmed this news by telephone. At 4 P.M. I arrived at Tempelhof airport to greet Goebbels. The chief of the Eastern Department of the A.A., Meyer, brought a telegram from Moltke about Pieracki's death. Goebbels was shocked by the news of the assassination, and from what was said by his entourage I surmised that they were worried lest the assassination in some way be connected with the Goebbels-Pieracki meeting in Warsaw. Foreign correspondents in Berlin, ill-disposed to the idea of the Polish-German rapprochement, gave wide circulation to this version. Our Legation had to counteract this propaganda. In the following days I began to receive from Warsaw news of reprisals applied by the government of Prime Minister Kozłowski against nationalists suspected of possible participation in the attempt, of the creation of a camp at Bereza, and of a great ferment in Polish public opinion. I could not believe that a Pole could have murdered Pieracki. An argument against the hypothesis that the deed had been done by the Ukrainian terrorists was that they had hitherto (as I was informed later) performed these acts of terror only in territories inhabited by Ukrainians. An investigation starting from similar assumptions at first went astray. Several days after the assassination I received an anonymous letter, written in Ukrainian from the vicinity of Szczecin [Stettin], pointing to the killer, who was allegedly a resident of a Ukrainian settlement near that city. I sent this letter to Warsaw immediately. However, I was later told that it did not aid in the investigation.

A few days later, when I had guests at the Legation, I received a telephone call at 11 P.M. from Warsaw from Minister Schaetzel, chief of the Eastern Department of the Ministry of Foreign Affairs. He told me that at 7 P.M. that day the alleged killer of Minister Pieracki had left Danzig aboard the ship *Preussen*. The ship was to land at Swinemünde at about 6 A.M. without stopping on the way. Schaetzel gave me a description of the person, asking me to do my best to arrange for his arrest. There was not a single moment to lose. Taking leave of my guests, I detained only Dembiński, the director of the Polish Telegraph Agency, and made a direct call to the headquarters of the Gestapo in Berlin, circumventing the A.A. At that late hour I would probably find no one present at that office; besides, I had no doubts but that the old Prussian clerks would take a negative attitude toward my intervention.

The officer on duty took my telephone call. Fortunately, no senior functionary was present. I gave the officer the details communicated to me from Warsaw, laying particular stress on the necessity of arresting the man upon his landing in Swinemünde. As the Gestapo functionary did not contradict me, and to all my demands replied in a dutiful tone, "Jawohl, Excellenz," I told him that in a few minutes Mr. Dembiński would come to assist him in this matter. We also called Counselor Lubomirski and started on a full night's work at the Legation. I issued personal telephone instructions to Polish Consul Sztark at Szczecin to proceed immediately by car to Swinemünde and call on Chief Police Commissary Opitz, who on orders from Berlin was to perform the arrest of the murderer upon his landing. Consul Sztark was further instructed at all cost to be present at the interrogation of the criminal. Dembiński acted very efficiently. He suggested that we send a radio message to the ship *Preussen* to confirm that the person in question, as described in our report, was indeed among the passengers and asking that he be watched and prevented from escaping. Upon further instructions from Warsaw, we obtained permission from the Gestapo for our agent Budny, who had trailed the murderer until the moment he boarded ship, to cross the frontier post near Wielkie Boże Pole that same night.

About 7 A.M. I received a telephone report from Consul Sztark about the arrest of this man. It took place in the following circumstances: The

captain of the *Preussen* replied to the radio message that there was a
person answering the description aboard ship and that he showed signs
of considerable nervousness. Even before the landing at Swinemünde,
several police functionaries arrived by motorboat and arrested the man,
taking him ashore discreetly. The interrogation took place in the presence of the Polish Consul. The man proved to be a Ukrainian. With
obvious satisfaction he learned that he was already on German soil. A
search of his travel documents revealed a brand new passport from the
consulate general of the Reich in Danzig. His name was Mikolaj
Łebed, and he had been the organizer of an earlier attempted sabotage
on a train at Gródek Jagielloński. The faces of the German functionaries
showed embarrassment at this obvious gaffe, since the Polish Consul
was present and wrote down a protocol.

In the morning hours I informed Warsaw about the arrest and received instructions to undertake steps for extradition immediately. Upon
consultation with my staff (Counselor Wyszyński) I decided not to take
the official routine channel through the A.A. but instead to approach the
top Party authorities directly. I ordered my secretariat to arrange a
meeting for me with the chief of the Gestapo, Himmler. The meeting
was fixed for 12 noon. A quarter of an hour before I was to leave the
Legation, Himmler telephoned that he had been suddenly summoned by
Hitler and on his way back from the Reich Chancellery would come to
the Legation.

About 1 P.M. Himmler arrived at the Legation with a large retinue.
Upon entering my office he was the first to mention the affair, declaring
in the Chancellor's name that it had been decided to hand over without
delay to the Polish authorities the Ukrainian arrested that morning. Herr
Himmler added that he had interrogated the person in question. The
man was the chief organizer of Pieracki's assassination, and he was to
be deported about 2 P.M. that day by plane to Warsaw. Himmler then
shifted the conversation to broader topics of Polish-German relations,
suggesting an understanding between the security organs of the two
countries.

Upon informing Warsaw of these developments, I gave instructions to
watch for the announced flight. At the hour fixed for the departure, I
received a telephone call from a representative of a Polish airline who
was present at the airport, informing me that the departure would not
take place. Upon confirmation of this news, the Legation was advised

that the departure would not take place that day. Our apprehensions that the German Intelligence Department, engaged in schemes with the Ukrainians, would object to turning the criminal over to Poland thus proved to be justified. It was also clear to me that the A.A., as well as the Reichswehr, was opposing the Chancellor's decision. I obtained a telephone connection with Himmler's office. I was first told that he was absent, and that he had left, but when I firmly insisted on the necessity of speaking to him immediately, Himmler took the call. I told him that I was calling him with reference to the information I had received that the plane had not left at the hour fixed for the departure. Himmler began to explain that a delay had occurred because the matter was more complicated than appeared at first. The man arrested was mixed up in other cases on German territory, which required further long investigations. However, he assured me that within a few days the man would be delivered to the Polish authorities. I replied firmly that I had already communicated the Chancellor's decision to Marshal Piłsudski, and that it was impossible for me to accept a change in the decision. I could not risk it, because this might have disastrous consequences for Polish-German relations. I let it be understood that under such circumstances I would consider my mission as ended. As far as German interests were concerned during legal proceedings, I assured Himmler that everything possible would be done to avoid unnecessary friction. I added that the German side would be free to obtain all information in the course of the proceedings through normal legal channels. In view of my very firm stand, Himmler weakened and declared that he would approach the Chancellor once more. It was obvious that if the matter were not settled immediately it would be impossible to obtain the extradition at a later date. Poland's political interest was at stake, since it was imperative to appease public opinion by showing that the coup had been organized by foreign terrorists and not by Poles. After a rather long wait, Göring telephoned at 4 P.M. He stated that as chief of the German Air Force he was not opposing the departure of the criminal to Poland, and that he had given orders to this effect. A moment later Himmler informed me that the matter had been settled and agreement secured for the immediate departure of a Polish plane to Poland with the arrested man aboard. Himmler added that at the earliest opportunity he would explain to me the causes for the delay.

Shortly before the purge of June 30, Funk, the secretary of state at the Propaganda Ministry, threw a large party at his villa near Berlin for the diplomatic corps and the Party. When we sat down at the table, I was astonished to see that a number of places were empty. Our hosts were obviously taken aback by the absence of their guests. It developed that the missing visitors were Röhm's adherents. Himmler arrived late, almost at the end of the dinner. In a casual conversation after dinner he began to explain why the departure of the plane to Poland had been delayed.

He put the blame for this on elements of the old regime who had allegedly collaborated with the Ukrainian terrorists against Poland. He solemnly declared that he had severed all ties with the terrorists. However, when after this conversation Warsaw forwarded a number of names of Ukrainian terrorists who were leading diversive anti-Polish action in the Reich, the Gestapo made no reply for a long time, or else just issued casual explanations. The extradition of Łebed took place only because the German government had been compromised by the collaboration of its consulate general in Danzig in Łebed's escape to Germany.[1]

[1] M. Łebed was tried in Poland and was sentenced to death, but the sentence was reduced to life imprisonment. When Poland was occupied by Germany, he was released from prison. At present he is in the United States.

See Wojciechowski, *Stosunki Polsko-niemieckie, 1933–1938*, pp. 235–37, Roos, *Polen und Europa*, p. 154, and Szymanski, *Zły sąsiad*, p. 152.

# The Eastern Pact
## *May—December, 1934*

The declaration of nonaggression between Poland and Germany of January 26, 1934, resulted in a further *détente* in relations between the two countries, so that by February 7 a commercial agreement had already been signed by them. The German offer to coordinate with Poland the problem of the construction of the superhighway (autobahn) to East Prussia, as presented by von Moltke in his conversation with Beck on May 25, 1934, was probably connected with this agreement. Four years later the problem of a German superhighway across Polish Pomerania became one of the principal causes of the Polish-German conflict.

The matter of regional pacts of mutual aid was initiated by Louis Barthou, who became the minister of foreign affairs of France in the cabinet of Gaston Doumergue (this government was formed on February 9, 1934). He attempted to include Poland in this system during his visit to Warsaw (April 22–24). However, Poland did not support his plan of an Eastern Pact. The pact, in which Poland, the Soviet Union, Germany, Czechoslovakia, Lithuania, Latvia, Estonia, and Finland were to participate, was discussed by Barthou with Litvinov at Geneva (May 18–19). Von Moltke referred to this conversation in his discourse with Beck on May 25, 1934.[1]

The visit of the Reich propaganda minister, Dr. Josef Goebbels, to Warsaw on June 12–15 was a further sign of improved Polish-German relations. He came at the invitation of the Polish Intellectual Union and on June 13 delivered a lecture entitled "National Socialist Germany as an Element of European Peace." In the course of this lecture Goebbels declared, in part, that there was no problem in Europe which would necessitate a solution by war. The press in Danzig stated that this speech was also addressed to Paris, Moscow, Prague, and all countries which feared that National Socialism had imperialistic features and aggressive tendencies. Goebbels' speech had a favorable reception in Poland.

Lipski's report of June 22 gives an illustration of the general situation in European relations at the beginning of the summer of 1934.

[1] *DGFP*, Series C, Vol. II, No. 465.

DOCUMENT 28   Lipski to Beck

NO. N/49/78/34                                    Berlin, June 22, 1934

In connection with the telegram of June 21, in which I informed you about explanations given to me by the A.A. with regard to conversations of Hitler with Mussolini and of Neurath with Litvinov, I am now presenting the following information.

I have been able to observe recently a considerable increase in German diplomatic activities. In Polish-German relations, this was illustrated by Herr von Neurath's initiative in meeting you in Berlin and by Herr Goebbels' trip to Warsaw; in relations with other nations, by the Chancellor's meeting with Mussolini in Venice, by the travels of von Ribbentrop, the delegate for disarmament problems, to London and Paris, and, finally, by the conversation between Litvinov and von Neurath in Berlin as disclosed by the press. Beyond any doubt, this increased activity is due to the international situation of the Reich at present—namely, to its rather considerable isolation. At the same time the Reich strives to counteract French policy, which, since Barthou became minister of foreign affairs, tends to strengthen the French position by more pressure on London, an approach to Russia, reactivization of relations with Poland, and a tightening of links with the Little Entente.

Under these circumstances, I thought it desirable to obtain authoritative comments on moves in German politics which have taken place since your last conversation with Minister von Neurath.[2]

At the A.A. I was told that inquiries had come from various quarters about whether there was any connection between Hitler's trip to Venice and Goebbels' visit to Warsaw. As the dates coincided, they could not accept the fact as sheer coincidence. In spite of assurances by the A.A. that the day of Goebbels' arrival had been fixed long in advance, before it was known when Hitler would be able to leave for Italy, no one was willing to accept this explanation.

With regard to Hitler's meeting with Mussolini, the A.A. confirmed that the aim of this visit was, in the first place, to establish personal contact between the two dictators and to offer the opportunity for free discussion of the complex of international problems of interest to both

[2] *Ibid.*, No. 485. The meeting of Hitler with Mussolini in Venice took place on June 14.

countries. There was no question of any binding agreements. The German side is very well satisfied with the results of the meeting, since besides allowing for personal contact between the two statesmen, it also demonstrated a far-reaching community of opinion on international matters.

As for Austria, the A.A. communicated to me in strictest confidence that the Chancellor presented the matter to Mussolini in the following vein: any attempt to calm the situation in Austria would be impossible to achieve with the present Dollfuss government. The Chancellor observed that a neutral person should be placed at the head of the government. Under such neutral rule elections should be held, and only then would peace come to Austria.

The A.A. did not comment on Mussolini's point of view on this question, and it was impossible to press further for comment owing to the fact that the matter was rather ticklish. From other quarters, however, I learned that German government circles consider elections in Austria a possibility as a result of the Venetian talks. From the Italian press and correspondence in the *Temps* of Rome it could be concluded that Mussolini had won a victory over Hitler on the Austrian question. The German government supposedly is for the independence of Austria, and will coordinate its actions with the Italian government.

From the A.A. statements it is obvious—in my opinion—that Hitler is standing firm on the position he has repeatedly stated, which in short is that he is not acting against Austria's independence, but only requests that the population have the right to vote freely for the government of its choice. He is counting on a *Gleichschaltung* after the elections.

In the light of the A.A. statements it is also obvious that the present terrorist methods applied by Austrian Hitlerites are designed to prepare the way for the overthrow of the Dollfuss government.[3]

According to the A.A. information, during Hitler's conversations with Mussolini the question of Germany's relations with the League of Nations, as well as the matter of disarmament, was also touched upon, and

---

[3] For some time Austria had become a stage for many acts of terror, such as the destruction of roads and bridges and assassination attempts in public places. These acts were part of a systematic and organized action designed to wreck security and create difficulties for tourists, who contributed considerably to Austria's income. The action was conducted by Austrian National Socialist organizations under direction from Munich. In order to overcome the terror and sabotage, the government of Chancellor Dollfuss extended the competence of Austrian martial law, introducing the death penalty for these criminal offenses.

it was ascertained that the views of the two leaders are similar on these subjects.

With regard to the question of disarmament, Hitler referred to the stand taken by the German government in the known notes addressed to the Great Powers, which stressed that German demands should be considered an indispensable minimum.

Relations with the Western Powers—that is, with France and England—were also discussed, the problem of the Four-Power Pact, relations with Russia, the question of the Far East, but there was no mention of the Balkan pact or the triple agreement [Italy, Austria, Hungary].

Giving me further information on the plan of the Litvinov pact, which was also discussed in Venice, the Auswärtiges Amt described the situation as follows:

A few days before Litvinov's visit to Herr von Neurath, François-Poncet called at the A.A. and communicated the plan for the pact, based on the principles of consultation, nonaggression, and reciprocal aid with the participation of Russia, the Baltic states, Poland, Czechoslovakia, and perhaps also the Little Entente. The plan provided for a guarantee by France, without its actual participation in the pact. In return for the guarantees obtained by this pact, the Soviet Union, for its part, had to guarantee the Rhineland Pact.

On the very day of Neurath's departure for Venice, the Soviet Embassy called unexpectedly, suggesting that, on his way back from Geneva via Berlin, Litvinov be received by von Neurath. Neurath replied that he was leaving in a few hours, but, bowing to pressure, he received Litvinov.[4]

In the conversation with Litvinov the question of the pact was brought up. Litvinov did not present any plan in writing. The A.A., after its talks with Poncet and Litvinov, has some misgivings as to the authorship of the pact. The A.A. hints that the pact is rather a French product. Neurath told Litvinov that the plan for the pact is receiving careful attention. He stated that it possesses some positive elements, such as consultation and nonaggression. However, he stressed that the German government is negatively disposed with regard to the grouping of states involved in mutual assistance, since this means a return to the policy of alliances. Besides, owing to the restrictions in armaments, the German government would be unable to accept obligations under such a pact.

[4] On June 13, 1934.

The same explanations were repeated by the German chargé d'affaires in Moscow. Consequently, the press rumors that the German government had rejected the plan for the pact "purement et simplement" are not accurate. In his discussion with Litvinov, Neurath once more explained the stand of the German government toward the plan of the Baltic Pact as presented by Moscow some time earlier.

Herr von Neurath also implied to Litvinov that he desires good relations with Moscow.

Coming back to the Hitler-Mussolini conversations, I was told that the question of reciprocal assistance was also under discussion and that the Italian government shared the opinion of the German government on this matter absolutely.

The German government thought that the pact would grant the Franco-Russian alliance special influence. Also, by entering into the pact, Germany could be dragged into conflicts—as it was put—at the cost of money and blood.

It was further noted that Belgium would in principle be against the guarantee of the Rhineland Pact by Russia, as well as by Italy and England. According to the A.A. information, Finland is also negatively disposed to this project. The Finnish foreign minister, who was passing through Berlin, allegedly spoke of Soviet propaganda spreading news of a threat of German invasion of the Baltic states.

At the end of my interview I also asked about the recall of Nadolny from Moscow. This news was confirmed to me, but it was stressed that this was purely a personal matter and had nothing to do with a difference in political opinion, as was hinted by the foreign press. He will be succeeded by Count von Schulenburg, the envoy in Bucharest.

I must stress that the chief of the Eastern Department, who in the absence of the secretary of state was my informer, asked for my discretion and added that the German government would like to continue a permanent contact with the Polish government on the question of Litvinov's planned pact. Herr von Moltke will call on you next week to discuss this problem. Also von Bülow, the secretary of state, would like to see me upon his return to the office.

Finally, I am taking the liberty of making the following observation on the background of German-Russian relations:

According to information in the *Temps,* Mussolini pressed Hitler to modify his position toward Russia, to stop Rosenberg in his anti-Russian propaganda, which is highly irritating to Moscow, and to do this independently of the negative stand taken by Italy toward the mutual aid pact.

I presume that this was really so, and that Italy undoubtedly was using the argument that the anti-Soviet tendency of the German policy is contributing to the Soviet-French rapprochement, forcing Litvinov to look for guarantees.

I have reason to believe that the elements in Germany that are basically oriented toward the Soviets (primarily the circles close to the Reichswehr and the former Hugenberg camp) are using such arguments in order to ease German-Soviet tensions.

*Józef Lipski*

The problem of the Eastern Pact or the Eastern Locarno was the topic of a number of diplomatic conversations in Berlin and Warsaw, at the League of Nations, and in other capitals. On July 13 von Neurath informed Lipski about the French and British proposition.

### DOCUMENT 29   Lipski to Beck

NO. N/49/100/34                                          Berlin, July 13, 1934
                                                        *Top Secret*

This afternoon, quite unexpectedly, Neurath asked me to call on him without delay. Apologizing for summoning me to the A.A. so suddenly, von Neurath said that he was already anxious yesterday, after his talk with the British Ambassador [5] about the Eastern Pact, to inform me of its course, but his secretary forgot to telephone, and this was the reason for his asking me to call today.

Herr von Neurath submitted for my information two texts handed to him by Sir Eric Phipps, one containing the original French plan, and the other with British propositions accepted in London by Barthou. I am attaching copies herewith.[6]

He told me that, according to his information, Sir William Erskine presented a similar *démarche* to you.

[5] *DGFP*, Series C, III, 164–68.
[6] *Ibid.*, No. 85, enclosures 1 and 2.

Discussing the texts, von Neurath stressed their knottiness and the difficulty in deducing the consequences which might follow for the signatories of such agreements.

Regarding Part I, point *a,* he observed that the obligation of the participants of the pact to offer mutual assistance might result in the presence of the Red Army on the territory of Germany or Poland, which—as he jokingly remarked—would be no pleasure for either country. Neurath further called my attention to the fact that, according to the text, assistance would be extended immediately without consultation.

He especially stressed point 2, concerning the Franco-Russian agreement for mutual aid, as well as letter C of point 3, dealing with Russia's joining the League of Nations.

With regard to the counterpropositions on the British side, Neurath pointed to the very involved wording of point 3, dealing with equality of rights for Germany. In reply to the *démarche* of the British Ambassador, von Neurath replied that both texts would receive careful investigation. Without approaching the matter *ad meritum,* he limited himself to three questions posed to the Ambassador: namely, whether Great Britain intends to join the pact, which would endow the pact with special value; whether the Ambassador does not foresee that such a pact could turn against Great Britain, that is, in case of a conflict in India; and, finally, how the matter of *Gleichberechtigung* [equality] for the Reich in the field of armaments in connection with point 3 of the British plan should be understood.

With regard to this last question, von Neurath observed that point 3 of the British plan is constructed in such a way that only upon the conclusion of the pact could negotiations be started on the convention providing the acceptance of the principle of *Gleichberechtigun*g for Germany. He added that it is beyond his comprehension how the German government could join such a pact prior to the settlement of the armaments problem.

The whole course of von Neurath's thinking was definitely negative to the project. Neurath wants to deal with the whole matter slowly and to withstand the pressure of the Great Powers. He made this obvious by planning to go on leave the following week. He stressed that even the threat that a Franco-Russian alliance would be concluded in case of a negative attitude by Germany toward the pact would not force the German government to abandon its position. A Franco-Russian alliance is no threat to us, he added, since we have no aggressive intentions. Besides, von Neurath thinks that if the French government had to defend the alliance with the Soviets before the Chamber of Deputies it would encounter serious opposition.

Neurath described the pact as a hegemony of strongly armed powers, making an allusion to France.

Since the afternoon press brought news of Sir John Simon's communication to the House of Commons on Mussolini's stand toward the pact,[7] I asked for Neurath's opinion regarding the Italian declaration. Von Neurath replied that he was also taken aback by the press announcements; only upon reading Mussolini's statement did he get the impression that this was a very skillful retreat by the chief of the Italian government from probable British pressure that he participate in the Eastern Pact.

Mussolini's declaration is not in the least contradictory with his basically negative point of view toward the pact, as he clarified it in his conversations with the Chancellor at Venice.

Neurath also told me that, in view of the information in the London press that Simon's speech was made in time to enable the Chancellor to take a stand during his speech tonight on the question of the pact, he had immediately contacted Hitler and asked him to keep silent on this point.

Closing the conversation, von Neurath promised to keep me further informed about developments in this matter.

From my side, I gave him to understand that we are rather critical toward these plans, and that we shall have to investigate them thoroughly.

*Józef Lipski*

Eighty-seven-year-old President Hindenburg died on August 2, 1934. Three hours later, a directive dated August 1 was issued stating that the offices of Chancellor and President had been combined and that Hitler had taken power as the head of state and commander in chief.

A plebiscite was held on August 19, and 90 percent of the people voted in favor of the above directive.

[7] In his speech in Commons on July 13, Sir John Simon read a telegram just received from Mussolini, who informed the Foreign Secretary that the attitude of Italy toward the Eastern Pact was identical with that of Great Britain.

In a private letter of August 17, Lipski wrote to Józef Potocki, vice-director of the Political Department of the Ministry of Foreign Affairs, as follows:

More than ever before Chancellor Hitler is the dominant figure in the Reich's political life. Since the passing of the decree of August 1, fusing the functions of President and Chancellor, Hitler grasps the maximum of power in his hands. This is a fact which is worrying more than one politically-minded German, since the whole system depends on one man, with the attendant dangers.

If one takes a better look behind the scenes, it is clear that the events of June 30 aggravate the internal situation even more, and their results may be felt as time goes on. Nevertheless, viewing the events of June 30 from the vantage of the most recent moves connected with the succession of Hindenburg, it must be admitted that Hitler came off well, liquidating Röhm and getting rid of Schleicher before the death of the Reichspräsident. I have even met with the opinion that Hitler, who has known for more than three months about the possibility of Hindenburg's sudden death, rushed things through.

In this connection, it seems quite significant that the last published testament of Hindenburg is dated May 11. Since June 30 Hitler has systematically taken advantage of all developments to further his ends. His rapprochement with the Reichswehr facilitated his take-over of presidential power and his control over the armed forces. All the moral credit enjoyed by the late President in Germany is utilized for the aims of the National Socialist Party. Hindenburg is made out to be the spiritual father of Hitlerism. Hindenburg's testament is announced a day before the plebiscite.

It is immaterial whether the rumors (rather unconvincing) making the rounds abroad, that the document was allegedly forged, have a basis in fact or not. It is a fact that German public opinion believes that Hindenburg's testament favored Hitler. Even in Austrian-German relations he evokes the ghost of Hindenburg. Papen calls on Hindenburg's authority and wishes in carrying out his mission.

Hindenburg is to be buried in Tannenberg with full honors. They have taken over his glory, and his body remains in the distant East Prussian soil. It is better not to have a new Mecca too close to the capital.

In connection with Bülow's note, about which I write separately, the law of August 1, gives rise to interesting reflections. The title *Führer und Reichskanzler,* and abroad *Der Deutsche Reichskanzler,* seems somehow to be less than the idea of the head of state in other countries. One automatically feels that something is still missing. It is possible that Hitler did not want to forejudge the matter, but left possibilities open for the future.

How does the matter of the monarchy look? In my opinion, it is not of present interest, especially until Hitler's program of uniting Germany, in the wide meaning of the word, that is, with Austria, is realized. The monarchy would be a stumbling-block that would probably make unification impossible. The monarchy could only be the crowning achievement of a *fait accompli*—a definite stabilization. Meanwhile, we are in the full process of evolution. Of course, the trump card of the monarchy could be thrown in as the last hope in case of the collapse of Hitlerism. But this possibility is not being considered at present.

In conclusion, I may say that I do not see the monarchy as a current problem, but I do feel that, as the internal situation in Germany develops, it is imperative to watch this aspect closely. A plebiscite is strictly a touch à la Hitler, a means of clearing the atmosphere. Also, it is an absolution for the events of June 30, the acceptance of the law of August 1 by the nation, a demonstration to foreign countries that, in spite of what is said, the Germans back Hitler and his regime. What are the horoscopes? Most of them, in my opinion, are assured in advance. An element in the election struggle is the lack of a strong S.A. as an agitating agent in the elections. There may be surprises there. I expect that those who come to the polls will vote "for." Nevertheless, there may be a sizable number of abstainers, although the authorities are trying to counteract this possibility by special implementing orders. One would have to have comparable figures from previous elections at one's disposal to evaluate the results. A few more words about Hitler himself. I saw him during the funeral ceremonies for Hindenburg and I spoke with him. Outwardly he has changed a lot; the smile has disappeared from his face. He looks gloomy. His closest collaborators say that the Führer is suffering inside because of the betrayal of June 30. There is a certain atmosphere of *unheimlich.* Past and future assassination attempts are constantly discussed.

If it is very successful, the plebiscite will serve to clear the atmosphere.

DOCUMENT 30   Lipski to Beck [8]

N. 128/20/34

Berlin, August 27, 1934
*Strictly Confidential*

On Thursday, August 23, the secretariat of Minister von Neurath telephoned to the Legation asking whether I would be in Berlin next Monday. Next day I was advised that the Minister for Foreign Affairs of the Reich would like to have a conversation with me on August 27 at 11 A.M.

Expecting that the problem of the Eastern Pact would be raised in the conversation, I asked for your eventual directions, which I received yesterday.

Minister von Neurath broached the question of the Eastern Pact, remarking that he would like to have Polish-German collaboration in this matter. He thought this should be done discreetly to avoid false rumors, which are already being circulated abroad by hostile propaganda. Herr von Neurath alluded here to the allegations in *Echo de Paris* about supposed secret Polish-German clauses. The German government had the project of the pact carefully investigated by its jurists, with the result that its reservations were rendered even more justified. The German government intends to issue an answer to the authors of the project, who, in von Neurath's opinion, use camouflage. Such a reply, expressing German reservations, would be handed to the British government.

The German government would like to check with us on this matter and therefore the Chancellor of the Reich desires to see me today at 2 P.M.

He is now in Berlin for a few hours and returns in the afternoon to Berchtesgaden by plane. Neurath also leaves tonight.

Last week the idea of inviting me to Berchtesgaden was discussed. However, it was necessary to conceal it from the press. Herr von Neurath asked me to be discreet about what he told me with regard to the pact, until my conversation with the Chancellor. On my side, when talking about the pact, I followed your latest instruction, pointing to our

[8] Lapter, pp. 314–18.

unchanged attitude and stating that we had not made much progress in studying this problem, which appears obscure from many angles.

Herr von Neurath also informed me that the Chancellor will present to me the question of establishing embassies in Warsaw and Berlin.

He closed the conversation with a sigh alluding to Pless. I presented to him a number of arguments pointing to absolutely improper dealing by Pless with his income tax duties.

I came to von Neurath before 2 o'clock and went with him to the Chancellery. The Chancellor thanked me in the first place for my greetings on the results of the plebiscite. He then declared it to be his wish to raise the German Legation in Warsaw to the rank of an embassy.

Next the Chancellor remarked that he would like to discuss with us very frankly the subject of the Eastern Pact.

Parental claims upon this project seem to be rather ambiguous. The Chancellor's attitude to the pact is negative in principle. In the problem of equality the pact offers no solution, although here there is a certain difference of opinion between the British and Italians on one side, and the French on the other.

From what the Chancellor said, I gathered that something might be hammered out in connection with the pact.

The Chancellor further pointed out that, in accordance with the pact, the Soviets would come to the aid of the Reich in case of a French attack on Germany. The Chancellor said that this is not without a certain irony. He cannot imagine what country would welcome the Red Army on its territory. Germany is quite content with the Locarno British-Italian guarantees, as is Russia. Besides—the Chancellor observed—in case of a French assault the real defense will rest on the Germans alone. In his opinion, this is true of all states; that is, they can count only on their own forces.

The Chancellor further stated that the whole conception of the pact involves Soviet Russia's interest primarily.

He observes Russia from two angles, from its drive for expansion and its military power.

In the Chancellor's opinion the whole might of the Soviets is based on their Communist doctrine of international scope. Contrary to Hitlerism or Fascism, Bolshevism does not respect national frontiers. It is an illusion to think that Bolshevik expansion reaches a terminal point. He quoted the example of America, where they are again having trouble with Moscow. In every country the Soviets have their organizations that would start action on behalf of Moscow in case of a conflict. That is why he, Hitler, was ever against the policies of former German governments that strove to rely on relations with the Soviets.

Russia is a colossus of unlimited resources. To think that in a few oncoming years something might change in Russia is an error. A doctrine never changes.

Russia's military progress is enormous. The Chancellor quoted figures of planes, tanks, people under arms. He does not belong to those who close their eyes in the face of danger. He never ceases to point out this danger of Russia to his people. Presently a commotion is boiling up in the Far East. Nobody can foresee whether a conflict with Japan will take place. However, the Chancellor thinks that Russia's whole policy—to join the League, to sign the Eastern Pact, to remove prejudices against collaboration with capitalist states—points to the intention of the Soviets to safeguard themselves in the West in case of a conflict in the Far East. Hence to sign the pact would mean to support the Soviets. This obviously does not please the Chancellor in the least. German guarantees for Russia are against his point of view. In a raised voice he declared: No German soldier will fight for Russia, at least as long as I live. In his long deliberations the Chancellor said many things about Poland. He declared that he had decided to change his policies toward Poland when he saw the danger coming from the East. For Europe— and particularly for Germany—Poland is a shield against the East. He always says that to his people. In relation to this ominous problem, any Polish-German divergences under the treaty fade away. These, of course, are unpleasant matters for Germans, but they retreat to the back of the stage. Thus, for example, if Poland's access to the sea had been pushed eastward from East Prussia at Versailles, then the two states would long ago have become allies. Poland to the east—Germany to the west. Germans and Poles have to live side by side and they should know better than to Germanize or Polonize. France's rapprochement with Russia is not a surprise to the Chancellor. For many years he was of the opinion that, when Russia took on weight, France would seek an alliance with Russia at the expense of its friendship with Poland. That is why he opposed the Reichswehr's politics toward Russia.

Coming back to the Eastern Pact and reiterating his ideas, the Chancellor confirmed that Germany's joining the pact would reinforce the

Soviets, which he does not want in principle, and which he regards as detrimental not just for Germany but for Europe too.

In this situation Poland's position is crucial. If Poland, in spite of being a neighbor, would join the pact, this would deprive him of his main argument. He would then be obliged to revise his position, eventually to bargain to some extent with the Great Powers (he is not precise but it is clear that he has the *Gleichberchtigung* in mind). On the other hand, if he could be sure that Poland's attitude to the pact is also negative, then merely a tactical arrangement would suffice, which would be relatively simple.

Here von Neurath explained that the German government would reply to the British government prior to Geneva, itemizing its negative attitude. The Chancellor mentioned your possible meeting with von Neurath prior to the Geneva session.

In reply to the Chancellor's deliberations I stated that I would communicate them to my government. With regard to the pact I added that you had a discussion with Herr von Neurath some time ago and that a series of conversations had taken place between the two governments. I confirmed that nothing had changed in our attitude toward the pact, which was not especially enthusiastic, and that we saw a number of complications.

At the end of the conversation with the Chancellor I left with von Neurath for the Auswärtiges Amt to render its results precise.

1) In von Neurath's opinion the question of the embassy should now be positively settled. This decision of the two governments could be realized at a suitable moment, and the German government would conform to the desire of the Polish government.

2) Von Neurath asked me to communicate to my government the contents of the conversation with the Chancellor and obtain a reply of the Polish government as to its basic standing regarding the pact. In case the reply from Warsaw would confirm as negative a standing as that of the German government, he would in all probability still forward a reply to London at the end of this week. Von Neurath thinks it very advisable to specify reservations toward the pact to the Powers prior to the Geneva session, in order to prevent sudden undesirable decisions in Geneva. Neurath thinks that the best thing to do would be to have the pact dissolved. The Polish-German understanding should not—in his opinion—be outwardly revealed. He also understands that arguments used by each of the governments would be different.

As to meeting you prior to Geneva, von Neurath does not see any possibility of meeting in Berlin. He suggested your eventual transit through Stuttgart on your way to Geneva via Berlin, where the meeting could take place on his estate situated at 20 minutes' distance from the former town. Herr von Neurath is leaving today for Berchtesgaden with the Chancellor. He requests that the reply about the pact be forwarded to the Secretary of State. Owing to shortage of time before the departure of the courier, I have made only a brief résumé of the most important points of the conversation with the Chancellor.[9]

*Józef Lipski*

On August 30, in his conversation with Secretary of State von Bülow, Lipski announced the approval of the Polish government regarding the question of embassies (which went into effect on November 1) and presented the initial Polish opinion regarding the Eastern Pact.[10]

On September 6 Beck discussed the question of the pact with von Neurath.[11]

The assassination of Minister Barthou on October 9 temporarily held up conversations on the Eastern Pact, but his successor, Pierre Laval, renewed discussions and started diplomatic action in this matter.

DOCUMENT 31   Dębicki to Lipski

Warsaw, December 2, 1934

Following the instructions of Minister Beck, I am taking the liberty of quoting below his remarks, which, together with the text attached herewith, plus possible verbal comments of the bearer of this letter, Mr. Skiwski,[12] might help you, Mr. Ambassador, in your informative action, which is at present of great importance to Minister Beck.

I. (*a*) The reply of the French government to the Polish exposition of the Eastern Pact (both documents enclosed),[13] presented by Ambassa-

[9] For the German version, see *DGFP*, Series C, Vol. III, No. 177.
[10] *Ibid.*, Nos. 184 and 187.
[11] *Ibid.*, No. 194.
[12] Wiktor Skiwski was chief of the Press Department at the Ministry of Foreign Affairs.
[13] For the text of the exposition, see *DGFP*, Series C, Vol. III, No. 226; for France's reply, *ibid.*, No. 379.

dor Laroche on November 26, brings no new elements to the basis and system of the pact. It only contains concessions for the Polish thesis regarding Czechoslovakia and Lithuania. The Minister considers this reply a product of the bad traditions of the old Quai d'Orsay. He declared to the French government that he would have to make a study of it, and is keeping to his present position of reserve toward the planned pact.

(b) A further stage of this question is the Minister's conversation with Ambassador Laroche, a *compte rendu* of which I am enclosing herewith.[14]

(c) Finally, I am enclosing a memorandum of the conversation of Director Potocki with Herr von Schliep, held in consequence of the inquiry made by the German Chargé d'Affaires regarding the text of the French reply.[15]

II. Germany's stand on this question remains of essential importance for Minister Beck. Any shift in this stand would create a really new situation and force us to change our tactics. Therefore, it is most important and most urgent to obtain information about anything pertaining to German opinions on the whole problem of the pact. In order to collect such information, the Minister thinks it is indispensable that you, Mr. Ambassador, remain in Berlin. Although from conversations held so far with Herr von Moltke it develops that the German government still retains its negative attitude toward the pact, the impact of a possible change in this stand would result in such serious consequences that it is of the utmost importance to follow this problem as closely as possible, since it is the foremost problem facing us at present.

On the other hand, we are trying to find out whether the British campaign to legalize German armaments (resulting from recent speeches of Baldwin and Simon in the House of Commons) is at all connected with the question of the Eastern Pact, or whether it is being undertaken independently of it. If it turns out that the action of the British government and France's renewed efforts for the realization of the Eastern Pact have no interconnection and are being conducted independently, then this, in the Minister's opinion, could weaken the concept of the Eastern Pact. If, on the other hand, French policy succeeds in combining its efforts toward the realization of the plan with England's

---

[14] Enclosure missing. For the text of the conversation, see Laroche, p. 187.
[15] Notice missing.

initiative to legalize German armaments, the observation of the German position will become all the more important, since if both actions were combined, one of the chief German objections to the pact would fall and it could become for Germany the first genuine objective of political bargaining.

III. In the light of the above, strictly internal, considerations, Minister Beck requests that you declare to Herr von Neurath at the first opportunity that we made no promises as to the revision of our stand on the question of the pact, and that we are investigating the French reply, reserving judgment for the present. Up to now, the results of our studies on this reply are not very satisfactory. We are asking what the German stand is, declaring that we are ready to continue an exchange of opinions on this subject.

*Dębicki*

DOCUMENT 32   Lipski to Beck

Berlin, December 5, 1934
*Strictly Confidential*

On Monday, on the 3d inst., Skiwski brought me your verbal instructions regarding the Eastern Pact, as well as the letter of Director Dębicki, dated December 2, together with its enclosed texts and informative material.

I asked Reich Foreign Affairs Minister von Neurath for an audience on Tuesday and received a reply that, owing to important cabinet sessions, the Reich Minister was asking me to come on Wednesday at 12 noon.

At the cabinet session Minister von Neurath reported on foreign policy problems, particularly questions of the Saar. On Tuesday evening at Kiepura's concert I talked casually with Herr von Neurath, and we agreed that on the next day we would talk politics.

Arriving at Herr von Neurath's on Wednesday, I told him that I would like to discuss the question of the Eastern Pact, which had again become timely. I recalled that after your meeting with von Neurath at Stuttgart you had a conversation with Barthou at Geneva on the Eastern

Pact. At the request of the French Minister of Foreign Affairs you handed him an exposition in writing, not destined for publication because of the form of the document, since it was not a formal note but merely a summary of verbal explanations. Consequently, you informed Herr von Moltke about the contents of this document. I then handed this very document to Herr von Neurath, asking him to regard it as confidential.

I next stressed that after Barthou's death it seemed that the problem of the pact lost some of its timeliness; this was also the opinion of the A.A. I came across such statements in the course of several conversations. At present M. Laval is again taking up the problem of the pact. The French ambassador in Warsaw handed you a reply to his exposition of September 27. According to your instructions contained in Mr. Dębicki's letter, I mentioned that we did not make any promises to the French government so far as our attitude toward the pact was concerned, and that we are studying the French reply, reserving our opinion. I added that, although with regard to guarantees to Czechoslovakia and countries that have no diplomatic relations with us the French reply attempts to observe Polish restrictions, nevertheless, upon investigation of the text, no changes in the essence of the pact itself were discovered.

Here Herr von Neurath quickly rejoined that he had received the same impression, that nothing had changed in the very foundation of the pact.

At the end I remarked that it seems that our study of the French reply will take some more time; that we would like to know what the stand of the German government is and to remain in contact with them on this matter.

In reply Herr von Neurath said that he knows from Ambassador Köster that the French government intends to communicate to the German government the wording of the reply to Poland, and that it only awaits Warsaw's consent.

I explained that we gave a positive reply to Paris, which was obvious in itself.

Herr von Neurath firmly verified that the stand of the German government on the problem of the Eastern Pact was unaltered. He said he is quite sure that there is no possibility of any change, unless the essential foundations of the pact are altered, for the German government has no intention of being drawn into guarantees which might expose it to unpredictable conflicts.

This declaration was rather characteristic, since Neurath passed over in silence the question of equality of rights, but instead used the question of obligations for reciprocal assistance as an argument against the pact.

Herr von Neurath added that he would like further to keep in contact with me, and upon receiving the French reply to Poland he would like to take up this question again.

Herr von Neurath mentioned that he saw from the press that Mussolini is pushing his new idea. Knowing Mussolini, he is not surprised, for in such international situations the chief of the Italian government is trying to get into the forefront in the character of superarbiter. Herr von Neurath is only *au courant* of Mussolini's plan from the press. It would appear that a great many countries would be united in a pact of friendship. However, Herr von Neurath thinks that this apparently innocent concept conceals a hidden catch in the form of an obligation to limit armaments on the basis of the present status. This means that Germany would be granted its presently achieved armaments, thus limiting its ceiling, which is against its interests.

It was clear from the conversation with Herr Neurath that the German government's stand with regard to the Eastern Pact is still negative, and that it is rather satisfied that Warsaw received the last French reply with reserve, considering that the essence of the pact was unchanged.[16]

It was rather significant that von Neurath called the pact *Russenpakt.* May I remind you that Chancellor Hitler, in his conversation with me on August 27, 1934, stressed his reluctance to reinforce the Russian position in Europe as his main argument against the pact. At an audience of November 14 last, Hitler firmly assured me that his government, outside of economic relations, will not enter into any further understandings with Soviet Russia. Although I am aware that the circles of the Reichswehr and industry are drifting in the direction of a rapprochement with Russia, I nevertheless do not conceive the possibility that influence could be exerted on the Chancellor—given the present structure of power inside the Reich—to make him abandon his guiding policy line,

---

[16] The stand of the German government regarding the Eastern Pact was defined in the instructions to Ambassador von Moltke in Warsaw on December 15 (*DGFP,* Series C, Vol. III, No. 392), which he carried out in his conversation with Beck on December 20 (*ibid.,* No. 397).

all the more so since he regards the Eastern Pact as a trend toward French-Russian hegemony in Europe. Though the German-Russian rapprochement might have some attraction for certain German circles, a *détente* with Russia effected by the Eastern Pact cannot be advantageous to any German movement.

In his letter Mr. Dębicki asked whether British action to legalize German armaments has any connection with the Eastern Pact, in short, whether the Great Powers would agree to concessions on the armaments problem provided Germany joins the pact.

I shall keep you informed about all observations on this matter that I am able to make here. I did not want to take up this matter with Herr von Neurath, since I am very careful to avoid any topic with the Germans which would bring up the problem of equality of rights. I will only mention that von Neurath dealt with the matter of the pact independently of considerations of equality of rights. We could ask ourselves to what extent Germany is interested in the legalization of its armaments and what price it would be willing to pay for this move. Now, since the German government offered a certain ceiling in its notes to Great Britain and Italy, the situation has changed drastically. Germany has clearly contravened the provisions of Part V of the Versailles Treaty by arming, while the reaction of the Great Powers turned out to be just a platonic one. Public opinion has become used to German armaments, as could be observed even from the last debates in the House of Commons. If one of the leading British objections is that nothing precise can be learned about the state of German armaments, I presume that this objection is rather welcomed by the chief of the General Staff of the German Army. I think that, for the German government in the present period of Army expansion, it is more convenient to arm now, even against the letter of the treaty, than to agree to a restriction of armaments on a certain level, which would undoubtedly bring about controls.

If the tempo of German armaments has been accelerated during the last months, we have to assume that, besides other considerations, this is due precisely to a desire to create a *fait accompli* in face of the attempts of the Great Powers to limit the armed forces of Germany to a certain level.

*Józef Lipski*

# Introduction of Conscription in Germany
## January—May, 1935

---

NO. 49/1/5/35                                  Berlin, January 24, 1935
                                                *Strictly Confidential*

The annual dinner for the chiefs of diplomatic missions accredited in
Berlin took place on January 22.

After dinner Chancellor Hitler conversed with several ambassadors,
among others with me.

I began by declaring that I was very glad that in a few days Reichspräsident Göring will take part in a hunting party in Poland. The Chancellor was visibly pleased with this.

Next, the conversation turned to Polish-German relations in connection with the anniversary of the nonaggression declaration signed a year
ago, on January 26. The Chancellor stressed in very cordial terms the
importance of the rapprochement between the two nations. Deliberating
on this topic, he said how false the thesis of Polish-German *Erbfeind-
schaft* had proved to be. Hitherto in our history there were periods when
we collaborated, opposing the common danger from the east. We also
had some dynastic ties. Here I mentioned the last visit of the lord mayor
of Dresden, Zoerner, to Warsaw and Cracow and how warmly he was
welcomed. The Chancellor—developing this theme—remarked that in
some eight or nine years utterly different relations would prevail, when
the two nations would get to know each other and would rid themselves
of former prejudices. He added that of course there are some elements
in Germany acting against Poland. These are the elements which, as he
put it, would like to prevent his government from being successful in its
foreign policy. Such elements undoubtedly exist in Poland also, the
Chancellor remarked.

The Chancellor then went on at length about Russian problems and the danger from the east. He pointed to the information obtained from his military circles and the intelligence service that Russia had made enormous progress in the military field. A moment might come when both countries would have to defend themselves against invasion from the east. In his opinion, the policy practiced by the governments of his predecessors, and especially by the Reichswehr, based upon alliances with Russia against Poland, was sheer political nonsense. He himself at one time had clashed very bitterly with General von Schleicher, who wanted to get closer to Russia at Poland's expense. The Chancellor told him at that time that such a policy, even if it resulted in wrenching some territories from Poland, would lead to the resurgence of the worst danger for Germany, that is, the Soviet threat. He himself knows Bolshevism and has been combating it from the beginning, and here he brought up his struggle with Communism in Bavaria.

Talking about Marshal Piłsudski, the Chancellor said that he feels ashamed that only recently has he had the opportunity to learn more about the Marshal's life, and his esteem for the Marshal as a great statesman has increased even further. I took this occasion to thank the Chancellor for the kind gesture of sending Secretary of State Meissner to me to inquire about the Marshal's health, as a result of some press reports which had appeared a few weeks earlier.

Next, Hitler inquired about our stand toward the Eastern Pact. I replied, according to your instructions, that, as there were no changes in the basic structure of the plan for the pact, we are still reserving judgment. Finally, the Chancellor said a few very cordial words about Ambassador Wysocki.

We also talked about the Weisser Hirsch sanatorium near Dresden, and I thanked the Chancellor for his concern about my cure when he visited General Blomberg there.

At the close of the conversation, to which the Chancellor obviously wanted to lend a hearty tone, I said a few complimentary words about the results of the Saar plebiscite.[1] I remarked that this result is dispersing some false rumors peddled by the international press after the elections held in the Reich.

[1] A plebiscite was held in the Saar on January 13, 1935. The large majority of inhabitants (477,000 against 48,000) voted for the union of the Saar with the Reich. Hitler then declared that he had no territorial claims on France.

In connection with the above, I am also taking the liberty of stressing that at the same reception the French Ambassador expressed his conviction that he has lately felt a certain stiffening on the part of the Germans regarding the equality of rights. He also criticized the last speech of the Chancellor, stating that Hitler's previous public appearance was more moderate, since it was first discussed with von Neurath. M. François-Poncet was visibly disturbed by this state of affairs, and remarked that in the present situation reciprocal concessions and the search for a formula, etc., should be under discussion.

Also from other quarters I can detect a certain intensification of German demands regarding armaments since the settlement of the Saar problem. I refer to my report of the 8th inst., No. N/49/I/1/35, where I stressed that, in my opinion, military elements would not be willing at present to limit the ceiling of armaments and to allow controls. However, it is still difficult to judge what Germany's stand will be, and one can only make certain conjectures. Nevertheless, even now we can state that Germany will not be in a hurry to enter into negotiations and will rather keep to a position which would play into their hands from a tactical point of view.[2]

*Józef Lipski*

DOCUMENT 34   Lipski to Beck

NO. N/49/I/10/35

Berlin, February 5, 1935
*Strictly Confidential*

Referring to my telegrams of the 4th inst., I would like to report that on February 3 in the evening, when I met the French Ambassador at the races by chance, I learned that, together with the British Ambassador, he had presented the London resolutions to Hitler. The French Ambassador remarked that the text of the London resolutions was so cautious and subtle in wording that it should not have evoked any controversy from the German side. Nevertheless, the Chancellor strongly objected to two items, on which the Ambassador did not elaborate further. As far as

[2] The *Polish White Book* presents this report (No. 13) in an extensively abbreviated and considerably deformed version.

the plan of the air agreement was concerned, the Chancellor had a rather favorable opinion. The French Ambassador did not conceal his anxiety that the German government might jeopardize these negotiations, the results of which might prove so important, by its overly prejudiced stand. M. François-Poncet is of the opinion that this is the crucial moment for the shaping of international relations in Europe. Either Germany will accept international collaboration along the lines presented by the Great Powers, or a system of blocs and an armaments race will persist. Here the French Ambassador assumed that Poland would also have an interest in the success of the negotiations, since otherwise it would be compelled to abandon its present convenient position and declare itself on one side or the other. The Ambassador made a slight allusion to the fact that the Polish government, since it holds such an influential position in Berlin, could now render a useful service to the cause of peace.

I would also like to add that François-Poncet, who has read the protocol of Laval's conversation with you, told me that Laval is positively impressed by these talks.[3]

Talking about your last speech,[4] François-Poncet remarked that the German press is constantly intriguing to create friction between two allied nations. For example, it was stressed that the passage about France was especially brief as compared with the number of words you devoted to the relations with the Germans, etc. However, François-Poncet thinks that what is most important is that you confirmed the existence of a Franco-Polish alliance, which should be quite sufficient for his government.

On the following day the chief of the Eastern Department at the A.A. quite confidentially, informed me, on behalf of von Neurath, about the Chancellor's conversation with the ambassadors of France and Great Britain, which, as I mentioned before, was held on February 3. He handed me the text of the London resolutions in English, which had been presented to the Chancellor on this occasion. The text is nearly identical with the communiqué published the following day in the European press. I am enclosing a copy of the English text herewith.[5]

[3] For Beck's note of conversations with Laval on January 16 and 19, 1935, see *Diariusz*, I, 466–69.
[4] For Beck's speech of February 1 at the Commission for Foreign Affairs of the Diet, see Beck, *Przemówienia, deklaracje, wywiady, 1931–1937*, pp. 142–50.
[5] For the text, see *British Blue Book*, Cmd. 5143 of 1936, No. 5.

Minister Meyer declared that upon receiving this text the Chancellor in the first place firmly refuted the allusion that Germany has reputedly violated the armament clauses of the Treaty of Versailles. He declared that it was not Germany but the Great Powers who did not keep their respective obligations. As for Germany's joining the League of Nations, the Chancellor was supposed to have repeated his well-known position. Regarding the Eastern Pact, he took exception to the obligation of reciprocal aid.

Declaring that at present he was simply making a few comments based on superficial initial investigations that had taken place at the A.A. on the morning of February 4, Herr Meyer remarked that the text, which he considers quite interesting, will be given careful attention. As for the question of reciprocal aid in the Eastern Pact, Herr Meyer— evidently acting on instructions from the top—declared very explicitly that the German government would under no circumstances accept such stipulations. Herr Meyer stressed as a certain *novum* that it was noted in the text that Great Britain would take part in the consultations provided for by the Roman agreements in case the independence of Austria is threatened.

Regarding the accession to the air convention which was proposed to Germany, Herr Meyer gave me to understand that the stand of the German government might be positive. He added that such an agreement concluded between Great Britain, France, Italy, Belgium, and Germany could logically result from Locarno obligations which bind these states.

I am taking the liberty of remarking that the proposition of an air agreement is rather convenient for Germany, only because it grants the Germans an *a priori* military air force. Besides, it guarantees a possibility of removing from German-British relations the most drastic cause of friction.

Closing our conversation, Herr Meyer said that the German government would continue to keep me informed about these matters.

Not declaring myself at present as to the chances of success or failure of negotiations started between Germany and the Great Powers, I would just like to observe that the scope of the talks has become extensively broader, inasmuch as all problems (equality of rights, disarmament problems, Germany's entrance into the League of Nations, the Eastern Pact, the Central European Pact, Austria) are under discussion.

Here I shall recall the position presently held by Germany with regard to the particular problems encompassed by the negotiations.

*The problem of the Eastern Pact.* In principle a negative stand. The main argument used against the pact is the question of obligatory reciprocal assistance to the signatories of the pact.

*The problem of the Central European Pact.* Germany's position is declared in the memorandum to Italy and France, on which I reported in No. N/49/I/9/35 on the 5th inst.

When investigating this problem, it should be kept in mind that the German government would oppose anything that could in the future be an obstacle to its free action in relation to Austria.

*Disarmament problems.* Theoretically would demand absolute equality of rights with the Great Powers. As far as the limitations which would be accepted by the German government, it is doubtful whether it would still keep to its stand, as revealed in its last note in the spring of 1934. It is probable, as I mentioned in my previous reports, that Germany's demands were henceforth raised, and that military elements would oppose the establishment of limitations and controls.

*Western air agreement.* Stand of Germany positive in principle.

*Germany's entrance into the League of Nations.* Germany's stand is that the return of Germany depends on first obtaining equality of rights. Whether besides equality of rights the German government would also bring up the question of the League's reorganization is not yet quite clear, but my guess is that such a possibility might occur.

When evaluating the chances of negotiations so broadly conceived as a topic of conversations between the Great Powers and the government of the Reich, two points should be considered. First, that present-day National Socialist Germany is in a dynamic and not a static state. Therefore, a formula presented by the Western states that is too restrictive for Germany cannot be in line with the present development of Germany. Also, a too-extensive connection with democratic organizations in the West in the field of international collaboration, as for instance in the League of Nations, could not be very tempting to the regime. These *imponderabilia* will undoubtedly have an impact on the decision of the Reich government.

*Józef Lipski*

DOCUMENT 35 Lipski to Beck

NO. N/49/I/9/35 Berlin, February 5, 1935
*Strictly Confidential*

Referring to my telegram of the 4th inst., I am taking the liberty of reporting as follows:

During my stay in Poland with Prime Minister Göring,[6] the chief of the Eastern Department of the A.A. telephoned the Embassy, expressing the wish to see me. As he explained to me on the 4th inst., he wanted to hand me a memorandum addressed by the German government to France and Italy in connection with their *démarche* in Berlin regarding the Roman agreements.[7] Director Meyer declared to me that Ambassador Moltke was instructed to present this memorandum to you.

The memorandum, a copy of which is attached herewith,[8] contains a statement in the introduction that the German government accepts as self-explanatory the principles agreed to in the Central European Pact: namely, nonintervention into the internal affairs of other states; interdiction against the preparations on its territory of acts of terror directed against another state. On this basis the German government expresses its consent to undertake conversations to conclude an agreement which would define the above principles.

The memorandum further poses five questions to the French and Italian governments, to which I would like to add the following explanations:

*ad* 1) The demand for a precise definition of the idea of nonintervention into another state's affairs is made in connection with the Austrian situation. Already in my previous talks at the A.A. I heard musings on whether financing of the Heimwehr should be regarded as mixing into Austria's internal affairs. I presume that this point might serve the German government as a basis for bringing up the question of the Great

---

[6] Göring stayed in Poland at a hunting party from January 27 to January 31. Besides hunting he had several conversations with Marshal Piłsudski, Beck, Szembek, and others (see *Diariusz*, I, 218–21, 223–25, 230–31). For the German version of this visit, see *DGFP*, Series C, Vol. III, No. 474.

[7] The Roman agreements were a series of agreements regarding Danubian problems and African questions, signed in Rome on January 7, 1935, by Laval and Mussolini.

[8] See *DGFP*, Series C, Vol. III, No. 460, enclosure on p. 866.

Powers' not opposing the right of a free vote for the Austrian population and not pressing for the suppression of the Hitlerite Party in Austria.

*ad* 2) Objections against the so-called *accords particuliers* were raised by the German government from the moment it had been informed about the contents of the Roman agreements. Undoubtedly, the Germans particularly fear any ties of Austria with other states, for example, with Italy, and therefore they introduce the restriction that such separate agreements have to be previously accepted by all signatories of the pact.

*ad* 3) The suggestion that Switzerland, and especially Great Britain, should be partners in the pact was probably caused by two reasons. It could be that the German government wanted to weaken the Central European Pact by expanding the number of signatories, thus neutralizing individual influences, or that it wanted to burden the negotiations with further demands.

*ad* 4) The Italian-French consultative agreement concerning Austria, as we know, evoked the strongest objections of the German government, which regarded it as a sort of protectorate over Austria. Hence the demand that, if the consultative pact were to be continued during the period of the Central European Pact, it should be extended to the full extent to cover reciprocal relations of all signatories of the Central European Pact.

*ad* 5) The fifth question derives logically from Germany's walkout at the League of Nations. However, bringing up this point makes it doubtful that Germany could enter the Central European Pact prior to its return to the League.

Recapitulating the above, one cannot help having the impression that by posing these questions the German government not only did not facilitate negotiations but actually complicated them, for these questions require solutions of problems pending between Germany and the Great Powers, such as equality of rights and the return of Germany to the League of Nations.

*Józef Lipski*

DOCUMENT 36 Lipski to Beck

NO. N/128/8/35
Berlin, February 14, 1935
*Strictly Confidential*

Referring to my telegram, dispatched tonight, I am taking the liberty of reporting as follows:

This afternoon Foreign Affairs Minister von Neurath handed to the ambassadors of France and Great Britain the reply of the Reich government to the London resolutions. At 6 P.M. I was received by von Neurath, who declared that in accordance with his promise to keep us closely informed about the negotiations with the Western Powers on the above matters he would like to hand me the text of the German reply.[9]

Leaving me some time to acquaint myself with the text, Herr von Neurath added the following verbal comments:

The German government was rather pleased that the British and French governments informed it of the results of the London consultations, even prior to issuing a joint communiqué. Therefore, the German reply is maintained in a tone of courtesy and marked with the desire to reach an understanding.

Herr von Neurath further confirmed that the German government found in the text of the resolutions communicated to it, first of all, reference to a number of problems previously discussed by the Powers and the German government. Herr von Neurath enumerated here the question of the Eastern Pact, the Roman agreements, and disarmament. The German government did not deem it advisable to return to these particular questions in its present reply. This reply is therefore general in character, for as far as the Eastern Pact is concerned, the German government has already explicitly stated its point of view and has nothing further to add. It regards this pact—and especially the clause of reciprocal assistance (*assistance mutuelle*)—as not acceptable. The French reply to the German government brought nothing new to this problem. Therefore, the German government had nothing to add regarding the Eastern Pact; it would only have had to declare its negative attitude.

With regard to the Roman agreements, Herr von Neurath referred to questions already known to us, posed by the Reich government to the

[9] For the text, see *British Blue Book* for 1936, No. 6.

governments of Italy and France. Here too there was nothing more to say.

Regarding the disarmament problem, Herr von Neurath told me that it was certainly the French government and not the German government which broke off negotiations carried on last spring on this subject.

Therefore the Powers had to say the last word here, and not Germany.

Finally, von Neurath declared that the only *novum* is the proposition of the air pact. Therefore, this item was treated in detail in the German answer, and their stand on this matter was positive.

To my question as to the meaning of the statement in the German reply that the Reich government would like to negotiate in a more restricted group on the air pact, Herr von Neurath remarked that this passage, which, in his opinion, evoked a reaction on the part of the British ambassador, Sir Eric Phipps, was meant as a certain preparation for negotiations. Herr von Neurath, stressing that this is only his own opinion, remarked that the air pact, as an outgrowth of the Locarno agreements, would present no editing problem. It could be contained in two articles. In one it could be stated that the signatories of the agreement agree to mutual assistance without prior recourse to the League of Nations in case of attack by air. The second article could contain certain resolutions of a technical nature. Of course, Herr von Neurath has no illusions that considerable difficulties might arise in this matter.

Talking about the air pact, Herr von Neurath told me that he had a conversation with the Chancellor yesterday, during which the latter informed him of our discourse during the dinner for the Papal Nuncio.[10]

In this connection, Herr von Neurath asked me to inform you that he thinks it would be desirable at the present time to bring about a Polish-German conversation regarding the air pact, because he fears that if the question is raised about Polish-German mutual assistance in case one of these states is attacked by air, the problem would become timely and lead directly to the Eastern Pact. Russia undoubtedly would place a request for mutual assistance in air matters. Therefore von Neurath thinks it is better, in the present circumstances, to leave this question alone in Polish-German relations and await results of the conversations with the Western Powers. From the practical point of view, von Neurath repeated twice that in case of an air attack on us from the only side to be considered, that is, by Russia, we can count on the stand of Ger-

[10] In the Lipski documents the report of this conversation is missing.

many. Herr von Neurath remarked that in his conversation with the Chancellor he had told him the same thing.

I told Herr von Neurath that I could not give the Chancellor an authoritative reply the day before at the Nuncio's dinner to his concrete inquiry as to whether we would accept an air pact without Russia or not. I added that I had informed you about my conversation with the Chancellor.

Herr Neurath remarked that obviously I could not declare myself without consulting my government on such a matter—and that he was well aware of this. He repeated again his opinion that it would be better not to actualize the Polish-German air agreement. It was better to await further developments in the situation, and he added that the moment might come when it will become timely.

The above explanations of Herr von Neurath answer the question I put to myself after my conversation the day before with the Chancellor. I referred to it in my telegram of the 13th inst. I see from it that the idea of mutual air assistance in Polish-German relations came from the Chancellor and is not a result of suggestions from any third state. The Chancellor, who in the matter of security takes the Polish problem seriously, and probably taking into consideration the air negotiations with the Western Powers, did not want to leave a void on the Polish side.

Owing to a lack of time because of the courier's departure, I would only like to draw your attention to several issues in the German reply.

I seriously doubt whether passing over in silence the question of the Eastern Pact, the Roman agreements, and the disarmament problem, which Herr von Neurath tried to present as tactical moves, would meet with much enthusiasm on the part of the Western Powers, especially France, which tied all problems into one tight bundle.

The passage stating that the armaments race was caused by the policy of the Powers who were against disarmament as foreseen by the Versailles Treaty is a reply to an item in the London resolutions: namely, that the Powers cannot admit a one-sided violation of the treaty's disarmament clauses.

The suggestion to undertake direct German-British talks on the air pact is obviously a tactical move destined for public opinion in England.

In conclusion, it might be stated that the reply of the German government, as it is given, poses even more questions over the whole of the negotiations. It is most improbable that the air pact can be separated from the bulk of questions, and that Great Britain upon reaching an understanding with France in London would like to deal with this matter independently of the whole complex of other problems in the field of security covered by the forthcoming negotiations.

I stress that the text will be published on Saturday. Today the German press received only general information.

*Józef Lipski*

DOCUMENT 37   Lipski to Beck

N/128/12/35                                        Berlin, February 25, 1935
                                                            *Confidential*

Referring to my telegram reporting on the conversation I had with Herr von Neurath on the 21st inst., I am taking the liberty of communicating as follows:

To begin with, I declared to Herr von Neurath that, in connection with my conversation with the Chancellor at the Nuncio's reception and the explanations von Neurath later furnished me with, I had written to you and had received your reply, which I would like to acquaint him with. I remarked that we very much appreciate the open and sincere manner of the Reich Chancellor's declaration regarding the possible extension of the air pact to Poland. I added that we shall adjust our relations with Germany in this matter accordingly.

Passing *ad meritum* of the problem, I pointed out that the air guarantee is quite a *novum* and that, as far as the wording of such an agreement is concerned, no precedent exists. We have had no possibility as yet to investigate fully the problem regarding the application in practice of this guarantee. I further added that we shall follow the negotiations closely, and in case attempts are made to extend the air pact to other groups of states also, we will discuss this matter with the German government.

With regard to my previous conversation with Herr von Neurath, I said that you had not as yet received any proposition from the Russian side to this effect. Nevertheless, you share the opinion that the Soviets will strive to bring up the Eastern Pact in other ways. I declared that our stand on this matter is unchanged.

In a discussion that followed the above explanations, Herr von Neurath remarked that he fully understands that Poland cannot at present declare itself regarding the air pact. The Chancellor's suggestion aimed in the first place at assuring Poland that in negotiations conducted in the West on this matter Poland would not be left out by the Reich.

I replied that it was just because of this idea of the Chancellor that I declared, on your behalf, at the start of this conversation, how highly we appreciate his approach to this matter.

Herr von Neurath's comment regarding the reception of the German note in London and Paris was that criticism stating that Germany allegedly grasped at the negotiations of the air pact while omitting other issues contained in the Anglo-French declaration was groundless. The Reich's stand regarding other issues, such as the Eastern Pact, Roman agreements, or equality of rights, has been explicitly stated in the course of the Reich's conversations with the Powers, which have been under way for some time. The only *novum* is the air pact. The Anglo-French declaration stated that negotiations on this subject should be begun promptly. It was therefore evident that in its reply to the declaration the Reich government gave priority to the air pact.

Regarding Simon's trip to Berlin or Neurath's to London, the Reich Foreign Minister observed that, unless such visits are properly prepared, the meeting of the ministers to discuss such difficult and intricate matters might be prejudicial if no positive result is attained.

Herr von Neurath promised to keep us *au courant* on this matter.

He then spontaneously touched on the question of Schuschnigg's trip to Paris and London. He told me that according to information he received it is not impossible that the problem of the future regime in Austria will be discussed to consider the idea of the return of the Hapsburgs. For the idea prevails of creating a *Reichsverweserschaft* as it existed in Hungary. Until the return of the Hapsburgs, supposedly Starhemberg would take this post. Now, von Neurath confided in me that in the Hapsburg question the German government is taking a stand of total *désintéressement* and has issued instructions to whom it may concern accordingly. The constitutional form the regime in Austria will wish to adopt is its own affair, so that the Reich has no intention of interfering.

In my further conversation with Herr von Neurath on this issue, I had the strong impression that this stand of the Reich is rather opportunistic, since Neurath is of the opinion that the Hapsburg question will render the situation still more confused. Of course, he does not believe that Austria can achieve normal relations. It was rather characteristic that in connection with this question Herr von Neurath made a slight allusion to the Italian-Abyssinian conflict.

*Józef Lipski*

On March 16, 1935, a bill was published in Germany introducing conscription and a build-up of the army.[11] In peacetime it was to be developed to twelve army corps and 36 divisions, totaling about 500,000 men. This was a final violation of Part V of the Treaty of Versailles.

Von Moltke, in his telegram of March 18 (*DGFP*, Series C, Vol. III, No. 536), reports how public opinion in Poland reacted to this news. (See also *Diariusz*, I, 242–43.)

DOCUMENT 38    Lipski to Beck

NO. N/133/a/10/35                     Berlin, March 16, 1935
                                       *Strictly Confidential*

Today I was asked to call on Chancellor Hitler, who received me at 5:45 P.M. at the Chancellor's palace, with Herr von Neurath present.

Entering the palace, I met the British Ambassador, whom the Chancellor had received before my audience.

Chancellor Hitler opened the conversation by declaring that I was probably already informed about the conscription bill issued by the Reich, dealing with the build-up of the army. (Here I must note that before my departure for the Reich Chancellery I was informed by the representative of the Polish Telegraph Agency that Goebbels had just advised the press about the publication of the bill.) Chancellor Hitler stated to me that the issuing of the bill was due to the general situation that prevailed as a result of the Powers' armaments. He added that what is contained in the bill more or less corresponds to the actual state of the Reich's armaments. He further emphasized that this step of the Reich is

[11] For the English text, see Royal Institute of International Affairs, *Survey of International Affairs, 1935*, pp. 141–42.

devoid of any aggressive tendencies, since it is only of a defensive nature. Besides, the effective forces themselves defined in the bill by the Reich, as compared with those of its neighbors, manifest the peaceful tendencies of the Reich. Here the Chancellor cited 101 divisions in Russia, 41 divisions in France, and 30 divisions in Poland. He further stressed that the government of the Reich—provided conditions permit —will not try to avail itself of the figures drawn up in the bill. The bill, as the Chancellor conceives of it, would in no way mean a cancellation of talks with the Powers on limitation of armaments, which the government of the Reich is anticipating. The Chancellor also gave me to understand that he regrets handing this text to me so late, and without a Polish translation. It was obvious from his words that the decision of the Reich government must have been taken very hurriedly, probably in connection with yesterday's debate in the French parliament. Besides, the Chancellor told me that he interrupted his rest leave at Berchtesgaden and arrived in Berlin today.

Next the Chancellor took up the subject of future Anglo-German conversations. He stated that the Eastern Pact is for him the most difficult point in the program of talks, for the government of Great Britain exerts very strong pressure on the Reich government to bind itself to the Eastern Pact by a clause of mutual assistance. Now, under no circumstances will the Chancellor accept the clause of mutual assistance in relation to Russia. To confirm this stand of his, he told me that in the first place the Reich has no frontier with Russia. Furthermore, it is inconceivable for him that divisions of the National Socialist army could bring assistance to Communist Russia. Finally, he thinks that the whole construction of extending mutual assistance could of itself result in a situation in which Russia, supported by France, could start a conflict and shift the responsibility to Poland, for example. In such a case, it is inconceivable that, in accordance with the obligations of the Treaty, the German Army would have to act on the side of Soviet Russia. The Chancellor is ready to enter into pacts of mutual assistance with any other neighbor. He then cited Holland, Belgium, Poland, France, and even—adding that this would not be easy for him—Austria. In connection with Russia, such an obligation is out of the question.

Poland's position regarding the Eastern Pact is—in the Chancellor's opinion—of utmost importance. The Chancellor gave me to understand that he is very much concerned that we should maintain our position without change.

I explained to the Chancellor that Poland's stand toward the Eastern Pact—as is well known to the German government—is replete with reservations. I told him that we still have a pact of nonaggression with Russia.

Both the Chancellor and Neurath pounced on this point, stating that this pact should be enough.

In a discussion on this point, I said generally that we recognize all elements, such as nonaggression, consultations, and nonintervention, and that our pacts are based on these principles. Neurath, together with the Chancellor, eagerly agreed with me.

When the Chancellor once more stressed that the Eastern Pact will be the most difficult point to discuss with the British side, Neurath, addressing me, remarked that the best solution would be to oppose the British firmly on the idea of mutual assistance. The Chancellor then observed that the English would break their heads and find some solution.

I would also like to add that, in broad terms, the Chancellor described his conversation with the British as follows:

He said that in the field of armaments he foresees possibilities of discussion, and that the Reich government is in favor of the air triangle with England and France. Regarding the Danubian point, the Chancellor thought that on this also a settlement could be reached in spite of considerable difficulties with the problem of the definition of intervention.

When discussing the Eastern Pact, the Chancellor said that he does not understand why France, instead of agreeing to direct talks with Berlin in which Poland would possibly be included, was seeking channels via Moscow. Was it not easier, observed the Chancellor, to talk directly with Berlin after its declarations about Alsace and Lorraine? Here the Chancellor reiterated again that, regarding the Saar, he obviously had to claim the return of this territory to the Reich, since the population was totally German, while, with regard to Alsace and Lorraine, he went so far as to renounce any revindication. In his words, the population of Alsace and Lorraine draws toward Germany when it is under France; when under German authority, it is attracted toward France.

The whole misfortune of France, Hitler said, is that it has no Marshal Piłsudski. The parties are gambling politically with international problems. As an example of how a solution can be found to difficult problems, he pointed to Polish-German relations. He remarked that here it was psychologically impossible to waive so clearly a revindication of territories—as could be done regarding Alsace and Lorraine. We therefore had found a formula to renounce the use of power in our mutual relations.

I must add here that in justification of the conscription bill there is a passage regarding Polish-German relations on which, for lack of time, I do not dwell any longer.

Taking leave of the Chancellor, I asked about his health. I must add that in the course of the whole conversation he tried to speak in lower tones because of a sore throat. The Chancellor said that false rumors were spread by the press that he had caught a cold during the Saar demonstrations, for he had not been too well and the Saar affair aggravated his condition. The worst of it is that he has to deliver speeches, and this affects his vocal cords. "Breaking off my rest and leaving Berchtesgaden," said the Chancellor, "was not fortunate either, and I am not feeling very well."

When I took my leave, he asked me to present his respects to the Marshal.

The assistant of the military attaché—owing to the late hour and the departure of a special courier—is forwarding to the General Staff only the bill with the justification. He is also reporting to the chief of the General Staff that I had a conversation with the Chancellor on this subject. It is therefore possible that the chief of the General Staff will contact you for information about the contents of my report.

*Józef Lipski*

DOCUMENT 39   Lipski to Beck

NO. N/133/14/35                                  Berlin, March 23, 1935
                                                *Strictly Confidential*

Referring to my telegram of today, I am taking the liberty of communicating that, following your instructions contained in the telegram of March 22,[12] I had a conversation with Reich Foreign Minister Herr von Neurath at 12 noon today.

I told him that I had informed my government of the decision com-

[12] See *Diariusz*, I, 248–49 (conversations with Laroche of March 23 and 24); also Laroche, p. 207.

municated to me by the Chancellor on March 16 about the introduction of conscription. The Polish government instructed me to call the attention of the German government—in a quite friendly way—to the fact that the situation created by the introduction of conscription by the Reich government might result in complications in international relations. I added that these complications can at present not be evaluated. I also called Herr von Neurath's attention to the fact that, in case the League of Nations handles this problem, difficulties will naturally increase considerably. I gave Herr von Neurath to understand that the Polish government is concerned about the international situation caused by this problem. I then added a few words to the effect that the Polish press kept a quiet and reasonable tone in this difficult moment.

Herr von Neurath was evidently prepared for this statement of mine for, as I could observe, he had very precise answers to each particular item. First of all, he stressed that the League aspect is of the least concern to him. Of course, opening proceedings against the Reich government would not encourage him to join this institution (Germany will undoubtedly use this argument with Simon). He is quite aware that the situation might become rather embarrassing for some members of the Council. However, as far as the *meritum* of the matter is concerned, the League of Nations can only pass a declaration that the Treaty was violated. Such a declaration, however, would be merely a paper without further consequences.

Herr von Neurath further stated that in taking such a decision the German government naturally realized what difficulties it might encounter. However, the development of events compelled it to take such a step. He mentioned that the prevailing confusion was unbearable *à la longue*. Besides, even the British government claimed that it is known that Germany is arming, but it knows nothing definite about it. The German government was alarmed that Sir John Simon is setting out on his trip to Berlin totally misinformed, convinced that he will be able to bargain for too high stakes in particular fields of national defense. It was therefore better to play an open hand.

As to the results of Simon's trip, von Neurath was of the opinion that they might be meager. He added that he sees no possibility of discussing Germany's military forces, which are essential for the Reich's national defense, as drawn up by the bill. I could not be sure whether this declaration by von Neurath meant that any discussion regarding the ceiling on armaments was excluded in principle, or whether it was just a tactical statement designed to keep us from making a hint to the British side regarding any hopes for possible German concessions in this field.

Further, von Neurath mentioned that, as far as pacts are concerned, some solution might be found. However, he strongly confirmed that guarantees for mutual assistance are out of the question. Simon's trip—as von Neurath put it—will be rather of an informative nature. The British Foreign Secretary, in contrast to other Powers interested in this problem, such as France and Italy, is handicapped in his competence.

Passing to more general topics, Herr von Neurath stated that it should now be expected that France might dress up its understanding with Soviet Russia to take the form of a treaty. He thinks it would have come to this anyway.

He began to deliberate on the growing Russian imperialism. For the moment it might still be devoid of elements of immediate threat, but its aims are quite obvious. He remarked that it is quite clear that sooner or later this imperialism will reach for the Baltic states, for it is fluctuating either eastward or westward. Herr von Neurath even presumes that the aggressive tendencies of Russia, following in the footsteps of tsarist Russia, will also spread to the Balkans, so that the prewar situation will be restored with only a changed internal Russian constellation. Poland and Germany are the two states most threatened by this development of Russia, which is now showing the wish to intervene in European matters.

Closing our conversation, Herr von Neurath said that he will keep me *au courant* of his talks with Sir John Simon.

As I mentioned before in this report, I have the impression that Neurath—possibly because of your conversation with Moltke—was already prepared for our *démarche*. In spite of the fact that, in accordance with your instructions, I kept my statement in a friendly tone, the German Minister of Foreign Affairs must have understood the meaning of the expression of the Polish government's concern over the tide of international events as a discreet reminder that a violent decision by, and obstinate action on the part of, the Reich creates a rather awkward situation for us also.

As for Neurath's suppositions that in the field of pacts some settlement might be reached in the talks with the British, this explanation to some extent coincides with information forwarded by me in the letter of the 22d inst. addressed to Director Dębicki. On the other hand, I was rather astonished by the stiff approach of the Reich Foreign Minister regarding the possible discussion of the ceiling on German armaments, as based on the newly published bill. Since the bill did not precisely define the actual figures (and besides, information obtained by Captain Steblik showed that not all divisions were completed), it could be assumed that a margin for negotiations might be placed between the present actual state of build-up of the German Army and the full figure of armaments foreseen within the frame of the bill. Neurath's declaration seems to disperse this illusion. However, I must stress that the Reich Minister, who did not explicitly mention the ceiling, saying only in general terms that on the problem of equality of rights and of national defense as fixed in the bill there will be no bargaining, was so firm on the problem for tactical reasons only. [13]

*Józef Lipski*

### DOCUMENT 40 Lipski to Beck

NO. N/128/30/35 Berlin, April 13, 1935
*Strictly Confidential*

In the afternoon of April 12 I was informed that Herr von Neurath had asked me to call at the A.A. on Saturday at 11:30 A.M. In the evening Ambassador von Moltke came to dinner to discuss certain economic matters in Polish-German relations. During the dinner I received your telephone call regarding Sir John Simon's declaration at Stresa concerning Herr von Neurath's explanations given to the British Chargé d'Affaires in Berlin about the Eastern Pact.[14] At the same time a repre-

[13] For the German version of this conversation, see *DGFP*, Series C, Vol. III, No. 553.
[14] The Stresa Conference of the ministers of Great Britain, France, and Italy lasted from April 11 to April 14. On April 12 Beck received news in Warsaw that Minister Simon allegedly declared that, in the conversation between Neurath and the British Chargé d'Affaires in Berlin, the German Foreign Minister had confirmed Germany's consent to join in a general pact of nonaggression. This pact foresaw the possibility of particular signatories of the pact contracting additional agreements of mutual assistance. Upon receiving this information, Beck instructed his cabinet director, Dębicki, to contact the Polish Embassy in Berlin immediately in order to obtain from Lipski the information whether the above news from Stresa was duly confirmed in Berlin. *Diariusz,* I, 267.

sentative of the Polish Telegraph Agency in Berlin confirmed the declaration of the British Foreign Secretary, with an annotation that both the Deutsches Nachrichtenbüro and the A.A. declined any clarification in this matter.

Herr von Moltke, whom I have informed to this effect, and who, besides, saw that I had been called on the telephone by you, told me that Herr von Neurath just wanted to inform me tomorrow about his conversation with the British representative. Moltke was of the opinion that Simon's declaration was an indiscretion. When I told von Moltke that you are leaving for Geneva this morning, he was even more upset by the fact that the Polish government was not informed in time. He even tried to arrange an interview with Neurath for me during the night, so that you could be informed before leaving Warsaw. As he did not succeed in reaching von Neurath, he advised Director Meyer to give me precise information, which I duly cabled to you on the same night.[15]

This morning von Neurath asked me to call at the A.A. an hour later, that is, at 12:30 P.M. and right from the start, apologizing that owing to a misunderstanding he could not see me immediately after his conversation with the British Chargé d'Affaires, he declared that Chancellor Hitler wanted to see me at once. Herr von Neurath explained briefly that some inaccurate information appeared in the press regarding the reply he gave to the British Chargé d'Affaires concerning the Eastern Pact. He then read to me his own note from the conversation with Newton, approved *post factum* by the Chancellor, and handed me one copy for your strictly confidential attention. This copy is enclosed herewith.[16]

Then, accompanied by Herr von Neurath, I went to see the Chancellor, who told me more or less as follows:

He wanted to inform me personally about the actual situation in connection with the conversation held yesterday between the Reich Foreign Minister and the British Chargé d'Affaires, because some of the daily papers published misleading information, thus creating confusion. For this reason the Chancellor this morning ordered that the British representative be presented a *mise-au-point* in writing. It will appear in the press, possibly tonight or tomorrow morning.[17]

The Chancellor then read to me the text of this document. The docu-

[15] See *DGFP,* Series C, Vol. IV, No. 28.
[16] See *ibid.,* No. 24.
[17] *Ibid.,* No. 29.

ment states that during the conversation with Simon in Berlin Chancellor Hitler, as requested by the British side, communicated principles which might serve as a foundation for a nonaggression pact in Eastern Europe. These principles were limited to nonaggression, consultation, arbitration and conciliation, and nonassistance to the aggressor. Questioned by Simon as to whether the German government, having rejected mutual assistance in the Eastern Pact, would be prepared to agree that, within the frame of the nonaggression pact as proposed by the Reich, particular signatories could contract agreements of mutual assistance, the Chancellor gave a negative reply.

The document then passed to the last conversation of Neurath with Newton, stating clearly that the German government maintains its proposition for a nonaggression pact in Eastern Europe. This offer is made irrespective of whether particular signatories of the pact would contract additional agreements for mutual assistance. However, the German government made a reservation that it would not agree to any mention in the text of the pact about such agreements, and would not accept any notification that such agreements were contracted. Finally, the document confirms that agreements of mutual assistance are logically contradictory to the very idea of nonaggression pacts, anticipating in advance the bad will of the contracting parties. When reading this document, the Chancellor observed that after the last move on the British side he wonders whether it would not be best to withdraw the offer of the nonaggression pact made to Simon. Psychologically this would suit him best in the face of tactics applied by the Powers, who press for military agreements, disguising them in a formula of mutual assistance. However, if he did this, the whole world would denounce him as a warmonger. That is why he decided to give the above reply to the British side. The Chancellor stressed firmly that he is definitely unwilling to legalize such agreements, and that is why he excludes the possibility of formally binding them with the nonaggression pact in any way.

Here I mentioned that in my opinion, besides the formal side of legalizing such agreements, the danger exists of Soviet Russia's pressure on smaller states for contracting such agreements. I pointed precisely to the Baltic. Both the Chancellor and von Neurath very openly seconded my concern.

I thanked the Chancellor for his gesture, obviously designed to remove any resentment on our part for not being informed in time by the

German government regarding its last *démarche* to Great Britain. I also availed myself of the occasion to carry out your instructions conveyed to me yesterday by telegram. I said that you will pass through Berlin today on your way to Geneva, and that your intention is to observe the international situation, which in our opinion is far from clear, at firsthand. I further stated that the foundation and principles of Poland's foreign policy, known to the German government, will remain unaltered. Further, referring to one of your recent talks with Ambassador von Moltke, I said that you anticipate an extensive action on the part of the Soviets in Geneva to save at least some semblances of the Eastern Pact, and that probably they will exert strong pressure on smaller East European states to this end. I finally said that the Soviet-French bilateral pact is not a subject of special concern to us. Following your instructions, I added with some emphasis, so that both the Chancellor and von Neurath would realize our intentions, that the Polish government is not inclined to link Franco-Polish problems with Franco-Soviet problems, and that we shall follow this line in our relations with France.

After listening to these explanations of mine, the Chancellor passed next to considerations of a general nature. They would be rather difficult to render in detail in this report. As usual, the very basis of his deliberations was Soviet Russia. His attitude toward it is clearly negative.

He analyzed Russia from many angles, including economic expansion, and stated that it is a power which will be a serious threat to European civilization. That is why—in his opinion—and here he added that he was not talking now as a Chancellor but rather as a professor, a logical idea would be for all states to unite on nationalistic grounds in the name of solidarity and common effort to overcome this danger. Of course, he was talking only in a hypothetical sense.

I am taking the liberty of quoting some interesting points of his deliberations.

He said, for example, that if someone in Germany thinks that the Russian danger is meaningless, since Poland separates Germany from Russia, this problem should be viewed from a long-range historic perspective. In his opinion, Russia will be a danger for the whole West. If the West does not wake up—in his opinion—it may pay the price of its whole culture and civilization. Poland, of course, could—as he put it—keep its position in the east for some ten to fifteen years. However, for an effective opposition, the solidarity of all concerned is needed. From

this broad point of view all frictions between the states of Europe become unimportant.

Talking about war, he said that in his meditations he came to the
conclusion that Germany, if you consider the last centuries, lost millions
of people in wars, and the best ones too, reaching no goal and remaining
practically in the same spot. By contrast, England lost very few people.
Instead of spilling blood, England dominated the world. The best human
element, lost in Germany for nothing, remained in England and contributed to the realization of its great world policy.

Then the Chancellor talked about expansion being impossible in relation to Germany's neighbors, quoting figures of overpopulation. He
mentioned here that this has induced him to raise the colonial question
with the British. He needs an outlet for the population and also raw
materials. When Germany has access to raw materials from the colonies,
it will be able to increase its exports, which will allow it to import more,
and this will have only positive results for other countries trading with
the Reich. He said that he had to raise the colonial problem, since this is
a master problem. Of course, he is not for an immediate solution of this
problem.

Pointing out that Germany is not striving to enlarge its possessions,
he cited the fact that the Saar annexation cost the Reich a great deal.
Fifty thousand unemployed in the Saar took jobs away from half a
million people of the Reich. The deplorable economic condition of the
Saar is a heavy burden for the Reich today.

As far as Austria is concerned, the Chancellor said that his desire is
only to enable the population to express their will freely. However, if
this occurs, it would be impossible for the Reich to take over the burden
of a state of six million in such a deplorable economic condition. There
are some things, the Chancellor continued, which demand a strict ac-
counting. He stressed here that he has quite enough problems and difficulties on the territory of the Reich.

Returning again to the question of Europe's relation to the Russian
problem, the Chancellor said that there is one method, which I have
already mentioned, namely, a certain solidarity in the stand of all states
of Europe toward this problem. There is also another method, he remarked, the one cherished by the British—which consists in shoving
away danger and in tactical gambling. England is playing with Russia
here in the sense of not allowing it to expand too far either eastward or

westward. The Chancellor said that such policies are clearly short-sighted. There are some people in England who understand the whole problem. They are not to be found, however, either in the government or in the Foreign Office.

Next the Chancellor raised the question of the Far East and the role of Japan as a dynamic factor, dangerous not only in the Far East but also, owing to its great vigor in economic competition, for the countries of Europe. He explained that in this respect Japan, though for different reasons, is as dangerous as Soviet Russia.

I must stress here that the above deliberations of the Chancellor were made to me, to some extent confidentially, with the provision that they not be revealed as some of his more deep-seated views.

Taking leave of the Chancellor, I thanked him for the audience and for giving me explanations regarding Germany's approach to the nonaggression pact in the east.

Herr von Neurath remained with the Chancellor alone for a moment, and later accompanied me to the A.A. for a short conversation. I talked with him for a moment about items contained in your instructions. I again stressed possible attempts by Russia with regard to smaller states situated in Eastern Europe. Talking about Hungary, whose position is somewhat delicate, Herr von Neurath said that he has persistently exerted pressure on Budapest to bring about an understanding with Yugoslavia. Before the assassination of the king the situation was easier. Neurath is of the opinion that Hungary will not find a common language with Czechoslovakia and Rumania. With Yugoslavia the object of contention is not so important. Besides, within the frame of the Little Entente, Yugoslavia represents a real value of strength.

At the end of our conversation Herr von Neurath asked me to present his respects to you, and to tell you that in case you return via Berlin he would be very glad to meet you. I will await your instructions in this matter.

Herr von Neurath and the Chancellor, in order to make a sort of demonstration for Geneva, are leaving today for vacations, but, as the Minister confided to me, he will probably be obliged to interrupt his leave several times.

Recapitulating the above conversations held today, I am taking the liberty of stressing that the declaration presented to the British Chargé d'Affaires yesterday did not formally change the stand of the German government regarding the question of the Eastern Pact. *Ad meritum,* however, by declaring its *désintéressement* in agreements of mutual assistance contracted outside the nonaggression pact in the east by its signatories, the German government has taken a step toward conceding compromise. It is essential to realize that the German government fully maintains its negative approach regarding the signing of a pact of mutual assistance between the Reich and the Soviets. Nevertheless, by the concession mentioned above, it undoubtedly opened the door for Russia to attempt to put pressure on the Baltic states in order to induce them to contract agreements of mutual assistance, and also rendered easier Franco-Russian action in relation to the Little Entente. That is why I raised this aspect of the problem in my conversation today.

*Józef Lipski*


The problem of Hitler's introduction of conscription and German violation of Part V of the Treaty of Versailles was placed before the Council of the League. Beck delivered a speech on April 16 at the Council, stressing the role played by Poland in the build-up of peace in Eastern Europe by the stabilization of Poland's relations with its neighboring Great Powers. On April 17 the Council of the League passed a resolution condemning the German action.[18] Poland voted for this resolution.


DOCUMENT 41    Lipski to Beck

NO. N/49/28/35                                        Berlin, April 25, 1935
                                                     *Strictly Confidential*

As I already reported to the Vice-Director of the Western Department in my letter dated April 20, I was invited by Prime Minister Göring for Thursday, April 25, to his forest pavilion at Schorfheide. Minister Göring showed me a document, beautifully bound in silver, destined for the President of the Polish Republic as a member of *des Reichsbundes deutscher Jägerschaft.* He also displayed several other gifts for people participating in the hunting party at Białowieża. These objects will be

[18] For Beck's speech and the text of the resolution (both in French), see *Diariusz,* I, 496–501. For von Moltke's opinion on this matter, see *DGFP,* Series C, Vol. IV, No. 41, No. 49, and partly No. 75.

taken to Warsaw in the coming days by an aide-de-camp of Göring so that they may be handed out by Ambassador von Moltke.

During my stay of several hours at Schorfheide, Herr Göring expressed his desire to have a longer political talk with me. He declared that last Saturday he had a conversation with Hitler, who suggested that, independently of official Polish-German relations, he should take the relations between the two countries under his special protection. Herr Göring gave me to understand that this does not mean that he will do this officially. In his opinion, however, in such important matters a discussion might often be useful with persons on the German side who are not encumbered by the Reich's policies toward Poland as conducted by previous governments.

Herr Göring stressed that Foreign Affairs Minister von Neurath is a person thoroughly loyal to the Chancellor. On the other hand, he stated that he is not 100 percent sure whether other officials of that office strictly observe the line toward Poland as drawn up by the Chancellor. Here Göring added that, if it were up to him, he would have cleaned up the Auswärtiges Amt long ago. However, the Chancellor is perhaps too indulgent, and pays too much attention to the services rendered in the past by some of his collaborators who cannot adapt themselves to the new situation. Referring to the Chancellor's policy toward Poland, Herr Göring firmly stressed that it is not dictated by any premises of a tactical nature but is the result of a very deep grasp of this problem. On this point the Chancellor will not stand for any fluctuations or changes in direction.

Passing to the last Geneva session, Minister Göring said that the Chancellor fully understands the position taken by you. He asked Göring to bring this to my knowledge. In my conversation with Göring, I stressed the fact that your speech gave a clear and precise idea of our basic political line. Minister Göring agreed completely. He said that personally he admires the independent position taken by you in your speech, which was even more than they expected. As for voting for the Geneva declaration, I said that this was just a formal act, which was obvious both from your speech and your statements given to members of the Council. To this Göring replied that he understood the difference between the speech and the voting in a similar way. Finally, talking about Franco-Russian relations, I referred to the declaration [19] pre-

19 *DGFP*, Series C, Vol. IV, No. 30.

sented to the Chancellor on your behalf and stated that we do not in the least intend to link our relations with France to Franco-Russian relations. Here I remarked that it was not in the interest of Poland, nor indeed of Germany either, to slam the door definitely in the face of Laval at Geneva, pushing him permanently into the arms of Russia. Göring understood our tactics on this point. He remarked that this might possibly contribute to a certain extent to some reaction in France against too far-reaching relations in its alliance with Russia.

I discussed more extensively the question of the Geneva session with Göring, since I assumed that the Chancellor may need some arguments for orienting himself to our position. Göring added that von Moltke was instructed to lodge a protest in Warsaw similar to the one lodged with other members of the Council, although this should be regarded as a purely formal act, without any further consequences. Göring spoke well of von Moltke, stressing that he is a loyal person, devoted to the Chancellor's policy toward Poland. In his further comments about certain elements who cannot adapt themselves to the new policy of the Chancellor, Göring pointed out that they took advantage of the voting in Geneva and some incidents in Pomerania to create an unfriendly atmosphere for Poland in Germany. However, the Chancellor reacted very firmly, issuing suitable instructions. From Göring's words I had the impression that it was precisely because of a certain reaction among these elements that the Chancellor had decided to entrust Göring with the special mission of taking an interest in Polish-German relations. Göring stated that on his part he had issued most strict orders to local authorities to avoid any drastic demonstrations against the Poles. Here I told him that you are acting in the same way with our local authorities. Göring even added that, in case we observe some shortcomings on the German side in this respect, he requests that we bring them to his attention, even if from our point of view it should be a matter of some undesirable German activity on the territory of Poland.

At the conclusion of our talk Göring once more very emphatically stated that the Chancellor wishes to maintain the best possible relations with Poland. Deliberating on the question of Polish-German relations, he repeated all the things he said during his stay in Poland. Therefore, there is no need to repeat them here. I would just like to stress that Göring declared again that the Chancellor is fully aware of the necessity of Poland's access to the sea, and that for him the problem of the Corridor does not exist in the field of close Polish-German relations. As usual strong anti-Russian note could be detected in Göring's deliberations, both toward the Soviets and toward any other possible regime in Russia.

Minister Göring laid stress on the fact that, in accordance with information received by his intelligence agents, he sees how efforts are made from many quarters to interfere with good Polish-German relations. He mentioned that Mussolini—obviously for fear that Germany allegedly has aggressive intentions toward Austria—is trying everywhere to act against the Reich. Göring vented sharp criticism of the policies of the Italian government. He mentioned here that he is aware of the overtures made by Rome to the Polish government. Although Göring tried to deal with this question rather casually, some anxiety could be noted in his words.

Passing to some practical action in Polish-German relations, Göring mentioned how pleased the Chancellor would be to welcome you at a convenient opportunity in Berlin. He added that after the visit of the British ministers in Berlin and your meeting with Suvich [20] in Venice, he thinks that such a visit would be very desirable, for two great nations who are neighbors should from time to time demonstrate their good relations by such contacts. Here I remarked that you had stopped in Germany on two occasions to converse with Foreign Affairs Minister von Neurath. However, on the advice of the A.A. these meetings were not publicized, and you mentioned to me that in case any further meetings were to take place it would be much better to give them some publicity. Herr Göring was of the same opinion, and discreetly observed that your visit in Berlin on some convenient occasion—for example, on your way to Geneva—would be very advisable.

The main aim of such a visit would be a direct contact with the Chancellor. Therefore, Göring thinks that it would not be so important to bestow on it a strictly official character, since this is always very burdensome for the guest, but it should rather be made an informal affair. Finally, in connection with contacts he made in Białowieża with General Fabrycy, General Sosnkowski, and other ministers, Göring said he would take great pleasure in being able to reciprocate for the hospitality extended to him at Białowieża by inviting some of these people for a stag hunt at Schorfheide in the fall. I promised that I would take this matter up in Warsaw.

At the close of our conversation I thanked him for his valuable expla-

---

[20] Fulvio Suvich, undersecretary of state at the Italian Ministry of Foreign Affairs.

nations and expressed my satisfaction that by authorization of the
Chancellor I shall be able to address myself directly to him in case any
difficulties arise in matters of interest to both our countries. I remarked
that I would inform you about this conversation, adding that in the
coming days I shall be in Warsaw, and upon my return I shall call on
him again.

Recapitulating this conversation, I am taking the liberty of observing
that the most important element is that the Chancellor, in spite of some
rumors spread by elements rather unfriendly to us, understood Poland's
position at the last session at Geneva. I consider the fact that Göring
was entrusted with a mission to take care of Polish-German relations as
positive for us. His position as prime minister of Prussia will enable him
to assist us not only in the field of general politics but also in practical
territorial matters.

From Göring's further comments it is worth noting that he expressed
some anxiety about Italian efforts in Warsaw. Undoubtedly, fear can be
detected that Italy may obtain from us some obligations regarding Austria, for this matter is of basic importance for the National Socialist
Party.

A statement inside the Reich that the Chancellor's policy toward
Poland is consistently pursued, and that in the field of international
relations no essential difference of opinion exists on problems of basic
importance for Germany, evidently makes the Chancellor even more
willing to meet you.

*Józef Lipski*

### DOCUMENT 42   Lipski to Beck

NO. N/128/38/35                                   Berlin, May 5, 1935
                                                  *Confidential*

Upon my return from Warsaw I had, on May 3, my first conversation
with Herr von Neurath, foreign minister of the Reich, since the last
Geneva session. Following your verbal instructions, I declared to him
more or less as follows:

I remarked that I had returned from Warsaw, where I had the opportunity of discussing with you at length your trip to Geneva. I stressed, as

I had already mentioned to Herr von Neurath in our talk on March 23, that you were anticipating beforehand that the situation in Geneva would be particularly awkward. You decided to go to Geneva because you thought it to be unavoidable to state explicitly in your speech Poland's stand in connection with the international situation, inasmuch as the Soviets displayed an obvious tendency to save at least the appearances of the Eastern Pact, and pressure to this effect could be felt especially in relation to smaller states. After your conversation with Mr. Eden, the British delegation did not conceal any longer that it regards the concept of the Eastern Pact as dead and buried. Nevertheless, in view of the efforts made by the Soviets, you thought it necessary once more to define the negative position of Poland toward the Eastern Pact before the forum of states present at Geneva. Besides this, I stated that in your speech you presented existing Polish-German relations as a fully realistic, positive international element to be seriously taken into account by all states.

Regarding the Geneva resolution, I remarked that, both in your speech and in your conversations with some members of the Council, you expressed your *désintéressement* as to its text, considering it merely a formal act. Thus your speech was a competent expression of the stand taken by the Polish government.

I also made it clear that extending the discussions in Geneva would not serve Germany's interest; the best thing would be to close the problem. I also stressed—feeling that this argument is most agreeable for authoritative elements here—that breaking all ties with Laval would only serve to push the French Foreign Minister definitely into the Soviets' embrace.

In his reply Herr von Neurath remarked that he also understood the stand taken by you in Geneva in this way. He understood that Poland's position would be especially delicate and difficult. Public opinion in Germany was somewhat taken aback by the vote of Poland, but this did not last long. Herr von Neurath stressed that the resolution is unpleasant for the German government and that the Powers could word it differently, introducing, for example, an adequate preface. Herr von Neurath told me that immediately after the Geneva decision he went to the Chancellor to discuss with him future tactics. I could detect from his words that he was acting to prevent too violent a reaction to the Geneva resolution. Herr von Neurath remarked that the Chancellor would shortly deliver a speech on the Reich's foreign policy, referring to the note presented to the members of the Council, and would then bring up the whole matter. (As I found out, the Chancellor's declaration will probably be delivered on May 14.) [21]

Herr von Neurath also remarked that Moltke's protest in Warsaw was just a formality. The words of the Reich Minister of Foreign Affairs resulted—if in more diplomatic terms—in a confirmation of the comments I heard from Göring, which I reported on April 25, No. N/49/28/35; that is, that the Chancellor completely understood the stand taken by Poland in Geneva.

Next, Herr von Neurath rather casually talked about developments in the international situation. First of all, he stressed that from MacDonald's speech [22] it was clear that the British government still stands firm in its position of the resolution of February 3. Here he observed that since February 3 many things have changed. He added that MacDonald is again talking about the Eastern Pact which Germany should join. This point of the British Prime Minister's speech is not clear for the German government, since the German side has already said all it had to say on this matter. By the way, Neurath mentioned that the concession he made to Simon at Stresa, about which I reported on April 13, No. N/128/30/35, when he said that the German government maintains its offer for a nonaggression pact in the east regardless of whether agreements of mutual assistance will be contracted between particular signatories of the pact, had no effect whatever. At the given moment he might have rendered Simon's task at Stresa easier, but no consequences were drawn from it. Neurath's avowal that as a matter of fact he did then make a useless withdrawal from the position taken by the Chancellor toward the British Minister was sincere and quite disarming.

In acknowledging that since February 3 quite a lot has changed, Neurath pointed to the development of the situation regarding the

[21] Hitler's speech was delivered on May 21.

[22] On May 2 Prime Minister MacDonald delivered in the House of Commons a declaration expressing concern about German armaments, calling on Germany to join in international collaboration. Great Britain would not accept any new obligations on the continent, he declared. The British government was of the opinion that Hitler's proposal for a collective nonaggression pact in the east should not be rejected, but it felt that this offer should be balanced with the Franco-Soviet pact then being negotiated. Germany's stand regarding armaments rendered questionable the frankness of the Reich's declaration. The British government was trying not to create military alliances but to get the Powers to collaborate for peace. The understanding between Great Britain, France, and Italy meant just this.

Danubian plans. He has not as yet received from Simon the promised definition of "nonintervention." A few days ago he reminded the British Ambassador of this when the latter brought up the question of the Danubian agreement.

Regarding the conference presently taking place in Venice,[23] von Neurath said that its final result cannot be foreseen; even the date when the conference is to be held in Rome is as yet unknown. He laid some stress on certain misunderstandings between the partners of the proposed pact. According to information obtained from the Yugoslav minister, Yugoslavia would join the pact under the condition that the restoration of the Hapsburgs be excluded.

Regarding armaments, Herr von Neurath remarked that the Powers now have the last word, since Germany has nothing more to request in this field. He stressed that the forthcoming German-British sea conferences will be only of a preliminary character.

Upon these casual remarks of Herr von Neurath, I gave him some information about your meeting with Suvich in Venice.[24] I mentioned that this meeting was not planned in advance. When you decided to spend a short Easter vacation with Mrs. Beck in Italy, Signor Suvich proceeded to Venice. I explained that the conversation was of a general character. Besides, following your instructions, I stressed that in general Polish-Italian relations, with perhaps the exception of the period of the Four-Power Pact, have always been friendly. However, the two countries have no interests in common which would constitute a link between them. Adriatic problems, for example, and other matters of primary concern to Italy are of little interest to us.

I added that only in our relations with Hungary do we find a certain platform of common interest, since neither Warsaw nor Rome would like to see Hungary in complete isolation from the Little Entente.

Later in our conversation I hinted quite casually that, as far as I can see from the reports of our ambassador in Rome, it is rather characteristic that some sort of anxiety might be detected in Italy with regard to a possible expansion of Russia at the expense of the states of the Little Entente. Herr von Neurath took up this point, remarking that the Ital-

[23] On May 4 a conference began between the ministers of foreign affairs of Austria and Hungary and the Italian vice-minister, Suvich, in Venice, to discuss political problems in connection with the proposed Roman conference regarding the Central European (Danubian) Pact.
[24] On April 19.

ians are quite right; he is also of the opinion that modern Russia, acting within the pattern of the old tsarist Russia, will strive to spread its influence over the Balkans.

I then said to Herr von Neurath that you regret that on your way back, which was not via Germany, you could not avail yourself of Herr von Neurath's suggestion for a meeting. Nevertheless, on the occasion of passing through Germany, you would be very pleased to have an opportunity to talk with Herr von Neurath and present your regards to the Chancellor. I also added that this time it would not be advisable to keep the meeting secret; it should be revealed to the press.

Herr von Neurath eagerly agreed with this idea, adding that this very morning he had a talk with the Chancellor, who personally stresses the necessity of maintaining friendship with Poland. Therefore Herr von Neurath thinks that your meeting with the Chancellor would be most desirable. I did not mention any precise date for your visit, but only mentioned in passing that such an occasion might arise in the future. Von Neurath asked whether you will be in Geneva on May 20, and I replied that I did not know.

Closing my conversation with Herr von Neurath with a reference to some claims I have encountered in Warsaw regarding the alleged German agitation in our western provinces, which may possibly be inspired by the Reich, I laid stress on the necessity of avoiding any friction in relations between us. By the way, I mentioned that upon resolving the new Constitution [25] we are approaching elections and that on such occasions any irritating incidents should be avoided. I mentioned in passing that, acting accordingly, you had used your influence to put off demonstrations of the Silesian insurgents planned for May 3, and I learned with satisfaction from Prime Minister Göring that he on his part had issued strict orders on the German side.[26]

[25] The new Polish Constitution was signed by President Mościcki on April 23, 1935.

[26] On May 3, Poland's national holiday, a demonstration was to be held in Warsaw to commemorate the anniversary of three Silesian insurrections against Germany in 1919–21. About 5,000 uniformed insurgents were to attend. The Prime Minister, the Minister of the Interior, and the Vice-Minister of War were to be sponsors. In his conversation with Vice-Minister Szembek on April 24, Ambassador von Moltke called attention to the consequences of such demonstrations for Polish-German relations (*Diariusz*, I, 274). At the end of April, while in Warsaw, Lipski stressed that at this time such a demonstration was not advisable (*ibid.*, p 277). In spite of pressure on the part of Silesian deputies in the Diet, the Polish government canceled the insurgents' rally.

Agreeing with me, Herr von Neurath said that he had talked with Hess on this matter, and that orders were issued to this effect. Referring to the situation of Germans in Poland, Herr von Neurath observed that party quarrels among Germans in our country bring about certain frictions.

Next, I pointed out that I had handed to the Press Department of his Ministry material pertaining to some transgressions on the German side regarding the Polish-German press agreement, and I stressed the problem of demands about inscriptions on monuments.

Finally, I told Herr von Neurath that I shall be in Munich on May 12 to attend the opening of the Polish Exhibition, and on the 14th I will be in Hamburg. Regarding my stay in Munich, I mentioned that I shall of course pay a visit to Governor General Epp and that I also intend to call on Cardinal Faulhaber. I presumed that this courtesy visit of mine would not be misinterpreted. Herr von Neurath replied that he naturally has nothing against such a visit. However, he warned me against any contact with the Papal Nuncio in Munich, whose situation in relation to the German government is irregular.[27]

On the same evening I went with Prime Minister Göring to Spreewald for blackcock tooting. I took this opportunity to give Göring the explanations he asked for in our conversation of April 25.

First of all, I stated that you were very pleased to learn that the Chancellor had entrusted Prime Minister Göring with special care over Polish-German relations. On this occasion I repeated what I had already said to Neurath: that you would like to stop in Berlin at a convenient opportunity to see the Chancellor, and that such a visit—according to what we agreed to previously with Herr Göring—would be publicized by the press.

As to the invitations to the stag rutting in the fall, Göring would like to extend invitations to some personages who participated in the hunting party at Białowieża; I said that I had taken this matter up with you. You mentioned the names of General Fabrycy and Maurice Potocki. We will let him know about other possible names.

Finally, I once more discussed the Geneva problem with Göring. Göring again declared to me that the Chancellor fully understands our

[27] The Papal Nuncio officially recognized by the German government was Monsignor Cesare Orsenigo in Berlin. The Nuncio in Munich, who was there in accordance with the old concordat between Bavaria and the Vatican, was not recognized by the German government.

point of view; besides, he will talk it over with me at an available moment. According to Göring, the Chancellor is satisfied that you did not want to give France a definite push into the arms of Russia at Geneva.

I also gave Göring some information about your meeting with Suvich. It was typical that Göring told me that he negotiated on behalf of his government with the Italian government on the Four-Power Pact. He told Mussolini that Germany is not in the least interested in concluding this agreement. It is doing so just for the sake of German-Italian friendship. I could detect in Göring quite a lot of suspicion and dislike for Italy. When I mentioned to him some common Polish and Italian opinions regarding the Hungarian problem, Göring remarked that for Hungary the most appropriate thing to do would be to approach Yugoslavia. He himself is going to Yugoslavia in the near future, and he intends to act along these lines in Belgrade. In his opinion the differences between Hungary and Yugoslavia are insignificant as compared with the situation between Hungary and Czechoslovakia. That is why the German government is putting pressure on Budapest to relinquish its secondary demands on Belgrade. Göring mentioned that he is very well liked in Yugoslavia, and to prove it he said that he received many letters and telegrams on the occasion of his wedding, not only from official quarters, but also from a multitude of the local population.

I am taking the liberty of reminding you that I had already heard about the concept of Hungarian-Yugoslav rapprochement from the Reich Foreign Affairs Minister and duly reported it to you some weeks ago.

I next told Göring that you were very glad to hear that Göring will issue special orders to prevent German-Polish frictions. I mentioned the cancellation of the insurgents' rally, which was acknowledged with great satisfaction. He then said that, if we let him know about any anti-Polish action in Germany, twenty-four hours later he will issue orders and they will be carried out, whereas things are more difficult if claims concern the German minority in Poland. There, of course, the German government has no direct executive power. Besides, as Göring confided to me, very often elements prevail among this minority who are at odds with National Socialist tendencies. They think that Chancellor Hitler's government, through its understanding with Poland, abandoned the minority to the mercy of fate. I did not pursue further discussion with Göring on this subject. However, in my opinion, if adequate orders are issued for state and Party organs in the Reich to avoid any clash with Poland, this might also reflect on the behavior of Germans in Poland.

I was also interested in what Göring confided to me about Danzig. He said that it is only owing to the fact that the National Socialist majority is in power in Danzig that relations between Poland and the Free City are good. If the old parties had won the elections, the same quarrels and contentions would undoubtedly exist and the same methods would be applied as prior to Hitler's coming to power, since all the old parties continuously leaned toward dissension with Poland, opposing any kind of understanding. I fully agreed with this opinion of Göring.

Finally, I am taking this opportunity to mention that, during the declaration with regard to air-force problems made by Göring to the foreign press, Mrs. Męcińska, correspondent of the *Kurier Warszawski,* addressed several questions to him. These questions were so undiplomatic and nonpolitical that the Prussian Prime Minister lost his temper and reacted with a rather sharp reply. Göring commented at length about this, cursing the lack of tact on the part of the Polish lady correspondent. She later declared in the presence of the *Havas* representative and others that Göring is making very light of Poland's role in Eastern Europe.

I appeased the Prussian Prime Minister by stating that I personally and the whole staff of our Embassy have a well-established opinion regarding Mrs. Męcińska's political experience. Besides, I told him that I had already expressed my highest disapproval of the correspondent through the intermediary of the chief of the press of the Embassy.

*Józef Lipski*

# The Death of Marshal Piłsudski
# The Currency Conflict with Danzig
### *May—July, 1935*

---

DOCUMENT 43   Lipski to Beck

NO. N/421/15/35

Berlin, May 15, 1935
*Strictly Confidential*

News of Marshal Piłsudski's death was received in Berlin on Sunday, May 12, at 10:30 P.M.[1] According to information I received on the next day from Secretary of State Meissner, the Chancellor of the Reich, who was informed during the night, was deeply shocked by this news. He immediately addressed a telegram of condolence to the President of the Polish Republic in words of high esteem for the late Marshal of Poland and sympathy of the German nation for the Polish nation. The Chancellor laid special emphasis on the fact that the Marshal's policy toward Germany brought about profound advantages for both nations and served the cause of peace. Orders were given to lower flags to half-mast on all government buildings in the Reich on May 13 and on the day of the funeral; General Göring was delegated to be a representative at the funeral in Poland; and it was announced that, contrary to all traditions hitherto observed, the Chancellor would personally attend services in Berlin: all these were Hitler's personal spontaneous decisions.

I will take the liberty of presenting a special report illustrating in detail the reaction in the Reich to the death of the Marshal. In the meantime I would only like to confirm that the reaction was very strong in governmental circles as well as in the wider spheres of the German community.

Yesterday, on the occasion of Göring's condolence visit at the Em-

[1] Marshal Piłsudski died on May 12, 1935, at 8:45 P.M.

bassy, I had a long conversation with him, and I am anxious to report to you on this without delay.

Minister Göring, who was delegated as a personal representative of the Chancellor, will attend the funeral of the Marshal escorted by a brigadier, an admiral, and two aides-de-camp. He expressed his desire for a meeting with you in Warsaw on Sunday, after the Friday funeral services in Warsaw and the Saturday ceremonies in Cracow. He also told me that he would like to obtain an audience with the President of the Republic and establish contact with General Śmigły-Rydz.

I could detect in Göring, who discussed these things with the Chancellor, a certain undertone of concern with regard to our future policy toward Germany. Of course, I did not fail to disperse all his doubts in this respect. General Göring, who spoke very openly, expressed his opinion that France will now do all in its power in order to draw Poland away from its policy toward Germany. In Göring's opinion, without Poland the Franco-Russian alliance will be of little use. Here Göring stressed with great satisfaction that, according to information the Chancellor received from Warsaw, in your conversations with Laval you stood your ground firmly as to your earlier point of view, excluding any possibility of Soviet troops crossing the territory of Poland. Herr Göring declares that the key to the peace situation is in the hands of Poland, and that, in case Poland goes over to the side of the Franco-Soviet alliance, an armed conflict will be unavoidable. Göring obviously spoke with me very frankly, stressing that he feels himself authorized to do so, owing to the fact of our long collaboration.

For my part, I told Göring that to my mind such an open exchange of opinion, free of diplomatic protocol, is most useful for our mutual relations. I confirmed that Marshal Piłsudski had defined so clearly the goals of Poland's policy in the fields of internal structure, organization of the armed forces, and foreign policy that Poland's idea of a nation is very strictly delineated for the future executors of the Marshal's policy.

Minister Göring also mentioned to me that on his shortly anticipated trip to Yugoslavia he would like to press for a Hungarian-Yugoslav rapprochement, and later on also for a Yugoslav-Bulgarian understanding. On this problem he would in all probability like to have an exchange of opinion with you to be quite clear as to whether this concept is in accordance with Poland's stand.

Talking about Czechoslovakia, Göring assumed that the Czechs are under the influence of Russia in the military field and that certain preparations of the air force in Czechoslovakia are directed not only against Germany but also against Poland.

As far as Rumania is concerned, Göring is very skeptical with regard to Minister Titulescu's moral caliber. Göring told me that, according to information in his possession, Rumania would agree to the possible crossing of Soviet troops across Rumania.

From all these considerations the result is that the Chancellor is very much concerned about Poland's stand, since he regards it as a central focus of further developments in the east.

Göring mentioned that if Laval is present at the funeral services in Poland he will not fail to contact him.[2]

Finally, Herr Göring returned to what he had already said during his last conversation with me, stressing very intensely the necessity of a meeting between you and Hitler in the near future.

In the end I would like to point out that, owing to the funeral of the Marshal, the Chancellor has postponed the date for convening the Reichstag from the 17th to the 21st of this month.

*Józef Lipski*

DOCUMENT 44   Lipski to Beck

NO. N/52/3

Berlin, May 23, 1935
*Strictly Confidential*

When I took leave of Chancellor Hitler after the funeral services for the Marshal at Saint Hedwig's Cathedral, he expressed the wish to see me in the next few days. On Monday morning, May 20, I asked Secretary of State Meissner to let me know when I could be received by the Chancellor, and we agreed that this could only take place after the session of the Reichstag called for Tuesday evening. Early in the evening of Wednesday, May 22, I was advised that the Chancellor had invited me for 8:30 P.M.

[2] The conversation between Göring and Laval was held in Cracow on May 18. See *Diariusz*, I, 295–99 and 304.

Chancellor Hitler received me very informally; Neurath was not present, and the usual protocol was dispensed with.

He looked overtired after the oratorical exertion of the day before at the Parliament, where he talked himself hoarse. He told me that he has a gland in the throat which makes him hoarse when his voice is strained. He is considering the possibility of an operation to get rid of this gland.

I subsequently expressed to the Chancellor, in very cordial tones on behalf of the President of Poland and the government, our thanks for the token of sympathy extended to Poland by him, government circles, and the German community in the face of the mourning into which our country was plunged at Marshal Piłsudski's passing.

The Chancellor said that the death of the Marshal has moved him deeply. The figure of the Marshal always had a great attraction for him, and his desire was to meet the commander of the Polish nation.

He even considered the possibility of a meeting to take place in a train at the Polish-German frontier, although he understood what a sensation this would create in world opinion.

Hitler was also anxious to meet Mussolini, whom he considers one of the great national leaders, in spite of a deterioration in German-Italian relations.

The Chancellor also mentioned that he would like to meet Kemal Pasha.

Coming back to the subject of the Marshal, the Chancellor remarked that the death of the Marshal has become a cause for concern in connection with the continuance of the line of Polish foreign policy. However, Minister Göring gave him reassuring information upon his return from Warsaw.[3] I declared to the Chancellor that I am in a position to assure him very firmly that no change will occur in our policy toward Germany.

The Marshal defined very clearly the goals for internal administration, as well as the organization of the armed forces and foreign policy. For many years he had been training his collaborators for independent work following his instructions. The Marshal's teachings are obligatory rules for all of us.

[3] Göring stayed in Poland on the occasion of the funeral of Marshal Piłsudski from May 17 to May 24 (see Moltke's report of May 21, *DGFP*, Series C, Vol. IV, No. 98, and parts of his report of May 28, *ibid.*, No. 115, p. 223).

The Chancellor accepted this statement with satisfaction.

I further declared that the Marshal's policy was always based upon the genuine interest of the Polish state, rather than on abstract ideas, thus guaranteeing the absolute durability of his policy.

In his further deliberations, the Chancellor remarked that the Marshal was one of those exceptional statesmen who understood the reality of the international situation and steered the policy of his country in accordance with this concept.

Subsequently the Chancellor began to analyze his policy toward Poland. He declared that he was the first to get rid of the previous negative political attitude toward Poland, the so-called Rapallo policy, represented by the Reichswehr, headed by Groener and Schleicher. Even prior to his coming to power, he exerted pressure on Schleicher to break his relations with the Soviets, but in vain. The fact alone that Schleicher contributed to Soviet Russia's becoming a military power is sufficient justification for the end that he met. The Chancellor said that much worse things were also weighing against Schleicher, and it was embarrassing to talk about them now. It was a shame even to think about them. It could be concluded from these words that Schleicher's policies were not disinterested.

The Chancellor further stated that the opinion of the Reichswehr then was that a militarily strong Soviet Union could be a threat to Poland only, but not to Germany. This was a shortsighted policy. The only man who at that time understood the Chancellor's opinions was Blomberg. As commander of a corps in East Prussia, he was well versed in the problems of the East, in contrast with the men sitting in the offices of the Reichswehr in Berlin. Also General Reichenau, in the Chancellor's opinion, was well informed.

Talking about Russia, the Chancellor pointed to the danger threatening from that side. Then he stressed that the Marshal understood the Russian reality, just as the Chancellor—according to what he said at the Parliament yesterday—had a knowledge of Bolshevism. Statesmen in the West, I added, are commonly acquainted with Russia only through literature. This generality obviously pleased the Chancellor, since he repeated it several times during the conversation.

In his Eastern policy the Chancellor has taken the stand that a rapprochement with Poland gives much more to the Reich than dangerous relations with Russia. For Germany there exists the problem of finding territories for economic expansion—or room for its population—which Poland does not possess and cannot offer. He was reproached on the question of the Corridor, to which he retorted that compared with these enormous problems the Corridor is of no importance. What harm is there, if Polish-German relations are good, in crossing several tens of kilometers of Polish territory? In a few dozen years of good relations, they will forget about the Corridor in Germany, and in Poland also this problem will become less acute.

The Chancellor has an idea, about which it is too early to speak today, but which could be put into life in some fifteen years: namely, to establish a special railroad and a highway through Pomerania for transport purposes.

The Reich's policy toward Poland will not change, even if he is no longer here, for he has passed his ideas on to his collaborators. In case of his death, which may occur at any time—some idiot (*ein Narr*) can throw a bomb—he has two successors named.

The Chancellor says that his policy is shared by the whole nation. He confirmed that as a result of his speech yesterday [4] countless numbers of letters of congratulations are arriving from all sections of the country.

Who else opposes his policy? Certain aristocrats, some groups of the clergy, and a few old *Deutschnationale*, the last only because he removed them from power, since they have no arguments against his program. He considers Hugenberg to be a loyal man, while his opponents on the right wing are such people as Oldenburg-Januschau.

Next the Chancellor approached the armament problem. He says that some restriction of armaments should be introduced. He states that in some cases the technique of war has gone so far as to render its application impossible.

As an example he noted that close to the end of the war the Germans discovered the *Brandbomben*, but they could not take the decision of using them for fear that the same weapon might be used against them. The present inventions in the field of incendiary bombs make it possible to destroy whole cities, burn out whole forests, etc. Mutual struggle would thus end in complete ruin on both sides, and the future victor would find himself facing a desert, which would result in a catastrophe for him as well. Therefore, banning the use of certain military weapons is in the interest of all nations.

[4] For extracts from Chancellor Hitler's Reichstag speech, see *Polish White Book*, No. 18.

He also mentioned that the Russian factor will obstruct the restriction of armaments.

In the course of the conversation I also had the opportunity—following your instructions—to touch upon our general reservations as to the motives guiding many international circles when they promote plans for multilateral pacts. I stated that in all combinations of this kind we shall be very cautious, in order that real results obtained in our mutual relations are not jeopardized in any way.

The Chancellor also mentioned that he sees from Baldwin's words uttered in the British Parliament that his speech was received with some understanding by the British government.

I would like to stress that the whole conversation was of an informal character and that the statements were rather general, without exactness in separate items.

Owing to the Chancellor's intimate confidences concerning the internal affairs of the Reich, I am sending this report exclusively for your information.[5]

*Józef Lipski*

## DOCUMENT 45   Lipski to Beck

NO. N/128/54/35                                    Berlin, June 7, 1935

In view of the cabinet crisis in France, which has been dragging on for some time already,[6] I was not in a hurry to contact the Auswärtiges Amt upon my return to Berlin, assuming that it would be convenient for you not to actualize your trip for the time being. I limited myself at present to a single informative talk with the chief of the Eastern Department, in the course of which I stated that in principle, according to what was discussed with Neurath and Göring, you would like to come to Berlin to meet the Chancellor and the Foreign Affairs Min-

---

[5] Inserted in the *Polish White Book*, the text of this report (No. 19) is incomplete and very distorted.

[6] On May 30 the Chamber of Deputies rejected the plan of granting financial power to the government, causing the resignation of the Flandin cabinet. On June 1 the Buisson cabinet was formed, but was overthrown June 4 in connection with a demand for economic warranties. On June 7 Laval became prime minister and minister of foreign affairs, with parliamentary support.

ister of the Reich. I added, however, that I was as yet unable to declare myself as to the date and form of this visit.[7]

On current affairs now under discussion by the Reich government with the Western Powers in connection with Hitler's last speech, I would like to give the following explanations, since they result from the above-mentioned conversation:

## 1. The Problem of the Conformity of the Franco-Soviet Agreement with Resolutions of the Rhineland Pact

On this matter the German government presented a memorandum to the French government on May 25, a copy of which was handed to you by Ambassador von Moltke.[8] As was announced in Paris, the German government is to have the reply of the French government in the next few days. The Auswärtiges Amt seems to attach a great deal of importance to this matter and is looking forward with great interest to arguments of the French government, since it feels that it will be very difficult to confirm that the two agreements are not in conflict with each other.

## 2. The Problem of the Eastern Pact

The French government, referring to the proposition of a nonaggression pact in the East presented by the Chancellor of the Reich to Simon during his stay in Berlin,[9] as well as the explanations on this problem offered by the German government to the British government during the Stresa Conference, handed to the German ambassador in Paris an *aide-mémoire* expressing the intention of undertaking negotiations with the German government on this matter.[10] Ambassador von Moltke was instructed to communicate to you the text of the French memorandum. In the meantime the Auswärtiges Amt is investigating the document, and I was advised that the matter of conformity of the Franco-Soviet pact with the Locarno agreement is being given priority.

## 3. Naval Negotiations under Way in London

As is known, these are preliminary talks, not destined to reach any final solution. Nothing special was communicated to me on this matter, be-

[7] For the German version of the conversation with Meyer, see *DGFP*, Series C, Vol. IV, No. 142.

[8] *Ibid.*, No. 107.

[9] *Ibid.*, No. 29.

[10] *Ibid.*, No. 127.

yond a general assumption that the conversations are following the normal line, and that after a short vacation period they will continue once more. However, it can be felt here that precautions will be taken to spare any irritation to Great Britain, for the local political spheres are concentrating on a solution to the impasse by means of an improvement in German-British relations.

### 4. Problem of Italo-German Relations

I was informed just in a general way that some sort of relaxation might be observed, appearing primarily in press relations. Nevertheless, it was stated that nothing happened which would go beyond normal diplomatic talks between the two countries, and that all rumors spread abroad about trading Austria for Abyssinia are of course a product of sheer imagination.

*Józef Lipski*

Poland's relations with Danzig did not enter into the sphere of activities of the Polish Ambassador in Berlin. Poland was careful to settle Danzig problems directly with the Senate of the Free City. It was only in emergency cases that Warsaw issued instructions for Lipski to negotiate on these matters from Berlin.

Such an emergency case was the tension in Poland's relations with Danzig in the summer of 1935.[11]

The conflict began on May 2 when, owing to financial difficulties in Danzig, the Senate of the Free City devaluated the Danzig gulden by 42.3 percent. This caused heavy losses for Poland, since customs income collected by Poland decreased automatically by an equal percentage. The Polish government made a proposition to balance the Danzig gulden with the Polish złoty. However, Arthur Greiser, the president of the Danzig Senate, opposed this proposal vehemently for fear that the złoty might completely replace the gulden.

This catastrophic situation in Danzig's finances constituted a grave political threat for Hitler, inasmuch as it could bring about the downfall of the National Socialist movement in the Free City. In their anxiety to avoid this calamity, political circles were ready to extend financial assistance to Danzig. On the other hand, however, these same political sponsors were well aware that in order to push Germany to the forefront as a large European power they had to continue expensive armaments, and they were reluctant at that

[11] See *Diariusz,* I, 320, 323–25, 522–25.

time to entangle themselves in the Danzig problems. At the same time economic circles (represented by Schacht, president of the Reichsbank) were unwilling to increase the normal monthly subsidy allotted for Danzig.

On June 11 Danzig introduced a currency control which constituted a direct blow to Polish industrialists who used the harbor of Danzig. Besides, this measure was illegal on the part of Danzig, since it was contradictory to the Polish-Danzig convention of November 9, 1920.

Under these circumstances the Polish-Danzig conflict deepened, with Hitler's obvious support and his promise of all possible aid in money and food in case Poland shut its frontier.

Two reports by Lipski dealing with the conflict follow.

DOCUMENT 46   Lipski to Beck

NO. G/3/8/35                                        Berlin, June 13, 1935
                                                    *Strictly Confidential*

In accordance with your recommendation received yesterday by telephone,[12] I called on Schacht this morning at 11 A.M. and made the following declaration:

I learned from the press that Herr Schacht is to proceed in the next few days to Danzig. I am calling on him in this connection to discuss the financial and economic situation in effect in the Free City at present, noting that my action is not an official *démarche* because—if for no other reason—Danzig is beyond the sphere of direct Polish-German relations.

I subsequently stressed that I would like to present to Herr Schacht our point of view on this problem, assuming this might be of assistance to him. I began by declaring that the relaxation in Polish-Danzig relations was the first stage heralding a Polish-German rapprochement. The Polish government accepted, as a principle, nonintervention in Danzig's internal affairs. Our stand in the face of internal political struggles waged on the territory of the Free City during the last years might serve as sufficient proof here. What Poland is pressing for is that its rights in Danzig, based on a number of agreements, be respected.

I was recently approached by top political spheres of the Reich, who expressed some anxiety about the situation now prevailing in the Free

[12] *Ibid.,* p. 316.

City, for fear of repercussions on Polish-German relations. I was requested to watch over this problem within the frame of my opportunities. Availing myself of this occasion, I had come today to have a talk with Schacht.

Coming back to the financial situation in Danzig, I stressed that it is causing justified anxiety. I confirmed that a successful economic development of the situation in Danzig is also of concern to Poland. Therefore, I stated that we would be ready to extend financial and economic aid. I added that this aid would take a form that would be politically unobtrusive for the government, under the condition of loyal economic collaboration with us. Finally, I pointed to the fact that it would be regrettable to have something go on in Danzig which is contradictory to Polish-Danzig agreements.

Here Herr Schacht inquired which acts of Danzig, in our opinion, are in contradiction with the agreements, to which I replied that I had in mind currency restrictions which, besides being contradictory to Article 195 of the Warsaw Convention, in practice are bound to expose to difficulties Polish interests in their transactions with the Free City and via the Free City. Herr Schacht reacted strongly to this point and tried to persuade me that the introduction of currency restrictions in the Free City, as a matter of fact differing from those issued in the Reich and aimed solely at stopping the exodus of gold from the Bank of Danzig, is not designed to hurt Polish interests. As for the contradiction with Article 195, he did not deny that it might be against the law, and he said that he would give this matter his attention.

Herr Schacht replied as follows: He is proceeding to Danzig in his capacity as president of the Reichsbank, at the invitation not of the Senate of the Free City but of the president of the Bank of Danzig. He will not have any contacts with the Senate, a political institution. The goal of his visit is to reinforce the position of Schäfer, whom he regards as quite a competent person. In his conversations he will obviously avoid any subjects embarrassing for Poland, since maintaining good relations with Poland is his heart's desire, as well as that of other members of the government. Although several years ago a rapprochement would have seemed unrealistic and impossible, such a fact had occurred in a form positive for both partners.

Schacht declared that the situation of the Bank of Danzig is quite good. The balance sheet shows that on 32 million gulden in assets (*Aussenstände*) there are bills worth 29 million gulden in circulation

(*Notenumlauf*). His opinion is that the crisis is purely psychological. Stronger nerves will restore a perfect currency situation in Danzig in two months. The gulden will become the most sought-after currency. That is why he wants to inject psychological resistance into the Bank of Danzig. He deems it to be necessary to introduce currency restrictions for a time. This might be a painful blow for some individuals, but it will have an immediate positive effect. In his opinion the whole matter is exaggerated and a result of artificial excitement. He is aware, of course, that the Senate of the Free City found itself in a difficult position with the elections over and the necessity of introducing the devaluation of the gulden immediately afterward.

With regard to Poland's financial and economic aid, Herr Schacht asked if we would be ready to give gold from the Bank of Poland to cover the gulden. I replied that some aid of this sort could be extended. In the field of economics, I answered Herr Schacht by stating that I understood that, in view of the complex of Polish-Danzig economic relations, some way might be found to reach out a helping hand to the Free City.

At the end of my conversation with Schacht, I stated that I only wanted, quite informally, to draw his attention to the Danzig aspect as observed from Warsaw. For his part, Herr Schacht stressed that in his opinion the financial situation should not be considered too tragically, that it will improve very soon, that he understands Poland's concern to have its interests in Danzig respected, and that certainly nothing will be done by the German government to jeopardize Polish-German relations.

In view of the position taken by Herr Schacht and his very strong dissociation from any political elements, both here and in the Free City, I did not deem it necessary to ask him to meet our representative in the Free City.

I would like to add that on my return to the Embassy I received a telephone call from the Auswärtiges Amt, informing me that they were advised of my conversation with Schacht and that they shared the point of view of the Reichsbank President. I replied that I had spoken with Schacht privately, since I had no authority to hold talks with the Reich government on the subject of Danzig.[13]

I quite understand that the German government was compelled to support Danzig financially in view of the difficult financial situation there. Undoubtedly, the mission of investigate the problem was en-

[13] See *DGFP*, Series C, Vol. IV, No. 149.

trusted to the most responsible factor in the Reich, namely, to Schacht. As far as I can see, the restoration work is proceeding on the following lines:

1) Compression of the inflated budget. Here, as was already confirmed by Greiser in his speech, the Reich is granting assistance in order to meet individual claims.

2) The Bank of Danzig, following Schacht's advice, will try to stop the exodus of the gulden by currency restrictions. Schacht thinks that, if the gulden remains as the only currency in the Free City, its exodus will stop as a result.

3) The assistance has become a matter of prestige, owing to the fact that the Reichsbank President is paying a visit to Danzig.

4) It is at present difficult to ascertain whether there are other invisible subsidies coming to Danzig from the Reich.

Regarding our assistance for the Free City, I am of the opinion— observing the situation from Berlin—that this matter is being used by the opposition elements in Danzig as a trump card to fight the National Socialist government, especially with regard to introducing gold currency in Danzig. Therefore, I imagine that it would be extremely awkward for the Senate to approach Poland with a proposition for aid.

Although my conversation with Schacht did not result—in my opinion—in any positive end with regard to our participation in extending aid to Danzig, nevertheless a concrete advantage was obtained, since it revealed the method of action of the Reich government regarding the financial crisis in the Free City.

*Józef Lipski*


DOCUMENT 47    Lipski to Beck

NO. G/3/11/35                                    Berlin, June 17, 1935
                                                *Strictly Confidential*

Owing to the absence of Reichspräsident Göring from Berlin, only this morning could I discuss with him the situation in Danzig.[14]

With reference to what Göring declared to me on May 21 concerning Danzig problems, I opened the conversation by saying that I had wanted

14 See *ibid.*, No. 158.

to talk with him on this subject for several days. Unfortunately, this was not possible because of his absence from Berlin. I added that I had had a conversation with Schacht before he left for Danzig, but the President of the Reichsbank saw this matter from a purely financial angle. Göring replied that Schacht indeed does consider this question only as a currency problem.

I further declared to Göring that, realizing that a National Socialist Senate in Danzig is also most desirable from our point of view, since it brought about a rapprochement between the Free City and Poland, I would like to remind him that we have always kept aloof from internal Danzig problems. In spite of approaches repeatedly made by the opposition parties, we rejected any attempt to draw us into action against the Senate. I mentioned quite confidentially that the Polish minority in Danzig was advised not to join forces with the opposition at the time of the elections. Deliberating on this point, I pointed to our basic attitude regarding the situation of the National Socialist Senate.

Subsequently, I stressed that, owing to the introduction of the currency order without our knowledge, we were presented with a *fait accompli* that constituted a serious blow to our economic interests. I further illustrated with examples to Herr Göring how detrimental the currency regulations are both for our economic interests and for the genuine interests of the Free City. I mentioned that we had the possibility of taking this matter to the League but that you abstained from doing so, realizing that on the platform of the League such a case could be exploited by a number of elements to the detriment of Polish-German relations. I added that for the time being you had settled for a protest presented on the 13th inst., that the strongly worded protest was purposely softened for presentation to the press, and that, counting on the possibility of direct talks with the Senate, we had not as yet introduced any retaliatory measures. I said again that the only way out of this situation would be direct conversations between Poland and the Free City. Poland would then be able to offer certain financial and economic aid to the Free City, and I added in this connection that Mr. Roman is leaving tomorrow for Danzig with this aim in mind. I remarked that Mr. Roman is well known to the German side as a very able and reasonable negotiator, who conducted negotiations with the Free City for many years.[15]

[15] At this time Antoni Roman was Polish minister in Stockholm.

In the course of my deliberations Herr Göring several times gave me immediate explanations which, in brief, are as follows:

He stated that the Chancellor is taking a firm stand that the Danzig problem should under no circumstances create difficulties in Polish-German relations. Both Greiser and Forster are well aware of this. The Chancellor insists on supporting the National Socialist Senate in Danzig, not only for prestige reasons, but primarily because he knows that, if power in Danzig were seized by the opposition, this would be harmful for the Free City's policy toward Poland. The opposition parties would obviously immediately revert to the old policy against Poland.

Regarding currency regulations, Göring said that the Senate was ordered to advise the Polish government. As a proof of how the Chancellor is keeping watch over this matter from the point of view of Polish-German relations, Göring cited the fact that, when Greiser asked that a battleship be sent to Danzig to boost the Senate's prestige, the Chancellor replied that he would not do it, since a visit of the Germany navy to Gdynia should have priority. Also, Schacht's trip was solely aimed at keeping up spirits at the Bank of Danzig.

Regarding assistance for Danzig, Herr Göring said that, of course, both Germany and Poland are not very well off at present, and therefore assistance on a large scale is difficult. I mentioned here that, with good will, we might on our part find some means of easing Danzig's situation. Here I made the reservation that we are well aware that this aid should be devoid of any aspect which would compromise the National Socialist Senate in the eyes of the opposition.

Göring expressed great satisfaction over this clarification. He added that Greiser told him that it was apparently stated by our side that, in case the Free City does not accept Polish conditions, it would be economically ruined, and that it was also said—between the lines—that time has now come to cancel some of the rights of the Free City. When this was related to him, Göring allegedly declared in the presence of the Chancellor that he does not know what was said in Danzig; but he was in Warsaw and spoke with competent elements there, and he is well aware of the atmosphere in the Polish government, which is trying to maintain good relations with Germany. Here I remarked to Göring that possibly opposition circles are intriguing on both sides. We are not in the least interested in depriving the Free City of any rights whatsoever, and in economic talks certain ways can be found financially to support the currency.

Talking about Greiser, Göring said that Greiser does not please him, since his position is visibly turning his head a bit. But he praised Forster, stating that it was worth while to talk with him, since he is absolutely in favor of the maintenance of good relations with Poland. He therefore advised that Minister Roman should also talk with Forster.

Herr Göring during this whole conversation stressed authoritatively that nothing would be done by the German government to create difficulties in Polish-German relations, but that, on the contrary, pressure would be exerted on the Senate in this matter. In conclusion he said that he would immediately call Greiser and Forster by telephone in order to induce them to conduct their talks with Minister Roman in this spirit. He will also advise the Chancellor of our conversation.

Parenthetically I might add that Göring thought that you had a conversation with Greiser in Danzig. Herr Göring asked me to extend to you his thanks for approaching him on these matters and to assure you that the previous line is not subject to fluctuations. He remarked that it would be sheer nonsense if such a nutshell as Danzig were to complicate the all-important Polish-German relations.

Finally, Herr Göring said to me that he is very anxious for you to come to Berlin now. He has already announced this to the Chancellor. I replied that in principle you would be pleased to come, and that the Danzig problem, as well as Göring's absence from Berlin, has simply delayed your arrival a bit. Herr Göring also added that he counts on an understanding being reached in direct talks in Danzig. If any difficulties should arise, he is ready at any time with personal intervention, and thinks that in case of necessity you could take this matter up with the Chancellor.

I would like to add that the local press—in all probability inspired—passed over in silence the whole Danzig affair. The D.N.B. [Deutsches Nachrichtenbüro] is very thrifty with news to be circulated in Germany.

*Józef Lipski*

On July 18 the Polish government, having authority on customs problems, ordered that duty be levied in Danzig only on goods destined for the internal consumption of the Free City, while duty on goods bound for Poland via Danzig should be collected in Poland. This order could have resulted in economic catastrophe for Danzig, and certain German elements reacted by urging that Danzig be detached from Poland and united with the Reich. Von

Moltke, in a conversation with Beck, strove to iron out the situation, but the Danzig Senate aggravated the conflict still further by its order (on August 1) to admit customs-free those goods destined for internal consumption in the Free City.

Immediately following this order, Lipski, who at that time was in Warsaw, received instructions to return to Berlin for orientation on whether the government of the Reich supported the decision of the Danzig Senate.

On August 2 Lipski had a conversation with Secretary of State von Bülow. Bülow criticized sharply the action of the Senate and expressed the opinion that, in spite of this, Polish-Danzig negotiations would succeed in achieving the liquidation of the conflict (*DGFP,* Series C, Vol. IV, No. 244).

On the next day Lipski proceeded to Berchtesgaden, where Göring was taking part in a hunt. In his conversation with Lipski on August 4, Göring had words of sharp criticism for the order by the Danzig authorities, as being contrary to the Chancellor's guiding line. Their action had absolutely nothing to do with the Reich government. Göring was of the opinion that the conflict must be liquidated immediately. He was ready to summon Greiser to Berlin in order to use his influence on him to this effect. To Göring's question how this strife could be ended, Lipski explained that the Danzig authorities should withdraw their order and, in consequence, upon agreement that customs would be levied in a fixed currency, the Polish government would withdraw its order of July 18. Göring approved this solution and promised Lipski to arrange a meeting with Hitler.

This meeting took place on August 5 (*DGFP,* Series C, Vol. IV, No. 25). When the Ambassador outlined the course of the Danzig problem to the Chancellor, as he had previously to Göring who was also present, Hitler declared that his argumentation was quite clear and convincing. Hitler said that in his policies he gave priority to essential problems, subordinating second-rate problems to them. The Chancellor regarded good Polish-German relations to be of primary importance. With the situation developing in the east, the two states might face an omnific moment, and they should therefore coexist in friendship. Compared to these great interests, the Corridor question was of second-rate importance. Poland needed access to the sea; if deprived of it, the whole Polish nation would then turn against Germany. Returning to the Danzig question, the Chancellor stated that he was in favor of absolute respect of the *status quo* in the Free City by both Germany and Poland. This was the only way to avoid unnecessary conflicts. The problem of Danzig was a second-rate problem; it should not encumber Polish-German relations.

Bringing the conversation to an end, the Chancellor urged a prompt liquidation of the Danzig conflict, asking on what level this could be achieved. Göring quoted conditions of the agreement as discussed with Lipski. Without bringing up further details, the Chancellor thanked the Ambassador for coming to Berchtesgaden and asked him to communicate their conversation to Beck.

Once more, on August 6, Lipski had a conversation with Göring, first getting authorization from Beck by telephone to settle the conflict. Forster and Greiser accepted the Polish formula upon Göring's inquiry by telephone.[16] Beck's conversation with Greiser at Gdynia on August 8 (*DGFP*, Series C, Vol. IV Nos. 257 and 258) brought this conflict to a close, and aggressive orders on both sides were withdrawn. A number of relevant documents are cited in *DGFP*, Series C, Vol. IV, Nos. 65, 92, 97, 103, 112, 123, 126, 130, 133, 134, 143, 149, 150, 158, 214, 215, 224, 226, 227, 240, 244, 245, 247, 250, 251, 254, and 256.

[16] In his report to the Foreign Affairs Ministry dated August 15, Lipski presented the whole of this action from August 2 to August 6, as well as his conversations with von Bülow, Göring, and Hitler. This report is missing from Lipski's papers. Halina Trocka quotes from it and summarizes it in *Gdańsk a hitlerowski "Drang nach Osten"* (Danzig, 1964), pp. 58–60, while sentences from the conversation with Hitler are quoted literally as per Lipski's report, although with omissions.

# German Refunds for Transit across Polish Pomerania
## July, 1935—March, 1936

---

MINISTER BECK'S official visit to Berlin on July 3 and 4, 1935, was an important event in Polish-German relations. Beck, accompanied by Lipski, had his first long conversation with Hitler at that time. For details according to the German verson, see *DGFP*, Series C, Vol. IV, No. 190, pp. 398–407, and No. 192. For the Polish résumé of this conversation, see *Diariusz*, I, 330–32, 344–45, and 526. The official communiqué about this visit appears in *Polish White Book*, No. 20.

On June 20 negotiations were started in Berlin on the Polish-German trade agreement, which was signed in Warsaw on November 4, 1935.

### DOCUMENT 48   Lipski to Beck

NO. N/52/4/35

Berlin, July 15, 1935
*Strictly Confidential*

Before my departure tomorrow for a three-week vacation, I called today on Secretary of State von Bülow, who is substituting for von Neurath during the latter's absence from Berlin.

Von Bülow expressed the German government's satisfaction with the results of your visit to Berlin, stressing that good Polish-German diplomatic collaboration in Warsaw and Berlin was developing so successfully as to render new achievements dispensable.

For my part I referred to the question of the current Polish-German trade negotiations. I pointed out that, following the suggestion for a broader understanding made by the German representative, Directors Sokołowski and Rose left for Warsaw to obtain authorization to negotiate on the basis suggested by the German side.

I remarked that this was not an easy problem, especially with regard to granting Germany the most-favored-nation clause.

I confirmed that naturally we are most interested in satisfying agricultural demands. Here I emphasized that, in accordance with the suggestions of the delegation, our demands in this field cannot be reduced. I especially laid stress on the point that our total calculation is based on obtaining sufficiently high prices.

I said that both Herr Hemmen and Herr Ritter understand and support our stand; however, they are concerned about possible opposition from Herr Schacht's department. Therefore, I asked Herr Bülow to give his careful attention to this problem. Von Bülow, who agreed with my explanations, stated that he also understands our interest in striving to obtain the highest possible prices for agricultural products, and that this is a basis for a possible agreement.

I also asked Herr von Bülow, in case any difficulties arose, to receive Counselor Lubomirski in my absence, and if necessary to extend his assistance to him, which he willingly promised to do.

I subsequently took up the question of Sir Samuel Hoare's speech in the House of Commons.[1] The Secretary of State replied that Hoare's speech made an unfavorable impression on the German government; here he obviously had in mind the appeal made to the Chancellor to agree to the Eastern and Danube pacts. This is even more unpleasant if one bears in mind that the British government was well aware what was cooking backstage. It is obvious that the British, French, and Italian governments distributed parts between them. England is pressing for the air pact, France for the Eastern Pact, and Italy for the Danube Pact. At present Italy has ceased its pressure for the Danube Pact; the problem of the Eastern Pact, viewed from the angle of Franco-German relations, is more complicated. The British appeal calling on Germany to accept these pacts was very tactless under these circumstances. Such was the reaction of the German press. Herr von Bülow remarked further that he has spoken only with Herr von Neurath, who has not yet seen the Chancellor since Hoare's speech. Neurath and Bülow took a stand—which they expect will be shared by the Chancellor absolutely—that the appeal of the British Secretary of State should be dismissed without any reply.

Herr von Bülow stated that the German government will not stand for blackmail (he used a milder expression) by Great Britain in connection with the air pact. If he followed Britain's course, then after the Eastern

[1] July 11, 1935.

Pact the Danube Pact would be brought forward, and after the Danube Pact the return of Germany to the League of Nations, etc., etc. If the air pact is not concluded, it cannot be helped. Germany will continue to build up its air force; this build-up, von Bülow added, will be conducted only in accordance with real needs.

With regard to the Eastern Pact, Herr von Bülow remarked that he had recommended to the German ambassador in Paris, Köster, that he ask Laval informally whether France really intends to participate in the suggested Eastern Pact. Herr von Bülow stressed that Barthou's original proposition included France's participation, but in subsequent plans this participation was not explicitly mentioned. Bülow thinks that this will be a convenient tactical question, since it might open the possibility for a series of new arguments against the pact.

Next, observing that he would like to discuss a timely matter of importance, Herr Bülow referred to the question of the recent meeting of the representatives of the Baltic states at Riga.[2] He confirmed that the Auswärtiges Amt had received news that strong pressure was exerted from the Soviet side on the Baltic states to draw them, like Czechoslovakia, into the Franco-Soviet agreement. This was the subject debated at Riga, and the German Envoy reported from Riga, following his conversation with the Latvian Foreign Affairs Minister, that Latvia is beginning to lean toward the Russian-French plotting.

Herr von Bülow stressed that Ambassador von Moltke was instructed to inform you about this state of affairs.

Today, prior to my visit, the Latvian Envoy called on the Secretary of State and communicated to him the text of the resolutions passed at the conference of Baltic states in Riga.[3]

One of these points states that, in case the German government does not support its earlier declaration made at Stresa with regard to the Eastern Pact and the pact is not concluded, the Baltic states will then be compelled to join the Soviet-French agreement. The Secretary of State allegedly reacted very strongly to the point of view expressed by the Latvian Envoy. He said, in the first place, that in Stresa the German government only expressed its opinion, without taking on any binding obligations. Since the problem of the Eastern Pact is very complicated, it

[2] This was a conference of thirteen Latvian envoys from various countries that lasted from June 28 to July 3.
[3] See *DGFP*, Series C, Vol. IV, No. 208.

is not possible to present motions, as the Baltic states are prepared to do, basing themselves on explanations supplied by the German government to the Western Powers at one time. Von Bülow supposedly then pointed out that the Eastern Pact is nothing but a cover for a Soviet-French alliance.

He further declared to the Latvian Envoy that the German government is very positively disposed toward the Baltic states and their independence.

Although he could not agree to the conclusion of an agreement of mutual assistance with these countries, this did not indicate in the least his *désintéressement* in case other Powers threatened the independence of the Baltic states. Finally, von Bülow warned the Latvian Envoy against joining the Soviet-French system, which constitutes a threat for the independence of the Baltic states. He stressed that, faced with such an emergency, the German government could be compelled to revise its present attitude toward these states. Herr von Bülow told me that he strove to influence the Latvian side not to succumb to pressure exerted by the Soviets. He remarked that this pressure also has its basis in the field of economic relations. Herr von Bülow concluded by asking me to support, for my part, Ambassador Moltke's *démarche* to you aimed at obtaining the collaboration of the Polish government in taking action in Riga and Tallin to keep them in the present state of balance.

I remarked that, owing to my departure for a vacation tomorrow morning, I would write my report on the conversation with the Secretary of State today and dispatch it without delay for your attention.

I declared that in my opinion the wisest policy for the Baltic states would be to maintain their neutral position toward the Great Powers, and that such a stand is the best guarantee for their independence.

I stressed that our activities were always aimed at the preservation of independent Baltic states, without binding them with agreements which could prove detrimental to their independence. I also made allusion to the fact that Estonia's policy was the most forthright and well balanced.

The Secretary of State agreed with my opinion. He also added that the German envoys in Riga and Tallin had received appropriate instructions. As far as Kovno was concerned, in his opinion it was hopeless.

I also had a casual talk with Director Meyer. As far as I can judge, news coming from Riga has rendered the Auswärtiges Amt somewhat nervous. Probably this is due also to the absence of Neurath.

In order to inform you without delay, I took the liberty of sending a special courier.

*Józef Lipski*

DOCUMENT 49    Lipski to Szembek

NO. 1/3/45/35                                    Berlin, October 18, 1935
*Confidential*

I am forwarding the enclosed report on a conversation held on October 11 between Minister Beck and Minister von Neurath after dinner at the Polish Embassy. This report gives only a general outline of the conversation, which was conducted in a very subtle manner.

I would like to add that on the same day at 7 P.M. Minister Beck called on Minister President Göring, by special invitation. The conversation also dealt with the Abyssinian question, and Herr Göring's arguments, if not so detailed, were more or less in agreement with von Neurath's opinions.

Herr Göring expressed his concern about progress made by the Soviets in Rumania, remarking that, in case a Soviet-Rumanian pact is concluded, he is convinced that the question of allowing Soviet troops to march through Rumania would be settled positively as well. Minister Beck, without involving himself in further discussion on this point, said only that the situation in Rumania is difficult indeed, and that the King seems to be more and more under the influence of Mr. Titulescu's policy.

*Józef Lipski*

Report on the Conversation of Foreign Affairs Minister Józef Beck with
Reich Foreign Affairs Minister von Neurath,
*held on October 11, 1935, in Berlin*

On October 11, on his way from Geneva to Warsaw, the Foreign Affairs Minister met with Reich Foreign Affairs Minister von Neurath at a dinner at the Embassy. The course of this conversation was as follows:

Both Minister Beck and Herr von Neurath agreed that the situation in connection with the Abyssinian conflict is very serious, more than a local struggle, and that in the long run it might constitute a danger for Europe.[4]

Minister Beck remarked that this time the impact of the situation could be felt at Geneva. He stressed that one thing has become obvious, namely, that the Second and the Third International had acted jointly, striving to regain their positions. Minister Beck had called the attention of the British delegation to this fact. Herr von Neurath was absolutely of the same opinion. Both ministers agreed in their supposition that the conflict could extend further owing to a miscalculation of the British situation by the Italians and vice versa.

They both realize that Italy's position is rendered more difficult because broad public opinion in all countries is taking the part of Abyssinia as a country attacked. Here Herr von Neurath quoted facts from Germany, remarking that he can hardly stop the press from attacking Italy.

Both ministers do not at present see any way out for Mussolini. They share the opinion that an Italian defeat would be very dangerous for relations in Europe and would only contribute to the reinforcement of the Third International.

Minister Beck stated that, although in principle Poland abstains from interfering with matters of no direct concern to our state, in this particular case, in the face of the seriousness of the situation, he did not shrink from participation in the Committee of Five, which is striving, within the limits of existing possibilities, to assist in settling the conflict.

Minister Beck emphasized the efforts made by Laval to find a way out of the situation. Herr von Neurath remarked that, if Laval were defeated, power would go to Herriot. Both ministers shared the opinion that too-strong British pressure on France, with the consequent downfall of Laval, would only bring about a closer Franco-Soviet association.

Herr von Neurath, remarking that he had had a conversation with the Chancellor that afternoon, declared that the German government considers the developing situation as a serious danger for Europe and is interested in the speediest possible settlement of the conflict. In this matter the German government is not following its own secondary inter-

[4] On October 2 Italy mobilized, and on the 3d Italian troops marched into Abyssinia. On the 5th the Council of the League of Nations was in session, and on the 7th the Council unanimously proclaimed Italy an aggressor. Poland voted for this motion.

ests but is taking a broader European point of view. Herr von Neurath stated that since the German nation lives in Europe it must take care of the development of this part of the world. Bearing these issues in mind, Herr von Neurath believes that at the right moment this point might be communicated to public opinion, thus favorably affecting the general situation. He thinks that if, for instance, the German government were approached with regard to sanctions, this could possibly be the occasion for this sort of action.

Minister Beck noted with appreciation the stand of the German government regarding the Anglo-Italian conflict. On this point he stressed that, as a result of his conversation with the Chancellor, he had expressed to the English his conviction that the government of the Reich desires its relations with Great Britain to take the best possible turn.

Herr von Neurath went on to confirm that, in the light of these issues, he could assure Minister Beck that nothing would occur with regard to Kłajpeda [Memel]. The fate of several thousand Memel Germans is a secondary issue compared with wide European interests. The German government, even now after the elections, will endeavor—if a reasonable reaction by the Lithuanian government prevails—to normalize its relations with Lithuania if possible.

Minister Beck, remarking casually that negotiating with the Lithuanian government is not an easy task, referred to his conversation with Lozorajtis. He stated that he told the Lithuanian statesman that for Poland to establish relations with Lithuania it is essential to know whether Lithuania has a self-governing policy. Minister Beck stressed to Herr von Neurath that a certain reaction can be detected in Lithuania against total surrender to Moscow's supremacy. Herr von Neurath agreed with this.

With regard to the Baltic states, both ministers were of the opinion that a certain amount of calmness and sobering down could be noted in these countries. Minister Beck thinks this is due partly to the fact that representatives of these states could observe in Geneva that the importance of Moscow in Western Europe is not so considerable as it seems locally. Mr. Beck stated that he appraises positively the visits of Scandinavian statesmen to the Baltic states.

Coming back to current Polish-German economic matters, Herr von Neurath stressed that he was advised that the delegation which is to negotiate with Poland is to leave for Riga. He asked if it would not be advisable that they go via Warsaw. Ambassador Lipski replied that in his opinion this is desirable, suggesting that the stopover take place next week.

Ambassador Lipski referred to the question of railway payments.[5] Minister Beck remarked that this matter is not exclusively a financial one but has a political aspect as well.

DOCUMENT 50   Lipski to the Ministry of Foreign Affairs

NO. N/51/58/35                           Berlin, November 7, 1935
                                         *Confidential*

On October 28, I was summoned by telephone by the Vice-Minister of Foreign Affairs to come to Warsaw on October 30 in connection with the question of German arrears in refunds for transit through Poland. On October 30 and 31, I was present at consultations on this matter conducted in the presence of Vice-Minister Szembek, Vice-Minister of the Treasury Koc, Director of Financial Turnover Baczyński, Director Potocki, and others. On November 1, I proceeded to Rabka with Vice-Minister Szembek and Director Baczyński in order to receive from Minister Beck final instructions for my conversations with the German government.[6]

Upon my return to Berlin, on November 3, I was received by Foreign Affairs Minister von Neurath on November 4 at 11:30 A.M. After a preliminary exchange of opinion regarding rumors about the alleged deviation from our present political line and my reassurances on this point, I passed to the subject of arrears in railway refunds. I declared that this matter had reached such dimensions that besides its financial aspect it now assumed a conspicuous political character. I pointed to the very negative reaction in the Polish government to Germany's tardiness in settling these refunds. I remarked that the economic department decided that granting further credits to German railways is impossible and that the only solution would be to issue orders to collect the arrears for transit on the frontier. In order to prevent this extreme solution, I tried

[5] These payments were connected with transit from Germany through Polish Pomerania to East Prussia. Contrary to the binding Paris Agreement of 1921, Germany withheld payment, which by the end of September, 1935, amounted to 29,500,000 zlotys. Germany tried to combine this question with other economic matters in the current trade negotiations; the Polish side requested that these debts be settled separately.

[6] For Lipski's conversations in Warsaw, see *Diariusz*, I, 391–95.

to find a way out in my conversations with the ministers. I stressed that the present government, whose main concern is to stabilize the budget, and which for this reason will have to increase the tax burden on the population, is even more reluctant to let such arrears jeopardize its recovery plans. I subsequently presented our suggestion requesting the immediate repayment of 42 million zlotys, indicating that after this refund is made we would be prepared to credit the German government for two years with an equivalent sum from the future flow of transit dues. The balance would be transferred to the German-Soviet-Polish triangle. I told Herr von Neurath that we would thus enable Herr Schacht to shift payments for raw materials, for example. I made it explicitly clear that the refund is indispensable and that nonpayment would have bad consequences for our relations.

Herr von Neurath replied that, as far as the field of foreign policy is concerned, this whole problem has been weighing heavily on him for months, and that he is doing his utmost to liquidate it. Of course, in this case he has to confer with the Chancellor and with Schact.

I added that up to now I had never embarrassed the Chancellor with either economic or financial matters, confining myself to purely political matters of a general nature. However, in view of the importance of this particular case, I would like him to advise the Chancellor that I am at his disposal for discussion on this problem.

In the course of the conversation, von Neurath also mentioned that the matter of our later crediting the sum of 42 million zlotys, upon repayment of the present arrears, is not too convenient a solution, for it still leaves a debt. In his opinion, the problem should be solved completely, in order to prevent its reoccurrence.

I laid stress on the urgency of the case, asking Herr von Neurath for a reply, possibly in the next few days, which he promised to give me.[7]

On the 5th inst., Counselor Gawroński was interpellated at the Auswärtiges Amt by the economic desk officer, Herr Bräutigam, about this matter in connection with my conversation with Herr von Neurath. Counselor Gawroński also took a determined stand.

Realizing from this conversation that the matter is receiving attention inside the department, I had a talk yesterday, on the 6th inst., with Minister President Göring, in the course of which, acting as I had previ-

[7] For the German version of this conversation, see *DGFP*, Series C, Vol. **IV**, No. 392. See also *ibid.*, No. 409.

ously with von Neurath, I insisted on the necessity for the refund of railway arrears.

Herr Göring noted all the details, remarking that he will have a talk with Schacht right away and will give me a reply, possibly on Monday.

On this occasion Göring told me that, when at the Council of Ministers the question of payment of membership fees to the League of Nations by the Reich government was presented, he strongly urged that this sum be given to Poland instead of to the League. The argument presented against this was that, if Germany does not cover its indebtedness to the League of Nations, it might still be regarded as subject to membership obligations, and this would be a political handicap for it.

As I wired yesterday, I am leaving for Munich for two days. I therefore assume that I shall not be in a position to give you further information on this problem before Monday.

*Józef Lipski*

DOCUMENT 51   Lipski to Beck

NO. N/320/151/35                                Berlin, November 24, 1935
                                                *Strictly Confidential*

My nearly two years of observations and experience in the field of so-called Polish-German moral disarmament found application in the declaration of January 26, 1934, and especially in the press agreement concluded on February 24, 1934.[8] These, in my opinion, can be of assistance in evaluating results achieved as well as obstacles continually manifested in this matter. A synthesis of this matter would also contribute to a proper orientation regarding our future action and tactics.

It should be taken into consideration that, in the post-Versailles pe-

[8] In February, 1934, press conversations were held in Berlin between Poland and Germany in connection with the nonaggression declaration of January 26, 1934. Participating on the Polish side were Wacław Przesmycki, chief of the Foreign Ministry Press Department and his deputy, Emil Rücker; on the German side, Director of the Press Department of the A.A. Aschmann and Counselor Jahnke of the Propaganda Ministry. The conversations concluded with a secret protocol established by the two sides on February 24 which defined a series of resolutions aimed at creating a friendly atmosphere and good-neighbor relations in the fields of the press, radio, theater, cinema, and periodicals. This protocol was supplemented at the next conference in Warsaw.

riod and until conversations were undertaken with Chancellor Hitler, German governments, regardless of their party line, systematically rejected all our suggestions that they abandon German press and propaganda action against Poland. The Polish government's endeavors, both during the period of Locarno and during the rule of Chancellor Brüning, took a very concrete form. We were permanently vigilant in this matter, approaching the Geneva institution with our claims and using the governments of France, England, and America as intermediaries. German propaganda against Poland, active inside the Reich, spread abroad to other countries.

It served two principal goals:

a) on the assumption that Poland is a foe of the Reich, to counteract our interests in all fields;

b) through a permanent revisionist action against Polish frontiers, to maintain, both in German and foreign minds, the concept that a peaceful coexistence between the two nations is impossible without territorial changes.

Starting with conversations with Chancellor Hitler, action described under (a) necessarily subsided and became pointless when, after the declaration of January 26, 1934, the German government accepted for propaganda use abroad the principle of displaying correct and friendly relations with Poland.

It was and will remain much more difficult to find brakes for the multicolored German propaganda generally labeled as revisionism. Here the Polish side, realizing that leaving this problem to the normal exchange of opinion through diplomatic channels (which would make permanent contacts necessary) would result in the need for a permanent objective procedure and definitely defined principles to oppose this action, suggested a press and propaganda understanding inaugurated by the signing of respective protocols on February 24, 1935.

The above press understanding, supplemented by protocols confirmed at the following conference in Warsaw, gives, according to the present *status quo*, a general outline of credit balance in our favor:

a) a generally correct stand and tone toward Poland by the popular daily German press;

b) cessation of the revisionist campaign against our frontiers by this press, especially against Pomerania. This is a positive result for us, particularly outside the Reich's frontiers. On the other hand, in spite of continuous efforts by the Embassy, we could not succeed in general in stopping harmful publicity in the local press, especially in the east. Of concern here are the publication of maps and other items sponsored by such organizations as the B.D.O. and V.D.A.,[9] demonstrations at the frontiers, etc. The results achieved in this sector are rather modest. Therefore, an even greater need exists to find ways and means to render this action as harmless as possible.

The resolutions of the present Polish-German protocol may sometimes be an insufficient basis for intervention. Of course, the Embassy is trying to extend the application of press protocols even to such fields as activities by the V.D.A. and B.D.O., although par. 2, section III, of the protocol gives little formal basis for this.

Closing these general remarks, I present below a synthesis of particular sections of German propaganda, asking that you give your careful attention to the following items:

## *I. Press*

The popular political press is generally taking a correct attitude. Only one case of a serious deviation could be noted (the *Frankfurter Zeitung* on the occasion of the Danzig conflict). In the provincial press, especially the East Prussian press, the frontier press, and the Silesian press, anti-Polish notices and articles are still being printed.

Commenting very broadly on par. 9, section I, of the protocol, the Embassy protests the use of terms such as *Korridor* and even *abgetretene* (ceded) and/or *abgetrennte* (separated) *Gebiete*. The Embassy succeeded in obtaining some positive results here. *Der Gesellige* at Piła, a daily well known for its anti-Polish campaigns, recently began to use the term *Pomerellen* (No. 235 of October 8, 1935). Also, the Deutsches Nachrichtenbüro ceased to use the term *Korridor*.

An explicit definition of the Ministry's demands with regard to the use of the above-mentioned terms by German propaganda would greatly contribute to a further exploitation of the press protocol to our advantage. As for the terms *geraubte* or *entrissene Gebiete,* these are undoubtedly in contradiction with the contents of the press protocol. However, the same cannot irrefutably be deduced as far as such expressions as *Korridor, abgetrennte,* or *abgetretene Gebiete* are concerned.

[9] B.D.O.: Bund Deutscher Osten. V.D.A.: Volskbund für das Deutschtum in Ausland.

The number of press interventions initiated by us is therefore the result of a very broad interpretation of the protocol.

## II. Books, Pamphlets, and Periodicals

In the course of the last year several books were published with anti-Polish tendencies, such as *Volk ohne Heimat,* by Christoph Kaergel; *Volk an der Grenze,* by Rudolf Fitzek; and *Annaberg,* by Kurt Eggers.

As the result of very scrupulously kept records at the Embassy, and based also on collaboration with the consulates, the number of interventions on this matter at the Press Department of the Ministry of Foreign Affairs reached the figure of 131. It would be useful if the press conference could determine more precisely the technique to be employed, as a guarantee of fuller consideration of our claims.

## III. Schoolbooks

Obtaining changes in anti-Polish passages can only take place through a resolution passed by a mixed commission called on the basis of the press protocol. This is due to the fact that the Ministry of Education is the competent authority. Neither prompt nor sufficient results may be obtained simply by bringing to the knowledge of the German side questionable passages or books.

## IV. Meetings, Demonstrations, Excursions to the Borderland

Centers dealing with problems in the east, particularly pertaining to Poland, are the V.D.A. and B.D.O., with affiliated organizations such as the Bund Heimattreuer Oberschlesier, Westpreussen, Thorner, Posener, etc. The whole complex of activities of these organizations is subject to control by the staff of the Führer's deputy, Reich Minister Hess. The Embassy is trying to deal with these activities within the frame of the press protocol, in the face of a determined stand by the German side and the very vague formulation of par. 2, section III, of the Warsaw protocol.

A check on V.D.A. and B.D.O. activities might be achieved by way of further special negotiations and utilization of the material accumulated by the Embassy.

## V. Maps

Par. 1, section III, of the protocol regulates the question of maps with revisionist tendencies. The German side continues further to violate these resolutions, but recently, especially on official occasions (as, for example, the Reichsautobahnen propaganda map displayed abroad), the resolutions of the protocol have been observed in various instances.

### VI. Films, Theater, Radio

In this sector anti-Polish propaganda cases are quite exceptional, and the *status quo* might be considered satisfactory.

### VII. Monuments

The removal of monuments in existence for several years that were erected in connection with the loss of Polish territories by Germany should be the subject of special discussions at a Polish-German press conference, and if possible at the earliest opportunity. The press protocol, as I have already pointed out, still has many gaps, and efforts should be made to fill them in at future conferences. Hitherto, these conferences proved in practice to be of assistance in promoting some of our basic claims. Of course, the German side will not fail to display a whole arsenal of claims, directed mainly against our daily press. It is difficult to control our local press, while in Germany the local press is subject to absolute censorship by the government. When I compare the scope of anti-Polish action in Germany with anti-German tendencies in Poland I come to the conclusion that spontaneous rather than organized impulses may be noted in the press columns in Poland. On the other hand, where organizations exist subject to control by governmental censorship, principles of the agreement are observed. In Germany under the present regime there is no room for spontaneous reactions. The popular press observes the rules of the agreement, while the organizations whose goal it is to propagate revisionist ideas continue their task. They do this, however, with less impetus and without broad external propaganda effects. It should be added that, as far as the local press is concerned, it often commits sins against the agreement, particularly in the eastern region bordering Poland.

When the Ministry takes up the preparation of material for the press conference, I would appreciate it if the press desk officer of the Embassy would be summoned to Warsaw.

*Józef Lipski*

DOCUMENT 52   Lipski to Beck

NO. 51/62/35                                   Berlin, November 30, 1935
                                              *Confidential*

As I informed you in my telegram of November 25, I asked for an audience with Minister von Neurath to take place on November 28, immediately after his return from a short vacation, in order to receive a final reply with regard to railway refunds. I put the Auswärtiges Amt on notice that, since I was not in a position to wait any longer, I would place my inquiry very explicitly and precisely.

I still tried to influence the Chancellor indirectly. Specifically, I instigated a direct report to the Chancellor by General von Massow, a member of the S.S. with whom I am personally well acquainted. In his report the General referred to his conversation with me on the situation arising in connection with nonpayment by Germany of arrears in railway payments. As a result of this step, on November 28, I received a telephone call from the president of the Prussian Council of Ministers, Göring, whom I once more pressured strongly on this matter. I obtained a promise that he would take further steps in this respect.

I called on Herr von Neurath today at 11 A.M. Herr von Neurath declared to me that unfortunately he is not in a position to give me a positive answer. Efforts made by him to bring about the refund of these arrears have so far been unsuccessful, in the face of Schacht's declaration about a complete lack of foreign currency. Herr von Neurath seemed to me to be embarrassed, and he emphasized, from the point of view of his department, how awkward this matter is for him. The Chancellor, in his opinion, is well aware of this.

I answered Herr Neurath that the only thing I could do now was to report this negative stand to the Polish government. I remarked that on Wednesday of this week the Council of Ministers was to debate on the question of refunds. At your request this subject was postponed, awaiting the reply of the German government scheduled for the week-end. I pointed to serious complications caused to the Polish government by the nonpayment of such a considerable sum, and mentioned the heavy burdens laid on the population in order to balance the budget. I made allusion to the fact that the shortage of such an amount in foreign currency compels the Polish government to seek security elsewhere.

Finally, I said that I must warn Herr von Neurath that the Polish government will undoubtedly be obliged to undertake preventive measures.

Herr von Neurath replied that this is significant and that he understands the necessity. He added that, when the situation reaches a crucial point, the possibility of a concrete solution might arise. He also added that he personally is persisting in his efforts, but he hinted that his proposals up to now have been rejected by Schacht. At a convenient moment he plans to take the next step.[10]

From my conversation with Herr von Neurath today I concluded that, considering the opposition of Schacht, who is using the excuse of a shortage of foreign currency, the Reich Minister of Foreign Affairs has failed to enforce the solution for repayment of railway arrears in our favor. It is quite clear to me that in this situation it might even be convenient for von Neurath to have us undertake steps which would compel Schacht to change his point of view. That is why he so frankly stated to me that his endeavors had failed, and why he did not try to maintain the present situation, which he also considers untenable.

For my part, I did not make any further suggestions, in order to leave us a free hand in negotiations.

While I was dictating this report I received your instructions to be in Warsaw on December 2. I am therefore withholding further conclusions that I intended to suggest when I sent Counselor Lubomirski to Warsaw in connection with tactics to be applied.

I shall present these conclusions to you personally.

*Józef Lipski*

DOCUMENT 53   Lipski to Beck

NO. 1/90/35                                        Berlin, November 30, 1935
                                                        *Confidential*

In the course of today's conversation with Minister von Neurath regarding railway refunds, we also took up several matters of general policy.

In connection with the latest conversation of French Ambassador François-Poncet with Chancellor Hitler, Herr von Neurath said that this

---

[10] For the German version of this conversation, see *DGFP*, Series C, Vol. IV, No. 436. See also *Diariusz*, I, 412, 413, 416, 423–25.

meeting produced no practical results.[11] The French Ambassador raised several points. With regard to the Soviet-French pact, M. François-Poncet supports the thesis of its conformity with prevailing international obligations. He was anxious that the German government should withdraw its reservations and, as Herr von Neurath put it, give the pact its "blessing." However, the Chancellor, although he expressed confidence in Laval's peace policy, did not satisfy the above-mentioned wish of the Ambassador.

Subsequently the French Ambassador suggested that the German government should make a declaration that it has no aggressive intentions toward Soviet Russia. In reply, the Chancellor stressed that in the first place Germany has no common frontier with Russia. He jokingly observed that he would have to embark on a sort of "Argonauts' expedition." He further pointed to declarations he had already made many times. Von Neurath thinks that the French government is anxious to obtain such a declaration in connection with presentation to the French Chamber of the ratification of the Franco-Soviet agreement.

Finally, the French Ambassador asked whether the German government is still in favor of reduction of armaments and the conclusion of the air convention. Declaring his readiness in principle, the Chancellor considered the present moment to be rather untimely for such negotiations, owing to the general political situation and frantic rearmament by the countries concerned. On the other hand, he reiterated his statements made in the May speech [on May 21, 1935] with regard to restrictions of a number of means of waging war.

The communiqué which appeared after the conversation was published at the request of the French side. Its editing was not easy, since none of the concrete points raised by the French side met with a solution.

Von Neurath gave me to understand that he had the impression that the French initiative for the conversation was dictated by tactical reasons with regard to the British government. Von Neurath then deliberated on the internal political situation in France and on the chances of Laval's government remaining in power. He thinks that the fact of the approaching elections is playing into the hands of the Prime Minister, since no other statesman would venture to seek power under such circumstances.

[11] This conversation took place on November 21. After the conversation, on the same day, identical official communiqués appeared in the Paris and Berlin press, giving special importance to these talks.

In accordance with your telegram of November 27, I asked von Neurath about his opinion regarding England's relations with the Soviets in connection with the developments in the Far East. I said that you are taking an interest in this point. Herr von Neurath, also showing great interest in this question, told me that up to now the German government has not been informed of any actual political, or even financial, agreement between the British and Soviet governments. Von Neurath thinks it is too early for that. Nevertheless, the thesis of the German Foreign Affairs Minister is that the British government has a method of far-reaching calculations. Therefore, upon the liquidation of the Mediterranean problem, it will necessarily have to make a shift to Far Eastern problems. Besides, the situation developing there constitutes a serious threat for British interests. That is why the British government is already paying a good deal of attention to the countries which in a future showdown might become considerable trump cards in its hands. Russia, in his opinion, might be one of these countries. Herr von Neurath has already been struck by the fact that during Mr. Eden's trip to Moscow the British government suddenly began to proclaim a theory that Russia is not a danger from the point of view of Bolshevism. This, in Herr von Neurath's opinion, is a very characteristic symptom of the psychology of British policy. At the moment that a distant possibility appeared of a need for the Russian trump card, the hitherto proclaimed slogan of Bolshevik danger was brushed aside.

Von Neurath is watching this problem, as I have already pointed out, from a further and broader perspective; nevertheless, he thinks this matter should be closely followed. Herr von Neurath also feels that the strong position taken by the British government in the Mediterranean question—specifically, keeping full freedom of transit in its hands—is a symptom which can also be explained in connection with the future contest in the Far East. Von Neurath thinks that Great Britain will now liquidate Italy's action. He is pessimistic as to Mussolini's situation. If Great Britain succeeds in enforcing sanctions on oil, the power of Italy's national defense will be undermined. Besides, in von Neurath's opinion, the Italians, after their first easy successes on the territory of Abyssinia, are now encountering real opposition. Ending the conversation on this point, von Neurath said that in his opinion the only narrow escape for Mussolini in case he realizes his defeat, although a very risky one, is to address his nation with a declaration that the Great Powers stood in the way of the realization of the Italian program. In short, to shift all responsibility onto the Great Powers at the right time. Of course, von Neurath sees an ominous danger in such a step from the internal point of view of the Italians.

*Józef Lipski*

DOCUMENT 54   Lipski to Potocki

NO. N/51/66/35                                    Berlin, December 14, 1935
                                                  *Confidential*

Upon my return from Warsaw, in accordance with instructions received from Minister Beck,[12] I advised the Auswärtiges Amt on the 7th inst. through the intermediary of the Commercial Counselor that Herr Neurath's reply, which contained no counterproposition of any sort, will make a very bad impression in Warsaw. The Commercial Counselor also informed him that the question is now being discussed in Warsaw of putting into effect the disposition to collect dues for railway transit at the frontier. A copy of the memorandum on this conversation is enclosed.[13]

On the same day, during a dinner at the Embassy, I had a conversation about railway refunds with a member of the cabinet, Minister Frank, who, as is known, is the legal adviser of the Party and the government. I have close and friendly relations with Herr Frank. He told me confidentially that Schacht approached him with a request that he investigate the legal aspect of this problem. Frank was of the opinion that Poland's right to claim refunds is indisputable, despite the fact that this might cause a considerable burden for German finances. Herr Frank added that from his conversation with Schacht he had the impression that the latter considers Poland's currency position strong enough to meet a period of nonpayment.

In reply I pointed out how wrong Herr Schacht was in his calculations on this, stressing the burdens the Polish government has had to impose on the population in order to balance the budget and maintain the currency. Finally, discussing a possible way out of the situation, I sug-

[12] See *Diariusz,* I, 428, 432, 437–46.
[13] Enclosure missing.

gested that the German government pay a certain considerable sum and find a practical solution for the balance.

In principle, Herr Frank thought this suggestion was acceptable. For his part, simply as a suggestion, he cited the sum of 10 million reichsmarks for immediate refund. Obviously concerned over the refund for arrears, Herr Frank promised me personally to exert strong pressure and to discuss the problem with the Chancellor.

During the hunting party at Springe on the 9th inst., I had the opportunity to discuss this subject with Herr von Neurath. I told him that, according to information in my possession, Reich Minister Schacht is not quite aware of the difficulties the nonpayment of amounts due for railway transports is causing to our finances. Neurath was quick to answer that he gave Schacht adequate information. As a result, I agreed with Neurath that the German government should make a counteroffer, and I pressed for immediate payment of a certain sum.

On December 12 Counselor Lubomirski discussed this problem with the chief of the Polish Desk, Herr von Lieres. The latter was already in possession of Moltke's report on his conversation with you.[14] Lieres said that Moltke called his attention to the fact that the situation is serious, with the refund of amounts due still being dragged out. Herr von Lieres once more referred to measures taken on this matter by the A.A. These efforts have up to now been to no avail in the face of Schacht's declaration that he has no foreign currency (Schacht used the expression that he is *ganz nackt*). At present the Auswärtiges Amt is working on the plan of a counterproposition to be presented to us before the holidays. The Commercial Counselor was also informed accordingly.

As far as I could observe the attitude of all competent elements regarding this problem, a certain confusion and desire to make up for the bad impression can be noted. Reich Minister Frank took the longest stride in this direction when he declared to me outright that the situation as it stands today is *untragbar* from the point of view of the prestige of the Reich. Nevertheless, as I am being informed from all quarters, the foreign currency situation has deteriorated seriously, and endeavors to obtain a loan ended in a fiasco. Official *démentis* published to this effect are but a further confirmation that endeavors were undertaken.

In my opinion, it would be advisable to undertake concrete planning on our side as to how we could possibly use finances frozen in the Reich.

14 See *DGFP*, Series C, Vol. IV, No. 455.

We could, for instance, buy up certain industries in Silesia, such as Wspólnota Interesów [Interessen Gemeinschaft], Pless, etc.; or make some purchases in Germany, for which amounts are earmarked in the budget of the Polish state; or, finally, investigate deals with the Russian triangle, a tobacco loan, etc.

*Józef Lipski*

DOCUMENT 55    Lipski to Beck

NO. N/128/86/35                    Berlin, December 16, 1935
                                   *Strictly Confidential*

Today I was received by Reich Foreign Affairs Minister von Neurath at his request. Herr von Neurath opened the conversation by stating that he would like to inform me about the conversation which took place on the 9th inst. between the Chancellor and the British Ambassador.[15] Chancellor Hitler would like to see me on Wednesday, at 12:45 P.M., to renew our contact after a long interval. In the course of this audience he will probably give me more detailed information about the above-mentioned conversation. Herr von Neurath therefore limited himself to a brief outline of its essential points.

I stressed that I was grateful for today's reception in connection with your stop in Berlin this evening on your way from Geneva.

In a brief résumé of the Chancellor's conversation with the British Ambassador, Herr von Neurath said that Sir Eric Phipps asked whether the German government still intends to conclude an air pact with the Locarno states, as well as a disarmament agreement. The Chancellor said that he is positively disposed toward the concept of an air pact and the idea of disarmament. Nevertheless, with regard to armaments, the Chancellor's opinion is that time should not be wasted in general vague discussions. He formulated his claims for concrete restrictions of a certain category of weapons in his speech of May 21.

The British Ambassador further inquired whether the German government would be prepared to enter into an air convention with the Locarno states if some of them were linked by special agreements of the

_____
[15] For Neurath's version of this conversation, see *ibid.*, No. 462.

same category. Questioned by the German side as to the meaning of such special agreements, the British Ambassador explained that in this case the creation of bases for the Royal Air Force on the territory of France and Belgium should be taken into consideration. The British Ambassador cited as the motivation for this necessity the distance separating England from the European operational base under the obligations of the Locarno agreements. To the question by the German side, which, I understand, was made ironically, that is, whether the British government would consider it necessary, owing to its Locarno obligations, to establish similar air bases on the territory of the Reich, the British Ambassador answered that such a necessity would not arise owing to the fact that, in case England's guarantee under the Locarno obligations would have to turn against France, the distance from the operational territory would be much shorter from the point of view of the Air Force.

With reference to the above question of Sir Eric Phipps as to whether the German government would agree to an air convention in case it were supplemented by separate agreements of the Locarno signatories, the Chancellor took an absolutely negative stand. He further added that, in case Great Britain engaged in building operational air bases on the territory of Belgium and France, the German government would be compelled consequently to move its operational air force bases westward. Herr von Neurath explained this to me as a cancellation of resolutions pertaining to the demilitarized zone. Besides, the Reich Chancellor declared to the British Ambassador that the concept of such bilateral agreements serving as an instrument for coordination of air forces with the Locarno states in the West should also be applied to the Franco-Russian alliance, in case it becomes a reality; for the German government in its evaluation of the question of armaments restrictions of air forces by means of a pact with Locarno signatories must give a lot of thought to the fact that Soviet air force bases were built on the territory of Czechoslovakia as a result of the Soviet-Czech agreement. The British Ambassador allegedly rejoined by referring to the German government's agreement expressed in Stresa. He received the answer that the Franco-Soviet agreement, which is undermining the Locarno principles, in the opinion of the German government, brought about a change in the situation. Deliberating at length on this subject, the Chancellor allegedly told Phipps that if, for instance, the Soviets attacked Poland, the German government could not remain passive. In that case France, under its agreement with the Soviets, would have to come out against Germany.

At first no communiqué was supposed to be issued on this conversation with Phipps. Herr von Neurath observed that in his opinion it would serve no purpose to issue a communiqué after each conference of an ambassador with the chief of the government, and that my conversation of Wednesday would not be communicated to the press. After the Chancellor's conversation with Phipps, the English press started to disseminate information, so that it became imperative to issue a communiqué. This communiqué appeared in a form similar to that published after the conversation of François-Poncet with the Chancellor.

To my inquiry as to whether Sir Eric Phipps had brought up the question of the Eastern Pact, Herr von Neurath replied that he had not. He added that, bearing in mind the Chancellor's point of view with regard to the Franco-Soviet agreement in connection with the air convention, the question of the Eastern Pact is probably buried for good; it already displayed very few signs of life.

I subsequently asked Herr von Neurath what had impelled the British Ambassador to approach the Chancellor at this particular moment. Herr von Neurath replied that he had also given some thought to this question and that, in his opinion, it was a sort of maneuver in connection with the previous conversation with Poncet.

I then directed the conversation toward the latest developments in the Abyssinian conflict. Neurath did not conceal his critical attitude with regard to the agreement between England and France.[16] He thought this lent a flavor of melodrama to the whole problem, administering a fatal blow to the prestige of the League. He is seeking an explanation for this unexpected change in Great Britain's position. He thinks that this might have been brought about by Laval's declaration that the French

[16] Prime Minister Laval reached an understanding with Great Britain's foreign secretary, Samuel Hoare, on December 8, 1935, regarding Abyssinia. Upon approval by the British government on December 13, this agreement was presented in the form of a note to the Italian government. The Anglo-French plan recommended that the Abyssinian government agree to cede to Italy a portion of its country, rectify the frontier, and create in South Abyssinia a zone for economic expansion and immigration for Italy. This plan met with violent reaction in England as being contradictory to the pact of the League of Nations and the concept of justice. It was the cause of Hoare's resignation on December 18. Prime Minister Baldwin declared on December 19 in the House of Commons that the government considered the Laval-Hoare pact nonexistent, and on December 22 the portfolio of foreign affairs passed to Anthony Eden.

government would not condone oil sanctions. This shifted the whole burden to the government of Great Britain, with all the ensuing consequences.

It might be considered a fact not without its amusing side that the recent developments in the Abyssinian situation have been exploited by local public opinion to express taunts on the subject of the blow that the Great Powers dealt to the high ideals of the League of Nations. Of course, the settlement of the conflict by means of an agreement between the Powers would deprive the German government of the very convenient situation it is presently enjoying in the midst of international turmoil.

*Józef Lipski*

DOCUMENT 56   Lipski to Beck

NO. N/52/11/35                                   Berlin, December 18, 1935
                                                 *Strictly Confidential*

Following my report of December 16, N/128/86/35, I am taking the liberty of communicating to you that I was received today at 12:45 P.M. by Chancellor Hitler. The conversation lasted for over an hour.

The Chancellor started with a statement that, in view of developments in the political situation and in particular his conversations with the ambassadors of France and England which were so widely commented on in the press, he would like to have an informative talk with me. He observed that the press greatly exaggerated the real meaning of these conversations. Analyzing the purpose of the interventions of both ambassadors, the Chancellor thinks they were undertaken for reasons of diversion.

The Chancellor then gave a general outline of his conversations with the two ambassadors. His deductions are in accordance with what I related after my conversations with Neurath in my reports of November 30, No. N/1/90/35, and December 16, No. N/128/86/35. I am therefore limiting myself to communicating only the more important parts of these conversations, or those that Herr von Neurath did not mention to me.

Referring to his conversation with François-Poncet, the Chancellor remarked that the French Ambassador was anxious to push to the forefront the question of Laval's meeting with him. However, at the Chancellor's request, Neurath advised the Ambassador to drop this suggestion. In this connection the Ambassador confided to me that it is obvious that in the prevailing situation a meeting with Laval is out of the question. Under the present circumstances the Chancellor cannot meet with Mussolini, for example. The German government is taking a purely neutral stand toward the Abyssinian conflict. However, the Chancellor is rather anxious to maintain good relations with Great Britain, with whom he signed a sea pact. On the other hand, in spite of the unfriendly attitude of the Italian side, the Chancellor considers Mussolini and the Fascist regime positive elements. The Chancellor explained the anti-German attitude taken by the Italian government at the Stresa Conference as an effort to cajole the Great Powers in connection with the already planned action in Abyssinia. According to the Chancellor's words, the German government has no interest whatsoever in taking the part of one side or the other but wishes to remain totally aloof from the conflict. That is why it rejected the British suggestion that it participate in sanctions, as well as their demand to introduce certificates of origin. As far as coal supplies for Italy are concerned, the German government must consider the economic situation of the mines, where each ton of exported coal contributes to the reduction of unemployment. Germany has no intention of drawing any special profit from the present conflict. Export of arms to the belligerent countries was stopped in advance. The French, as the Chancellor put it, replied to this that Germany was not even in a position to supply arms, since it needs them for its own armaments. However, this is a misleading argument, for these small-scale orders could be executed. After all, the Chancellor continued, it is evident that any war industry, in order to maintain itself, has to export. That is why the German war industry is also exporting. If it is assumed that Germany, because of its withdrawal from the League of Nations, is drawing a profit from the present conflict, the Chancellor's reply is that he walked out of the League for quite different reasons than the Abyssinian question, which at that time was still unknown. He also ordered conscription without any knowledge of the oncoming conflict. To make a long story short, all his undertakings had nothing to do with the present development of the Abyssinian question. Certainly, the Chancellor draws some satisfaction from the fact that he is not obliged to sit in Geneva at this moment. As an illustration he noted that quite recently the English pressed him on the problem of sanctions, requesting the introduction of certificates of origin. Today, quite unexpectedly, they made a *volte-face*.

In the ensuing discussion on this subject I said, following your instructions, that we would describe our attitude toward the present situation as follows:

We are not tied to any special doctrine in relation to the League of Nations, that is, with regard to the limits of its competence in general or pertaining to certain regions. However, we deem it to be unquestioned that we are faced with *faits accomplis* enforced on us by certain rules passed in the course of events. I added that this, of course, has nothing to do with our relations with Italy, which are known to be friendly. On this occasion I also mentioned the efforts undertaken by you within the frame of the Committee of Five.

The Chancellor replied that he certainly understands our point of view, which lies beyond the sphere of our relations with Italy and pertains to certain methods of action of the Powers.

The Chancellor remarked in passing on the subject of the League that he sees from today's news that a plan is now being launched, possibly aimed also against Poland, to create a directorate of Four Powers in the League, including Germany. The Chancellor emphatically declared that he has not the slightest intention of entering such a combination.

Deliberating further on his conversation with François-Poncet, the Chancellor remarked that, in order to reinforce Laval, the Ambassador was eager to obtain the blessing of the German government for the Franco-Russian pact. The Chancellor called one of his previous conversations with the French Ambassador (already known to you) when the latter begged that Laval be saved at the cost of the Eastern Pact. The Chancellor then asked the Ambassador how long Laval might remain in power, to which he got the reply that it might be until the fall. The Chancellor then pointed out to the Ambassador that he deemed it impossible to bind his country to a harmful pact in order to prolong the life of a French prime minister by a few months. It was clear from the Chancellor's words that in the course of the last conversation François-Poncet used a similar argument, for Hitler reiterated that in spite of his esteem for Laval he could not jeopardize his vital interests. For this reason he denied the French Ambassador his consent for the Franco-Russian pact, motivating his refusal, first of all, on the fact that the definition of the aggressor remains in the hands of the countries involved. He illustrated this by the fact that in the Oual Oual case the aggressor is still not defined.[17]

With regard to the French Ambassador's wish that the Chancellor make a declaration that the German government has no aggressive intentions toward Russia, the Chancellor in the first place allegedly pointed out that he has no common frontier with Russia. On the other hand, he is not inclined to engage in erratic adventures.

From the conversation with the British Ambassador the following passages are worth commenting upon:

The Chancellor first of all told me that he was surprised that the British Ambassador did not utter a single word, as would quite naturally be expected, about Great Britain's *volte-face* on the Abyssinian problem.

With regard to the British Ambassador's question as to whether the German government is positively disposed to the idea of the air pact and the disarmament problem, the Chancellor's reply was affirmative. He cited a series of arguments in support of this, such as heavy expenses resulting from excessive armaments, etc. On the other hand, the Chancellor criticized the British Ambassador's idea of the application of bilateral agreements within the frame of the air pact. This point was analyzed by the Chancellor in more detail than in my conversation with Herr von Neurath. Specifically, Sir Eric Phipps allegedly suggested an air pact mentioning England, France, and Germany. Other states, it seems, were not mentioned by the Ambassador. But he ventured to suggest an idea that within the frame of this pact special air agreements could be included, such as, for example, French-English and French-Soviet. The Chancellor assumed that with such a concept the general pact would be just a purely formal act. On the other hand, only special pacts would be in force. In practice this could mean Germany's authorization for Soviet air bases in Czechoslovakia or Lithuania, for example. On this occasion the Chancellor said—and this is very significant—that for him Czechoslovakia is the great unknown, if only because of its internal political situation. For instance, he fears that Czechoslovakia may adopt the form of so-called National Communism.

---

[17] On December 5, 1934, there occured an encounter near Oual Oual on the Abyssinian-Italian Somaliland frontier. The Abyssinian government maintained that Somalis under the command of Italian officers were the aggressors. The Italians claimed that their troops were attacked by the Abyssinian Army which penetrated into Somaliland territory. The problem was never cleared up.

Hitler allegedly told Phipps that he cannot understand the French policy, which binds itself with Soviet Russia. But France is certainly safeguarded by England, and *besides it has a "Ruckversicherungsvertrag" with Poland.*

I consider this declaration of the Chancellor to be very significant.

In his further deliberations the Chancellor stated that he is firmly opposed to drawing Russia westward. As a National Socialist, he sees an ominous danger in Bolshevism. No matter how other states consider this problem, Germany would pay for the rapprochement with Soviet Russia with a social revolution. He is afraid that other countries would also pay for it heavily. He is for European solidarity, but such solidarity ends at the Polish-Soviet frontier. The air pact should have a more general scope, but only those countries should be admitted which are bound by the same principles of international policy. How is it possible to bind oneself to Soviet Russia, which preaches a world revolution?

Finally, the Chancellor also added that his answer to the British Ambassador's question whether nonactivation of the French-Soviet agreement would not change the situation was affirmative.

The above deliberations of the Chancellor could be viewed as general political considerations. I thought it also desirable in this connection to spell out to him certain points of ours.

I said in the first place that I would like to confirm my previous declaration made to the Chancellor that we are dealing with France irrespective of French-Soviet relations. I added that M. Laval was well informed by you about our stand in this matter. I confirmed that we shall not let ourselves become entangled in any deals. Following your instructions, I mentioned your conversation with Hoare during the last session in Geneva. In this conversation, in connection with a reference made by the British Minister to Franco-German relations, you remarked —in the form of a personal opinion—that France's Russian policy is a handicap for these relations. I mentioned in passing that some influences from Russia often cause a certain amount of nuisance for us.

Subsequently, passing to direct Polish-German relations, I remarked that it had not surprised us when, after the first change in the Polish government following the death of Marshal Piłsudski, a number of international elements spread various rumors with regard to a change in our foreign policy line. I stated that Poland's foreign policy, as outlined by Marshal Piłsudski, is primarily an independent Polish policy based exclusively on our interests. Therefore, all competent circles in Poland will follow this policy line. I added that it is quite understandable that opposition to good Polish-German relations exists in many international quarters. The campaigns opposing our rapprochement serve as a proof of this. But in order to avoid feeding this alien propaganda, we should immediately remove any possible friction from our relations. I said that in my estimation the last year had contributed to a successful development in our relations in the general political field, and that positive results had been achieved in cultural and social contacts.

The Chancellor approved this statement with satisfaction and remarked that, of course, a few years are needed to reach a broader *détente*.

Referring to the necessity of avoiding all possible difficulties, I stressed to the Chancellor that I had a question causing us considerable trouble and concern in the financial field.

Neurath, addressing the Chancellor on his own initiative, said that this concerned railway refunds.

The Chancellor replied that he had already heard about this matter and that, in his opinion, its settlement is indispensable. He will use his influence on Schacht.

I took advantage of this occasion to inform the Chancellor of our financial measures striving to balance the budget and stabilize the currency. I explained to him, well aware that such arguments impress him, the patriotic zeal displayed by the officials and the population in accepting the burdens imposed. However, I observed that under these circumstances the Ministry of Railways cannot be exposed to a permanent deficit from arrears for dues for transit.

The Chancellor asked if a portion could not be compensated by goods. Before I could reply, Neurath explained why this would not accommodate Poland, and the Chancellor understood. On the other hand, Neurath, stressing the necessity of presenting a counterproposition to the Polish government, remarked that a certain portion could be covered by the Soviet triangle, or some other deal, as, for example, Italian, etc. It was agreed that the Chancellor would speak with Schacht.

Subsequently we touched slightly on Rumanian and Baltic questions. Following your instructions I mentioned on the subject of Rumania that some reaction by public opinion could be observed against the excessive pro-Soviet tendencies of Mr. Titulescu. Neurath said that he had heard similar rumors and had received reassuring information a few days ago.

With regard to the Baltic states we also agreed that the problem has abated to a certain extent, and the Chancellor added that relations with Lithuania have also improved a little. He said that the problem of Kłajpeda [Memel], which is of secondary importance as a matter of fact, was to some extent embarrassing, evoking constant tension in German public opinion. But it was awkward for him to stop the press from commenting on persecutions of Germans at Kłajpeda.

At the close of the conversation, the Chancellor suddenly addressed this question to me: "Tell me, why did the British government retreat in the Abyssinian problem?" I replied that, according to information from London, the British Admiralty had certain misgivings as to the advisability of maintaining a concentration of the British fleet in the Mediterranean. Neurath interjected that he had similar information. I also thought that the situation in Egypt and the events in the Far East all compelled Great Britain to cut short the Abyssinian conflict. And finally I added that I had heard from Paris that Hoare allegedly surrendered to Laval.

Taking leave of the Chancellor, I extended New Year's wishes to him and thanked him for his support, which had facilitated me to carry out my mission during this year.

The Chancellor replied very warmly to the greetings, thanking me and my predecessor for such loyal cooperation with him.[18]

I dictated this report in a great hurry owing to the departure of the courier. In summary, I would like to call your attention to the following more important declarations of the Chancellor:

1) His assumption that the Polish-French agreement constitutes a safeguarding element for France. Together with our statement that Poland's relations with France are dealt with by us independently of French-Russian relations, it might be considered to a certain degree an acceptance by the German government of the French-Polish agreement as a *Rückversicherungsvertrag,* for France and for us, without encumbrances to our relations with Germany.

2) The emphatic declaration of the Chancellor that he will not go in for any deals such as the Four-Power Pact or a reorganization of the League of Nations.

3) Clarification at the very source that the problem of railway ar-

[18] For the German version of this conversation, see *DGFP,* Series C, Vol. IV, No. 470. A very condensed text is in the *Polish White Book,* No. 21.

rears is not viewed by the Chancellor from the political angle but simply as a financial difficulty, which does not take for granted what is going through Herr Schacht's head on this matter.

*Józef Lipski*

The problem of frozen German refunds for transit through Pomerania became considerably complicated at the beginning of 1936.

In Lipski's papers there is a handwritten notice on this matter:

In the first months of 1936 the problem of frozen railway arrears took a very sharp turn, threatening an open Polish-German conflict. On the Polish side the strongest pressure was exerted by the Bank Polski and the Ministry of Finance purely from a currency angle. Through my interventions (conversation with the Chancellor on December 18, 1935, and also with von Neurath),[19] my conversation with Schacht took place on February 15.[20] Schacht clearly gave me to understand that he was ready to liquidate the frozen amount, paying a certain portion in foreign currency and liquidating the balance by way of credits for goods or advancing the amounts due to the German side for the Polish government's take-over of German industrial companies in Upper Silesia (Wspólnota Interesów—Interessen Gemeinschaft).

As a result of this positive conversation with Schacht, I was to continue further conversation with him. However, I contracted a severe cold, and in consequence Warsaw was approached with a proposition to delegate someone else for these conversations. Mieczysław Sokołowski, vice-minister of the Ministry of Industry and Commerce, was appointed and arrived in Berlin. On the eve of the Rhineland occupation on March 6, 1936, Schacht took an absolutely intransigent stand as to payment of a portion of the refund in foreign currency, causing a breach in negotiations and the departure of Sokołowski. I asked for a meeting

[19] For the Beck-Neurath conversation of January 25, see *DGFP*, Series C, Vol. IV, No. 521; for the Lipski-Bülow conversation of January 30, *ibid.*, No. 528; for the Lipski-Neurath conversation of February 4, *ibid.*, No. 537.

[20] *DGFP*, Series C, Vol. IV, Nos. 551 and 567. It should be noted that on February 7 an order was issued by the Polish Minister of Communication limiting transit through Pomerania owing to arrears of refunds by German railways. Whereupon the German government announced a change in railway communications and the opening of permanent communications by sea between East Prussia and the Reich.

with Neurath for the next day. I received the answer that the Reich Minister asked me to meet instead with Secretary of State von Bülow, since he would be very busy that morning. Bülow received me on March 7, at 11 A.M.[21] At 12 noon the Chancellor was to deliver a speech at the Reichstag and it was presumed that the Rhineland problem would be the subject of the declaration.

On the evening of the 5th I gave a large dinner for Herr Goebbels and his wife. Mrs. Betka Potocka and Alfred [Potocki] were also present. The Germans gave no hint as to the text of the Chancellor's speech, in spite of the fact that all conversations revolved around this subject.

Coming back to my conversation with von Bülow, when I informed him that on the previous day a breach in the negotiations had occurred owing to Schacht's intransigent stand, this very stiff and unfriendly-to-us diplomat displayed an animation rare to him and expressed a desire to iron out the impasse. He promised to contact Schacht immediately and in general gave me the impression of being taken completely aback by this turn of events. His embarrassment was very obvious when I pointed out to him that this nonsettlement of the problem of arrears in railway refunds was forcing us to close the transit through Pomerania to East Prussia. Bülow's attitude became clear to me when, upon closing this point of the conversation, he handed me, at Neurath's request, the text of the declaration with regard to the remilitarization of the Rhineland to be presented by the Chancellor during his speech at the Reichstag at 12 noon. I maintained an absolutely noncommittal attitude; von Bülow emphasized that German detachments would only symbolically occupy the Rhineland.

I told Herr von Bülow when I took leave of him that, owing to pneumonia from which I had just recovered, I would not be present at the Reichstag. Immediately upon my return to the Embassy I telephoned Minister Beck to inform him in brief of the text of the declaration that Hitler would present to the Reichstag, even before the Chancellor's appearance. I wired to Warsaw at once the full text of the declaration handed to me by von Bülow.

Together with Counselor Lubomirski I decided to take advantage of the crisis caused by Hitler's breach of the Locarno Treaty to approach the German side with a proposition favorable for us in the settlement of railway arrears.

[21] *DGFP*, Series C, Vol. V, Nos. 22 and 62.

On the evening of the same day, March 7, Lubomirski met Koerner, Göring's secretary of state, at a dinner, and presented in a very dramatic way the consequences of Schacht's breach of negotiations for Polish-German relations against the background of the international crisis caused by the remilitarization of the Rhineland. He observed considerable nervous tension on the part of his German collocutors and a desire to settle the dispute with us. Consequently Göring took over the problem of the frozen railway arrears. . . .

During those critical days of March I had several long conversations with him. It was quite obvious that, under the threat of a conflict in the Rhineland case, he was anxious to make any sacrifice in order to settle the question of railway arrears to our satisfaction, and thus avoid a conflict on the Polish-German sector. He offered, without bargaining, a sum of several tens of millions of zlotys in foreign currency, with the balance of the debt to be liquidated in goods. The results of this understanding, jointly with an agreement for the future, were fixed under the supervision of Göring, who exerted decisive pressure on the German economic agencies. Technical negotiations finalized by an agreement lasted for some time.

The problem of German refunds for transit through Pomerania was settled on April 7, 1936, by a provisional agreement which was to remain in force to the end of 1936. It was agreed therein that beginning with March 25 current dues were to be paid by the Germans every month by way of a cash transfer amounting to a million and a half reichsmarks in gold. Two commissions were also formed to define the size of transit through Pomerania and the method of liquidation of the arrears. In the latter case the possibility of Germany's taking over refunds of the Polish tobacco loan in Italy was to be considered, as well as readjustment of accounts in connection with Poland's take-over of Wspólnota Interesów (Interessen Gemeinschaft) in Upper Silesia.

The settlement of the problem of refunds for transit through Pomerania took place on August 31 and December 22, 1936. Delegates of the ministries of Communication of Poland and Germany signed an agreement in Berlin for regulation of transit between East Prussia and the rest of the Reich, which was to become binding for 1937.[22]

[22] See *Diariusz,* II, 65, 386–87, 70, 72, 74–75, 79–80, 88–89, 91, 101–2, 105–6, 113–15, 138–41, 143–44, 150–54, 156–57. See also *DGFP,* Series C, Vol. V, Nos. 82, 107, 151, 261, 264, 276, 356, and 491.

# Remilitarization of the Rhineland (March, 1936) and Blomberg's Directive (June, 1937)[1]

IN LIPSKI'S ARCHIVES there are no materials relating to the problem of the remilitarization of the Rhineland. At that time (February–March, 1936) Lipski was seriously ill with pneumonia; this might explain to some extent the lack of his reports. However, he had some contacts with certain persons in the Reich government and the diplomatic corps, as can be seen from his handwritten notes.

Lipski wrote an article about the Rhineland, which is quoted below. Although it relates to General Blomberg's operational directive of June 24, 1937, fully a year after the remilitarization of the Rhineland, it contains a number of interesting details illustrating the events of March, 1936.

It should be mentioned, as far as Blomberg's directive is concerned, that it pertains to the period of time from July 1, 1937, to approximately September 30, 1938. At that time the directive was still not planned as a German offensive action but was limited to defense in the east and west. This directive was changed by Hitler's order dated May 30, 1938: "to smash Czechoslovakia by military action in the near future." [2]

In Lipski's handwritten notes the following remarks may be found relating to the remilitarization of the Rhineland:

A few days prior to the marching of troops into the Rhineland, the Italian ambassador, Signor Bernardo Attolico, paid me a visit. It was an extremely difficult period for Italy because of sanctions imposed for the aggression against Abyssinia. Italy's vital interest was to see Germany engaged in a conflict with Great Britain and France on the Rhineland problem, thus relieving its own front.

Signor Attolico, using veiled language, touched on the Rhineland question, giving me to understand that the Reich now found itself in unexpectedly favorable circumstances to risk a step allowing it to get rid

[1] This article, entitled "Blomberg's Directive of June 24, 1937," was published in *Sprawy Międzynarodowe* (London), 1947, Nos. 2–3.
[2] *DGFP*, Series D, Vol. II, No. 221, enclosure.

of the treaty clauses pertaining to the demilitarization of the Rhineland.

I had the impression from Signor Attolico's words that he was probably in possession of some inside information on Germany's intentions, and that possibly Mussolini's advice might play a certain role in them.

With regard to Göring's opinion on the Rhineland question, Lipski notes the following remarks:

Göring was visibly terrified by the Chancellor's decision to remilitarize the Rhineland, and he did not conceal that it was taken against the Reichswehr's advice. I had several talks with him then. I found him in a state of utmost agitation, and this was just at the time of the start of the London Conference.[3] He openly gave me to understand that Hitler had taken this extremely risky step by his own decision, in contradiction to the position taken by the generals. Göring went so far in his declaration as to say literally that, if France entered upon a war with Germany, the Reich would defend itself to the last man, but that, if Poland joined France, the German situation would be catastrophic. In a broken voice Göring said that he saw many misfortunes befalling the German nation, bereaved mothers and wives.

In the course of these deliberations an aide-de-camp entered with news from London that Germany was to be invited to the London Conference. In his excitement Göring asked for my advice on what to do. I replied that of course I would accept the invitation.[4]

Göring's breakdown during the Rhineland period made me wonder about his psychological stamina. I thought this might be due to his physical condition, since he was using narcotics.

Here begins Lipski's article:

When on June 24, 1937, General Blomberg issued his "Directive for standardizing the preparation of the German armed forces for war," he already had several years of experience and of strenuous efforts to build up Germany's military potential behind him. Hitler cleared his path by his political moves. The declaration of the bill for general conscription, issued on March 16, 1935, contrary to the provisions of the Treaty of Versailles, met with only a formal protest on the part of the Great

[3] The London Conference of the Council of the League of Nations opened on March 14. It was decided to invite Germany to take part in the debates on the Franco-Belgian claim concerning the breach of the Locarno agreements.
[4] *Diariusz*, II, 411–14.

Powers that was agreed to at the Council of the League of Nations with Poland's participation. An understanding between the three Western Powers reached at Stresa,[5] aimed at forming a common front against Hitler's Reich, was a short-lived undertaking. Relations between France, Great Britain, and Italy were rapidly deteriorating because of the Abyssinian conflict. With the British government's rejection of the Hoare-Laval agreement of December, 1935 [6]—the last sheet anchor for keeping Italy on the side of Great Britain and France—the policy of sanctions prevailed, creating broad perspectives for German diplomacy. A rapprochement between Berlin and Rome followed that later took the form of a formal alliance.

Availing himself of this favorable international situation, Hitler decided to take another still more risky step, in spite of strong warnings by the Reichswehr. On March 7, 1936, German detachments marched into the demilitarized zone of the Rhineland. This came as no surprise to Paris, London, and Warsaw, since for a long time some new violent stroke by Hitler threatening the safety of France had been anticipated in connection with Germany's interventions against the Franco-Soviet agreement. From the top French military quarters Warsaw received assurances that the French government would counter by force any attempts to remilitarize the zone.

Shortly before March 7, 1936, upon his return from Paris, M. François-Poncet declared to me that, in case of a breach by Germany of the Rhineland Pact resolutions, France would resort to general mobilization. This would result in an armed conflict: "Ce sera la mobilisation générale, ce sera la guerre." The French Ambassador empowered me to make use of this declaration, which he defined as most authoritative. I immediately advised Warsaw accordingly.

In consequence of reports received as to Hitlerite intentions in the Rhineland, Marshal Śmigły-Rydz delegated a trusted officer of the General Staff to get in touch with our military attaché and investigate the condition of German preparations.

Therefore, it was not a surprise to Minister Beck when, upon receiving from Secretary of State Bülow on the morning of March 7 the text

[5] The understanding reached at Stresa by Italy, France, and Great Britain on April 14, 1935, established their common front against the breach of treaty obligations by Germany.

[6] See p. 240, footnote 16.

of the declaration that Hitler was to present an hour later to the Reichstag, I immediately got in touch with Warsaw by telephone and communicated to the Minister that German troops had begun to occupy the Rhineland.

The Polish government's reaction is known from various diplomatic publications. It was expressed in the immediate declaration of *casus foederis* to the French government.[7] France did not venture independent action, as Poincaré had in 1923.[8] The French government decided to approach Great Britain. The British government, under pressure of pacifist tendencies in British society, pursued a policy of appeasement toward Hitlerite Germany. Under these circumstances, armed action was not taken against Hitler, nor was his offer exploited as a basis for setting up concrete claims.

The prestige of the Western Powers suffered a serious setback in Europe as a result of the Rhineland problem, expecially in such smaller countries as Belgium, Yugoslavia, and Poland.

Other events in the international field also contributed to reinforcing the German situation at that time. In July, 1936, civil war broke out in Spain. This drew Italy closer to Germany. Ciano's trip to the Reich in October of 1936 brought about the signing of a protocol by the Italian

[7] On March 7, 1936, Polish Foreign Affairs Minister Beck summoned the French ambassador in Warsaw, Léon Noël. "I declared to the Ambassador that in view of the information received on the action of the German troops, which in certain circumstances might threaten to become a French-German conflict, I asked him to inform his Government that should it come to any clash under conditions in accordance with the spirit of the alliance, Poland would not hesitate to carry out her obligations as an ally." (Beck, *Final Report*, p. 110.) Noël's version of the same conversation reads: "At the fixed hour I entered the elegant Raczynski Palace . . . . 'This time it is serious,' the Minister said to me. . . . Colonel Beck presently requested me, not without solemnity, to make the following communication to my government on his behalf and in the name of 'high authorities' of the Polish state: Poland is anxious under the circumstances to assure France that she will be true, in case of emergency, to the engagements binding her to your country." (Noël, p. 125.) See Noël's telegram to the French Ministry of Foreign Affairs on the same day, where Beck's declaration was presented in a very camouflaged form (*Documents diplomatiques français, 1932–1939*, 2 Série, Vol. I, No. 303; also Vol. II, No. 214). See also *Diariusz*, II, 110–11, and *DGFP*, Series C, Vol. V, No. 106.

[8] In December, 1922, when Raymond Poincaré was prime minister of France, the Reparations Commission agreed, against the opinion of Great Britain, that Germany was not carrying out delivery of coal and coke provided for in the reparations agreements. At that time Poincaré presented the question of sanctions against Germany, and, contrary to Great Britain's stand, French and British troops occupied the Ruhr basin.

Minister with Neurath and the approval by Germany of the Italian Empire.

News from Soviet Russia about Stalin's purge within top military ranks, including even Marshal Tukhachevsky, was evaluated by governing circles of the Third Reich, and particularly by the Reichswehr, as a serious weakening of possible Soviet war activities.

This explains why General von Blomberg, when he issued his orders, was inclined to draw an optimistic picture of Germany's international position.

"The general political position," wrote Blomberg, "justifies the supposition that Germany need not consider an attack from any side. The chief grounds for this are, in addition to the lack of desire for war in almost all nations, particularly the Western Powers, deficiencies in preparedness for war on the part of a number of states and of Russia in particular.

"Germany has no intention of unleashing a European war. Nevertheless, the politically fluid situation, which does not preclude surprising incidents, demands a continuous preparedness for war by the German armed forces (*a*) to oppose attacks at any time and (*b*) to enable the military *exploitation of politically favorable opportunities should they occur.*" [9]

Blomberg's directive provided for various hypotheses of war entanglements for which concentrated plans had to be drawn.

In general, military orders are drawn to meet various alternatives of action. The starting point, as a rule, is an evaluation of the political situation by authorities in control of the state's defenses. In the Third Reich, Hitler's word was law. From military orders we therefore can guess the general attitude of the dictator of Germany at that time. Blomberg's disposition was rather defensive in character. This was still before the storm. The marching of German troops and occupation were contemplated only in case of the Hapsburgs' restoration.

In regard to the hypothesis of a war on two fronts—with France in the west, and with Russia and perhaps Czechoslovakia in the east—the directive anticipated that Poland would at first remain neutral, or might assume a wait-and-see attitude. Poland's participation in the war on the side of Russia was considered improbable from the very beginning.

[9] *Trial of the Major War Criminals,* Vol. XXXIV, No. C-175. Emphasis added by Lipski.

The Lithuanian attitude was evaluated along the same lines. It was assumed that Lithuania would only take arms against Germany jointly with Poland, or if Soviet armies marched into its territories.

Regardless of this appraisal, the German command also made preparations in case Great Britain, Poland, and Lithuania entered the war at the outbreak of hostilities. Considering such a state of affairs as a calamity from the point of view of Germany's defenses, the leadership assumed that German political leaders would do their utmost to maintain the neutrality of Great Britain and Poland.

# The Battleship *Leipzig* in Danzig and Danzig Problems[1]
## *Summer, 1936*

IN SPITE OF the *détente* in relations between Poland and the Free City which could be noted in the second half of 1933 and following the Polish-German declaration of January 26, 1934, the entire period until the outbreak of the war was marked by continuous incidents in Danzig, often necessitating firm protests lodged by the Polish side in Berlin.

In the summer of 1936 a serious Danzig problem arose in the forum of the League of Nations, this time with the indirect participation of the Reich government. The very roots of the crisis were linked with the struggle of Nazi elements against the Geneva institution, represented in Danzig by Sean Lester, who protested against the *gleichschaltung* of the Free City in the form of liquidation of opposition parties. However, the immediate cause of the conflict was the visit of the battleship *Leipzig* to Danzig on June 25, 1936. In paying an official call, the commander of the *Leipzig* ignored the High Commissioner of the League of Nations. Lester referred the matter to Geneva, claiming a breach of binding agreements. The German side explained the behavior of the commander of the *Leipzig* by the fact that during an earlier visit to Danzig of the battleship *Admiral Scheer* in August, 1935, the commander of that ship had met representatives of the Danzig opposition, vehement adversaries of National Socialism and its Führer, at the reception given by the High Commissioner of the League of Nations, thus creating an embarrassing situation for the representative of the German Navy.

Arthur Greiser, president of the Danzig Senate, was summoned by the Council of the League of Nations on July 4, 1936, to explain the Danzig

1 Published in *Bellona* (London), 1950, No. 1, under the title "Danzig Problems. From the Appearance of Senate President Greiser before the Council of the League of Nations in July, 1936, to Lord Halifax's Visit to Berchtesgaden in November, 1937."

problem. As far as the form and content of his appearance was concerned, it constituted an attack against the Geneva institution unprecedented in the international forum. Finishing his speech, Greiser walked out of the hall, provokingly sticking his tongue out at those present.

This escapade of Greiser caused general consternation. It was interpreted as the intention of the Free City to break relations with the League of Nations by way of *faits accomplis,* and with the Reich's blessing. However, the representatives of the Great Powers sitting on the Council did not manifest a desire for more serious engagements in defense of the statute of the Free City.

Under these critical circumstances, Minister Beck tried to determine to what extent Great Britain's support could be expected in Danzig matters. In a conversation with Minister Eden at the Carlton Hotel, with Tadeusz Gwiazdoski, vice-director of the Political Department of the Polish Foreign Affairs Ministry also present, Beck discussed the possibility of applying measures to prevent further possible action by the Senate and the German government aimed against the authority of the High Commissioner and the League of Nations. With this discussion under way, Beck addressed a question to Eden as to whether the British government would be willing to send a battleship to Danzig under the pretext of a normal visit of the fleet. This step, in Beck's opinion, would be the best measure to display to the German side the importance Great Britain attached to respect for the authority of the League of Nations in the Free City. However, Eden did not think it at all possible to approach his government with such a proposition.[2]

Finally, it was decided in League of Nations circles to entrust Poland with the settlement of this matter. The Council issued a resolution to confer a mandate on the Polish government for clarification of the *Leipzig* incident with the Reich government, as well as to obtain adequate assurances for the future.

On July 5 I received the following instructions by telegram from Minister Beck in Geneva:

[2] Memorandum by Gwiazdoski in Lipski's papers, File 9. The problem of the battleship *Leipzig* is related in more detail by Szembek, *Diariusz,* II, 231, 454-55, 457–72, 241–42, 476–80, and in *DGFP,* Series C, Vol. V, Nos. 419, 429, 430, 434, 435, 436, 437, 438, 443, 458, 467, 472, 473, 476, 524, 557, and 566.

DOCUMENT 57   Beck to Lipski

July 4, 1936

Today's appearance of Danzig Senate President Greiser definitely points to a German attack on the League of Nations. Simultaneously, a wish to respect our rights in Danzig was expressed in his speech. At today's open and secret meetings of the Council of the League of Nations I *still* gained the support of the League of Nations and of the Powers for the *present statute of the Free City.* The ambassadors of Great Britain and France will make a warning *démarche* in Berlin and we are faced with either a disagreement or an understanding with Germany. I shall dispatch additional details. Please obtain an immediate audience with the Chancellor, Göring, or Neurath and declare that in the Polish-German agreement we agreed to consider the problem of the Free City as a measure of our relations.

The visit of the battleship *Leipzig* and the appearance of the President of the Senate at the Council of the League of Nations indicate that Greiser has chosen the method of *faits accomplis* in violation of our agreement that Danzig should not become the object of strife between Poland and Germany. The Polish government is ready to consider the most complicated matters by way of direct discussions, but it would react immediately to any breach of the afore-mentioned agreement.

The statute of the Free City is undoubtedly clumsily formulated; however, it has served hitherto as a basis for Polish-Danzig and Polish-German relations. The breach of this statute must bring on conflict in case a change is not achieved by means of a mutual agreement.

The Polish government deems it possible to deliberate on this matter with Germany prior to the occurrence of events precluding in advance any such contact.

*Beck*

On the same day I had a long conversation with Göring, on which I reported to Minister Beck:

DOCUMENT 58   Lipski to Beck

NO. G/3/26/36            Berlin, July 5, 1936
*Strictly Confidential*

Following your telegraphic instructions dated July 5,[3] I had a conversation with Minister President Göring at 2 P.M. today, in the absence of the Chancellor from Berlin.

As a preamble to the execution of your instructions, I stated that on June 19 in my conversation with Secretary of State Koerner I had already raised the question of incidents in Danzig between the National Socialists and the parties of the opposition. On the next day, that is, on June 20, Herr von Neurath on his own initiative informed me about the attitude of the Chancellor with regard to the recent Danzig incidents and stressed that it was a matter of concern to the German government that the Danzig problem should in no way aggravate Polish-German relations. After these soothing explanations I left for a cure at the Lahmann Sanatorium where I read in the papers about Forster's article and the incident caused by the arrival of the battleship *Leipzig*. Yesterday—I continued—a bombshell exploded at Geneva and I received from Minister Beck instructions to present a certain declaration to Minister President Göring requesting him to inform the Chancellor accordingly.

Here Göring interrupted, remarking that the incident in Geneva was by no means directed against Poland's interests. It is a firm policy of the German government as well as of the Senate of the Free City not to infringe upon the rights of Poland and its citizens in Danzig. If during the recent incidents some Polish citizens were hurt, the offenders will be prosecuted. In spite of the fact that some Polish Communists demonstrated in Danzig, orders were issued that they should be left alone. Instructions were also issued to ignore the fact that the German opposition in Danzig used training premises belonging to Polish companies in Danzig. As far as Greiser's performance in Geneva is concerned, it was directed against Lester, who maintains contact with the opposition to the National Socialist Party in Danzig. Allegedly there is proof that Lester coordinates his action with Ziehm. Greiser's speech in the forum of the League was a sort of unloading of grievances accumulated for many years. The German government did not restrain him from this.

[3] The date should be July 4.

However, Göring assured me that, outside of this speech, nothing further will happen.

Here I interrupted Herr Göring to ask him to hear out your instructions. When I finished reading them, Göring promptly referred to the sentence that the Polish government assumes that no events whatsoever could take place to render Polish-German relations impossible to be continued. He stressed that he is in a position to declare most emphatically in the name of the Chancellor and on his own behalf that nothing will happen on the part of the German government and Danzig besides the Greiser speech. He is authorized to declare, in the name of the Chancellor, that, if requested by the Polish government, he can assure us quite categorically on behalf of the German government that

1) neither from the side of the Free City nor from the side of the German government will the Danzig statute, and particularly laws pertaining to Poland, be undermined in any respect;

2) there will never be any question of steps aimed at uniting Danzig with the Reich.

Here Göring once more confirmed that Greiser's whole performance resulted from Lester's behavior and from the fact that Greiser was summoned to Geneva in order to make an explanation, which was embarrassing from the German point of view.

In the course of the conversation I repeatedly underlined the fact that Poland, as a member of the Council, has certain obligations, and I mentioned the resolution of the Council dealing with the *Leipzig* incident. Herr Göring remarked that the Chancellor feels personally offended by the problem of the *Leipzig,* for Lester is blaming him, as commander of the armed forces, that the commodore of the fleet did not call on the High Commissioner, who only last year, in a most tactless manner, compelled a commodore of the German fleet to meet under his roof with a representative of the Danzig opposition who vehemently fights against National Socialism. Herr Göring confided to me that the Chancellor ordered him to declare to the British Ambassador that, if a diplomatic intervention takes place on the *Leipzig* problem, the Chancellor will withdraw his promise to join the League of Nations, for the Chancellor does not want to enter a League which deals in such a manner with orders he delivers to units of the German fleet.

Herr Göring repeatedly asked me to bring his argumentation to your attention and to assure you that not only will the statute be respected but also that other rumors spread all over the world about German aggressive tendencies are absolutely groundless. He also sought a formula for a solution which would avoid any complications of the situation in case I make a *démarche* in Berlin in consequence of the Council's resolution. So, for instance, he mused aloud on my possible questions to the German government (1) respecting the Danzig statute and (2) respecting the rights of Poland and its citizens, to which positive answers were given by the Chancellor.

*Lipski*

On the same day, July 5, 1936, Beck stopped in Berlin on his way back from Geneva and met with Göring in the evening at a dinner at the Embassy. In spite of Göring's endeavors to pour oil on troubled waters, the atmosphere was rather tense, since it was quite obvious that Greiser's behavior in Geneva was coordinated with the top authorities of the Reich. Göring's statements made to Beck did not differ from those he made to me during our afternoon meeting. It was evident that, in view of the great commotion in international opinion and Poland's firm stand, Berlin would content itself with that drastic anti-League demonstration and would abstain, at least for the time being, from further steps.

The next day the ambassador of France and the British chargé d'affaires intervened at Wilhelmstrasse, in accordance with what was agreed to in Geneva. They both received appeasing explanations. I informed the Ministry of Foreign Affairs accordingly in my report of July 6, 1936.[4]

DOCUMENT 59   Lipski to the Ministry of Foreign Affairs

NO. G/3/27/36                                         Berlin, July 6, 1936
                                                      *Strictly Confidential*

The Counselor of the French Embassy telephoned Counselor Lubomirski today, stating that the French Ambassador, having received instructions to make a *démarche* on the Danzig problem to the German government, would like to coordinate his action with my intervention.

[4] *DGFP*, Series C, Vol. V, Nos. 436, 437, and 438.

On my direction, Counselor Lubomirski called on the Counselor of the French Embassy and communicated to him that yesterday I had had a conversation with Reichspräsident Göring concerning Greiser's last appearance in Geneva and had received appeasing explanations with regard to respect for the statute and abstention from any *faits accomplis.*

During this conversation at the French Embassy, Ambassador François-Poncet returned from the Auswärtiges Amt, where he had made his *démarche* to the counselor of the Ministry, Dieckhoff, who was in charge in the absence of von Neurath. The French Ambassador informed Counselor Lubomirski that Herr Dieckhoff also gave him reassuring explanations, remarking, however, that the problem of the revision of the Danzig statute was raised by Greiser's speech. Thus, Dieckhoff's statement is to some extent contradictory to Göring's declaration yesterday.

The British Embassy had also tried to contact me since morning. I received the chargé d'affaires, Minister Plenipotentiary Newton, who informed me that he had received instructions from his government to put pressure on the German government in order to obtain from it reassuring statements as to possible further occurrences to follow Greiser's action; and to mention the mandate granted to Poland to clarify the problem of the battleship *Leipzig,* expressing the hope that this might settle the dispute.

Mr. Newton tried to contact Dieckhoff yesterday, and this morning he called on him at the A.A. Herr Dieckhoff first of all made accusations against Lester for his activities in Danzig; he also complained about summoning Greiser to face the forum of the League. Herr Dieckhoff, contrary to what he allegedly said to the French Ambassador, assured Mr. Newton that the revision of the Danzig statute is at present not considered.

For my part I told Mr. Newton that yesterday I had had a conversation wtih Reichspräsident Göring, who also gave me some reassuring explanations. To Mr. Newton's question as to our stand with regard to the statute, I replied that it certainly is the very basis of the whole legal position at present. Mr. Newton also asked whether in our opinion the High Commissioner should safeguard the statute, as Lester did. I gave an affirmative reply, and said casually that the behavior of the High Commissioner in the field is naturally a matter of his personal methods.

In my discussions with the French and British embassies I followed the line of the position you took at Geneva; that is, I did not want to be pushed into a joint *démarche*. That is why I mentioned that I had already had a conversation with Göring yesterday. On the other hand, I maintained a friendly contact with the two ambassadors.

Analyzing yesterday's conversation with Göring, I conclude as follows:

Undoubtedly, Greiser's action in Geneva—coordinated, as we positively know, with the Chancellor and with Göring—was aimed at actualizing the problem of some revision of the statute. Fearing to jeopardize Polish-German relations in view of the reaction of Poland, Herr Göring yesterday deprecated the revision of the statute, at least for the near future. He probably assumed that such a moment would come, and possibly under circumstances more favorable for Germany, in the fall. Some contradictory explanations by Dieckhoff might be due to his misinformation in Neurath's absence, or perhaps he engaged on purpose in tactics which would lead to the question of revision.

Beyond any doubt, the French on their part, as I can see from their press, will bring this problem to the forefront.

*Lipski*

Obtaining formal assurances from the German government with regard to the *Leipzig* incident was a very embarrassing procedure. Following several burdensome conversations with Neurath, he informed me that Hitler finally agreed to the exchange of notes as proposed by the Polish government; the exchange took place in Berlin on July 24, 1936. The German note ended with a declaration that there was no intention to act against the statute and Poland's rights in the Free City. The Council of the League of Nations accepted the note as the execution of the mandate entrusted to the Polish government.

DOCUMENT 60   Lipski to the Ministry of Foreign Affairs

NO. G/3/46/36                                     Berlin, July 23, 1936
                                                 *Confidential*

In accordance with my telegram sent yesterday to the Ministry of Foreign Affairs, I was received at 12:30 P.M. by Director of the A.A. Dieckhoff, who is replacing von Neurath during his absence from Berlin.[5]

[5] *Ibid.,* No. 473.

Dieckhoff communicated to me that Chancellor Hitler expressed his agreement to the exchange of notes proposed by me regarding the incident with the battleship *Leipzig.* Herr Dieckhoff showed me a note signed by Herr von Neurath as a reply to our question. This note is identical with the text proposed by me to Neurath in my second conversation with him on July 9 (No. 6/3/30/36); only the last paragraph contains a slight, but not vital, alteration. This paragraph now reads:

"Hence no intention was suggested of acting against the Statute of the Free City or Poland's rights."

Herr Dieckhoff declared that he is authorized to exchange the notes with me immediately.

We agreed that the exchange of notes would take place tomorrow at 12:30 P.M.[6]

Herr Dieckhoff then communicated to me that Herr Neurath had confidentially expressed the desire that Minister Beck would use his influence in Geneva to induce a change in the post of the high commissioner of the League of Nations in Danzig. I availed myself of this occasion to remind Dieckhoff discreetly that this spring, at Greiser's request as related to me by Göring, Minister Beck had already arranged that Lester's mandate would not be prolonged beyond the fall. However, Greiser later expressed to the British his consent that the mandate be extended for another year. Herr Dieckhoff, deploring Greiser's unwise action, remarked that certainly with the extension of Lester's mandate only until fall the situation concerning the change of commissioners would have been much easier than at present.

Finally, Herr Dieckhoff remarked that he understands that the exchange of notes will not be reported in the Berlin press, since their publication will take place in Geneva.

Herr Dieckhoff plainly stressed in the conversation that the German side is anxious to have the matter settled as promptly as possible, and he gave vent to his concern that Polish-German relations might be endangered by the Danzig incidents. I mentioned in passing yesterday's talk of Greiser with Papée. However, since I had no information on this matter, I abstained from any comment.

I would like to add that, although the press here in general passed over in silence the anti-Danzig demonstrations on Polish territory, in competent circles they gave rise to a certain amount of agitation.

[6] For the text of the notes exchanged on July 24, 1936, see League of Nations, *Official Journal,* November, 1936, p. 1334.

Finally, I am taking the liberty of communicating to you a copy of a rather significant letter received by me from Staatsrat Boettcher of Danzig, who invites me, in Greiser's name, to Zoppot for the Wagnerian plays on July 26 to 28. Of course, I shall refuse.[7]

*Józef Lipski*

Further appeasing reassurances regarding Danzig were made by Hitler to the undersecretary of state at the Foreign Affairs Ministry, Count Szembek, on August 12, 1936, during his visit to the Olympic Games in Berlin.[8]

At Nuremberg in the trial against Weizsäcker a memorandum was presented on Danzig matters, signed by him on October 15, 1936, when he was still director of the Political Department.[9] It is written from the angle of negotiations to be started between the Senate of the Free City and the Polish government and illustrates the A.A.'s point of view on this problem at the time.

Weizsäcker poses the principle that the problem of Danzig cannot be dealt with separately from the Reich's foreign policy, for the relaxation of possible tension in Polish-German relations depends on how matters are treated in Danzig. Here he is drawing a practical conclusion that the Senate and the unruly Gauleiter Forster must act in close direct contact with the Auswärtiges Amt. The aim of the Danzig policy must be the return of the Free City to the Reich. Under present conditions this is impossible, unless a *coup d'état* is arranged. A *coup d'état* is at present not envisaged, since this would actualize the hitherto unsolved question of the Corridor. In his further deliberations, Weizsäcker considers the subordination of Danzig to the League of Nations as an inconvenient solution. Analyzing the possibility of transferring to Poland part of the League of Nations' right, or possibly even of nominating a Pole to the post of high commissioner, he reaches a negative conclusion. Under the prevailing good Polish-German relations, this would possibly cause a relaxation in the situation but, with a change for the worse, the

[7] Invitation not enclosed.
[8] *Journal*, pp. 196–98; *Diariusz*, II, 259–61; *DGFP*, Series C, Vol. V, Nos. 506 and 513.
[9] The text of the memorandum is in *DGFP*, Series C, Vol. V, No. 605. See also No. 609.

hand of Poland would weigh over Danzig, especially since the high commissioner is authorized, on his own responsibility, to call on the Polish armed forces to restore order to the Free City.

Weizsäcker confirms that under the legally binding statute the high commissioner is authorized to intervene in the Free City's internal affairs.

In his conclusion, he recommends that the Senate seek jointly with Poland a neutral successor to Lester; that it bring about a calming down in the internal situation of Danzig, so that at the next session of the Council of the League of Nations Poland would be able to declare that peace has been restored to the city; that it not grant any concessions in the negotiations with Poland which might in the future create difficulties for the return of Danzig to the Reich; and, finally, that permanent contact be maintained with the A.A. during the negotiations.

In 1937 a change occurred in the post of the high commissioner of the League of Nations in Danzig. Lester was succeeded by Professor Burckhardt, a Swiss (Swiss envoy in Paris, 1945–49). His candidacy—as is now obvious from German documents—was discreetly supported by Weizsäcker. They had been acquainted since 1920 and maintained close contacts until the outbreak of the war. At the Nuremberg trial Burckhardt presented an affidavit in defense of Weizsäcker.

At the Nuremberg trial Weizsäcker, when questioned about the memorandum on Danzig matters, replied verbatim as follows: [10]

"The later incorporation of Danzig as the final aim was justified not only because without a plebiscite Danzig had been taken away from Germany and was almost completely German, but also in a political sense this aim was justified because there was not one problem during the years beginning with 1920 with which the League of Nations had to make such constant and such useless efforts as the Danzig problem. A complete clarification of the Danzig question was essential for any practical European peace policy. I remind you that the Danzig problem at that time was somewhat similar to the Trieste problem, and I don't think that I am the only one who holds that opinion because the British foreign minister, Lord Halifax, one year after I wrote this memorandum, that is, in 1937, in autumn 1937, stated publicly that changes in the European order would have to come sooner or later and that one of

[10] At the session of the court on June 9, 1948 ("Trials of War Criminals," mimeographed transcript, p. 7835, Lipski's Papers, File 23).

these changes for him was Danzig, while another one was Austria, and so on and so forth."

This declaration of Weizsäcker is connected with Lord Halifax's mission to Hitler in November, 1937.

In the disclosed German documents we find a full report of the conversation that took place on November 19, 1937, at Berchtesgaden.[11]

The aim of Halifax's trip was to investigate possibilities for a large-scale British-German understanding, which was the goal of Neville Chamberlain's policy. Toward the end of 1937, with Hitler's power in a state of constant growth, the West showed an increased tendency toward a rapprochement with the Reich. This tendency was apparent not only in Great Britain but also in France. On this subject there is an interesting report by von Papen, dated November 10, 1937, on conversations he had with Minister of Finance Georges Bonnet, Prime Minister Chautemps, François Pietri, Champetier de Ribes, and a number of other politicians.[12]

In his conversation with Hitler, Lord Halifax in principle was of the opinion that the British-German rapprochement should not put a stress on Great Britain's relations with France and Germany's with Italy. He had the idea that, when an understanding between Berlin and London was reached, the four Western Powers would be called on to create common foundations for a lasting peace in Europe; in other words, a reversion to the Four-Power Pact.

Referring to the friendly attitude taken by the British government toward Germany on the problem of the premature evacuation of the Rhineland in 1930, on the cancellation of German war indemnities, and on the remilitarization of the Rhineland (in March, 1936), Lord Halifax remarked that the British side would not insist on maintaining the status quo in Europe as a condition sine qua non. Great Britain understood that it might be necessary to consider balancing the situation in the light of new conditions and correcting errors committed in the past. Great Britain was only concerned that such changes should be carried out peacefully without resorting to the threat of war. Referring to possible changes in the European system, Lord Halifax at one time pointed concretely to Danzig, Austria, and Czechoslovakia.[13]

In his reply Hitler engaged in a discussion on Czechoslovakia and

[11] DGFP, Series D, Vol. I, No. 31.
[12] Ibid., No. 22.
[13] Emphasis added by the author.

Austria, while he passed over in silence Halifax's allusion to Danzig. Referring several times to Poland in the course of this lengthy exchange of opinion, the Chancellor expressed satisfaction with the good relations he had succeeded in establishing with this state in spite of difficulties inherited from the past.

It should be recalled that a few weeks before Halifax's visit, on the occasion of Polish-German declarations dealing with the treatment of national minorities (November 5, 1937), Hitler made a solemn declaration to the Polish Ambassador on the inviolability of the statute of the Free City and respect for Poland's rights in Danzig.[14] The government of Great Britain was duly informed about this.

Lord Halifax's stand was understood in Berlin as a sort of *désintéressement* on the part of Great Britain in the problem of Austria and the Sudeteland, and had a serious impact on Hitler's future decisions.

I do not know whether Warsaw at that time received any alarming news in connection with Halifax's mission. It is a fact, however, that the Ministry of Foreign Affairs, referring to the forthcoming visit of French Foreign Affairs Minister Delbos to Warsaw, urgently requested the Embassy in Berlin to supply more detailed information on Halifax's conversations with Hitler. At first Weizsäcker was reluctant to give such information, describing the meeting as personal and confidential, the results of which were transmitted only to Paris and Rome. When Lubomirski insisted, he referred the matter to Neurath, and with the latter's consent on the same day he gave a general outline of the conversation and characterized Halifax's opinion about Danzig as a vague remark to which Hitler did not react.

When Beck passed through Berlin on January 13, 1938, the Chancellor repeated to him word for word the declaration on the matter of respecting the legal situation in Danzig as made on November 5, 1937. In connection with rumors about the possibility of the withdrawal of the League of Nations from Danzig, Hitler confirmed during this conversation that his declaration was binding independently of the fate of the League of Nations.[15]

Here Lipski's article ends.

Coming back to the Danzig problems at the end of 1936, it should be stressed that Nazi elements in the Free City permanently maintained the

[14] *DGFP*, Series D, Vol. V, No. 19.
[15] *Ibid.*, No. 29.

explosive state of Polish-Danzig relations, in spite of the many promises made by Hitler and Göring.[16] For example, in October, 1936, the Danzig Senate issued a number of rulings of a commercial character detrimental to Poland's interests. On October 31 an armed Nazi band attacked a Polish home at Schönberg (near Danzig). The Commissioner-General of Poland in Danzig intervened in this case, and the Senate promised to investigate.

The Danzig Senate also created the Landesarbeitsamt, a labor exchange office, designed to render it impossible for Poles to obtain work. And again on November 7 the Commissioner-General had to intervene in this matter.

These incidents met with a strong reaction from the Polish community, especially at Gdynia, as well as from the Polish press.[17]

At this time Lipski twice discussed the problem of conflicts in Danzig with Göring (these reports are missing from Lipski's papers). According to what Szembek notes in his journal (*Diariusz*, II, 326), Göring "expressed a wish to remove all misunderstandings which had occurred in this matter. Next, in a most confidential manner, he told the Ambassador about Hitler's opinions on the problem of Pomerania and Germany's connections with East Prussia. Specifically, the Chancellor would wish—against compensations to be granted to Poland in another field—to obtain easier access for Germany to East Prussia. This might be achieved by the construction of a superhighway through Polish territory, as well as the creation, under Poland's supervision, of transit for German railways across Pomerania. Hitler thinks these plans cannot be realized at present, but he envisages them as projects for the future."

This inflammatory situation is described in the conversation of Beck with Ambassador von Moltke in Warsaw.[18]

At the beginning of September there was held in Nuremberg, as usual, a congress of the National Socialist Party. Lipski was there, together with the heads of other diplomatic missions.


DOCUMENT 61     Lipski to Szembek


NO. N/7/121/36                          Berlin, September 16, 1936
                                         *Strictly Confidential*


I returned yesterday from the Congress at Nuremberg and I shall dispatch a detailed report by the next courier.

Following up the conversations you had with authoritative German elements during the Olympic Games in Berlin, I tried to present the

[16]*Ibid.*, Series C, Vol. V, Nos. 623, 628, 635, 636, and 639.
[17] See *Diariusz*, II, 314–16, 521–26, 325, 330, 534–35.
[18]See *Polish White Book*, No. 26, where the conversation is given in abbreviated form. The full text is in Lipski's papers, File 9.

results of General Śmigły-Rydz's trip to France in a suitable light.[19] I laid stress on the fact that Poland's foreign policy has remained absolutely unaltered, and that conversations were held on a purely bilateral military Polish-French ground. Easiest to digest for the German side is the argument that the revival of the Polish-French alliance contributes to the devaluation of the French-Soviet alliance, and also that it has an impact on the nationalistic shift in focus of the internal policy in France. This argument is most persuasive in the present psychological atmosphere of anti-Bolshevism in Germany. The press attaché of the Embassy, Mr. Wnorowski, followed this line in his interviews with the local press at Nuremberg. . . .

Although competent German circles allegedly understand and properly evaluate our recent moves in relation to France, popular reaction is rather unfavorable. A similar reaction may be observed among those personalities who after all were wrong in their assumption that contracting good Polish-German relations would once and for all definitely cut off the link uniting Warsaw with Paris.

A particular touchiness with regard to all symptoms in Poland's relation to Germany may be observed from press articles—acting as an instrument of public opinion—especially those against our press. In a number of communications from Warsaw in the local press yesterday and today, annoyance is obvious because of negative comments in our press with regard to the political meaning of the Nuremberg Congress. Here Smogorzewski's telegram in *Gazeta Polska* is an exception.

Under these circumstances I am taking the liberty of suggesting that influence be exerted on the Polish press (if possible on all its segments) to inspire it to comment most cautiously on German matters.

I would like to remark that the thesis of foreign correspondents attending the Nuremberg Congress as disclosed in the course of the first

[19] In connection with Polish-French military relations, two visits took place in August-September, 1936. General Gamelin, chief of France's General Staff, visited Poland on August 12–18, and General Śmigły-Rydz, general inspector of the Polish Army, visited France on August 30-September 6. He participated in the grand maneuvers of the French Army and had a number of conversations, finalized by the Rambouillet Agreement of September 6 with regard to Polish-French technical and financial collaboration. On the basis of this agreement Poland received a loan of 2 billion French francs, half of which was in gold and the other half in matériel. Of this second portion Poland received only 13 percent before the outbreak of the war. Problems of the military alliance of Poland with France are related in *Diariusz*, II, 433–39; for the stay of Śmigły-Rydz in Paris, see *ibid.*, pp. 488–97.

days of the conferences—that the Chancellor in his anti-Bolshevik declaration tried to impose on particular states the choice of either Communism or Fascism—does not correspond with the actual situation. I shall return to this question in my report. The Chancellor stated that Italy, a state which definitely threatened Bolshevism, is sympathetic to the National Socialist movement. The same is true of all other states which in their own way oppose the destructive action of Moscow. Nevertheless, he made the reservation that he is not imposing the system of National Socialism, labeled "made in Germany," on any foreign state.

I was invited to Rominten for September 28 and 29 by General Göring, with whom, unfortunately, I could not get in touch at Nuremberg. Neurath told me that he would also be at Rominten. I think that I should then talk more authoritatively with the ministers of the Reich. I would therefore like to be in Warsaw prior to this date and to have an audience with General Śmigły-Rydz, owing to some prejudices in this territory which are well known to you. I shall talk this over with Minister Beck tomorrow when he passes through Berlin on his way to Geneva.

*Józef Lipski*

From November 25 to November 28, 1936, Mr. Victor Antonescu, who became foreign minister of Rumania after Titulescu's resignation,[20] paid an official visit to Poland.

In the same month, two eminent Rumanian politicians, who were in opposition to the government, proceeded on a political trip to Western capitals.

In Berlin they called on Ambassador Lipski, about which Lipski writes in the reports that follow.

### DOCUMENT 62   Lipski to Beck

NO. N/52/9/36                                          Berlin, November 20, 1936
                                                      *Strictly Confidential*

From reports of our Legation in Bucharest dated October 28, No. 52/R/83, and October 30, No. 52/R/85, I learned of the planned trip of Messrs. George Bratianu and Atta Constantinescu to Berlin, Brussels, and Paris.

[20] *Diariusz,* II, 342–43, 553–54.

The politicians paid me a visit at the Polish Embassy on November 5. I had not seen either Bratianu or Constantinescu since our meeting in January of 1936, on which I reported at that time to the Ministry of Foreign Affairs in my letter dated January 27. Mr. Bratianu expressed satisfaction over the improvement in Polish-Rumanian relations since Titulescu's departure from government. He informed me about his recent conversations with the foreign minister of Rumania, Mr. Antonescu, and with Count Ciano in Rome. These have already been related in the above-mentioned reports of our Legation in Bucharest. He was visibly disturbed by Mussolini's last speech delivered in Milan,[21] a paragraph of which is devoted to the support of Hungarian revisionism. In connection with Count Ciano's visit to Berlin, Bratianu is wondering whether this speech is the result of opinions duly coordinated between the Italian and German governemnts.

In the course of a long debate I expressed the opinion that during Ciano's conversations with German statesmen they defined their points of view only with regard to Austria. This had been made clear in the press declaration of Italy's Foreign Minister at Munich, while no agreement—in the broader sense of the word—had been reached with regard to the Danubian basin. I am confirmed in this belief by the fact that governing spheres of Germany were rather critical of Mussolini's speech.

Mr. Bratianu told me that this time he would like to be received by the Chancellor of the Reich, especially since Mr. Goga, the head of another political party, had already obtained an audience with Hitler during the Olympic Games. He stressed that he would remain in constant contact with me and would inform me extensively about all his conversations in Germany, as well as about his impressions from Paris and Belgium.

After his talk with Göring, Mr. Bratianu is even more convinced that, as far as the Rumanian and Hungarian problems are concerned, no conformity exists between the Italian and German points of view. Rather, a rivalry prevails. Göring is definitely critical of Mussolini's speech. Göring also mentioned that while he was in Budapest for the funeral of Gömbös [22] he could see Ciano's obvious reserve toward any particularly friendly manifestations shown to him by the Hungarian side. Göring defined his attitude toward the Rumanian question by stating that

[21] The speech was delivered on November 1, 1936.
[22] General Julius Gömbös de Jákfa was prime minister of Hungary from 1932 to 1936.

the German government is ready to safeguard Rumania from Hungarian revisionism in the same way it protected Yugoslavia against it. But this on the condition that Rumania frees itself from commitments to Soviet Russia. Besides, Herr Göring drafted plans for possible German-Rumanian economic collaboration. He would be prepared to consider during the next six months all more concrete prospects for such collaboration with Rumania, within the frame of his four-year plan now under elaboration. Finally, Göring promised Bratianu that he would arrange a meeting for him with Hitler.

Messrs. Bratianu and Constantinescu left for Paris for a few days, and returned to Berlin on November 15. The next day Bratianu was received by Neurath, whose deliberations followed the same line as Göring's, but in a more prudent tone. Later, Bratianu was received by the Chancellor.

The Chancellor's deliberations can be recapitulated in the following three points:

1) The Reich would be prepared to influence Budapest to restrain its revisionist aspirations toward Rumania when it is assured that the Rumanian government would free itself from the influence of Soviet politics.

2) When Bratianu explained that they have an alliance with France and Poland, the Chancellor took the stand that these agreements create no obstacle for German-Rumanian collaboration.

3) The Chancellor laid special stress on tightening German-Rumanian economic relations.

In the Chancellor's reasoning there were also comments about Poland. He said, for instance, when he stated that the Reich cannot claim reunion of all regions inhabited by Germans beyond its frontiers, that for the sake of about 300,000 Germans living in Poland there is no reason to create difficulties in the relations between Poland and Germany.

The Chancellor also mentioned the Corridor, stating that, since a nation of 35 million needs access to the sea, this problem has been removed from the agenda.

These two passages dealing with Poland—mentioned to a Rumanian statesman—are, in my opinion, of great positive meaning, especially since they were uttered at a moment of persistent tension over Danzig problems.

About France the Chancellor allegedly repeated his previous arguments that he has no territorial quarrels with that country. Here he made a rather characteristic allusion—with regard to raw materials and colonial aspects—to a possible compromise with France in that field, not in the sense of territorial expansion in French colonies, but in the spirit of economic collaboration with France and its colonies. I am laying special stress on this point because this is the first time such an idea of the top German authorities has been brought to my knowledge.

On the next day Mr. Bratianu left Berlin, proceeding to Brussels for an audience with the King. He will then go to Paris to be received by Prime Minister Blum.

Mr. Bratianu also shared with me his impressions from an earlier stay in Paris for a couple of days. As a positive element of the situation in France he considered the fact that M. Daladier, minister of war, is to some extent purging the army of Communist elements. As far as the internal situation of France is concerned, Mr. Bratianu's opinion is rather pessimistic. French policy shows symptoms of considerable deterioration.

High-ranking factors in France made it clear to Mr. Bratianu that under the present circumstances Rumania cannot count on any kind of military assistance from France. As a symptom of France's reaction, March 7 was cited to Mr. Bratianu, followed by a declaration that the French soldier would only take up arms if the enemy crossed French frontiers.

Mr. Bratianu was rather impressed by the evaluation of the Czechoslovak situation made to him in Paris. The French are of the opinion that the position of Czechoslovakia is tragic, with the bulk of Hungarian revisionism concentrated in its direction. But competent spheres in France did not deem it possible to give assistance to Czechoslovakia in case of emergency.

The above conversations held in France and Germany further confirmed Mr. Bratianu in his basic thesis that Rumania must undertake a more independent policy based upon purely national interests. In his opinion, both Rumania and Poland should stay aloof from the struggle of the two blocs devoted to different ideologies. He first defined this policy line as neutral politics, evidently having Belgium in mind. However, he corrected this definition as inaccurate, referring to alliances his country is partner to. Mr. Bratianu thinks that it would be advisable to start a more active policy against Germany. Yugoslavia evidently represents some sort of bait for him as far as safeguarding Rumania against Hungary's revisionism is concerned.

When discussing all these problems, I tried to point to the fact that in the economic field no particularly positive results should be anticipated from collaboration with Germany, since the Reich finds itself on the path leading toward ever-tightening autarchy. Also, when Mr. Bratianu mentioned possible collaboration with Germany in the field of armaments, I tried to make it clear to him that regardless of the increase in economic turnover between the two countries, which in his opinion would be profitable for Rumanian export, certain caution should be observed, bearing in mind that Rumania, as well as Poland, should take into account its proximity to Soviet Russia.

Apart from these conversations with Messrs. Bratianu and Constantinescu, which must be kept in strict confidence, a few days ago I had a visit from the Rumanian envoy, Mr. Comnen, who just returned from Bucharest. From the long conversation I had with him I could deduce that Mussolini's last speech evoked strong dissatisfaction in Rumania. These ill-feeling will probably be exploited by Germany for its own ends.

*Józef Lipski*


DOCUMENT 63    Lipski to Beck

NO. N/52/10/36                              Berlin, November 28, 1936
                                            *Strictly Confidential*

With reference to my report of November 20, No. N/52/9/36, I am taking the liberty of communicating that I received further information pertaining to Mr. Bratianu's conversations with the King of Belgium and M. Delbos, the foreign minister of France.

The Belgian King allegedly laid special stress on Belgium's tendency to conduct its own independent national policy. Therefore it will form its relations with particular states in accordance with its own national policy. The Belgian King referred here to Poland as a state that succeeded in basing its foreign policy on the interests of the country. The King of Belgium further stated that he is at present finalizing an agreement with Holland based on such principles. In his opinion, Rumania, through its alliance with Poland, should follow a similar policy.

The King was allegedly satisfied with Hitler's statement made to Mr. Bratianu with regard to the fact that the Reich would fully respect Belgium's sovereignty.

Mr. Bratianu was impressed very positively by his conversation with the Belgian King.

In his conversation with M. Delbos, Mr. Bratianu referred in the first place to his previous meeting with the French Foreign Minister several months ago, stating that Mr. Titulescu's resignation from the post of foreign minister resulted from Rumania's reaction—as foreseen by Mr. Bratianu—to the attempt to draw it into the orbit of Soviet Russia. Allegedly Mr. Bratianu quite bluntly declared to Delbos that pushing Rumania into an agreement with Russia had to be obviously understood in his country as a desire to shift to Russia obligations deriving from the French-Rumanian alliance. To this M. Delbos retorted that the chief aim of the French-Russian agreement was to draw Germany away from Soviet Russia, that is, to counteract a possible renewal of the Rapallo policy. At present the signing of the German-Japanese agreement, in the opinion of the French Foreign Minister, definitely canceled such a possibility. Therefore, the attitude of the French government toward an agreement with Russia might also be subject to certain alteration. M. Delbos, aware of the fact that 60 percent of the French nation desires an understanding with Germany, cannot oppose the establishment of closer contact between Rumania and the Reich. In his opinion, Rumania should follow the line of policy as pointed out by Poland. Here M. Delbos laid special pressure on his statement that, in spite of all appearances, the line of the French-Polish alliance had been constantly maintained, and that complete accord prevails between your opinions and those of the French government. A certain superficial misunderstanding has been removed by the trip of Marshal Śmigły-Rydz to France. This trip evoked symptoms of friendship for Poland in the French nation.

Mr. Constantinescu, who reported on the two above-mentioned conversations to me, stressed how deeply both he and Mr. Bratianu were impressed by the fact that the Belgian King, as well as M. Delbos, cited the foreign policy conducted by Poland as an example to be followed and laid stress on the alliance between Rumania and Poland. Mr. Bratianu stated that the closest possible collaboration with Poland is the basic foundation of his policy. Starting from this premise, he fought against Titulescu.

The above reports are evidently only fragmentary, since the conversations were only briefly reported to me by Mr. Constantinescu.

Expressing their satisfaction over the trip of Foreign Minister Antonescu to Warsaw, Messrs. Bratianu and Constantinescu declared their intention to visit Poland at the beginning of next year.

My observations with regard to the reception offered locally, as well as in Belgium and France, to Mr. Bratianu, in spite of the fact that he is going as a private individual, confirm my opinion that his position abroad has gained considerable weight since last year. Perhaps Titulescu's resignation contributed to this, since it forces the government to seek a factor to play a leading political role in Rumania.

*Józef Lipski*

# Beck's Conversation with Neurath
## *January, 1937*

WHEN HE WAS in Warsaw at the end of 1936 (on December 10), Lipski informed Vice-Minister Szembek about the internal situation in Germany, which he considered very difficult in the financial and economic fields.[1]

On January 11, 1937, at the annual reception of Chancellor Hitler for the diplomatic corps, Hitler, talking with Ambassador Lipski, expressed his hope for a positive solution to the Danzig problems and stressed the importance of the Polish-German agreement of January, 1934.[2]

Ten days later Minister Beck, on his way to Geneva to a session of the Council of the League of Nations, stopped for one day in Berlin and had a conversation of a general character with Minister von Neurath.

DOCUMENT 64 Memorandum on the
Conversation of Minister Beck with von Neurath,
the Reich Minister of Foreign Affairs,
*held on January 20, 1937 (11:30 A.M.–1 P.M.)*
*in the presence of Ambassador Lipski*

### *1. Danzig*

Herr von Neurath began the conversation by stating that the first matter to be discussed would be the problem of Danzig. He added that, as he was informed, a Polish-Danzig agreement had been reached, thus bringing about a *détente* in the situation.[3]

[1] *Journal*, pp. 218–19.
[2] *Polish White Book*, No. 27.
[3] On January 6 negotiations were terminated in Danzig concerning Poland's rights in the Danzig harbor. The Senate of Danzig made a declaration confirming its readiness to respect all political and economic rights of Poland under the treaty and the agreement. The Polish government on its side stressed its readiness to respect and not to transgress on economic and legal relations binding under the statute of the Free City and obligatory agreements.

Minister Beck confirmed this, adding that additional talks on technical issues would follow. He did not wish to deal immediately with these matters under the new agreement, so that it would not look as though Poland was trying to exploit the situation because of its mandate in the League of Nations. Minister Beck underlined the fact that the Danzig problems evoked quite an uproar in public opinion recently, and he therefore deemed it advisable to deal with them from a proper angle in his speech delivered at the Senate Commission.[4] He stressed in this speech how necessary it was to respect mutual rights.

Minister Beck further told von Neurath that Poland was not demanding an extension of its rights, since it was only concerned with the maintenance of the balance.

Passing to the question of the high commissioner, Minister Beck stressed that he presented the principle that the new candidate should not have connections with the secretariat of the League of Nations. Herr von Neurath readily shared this opinion. In Mr. Beck's opinion the candidate should be a person belonging to a neutral country, independent and not subject to influence from the outside. Perhaps an army man with a good record of service.

As to the attributes of the commissioner, von Neurath mentioned casually that it would be desirable that he should keep aloof of internal matters.

Minister Beck replied loosely that some formulas for this have been provided.

The [Polish] government contacted the Senate formally with regard to the candidates, and some of these candidacies were discussed: two Norwegians, one Portuguese. Of course, the problem will be settled definitely in Geneva. Minister Beck added that, since he is in touch with Eden, he has reason to believe that the British Foreign Secretary shares his concept of the type of candidate.

Herr von Neurath stressed that these particular candidates are not known to him, and he thinks that Eden, in his capacity as *rapporteur,* would only welcome an agreement between Poland and Danzig which would relieve him of further difficulties. However, he agreed with Mr. Beck that some unexpected complications might, as always, be in store

[4] Beck's speech at the Commission for Foreign Affairs of the Polish Senate on December 18, 1936. See J. Beck, *Przemówienia, deklaracje, wywiady, 1931–1937,* pp. 272–73.

for us in Geneva. He therefore advised Greiser to be present in Geneva and to contact Minister Beck personally if necessary.[5] As for Forster, whom he considered a very unruly individual, von Neurath remarked that he had taken measures to keep him within the proper limits. Von Neurath requested that Forster should communicate with him, and he now does this when he comes to Berlin.

Forster intended to call on Minister Beck presently in Warsaw. Von Neurath had restrained him for the time being, since he thought this might not be convenient for Minister Beck. However, both Minister Beck and von Neurath were of the opinion that such a visit by Forster to Warsaw might be advisable at the right time. Herr von Neurath, confirming in principle that the Danzig problems should not weigh on Polish-German relations, referred to Hitler's statement on these lines made recently to Ambassador Lipski at the New Year's reception of January 11. Minister Beck also expressed the hope that Polish-Danzig relations would now take a normal course and he indicated that, acting in Danzig's favor, he had taken up the question of lowering the high commissioner's salary, which weighed so heavily on the modest budget of the Free City. Von Neurath stressed the importance of this measure, since the high figure of the salary aroused criticism.

## 2. The Problem of the Raw Materials Committee in Geneva

Minister Beck explained that he had received information that the secretariat of the League of Nations omitted Germany when it investigated chances for collaboration in this committee of some countries who were not members of the League and when it consulted these countries. Minister Beck, as a *rapporteur,* firmly took exception to such discriminatory methods. Minister Beck stated on this occasion that he would discuss with Herr von Neurath Germany's attitude toward the Committee of Raw Materials.

Herr von Neurath replied that for the time being the German government is not prepared to participate in the works of the Raw Materials Committee. The Chancellor, whom von Neurath asked some days ago about his opinion on this question, took the same point of view. Although von Neurath was not expecting much from the committee's activ-

[5] The chairman of the Council of the League of Nations nominated a Swiss, Professor Charles Burckhardt, as high commissioner of the League of Nations on February 17.

ities, he preferred not to slam the door for the future but just to wait and see how things develop.

Summing up his present activities on the problem in relation to Germany, Mr. Beck stated that there are two possible alternatives. Either he should declare at Geneva, referring to his conversation with von Neurath, that the German government will not join the committee, or he should admit a formal consultation, to which the German government will give its reply.

Following Herr von Neurath's idea not to slam the door on this matter, Minister Beck suggested the following solution: he will state in Geneva that in his talks with the German government he noted interest in the problem, but he is not certain whether under the present circumstances, if a consultation followed at a later stage, the Reich government would define its stand more precisely. Von Neurath expressed his appreciation for this suggestion and accepted it, remarking that at the consultation he would reply so as not to exclude further possibilities.

### 3. The Geneva Convention

Herr von Neurath, remarking that the term of the Geneva Convention on Upper Silesia expires in July, stated that it will be necessary for the two governments to give attention to this problem in order to find some solution.

Minister Beck replied that from the political point of view it is better that the situation prevailing thus far come to an end, and that the situation is becoming clear.

Von Neurath shared this opinion.

Minister Beck stated further that in case of technical problems requiring settlement prior to the expiration of the convention, such as in railway or mining matters, they should be discussed.

Ambassador Lipski stressed that he had just received such instructions from Warsaw dealing with railway questions, which he will submit to Herr von Neurath or, as they are of a purely technical character, to the Secretary of State.

Herr von Neurath, not going into details, limited himself to the remark that discussions on such technical and economic problems should be undertaken because they are so essential for the local population.

Minister Beck again laid stress on the fact that technical matters will have to be negotiated.

## 4. Spanish Matters

Herr von Neurath gave some explanations on this matter. He reported that the German government will give an answer to the British government in the coming days regarding volunteers. This answer, as well as the first one, will be positive. Herr von Neurath stated confidentially that the German government had already issued an order to stop shipments of volunteers. The Italian government allegedly is considering a similar prohibition. Von Neurath also mentioned similar British dispositions and the latest French law.

In von Neurath's opinion the next step will be the problem of controls, which is under discussion in the nonintervention committee. By these means, as he put it, they would reach "zur Einkapselung" of Spain. The Civil War would probably still go on, but without participation from the outside. Spain, which in von Neurath's opinion has no elements for becoming a Fascist state, would find some way to rule itself. There is just one thing that neither the German nor the Italian government would stand for, and that is a Communist state in Spain. This stand of the two governments is in the interest of the whole of Europe. Here Herr von Neurath, asking if Mr. Beck shared his opinion, stressed that it seems as if the Soviets have recently been backing out of the Spanish affair.

Referring to the recent tension in the case of Morocco, von Neurath declared that this whole anti-German campaign had no foundations whatever and that a talk between Hitler and François-Poncet had put an end to it. He agreed that naturally Germany receives, as compensation for war matériel, raw materials from mines in the zone occupied by General Franco (Rio Tinto and Morocco). He mentioned brass as an example. However, he remarked that with the end of war supplies, which of course is inevitable, the flow of raw materials from Spain to Germany will also cease.

## 5. Italy and England

Herr von Neurath corrected the current opinion that the newly reached understanding between Italy and Great Britain is not convenient for the German government. Without this understanding, he added, our whole friendship with Italy would be worthless. He personally persuaded Ciano to negotiate with England. Hitler, without contacting him, made a statement along the same lines to the Italian Foreign Affairs Minister.

Herr von Neurath was of the opinion that the Italian-British agreement did not remove basic controversies, which still exist. But it contributed to a clarification of the atmosphere of British-Italian relations, which at any moment, even for a trifle, could result in a conflict. Such a situation was a hindrance to any policy.

### 6. French-German Relations

Herr von Neurath noted a certain *détente* in the sector of French-German relations. He remarked that he could feel some inclination in Blum as well as in Delbos for a rapprochement with Germany. Presently it will be started by a resumption of French-German trade negotiations. But he cannot predict whether concrete results will be obtained in French-German relations. As usual, when dealing with France, Herr von Neurath thinks that, even if the French government desired an agreement with Germany, it might not be able to achieve it, since this could result in the downfall of the cabinet.

### 7. The Western Pact

Herr von Neurath observed that the events in Spain pushed the problem of the Western Pact into the background. It might, however, again become timely as the result of a certain relaxation in French-German relations.

Minister Beck made a longer statement defining our general concepts with regard to the Western Pact.

He pointed out that in principle we conceive of this pact as an understanding with Germany, and not against Germany. That is why he directed Ambassador Lipski to establish contact with the German government on this problem.

Bearing in mind that the old Locarno concept is no longer timely, Minister Beck stressed the available possibility of finding other forms of understanding. Realizing the difficulty created by the French-Soviet agreement, Minister Beck remarked that a certain reaction might be observed in French public opinion against excessive engagement with Soviet Russia. Here the Polish-French alliance is an instrument enabling French opinion to evolve in this respect. The defensive and bilateral character of this alliance is well known to the German government. Herr von Neurath agreed with this. In the Western Pact this Polish equivalent could relieve the situation. The fact that the Polish-French alliance was concluded before Locarno is an argument in support of this concept.

In his deliberations, Herr von Neurath also laid stress on the fact that the old Locarno concept is now out of date. The British, as he remarked, are holding on tight, as usual, to the old ideas, and therefore some time may pass until they change their minds. Herr von Neurath sees a considerable difference of opinion in the British and Italian points of view.

Von Neurath listened to Mr. Beck's statements with great interest. He remarked that the problem requires long-lasting negotiations, and added that he will maintain close contact with us.

### 8. Austria

Minister Beck stated that he would like to raise a point which Herr von Neurath might not be prepared to answer. Namely, he would like to have some idea as to the relation of the Reich toward the present Austrian government. Minister Beck stressed that this question is connected with a certain possibility of visits. He made the reservation that Poland has no special political interest in Austria. The two countries, however, have considerable economic ties, if only resulting from earlier trade between Małopolska [Galicia] and Vienna.

Herr von Neurath remarked that the best reply would be if he informed Minister Beck, for the time being quite confidentially, that in a month he intends to go to Vienna. Von Neurath confirmed an improvement in relations with Austria, defining it as the return to a normal situation. He stressed correct relations with the Austrian government.

In this connection, Minister Beck pointed to our unchanged stand with regard to the Danubian basin, which was defined at the time of the plan of the Danubian pact.

### 9. Rumania

Herr von Neurath pointed to a certain noticeable improvement in German-Rumanian relations, which occurred after Titulescu's departure. The only thing that causes him some anxiety is that Titulescu is allegedly recovering from his illness.

Minister Beck strongly lauded the very logical and quiet activty of Minister Antonescu.

10. Minister Beck brought up the problem of the D.N.B. [Deutsches Nachrichtenbüro] communiqué regarding the Kiel Canal.[6]

Herr von Neurath replied that this is not a new step concerning the canal; the problem was contained in the Reich's declaration on the Versailles Treaty resolutions with regard to water communications.

For in practice battleships passing through the canal were as a rule always reported to the German government. At present the only change consists in the fact that in answer to the notification the Reich government grants its consent.

Herr Neurath does not know for sure why the navy issued such a communiqué. It is possible that the communiqué was issued in answer to an inquiry by one of the Scandinavian countries.

11. Herr von Neurath touched casually on the matter of the unfriendly tone of the Polish press in relation to Germany, remarking that this also refers to newspapers close to the government.

Ambassador Lipski replied that Herr Neurath probably had in mind the *Kurier Poranny,* which cannot at present be regarded as a governmental press organ.

Minister Beck remarked that the solution of Danzig problems, so irritating to Polish opinion, will undoubtedly contribute to the calming of the tone of the Polish press.

Ambassador Lipski remarked that recently such a calming was already under way.

12. Minister Beck informed Herr von Neurath that the German Embassy in Warsaw obtained the agreement of the Polish government to the purchase of land for the building of new premises, by way of compensation for goods.

In February, 1937, Göring arrived in Poland for a hunting party. On February 16 he paid a visit to Marshal Śmigły-Rydz with Vice-Minister Szembek and Ambassador von Moltke also present. (For the contents of the conversation, see *Journal,* p. 221, and *Polish White Book,* No. 29. The final part of the conversation containing Marshal Śmigły's statement is missing from both summaries.) The Marshal stressed that he was determined to follow the policy line initiated by the late Marshal Piłsudski. He thought that

[6] The Kiel Canal was internationalized according to articles 381–86 of the Treaty of Versailles. The passage was open to all commercial and navy ships. On November 14, 1936, Germany unilaterally repudiated the international status of the canal.

Polish-German relations were slowly but steadily developing in a positive way. However, the Polish government was not in a position to exert its influence on public opinion to such a degree as the Reich government. The Marshal thought also that in this respect an improvement was shortly to be expected. The Marshal called attention to the fact that the youth in Germany was brought up in an anti-Polish spirit. He shared the opinion of Prime Minister Göring that, in case misunderstandings arose, they should be frankly clarified between the two parties.

As far as the attitude toward the Soviets was concerned, the Polish nation would not succumb to Communist influence. This was proved in a gallant way when Polish soldiers fought the Bolsheviks in 1919–20.

The Marshal, like Prime Minister Göring, did not think the Soviets would plan aggression. Nevertheless, he had the impression that in case of complications in Europe the Soviets would avail themselves of the situation to spread social disturbances in weak and more unsteady sectors. It was beyond conception that Poland would be on the side of the Bolsheviks in case of international conflict.

With regard to the alliance with France, the Marshal stressed that it was purely a defensive one, and he added that since Marshal Piłsudski's death this alliance had been neither extended nor altered. Prime Minister Göring declared that he was happy to have heard the above statement from the Marshal and that he would be able to repeat it to the Chancellor.

Later in the course of the conversation Göring supplied information about the war situation in Spain, where, in his opinion, the Soviets had already lost their game. Giving this information, he did not conceal the large number of German and Italian troops and armaments in the Spanish fighting.

In his notes Lipski complains of difficulties over the visits of Polish ministers to Germany. Fearing public opinion, they did not wish to engage themselves in German politics. Such was the case of the minister of justice, Witold Grabowski, whom Minister Frank invited to deliver a lecture in Berlin. He first agreed to come but later refused, and only decided to go to Berlin at the urging of the Ministry of Foreign Affairs and Marshal Śmigły-Rydz. In Berlin, besides holding other conversations, he was received by Chancellor Hitler.

# Declaration about National Minorities
## June—November, 1937

IN THE SUMMER and fall of 1937 negotiations were conducted by Poland and Germany on the situation of national minorities. The talks began on the initiative of the German government, which strove to find a legal way to increase the rights of the German minority in Poland. This minority, numbering about 740,000 (in 1931), was very well organized, was generally economically prosperous, had a system of German schools on a large scale, had its representatives in the Diet and Senate in Warsaw, and was constantly supported financially by the appropriate institutions in Germany. Besides, this minority was protected by a minorities agreement which Poland was obliged to sign in 1919 and which was in force until 1934. Nevertheless, Germans in Poland fought determinedly for more rights.

As compared with this situation, the Polish minority in Germany, although much larger in number (about 1,300,000 in 1938), was economically destitute, had a lower degree of consciousness in the national and political fields and a modest school system, and was faced with all kinds of obstacles raised by the German authorities regarding its cultural and economic development. It was also exempt from the protection that Germans in Poland enjoyed for so many years under the minorities agreement of 1919.

Therefore, when the German government presented a proposition for an agreement on the minorities problem, the Polish government accepted this proposition in order to obtain similar rights for the Polish minority in Germany.

In the course of conferences on the minorities agreement, Ambassador Lipski discussed with the Polish Ministry of Foreign Affairs the necessity of binding this minorities agreement to a certain degree with the agreement defining the inviolability of Polish rights in Danzig. A distinct difference of opinion between the stand taken by the authorities in Warsaw and that of the Ambassador in Berlin could be noted. This difference is related in Lipski's reports and the instructions of Beck, who, although he desired to obtain an additional German declaration with regard to Danzig, did not want to bind it to the minorities agreement. Hitler's declaration of November 5, 1937, to Ambassador Lipski brought a solution to this problem.

DOCUMENT 65   Lipski to Beck

NO. N/52/11/37                                    Berlin, June 19, 1937
                                                        *Confidential*

Even before my return from Warsaw, Herr von Neurath, as you were
informed, asked me to call at the Auswärtiges Amt on Saturday the 19th
at 12 noon. In connection with news that submarine torpedo boats
belonging to the Red Spanish fleet had repeated their attack on the
battleship *Leipzig*,[1] Herr von Neurath informed me on Saturday morning that he had been summoned by the Chancellor for consultation.
Therefore the audience was postponed and the Foreign Affairs Minister
was pressed for time, which rendered difficult a detailed exchange of
opinion.

Herr von Neurath informed me that a few days ago the German
battleship *Leipzig,* on patrol duty in Spanish waters, had been torpedoed
by submarines of the Red Spanish fleet. On Friday, June 18, a similar
incident took place, rendering the situation serious. The German government cannot tolerate that its war units on patrol duty be exposed to
such risks. On this occasion the torpedoes missed their target. Nevertheless, at any time of such shooting the torpedo might hit the ship. As a
proof that the Madrid side did shoot at the German ship on purpose,
Herr von Neurath stated that although the Soviet navy remained silent
after the first shooting, the population on the side of the Reds was
informed about this fact. François-Poncet allegedly also confirmed this
to him. Under these circumstances the German government intervened
energetically at the London committee and is now awaiting measures to
safeguard the German side from such attempts.

Following such explanations, Herr von Neurath passed to the real
subject of our conversation.

I was invited to the Auswärtiges Amt to be informed that von Moltke
was directed by his government to present to you a proposition for a
declaration on minorities. Herr von Neurath observed that the minority
problems had become drastically complicated of late and he had great
difficulties in restraining the press and public opinion. This matter had

---

[1] The battleship *Leipzig* was attacked four times north of Oran on June 16–18,
1937, by Spanish submarines belonging to the government in Valencia.

reached the Chancellor himself. In von Neurath's opinion, such declarations would contribute to a relaxation of the atmosphere and would set an example for the local authorities to follow in selecting a proper line of conduct.

For my part, I mentioned that this matter is very ticklish for us, especially as compared with the situation of other minorities. I added that I already knew from von Moltke that he is awaiting proposals from Berlin to be presented to you. These proposals will be subjected to investigation by our side.

Next, we touched loosely with Herr von Neurath on the problem of negotiations now under way between Poland and Germany with regard to the expiring Geneva Convention.[2]

During the conversation Herr von Neurath mentioned his trip to the Balkans.[3] He stressed a positive development in the Yugoslav policy that is serving to improve relations with Yugoslavia's neighbors. He pointed to the considerable development of Belgrade in the last years, which impressed him even more since he had not visited this city since prewar times.

Then, following your recommendation, I invited Minister von Neurath, in the name of the Polish government, to visit Poland this summer. Herr von Neurath, requesting me to convey to you his thanks for the invitation, remarked that he had recently been traveling a good deal and that some interruption is advisable. He stressed that he was also compelled to give a negative answer at present to the suggestion of the French Ambassador that he visit Paris. He is going to London on the urging of the British government, without any definite program, and he knows that only a general exchange of opinion will take place. Moreover, he does not intend to take up any matters in detail, such as the Western Pact.[4] He asked that the date of his visit to Warsaw be postponed until autumn. Besides, in his opinion, there are no problems between us requiring settlement by way of such an official visit.

From the above pronouncements of Herr von Neurath I could draw

[2] On June 2, 1937, a new Polish-German railway agreement was signed following the expiration of the Upper Silesian convention of May 15, 1922.

[3] In the first half of June, Minister von Neurath paid official visits to Belgrade, Sofia, and Budapest.

[4] Von Neurath's visit to London, scheduled for June 23, was canceled on June 21 in connection with the *Leipzig* problem.

the conclusion that he thinks he has been traveling too much in the last period to various countries, and perhaps he feels overtired. At the same time he is somewhat concerned that the volume of his travels might reduce their prestige value. In the course of the conversation, in order to avoid the misleading impression that our invitation to Warsaw might in any way be connected with Herr von Neurath's visit to London, I mentioned his conversation with Minister Grabowski on this subject. Herr von Neurath agreed that on Minister Grabowski's suggestion he had expressed a desire to visit Warsaw, and that he still has such an intention.

Next I brought up the problem of the Western Pact, remarking that it might be noted that this problem is acquiring more concrete forms. I explained that hitherto we had not spelled out our point of view in writing but had simply conducted a loose exchange of opinions with particular countries. I stressed that, without prejudging our attitude of the future pact, I would like to state that the structure of agreements from 1925 on does not suit us, and I underlined among other aspects undesirable for us the excessive dependence on the League of Nations. I further explained that we see from the present exchange of correspondence between the Powers that an idea still prevails of concluding certain triangle agreements under the new pact between Great Britain, France, and Germany, and between Germany, France, and Italy. In this connection I observed that, under such a concept of triangles, a German-Polish-French triangle could be considered. Herr von Neurath quickly answered that in the first place, in his opinion, the whole idea of the pact is not yet ripe for realization. He referred to the difficulties existing between Great Britain and Italy, which encumber the possibility of reaching an understanding. As far as the concept of triangle agreements in the West is concerned, he does not see any real foundation for them, especially since the Italian government is against such a set-up. Herr von Neurath's attitude to the very idea of such triangles is negative, for in his opinion they would complicate the situation. He much prefers bilateral agreements, such as our agreement of 1934. The German government limited itself to conferences with the Western countries in order to avoid complications of the situation by other more extensive systems of pacts.

When I observed that our situation in the east is different, for besides our alliance with France we now have the 1934 agreement with the Reich, Herr von Neurath stressed that he considers the agreement with us to be of more importance than the concepts of some vague, more extensive pact. Bearing in mind this stand of the Foreign Affairs Minister, I confined myself to a statement that I only wanted to make a suggestion as to one of the possible variations.

With reference to the above report, I would like to explain that in my opinion Herr von Neurath's point of view does not preclude the possibility of further talks on this subject. I think that on the eve of his departure for London the Foreign Affairs Minister did not wish to commit himself to a more definite attitude toward us. On the other hand, this concept, which introduces quite a new element to the negotiations, might have taken him aback to a certain extent. Nevertheless, I may not exclude the possibility that the German government was told by the French government of our recent attempts in Paris. This seems even more probable, inasmuch as Herr von Neurath, in the course of the conversation, referred several times to his contacts with the French Ambassador; on the other hand, it is known to me that M. Delbos had a conversation with Ambassador Welczek with regard to the last French note. However, I must lay stress on the fact that Herr von Neurath's stand reflected a tendency well known to me—to separate the pact in the west from eastern problems.

This thesis recently appeared in the German press, and it could be observed in connection with the gradual growth of collaboration among the Four Powers in the London Committee of Nonintervention. In order to render the Minister of Foreign Affairs more conscious of the advantages to be gained by the German side from the concept of a triangle including Poland, eliminating the Soviets and Czechoslovakia from the pact, I chose an indirect way, by instructing Counselor Lubomirski to supply additional explanations on the problem to the office of the A.A. I intend to discuss these matters with Prime Minister Göring or other competent authorities of the Party at the next opportunity. I would begin these conversations from the angle that we on our part consider it desirable to maintain a friendly exchange of opinion and to collaborate with the German government on the problems of the Western Pact, and would like to know whether they reciprocate our point of view.

*Józef Lipski*

DOCUMENT 66   Lipski to Beck

NO. N/262/13/37                                          Berlin, August 6, 1937
                                                                *Strictly Confidential*

Last Tuesday, on August 3, I had the opportunity to discuss at length with Herr von Moltke the problem of the minorities and the Danzig declaration. Von Moltke expected a separate declaration by the Auswärtiges Amt on the subject of our counterplan on the declaration about minorities. However, the departments declared that they have to investigate the changes introduced by the Polish government into the German plan. A conference with the respective departments will take place on Monday, August 9. Until then, since he is not in a position to push the problem forward, von Moltke will remain at home in Silesia and will drop in for a day or two at Warsaw.

Availing myself of this occasion, I had a longer discussion with von Moltke about the difficulties encountered by our minorities in Germany in connection with the application of National Socialist rules. Only upon reading the memorandum on Polish minorities in Germany did Herr von Moltke realize the essence of the problem. However, he stated at the same time that there is a complete lack of orientation on this problem on the part of the central administration elements in Berlin. From this point of view he thinks that an interministerial consultation might be advisable, at which he will be able to expose this particular aspect of the problem. Herr von Moltke still has no clear idea for a solution to this problem. He considers that the question of exception to National Socialist rules would not be suitable for the declaration, and that the question should rather be solved by way of an internal German bill.

Referring to the fate of the German minorities in Poland, Herr von Moltke stressed that these minorities complain little about difficulties of a cultural character but instead claim a systematic economic pressure. Allegedly 80 percent of the minorities in Poland are unemployed. Herr von Moltke added that the central authorities in Warsaw are not quite aware of this, just as the central authorities in Berlin do not understand that Polish minorities in Germany suffer from the subjection to National Socialist laws.

Incidentally, I also referred in this conversation to the question of the high schools at Kwidzyń and Racibórz. Moltke replied that this question is quite clear, as far as its solution is concerned, in spite of difficulties with the application of a total system.

When I touched upon the Danzig declaration, Herr von Moltke answered that, unfortunately, this problem cannot be solved without von Neurath and the Chancellor. He added that personally he sees no objection to such a declaration, which in his opinion would have a favorable effect on bilateral relations. As Herr von Neurath is in the country and the Chancellor at Berchtesgaden, it is difficult to obtain a final decision. Neurath will probably have no opportunity to see the Chancellor prior to the opening of the Nuremberg Congress, which will take place on September 6.

When I mentioned the necessity of settling both matters and remarked that I am leaving for Monte Cattini on the 16th, Herr von Moltke observed that from your words he did not have the impression that the two acts should be connected and that, in his opinion also, this might not be advisable.

So, next week will bring a definition of the German point of view regarding alterations inserted by us into the German plan of the declaration and a possible coordination of the texts. On the 13th and 14th of this month Göring will be in Berlin for two days. I will avail myself of this opportunity to inform him about the state of negotiations and will take care to gain his support for the Danzig declaration.

I think that to present a declaration on minorities without obtaining at least an *accord de principe* with regard to the Danzig declaration would be dangerous. Therefore, if Moltke should return to Warsaw next week without a reply on Danzig, the solution to the minorities questions could be postponed until the Congress at Nuremberg. As I shall be in Nuremberg, I could take up the Danzig problem with von Neurath and the Chancellor.

*Józef Lipski*

DOCUMENT 67. Lipski to Beck

NO. N/262/16/37                                    Berlin, August 14, 1937

Following my letter of August 6, No. N/262/13/37, I am taking the liberty of reporting that Herr von Moltke, prior to his return to Warsaw on August 12, gave me a general idea of the results of local consultations on the counterplan of our declaration on the minorities questions. In the German insertions to the text I was most concerned about the desire to cancel the paragraph of our preamble stating that the minorities questions are the exclusive concern of the internal affairs of each country. Von Moltke justified this demand by saying that the German side does not recognize this thesis, and therefore does not want to declare it officially. Referring to the agreement of 1934 and our principles in this matter, I stated explicitly to von Moltke that such a demand will not be accepted by Warsaw. He then informed me that this stand of ours is no surprise to him, and that he did not fail to point out to the Auswärtiges Amt what difficulties might arise from such a German demand.

Von Moltke mentioned other alterations in a general way. On the item dealing with Church matters, I stressed the total neglect of Poles in Germany as far as the pastorate is concerned, quoting as an example that even our emigrants cannot obtain priests from Poland. I pointed to the last case when the departure to Saxony of a priest nominated by Primate Hlond was refused.

By the way, I would like to add that it would be useful to draw up a list of pastors in Poland who are citizens of Germany, in order that we may present this statistic to counter difficulties we have here concerning Polish priests.

As to my question on the application of National Socialist methods toward the minorities, von Moltke could as yet obtain nothing concrete; he only said that he had presented this problem *in extenso* to the representatives of the departments.

He did not mention Danzig at all.

It was obvious from the above that Moltke was working only with departmental clerks, without reaching competent authorities, who are on vacation. My meeting with Göring also did not materialize, since he did not return to Berlin as had been planned. All this makes me think that for the moment it is impossible to finalize the negotiations to our advantage, and that it is better to await the possibility of talking with competent authorities. Besides, I do not observe on the German side any special hurry in this matter, which was taken up on their initiative, and which could only be of interest for us if we obtain some positive results for our *minorities in Germany* and at the same time a clarification of the *Danzig question.*

Up to now the German text deals mostly with the demands of German minorities in Poland.

For the better orientation of the Ministry of Foreign Affairs I shall take the liberty of dispatching in the oncoming days a report prepared by the Association of Poles, dealing with the application of each of the particular National Socialist laws to the Polish minorities in Germany.

*Józef Lipski*

### DOCUMENT 68   Lipski to Beck

NO. N/262/22/37                                    Berlin, September 22, 1937
                                                   *Strictly Confidential*

Following your verbal instructions received on September 7 during the trip from Warsaw to Berlin, I had a conversation on September 11 with Foreign Affairs Minister von Neurath at Nuremberg dealing with Polish-German negotiations on the question of minorities.[5] I reported on it by telegram from Munich on September 11. This conversation, completed by explanations given to me by Herr von Moltke at Nuremberg and on September 14 in Berlin, yielded the following results up to now:

1) With regard to the declaration, it was decided that it will be published after your return to Warsaw, and that a date will be fixed to prevent other political moments, such as Mussolini's arrival in Germany, from absorbing public attention.[6] The two governments will therefore still have to agree on the date.

---

[5] For von Neurath's version of this conversation, together with the Polish plan of the declaration on the Danzig problem, see *DGFP*, Series D, Vol. V, Nos. 1 and 2.

[6] Minister Beck proceeded to Geneva on September 7 for the eighteenth session of the Assembly of the League of Nations, paying a visit on the way to

2) Herr von Moltke returned to matters *ad* point 1 of the declaration, suggesting the restoration of the wording in accordance with the Polish counterplan presented by you at the time. In my discussion on this subject with von Moltke on September 14, I introduced a formula most adequate for the interests of our minorities in Germany, which reads as follows:

"Mutual respect for the German and the Polish nationality in itself precludes any attempt to assimilate the minority by force, to question membership in the minority, or to hinder profession of membership in the minority. In particular, no pressure of any kind will be exerted on youthful members of the minority in order to alienate them from their adherence to such minority."

Herr von Neurath accepted the text of this formula, and the Auswärtiges Amt informed the Embassy accordingly on September 17.

I enclose the text of the declaration in German with the altered Article 1, together with a Polish translation of the first part of this article.[7]

3) In order that the German government would have in writing our restrictions regarding the consequences of some National Socialist laws for Polish minorities, on September 15 I forwarded the promised memorandum on this matter to Herr von Neurath. Copy enclosed.[8]

4) Regarding the Danzig formula, Herr von Moltke explained that von Neurath's statement to the effect that he allegedly understood from the Ambassador's report that we are interested in a one-sided declaration must be a misunderstanding, since as a result of his talk with you Moltke stated clearly in his report that the declaration is to be two-sided. Interpellated by von Moltke, Herr von Neurath did admit that the Ambassador's report raised no doubts in this respect, and that it was the Foreign Affairs Minister's own mistake. Herr von Moltke told me that the Chancellor will decide on this matter, and that it is a *novum* that we are now pushing forward the concept of a confidential exchange of notes on this problem instead of an official declaration. In spite of the fact that Herr von Moltke seemed to realize the purpose of a clarification of the Danzig problem between the two governments to be the appeasement of

---

Minister Delbos in Paris (September 8 and 9). The return to Warsaw took place on September 30. Mussolini's stay in Germany on an official visit lasted from September 25 to September 29.

[7] See *DGFP*, Series D, Vol. V, No. 18.

[8] Enclosure missing in Lipski's papers.

the competent authorities in Poland, nevertheless he was not quite sure whether the Chancellor would accept such a suggestion.

Under these circumstances I am trying to influence the Chancellor via Göring, with whom, however, it is difficult to establish contact, owing to the maneuvers and Mussolini's arrival, as well as his absorption with the Four-Year Plan.[9]

*Józef Lipski*

DOCUMENT 69   Lipski to the Ministry of Foreign Affairs

Telephonogram
NO. 107

Berlin, October 7, 1937
Received October 7, 7:50 P.M.
*Confidential: for the Minister
only*

Replacing the absent von Neurath and on his instructions, the Secretary of State declared to me that he cannot accept our suggestion for an exchange of notes on the Danzig problem. He referred to the principle which was accepted by the German government for nonconfirmation of particular resolutions of the Versailles Treaty. He tried to persuade me that the Chancellor's declaration of nonviolability of the Danzig statute should be sufficient for the Polish government.

In my reply, however, I explicitly stated why we consider the declaration to be necessary. I abstained from any discussion of the declaration on minorities.

I shall try to find out tomorrow through Göring whether the opposition stems from the A.A. or whether the Chancellor has really taken such a decision.[10]

*Lipski*

[9] Lipski talked with Göring on September 29, asking for his support in reaching a common declaration of the two countries on the Danzig question. Neurath presented this matter to Hitler, who accepted Neurath's stand not to link the declaration on minorities with the declaration dealing with Danzig (*DGFP,* Series D, Vol. V, Nos. 6, 7, 8, 9, and 10). See also the conversations between Lipski and Szembek of October 4 (*Journal,* p. 243).

[10] For Secretary of State Mackensen's version of this conversation, see *DGFP,* Series D, Vol. V, No. 11.

In Lipski's papers there is the following handwritten note:

After my conversation with Secretary of State Mackensen on October 7, I wanted to see Göring immediately. In his absence I had a conversation [on October 8] with Secretary of State Koerner [in Göring's office]. In very precise terms I criticized the negative German attitude with regard to the Danzig formula proposed by me. I went so far as to state that, if the Chancellor supported the negative stand of the Auswärtiges Amt on this problem, I would consider my mission as terminated. Koerner tried to iron out the problem and promised to discuss it seriously with Göring.[11]

DOCUMENT 70    Lipski to the Ministry of Foreign Affairs

Telephonogram                    Berlin, October 18, 1937
NO. 117                          Received: October 18, 7:30 P.M.
                                 *Secret*

Although during today's conversation von Neurath asked me to inform you that he will not be able to carry through the bilateral declaration on the Danzig problem proposed by us, he nevertheless showed willingness to find a solution in a different way acceptable to us.

He is also considering the following solution: that after receiving our minorities the Chancellor would, at a special audience, give me a verbal declaration on the Danzig question. In this connection, a communiqué appeared which followed the line of appeasing public opinion on Danzig matters.

I told von Neurath that I would communicate our point of view to him on Friday. I shall be in Warsaw on Thursday and relate to you another essential point for the conversation with von Neurath.[12]

*Lipski*

In a personal note on his conversation with von Neurath on October 18 and later with Beck, Lipski writes:

[11] For Koerner's version of this conversation related by Mackensen, see *ibid.*, No. 12.

[12] For von Neurath's version of this conversation, see *ibid.*, No. 13.

I referred to Forster's statement that Danzig is a *Zwergstaat* which sooner or later must disappear. I stressed the harmfulness of such statements by the Danzig Gauleiter. Herr von Neurath, as usual, said a few soothing words, alluding to the necessity of our having a special talk about this sometime.

I reported this to Beck. Beck instructed me to tell von Neurath casually, referring to his statement, that Beck also feels that the necessity may arise to discuss an understanding on the Free City of Danzig question.

DOCUMENT 71   Lipski to the Ministry of Foreign Affairs

Telephonogram
NO. 119                                        Berlin, October 23, 1937
                                   Received: October 23, 5:55 P.M.
                                   *Secret*

I communicated to Neurath your reply expressing agreement to the solution on the Danzig matter proposed in coded telegram No. 117. Following your wishes, I outlined verbally items of the communiqué from the anticipated conversation with the Chancellor. Neurath promised to work on the text and clear it with me.

Neurath will present the proposed solution to the Chancellor, who returns tomorrow, and will communicate the result to me.

Neurath said that, owing to the Chancellor's short stay in Berlin, the Chancellor's reception for the minorities and the audience with me, as well as the issuance of the declaration, will have to take place in the next few days.[13]

In this connection please advise the Civil Chancellery [of the President of Poland], since the receptions for the minorities by the Polish President and the Chancellor are to take place on the same day. Only after my next conversation with Neurath will it be possible to establish whether the reception by the Chancellor will take place prior to or after the declaration.

*Lipski*

[13] For von Neurath's version of this conversation, see *ibid.*, No. 16.

On November 3, 1937, Vice-Minister Szembek proceeded to Berlin to take part in the opening of the Hunting Exposition, where Poland also had a pavilion. Szembek handed Lipski Beck's instructions cited below for the conversation with Hitler, which was to take place on November 5.

After a luncheon at the Embassy on November 4, Szembek had occasion to have a talk with Göring, which Szembek related in his *Journal*, pp. 244–49. See also *Polish White Book*, No. 30.

DOCUMENT 72   Beck to Lipski

November 3, 1937

In your conversation with the Chancellor on the Danzig matters, I request you to declare that you are authorized by the Polish government to convey thanks for the declaration which was presented by Ambassador Moltke in the Chancellor's name to Minister Beck on September 6, namely, that neither the Chancellor nor the Reich has the intention of violating Polish rights in Danzig. The Polish government values this declaration highly, for the unanimous opinion of government authorities, as well as of the population at large in Poland, will always consider the Danzig problem a test case for Polish-German relations. And this in spite of the fact that the Danzig problem does not seem to have such objective importance. Please state further that we wish to explain that, if the Polish government raised this question on the occasion of the publication of the declaration on minorities, this was only due to the fact that it is not possible to create an atmosphere of confidence in Poland for relations between Poland and Germany without peace on the Danzig sector.

Please remind the Chancellor that, as far as the free development of the German population in Danzig is concerned, the Polish government abstained from participation in any international plotting, or any anti-German action by international elements.

Nevertheless, cardinal principles exist in respect to the life of the Free City to which the Polish government will never be indifferent. These principal Polish rights and interests, defined in the Polish-Danzig convention in Paris in 1920, seem to be threatened of late. Namely, we noted that the National Socialist Party in Danzig began to attack not only what was considered as the Geneva doctrine in Danzig but also the principles of the said Polish-Danzig convention.

The Polish Ambassador in Berlin has been working and continues to work for the great idea of a Polish-German understanding, but he must warn that the course of events in Danzig might spoil the positive effect of the present new effort (the minorities declaration) designed to consolidate Polish-German relations.

In case the Chancellor inquires what the crux of the matter really is, please answer that the rights and interests of Poland which you are referring to depend in the first place on the matter of the harbor and railways; next, on the situation of the Polish minorities; and, finally, on the customs system and the currency connected therewith. Also, forms of conduct of the Senate, considered from the angle of the afore-mentioned Paris Convention entrusting the foreign policy of Danzig to the Polish government, are of vital importance.

Regardless of the results of the conversation, I ask you to negotiate with Neurath the forms of the communiqué about the conversation with the Chancellor in such a way as to omit the paragraph with regard to conformity of opinion on the Danzig question.

*Beck*

On November 5, 1937, a declaration was published in Warsaw and Berlin by the Polish and German governments regarding treatment of national minorities. Simultaneously, President Mościcki received Ambassador von Moltke and a delegation of the German minorities in Poland, and Chancellor Hitler received Ambassador Lipski and a delegation of the Polish minorities in Germany. In the conversation with Lipski, Hitler made a declaration with regard to Danzig. Pertinent official communiqués were also issued.

Lipski's report which follows cites the wording of the declaration about Danzig. The text of the declaration on national minorities and other details may be found in the *Polish White Book*, Nos. 32, 33, 35. The text of Lipski's report of November 5 (*Polish White Book*, No. 34) is very much abbreviated. *DGFP* cites documents on this matter (Nos. 18 and 19).

DOCUMENT 73   Lipski to Beck

NO. N/262/31/37                            Berlin, November 5, 1937
                                           *Strictly Confidential*

I was received by the Chancellor at 12:15 P.M. today, with the Reich
foreign affairs minister, von Neurath, also present.

The Chancellor began the conversation by expressing satisfaction
with the finalization of the declaration on the problem of minorities. For
my part, I started my deliberations by remarking that the date of November 5 marks a certain anniversary. On that day four years ago I
received from Marshal Piłsudski basic instructions for my conversation
with the Chancellor of the Reich, which took place on November 15 and
which resulted in the agreement of January 26, 1934. I further stated
that, in spite of difficulties of an internal and external political nature,
the Polish government accepted the Chancellor's suggestion on minorities declarations designed to bring about a relaxation of Polish-German
relations in this sector. President Mościcki, together with Marshal
Śmigły-Rydz and Minister Beck, took a broad view of this matter. If in
the course of discussions on this subject we also referred to a relaxation
in the Danzig sector, it was because we strove for a general *détente*.
When, following your instructions of November 3, I then pointed out to
the Chancellor that his declaration presented by Ambassador von
Moltke to Minister Beck on September 6 relating to Danzig was duly
appreciated by the Polish government, the Chancellor for his part defined his stand, and he did so in a most precise manner. Specifically, he
stated point by point that

1) in the legal-political situation of Danzig no changes will occur
("an der rechtspolitischen Lage Danzigs wird nichts geändert werden");

2) the rights of the Polish population in Danzig have to be respected;

3) Poland's rights in Danzig will not be violated.

The Chancellor firmly declared that the agreement concluded by him
with Poland will be respected, and this applies also to Danzig. The
promise he makes will be kept. There is no question of any surprise
action. The Chancellor only desired the German population in Danzig to
adopt a system of rule most suitable for the Germans. Besides, such a
state of affairs is the best safeguard against possible complications, since

it is a protection against sallies by particular political parties. The Chancellor asked me to communicate the above declaration to the Polish government. He laid special stress on the fact that it is his desire that it should be known to Marshal Śmigly-Rydz. This undoubtedly relates to the fact that in my conversations I referred several times to the person of the Marshal and laid stress on the mistrust prevailing in these matters in our army command.

In reply, I acknowledged the above declaration, expressing my thanks for it to the Chancellor. In the course of further discussion on this point, I stated that we always abstained from intervention into the internal development of the German population in Danzig. We rejected all offers by the Danzig opposition. In the international forum we were careful to avoid entanglements in intrigues. I also mentioned that our rights and interests connected *with the existence of the Free City* are defined in the Polish-Danzig convention of 1920 as well as in later agreements.

Next, and just in a general sense, I added on my own that Danzig should certainly be a link—a center where Polish-German interests can work together. I pointed here to the important historic role Danzig played in olden times in trade with the Polish Kingdom and even far beyond its frontiers.

Here the Chancellor twice emphasized that Danzig is connected by its interests with Poland ("Danzig ist mit Polen verbunden").

Further, according to your instructions, I tried to shift the conversation to the domain of general politics. We first took up the subject of direct conversations, which had proved successful now and in the past, on Polish-German relations. And lately, as the Chancellor remarked, they had also yielded positive results with Belgium. Here the Chancellor called attention to the difficulties of applying such methods to regimes with overcomplex parliamentary systems, and he mentioned France. He illustrated by means of a number of his endeavors aimed at improving relations with France, as, for example, in the problems of disarmament. Unfortunately, they were of no avail, for at the moment of a possible understanding a part of the French press started a strong campaign.

About Czechoslovakia the Chancellor said that he cannot understand the government in Prague, which, in the situation in which it finds itself—surrounded by Germany and Poland, as well as by Hungary—has done nothing to settle the minorities question. A reasonable government in Prague would undoubtedly take the necessary measures to find a way out of the impasse by means of an agreement on these matters.

Regarding colonies, the Chancellor said that he is presenting the colonial thesis, and will realize it, but naturally not by means of war. Jokingly he remarked that he would not declare war even for the Cameroons. The colonial problem, in his opinion, has now passed from the European to the global level. If Germany is accused of the fact that the colonies would supply it with only 10 to 15 percent of its food and raw material needs, the Chancellor's reply to this is that this corresponds to the monthly consumption of the Reich, which is a very high figure. Today, in economic questions, the Reich government has to consider even the smallest states, and with some of these, as, for example, Belgium, relations are developing successfully. From the angle of economic interests, the Chancellor cannot remain indifferent to the internal development of these states, because in smaller states the Communist system immediately disrupts all commercial turnover; Red Spain might serve as an example. On the other hand, economic life in Spain under General Franco is developing to some extent.

Talking further about Spain, the Chancellor stated that he has no political interests there and that he does not intend to introduce National Socialism into Spain. In general, he will stay away from the problems of the Mediterranean, since they are very dangerous. If he were offered a portion of Morocco, he would willingly turn it down for the same reasons. If he had such possessions, he would have to build a tremendous naval war base, with all the risks this involves.

When discussing certain international diversions against the agreements, I pointed to the action of the Soviets, who still resort to this method. The Chancellor agreed with this, citing the incident of the Spanish submarines.

I would like to stress that the whole conversation was conducted on very friendly terms, and the Chancellor seemed to be very well satisfied with the understanding achieved with Poland.

*Józef Lipski*

DOCUMENT 74   Lipski to Beck

NO. N/52/22                                    Berlin, November 19, 1937
                                                      *Strictly Confidential*

Upon my return to Berlin I found an invitation from Göring for a
hunting party at Springe on November 18, which I attended before
leaving for my vacation. On this occasion I had the opportunity to
discuss political subjects with him at length.

As I had hunted in the Poznań region on November 15 with Marshal
Śmigły, to whom I once more related in detail my conversation with the
Chancellor on the Danzig problem, I told Göring that the Marshal accepted with satisfaction the Chancellor's declaration, which will undoubtedly also contribute to smoothing out the Danzig situation. I went
over again the items agreed to with the Chancellor. Göring, who now
seemed to be very well disposed toward us, said that he had talked with
Forster, who is very anxious to be received by you. In order to follow
strictly the guiding lines fixed in his conversation with the Chancellor,
Forster said that the prohibition against establishing parties in the Free
City does not apply to the Polish population. However, in his conversation with you he would like to find a solution which would render
impossible the infiltration of German Socialist elements into the Polish
parties in Danzig.

Göring thinks that in principle we should have nothing against this,
since burdening themselves with German Socialists does not seem to be
in the interest of the Danzig Poles.

I seized this opportunity to mention to Göring the present economic
negotiations between Poland and Danzig. I did this on purpose in order
to be able to exert pressure, via Göring, on the Party elements in Danzig, in case the need, as referred to me by Wachowiak,[14] should arise.

Today reprints appeared in the German press, nearly *in extenso,* from
*Political Information* on the subject of the last conversation with the
Chancellor about Danzig.

I think that our *mise au point* will have a very positive effect both
locally and abroad.

Among other subjects, Göring brought up the Russian problem, stat-

[14] Stanisław Wachowiak, former deputy to the Diet, was the Polish political
leader in Poznań and Silesia.

ing that the leaders of the National Socialist Party headed by the Chancellor profess the principle that Germany's attitude should be negative not only to Soviet Russia but also to a possibly nationalist Russia, which will always be a threat to the Reich as an unpredictable Asiatic colossus. He set this opinion against certain contradictory judgments prevailing in Reichswehr circles.

Next he said that Russia's military aspirations seem to be concentrated at present on the Rumanian sector and in the region of the Baltic states, including Finland. He posed the question whether Poland would remain neutral in case of some action on the part of the Soviets in these regions. I remarked that we have an alliance with Rumania. In relation to the Baltic states, our policy is that they should maintain their independence from Russia.

Göring was not yet prepared to discuss Halifax's mission,[15] stating that a decisive talk will take place at Berchtesgaden with the Chancellor. He only stated that Germany cannot afford to loosen its ties with Italy and Japan. Göring felt that support of Japan, in his opinion, would be a move in Poland's interest also, since it would check Russia in the Far East.

Göring quite openly counts on an invitation for a hunting party in Poland. I discussed this matter with General Fabrycy.

*Józef Lipski*

The following note (not dated) was found in Lipski's papers:

### The Problem of Marshal Tukhachevsky's Assassination [16]

Göring communicated to me strictly in confidence that Soviet Marshal Tukhachevsky, during his visit to London for the funeral of King George V, approached the Reichswehr through secret channels, offering

[15] Lord Halifax, at that time Lord President of the Council, came to Berlin on the occasion of the Hunting Exposition. Although his visit was of a private character, he was delegated by Prime Minister Chamberlain to establish contact with government authorities, and especially with Hitler. The conversation with the Chancellor took place on November 19 (*DGFP*, Series D, Vol. I, No. 31). Some information about this conversation was given by Weizsäcker to the Polish chargé d'affaires, Lubomirski, on December 2 (*ibid.*, Nos. 53 and 54).

[16] Mikhail Tukhachevsky, marshal of the Russian Army, was executed in June, 1937, together with seven prominent Soviet generals.

closer collaboration. This matter reached Chancellor Hitler, who emphatically rejected the offer.

Göring gave me to understand that the Reichswehr elements would have been more agreeable to an understanding with the Soviets, but Hitler prevented it.

I communicated this news to the Foreign Affairs Minister [Beck] who, so far as I know, did not make any further use of it. This indiscretion of Göring in front of the Polish Ambassador was, in my opinion, an attempt to persuade the Polish side that, as far as Hitler and the Party were concerned, it could be taken for granted that their attitude toward the USSR was negative. At the same time it served as a sort of warning that failure to join Hitler in an agreement against Russia might have grave consequences for Poland.

# Hitler Discloses His Designs [1]
## November, 1937

AFTER LONG and onerous Polish-German negotiations, the two governments promulgated simultaneously on November 5, 1937, the declaration regulating principles for the treatment of national minorities. In connection with the issuing of this declaration, I was received on the same day at 12:15 P.M. by Hitler in the Reich Chancellery, in the presence of von Neurath.

In the course of the conversation Hitler made a declaration ordering respect for the statute of the Free City of Danzig, the rights of Poland, and the interests of the Polish population in Danzig. During a later exchange I pointed to the role Danzig should perform as the natural harbor of the Polish hinterland, and recalled the importance of this city in old Polish times. Then Hitler twice firmly stressed that Danzig was bound to Poland ("Danzig ist mit Polen verbunden").

For several months the Polish government strove to bring about a clarification of the German stand on the Danzig problem. This became imperative in the face of the National Socialist campaign directed at that time against Polish interests in the Free City, with the knowledge and blessings of Gauleiter Forster. My concern was to induce an exchange of notes with the German government on this problem in order to give a more formal character to the pledge, which would be a bilateral commitment in writing. However, I met with obstacles on the part of the Auswärtiges Amt. At one time an acute clash resulted from Undersecretary Mackensen's refusal to accept my proposed text, previously confirmed by Göring. Mackensen hid behind von Neurath's decision. Under these circumstances it was necessary to clarify the Chancellor's stand.

Hitler's declaration was a sort of compromise solution, not very satisfactory.

[1] Printed in Sprawny *Międzynarodowe* (London), 1947, Nos. 2–3.

From the Reich Chancellery I proceeded to the French Embassy for a reception M. François-Poncet was giving for Göring and the international delegations visiting the Hunting Exposition in Berlin. At the entrance to the reception salons of the Embsssy I met the newly appointed British ambassador, Sir Nevile Henderson, whom Chamberlain entrusted with the mission to seek an understanding with Hitler. When I informed him of the result of my conversation with Hitler, Henderson, turning to his French colleague, remarked jokingly that Piłsudski had bought Hitler's shares at their lowest, while Great Britain and France wanted to buy them at the highest rate. This expression was very characteristic of the atmosphere prevailing at that time.

On the afternoon of the same day, a consultation was held at the Reich Chancellery that was enveloped in the deepest mystery. Hitler, Göring, Neurath, Blomberg, Fritsch, and Raeder took part in it. A report of this meeting written down by Colonel Hossbach fell into the hands of the Allies and was widely utilized at Nuremberg. It constitutes one of the most important documents of the prosecution, for it reveals the date when Hitler made the decision to choose the road of conquest.[2]

Opening the conference, Hitler remarked that he wanted to explain his principal idea for the necessity of German expansion. He requested that in case of his death this speech be considered his political testament. (Hitler often mentioned death when he spoke of his future plans. I heard such declarations of his several times.)

As usual, Hitler tried to explain his point of view in long and intricate deliberations. Analyzing the possibilities of finding a solution for the needs of the German nation and wondering if this could be achieved by autarchy or by an increase in Germany's share of foreign trade, or perhaps by increased international collaboration in the industrial field, Hitler concluded that, as far as raw materials were concerned, a system of autarchy might be applied to a limited extent only, for autarchy brings no solution when a nation has to be fed. Hitler's conclusions were also negative as far as the possibility of increasing Germany's share in the world's economy and the effectiveness of such a measure were concerned.

On the basis of these economic premises, Hitler concluded that the German nation, with a crowded population of 85 million, needed space to live (*Lebensraum*).

Illustrating with events from the history of the Roman and British

[2] *DGFP*, Series D, Vol. I, No. 19 (so-called Hossbach paper).

empires to show that those powers achieved accession of territories only by risky conquests, Hitler declared that Germany today faced the problem at a time when the *greatest conquests* could be achieved at the lowest risk.

This confession of Hitler renders his future actions more understandable.

In his further deliberations on the international situation, Hitler described Great Britain and France as potential enemies of the Reich. Besides these two states, Hitler also pointed to Russia and the smaller European states surrounding it as elements of power with which Germany must reckon. In this speech the dates for the war were fixed.

According to Hitler's calculations, the war was to take place in the years 1943–45. After this period Germany would begin to lose its ascendancy over its adversaries. The war could occur earlier in two cases: if social tension in France reached such a culminating point that the French Army would be unable to fight against the Germans, at which point the moment would come to occupy Czechoslovakia; or if a conflict erupted in the Mediterranean between Italy on the one hand and England and France on the other.

Hitler considered the necessity of occupying Czechoslovakia and Austria of primary importance. He explained this by a strategic need to remove the threat from the south in case of war with the West. However, it is quite probable that even then Hitler foresaw the possibility of subjugating Czechoslovakia without war, for he voiced the supposition that Great Britain and even perhaps France had ceased to count on Czechoslovakia. Besides, he was right when he argued that Great Britain's stand would be decisive for the behavior of France.

"If the Czechs were overthrown and a common German-Hungarian frontier achieved, a neutral attitude on the part of Poland could be the more certainly counted on in the event of a Franco-German conflict. Our agreements with Poland only retained their force as long as Germany's strength remained unshaken. In the event of German setbacks a Polish action against East Prussia, and possibly against Pomerania and Silesia as well, had to be reckoned with."

Elsewhere in the speech, when the probable reaction of France and Russia was considered in case of German warfare against Czechoslovakia and Austria in 1943–45, it was mentioned that Poland's position in such a conflict would depend on the dimensions and speed of German action.

Hitler presumed that Poland would not be inclined to stand up against a victorious Germany, with Soviet Russia at its back.

Hitler's deliberations on the Italian policy showed a striking lack of orientation. It turned out that he wanted to use his Italian ally as an instrument of his political strategy. He wished to bring about a conflict between Italy and France and England over the Spanish problems. He believed this war to be close at hand and even defined its anticipated dates. Neurath had some misgivings on this occasion. Blomberg and Fritsch were of the opinion that Great Britain and France should not be regarded as potential foes of Germany. They warned against taking lightly the military strength of France, and pointed to difficulties in conquering Czechoslovakia fortifications.

Hitler was not swayed by these arguments. Just a few months later, on February 4, 1938, Neurath, Blomberg, and Fritsch were relieved of their posts.

# Attempts to Draw Poland into the Anti-Comintern Pact[1]
## November, 1937

---

THE ANTI-COMINTERN PACT between Germany and Japan was signed in Berlin on November 25, 1936. [2] British political circles were amazed by the fact that on the German side the signature apposed to the act was that of Herr Ribbentrop, at that time the Reich's ambassador in London. Ribbentrop regarded the Anti-Comintern Pact as his achievement and his exclusive domain. He obstinately elaborated the concept of creating a league of states linked with the Third Reich against Communism and tried to gain Great Britain's consent to his plans. A special office in Berlin under Ribbentrop's leadership worked on anti-Comintern problems. Its activities were not controlled by the Auswärtiges Amt, thus creating a twofold policy that became a source of misunderstandings and frictions at the Wilhelmstrasse.

To the official pact between Germany and Japan a secret protocol [3] was attached which stated at the outset that Soviet Russia, supported by its armed forces, was trying to realize the goals laid out by international agencies. Article I provided that, in case of unprovoked aggression on the part of the Soviet Union against one of the participants of the pact, no action would be taken by the other side to reinforce the position of the USSR and that a consultation would follow immediately, aimed at safeguarding the common interests of the signatories. Article II contained an obligation not to conclude political agreements with the Soviet Union contradictory to the spirit of the pact.

A year later, on November 6, 1937, the Italian government joined the German-Japanese Anti-Comintern Pact,[4] under the clause providing

[1] Printed in *Bellona* (London), 1950, No. 1.
[2] For the text, see *Documents on International Affairs, 1936*, pp. 297–99.
[3] For the text, see *DGFP*, Series D, Vol. I, No. 463, footnote 2a.
[4] For the text, see *ibid.*, No. 17.

for the participation of other states. The problem of Poland's participation in the pact was discussed again and again by the original signatories, as can be proved by certain documents contained in *Documents on German Foreign Policy,* Series D, Volume I.

One of these documents [5] relates to a German-Japanese consultation in Berlin, organized on August 13, 1937, by the Ribbentrop office. This office delegated the following persons to the meeting: Dr. von Raumer, as director; Professor Langsdorf, as an expert on Rumania; and Dr. Kleist, as an expert on Polish problems. Representing Japan were these delegates: Count Mushakoji, ambassador in Berlin; General Oshima, military attaché in Berlin; General Sawada, military attaché in Warsaw; and Lieutenant Colonel Yoshinaka, representing the Japanese Foreign Affairs Ministry.

Opening the session, Dr. von Raumer mentioned the possibility of enlisting other states for collaboration against the Communist International, stressing the importance of drawing Rumania and Poland into the work. The Japanese Ambassador remarked that he had had a short conversation on this subject with the Polish Ambassador, and that he was convinced that a close collaboration with these two states would be very difficult to achieve. As far as Poland was concerned, its internal situation was not clear. Colonel Koc and his nationalistic camp encountered strong opposition from traditional right-wing circles, the adherents of which were opposed to the government and were now energetically fighting against Colonel Koc and his political group. Colonel Koc was supported, first of all, by the group of colonels and some of the left-wing circles. On the other hand, National Democrats, who were zealous adversaries of Communism and the Jews, and at the same time dogged foes of Germany, were now on the side of the national opposition.

Dr. Raumer agreed that these were difficult problems. However, in his opinion, it was necessary from the very beginning to choose the right path, and to act with energy. General Sawada suggested that a friendly atmosphere toward Germany be created in Poland and that pressure be exerted on Poland. He proposed a friendly gesture in the field of German minorities, an area so important for Poland, simultaneously suggesting that strong pressure be exerted by means of manifestations of power on the Polish frontier through a concentration of armed forces

[5] *Ibid.,* No. 479.

(maneuvers, fortifications), or even going so far as to occupy Kłajpeda [Memel] or possibly Lithuania.

Agreeing in theory with these tactics, Dr. von Raumer expressed doubt as to their consequences in practice. In conclusion, he suggested that one or more persons be found among the Poles to lead the anti-Communist drive, persons who at the same time would be in close contact with the government. He mentioned the name of Colonel Koc. Further, von Raumer suggested that the Japanese should exert their influence on the National Democrat circles in Poland, bearing in mind that the Germans had no connections whatever in those spheres. Those present agreed with this suggestion.

The attitude of the Polish government toward the anti-Comintern problem was determined in the circular telegram sent by Minister Beck on November 9, 1937, to representatives abroad. The instructions read as follows:

"No proposals to join the Italian-German-Japanese protocol [Anti-Comintern Pact] were hitherto addressed to Poland. Besides, Poland could not participate in such a protocol owing to its specific situation as a neighbor of the USSR and its basic stand against blocs. If asked, please inform accordingly."

The conversation held by the Polish ambassador to the Quirinal, Wysocki, with German Ambassador von Hassell on November 10, 1937,[6] follows these lines. Referring to his discussion with Beck before leaving Warsaw, Wysocki remarked that Poland wanted peace with Russia and that its participation in the Anti-Comintern Pact would be regarded by Moscow as a hostile demonstration. Wysocki's remarks on the reaction of the Italians to the agreement of November 6 are worthy of careful attention. He was taken aback by the optimistic judgments of Ciano, who was simply drunk with enthusiasm over the creation of such a powerful coalition. The Italian Minister thought that Great Britain would be so impressed by the fact of the coalition that it would seek to approach the Axis. Wysocki was even more surprised by the arrogant tone of the article in the semiofficial *Correspondenza Diplomatica* that attacked Chamberlain. This article, as Wysocki rightly supposed, was written by Mussolini himself. In the same report Hassell quoted a correct remark made by the counselor of the Soviet Embassy,

[6] *Ibid.,* No. 18.

confirmed by future events, that the pact was certainly an aggressive alliance against Russia; nevertheless, its first blow was destined for Great Britain.

In a later telegram of November 17,[7] Hassell reported on the conversation with Ciano on the subject of Poland's and Brazil's participation in the pact. Ciano thought that the United States would exert pressure on Brazil not to join the agreement. Poland would not take a positive decision because of its eastern neighbor. From Ciano's further deliberations it developed that for the time being he was not inclined to extend the partnership of the pact. He was anxious to maintain the full prestige of the coalition of the Three Great Powers. In any case, he did not intend to draw in smaller states such as Austria or Hungary. On January 12, 1938,[8] the German envoy, Erdmannsdorf, reported from Budapest that Ciano did not propose to Austria or Hungary to join the pact, since he was satisfied with their pledge of solidarity. Only large states should sign the pact. Ciano suggested that steps should be taken to get Poland and Spain to join. Drawing in Brazil, thus creating a breach in the ideological bloc of the democratic states on the American continent, would be very profitable. However, it was doubtful whether the President of Brazil could stand up to the opposition of the United States.

Upon taking over the Ministry of Foreign Affairs on February 4, 1938, Herr von Ribbentrop made some attempts to induce the Polish government to join the pact. Beginning in March, 1938, these endeavors lasted more than a year and came to an end when, following the March crisis in 1939, Poland and Great Britain provided each other with mutual guarantees. In order to get a full picture, it is worth while to establish a chronological chart of Ribbentrop's actions:

*March 31, 1938:* on the occasion of a general exchange of opinion on Polish-German relations, Ribbentrop suggested to the Polish Ambassador that Poland join the Anti-Comintern Pact.[9]

*September 27, 1938:* at the moment of the worst tension over the Sudetenland problem, Ribbentrop reiterated to the Polish Ambassador the question of Poland's attitude to the Anti-Comintern Pact.[10]

*October 24, 1938:* Ribbentrop proposed to the Polish Ambassador a

[7] *Ibid.,* No. 27.
[8] *Ibid.,* No. 97.
[9] See below, Document 83, p. 357, and *DGFP,* Series D, Vol. V, No. 34.
[10] See below, Document 109, p. 427.

broad Polish-German collaboration within the framework of the Anti-Comintern Pact in connection with a general settlement of Polish-German problems, the so-called *Gesamtlösung* offer.[11]

*January 26, 1939:* in his conversation with Ribbentrop in Warsaw, Minister Beck explained the reasons why the Polish government would not be in a position to join the Anti-Comintern Pact.[12]

Attempts to bind Poland more tightly to the Reich were not limited to Poland's joining a multilateral pact. Even before such a concept arose, beginning with 1935, the German side made a number of proposals, such as military cooperation, alliance against Russia, an air pact, etc.

To all these proposals Poland's attitude was negative.

[11] See below, Document 124, p. 453, and *DGFP*, Series D, Vol. V, No. 81, pp. 104–7.

[12] See *Polish White Book*, No. 56, and *DGFP*, Series D, Vol. V, No. 126.

# Weighty Decisions of the Third Reich [1]
### *November, 1937—February, 1938*

THE PERIOD from November, 1937, to February, 1938, was far-reaching in its consequences for the foreign policy of the Third Reich. On November 5, 1937, at a secret consultation in Berlin, Hitler, in the presence of Göring, Blomberg, Fritsch, Raeder, and Neurath, declared his decision to enter on the path of conquest. The war was to take place in the years 1943–45. It could be waged earlier in case the internal situation of France showed symptoms of debility, or if an armed conflict ensued between Italy and France and Great Britain. In the latter event, Austria and Czechoslovakia would become the first victims of Hitler.

The visit of Lord Halifax to Berchtesgaden opened perspectives to Hitler for an earlier solution of the Austrian and Sudetenland problems. He was faced with the problem whether to negotiate first with Great Britain, or whether to take immediate action for the realization of his plans. An understanding with Great Britain would indeed secure colonial advantages. Nevertheless, in Halifax's opinion, the colonial problem might only be settled positively within the frame of a global agreement, together with the security problem (disarmament), Germany's relation to the League of Nations, and an explicit definition of German claims in Central Europe, since this last matter was of special concern to France. At the consultation on November 5, speaking about the necessity of *Lebensraum* for the German nation, Hitler said, without mincing words, that Germany faced the problem of the greatest conquests with the smallest risk.

Still, other factors weighed on Hitler's decision. In spite of the power in his grasp as an absolute ruler of a populous and powerful nation situated in the heart of Europe, Hitler was afraid of the future (a symptom so very characteristic of political gamblers). He preferred im-

[1] Printed in *Bellona* (London), 1950, No. 1.

mediate solutions, which entailed great risks, to a long-term policy. His personal ambitions and a nervous, bouncing temperament also pushed him toward prompt solutions. His whole system was based on permanent dynamism.

His chief adviser, Ribbentrop, who enjoyed Hitler's ever-growing confidence, was opposed beforehand to the plan for Halifax's visit. He told me this already in September, 1937, at the Congress in Nuremberg. This was the period of the last months of his ill-fated mission in London, which made of him a dogged foe of Great Britain.

In a personal, strictly confidential memorandum of January 2, 1938, to the Chancellor,[2] Ribbentrop presented his point of view as to the future of German-British relations, recommending at the same time tactics of action. This important document provides a key to deciphering German political moves that followed.

I quote an extract of the conclusions reached by Ribbentrop:

1) Great Britain is lagging with its armaments and is therefore trying to gain more time.

2) Great Britain believes that in its competition with Germany time is playing into its hands. It plans to exploit its greater economic possibilities in the field of armaments, as well as to extend its treaties; for example, with the United States.

3) Halifax's visit should be considered as camouflage, just a pretext to investigate the situation. British Germanophiles on the whole play only such roles as are assigned to them.

4) Great Britain and its Prime Minister do not recognize in Halifax's visit the possibility of setting the basis for an understanding with Germany. Their trust in National Socialist Germany equals Germany's confidence in Great Britain. That is why they fear that they may some day be compelled to accept solutions detrimental to them. In order to counter this eventuality, England is making military and political preparations for a war with Germany.

The final conclusions of Ribbentrop are as follows:

1) Externally, further understanding with Great Britain to safeguard the interests of Germany's allies.

2) Keeping it strictly secret, to create with iron perseverence a coalition against Great Britain by tightening Germany's friendship with Italy and Japan, as well as by drawing in all other nations whose interests

[2] *DGFP*, Series D, Vol. I, No. 93.

correspond directly or indirectly to German interests. Establishing close and confidential collaboration of the Three Great Powers in order to reach this goal.

3) The question arises whether France, and as a result also Great Britain, will take up arms in case Germany engages in conflicts in Central Europe. This will depend on the specific conditions, on the speed with which the adversary will be conquered, and, finally, on the military situation. On this matter Ribbentrop wishes to present his personal point of view to Hitler.

In his final remarks there is an interesting paragraph relating to the role Ribbentrop attributed to Edward VIII in maintaining good German-British relations. After his abdication, which in the German Ambassador's opinion had a political foundation, Ribbentrop lost all hope for a possible agreement.

"Henceforth," writes Ribbentrop, "regardless of what tactical interludes of conciliation may be attempted with regard to us, every day that our political calculations are not actuated by the fundamental idea that England is our most dangerous enemy *will be a gain for our enemies.*" [Emphasis added by Ribbentrop.]

A month after dispatching this opinion, Ribbentrop replaced von Neurath, who was known for his pro-British sympathies.

The line drawn in the memorandum was of vital interest for the future formation of Polish-German relations. Ribbentrop's guiding idea was to create a coalition against Great Britain, in which, besides Germany, Italy, and Japan, smaller states whose interests corresponded with those of Germany were also to collaborate. Drawing Poland into the orbit of the pact was of obvious importance for Germany. Poland was to play the role of a bulwark in the East in case of Germany's conflict with the West, and of an ally in a war with Soviet Russia. This might explain Ribbentrop's endeavors in relation to Poland dating from March, 1938.

The Anti-Comintern Pact, created in principle against the Soviets, was gradually transformed into a tool of the German policy to check Great Britain. A great war alliance would grow out of it later on, while its two original signatories, Germany and Japan, would conclude non-aggression pacts with the Soviet Union.

# Beck in Berlin
## *January, 1938*

---

AMONG THE PAPERS of Józef Lipski there is a document (in Polish) written by him under the general title "Polish-Czech Relations, Observed from Berlin, in the Period from November, 1937, to the Conference in Munich." This work numbers twenty-two typewritten pages and was probably intended to be inserted in the memoirs of the author. It has never been published. It is included here in slightly altered form; the full texts of related documents, often given by the author in considerably abbreviated form, have been added.

In the second half of 1937, according to our information, we were in a position to assume that the moment was near when the Third Reich would actualize the Austrian and Czech problems on a nationalistic level.

On September 29, 1937, I was received by Göring at Karinhall in connection with our request for an exchange of notes on the Danzig problem on the occasion of the minorities declarations. Göring, who on the preceding day had received Mussolini at Karinhall, told me emphatically that the Duce stopped before a map showing Austria included in the Reich. Mussolini, without a single critical remark, simply said that the Reich was promptly realizing its program and, looking at Czechoslovakia, he added that this state was cutting deep into the German organism. Göring commented on this fact as a proof that Mussolini was taking the matter of the *Anschluss* for granted.

Minister Beck was of the opinion that Hitler, intending to settle the problem of Austria and the Sudetenland on the nationalistic level, wanted to exclude from this showdown the Polish-German minorities question, and that was why the Reich government intended to conclude an agreement with Poland on these matters. I, for my part, pressed for the necessity of binding the German side to an agreement on Danzig in connection with the minorities declaration. In case of the Reich's refusal,

I thought we should not finalize the minorities compromise. After extensive discussions with the Germans, the Danzig problem reached a semi-solution by means of Hitler's declaration of November 5, 1937. During the conversation with the Chancellor, when general problems were discussed, Hitler mentioned casually that he could not understand the rulers of Prague who, in their country's situation, surrounded as it was by Germany, Poland, and Hungary, did nothing to take care of the minorities question. A reasonable Czech government would, in Hitler's words, do all that was possible to take up these problems with its neighbors.

Although I did not know it at the time, on that same day, November 5, 1937, Hitler held a consultation with Göring, Neurath, Blomberg, Fritsch, and Raeder. The consultation lasted for four hours. Hitler concluded his deliberations by declaring that he had decided to gain living space (*Lebensraum*) for the German nation by conquests. From his detailed analysis of the plans it was clear that Austria and Czechoslovakia were at the top of the list in Hitler's aggressive strategy.

In the second half of November, Lord Halifax arrived in Germany on a mission from the British government. Halifax's conciliatory attitude toward German revisionist designs weighed considerably on Hitler's later decisions with regard to Austria and Czechoslovakia. During this period I was still unaware of the result of German-British conversations. Göring, whom I questioned on November 19 about the subject of these talks, was not able to give me an answer, since the decisive conversation of Halifax with Hitler was to take place that very day at Berchtesgaden.[1] He only said that Germany could not afford to loosen its ties with Italy and Japan.

On his way to Geneva for the session of the Council of the League of Nations, Beck stopped in Berlin on January 13–14, 1938, for an exchange of opinion with Hitler and the Reich's ministers. These conversations, besides covering Polish-German matters, dealt with all international problems. Beck, whom I accompanied to all the conversations, was able to see clearly the German plans for the near future. The conversations covered a very wide range of problems: German-French, German-British, and German-Soviet relations, the situation in Spain, the

[1] See *DGFP*, Series D, Vol. I, No. 31. On Beck's recommendation, Prince Lubomirski, chargé d'affaires in Berlin, questioned Weizsäcker on December 2 in Lipski's absence about the main subjects and viewpoints treated in the Halifax visit (*ibid.*, Nos. 53 and 54).

question of the Far East, and Germany's relations with the League of
Nations. The most important of the Polish problems under discussion
was the case of Danzig. . . .

From the outpourings of Hitler and the German ministers it was
apparent unequivocally that the Reich was approaching the realization
of its plans relating to Austria and Czechoslovakia.

Neurath's opinions were most characteristic; he always was more
reserved and more cautious than his colleagues. . . .

Göring, declaring that to the German way of thinking the Austrian
problem was an internal matter (he said so, without mincing words, to
Flandin),[2] stressed that Austria's annexation by the Reich must follow
sooner or later. . . .

In general, however, the Chancellor's stand was less adamant than
Neurath's and Göring's. He said, for example, that he would like to
arrive at an understanding with Czechoslovakia if, he added, he were
not compelled to act in a different way. . . .

Minister Beck listened to these deliberations, maintaining a certain
reserve in his pronouncements. Only with regard to Austria did he remark to Neurath that Poland had economic and transit but not political
problems with that country. He also expressed himself in a similar way
to Göring. He pointed to the difficulties in minorities problems encountered by Poland in Czechoslovakia. Referring to the forthcoming visit of
Horthy to Poland, Beck stated that he was acting in order to improve
Hungarian-Rumanian relations by trying to stiffen Rumania in relation
to the Soviets.

During Beck's visit in Berlin news came of the fall of Chautemps'
cabinet and the postponement of the meeting of the Council of the
League of Nations until the formation of a new government. Beck decided to stay in Berlin another day and to proceed later to Cannes, in
order to spend some time awaiting the meeting. On the day when Beck
was to depart for Geneva (January 15) the Yugoslav prime minister,
Stoyadinovich, arrived in Berlin. The Auswärtiges Amt approached me
with a suggestion that Beck take part in a dinner that night in honor of
the Yugoslav guest. The purpose of this invitation was obvious. On the
eve of the action against Austria, the German side was anxious to display the semblance of an East European bloc under Berlin's leadership.

[2] Pierre Flandin, who had been French prime minister (1934–35) and minister
of foreign affairs (1936), paid an unofficial visit to Berlin in the second half of
December, 1937.

I therefore advised Beck not to accept the invitation for dinner, and instead proposed his immediate departure for Cannes. In spite of technical difficulties made by the German railways administrations, evidently by order of the A.A., Beck succeeded in leaving Berlin in time.

The German government obtained from Stoyadinovich, who was closely tied to Germany, an agreement for the *Anschluss,* a promise that Yugoslavia would oppose the possible return of the Hapsburgs to Austria, and a promise that it would mobilize in case of a legitimist revolution in that country.

DOCUMENT 75    Report
on the Conversation of Foreign Affairs Minister Beck
with Reich Foreign Affairs Minister von Neurath,
*in the presence of Polish Ambassador Lipski,*
*on January 13, 1938, at 11:30* A.M.

NO. N/52/3/38                                        *Strictly Confidential*

1) Minister von Neurath opened the conversation by stating that he had observed Minister Beck's extensive activity of late. Minister Beck mentioned his exposition delivered at the Commission for Foreign Affairs of the Diet and yesterday's debate.[3] Such explanations serve the cause well. Herr von Neurath said that in the times of the old regime, when he had dealings with the parliament, the deputies were more reasonable when debating on problems in smaller groups, but in the forum of the parliament, when they addressed the electorate, demagogy flared up. Minister Beck remarked that it is our habit to have speeches delivered on foreign policy and national defense by members of the cabinet exclusively at the commission, since this renders matter-of-fact debate possible.

Minister Beck stated that in his exposition he wanted to describe precisely Poland's stand with regard to the problems of the League of Nations, even before the Geneva session.

A conversation ensued on the subject of the League. Neurath asked the Minister whether, in his opinion, some new plans for the League's

[3] Beck delivered his exposition on January 10, 1938, and participated in the discussion on January 12, 1938. See Beck, *Przemówienia, deklaracje, wywiady, 1931–1939,* pp. 331–40.

reorganization would be revealed at Geneva. The Minister thought this would not take place; Neurath shared this opinion.

Nevertheless, Minister Beck added that, bearing in mind that principal debates might always result from speeches of one of the delegates, he preferred in anticipation to define Poland's position.

Herr von Neurath pointed to a number of approaches made by the Western states to the German government (he also mentioned Halifax) actualizing the question of the League's reorganization. However, no concrete plans were presented; instead, endeavors were made to secure a plan of reorganization from the German government. To clear up the situation, after Italy's withdrawal from Geneva, the German government presented a declaration whereby it finally canceled its participation in the League. This was intended as a total blow to abolish the present structure of the League. ("The League of Nations must become completely kaput.") [4] Of course, Neurath was not excluding the possibility that some new form of international collaboration might be created in the future, replacing the present Geneva.

2) In connection with the discussion on the League of Nations, Neurath remarked that he had in mind a point and, not wishing to forget it, he wanted to bring it up immediately, namely, the problem of the Danzig flag.[5]

He wanted to assure us that this question is not at all timely and is of no importance to the German government. If in the future Danzig should desire, for example, to place a swastika on its flag, this would be the subject of a previous understanding between Danzig and Poland.

This gave rise to a conversation on Danzig in connection with the situation at the League. Minister Beck pointed to a certain improvement in Polish-German relations of late, adding that our relations are being discussed directly with the Senate. He mentioned recently concluded economic agreements. He remarked that Polish-Danzig matters were dealt with (in the last period) outside of the League's arbitrament. It might be necesssary, owing to the situation at the League, to investigate

---

[4] The Great Fascist Council decided on December 11, 1937, that Italy should withdraw from the League of Nations. The German Information Bureau proclaimed on December 12 a declaration by the German government supporting Italy's stand and stating that Germany's return to the League of Nations would never again be considered.

[5] Forster, the gauleiter of Danzig, wanted to add the swastika to the Danzig flag or to introduce a flag with a swastika.

(*überprufen*) this question, as mentioned at the time to Ambassador Lipski by Neurath. Herr von Neurath remarked that the present High Commissioner of the League in Danzig shows much more discretion and calmness in office, and does not sound the alarm for every petty detail. He heard from London that there is some intention there of withdrawing the Commissioner. He does not know whether this is still timely. He thinks that Danzig matters could be discussed either now or at a later date. He would appreciate it if Minister Beck would find out at Geneva what the consensus is there on this question.

Minister Beck remarked that it is essential that the League's withdrawal from Danzig should not coincide with a simultaneous aggravation of our relations. Von Neurath shared this opinion. For his part he exposed the thesis that, in case a revision of the League's situation in Danzig is undertaken, changes in the High Commissioner's rights should not be made. Minister Beck said that in this instance he is of the definite opinion that either the League will remain in Danzig under the present conditions or will withdraw from there entirely.

Neurath ascertained in conclusion that talks on this subject might be opened between Poland and Germany now or at a later date. From his words it was rather obvious that the German government is not in a hurry. Neither did Minister Beck insist particularly on expediting this solution.

3) Herr von Neurath touched upon the change in the cabinet in Rumania, asking the Minister's opinion. For his part, he thought that the government of Prime Minister Goga showed too much speed in its basic decisions.[6] Neurath had issued instructions to the German press to curtail their enthusiasm for the new government, which would only place a trump card in the hands of their opponents.

Minister Beck stated that two basic changes might be observed in the conditions in Rumania:

a) a definite withdrawal from the pro-Soviet policy propagated by Titulescu,

b) a structural change in the rule of the Rumanian state, which was based upon the old tradition of liberal prewar governments.

The Minister cannot predict what the fate of Goga's rule will be. With such radical changes in the system, he is afraid it might be safer to rely

[6] The Rumanian government of Tatarescu resigned on December 27, 1937. The next day a new cabinet was formed by Professor Octavian Goga.

on the organization emanating from below than to impose concepts from the top. It is therefore possible that, in case Goga fails, the King, who today is a competent factor in Rumania's politics, will choose a government with more middle-of-the-road tendencies. In his speech the Minister stressed Poland's attitude toward Rumania: nonintervention in internal affairs, but continued observance of the Polish-Rumanian alliance. On this level Polish-Rumanian relations cannot be exposed to any harm.

Herr von Neurath stressed that the German government, within the limits of its possibilities, also countered Mr. Titulescu's policy. If Mr. Titulescu claimed that he was for an understanding with Germany, von Neurath could confirm that such offers had been made; however, the German government had no confidence in the person of Mr. Titulescu and therefore all proposals made a few years ago through Envoy Comnen were rejected. Neurath remarked that German-Rumanian economic relations are prospering well.

4) With regard to Hungary, Minister Beck pointed to Horthy's trip to Poland,[7] stressing the friendship uniting the two countries. Referring to the paragraph of his speech wherein he mentioned the coordination of Laval's plan with Mussolini, Minister Beck remarked that he simply wanted to stress the positive aspect of this plan, which provides for certain collaboration of the Danubian states, placing them all on the same level, since this is exactly Poland's point of view. Herr von Neurath said that the German government's attitude toward this plan is a critical one, partly because it provided for Austria's independence. Besides, Minister Beck added, Poland does not conduct any *Grosspolitik* in the Danubian countries.

He stated that the Polish government is trying to assist in a certain rapprochement between Rumania and Hungary. He is of the opinion that Rumania would thus achieve more freedom in its policy with Soviet Russia; this might have a salutary effect on Rumania's internal situation.

Minister Neurath stressed that the German government also supports a Rumanian-Hungarian rapprochement.

5) With regard to Austria, Neurath complained that relations are not developing well, although on his part he has taken measures to improve them. However, he encounters a special personal resistance in Schusch-

[7] The visit of Regent Horthy to Poland took place February 5–9, 1938.

nigg, so that he is rather pessimistic as to the possibility of easing the situation. As a matter of fact, relations are so tense that Neurath does not exclude the possibility of an outburst inside Austria.

Minister Beck remarked that Poland has only economic relations with Austria; we have no special political interests there.

6) With regard to Czechoslovakia, Neurath called attention to the fact that relations with that country are not good. Attempts for improvement have yielded no results. A difference exists between the principles proclaimed by Mr. Beneš and repeated by the Czech Envoy with regard to the minorities in the Sudetenland and the real state of affairs.

Minister Beck stressed that, in spite of a liberal constitution, the Czechs are introducing the most drastic police-state forms with regard to the minorities.

Minister Neurath emphasized that, if the Czechs kept to the original Masaryk concept, they could exist at least for some time longer. But, as matters stand today, "This stump will have to be severed sooner or later."

7) Questioned about relations with the Western countries, Minister Beck said: "Im Westen nichts neues" ["All quiet on the Western Front"]. Neurath confirmed this. He remarked that there were loud repercussions on his fifteen-minute talk with Delbos at the station in Berlin.[8] Minister Beck confirmed this, remarking that Delbos had expressed to him satisfaction at this gesture of Neurath, a gesture that undoubtedly contributed to the easing of the atmosphere.

Minister von Neurath had a favorable opinion of Delbos. Minister Beck was of the same opinion, adding that in Warsaw Delbos showed the full understanding of a realistic statesman for Poland's need to carry on an independent foreign policy.[9]

Minister Beck remarked that he had the impression that Delbos desires to deal with all problems together, while Germany wants to settle each problem separately. Neurath replied that he had discussed this subject in a railway car with Delbos, and that he had the impression that the French Minister is not completely negatively disposed toward the German thesis.

On the other hand, Minister von Neurath expressed his very negative

[8] En route to Warsaw, Delbos had a short conversation with Neurath (at the latter's request) at the station in Berlin, *DGFP*, Series D, Vol. I, No. 55.
[9] Minister Delbos' official visit to Warsaw took place on December 3–7, 1937. Afterward Delbos proceeded to Bucharest, Belgrade, and, via Budapest, to Prague.

impression of his talk with Flandin. He said that Flandin belongs to the category of French ministers who have not learned anything. That is why Neurath did not arrange for an audience for him with the Chancellor.

8) About the Western Pact, Herr von Neurath said that this matter is not at all timely and that such a pact seems to be pointless, since it can be done without.

9) With regard to colonies, Neurath stated that it will probably be some time before England presents some proposals. He added that sooner or later this problem will appear in concrete form.

10) Spain: with regard to Franco's defeat at Teruel, von Neurath described this as an event which will postpone the settlement of the situation in Spain.

Minister Beck remarked that, according to information in his possession, the Red Spanish Army has improved considerably.

Neurath confirmed this, and added that because of this Berlin had advised General Franco to open the promised offensive as soon as possible. However, General Franco, as Mussolini declared to Neurath, is not taking into consideration two factors: time and money. Neurath added that in general it is not easy to deal with Spain.

Both von Neurath and Minister Beck agreed that today a defeat such as the one at Teruel might not create such misgivings as existed a year ago concerning the possible victory of the Reds and the spread of Bolshevism.

Minister Beck underlined that, in spite of Russia's internal isolation, the Comintern is still functioning very strongly abroad.

11) With regard to the Far East, Herr von Neurath described the situation as follows: for Japan it is not easy. Neurath does not consider the danger of Japanese entanglements with Soviet Russia, bearing in mind that, following Stalin's purge of the army, Russia's combat value is not sufficient for a conflict with Japan.[10]

Here Mr. Beck observed that the eastern Soviet Army was less affected by the executions.

Minister von Neurath maintained his opinion that he does not fear Russia's action against Japan; in his opinion, the difficulty lies in the dragging out of the conflict, which is also due to serious misunderstandings in Japan with regard to relations with China, in particular in the

---

[10] On June 11, 1937, Marshal Tukhachevsky and seven Soviet generals were sentenced to death in Moscow.

higher echelons of the army, the navy, foreign policy, etc. This renders the conclusion of peace with China very complicated. It should also be considered that Chiang Kai-shek remains an element of permanent anti-Japanese counteraction in the vast territory of China. He symbolizes China's national rebirth. Japan has taken up arms in order to put an end to this national revolution symbolized by Chiang Kai-shek.

In conclusion, von Neurath said that the Chancellor would like to see Minister Beck, if he could spare some time for this meeting.

Minister Beck replied that naturally he would consider it a great honor to be received by the Chancellor.[11]

DOCUMENT 76   Report on the Conversation of
Foreign Affairs Minister Beck at Lunch with General Göring,
*in the presence of the Polish Ambassador in Berlin, Lipski,*
*on January 13, 1938*

NO. N/52/3/38

The conversation with Göring was partially carried on during the luncheon, with Mrs. Göring present. This part was purely general in character. First of all, it concerned the development of the internal situation in Rumania. Minister President Göring has certain misgivings as to whether Goga is strong enough to realize his program. He thinks that in case he fails the Iron Guard will appear on the stage.

Minister Beck expressed an opinion similar to that he had described to Herr von Neurath.

They both agreed that the great danger which threatened as a result of Titulescu's policy of rapprochement with the Soviets had now been removed.

Further, the forthcoming visit of Göring to Poland was discussed. Beck invited him formally in the name of the Polish President. The date was fixed at about February 11, which was quite acceptable to Göring.

After lunch, when Mrs. Göring left, a political discussion began. Questioned by Göring as to whether any special political moves are expected to take place in Geneva, Minister Beck replied negatively. He

11 For the memorandum prepared for Neurath for his conversation with Beck, see *DGFP*, Series D, Vol. V, No. 25; for Neurath's version of this conversation, *ibid.*, No. 28.

referred to his speech at the Commission for Foreign Affairs of the Diet when he defined Poland's stand toward the League of Nations.

With reference to Danzig, Beck observed casually that a certain easing in the situation might be noted. Göring confirmed this, adding that we might count on him in these matters if necessary.

Minister President Göring pointed out that it would be desirable if Forster could be received by Minister Beck so as to disperse the last shade of misunderstanding. Minister Beck answered that this is being taken into consideration. Minister Chodacki is already in contact with Forster. Following the Minister's return to Warsaw, he will probably be in a position to receive Forster.

The last minorities agreement was described by Göring as a great *positivum,* and he gave voice to his satisfaction over such a successful development in Polish-German relations.

It is now essential that the lower ranks, such as mayors and voivodes, should conform to the governmental policy. He is always ready to help as far as the German side is concerned. Minister Beck mentioned that pertinent orders had been issued on the Polish side. Such problems as the release of members of German minorities sentenced at the Chojnice trial had also been settled.

Defining particular problems of the Reich's policy, Göring stressed that there are certain problems which in the nature of things should reach solution sooner or later. First among these problems is the reunion of Austria with the Reich. He illustrated by using this example: if in the place of Czechoslovakia a thoroughly Polish state existed, only ruled by factors other than those in Warsaw, would it not be quite natural that the whole Polish nation would long for reunion with the sister nation? That is why Austria, in the minds of the German people, is regarded as their internal affair. Herr Göring had presented this point in quite categorical form to Flandin, who asked for what price Germany would abandon the idea of annexing Austria. Halifax had shown much more understanding for this problem. Göring told him quite explicitly that the Reich government is striving for a peaceful union of Austria with the Reich. Nevertheless, he hinted that, if this way achieves no result, an outburst might occur. Germany, as Göring put it, will settle this matter without regard to others. It has no misgivings about France. In case of an Italian protest, any realistic politician in Europe will understand that, if Mussolini comes to Germany and delivers speeches binding for his policy, he will not act without contacting Berlin on the most important problem that could divide the two countries, namely, on the problem of Austria. Of course, it is rather awkward to publicize this. Here Göring cited the example of the map which he showed to Mussolini at Karinhall, in which Austria was united with Germany. To this Mussolini only observed that he could see on this map that Czechoslovakia was cutting too deeply into Germany.

Göring added that Schmidt [12] has been informed by him about this, so that the Austrian government is quite aware of the real state of affairs.

With regard to Czechoslovakia, Herr Göring observed that he cannot understand the Czech policy. This country, extended in a long line, lives in tension with Germany, Poland, and Hungary. The German minority in Czechoslovakia is not like the minorities in other countries, since it is well knit and numbers about four million people. He does not understand what the Czechs are counting on. French assistance is nothing but an illusion, the more so since new German armaments on the western frontier of Germany would render France's assault difficult even today. And in a year such an assault would be out of the question. Here Göring had critical words for the Maginot line, because soldiers in such fortifications are unwilling to leave them and fight. That is why the German government applied a system of dispersed defense points, which seems far better.

Herr Göring does not conceal that he considers the existence of the Czech state in its present form as impossible.

He inquired about Polish minorities inhabiting the Cieszyn [Teschen] region. When he talked about Hungarian-Czech relations, Minister Beck remarked that Hungary had failed in one point of its policy, namely, with regard to national minorities. Göring confirmed this, adding that Germans who went over to Yugoslav rule from Hungarian rule were of the same opinion.

As to the future of Polish-German relations, Göring declared that cutting Poland off from the sea would result in the thrust of a population of 40 million against Germany. Therefore, it would constitute political nonsense. In case of other compensations for Poland in the east, Germany would like in the future to have some convenient communication by railway through Pomerania. It does not aspire to anything else.

[12] Guido Schmidt, secretary of state in the Austrian Ministry of Foreign Affairs (July, 1936-February, 1938), later foreign affairs minister (February-March, 1938).

With regard to Austria, a subject to which Göring returned again, Minister Beck remarked that, as he had already told Neurath today, Poland has only economic interests there. Göring, who understood this allusion, replied that in the economic field an understanding will always be possible.

DOCUMENT 77   Report on the Conversation of
Foreign Affairs Minister Beck with Chancellor of the German Reich
Hitler *in the presence of Reich Foreign Affairs Minister*
*von Neurath and Ambassador of the Polish Republic in Berlin Lipski,*
*on January 14, 1938, from 12* P.M. *to 1:30* P.M.

*Strictly Confidential*

In very lengthy deliberations the Chancellor described his views on particular international problems and brought up the affairs of the Reich. In the field of international politics these deliberations concerned the relation of Germany to France and the internal French situation, German-British relations, with special stress on colonial affairs, the attitude toward Bolshevism and German-Russian relations, the attitude toward Austria and Czechoslovakia, the situation in the Far East, and the attitude of the German government toward the League of Nations.

In the course of these long deliberations, the Chancellor repeatedly referred to Polish-German relations and made a declaration with regard to Danzig.

### 1. Polish-German Problems

These problems are left out of this report for the whole of the conversation, to be dealt with as a separate point.

Minister Beck thanked the Chancellor for expressing a desire to see him during his stay in Berlin.

He found that Polish-German relations are developing successfully, and pointed to the agreement concluded on November 5, 1937.

The Chancellor said he was glad to see Minister Beck in Berlin and for his part repeatedly stressed during the conversation that the successful development of Polish-German relations constitutes one of the rare positive factors in the present inflamed international situation. On this occasion he confirmed his firm decision to keep to the same line of action. He expressed his sincere satisfaction with Minister Beck's last exposition at the Commission for Foreign Affairs of the Diet, and laid stress on the importance for the international situation of such a warning voice about the League of Nations.

In his general thesis the Chancellor confirmed his basic line that frontier corrections would by no means be commensurate with the sacrifices, and therefore would not make sense.

With regard to Danzig the Chancellor stated literally that on November 5, 1937, he had made a declaration to the Polish Ambassador. He would like to repeat this declaration to the Minister. He put it this way: that Poland's rights in Danzig will not be infringed upon, and that, moreover, the legal status of the Free City will remain unaltered. Polish-German relations, the Chancellor added, are of essential and decisive importance in this matter for him also. He only wished that the local German population could adopt a form of government which would suit it best, and which as a result would contribute to the maintenance of peace. The Chancellor gave firm assurances that the declaration made by him is binding. Further in the course of the conversation he mentioned that it is binding irrespective of the fate of the League.

With regard to the flag, the Chancellor assured us that this matter will be canceled. He added that he will talk it over with Forster and Greiser. He mentioned that he does not wish to complicate matters internally for the Minister by this question.

Minister Beck's statements can be recapitulated as follows:

Taking note of the Chancellor's declaration on Danzig, with a mention that he had discussed this matter with Neurath in order that our relations not be exposed to difficulties by a third party, such as the League, which today is the stage for surprises. It was mentioned that the Minister and Neurath went through a general review of problems of concern to the two states.

Affirmation that Polish-Rumanian relations are developing successfully. Mention of Horthy's visit to Poland and attempts to improve relations between Hungary and Rumania, thus reinforcing Rumania's resistance in its policy toward the Soviets. Underlining that in these problems the opinion of the Polish and German governments is uniform.

Stressing difficulties encountered by Poland with regard to its minorities in Czechoslovakia.

Underlining that besides this we are not conducting particularly large-scale politics in the Danubian basin.

## 2. *France*

The Chancellor remarked that he had just been informed that Chautemps' cabinet has fallen. Critical evaluation of the internal situation in France. Remark that if Blum would now seize power Communist tendencies would be strengthened. Fear of possible Communism in France, which would undoubtedly spread to Belgium and Holland. Opinion that the only nationalistic and stable element in France is the army; nevertheless, the army alone, without political leadership, cannot play a decisive role in the life of the country. If no political spheres will take the responsibility for engaging the army in politics, the army alone will not do so.

The optimistic opinions of people who say that there are right-wing movements in France are based on a false appraisal. These people only see the political pendulum swinging to the right and again to the left. They do not realize that the clock itself moves to the left.

From the egoistic point of view, Germany would welcome the weakening of France; however, wisdom and a well-conceived self-interest advise against it. With the present political and economic ties between the European countries, a breakdown in a neighbor's economy might signalize a Bolshevik revolution next door, and should therefore be cause for concern. Distant Spain is proof of this. Germany could not remain indifferent if Communism were to appear on its western frontier.

## 3. *Czechoslovakia*

Communism in the west is even more of a threat since there is a country bordering on Germany in the east which is yielding more and more to Moscow's influence. This country is Czechoslovakia. The Chancellor cited information received from there with reference to Soviet influence on the press, cinema, theater, etc. Czechoslovakia is one of the countries in the opinion of some in which a little flame (*Feuerchen*) might be fanned or extinguished at will. All those who argued this way were mistaken; when they want to extinguish the fire it is already too late and the fire overtakes them.

The Chancellor was very critical of Czech politics. He declared that Czechoslovakia is not a uniform nation, like, for example, Poland. The very name shows that Czechoslovakia is *ein Nationalitätstaat*. Its policy should be adapted thereto. But it is not, and this evokes conflicts with regard to the treatment of minorities. The Chancellor would like to find a peaceful solution here also, unless he is compelled to act otherwise.

## 4. Austria

Besides this difficult problem, as the Chancellor put it, there is another one which is causing him concern—Austria. If legitimistic attempts take place in Austria, the Chancellor declared with absolute firmness that he would not hesitate to march immediately into Austria. This would be done as quickly as lightning. By no means would he let the Hapsburgs in. This problem goes beyond Austria and concerns the territory of the Reich. In the Hapsburgs' entourage there is talk about an emperor of Germany. Religious considerations are also utilized here.

This passage of the Chancellor's statements is exceedingly decisive.

## 5. The Soviet Union

The Chancellor deliberated at length on his attitude toward Communism, stating very firmly that his negative stand is inviolable. In this connection he mentioned some opinions as to a possible national evolution in Russia. Similar opinions also prevailed at the Reichswehr. It was assumed that Soviet military elements would continue to impose their line. The opposite happened; Russia today is in the full swing of Communism and the generals are dead.

## 6. Great Britain

The Chancellor criticized Great Britain for misinterpreting the German situation. England refuses to understand the Reich's real need for colonies. This need results from the very structure of German economy, which cannot be fed without colonies. England grants the rights for colonies to everyone, even to the smallest states, except the Reich. The Chancellor illustrated Germany's need for raw materials by examples. In addition, he pointed to the fact that young vital elements of the Reich need territories for their expansion. In Germany everything is forbidden to them. They trample on each other's toes. Everywhere there are signs on what is prohibited. These young elements seek expansion in expeditions, for example, to Tibet. Sooner or later England will see how indispensable the colonies are for Germany. The old German colonies are not exploited by Great Britain. England's concept is that Germany should receive colonies from the smaller states. However, the German government has no claims on these states, which did not take the colonies from Germany.

France shows more understanding for Germany's colonial claims, but it is hiding behind Great Britain.

### 7. *The Far East*

The Chancellor is of the opinion that Japan will definitely win and that China will have to accept onerous peace conditions. He does not think that Russia, in its present situation, will constitute a serious threat to Japan. America and England, in spite of their loud promises, will certainly do nothing. China will be left to its fate. The Abyssinian situation will be repeated. There was a moment when Chiang Kai-shek had a chance to make peace. Then all the League spheres throughout the globe were shouting that China should fight to the very end, promising the assistance of other nations. In practice nothing came out of all this. The Negus also had a chance to make peace with the Italian government, saving a part of his state, possibly in the form of a protectorate. He trusted the League and lost.

### 8. *The League of Nations*

The Chancellor expressed sharp criticism of the system of the League, which consists in imposing far-reaching obligations on states. The Chancellor was very sarcastic, illustrating his opinion with examples. He declared that, with the prevailing League system, all those who trust it 100 percent, especially the smaller states, will always be made fools of, since the Great Powers always back out in time. That is why the German government will never again return to the League, and here the Chancellor was quite determined. There are moments when the League becomes more or less popular; this depends on the Great Powers' interests. At present Great Britain is again playing the card of the League in connection with the situation in the Far East. The League is the forum in which Great Britain furthers its interests.

### 9. *Germany's Internal Affairs*

The Chancellor pointed to economic difficulties in connection with the necessity of feeding 68 million people. Looking at things from this angle, he considered any convulsion in Europe to be of great danger. This dictates the necessity for a peaceful policy. He elaborated in detail on the subject of creating new raw materials.

He stressed the durability of his cabinet. Some of his collaborators have been at his side for fifteen years already. The ministers of his cabinet, with a few exceptions, are not being replaced.

About Schacht he said that, pressed by the Chancellor, Schacht had taken over the Ministry of Economy after Schmidt's illness. However, he had always shrunk from this department, since his profession is banking. Every six months since then he had handed in his resignation, since he was unwilling to take the responsibility for economic matters.

### General Remarks of the Chancellor

The Chancellor referred to the fact that his offers of disarmament, fixing the ceiling at 200,000 and later at 300,000 men, had not been accepted at the time. If a compromise had then been accepted, this fact would have had a favorable impact on Germany's economic life. Money would have been spent for productive aims instead of for armaments. As an illustration, he cited that the necessity to make armaments at such a pace delayed by four years the creation of a cheap motor car (the Volkswagen). Only now was its production being realized. This would be a gigantic enterprise, employing 65,000 people. The price of the car would not exceed 900 marks, which would be advantageous for the idea of savings. The Germans must be thrifty to meet the requirements of the national economy. With the goal of buying a cheap car in mind, an individual would be willing to save.

In connection with the cabinet change in France, the Chancellor stated that with a perpetual change of statesmen any kind of policy becomes impossible. Today there is one French minister with whom contact is established; tomorrow a new individual, a complete stranger, appears, with whom things have to be taken up from the very beginning. Hitler alluded to the fact that on the Polish side there was a permanent team of competent people.[13]

[13] See *Polish White Book,* No. 36, where this conversation is published in a very concise form. For the German version of the conversation, see *DGFP,* Series D, Vol. V, Nos. 29 and 30.

# Changes in the Reich's Top Rulers
# Conversations with Göring in Warsaw
# The Anschluss
### *February—March, 1938*

---

ON FEBRUARY 4, 1938, fundamental changes took place in the organization and staff of the top rulers of Germany. Dismissed from their posts were Reichswehr Minister Field Marshal von Blomberg, Commander of the Army General Fritsch, and Foreign Affairs Minister von Neurath, as well as seven Army generals and six Air Force generals. In addition, thirty-six generals were transferred to different positions.

Chancellor Hitler did away with the office of the Reichswehr minister and established the post of commander in chief, himself assuming supreme command over the armed forces. General Wilhelm Keitel was nominated chief of the General Staff, and General Walter von Brauchitsch became commander of the Army. At the same time Hitler promoted General Göring, commander in chief of the Air Force, to the rank of field marshal.

Joachim von Ribbentrop became foreign affairs minister, and von Neurath was relegated to the rather unimportant leadership of the newly created Secret Council for Foreign Affairs in the Chancellor's office.

These changes, worked out in the strictest secrecy, came as a total surprise to Germany itself, to other countries, and to the diplomatic corps in Berlin. In Lipski's papers the following personal note was found:

### *Note with Regard to the Events of February 4, 1938*

Following many insistent requests from Warsaw to introduce the Polish Ballet (created on the occasion of the *Exposition des arts décoratifs* in Paris) into the Reich, I approached Minister Goebbels to accept jointly with me the patronage of this enterprise. Goebbels accepted, agreeing to performances of the ballet not only in Berlin but also in a number of other German cities.

The gala performance at the Goebbels Opera in Berlin was fixed for a few days prior to the events of February 4, 1938. The Chancellor promised to attend. On the same day, an hour before the performance, I got a telephone call from the Secretary of State and the Reich Chancellery that Hitler, in spite of his best intentions, would be unable to attend. He hoped to have an opportunity to see the ballet in some other German city, for example, in Munich. At the opera I sat in a box with von Neurath, Goebbels, Rauscher, and Funk. I felt that there was something in the wind and that grave political complications were under way which prevented the Chancellor from attending. After the ballet there was a big reception at the Embassy, attended by von Neurath, Goebbels, and many high-ranking German dignitaries, as well as the whole corps de ballet. One half of the income from the first performance went to the Wintershilfe, and the other half for Polish needs. Goebbels presented me with a check.

Meanwhile, the Austrian problem was swelling into a crisis. On February 12 a meeting took place at Berchtesgaden between Austrian Chancellor Schuschnigg and Hitler, and on February 15 identical official communiqués were published in Berlin and Vienna, declaring that the two countries were determined to observe the principles of the agreement dated July 11, 1936,[1] and to consider them as a fundamental basis for mutual peace relations.[2] The terms presented in the form of an ultimatum by Hitler were accepted by Schuschnigg. In Vienna the cabinet was reshuffled, and Hitler's appointee, Seyss-Inquart, became minister of the interior and security. Amnesty was also proclaimed for political offenders (mainly for National Socialists).

On February 20 Hitler delivered an important speech at the Reichstag, presenting a detailed analysis of the Reich's foreign policy. He declared that Germany would never return to the League of Nations. With regard to Austria and Czechoslovakia, he remarked that 10 million Germans were living in those countries. A legal and governmental separation from the Reich could not result in a divorce so far as the rights of the population were concerned. With good will, as had been demonstrated, a solution might be found to problems of national minorities. However, a state which strove to prevent such an understanding in Europe by force might one day provoke an act of force.

With regard to Poland, Hitler laid stress on ever-increasing friendly relations. The Polish state respected national relations in Danzig, and the Free City and Germany respected the rights of Poland.[3]

In Lipski's papers there are two personal notes on these questions and a report to Beck dated February 19 (still prior to Hitler's speech).

[1] For the text of the agreement, see *DGFP*, Series D, Vol. I, Nos. 152 and 153.
[2] For the text of the communiqué, see *Survey of International Affairs, 1938*, II, 53–54.
[3] For the paragraph referring to Poland, see *Polish White Book*, No. 37.

*Austria*

On the afternoon of February 11 Austrian Envoy Tauschitz called by telephone, asking to be received immediately.

Showing some nervousness owing to the situation prevailing in Austria's relations with the Reich, he asked me if I was of the opinion that the changes which had taken place on February 4 in the top posts of the Reich's leadership were connected with Germany's intentions toward Austria.

In the course of a long conversation dealing with the political situation, I expressed my views as to the real plans of Germany with regard to his country.

When Tauschitz left, I received a report that Austrian Chancellor Schuschnigg was arriving the next day at Berchstesgaden. I think that when Tauschitz came to discuss this matter with me he had already been informed about the intended visit. However, a few days later he tried to persuade me that when he called on me he had known nothing about Schuschnigg's visit, and he begged me to believe that he had no intention of keeping this visit secret from me.

### February 15, 1938

Herr von Ribbentrop, nominated the Reich's foreign affairs minister on February 4, took office on February 10. He confined himself to leaving visiting cards with the ambassadors, instead of paying the usual personal call.

He established official contact with the chiefs of the diplomatic missions by inviting them to a reception at Kaiserhoff on February 15.

I had only a brief exchange of opinion with him. He was not enthusiastic when I mentioned Göring's visit to Poland, whence I was just returning. In general, even social contact with him was rather difficult, to say nothing of a political discussion, for he had the habit of monologizing without heed to the *meritum* of the arguments of his opponent.

DOCUMENT 78   Lipski to Beck

NO. 1/13/38                              Berlin, February 19, 1938

As of February 13, 1938, events in German-Austrian relations took such a rapid turn that I was obliged to communicate with you by telegram, almost on an hour-to-hour basis, on the more outstanding facts. I would like to report now on the fundamental stages of developments in this matter on the eve of the Chancellor's speech, which undoubtedly will concentrate on the outstanding political moment in the Reich's modern history: Hitler's conversation with Schuschnigg. This event is closely connected with the decisions taken on February 4.

From the conversation you had with the leading authorities of the Reich during your stay in Berlin on January 13–14, it was evident that the German government had decided to settle the Austrian problem in one way or another. May I just recall the statement of the usually reserved von Neurath, then in charge of the A.A., that, bearing in mind Schuschnigg's resistance, he saw no possible way of solving the situation by German-Austrian negotiations, and that therefore he was not excluding the possibility of an outburst inside Austria.

From these conversations, and especially from Göring's declarations, it was clear that, analyzing the reaction of the Western Powers interested in this problem, the German government came to the conclusion that Great Britain was leaving the Reich free to act (Halifax's conversations in Berlin).[4] France cannot afford any action, while the Italian government, as a result of Mussolini's conversations during his trip to Germany, also agrees with the idea of Austria's annexation to Germany. Finally, the Chancellor himself definitely stressed at that time that in case of an attempt to realize the legitimist idea he would not hesitate to march into Austria.

I am aware that the Austrian problem was discussed later on by German statesmen with Prime Minister Stoyadinovich when he visited Berlin. This occurred just after you left Berlin on January 15. A pledge was allegedly obtained from Stoyadinovich that the Yugoslav government would oppose the possible return of the Hapsburgs to Austria, and that Yugoslavia would mobilize in case of a legitimist revolution.

The consul general in Munich, [Konstanty] Jeleński, in his report dated February 1, No. 3/N/156, informed you about his conversation with Austrian Consul General Jordan. Herr Jordan was of the opinion that the legitimist movement in Austria would not be the only pretext for an open German intervention; he had most serious misgivings as to the possibility of an internal outburst through the National Socialist

[4] The Hitler-Halifax conversation of November 19, 1937 (*DGFP*, Series D, Vol. I, No. 31).

organizations in Austria. The Austrian Consul then pointed to a plan he was informed about—the creation of a provisional National Socialist government in Salzburg supported by the Austrian Legion, in order to seize power in Austria. He also mentioned the increase of financial subsidies granted by the Reich to Austrian National Socialists.

Here the question arises whether the changes ordered by the Chancellor in the army and the foreign service on February 4 were directly connected with the Austrian problem. It is impossible to prove beyond any doubt. I think that the complications caused by Blomberg's marriage were the very last straw that broke the camel's back, forcing the Chancellor to make a final decision in the domain of the commander in chief of the Reich's armed forces. However, it cannot be overlooked that the men who left on February 4, especially the military, represented the old Prussian, Protestant ideological trend, basically hostile to the reunion with Austria. It must also be added that the chiefs of the army, such as General Fritsch, who had to base their opinions on purely realistic considerations of the army's preparedness for war, often used their influence to mitigate decisions taken from the political angle. This was the case with remilitarization of the Rhineland, intervention in Spain, etc. So it is not impossible that in the Austrian problem also these elements would be in opposition to the use of the army as a trump card in the diplomatic gamble, at a moment when this army was not yet ready for action.

On the other hand, it was quite obvious that after February 4 Hitler was badly in need of a huge political showdown on the Austrian problem to erase the unpleasant memories of public opinion at large caused by changes in the leading posts of the army. Nevertheless, the following question arises, which I heard, for instance, from the Italian Ambassador: how was it possible that precisely at a time of weakness caused by changes in the top brass of the army the moment was chosen by the German side to hand an ultimatum to Schuschnigg, threatening him with consequences going so far as the use of force (*Machtpolitik*)? I think that in this case, as in the case of the remilitarization of the Rhineland when the risk was far greater, Chancellor Hitler took this risk, and won.

Whether, in case Schuschnigg refused the ultimatum, German armed forces would actually have been used for operations in Austria is still an open question. Besides this extreme, other means were at Hitler's disposal in case Schuschnigg rejected his conditions: the agreement of July,

1936, could be revoked; diversion could be started inside Austria by National Socialists supported by Party formations from the Reich. I was told here that Papen used the argument with Schuschnigg that the peace policy based on the July agreement would end at the moment he left Austria. Anyhow, the impact of the pressure exerted by Hitler's government, whether there was any bluff behind it or not, had its effect.

At any rate, this fact is worth noting, as far as concerns methods that the German government is now introducing to realize its plans in the field of foreign policy.

The atmosphere on the same evening at the reception the Chancellor gave for the diplomatic corps might serve to illustrate the state of tension which existed on February 15 until the German proposition was accepted. Even at 8:30 P.M., prior to the publication of the communiqué, General Field Marshal Göring took me aside and said how glad he was about his intended trip to Poland; however, he wanted to say as frankly as usual that this trip might have to be postponed if a row with Austria occurred ("Wenn wir mit Oesterreich krach bekommen").

The Chancellor, as I have already telegraphed, expressed to me his lively satisfaction with the agreement achieved, and headed very significantly that Czechoslovakia would now follow in the footsteps of Austria. However, in Göring I noted a certain dissatisfaction and concern on that day. From what I heard later, I had the impression—although unconfirmed—that, taught by experience, he preferred to go deeper into action immediately instead of pushing step by step, where some possible surprise might be in store that would cause long-term friction. Very characteristic was Secretary of State Mackensen's opinion that Schuschnigg's political suicide must have cost him quite a lot. Von Neurath, with a note of melancholy, observed to one of my colleagues that von Ribbentrop was now reaping the fruits of his work, for the initiative and the elaborated plan for Schuschnigg's meeting with Hitler were his. At the Auswärtiges Amt it was said that conversations on Schuschnigg's arrival at Berchtesgaden had already lasted for some weeks, and that the events of February 4 had brought about a certain interruption. . . .

*Józef Lipski*

Between February 23 and 26, 1938, Field Marshal Göring was in Poland at a hunting party. During this visit he had a conversation with Marshal Śmigły-

Rydz (see *Journal,* pp. 275–77, and abridged text in the *Polish White Book,* No. 38), as well as two conversations with Minister Beck.

DOCUMENT 79   First Conference of Minister Beck
with Göring in Warsaw, February 23, 1938

NO. N/52/6/38                    Berlin, February 28, 1938
                                 *Strictly Confidential*

On February 23, 1938, Göring had two conversations with Minister Beck. Résumé of the principal points of the first conversation held before noon at the Foreign Affairs Ministry, with Ambassadors Moltke and Lipski present.

### 1. Austria

On the Chancellor's recommendation, Göring informed Minister Beck, in strict confidence, about the circumstances of the Hitler-Schuschnigg conversation.

1) The German government had received of late information based on documents that the Austrian government was taking a new direction in its foreign policy, namely, that it was establishing close contact with the Czechoslovak government. There was the risk that through taking this path Austria would enter the orbit of Czech-Soviet politics. This situation called for prompt action.

2) Under these circumstances, the Chancellor was compelled first to take basic measures of an internal character in order to gain more freedom of action. This was achieved by centralizing in his own hand all the elements needed for the operation (events of February 4).

3) Without mincing words, the Chancellor communicated to Schuschnigg the information in his possession; he made him face the alternative—either to sever talks with the Czechs and make an agreement with the Reich, or to break with the Reich, with all the ensuing consequences. Schuschnigg chose the agreement.

4) Schuschnigg was told explicitly that the understanding achieved at Berchtesgaden was just the beginning of a rapprochement between the Reich and Austria.

5) The agreement consisted of granting power to the National Socialists (under Seyss-Inquart), admitting them to the *Vaterländische Front,*

and filling government posts with them; furthermore, granting an amnesty, a considerable economic rapprochement, for which the delegates to the economic negotiations with the Reich had already been nominated.

Göring mentioned ore when referring to the economic agreement. Czechoslovakia was to be eliminated from the Austrian market (coal) and was to be replaced by trade with the Reich. As a further step, a customs union was envisaged.

Austria's policy in foreign affairs was to conform to the Reich's guiding lines. For instance, persons who had acted or were acting to the detriment of the German ideology were to be dismissed from Austrian diplomacy. Göring said that there were people who had been forced by Vienna to act against German interests, as, for example, Tauschitz in Berlin. Those, of course, would not be purged. Closer military contacts, indispensable under such an agreement, were to be established between the two armies.

6) Göring declared that things had taken a more rapid turn in Austria than was foreseen by the German government. In other words, the idea of National Socialism was spreading ever more broadly.

7) In spite of a certain pressure from the Austrian side, Chancellor Hitler did not use the word "independence" in his speech at the Reichstag on February 20.

8) Göring pointed to a probable attempt on the part of Schuschnigg to shield himself in his speech from excessive attacks by the opposition. He thinks that Schuschnigg will say that Austria's independence was not encroached upon, since relations remained within the frame of the agreement of July, 1936. A certain anxiety could be detected in Göring in connection with Schuschnigg's forthcoming speech.

9) The French government had intervened through Ambassador Poncet with Ribbentrop on the Austrian problem. The Foreign Affairs Minister of the Reich replied that he was not in a position to answer his question, since this was *eine Familiengelegenheit* between Germany and Austria.

## II. Rumania, Hungary, Czechoslovakia

1) Göring pointed to the fact that the internal situation of *Rumania* is disturbing. He hinted that although Goga's cabinet was welcomed by the German government, nevertheless Berlin was aware that Goga went much too fast and had no support from the masses. The present gov-

ernment, with a patriarch at the helm, evokes some misgivings. The German government's main concern is that Rumania might fall under Soviet influence. In his opinion, Goga's downfall was certainly due to international intervention and Soviet threats.

Minister Beck, who was in possession of information from Envoy Arciszewski, [5] did not consider Rumania's internal situation so alarming. He thought that King Carol had trump cards in his hand with which to dominate the situation. At one time the King had decided to dismiss Titulescu, that is, the element most obedient to Soviet dictation. Minister Beck shared Göring's opinion that Goga had no mass support; besides, he wanted to carry out basic reforms through administrative channels. This, plus financial difficulties, had caused his downfall. As far as Soviet threats were concerned, the Rumanian government knew that it could count on assistance under the alliance with Poland.

2) Minister Beck stressed that, in order to stiffen Rumania against the Soviets, it was important that Rumania should feel at peace on the Hungarian frontier. Therefore, Minister Beck was endeavoring to procure a rapprochement between *Hungary* and Rumania.

Göring pointed to the difficulty in obtaining such an understanding, given Hungary's intransigent attitude. He allegedly heard from some Hungarians the thesis that, in view of the open Bessarabian problem, Hungary could, in case of a future Soviet-Rumanian conflict, grab Transylvania. When Göring answered the Hungarians that besides Transylvania and Bessarabia there still remained the former Rumania, he was told that the remaining part of Rumania could fall under Poland's protectorate. Göring declared that with such an atmosphere prevailing it was rather difficult to plan a rapprochement between Hungary and Rumania.

3) *Czechoslovakia* was touched on casually, and Göring remarked that it remains under the influence of Soviet Russia's policy. Minister Beck remarked that he does not see what other policy Czechoslovakia could adopt. It always adopts radical solutions. At one time it builds on the concept's of Beneš; if there is a reaction against this, it pushes Hodža and his thesis to the forefront.

In Lipski's papers there is a note with reference to his conversation with Beck after the first Beck-Göring conference:

[5] Mirosław Arciszewski, Polish minister to Rumania (1932–38); later he was assistant undersecretary of state in the Ministry of Foreign Affairs.

After this conference I had a conversation with Beck, at which time I returned to my idea of approaching the German side with some conditions with a view to stabilizing Polish-German relations. I assumed that upon the realization of German intentions toward Austria and Czechoslovakia the Reich's power would increase tremendously. We should therefore place our demands in advance. I suggested extending the declaration of nonaggression for twenty years, with an adequately worded introduction which would secure the *status quo* in our mutual relations. I suggested that this agreement could be signed on the occasion of Ribbentrop's visit to Warsaw. Beck agreed to this in principle, stressing additionally the necessity of securing an agreement on Danzig.

In addition, in view of the danger that in the Czechoslovak problem Germany might act over our head, I proposed definitely to declare to Göring our interest in that country, with which we have a long frontier-line. Such a reservation was to be made without going into details.

DOCUMENT 80   Second Conference of Minister Beck with Göring, in Warsaw, on the Evening of February 23, 1938, with Just the Two of Them Present, *after dinner at the Foreign Affairs Ministry*

Minister Beck said that, as far as *Austria* is concerned, as he had already stated at one time in Berlin, we have no political interests there, only transit and economic interests.

Göring replied that he had considered this point of view as it was communicated to him by the Minister in Berlin, and that Poland's interests would be adequately taken into account.

Beck stressed that, in contrast to Austria, we were seriously interested in the *Czech* problem from a twofold standpoint:

1) in a certain region of Czechoslovakia,

2) in the possible method of settling Czech problems ("die Art und Weise der eventuallen Lösung").

*ad. 1*) Göring replied that Poland's interests "in Mährish Ostrau" will not be infringed upon ("werden nicht berührt").

*ad. 2*) Göring acknowledged this statement, remarking that from the German side there would be no surprises for Poland. In case of any anticipated action in this respect, Warsaw would be informed in time.

Göring declared that the Chancellor had full confidence in Poland's foreign policy as directed by Minister Beck. The Chancellor wanted people in Poland to know that, as long as Poland's policy complied with the Marshal's [Piłsudski] guiding idea, the Reich would observe its line as agreed to with Poland.

Minister Beck replied that Poland would continue its line based on reciprocity, and he added that the leading authorities in Poland had no misgivings as to the development of Polish-German relations. But abroad our mutual relations were regarded as a temporary arrangement. Therefore the Minister suggested extending the act of 1934 on the occasion of Ribbentrop's possible visit to Warsaw.

Minister Beck remarked that this was just a vague idea.

Göring reacted in a very positive way to this idea, adding that the Chancellor had directed him to investigate how Polish-German relations could be reinforced in order to dispel the tensions existing on the Polish side.

Minister Beck remarked that he saw two possible ways:

1) by an adequate solution of the Danzig problem, adding that anything accomplished to appease the situation in the Free City would contribute to better mutual relations,

2) by the possible extension of the agreement of 1934, as mentioned above.

Göring declared that the agreement should be extended for 20–25 years, so as to make it clear that Polish-German relations were based upon a solid foundation. He suggested that, during the signing in Warsaw, the mutual tendencies of the two countries toward peace should be expressed in an adequately worded preamble, which would serve to influence public opinion at large.

Considering this matter to be strictly confidential, Göring will first discuss it with the Chancellor.

Events in Austria signalized that the dramatic crisis in the *Anschluss* problem was near at hand. On March 9 Chancellor Schuschnigg announced in his speech at Innsbruck that the plebiscite fateful for Austria's future would take place on Sunday, March 13.
Lipski noted on March 9:

On March 9, I had a farewell dinner at the Embassy for Mr. Comnen, the newly appointed foreign affairs minister of Rumania. Among others, the Austrian Envoy was present. Half an hour before dinner I received news by telegram from Gawroński [6] of the planned plebiscite in Austria. Gawroński got his information from President Miklas. As seen from Berlin, it was clear that the announcement of the plebiscite would push Hitler to occupy Austria. I kept this secret from my guests, and only after dinner did I disclose the news to them. Reaction to the news about the plebiscite had already started by 9 P.M. Participants of my party were receiving telephone messages from Berlin from their embassies there and their legations in various capitals. The evening came to an end in an atmosphere of general excitement.

On March 10 Hitler decided on a military occupation of Austria, issuing special orders to General Keitel. On March 11 Chancellor Schuschnigg tendered his resignation to President Miklas. On March 12 German troops marched into Austria.

DOCUMENT 81    Lipski to the Ministry of Foreign Affairs

NO. 39                              Berlin, March 12, 1938
                                    Received: March 12, 1938, 12 P.M.
                                    *Secret Code*

Göring told me that he counts on Poland's stand on the Austrian problem being the same as that taken by Minister Beck in Göring's conversation with Beck in Warsaw. He added that the Chancellor will be obliged to Poland for such a stand. I stated that our stand is unaltered and that we have only economic and transit interests in Austria. Göring replied that the German government will be all the more willing to consider these Polish interests.

Received: Warsaw, Rome

*Lipski*

The following is Lipski's personal note completing the telegram.

The conversation with Göring took place at a big reception given by him on the evening of March 11, 1938, at the Club for Airmen on the premises formerly occupied by the Prussian Herren Stube.

6 Jan Gawroński, Polish minister to Austria, 1933–38.

Before this reception I attended a dinner at Czech Envoy Mastny's, where an atmosphere of utter tension and depression prevailed. I went to Göring's reception together with Prince Olgierd Czartoryski. Göring told me that Mussolini had given his consent for the *Anschluss* in reply to Hitler's letter handed to him by Prince Philip of Hesse. He remarked that German troops were entering Austria to safeguard peace; that only in the industrial centers of Wilden and Wiener Neustadt might some local riots be expected. Otherwise, the whole of Austria was for Hitler.

He mentioned his conversation with Henderson, which had taken place just a moment before.[7]

During this reception bands were playing continuously and many couples danced in the large hall, while diplomats clustered at round tables were engaged in animated discussions. I sat at the table of ambassadors, presided over by Göring. Next to me sat Prince Bismarck, who rather tactlessly asked me repeatedly why I was so gloomy. He tried some ersatz merrymaking.

We left the reception with Czartoryski in a mood of utter disgust, convinced that the Reich was racing toward an inevitable catastrophe of war. In the Embassy we were on night-duty service. On my return to the Embassy I sent a telegram informing Warsaw of the entrance of German troops into Austria and reporting on my conversation with Göring. In a second telegram I described my answer to Göring's question about our stand. This declaration of Göring with regard to consideration of our economic interests in Austria I utilized later on in my trade negotiations with the Reich, gaining 800,000 tons of coal in export to Austria.

A decision on this matter was communicated to me, with Vice-Minister Sokołowski present, by the undersecretary of state at the Ministry of Economics of the Reich, Herr Brinkmann. (During the stay of Minister of Commerce Roman in Berlin this problem was not settled, and only after his departure did we ram through, together with Herr von Moltke, this principal Polish demand.) [8]

[7] Henderson, pp. 124–26.
[8] See also *DGFP*, Series D, Vol. V, No. 35.

# Resumption of Polish-Lithuanian Relations
## *Spring, 1938*

---

POLAND AND LITHUANIA had no diplomatic relations for twenty years, a striking anomaly for two neighboring states over such a long period of time. A frontier incident which occurred on the night of March 10, 1938, when a Polish soldier was killed, compelled the government of Poland to intervene. On March 17 an ultimatum was dispatched to Lithuania through the Polish Legation in Tallin, with an expiration date of March 19, requesting that diplomatic relations be resumed prior to March 31; the Lithuanian government accepted the ultimatum, and relations between Poland and Lithuania were established on the date fixed.[1]

In the papers of Ambassador Lipski there is a personal note on this matter.

### *Note with Regard to the Ultimatum to Lithuania*

Our action toward Lithuania was not coordinated with the Reich. The guiding idea of Poland's policy had been a constant tendency to normalize Polish-Lithuanian relations on the principle of the *status quo.* Beck tried to counteract the gradual growth of the Reich's power, and Poland's security became the axiom of his foreign policy.

I discussed this problem with him after his Berlin visit in the middle of January, 1938. The incident during which a Polish soldier, Stanisław Serafin, was shot by the Lithuanian frontier guards gave rise to Warsaw's large-scale action to exert pressure on Kaunas to resume diplomatic relations with Warsaw.

This action, which coincided with the *Anschluss,* quite erroneously gave the impression to international opinion that Warsaw and Berlin were acting jointly. This conviction contributed to a large extent to Kaunas' acceptance of the Polish ultimatum. Upon receipt of the Polish note fixing the date for an answer at March 19, the Lithuanian govern-

[1] See *DGFP*, Series D, Vol. I, Nos. 321–39; also *ibid.*, No. 33, and *Journal,* pp. 293–97.

ment addressed itself to the Great Powers, among others to Moscow, asking for advice. These Powers advised Kaunas to accept the Polish conditions, under the impression that Warsaw's step was covered by Berlin.

As a matter of fact, the situation in the sector of Polish-German relations was then as follows: on March 15 the tension in Polish-Lithuanian relations became so violent that a crisis could be expected at any time. A commotion within diplomatic quarters became very obvious; I could observe it at an evening reception at the Persian Embassy. Saulys, the Lithuanian envoy, approached me and, visibly excited, told me that Warsaw was seeking a conflict with Lithuania. I purposely kept my reserve.[2] In a longer conversation with me, Taffe, the Estonian envoy, stressed that this was the best occasion for the resumption of Polish-Lithuanian relations. A number of diplomats turned to me for information. The Soviet Chargé d'Affaires showed great excitement. He conversed with the Lithuanian Envoy.

Chancellor Hitler left for Austria. Göring was replacing him as head of state. Minister Beck was in Italy; his return was expected on March 16 at noon. On the morning of the 16th I received a telephone call from Göring at Karinhall inviting me to come over and inform him about the situation. I was without any instructions from Warsaw, and I could only act in accordance with the line of general political concepts and my personal intuition.

Göring told me that Ribbentrop had telephoned him from Munich, asking for information on the development of our relations with Lithuania, in order to transmit it to the Chancellor.

The German government was anxious to obtain more detailed information in view of the possible entanglements on Germany's frontier as a result of the Polish-Lithuanian conflict. Taking refuge in the lack of detailed instructions, I explained to Göring in general outlines the Polish-Lithuanian situation, stressing that it was impossible to maintain the present state on the frontier. I mentioned that the last frontier incident was proof that the void in Polish-Lithuanian relations threatened serious consequences at any moment. I was therefore of the opinion that the Polish government would be compelled to draw conclusions from this and to request that Lithuania resume relations. Göring showed understanding for our point of view. He stressed Germany's interest in Kłaj-

[2] See *DGFP*, Series D, Vol. I, No. 322.

peda [Memel], otherwise expressing his *désintéressement* with regard to Lithuania. Nevertheless, he came out with a question about Russia's stand and inquired whether the Polish government did not fear possible complications on that side. In accordance with general directives, I replied that we did not foresee any danger, adding that we were taking the Russian risk upon ourselves.

In addition, I promised Göring to keep him *au courant* of the development of events. Göring put through a telephone call to Munich and communicated our conversation to von Ribbentrop.

Our further exchange of opinion related to the assurances given by the Reich government to the Czech Envoy (see report dated March 16, 1938, No. 37/38) [3] and relations with Russia. Herr Göring came out with an open offer for Polish-German military collaboration against Russia. He stressed on this occasion that he could not conceive how Poland would be able, in the long run, to take the whole burden of Russia's threat on its shoulders. His present offer was even more detailed than those made previously.

Göring's stand on the Lithuanian question, confirmed by his telephone call to the Chancellor, enabled me to give a factual explanation to the Polish government upon Beck's return to Warsaw with regard to the position taken by the German government on our possible action against Lithuania.

This, in my opinion, had even greater importance when one bears in mind that this information could have an impact on the decision of the Polish government.

In reply to my telegram, the Ministry of Foreign Affairs forwarded to me a definition of the Polish stand with regard to the ultimatum to Lithuania, to be transmitted to Göring. A reservation was made therein that German interests in Kłajpeda would be respected by the Polish side, in case an armed Polish-Lithuanian conflict followed the rejection of the Polish request. I communicated this news to Göring in the late evening hours of March 17, when I retired unexpectedly for a short time from a dinner at the Embassy, leaving behind a large group of guests. I simply passed the news on to Meissner that I would leave for a moment to meet with Göring.

The next day, on March 18, Herr von Ribbentrop, who was back in

[3] See below, Document 82, p. 356.

Above left: Major Józef Lipski, London, November, 1951

Above: Józef Lipski, Berlin, October 3, 1933

Right: Foreign Minister Józef Beck and Ambassador Józef Lipski

Top: Ambassador Lipski showing the Wawel sculptured heads to German Chancellor Hitler at the Polish Arts Exhibition in Berlin, March 29, 1935. Between Lipski and Hitler, Professor Mieczysław Treter, organizer of the exhibition

Bottom: Conversation between Lipski and Hitler at the annual dinner for the chiefs of diplomatic missions, Berlin, January 22, 1935

Top: Memorial mass for Marshal Piłsudski on May 18, 1935. Ambassador Lipski greeting Hitler on the steps of St. Hedwig's Church in Berlin

Bottom: Alfred Rosenberg's monthly reception for foreign diplomats and foreign press at the Adlon Hotel, Berlin, March 7, 1938. Left to right: Lipski; Dr. Otto Dietrich, Reich press chief and secretary of state of the German Propaganda Ministry; Rosenberg; Hamdi Arpag, Turkish ambassador

Top left and right: Ambassador Lipski leaving the Auswärtiges Amt after his last interview with Ribbentrop on August 31, 1939

Bottom: Former Ambassador Lipski and Henryk de Malhomme (left), former First Secretary of the Embassy in Berlin, as cadets at Coëtquidan, Brittany's boot camp, October, 1939

Top: Private Lipski and "frères d'armes" at Guère, Brittany, May, 1940, before leaving for the Maginot Line

Bottom: General Józef Haller greeting Private Lipski at Coëtquidan, Brittany

This page: General Kazimierz Sosnkowski with Lieutenant Lipski in the Middle East, 1943

Opposite above left: General Władysław Anders and Major Lipski in Italy, 1944

Opposite above right: Major Lipski with commanding officer Colonel St. Zakrzewski after taking Ancona, 1944

Opposite: Major Lipski in a happy reunion with Colonel Antoni Szymański, former military attaché in Berlin, after the latter's release from prison in Russia

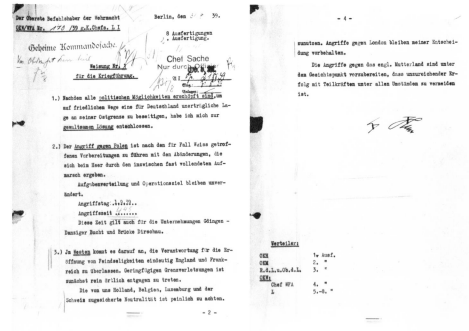

Der Oberste Befehlshaber der Wehrmacht

OKW/WFA Nr. 170 /39 g.K.Chefs. L I

Berlin, den 39.

8 Ausfertigungen
2. Ausfertigung.

Geheime Kommandofache.

Chef Sache
Nur durch Offizier

Weisung Nr. 1
für die Kriegführung.

1.) Nachdem alle politischen Möglichkeiten erschöpft sind, um
auf friedlichem Wege eine für Deutschland unerträgliche Lage an seiner Ostgrenze zu beseitigen, habe ich mich zur
gewaltsamen Lösung entschlossen.

2.) Der Angriff gegen Polen ist nach den für Fall Weiss getrof-
fenen Vorbereitungen zu führen mit den Abänderungen, die
sich beim Heer durch den inzwischen fast vollendeten Auf-
marsch ergeben.
    Aufgabenverteilung und Operationsziel bleiben unver-
ändert.
    Angriffstag .1.9.39..
    Angriffszeit ..........
    Diese Zeit gilt auch für die Unternehmungen Gdingen –
Danziger Bucht und Brücke Dirschau.

3.) Im Westen kommt es darauf an, die Verantwortung für die Er-
öffnung von Feindseligkeiten eindeutig England und Frank-
reich zu überlassen. Geringfügigen Grenzverletzungen ist
zunächst rein örtlich entgegen zu treten.
    Die von uns Holland, Belgien, Luxemburg und der
Schweiz zugesicherte Neutralität ist peinlich zu achten.

— 2 —

- 4 -

zunutzen. Angriffe gegen London bleiben meiner Entschei-
dung vorbehalten.

    Die Angriffe gegen das engl. Mutterland sind unter
dem Gesichtspunkt vorzubereiten, dass unzureichender Er-
folg mit Teilkräften unter allen Umständen zu vermeiden
ist.

Verteiler:

| | |
|---|---|
| OKH | 1. Ausf. |
| OKM | 2. " |
| R.d.L.u.Ob.d.L. | 3. " |
| OKW: | |
| Chef WFA | 4. " |
| L | 5.-8. " |

Top: Lipski after his arrival in the United States as the unofficial representative of the free Poles. At a reception in New York with Msgr. Felix Burant

Bottom left and right: The first and fourth pages (including Hitler's signature) of the German order for the attack on Poland at 4:45 A.M. on September 1, 1939. The time of attack was added in pencil at the last moment.

Berlin, got into the Polish-Lithuanian problem by inviting me for a conversation.

He declared [4] that Lithuanian Envoy Saulys had called on him and had tried to explore the German government's attitude with regard to Poland's demand dispatched to Kaunas. Herr von Ribbentrop told me that he had advised the Envoy to accept Poland's request.[5] He thought that Kaunas would do so. I expressed thanks to Herr von Ribbentrop for his position on this problem.

The French ambassador, M. Poncet, sent to me a well-known French journalist, Sauerwein, to explore the situation. It was rather difficult for me to play an open hand with him, since French journalists are known for their lack of discretion. I could not possibly reveal that our step toward Lithuania was dictated by our desire to shield ourselves in that region against Germany. I must admit that M. Sauerwein grasped our aims, sparing me the necessity of spelling out the situation, and he promised to refer the matter to competent French authorities.

Upon our dispatch of notes to Lithuania, Minister Saulys called me by telephone expressing his desire to see me without delay. In spite of the fact that I had a high opinion of Mr. Saulys as a patron of a rapprochement between our two nations, I could not comply with his demand. Meeting with him at a moment when Warsaw had sent a note requesting an answer by a fixed date, I could thwart the action of my government.

On the morning of March 19, I received news from Warsaw that the Kaunas government had accepted our request. I immediately approached the Lithuanian Envoy personally, asking to be received. We shook hands. He realized that I was sorry to have had to refuse his demand to see me a few days earlier. Very tactfully, he did not even mention it. The conversation now took a very friendly turn. This day of March 19 was a day of great satisfaction for me. . . .

The annexation of Austria by the Reich pushed the problem of Czechoslovakia to the forefront in international affairs. Lipski gives an account of this situation in his report dated March 16, 1938.

[4] *DGFP*, Series D, Vol. I, No. 334.
[5] *Ibid.*, Nos. 328 and 332.

DOCUMENT 82   Lipski to Beck

NO. N/37/38                                        Berlin, March 16, 1938
                                                         *Confidential*

Assurances received by Czech Envoy Mastny from Field Marshal Göring [6] and Minister von Neurath [7] that the German government has no
aggressive intentions toward Czechoslovakia were passed over in total
silence by the German press. This fact is characteristic, for it denotes
that it was not the intention of the German government to appease its
public opinion with regard to the Czechs.

The first spontaneous intervention by the Czech Envoy took place on
March 11 at a reception given by Minister President Göring, when news
came that German troops had marched into Austria. Later, Envoy
Mastny had a long conversation with von Neurath. He finally intervened
with Field Marshal Göring in connection with airplanes flying over the
territory of Czechoslovakia. [8]

Mr. Mastny, as he confirmed to me personally, was satisfied with the
assurances given, which were echoed in the speech of British Prime
Minister Chamberlain. [9] Field Marshal Göring, with whom I had a conversation today on Polish-Lithuanian relations, also confirmed his talk
with the Czech Envoy. He told me that not only did the Reich have no
aggressive intentions, but it is to be hoped that relations with Czechoslovakia may now improve. He asked Mr. Mastny if it was true that Czechoslovakia had taken some mobilization measures that might bring about
reaction on the part of Germany. Mr. Mastny, upon communicating
with Prague by telephone, advised him immediately that this news was
absolutely incorrect. [10]

As to the flight of German planes, Herr Göring remarked that there
was a lot of misinformation in the news in possession of the Czech side,
and that this matter had been cleared up in the conversation with Envoy
Mastny with an air expert present.

Deliberating on the Czechoslovak problem, Herr Göring told me that

[6] *DGFP*, Series D, Vol. II, No. 74.
[7] *Ibid.*, Nos. 78 and 80.
[8] *Ibid.*, Nos. 75–77.
[9] For the speech of Chamberlain on March 14, see *ibid.*, No. 84.
[10] *Ibid.*, No. 72.

the Reich government expects the Czech government to ease relations in the field of minorities and nonextension of Czech-Soviet relations. He added, however, that he does not think that in the long run Czechoslovakia can exist in its present form.

From the above deliberations of Göring it could be concluded that for the moment no violent action against Czechoslovakia by the Reich should be expected, provided that the basic line toward this state—known to you—is maintained in the future.[11]

It is very characteristic that the *Deutsch-Diplomatisch-Politische Korrespondez*, No. 49 of March 15, writing about recent events in Austria, mentions, for the first time so explicitly, that Hungary also still has unsettled national questions beyond its frontiers.

*Józef Lipski*

DOCUMENT 83     Lipski to Beck

NO. N/52/9/38                    Berlin, March 31, 1938
                                *Strictly Confidential*

With the Polish-Lithuanian conflict under way, I had just one conversation, on March 18, with the newly appointed foreign affairs minister, Herr von Ribbentrop, since he was traveling a good deal and I had no occasion to discuss with him in more detail problems pertaining to Polish-German relations. Last week Herr von Ribbentrop was also absent from Berlin, so that I could not be received by him until today.

To begin with, I would like to remark that the new minister continually stresses his positive and even friendly attitude toward Poland, which I have no reason to doubt. However, his personal style of holding office reveals that he is not quite *au courant* of particular problems and questions. The present secretary of state, von Mackensen, will leave the Auswärtiges Amt soon for the Embassy in Rome. Since his relations with Ribbentrop are not too friendly, the information service supplied to the Minister on the part of the A.A. leaves much to be desired.

May I add that von Mackensen's post will probably be filled by the present political director, Baron von Weizsäcker.

[11] See also the Lipski-Szembek conversation (*Journal*, p. 297).

Referring to my stay in Warsaw, I conveyed today your best greetings to Herr von Ribbentrop. When we touched casually on the successful liquidation of the Polish-Lithuanian conflict, I told him that you were obliged to Herr von Ribbentrop for the position he adopted on this matter at the time. I mentioned that the German Ambassador in Warsaw has already been advised accordingly.

Passing to Polish-German relations, I pointed to their successful development based on the declaration of January, 1934. I stressed that certain methods of action were established, based upon direct exchange of opinion in matters of interest to the two states. Thus, no surprises are in store, thanks to this system of mutual information. I added that, as the Chancellor confirmed in his speech at the Reichstag on February 20, this agreement had prevailed against many odds, facilitating a solution in the minorities question by a joint declaration of the two governments on November 5, 1937.

From these deliberations I went on to recall the conversation which took place in Warsaw on February 23 between you and Marshal Göring. At that time Göring said that the Chancellor had instructed him to investigate what could be done to reinforce Polish-German relations and to remove the tension which undermines Polish public opinion; to which you replied that anything that could be done to ease the situation in Danzig would have a positive effect on our opinion. I also mentioned that you promoted the idea of a possible extension of the agreement of January 26, 1934, hinting on my part that this could be done on the occasion of the planned visit.

To my great surprise, I noted that Herr von Ribbentrop had not yet been informed about this conversation. He explained that in the meantime the events in Austria had completely absorbed the whole government. Herr von Ribbentrop said that naturally he was not prepared to make a factual statement prior to consulting Göring. In the first place, he wondered whether such a well-functioning agreement contracted by the leaders of the two nations would not be weakened in the eyes of public opinion by an ill-timed extension.

I pointed to the fact that precisely by an extension would the provisional character of the agreement be removed; which, although it does not exist for competent authorities of the two states, is often exploited by international circles for opinion at large.

Herr von Ribbentrop, whose doubts might be due to a lack of orientation on the problem, promised to reflect on this question. Under these circumstances I did not insist further. Also in connection with Danzig, I simply referred to the Chancellor's declaration made to me on November 5, 1937, and repeated to you on January 14, 1938, as well as to the public statement contained in the Chancellor's speech of February 20.

As to the way the declaration of the two governments with regard to national minorities is working, Herr von Ribbentrop mentioned that he is not yet in a position to be acquainted with this matter. I gave him a general outline of this problem. I availed myself of this occasion to touch upon the census fixed for May 17, and now postponed because of Austria's annexation to the Reich. I did this presuming that, since the registration is being postponed and since as a result of the incorporation of Austria the bill calling for the census might be altered, the current moment is well chosen to present our reservations. I note here that I had already mentioned our objections to the head of the Political Department, Baron von Weizsäcker. Now, just in a general form, I presented the census problem to Herr von Ribbentrop, adding that I would forward to him an informative memo in the next few days.

Herr von Ribbentrop showed interest in Polish-German press relations. We discussed the departure of the German press delegation to Warsaw for a press conference on April 4–5. Herr von Ribbentrop remarked in general terms on the necessity of also influencing the opposition press in Poland. I stated that, as far as certain national organs of the opposition were concerned, they had recently changed their tone for a more positive view of the Polish-German policy.

For my part, I expressed the need of checking the German press in its propaganda campaign which exaggerates even the most insignificant minority incidents in Poland. I remarked that on our part we are hushing up such incidents concerning our minorities in Germany.

Herr von Ribbentrop also mentioned the unfortunate case of the correspondent of *Kurier Warszawski,* Mrs. Męcińska, with regard to the alleged German point of view on the Polish-Lithuanian conflict. He pointed to the Chancellor's dissatisfaction with this press incident, the more so since the German stand on this problem was correct and friendly toward Poland. I replied that Polish official quarters were most critical of this press release by a person who is also quite unqualified politically and is impressed by gossip. I stated that necessary steps have been taken by us to impress on *Kurier Warszawski* the necessity of recalling this correspondent from Berlin. In case this does not succeed, we would not protest if permission to remain in the Reich would be denied to her.

Finally, referring to the point of your conversation with Göring regarding the reinforcement of Polish-German relations, Herr von Ribbentrop made the reservation that he was not speaking officially but just as a friend, and asked me not to report the conversation to Warsaw. He took up a question which is weighing heavily on his heart: that of a wider anti-Comintern collaboration. He stressed that these matters are being worked on by a special bureau of his. Collaboration with Italy and Japan is yielding very interesting and positive results. At present a special commission has been formed to this end. Herr von Ribbentrop asked what Poland's reaction would be to this kind of collaboration.

With the reservation that I was also speaking quite informally, I stressed first of all that we are fighting Communism by all possible means inside Poland. We also react if it is infiltrated from abroad, and here I cited our last note to Czechoslovakia.[12] (By the way, my impression was that Herr von Ribbentrop only learned of this note from me, in spite of the fact that Ambassador von Moltke was duly briefed by the Polish government.) I further mentioned that we have a secret understanding with German security elements to this effect which is functioning satisfactorily, so that in practice we, like the Germans, are fighting Comintern activities on all sectors. Nevertheless, as far as outside manifestations are concerned, we must bear in mind our very special situation as an immediate neighbor of Soviet Russia, the more so since we are also under the obligations of our alliance with Rumania.

Herr von Ribbentrop said that naturally he brought up this issue quite informally, asking me again not to make any official use of it.

Since in the course of our conversation Herr von Ribbentrop was repeatedly called away from the office, I cut short the discussion and brought up no further problems of international politics.[13]

*Józef Lipski*

[12] In this note the Polish government made a firm declaration about Communist and diversive action directed against Poland from the territory of Czechoslovakia. In its reply of May 5, the Czech government declared that necessary steps would be taken to render this kind of action impossible in the future. The Polish government took due notice of the Czech declaration, provided that concrete results of action by the Czech authorities would follow.

[13] For the German version of this conversation, see *DGFP,* Series D, Vol. V, No. 34.

DOCUMENT 84 Lipski to Beck

NO. 7/70 April 9, 1938
*Secret*

With reference to my report of February 12, No. N/7/17/38,[14] I am taking the liberty of informing you that, in connection with the nomination of Herr von Ribbentrop on February 4 to the post of foreign affairs minister of the Reich, further changes followed in German diplomacy, published by the press on April 2, covering the head office of the Auswärtiges Amt and a number of posts abroad.

Former Secretary of State von Mackensen became ambassador in Rome, and his place was taken by Baron von Weizsäcker, formerly head of the Political Department of the A.A. When Herr von Neurath left the post of foreign affairs minister on February 4, Herr von Mackensen made no secret that he would not remain in his post. For the son-in-law of the former Foreign Affairs Minister, whose relations with Herr von Ribbentrop (as I mentioned in my report) were not too cordial, the situation at the A.A. became embarrassing, the more so since in his capacity as secretary of state von Mackensen would have to maintain contact both with Foreign Affairs Minister von Ribbentrop and Neurath as president of the Privy Council (*Geheimsrat*).

During his short stay in office as secretary of state, which lasted just a year, Herr von Mackensen did not cut a particularly remarkable figure. I was under the impression that he lacked technique, elasticity, and a quick grasp of matters indispensable in such a post. Herr von Mackensen and his wife genuinely welcomed the fact of their transfer to Rome, since they had become acquainted with that country some years earlier.

The newly appointed secretary of state, Baron von Weizsäcker, is a talented diplomat, highly intelligent and very flamboyant. He has always been well disposed toward nationalistic ideas, and he is a man of confidence of the Party. I would like to remark that an outstanding professional in the post of secretary of state was particularly needed by Herr von Ribbentrop, who is not a career diplomat and is not very fond of the technicalities of his office.

Herr von Ribbentrop transferred to the A.A. the former counselor of

[14] Not included in this series of documents. It contained details with regard to changes at the Auswärtiges Amt made on February 4, that is, the resignation of Minister von Neurath, the appointment of Ribbentrop to this post, and his biography.

the German Embassy in London, Herr Woermann, to become his new collaborator as head of the Political Department.

If we take into consideration that Herr Bohle is secretary of state at the A.A. for the problems of Germans abroad, that recently Herr Keppler was nominated to a similar post at the A.A. as secretary of state for Austrian affairs, we note that at present this ministry numbers four secretaries of state. This situation naturally evoked some misgivings on the part of the former ministerial directors, who were thus pushed into the background. It is more characteristic that the highest ranking director, Head of the Legal Department Gaus, was offered an autographed portrait of the Chancellor as a sort of compensation.

Vacant Embassy posts were now offered to Mackensen in Rome, von Dirksen in London, von Papen in Ankara, and General Ott in Tokyo.

As I mentioned before, the candidacy of Herr von Moltke was considered for London. Finally, the Chancellor decided to keep him in Warsaw, since he was well oriented in Polish-German relations and had a good reputation in Poland. I heard from people friendly with von Moltke that he was not very anxious to go to London. A large family and a landed estate in Silesia, which he often visits from Warsaw and looks after personally, probably influenced his decision.

Some circles close to the A.A. are of the opinion that Herr von Dircksen's nomination to London is not a very good choice, as he is allegedly much too bureaucratic for London.

In the last appointments, Herr von Ribbentrop did not neglect the chief of his special bureau, von Raumer, who was nominated minister plenipotentiary and will probably soon go into the diplomatic service.

Besides, I was informed that a number of young men from the Party would soon be introduced into the A.A. in order to "pump in some fresh blood."

*Józef Lipski*

DOCUMENT 85 Lipski to Beck

NO. N/L/82/38 May 19, 1938
*Strictly Confidential*

Rumors and unconfirmed reports are currently circulating here about the results of conversations during Chancellor Hitler's stay in Italy.[15] As the dictators of Italy and Germany were mostly conversing without witnesses, it is even more difficult to obtain reliable details. That is why I refrained for the time being from transmitting information not issued from official quarters. I was awaiting an occasion, upon my recovery from the flu, to discuss these topics with members of the German government. In the last days I took this subject up with the secretary of state at the Auswäriges Amt, von Weizsäcker, and the Chancellor's secretary of state, Lammers.

Herr von Weizsäcker limited himself to a few explanations of a general character, without going into details. In the first place, he stated that the visit did not, in principle, add any new aspects to German-Italian relations, or to the so-called Axis. No document was signed in Rome. Herr von Weizsäcker did not conceal the fact that there was some negative reaction to the *Anschluss* on the part of public opinion in Italy. Nevertheless Mussolini—a great statesman—considered this move to be a historic necessity. Chancellor Hitler's emphatic and so-well-justified declaration on the inviolability of the German-Italian frontier contributed to the appeasement of opinion in Italy. Besides, added von Weizsäcker, with the *Anschluss* already an accomplished fact, a tension permanently present in German-Italian relations was removed. At present a common frontier has become an element of rapprochement and further collaboration.

As for news spread by the press about the alleged dealing out of spheres of influence between the Reich and Italy in certain regions, as, for example, the Danubian basin, the Secretary of State called such rumors products of sheer imagination. In order to understand fully the very essence of German-Italian relations—von Weizsäcker said—careful attention should be paid to the speeches delivered by Mussolini and Hitler at the Venetian Palace. These texts reveal everything.

[15] Hitler's trip to Italy from May 2 to May 10 was to pay a return visit to Mussolini, who had come to Germany in September, 1937.

To my allusion about French-Italian relations, the Secretary of State only remarked that in this sector also an understanding would probably be reached, the more so since matters are not very complicated. Recent endeavors to extend the life-span of Red Spain were, in Herr von Weizsäcker's opinion, weighing on the relations of Italy with France. If once and for all a decision was taken to ease the situation in Spain, the conflict should not be prolonged by supporting the hopeless cause of the Red Army.

With reference to the reception of Ambassador Wysocki by Hitler, the Secretary of State explained that previous notice given to Ambassador Wysocki that the audience was not possible was caused by fear of establishing a precedent, especially since very high-ranking persons were also trying to obtain an audience with Hitler. I learned from a report from Rome that, upon refusal on the part of the German Embassy, a personal friend of Ambassador Wysocki, Secretary of State Meissner, obtained the audience for him. I therefore think that Herr von Weizsäcker tried to explain the behavior of the German Embassy in Rome. Von Weizsäcker also explained that Hitler made an exception for Ambassador Wysocki out of regard for his very positive role in the Polish-German rapprochement at the time National Socialism came to power.

If Weizsäcker in his deliberations did not throw too much light on the real meaning of the conversations in Rome, Secretary of State Lammers went a step further and was more explicit in his explanations. He stated that the journey to Rome was not just a demonstration but had resulted in concrete political advantages. In his opinion, the moment for the meeting—following the Italian-British agreement [16]—was well chosen, for otherwise Germany would be held responsible for possible difficulties in reaching this agreement.

Herr Lammers rather significantly stressed that the fruits of the Rome visit would only ripen in its aftermath. And he added that Germany is aware that Italy must have a free hand in the Mediterranean, just as Germany is striving to have freedom of action in some other regions.

With regard to the Chancellor's declaration as to the inviolability of the German-Italian frontier, Herr Lammers explained that the Chancellor launched upon a most emphatic and basic statement on the subject of German-Italian relations. He also added that the inhabitants of Tyrol

[16] The Italo-British agreement was concluded in Rome on April 16, 1938, clearing up a number of problems dividing these two states of late.

feel badly hurt by such a settlement. However, the greater good turned the scale in this case.

As Lammers is close to the Chancellor, I laid special emphasis on the fact that Ambassador Wysocki, as well as Polish governmental circles, greatly appreciated the fact that the Chancellor granted an audience to Wysocki. Herr Lammers replied that the Chancellor was pleased to grant it, owing to Ambassador Wysocki's merit in the cause of Polish-German relations.

As yet, I have had no opportunity to converse with Ribbentrop and Göring on the subject of the visit in Rome. However, it might be stated that, in spite of the *Anschluss* and certain negative repercussions caused by it to public opinion in Italy, the Axis is in full swing. Matters of overwhelming weight of interest were probably decisive for the maintenance of full collaboration between the two states. In my opinion this collaboration should be taken into consideration very seriously in concrete international situations. The last speech of Mussolini in Genoa is very characteristic in this respect.[17]

From what I could gather from a remark made casually to Counselor Lubomirski by Herr Woermann, the second secretary of state, it seems that the German government was warned and informed in advance about the tenor of Mussolini's speech in Genoa. The speech gives the impression of a certain challenge to France via Italy at a moment when the Sudetenland case is on the carpet. It is worth while to quote here from Hitler's speech at a banquet in the Venetian Palace, where he stated:

"Thus a bloc of 120 million people was formed in Europe ready to guard their eternal rights for life and to counter all forces which would oppose the natural development of these states."

*Józef Lipski*


DOCUMENT 86   Lipski to Beck

NO. N/L9L/38                                           Berlin, May 28, 1938
                                                       *Strictly Confidential*

With reference to my report of May 19, No. N/L/82/38, I am taking the liberty of informing you that lately I have had occasion to discuss

[17] Mussolini's speech of May 14 on Italian foreign policy.

the results of Hitler's trip to Italy with Italian Ambassador Attolico, who returned to Berlin after a long illness.

Signor Attolico spent the last period of his illness in Italy and was present in Rome during the demonstrations in honor of Germany's Führer. Chancellor Hitler paid him a courtesy visit at his Roman villa.

Signor Attolico told me, and I also heard this previously from Weizsäcker, that after the *Anschluss* the reaction in Italy was openly hostile to the Germans. During the first days of Hitler's stay in the Italian capital, this could allegedly be clearly observed. Even Mussolini and his entourage were visibly taken aback by this atmosphere. Only after Hitler's speech delivered at the Venetian Palace, and especially the passage stressing the inviolability of the Italian-German frontier, was the tension in feelings relieved, so that in Naples the reception was much warmer, reaching a diapason in Florence.

The Italian Ambassador thinks that, although the *Anschluss* was painful to take at the start, in the long run it removed a source of friction from German-Italian relations. In his opinion the words spoken by Hitler carry historic meaning. The Ambassador also explained that, since Mussolini's speech as a matter of course was less expressive, this shortcoming had to be balanced. Mussolini did so in the speech delivered in Genoa.

The Ambassador also strongly confirmed that nothing had been signed during the conversations between the two dictators. Questioned about Italian-French negotiations, Signor Attolico remarked that an error was possibly committed by not requesting an immediate nomination of an ambassador. On its side, the French government overloaded the negotiations with a lot of problems which, in the opinion of the Italian government, do not concern France in the least, as, for example, the Suez question, the Red Sea, etc. Besides, the French side started to mangle such delicate matters as Tunisia, thus making a mess of the negotiations.

*Józef Lipski*

# The Problem of the Sudetenland
*Summer, 1938*

A NUMBER of incidents occurred in the Sudetenland in connection with county elections in Czechoslovakia fixed for May 22–29 and June 12, 1938.

The tension reached its climax on May 19–21 when two Sudetenland Germans were killed by the Czech police near the town of Eger on the Czech-German frontier. The situation became so serious that the Czech government mobilized two classes of reservists on May 21. They were partially released on June 18.

The press in the West published news about the concentration of German troops on the Czechoslovakian frontier.

Lipski writes about these events in his memoirs.

Alarming news about the alleged German mobilization against Czechoslovakia came as a surprise to me. I had no regional reports dealing with the alleged German concentration on the Czechoslovakian border. Disturbed by the alarms sounded by the Western press, I approached the British Embassy and received the information that Henderson had ordered his staff to get ready to leave.[1]

At that time Minister Beck passed through Berlin on his way to Stockholm.[2] Upon discussing the matter, we decided that he should proceed with his trip. Owing to a longer stay at the station, Beck dictated in the car a reply to the French government's exposition addressed to us with regard to Czechoslovakia. (The text of Beck's telegram is not in my possession.)

On May 21 Ambassador Lipski noted his conversation with Göring:

At Göring's invitation I had a conversation with him.

Göring declared that the attitude taken by Great Britain and France on May 19–21 creates obstacles for a speedy realization of German demands with regard to the question of minorities in Czechoslovakia.

[1] This matter is related in Henderson, pp. 137–38.
[2] Beck left Warsaw on May 22 and arrived in Stockholm on May 24.

He suggested, rather casually and confidentially, the possible extension of economic pressure on Czechoslovakia on the part of Germany, Poland, and Hungary as a common action. The goal of this pressure was to be the realization of the demands of these states in relation to Czechoslovakia.

Keeping my reserve on this problem, I limited myself to the answer that the next time I was in Warsaw I would present this matter to the Foreign Affairs Minister.

Warsaw adopted a "wait and see" attitude in this matter. Beck, as usual, replied by a series of questions, which I was not able to present to Göring until our next meeting, held on June 17, 1938.

Lipski writes further in his memoirs:

As confidentially revealed by General Bodenschatz,[3] in answer to the stand taken by the Western Powers during the May crisis, Hitler gave orders for the building of fortifications on the western frontier of the Reich. And he wanted them built at full speed, fixing the deadline for a deal with Czechoslovakia at the fall of 1938. During my stay in Warsaw at Whitsuntide, I reported on this problem, asking the Minister to issue, in case of an emergency, evacuation instructions for the diplomatic posts in Germany. (The same instructions detailed at that time were applied later at the outbreak of the Polish-German war on September 1, 1939.) Besides this, I also warned the minister of the treasury, Eugene Kwiatkowski, about a possible conflict in the fall. Minister Kwiatkowski, disturbed by this news, which threatened his economic plans, told me half-jokingly that if I repeated the news to Marshal Śmigły the army would put an even greater strain on his budget. The top-brass of the army was, of course, informed about Bodenschatz's revelations.

DOCUMENT 87   Lipski to Beck

NO. N/52/18/38                                    Berlin, June 19, 1938
                                                    *Strictly Confidential*

Upon my return to Berlin after Whitsuntide, on June 7, I immediately called on Field Marshal Göring. I was informed that he was leaving Berlin the same day for about a week and would only be able to receive me upon his return.

[3] Karl Bodenschatz, a general of the Luftwaffe.

In the meantime I was able to draw a more precise picture of the situation which prevailed here following the events of May 19–21. I could do so on the basis of information received from a series of casual conversations with Minister von Ribbentrop and Secretary of State von Weizsäcker,[4] as well as with the ambassadors of France and Great Britain.

The position taken by Great Britain and France during these May days obviously contributed to the application of more circumspect methods in the Czech problem, in order to spare the Reich the risk of an international conflict.

During the debates which, as I heard, took place with the participation of representatives of the army, the Chancellor's opinion prevailed against more radical tendencies represented by some Party dignitaries. It is very characteristic that Ambassador Henderson, who plays first fiddle in this matter, told me that the only person showing moderation and reserve is the Chancellor himself. His entourage is, in the opinion of the Ambassador, fanatical and lacking in sufficient experience. The Chancellor personally, at a farewell audience for the Egyptian Envoy, firmly laid stress on his peaceful attitude, remarking that he would not wage war for the Sudetenland question.

Transition to more circumspect and to some extent more dragged-out tactics in the Sudetenland problem met with a certain disillusion in Party circles, not excluding, as I felt, even Göring himself. But especially disappointed was Himmler, who is very bellicose in his attitude toward Czechoslovakia. A glorification campaign by the West European press with regard to Anglo-French action on May 19–21, which compelled the Germans to retreat, was a severe blow for the Party elements to take.

This situation became a fertile ground for internal criticism which erupted against states supposedly hampering Germany's freedom of action. From a number of quarters information reached me that in circles close to the army rumors were being circulated that the unexpected attitude of Poland had rendered void Germany's undertaking in the Sudetenland problem, which was to have been settled in the above-mentioned days of May.

I am reporting these rumors, simply for the sake of information, without precluding whether they originated from actual ignorance of the

[4] See *DGFP*, Series D, Vol. II, No. 255.

real state of affairs or were spread intentionally by German or foreign factors hostile to us. As a matter of fact, I did not observe any such reaction on the part of the competent authorities.

Possibly there was just a temporary impulse of dissatisfaction caused by a failure in prestige combined with a desire to shift the blame to other states.

This passing wave of reaction in the face of the Sudetenland problem will, in my opinion, have no impact on the question itself in the long run, for German goals remain unchanged for the future. Besides, public opinion is being maintained in a state of tension by the press campaign, so as to actualize the problem inside Germany and abroad. A possible understanding by way of negotiations between representatives of Sudetenland Germans and Prague is excluded in advance. Secretary of State von Weizsäcker expressed his opinion to this effect to me.

On June 17, I was received by Göring at Karinhall. The conversation lasted for over an hour and consisted this time of a rather general exchange of opinion. From Göring's mood I had the impression that the Sudetenland matter, though still timely, had been to some degree slowed down, as if there were a lack of final decision as to what to do next.

I opened the conversation with a remark that immediately upon my return from Warsaw I had wanted to see Göring, but unfortunately, owing to his departure, our conversation had been delayed. Göring mentioned that he was in the west of Germany for a couple of days to inspect fortifications on the French frontier. I consider this detail to be of utmost importance under the present circumstances, and I shall return to it at the end of my letter. Next, I told Göring that, after our conversation of May 21, I had proceeded to Warsaw to report on it personally to you, since I was not prepared to deal with this problem in writing. Finally, following your instructions, I gave an answer to Herr Göring to his suggestion for possible economic pressure to be exerted on Czechoslovakia jointly by Germany, Poland, and Hungary.

1) Göring did not give a direct answer to your question as to what, in that case, would be the requests put to the Czech side. Only from his deliberations which followed could one get some idea of the German stand. Namely, he explained that, with regard to the realization of demands dealing solely with minorities, a total economic isolation of Czechoslovakia would be too costly an operation. Such action would only pay if the total disintegration of Czechoslovakia were considered.

Moreover, Göring did not conceal the fact that this is bound to occur some time, and he called Czechoslovakia an inconceivable creation.

Without further defining the German concept, in spite of my repeated attempts to question him, Göring referred to his conversation with you of February 24 and tried to learn something about our plans.

With matters at a standstill I also did not play an open hand, confining myself to referring to what you said on February 23. Still returning to the conversation with you, and recalling that the German government takes into consideration our interests in a certain region, Göring hinted in a very camouflaged way that the German side also understands our interests stemming from the geographical situation, and that in this case Hungary should also consider this aspect. Since we had previously discussed the subject of the excessively long stretch of Czechoslovakia on Poland's southern frontier, I think that Göring undoubtedly had in mind Carpathian Ruthenia.

2) With regard to possible gradual economic pressure, Herr Göring remarked that such an eventuality would be considered by the German side. On the basis of calculations he concluded that for Poland the greatest difficulty would consist in the problem of transit lines southward. Here I added that transit to our Baltic ports should also be taken into consideration. Herr Göring further stated, also in very general terms, that, with such an eventuality in mind, transit from Poland to Italy, for example, should be moved through the Reich's territory, and in such a way as not to burden Poland excessively. This operation would be most costly to Germany, with direct turnover disrupted, the more so since the Reich is importing many raw materials, such as wood, etc., from Czechoslovakia. No conclusion was reached, and the deliberations were rather general in character. Herr Göring ended his deliberations on this issue by a statement that this matter should be dealt with in a circumspect manner.

In our conversation we touched on a number of other questions. Göring mentioned, for example, that the Czech Envoy in Warsaw allegedly received instructions to declare confidentially to the Polish government that our minorities would receive more far-reaching rights than the Sudetenland. To this I replied that I had no information to this effect, and that some time ago Prague had assured us that our minorities would enjoy the same rights as those granted to other minorities. Herr Göring remarked that naturally Poland could not accept anything else. Göring further deliberated on the consequences that would follow if France attacked the Reich because of the Sudetenland question. On this occasion he tried to illustrate Germany's military power from the most favorable angle. In this connection he said that he had given orders to reinforce fortifications on the French frontier and extend them on the northern sector up to Holland in a wide belt. As far as the German air force is concerned, in the present state of development it is, in his opinion, nearly equal to Anglo-French aviation taken jointly. He did agree that great efforts are being made in England and France, but results are not expected sooner than in two years. He analyzed the productivity of an economic system at the disposal of a totalitarian state as compared with the difficulties in armaments encountered by democratic states. He cited England's problems with its air defense.

The conversation then shifted to Soviet Russia. Göring gave voice to rather serious concern that Rumania could panic under pressure from the Soviets and agree to grant transit to Soviet aviation, or even to let troops march across its territory.

I remarked that our collaboration with Rumania is designed to stiffen that state against Russia. I pointed to the recent visit to Warsaw of the Rumanian Chief of the General Staff.[5] I emphasized the necessity of safeguarding Rumania from the Hungarian side, and here as always Göring agreed.

I availed myself of this occasion once more to lay stress categorically on our stand against any attempt to use our territory for transit of Soviet troops. I confided to him that we had recently repulsed an attempted overflight of Soviet planes, which news he received with visible satisfaction. He also talked about international forces interested in the outbreak of a world war, which I on my part particularly stressed. Naturally the question of the Jews and Bolshevism was not left out of our discussion, and here Göring suggested that, in case the Jews and the Third International pushed Europe into war, then the Soviets, as *tertium gaudens,* would remain on the margin.

At the end of the conversation Göring especially underlined the common interest uniting Poland and Germany, which might in the future result in serious concrete advantages to be derived from their relation. He remarked that, in case of a Polish-Soviet conflict, Germany, in its own well-understood interest, could not refrain from giving assistance to

[5] The chief of the General Staff, General Jonescu, arrived in Warsaw on May 30, 1938.

Poland. He added that perhaps today Russia is comparatively weak, but who knows if in the future it would not become strong enough.

He insisted that Poland should understand that the Reich has no revisionistic designs whatever on Poland, for example, in Pomerania. Such ideas might dwell in the minds of small middle-class people, but never in the minds of responsible politicians. National Socialist Germany, as he put it, is not anxious to annex foreign nationals to the Reich. And that is why German aspirations in Europe come to an end with the settlement of the Austrian and Sudetenland problems. Afterward colonial problems might arise, said Göring.

My conversation with Göring was a further confirmation of my observations in the Sudetenland problem, on which I had the honor of reporting at the beginning of my letter.

*Józef Lipski*

We further read in Lipski's personal notes:

The German side was at that time seriously concerned about Rumania's reaction to Soviet requests of transit for their troops. Rumania's policy was similar to ours in this matter. This subject came up in every conversation with Göring. Germany began to threaten Rumania with its possible collaboration with Hungary in case Rumania yielded to Soviet pressure. Misgivings as to the alleged military agreement between Germany and Hungary grew deeper in Rumania with Keitel's visit to Budapest in June, 1938. I wrote about this in detail in my letter of June 21.

## DOCUMENT 88    Lipski to Beck

NO. N/52/23                                 Berlin, June 21, 1938
                                                    *Strictly Confidential*

In my report on my conversation with General Field Marshal Göring at Karinhall on June 17, I pointed to the serious misgivings of the President of Ministers that Rumania might be terrorized by Soviet pressure and agree to the overflight of Soviet aviation, and even to the marching of troops through its territory. I did not mention in my letter of June 19 that Herr Göring remarked in a discussion on this point that it would be worth while to influence Rumania to stiffen its stand against Soviet transit claims. The argument might be used that, in case Rumania grants a free hand to the Soviets, Hungary might stand up against it. This declaration of Göring, which I did not at first consider too seriously, is now taking on considerable weight in the light of the information I received yesterday from the Rumanian Envoy. Mr. Djuvara informed me that, according to news from Budapest, German-Hungarian military collaboration has been developing rapidly of late. There is circumstantial evidence that the Hungarian General Staff arrived at an agreement with German military authorities to coordinate their possible action against Czechoslovakia from the Hungarian side. This understanding was presumably so close that the Hungarians agreed to the marching of German troops through their territory. German action through Hungary would bestow a number of advantages on Germany: quicker and more effective action against Czechoslovakia, better protection in the Sudetenland from war operations, and, finally, better chances for an assault from the Hungarian side, where Czech border fortifications are not so strong as on the border facing Germany. The Rumanian Envoy also pointed to the recent visit of General Keitel to Budapest where, in his opinion, these matters were discussed. As you know, I have for years been on close friendly terms with the Rumanian Envoy, who is firmly in favor of the Polish-Rumanian alliance and categorically opposes the idea of the transit of Soviet troops through Rumania. He criticizes Minister Comnen's weak stand on this matter. I repeated to him what Göring told me: that he feared that Rumania may cede to Soviet pressure for transit of troops and overflight of planes. I added that I had no confirmation of Göring's information as to the allegedly far-advanced state of German-Hungarian military collaboration against Czechoslovakia. However, I called his attention to the fact that the evasive attitude of Bucharest with regard to the military transit of the Soviets might push Germany into military collaboration with Hungary against the Soviets. The Rumanian Envoy confided in me that he wants to report on this matter to the King, for in spite of the fact that the Soviet problem has been raised in his conversations with the Chancellor, Göring, and von Ribbentrop, Bucharest has not as yet given a definite reply that he could communicate to the German side.

Owing to my feelings of close friendship with Mr. Djuvara, I am very anxious to keep my report secret. I wish to add to the above information that I have as yet been unable to obtain more precise information about the German-Hungarian military collaboration. Questioned by me on this, the Hungarian Envoy here replied that General Keitel was paying a return visit for Hungarian Landwehr Minister Roeder's visit to Germany. My personal opinion is that, since Germany is concerned about the evasive stand of Rumania toward the Soviets (it might have heard about the overflight of planes), it is seeking support from Hungary.

*Józef Lipski*

In the period of June–July, 1938, the problem of Polish minorities in Germany and German minorities in Poland resulted in a series of conversations in Berlin and Warsaw. In Lipski's papers there are no documents on these events. They are dealt with extensively in the German version (*DGFP*, Series D, Vol. V, pp. 52–74).

We quote further from Lipski's personal notes:

On August 5 Beck passed through Berlin,[6] and I then had the opportunity to communicate to him my observations with regard to Czech-German relations. Too-strong anti-Czech accents in the Polish press were a handicap in my trump-card negotiations with Germany. My intention was to reach an understanding to stabilize Polish-German relations in the future.

Beck told me then that without pressure on the press on the part of the Foreign Affairs Ministry in support of our claims from Czechoslovakia, the press would engage in an opposite campaign, rendering our strategy impossible. I completed the information given to Beck verbally by means of a detailed letter dated August 11.

DOCUMENT 89 Lipski to Beck

NO. N/1/137/38 Berlin, August 11, 1938
*Strictly Confidential*

Since you passed through Berlin on August 5, when I had the opportunity of reporting to you verbally on the development of the situation in the Sudetenland as observed from the local angle, I obtained information that throws additional light on the matter.

Rather interesting is the opinion of the British Ambassador, who

[6] Beck paid an official visit to Oslo between August 1 and August 4 and was on his way back to Warsaw via Berlin on the 5th.

shows great independence of judgment. He recently told one of my colleagues that in his opinion Prime Minister Chamberlain took a great personal risk in sending Lord Runciman to Prague. The Ambassador laid special stress on the fact that Runciman's mission is taken most seriously by the British side, for a basic settlement is at stake and not just a short-term superficial solution. If Lord Runciman, in spite of his endeavors, fails to achieve an agreement, it will then become obvious that the Czech side is to blame, and that the Germans are right to state that in view of the unyielding attitude of the Czechs the only solution is to act by force. The British Ambassador let it be understood that in such case the British government would abstain from any further responsibility. It is also known to me that Sir Nevile tried to influence the Rumanian and Yugoslav envoys to have their governments exert pressure on Prague. He did this, as he confirmed, on his own responsibility, without being instructed by his government accordingly. Following further information, Belgrade and Bucharest duly intervened in Prague, advising the Czech government to make concessions.

I had further opportunity to converse with American Ambassador Wilson upon his return from Warsaw and Prague.[7] Owing to his acquaintance with Beneš when he was envoy to Switzerland, the President of the Czech Republic invited him to visit Prague for a conversation. Ambassador Wilson told me that Beneš, who in the past displayed self-confidence and composure, now impressed him as a man under pressure seeking for an emergency exit. Beneš denied the allegation that he is the main source of resistance against Sudetenland demands, and stressed his peaceful policy. Beneš was ready to approve a local self-government within the frame of the national electoral group, but he declared that the Sudetenland claim for territorial self-government could not be granted. In answer to my question Ambassador Wilson also explained that Beneš did not agree to the granting of *Staatsvolk* status to the Sudetenland Germans. The American Ambassador was rather surprised by the fact that, while competent elements in Prague are aware of how serious the situation is, public opinion at large seems to be insufficiently informed.

Finally Mr. Wilson, remarking that he was speaking from a personal point of view, said that he is under the impression that Chamberlain's choice of Lord Runciman, who belongs to the Liberal Party, was made

[7] See *Foreign Relations of the United States: Diplomatic Papers, 1938,* I, 540–44.

from the angle of England's internal politics, and possibly in accordance with French policy.

Yesterday at the reception given by the Italian Ambassador for Marshal Balbo, I had an opportunity for a casual conversation with General Field Marshal Göring. Göring said that he would like to talk to me in the next few days to discuss—naturally, as usual, privately and confidentially—the possibilities of a further Polish-German rapprochement in certain fields. He mentioned, as an example, the problem of discontinuing mutual spying action, in addition to some exchange of information regarding Russia and Czechoslovakia.

With regard to the Russian problem, he made a casual remark that this would become timely after the settlement of the Czech question. He referred to his idea that, should a Polish-Soviet conflict occur, Germany could not remain neutral and not come to the aid of Poland. He denied rumors that Germany would march into the Ukraine, stressing that the Reich's interests are concentrated in the first place on putting a stop to Bolshevik action. On the other hand, Poland, in his opinion, might have some direct interests in Russia, for example, in the Ukraine.

During the discussion on this point I informed Göring about Szembek's conversation with Comnen and the latter's emphatic statement against the transit of Soviet troops through the territory of Rumania.[8] Göring received this explanation with satisfaction.

Questioned about developments in the Sudetenland problem, Göring replied that it is now nearing its settlement ("die Sache geht jetzt zu Ende"). He is of the opinion that the Czech state will cease to exist as a creation made up of various nationalities: Germans, Slovaks, Hungarians, Ruthenians, and, finally, of some number of . . . Czechs. Göring mentioned casually that the moment is near when a decision should be taken and agreement reached on how to settle this matter. In Göring's opinion the Western Powers are beginning to realize how impossible the situation has become. In his opinion, England's mediation is just a *pro forma* affair. Prague's chief speculation is based upon its relation with the Soviets.

It was very characteristic that in the course of these deliberations Göring remarked that *Italy would naturally intervene* in case the Reich were attacked by France because of the Sudetenland conflict.

In view of the situation in connection with Lord Runciman's media-

[8] See *Journal,* pp. 325–26.

tion and the forthcoming visit of Regent Horthy to Germany, and bearing in mind the above statements of Göring that the Sudetenland problem is close to its crucial point, I thought it advisable to go one step beyond my usual limits in my conversation with Göring. With this in mind, I stressed that already at the Paris conference Czech policy strove for a common frontier with the Soviets, excessively stretching their territory on our southern border. This cut us off from our common frontier with Hungary, to the detriment of Polish-Hungarian interests based upon centuries of tradition of the two countries. Göring replied that he understands the necessity of a Polish-Hungarian frontier.

My further exchange of opinion with Göring was restricted to our immediate relations, such as the situation of our seasonal workers, whose efficiency is highly valued by the Field Marshal, and whose number he would still like to increase next year. We also touched on the successfully achieved Polish-German economic agreement, as well as the social insurance agreement.

At the same reception I had an opportunity to speak briefly with the Hungarian Envoy in Berlin. Following your directives, I referred to Regent Horthy's visit to the Reich, stating that I would consider it a great honor to be able to pay him my respects during his stay in Berlin. Envoy Sztojay seemed pleased and said that in all probability Horthy would receive me on August 24.

I further laid stress on the importance of the present moment for our common relations, adding that Warsaw and Budapest were in close contact. Asking him to keep this in strict confidence, I privately remarked that I had some misgivings as to whether in dealings on the question of the Sudetenland Hungarian and Polish interests in Czechoslovakia would not be overlooked. The Envoy seemed to share this opinion. I further added that I was observing Runciman's mission with a touch of skepticism in view of Prague's resistance to acceptance of the principal demands on the Sudetenland. However, I remarked that I did not yet see clearly a definite German line. I therefore thought that it would suit our interests to safeguard them in advance. Envoy Sztojay shared this opinion. He firmly stressed how important it is for Hungary to be sure of Poland's support. However, I could feel a certain hesitation when, for example, he expressed his concern about Yugoslavia's attitude, or Rumania's power of resistance with regard to possible Soviet claims for transit.

The following outline emerges from the conversations reported on above, which I shall take the liberty of turning into a factual report only after a longer talk with Göring:

The German government does not believe in the success of Runciman's mission, and the more radical elements, among whom I am also placing General Field Marshal Göring, are of the opinion that the problem can be settled only by force. If Beneš really rejects the claim for *Staatsvolk* and territorial autonomy, then the agreement seems to be more than doubtful. However, England could present Czechoslovakia with the choice of either accepting German conditions or facing England's retreat, which would leave Czechoslovakia in a tête-à-tête with the Reich. So, the moment of crisis might be close at hand. Chancellor Hitler, as I was informed from several reliable sources, declares to the outside that he would not wage war over the Sudetenland problem. This stand of the Chancellor corresponds with opinion at large, excluding more fanatical elements of the Party and youth, which is anxiously watching over the possibility of international war entanglements. Such information is reaching me from all over the territory. Nevertheless, among the older elements, memories of the great war lost in spite of the colossal preparations of 1914 carry a certain weight. At the same time, however, feverish preparations are being made to protect the Reich in case of a possible conflict with the West. This may be observed from fortifications built without regard to the material and human effort expended.

I would also like to call your attention to the recently very intensive contacts between Italian and German military spheres. May I just cite the recent visit of General Pariani, chief of the Italian General Staff, and the present visit of General Balbo. Besides the above-mentioned utterances of Göring with regard to the possible checking of France and Italy in case of a German-Czech conflict on the Sudetenland, I would like to lay stress on a rather characteristic passage in Marshal Balbo's speech delivered in reply to Göring's speech on the 10th inst.:

"Germany and Italy will remain unconquered if under the leadership of Mussolini and Hitler they will jointly realize their policy." ("Deutschland und Italien werden unbesiegbar bleiben, wenn sie, geführt von Benito Mussolini und Adolf Hitler, ihre Politik gemeinsam verfolgen.")

*Józef Lipski*

---

During the official visit of Regent Horthy in Berlin (between August 22 and August 28), Ambassador Lipski called on him on August 24 in the former Chancellor's palace. Lipski noted this conversation in his personal papers: [9]

This conversation, during which the Regent spoke very warmly about Poland, expressing the hope that the two countries might in the future share a common frontier, threw some light on his dislike of the National Socialist system and a certain concern over the risky policies of the Third Reich. He asked me confidentially to advise Warsaw that he would shortly send a trustworthy person to Poland to discuss the changing situation.[10] He emphasized that time was running short. He had a negative opinion about Rumania as our partner with regard to Russia. He was very much embarrassed by the commotion created by the publication of a communiqué from the conference in Bled.[11] The Regent labeled this matter an intrigue perpetrated against him in connection with his trip to Germany. He shifted responsibility for what happened to the Hungarian Foreign Affairs Minister.[12]

DOCUMENT 90   Note of Director Łubieński for Ambassador Lipski

August 25, 1938 [13]

### The Soviets

Mr. Ambassador has confirmation that the Polish government will always oppose Soviet intervention in European problems.

[9] See also *Sprawy Międzynarodowe* (Warsaw), 1958, Nos. 7–8, pp. 70–71.

[10] Count István Csáky. director of the cabinet of the Hungarian Foreign Affairs Minister, stayed in Warsaw on October 5–6 and held conversations with Beck.

[11] On August 23 a communiqué was issued by the conference of states of the Little Entente and Hungary at Bled. This communiqué stated that the provisional agreement reached "includes the recognition by the three States of the Little Entente of Hungary's equality of rights as regards armament, as well as the mutual renunciation of any recourse to force between Hungary and the States of the Little Entente" (text in *Documents on International Affairs, 1938*, I, 284). See also Horthy, pp. 162–63.

[12] "During the state visit Regent Horthy told the Führer informally that Hungary was prepared to advocate in Warsaw that Poland return the Corridor to Germany. The Führer requested the Regent to refrain from taking such a step." *DGFP*, Series D, Vol. V, No. 52. See also Horthy, p. 156.

[13] The date of the note is not correct. Michał Łubieński, director of Minister Beck's cabinet, must have delivered this note before August 24, for on that day the conversation between Lipski and Göring (Document 91) took place, during which the Polish Ambassador used the instructions contained in the note.

### Czechoslovakia

We do not believe that this country is capable of existing; we do not see any signs of change in its policy. The West is becoming tired of the Czech problem. The greatest obstacle for Germany in this question is that, in the West, German policy is described as a big adventure (Poland, of course, does not believe this). The dragging out of the Czech problem is creating an ever-increasing combustive situation.

### Hungary

The most stabilized element in that region, our eternal friends, etc. Are they capable of an effort? How far might they be relied on?

### Poland

Stress explicitly that various great efforts were made of late to draw Poland into some anti-German deals, but they were flatly rejected.

At present they are trying to use Danzig matters as a lever to undermine Polish-German relations. Danzig, it must be admitted, is now disorganized. We do not know with whom to talk there. Praise Greiser slightly, without blaming Forster.

### Czechoslovakia

Slovakia must at any rate get autonomy either from the Czechs or from the Hungarians. Carpathian Ruthenia is a junk pile of political intrigues not worthy of occupying oneself with.

### Poland-Germany

If there are some concrete proposals it should be declared that, since these are new aspects, they should be taken *ad referendum*. One thing, Mr. Ambassador, you have to say on behalf of your government: that nothing ever said in Berlin will be used by us against Germany. The initiative belongs to them, but we are not evading them.

According to the conversation, please investigate whether Minister Beck could not stop in Berlin for a personal conversation on his way to Geneva on September 7.

### Japan

Mr. Ambassador, you have to quote the words of Marshal Piłsudski, that for Russia a war with Japan would always be only a colonial war, and that a real national war might be only a European war.

*Poland*

Ever-growing consolidation of public opinion at large toward foreign policy (Arciszewski-Niedziałkowski).[14]


DOCUMENT 91  Conversation of Ambassador Lipski
with General Field Marshal Göring
*on August 24, 1938*

*Strictly Confidential*

Göring returned to the question of sending to Warsaw the hunting car presented by him to the President of the Polish Republic. His aide-de-camp, Captain Menthe, who will proceed to Warsaw with the chauffeur, will present the car to the President on his behalf. Göring thought this way might be more suitable than a letter from him to the President. He remarked that the technicalities will be settled by his aide-de-camp's office in agreement with the Embassy.

Göring stated that he had again issued orders regarding the overflight of German planes in the restricted zone near Hel. The last case reported to him by the Embassy (conversation of Lubomirski with Director Grutzbach on August 22, 1938) is subject to investigation. The airman was punished for violating the zone. On the other hand, it might be possible that he did not see the rockets fired as warning signals.

Göring remarked that he had not yet had an occasion to talk with Regent Horthy and his staff, who will only arrive in Berlin this afternoon. He wanted to stress that the German government exerted pressure on Budapest to conduct negotiations so as to avoid collective obligations with the states of the Little Entente but to enter into agreement separately with Belgrade and Bucharest, omitting Prague. Göring remarked that Stoyadinovich followed the line of these suggestions at the Bled conference (if I understood correctly). Thus, in Göring's opinion, Hungary would be free to act, as he put it, in the last stage, its action anticipated to follow only a few days after that of the Germans. Göring described Hungary's stand as somewhat soft (*flau*).

[14] Tomasz Arciszewski (1877–1955) and Mieczysław Niedziałkowski (born 1893; executed by the Germans in 1940) were leaders of the faction of the Polish Socialist Party before the war which opposed the Polish government.

He then began to deliberate on the Czech question. As he had in previous conversations, he pointed to tendencies prevailing in Czech military circles to bring on an international military conflict as the only solution to the situation. In case of a victorious war these elements believe that they would completely defeat the minorities which make up the Great Czech state.

Analyzing the position of the Western Powers from the angle of a possible international armed conflict, Göring remarked that England might be ready with military strength in aviation not sooner than at the end of 1939, especially in antiaircraft defense. He said that the British land force is minimal. Their navy is really powerful, but the new units are still under construction, since England, up to the moment of the Abyssinian war, neglected its armaments. Besides, England has a number of troubles; for example, in the Mediterranean, in Spain, and in the Far East. From Göring's words it resulted that international propaganda is spreading rumors overrating England's preparedness to take up arms.

Applying the same analysis to France, Göring pointed to the enormous fortifications built on the western frontier of Germany, where about 400,000 people are at work. In opposition to the Maginot Line, which is very deep, and therefore renders maneuvers by concentrated units very difficult, the Germans are creating a more elastic system by building a whole series of defense lines. Regarding French aviation, Göring observed that very considerable shortcomings have existed, and only recently have steps been taken to raise it to an adequate level.

On this occasion Göring stressed that in case of French mobilization Mussolini would also mobilize, and France is aware of this.

Agreements with the Soviets and the Czechs are becoming a burden to France.

General Vuillemin[15] told him that the French-Czech agreement operates exclusively via the League, should unprovoked aggression be confirmed. Göring answered General Vuillemin that, if this was the case, there would never be a war between the Reich and France, since the Germans will not be the aggressors. Very significantly Göring told me here that obviously either the Germans would be attacked or they would be provoked, as, for example, in case of riots in the Sudetenland.

Continuing his hypothetical deliberations about the war, Göring ob-

[15] General Joseph Vuillemin, chief of the French Air General Staff (after February 22, 1938), paid a state visit to Berlin on August 16.

served that some lessons of the world war were not wasted. So, for instance, the Germans would not open an offensive but would sit in their fortifications and repulse attacks, causing heavy losses to their enemies.

Returning to the Czech problem, Göring cited the British opinion that in a matter of time everything could be settled. He does not share that opinion. He cannot conceive how the Czechs could agree to any concessions, since their state is composed of so many nationalities. For instance, if in order to make things even with Poland they would grant it all concessions, then similar concessions would have to be made to all other minorities. Therefore, the situation is at an impasse.

Following your instructions, I replied to these declarations that we also do not believe the present Czech creation can exist any longer. Nor do we see any change in the Czech policy. I added that of late efforts have been made to draw us into anti-German deals but that the Polish government rejected these offers categorically. I ascertained that international propaganda presents German policy as pushing ever new claims and provoking conflicts. Poland, I added, does not believe this. Here Göring reacted very strongly, saying that indeed propaganda imputes to Germany intentions of new territorial demands.

He passed on to Polish-German relations, declaring that the German government would be ready to do anything in order to deny such groundless opinions. He mentioned that it was ready to extend the agreement of January 26, 1934, for twenty-five years. He described the foundation of German-Polish relations as based upon the Reich's decision to recognize Poland's territorial state, since this is to a certain degree more digestible for Germany, inasmuch as the territories ceded to Poland did belong to it prior to the partitions.

I returned to the Hungarian problem. I stressed Polish-Hungarian friendship, describing Hungary as an element of stabilization in the Danubian basin. Referring to the expression Göring used earlier—that the Hungarians are a bit *flau*—I came out with the question whether, in his opinion, they are mature enough for independent action. I remarked that the untimely death of Gömbös [16] was a heavy loss of Hungary. Göring confirmed my opinion, as well as my judgment that still not enough understanding might be observed in Hungarian statesmen on nationality problems (*völkisch*).

In discussion on this item, important opinions of Göring are worth

[16] Julius Gömbös, the Hungarian prime minister, died on October 6, 1935.

noting. First of all, he remarked that Germany has no precise understanding on this matter with Hungary, nor does it have any with Poland. On the other hand, Germany is aware of Hungary's interests in Czechoslovakia, and the same relates to Poland. The Germans envisaged that, in case Germany undertook any action, Hungary would join. Germany is taking on itself the task of restraining Belgrade from acting against Hungary. It expects that Warsaw would act along the same lines toward Bucharest in order to prevent any action. It would be most embarrassing if Hungary did not make a move, since Czech forces could then retreat to Slovakia. Evidently, Germany would not demand military assistance from Budapest or Warsaw, if only for the reason that this would look derisory in view of Germany's predominance over Czechoslovakia. But Germany understands that under such circumstances Poland would occupy the region of interest to it. In practice it might occur that Polish and German units would meet somewhere.

In connection with these deliberations of Göring, I stressed that Poland is closely united with Slovakia, owing to links of race and language. The ties are even closer since we have no claims to Slovakia. I observed that the evolution of the Slovak nation had progressed rapidly, especially in the last years, and I said that it is imperative that Slovakia be granted autonomy from either one side or the other—from the Czechs or the Hungarians.

Göring eagerly confirmed that this is a necessity. He added that Germany is fortunately in such a position that these matters are of no concern to it. On the other hand, there is the question of relations between Warsaw and Budapest, and Poland's good influence on Hungary. In his opinion Hungary should grant the autonomy which was refused by Czechoslovakia.

With regard to Sub-Carpathian Russia I observed, following instructions, that it is a place where international intrigues abound, adding that this land was taken away from Hungary solely for the purpose of giving Czechoslovakia access to Russia.

We further touched upon Polish-German relations. I followed my instructions on the Danzig problem. I stated that we observed a certain lack of organization in the territory of the Free City, and that this renders normal business difficult. I said that, although conversations with Forster were satisfactory, he has no executive power. I praised Greiser as a well-balanced person. However, I stated that the Commissioner is encountering obstacles, that some incidents are again poisoning the atmosphere, and that this situation is being exploited by elements hostile to a Polish-German rapprochement. Göring carefully noted my remarks.

Since during our conversation he implied that secret service action might be discontinued, I stressed, following your instructions, that we should both refrain from influencing minorities in such a way that they would take up political action.

Göring understood my idea, particularly since I casually mentioned the matter of the *Deutsche Vereinigung* at Bydgoszcz. He noted this point.

On this occasion he voiced some ideas as to whether it would not serve the cause best if German minorities in Poland were to return to Germany, and vice versa. He observed that in view of the shortage of workers in Germany he has given orders to make it easier for a number of members of the German minority in Silesia to return to the Reich. This evoked a loud protest from local German authorities, who objected to the weakening of the German element in Poland. To this Göring replied that, since the frontier is recognized, it is in the Polish-German interest to have as few minorities on either side as possible.

At the end of the conversation I asked Göring whether he would be in Berlin in the first half of September, in case you pass through Berlin and would like to meet with him. Göring said he would be in Berlin on September 6 and 7 and would be very glad if such a meeting could take place. On this occasion he would like to show you Karinhall.

### Supplement to the Report on the Conversation of Ambassador Lipski with General Field Marshal Göring on *August 24, 1938*

*Strictly Confidential*

The following points were omitted from the report:

1) To the passage dealing with Slovakia it should be added that, in case basic territorial changes take place in Czechoslovakia, Poland would naturally be entitled to request an agreement which would definitely settle the situation in the Danubian basin.

2) With regard to Polish-German relations, Göring remarked casually that there are people in Germany who declare that Poland intends to annex East Prussia. He personally does not believe that Poland would

be willing to absorb a larger number of Germans. In his opinion, Poland's legitimate aspirations would rather tend toward the fertile Ukraine. On this occasion Göring denied Germany's claims on the Ukraine.

3) Göring stressed that a certain rapprochement of Polish and German military spheres would be highly desirable.

4) Göring declared that upon settlement of the Czech question the Reich would issue a top-level statement to acknowledge the achievement of definite stabilization. Poland would also profit from this act.

5) Upon leaving at the end of the conversation, Göring expressed the hope that we might still have some peaceful times before us.

In his personal papers Lipski writes:

I had the impression from this conversation that this was the psychological moment to impress on Germany the necessity of accepting our demands. I thought that this could be done in connection with Beck's planned visit to Berlin. This inspired me to write on the 26th [of August] a letter to Director Łubieński.

DOCUMENT 92    Lipski to Łubieński

Berlin, August 26, 1938
*Strictly Confidential*

Dear Director:

With reference to our last conversation about the possibility of Minister Beck's stopping in Berlin on his way to Geneva, I would like to advise you that I must be in Nuremberg on September 7, for on that day Chancellor Hitler is giving a reception for the diplomatic corps. So the only date available for the Minister to meet with Göring and Ribbentrop would be September 6.

Perhaps under these circumstances it would be advisable to postpone this meeting to a post-Geneva period.

Reflecting on Polish-German relations in the light of my last conversations with Göring, I would like first of all to state that the German government is aware that unless Poland remains neutral the solution of the Sudetenland problem might take an undesirable turn. The Germans must also realize that, even with the most favorable settlement of the

Czechoslovak problem, our possible gains are infinitely less than Germany's. I therefore think this to be the moment to achieve some positive solutions in Polish-German relations. These are:

1) extension of the declaration of January 26, 1934;

2) some kind of declaration similar to the one issued by the German government regarding Alsace and the frontier with Italy and at present with Hungary.

I quote a passage from Hitler's speech delivered at a banquet in honor of Horthy:

"This steadfast *connection,* based upon an imperturbable bilateral confidence, will in the first place be of extreme value for both nations— when, following historical events, we shall as neighbors have found *our final historical frontiers.* I am convinced that it will not only serve the interests of our countries but that also, *in close cooperation with Italy, which is friendly toward us, it will become a pledge of a worthy and just common peace.*"

I noticed that Göring reacted to my statement that international propaganda is accusing Germany of having ever-increasing territorial aspirations. Göring kept repeating the words: What can be done to remove Poland's distrust? He mentioned, on his part, the extension of the 1934 agreement. Although I am not valuing highly declarations and texts in international relations, since only real power and interests remain the decisive factors, nevertheless there is a certain vacuum in territorial problems in our relations with Germany, especially since France, Italy, and Hungary received precisely termed declarations. It is rather worth noting that Göring mentioned for the first time Poland's aspirations with regard to East Prussia. This might be an occasion to take advantage of in order to endow such a declaration with bilateral features. However, considering our relations with the Western states, it would be awkward to stage such Polish-German demonstrations at present. Still, some sort of *pactum de contrahendo* could be obtained in both matters if presented at the proper moment.

Nothing definite was obtained on Horthy's case. Some *querschusses* were made to him here, probably by the Czechs and the French; for example, rumors were circulated yesterday that Prime Minister Imredy must return to Budapest immediately.

Yesterday, at the evening performance of the opera, Horthy again mentioned to me the possibility of sending a special trustworthy delegate to Minister Beck. However, he gave me a piece of advice, which I deem to be most characteristic and communicate very confidentially, not to use code when relating my conversation with him. Maybe you could make confidential use of this with our code service.

*Józef Lipski*

P.S. According to what I could observe, the Hungarians did not sign anything here and did not take on any binding obligations. I was informed most confidentially that Prime Minister Imredy allegedly confessed to a third party that in case of an armed German-Czech conflict in the Sudetenland they would not move unless they could join Poland's action.

*J.L.*

We continue from Lipski's personal papers:

In the first days of September I was in Warsaw, where I discussed all of these problems with Minister Beck. With regard to the Czech problem, Beck laid much more stress on the settlement of the Danubian problem than on the Teschen Silesia question, which he considered to be just a starting point. Although the problem of a common Polish-Hungarian frontier through Carpathian Ruthenia was more or less clearly defined, I could not find any clear concept about Slovakia. It was just stated generally that Slovakia should be granted autonomy either by the Czechs or by the Hungarians.

I also did not feel that Beck definitely wished to present our demands to Germany in order to stabilize our relations. Obviously, he did not want to bind himself to Germany by new agreements with regard to Czechoslovakia. In principle he was not against stopping in Berlin on his way to Geneva. However, bearing in mind that at that time his relations with the League were vacillating, since he feared the pressure of the Western Powers in Geneva he deferred a decision to come to Germany, preferring to stop in Berlin on his return trip.

I had inadequate information about our relations with Paris and London. At the Foreign Affairs Ministry the opinion prevailed that France, and consequently Great Britain also, would not move in aid of Czechoslovakia. With regard to preventing Soviet troops from marching through Polish territory, our stand was categorical. Our action in Bucharest followed this line.

DOCUMENT 93   Lipski to Beck

NO. N/52/30/38                                    Berlin, September 5, 1938
                                                     *Strictly Confidential*

This morning, upon my return from Warsaw, I had a personal telephone
call from Field Marshal Göring. He wanted to know how the matter
stands concerning your possible stopover in Berlin on your way to
Geneva, which I had mentioned in my last conversation with him.

I answered that, owing to a shortage of time, the meeting would have
to be postponed. I added that the chief of the Minister's cabinet, Director Łubieński, will be at Nuremberg.

Göring very emphatically informed me that he would have explanations for the Minister of the utmost importance ("Aufklärungen aller-
wichtiger Art"), which could not be dealt with via diplomatic channels,
and that the Chancellor, whom he advised of the planned visit, attached
considerable importance to it. Göring further questioned whether a
meeting could take place after Geneva. I said that I would immediately
contact you on this matter. Göring continued by saying that in the
aftermath of Geneva this meeting would be still more interesting for
him, since you would be informed about the position and attitude of the
Western Powers.

He fears, however, that considerable pressure will be exerted on Poland in Geneva by these states. According to his information, such
pressure is now being exerted by the Western Powers on Italy, Yugoslavia, and Poland. Italy, as he stated before, took a negative stand to
such propositions ("Haben eine kalte Schulter gezeigt"). Now the full
impact is on Belgrade and Warsaw. I told Göring that I was just back
from Warsaw and that I could assure him that our policy line remains
unaltered. Göring also remarked that the German side would be ready to
go far in Polish-German relations to our advantage.

I established with Göring that I would immediately contact you with
regard to the possible meeting. In case it could take place even now, on
which Göring did not insist so much in the course of the conversation,
the dates convenient would be Wednesday the 7th or Thursday the
8th.

For the meeting on your return trip, if the date could be September 20
or the next few days following, Göring suggests Rominten in East Prus-

sia, where he would stay during this period. In case you travel through Germany at a later date, Berlin. He thinks the meeting in East Prussia might be convenient for you, since it would cause no extra detour. He asked me, in that case, to accompany you as a guest at a hunting party. Göring stressed that this approach of his should be regarded as a direct unofficial contact with us owing to our close relations.

Since I have to leave for Nuremberg tomorrow evening, September 6, and since I have to give a reply to Göring before I leave, I am taking the liberty of sending Major Kowalczyk by plane to Warsaw; he can return to Berlin by night train.

For my part I would like to add to Göring's statements the following explanations:

The Chancellor and Göring, fearing that Poland's stand toward the German-Czech conflict might change in Geneva under pressure from the Western Powers, wanted to establish direct contact with you prior to the Geneva session. Undoubtedly in such conversations the German side would be likely to offer a gesture toward Polish-German relations.

The question is whether the German attitude toward us would be more expansive now or after Geneva? I think that, according to your opinion in our conversation yesterday, more favorable conditions might be available in the future, while at present, especially prior to Geneva, excessive obligations could be expected. Therefore I tried to persuade Göring to arrange the meeting for after Geneva. If, however, you would still prefer to see him now, there is a standing invitation for Wednesday or Thursday.

*Józef Lipski*


DOCUMENT 94  Łubieński to Lipski

Warsaw, September 6, 1938

In reply to the letter brought yesterday by Major Kowalczyk, I hasten, as instructed by the Minister, to communicate to you the following:

1) A meeting on the way to Geneva is out of the question, since the Minister does not know when he might be able to leave Warsaw (regardless of sleeping-car reservations).

2) On the other hand, the Minister seriously considers the possibility of the meeting after Geneva, probably just after September 20, and therefore perhaps at Rominten. The Minister would present the final proposal as to the date from Geneva, after seeing how long a period of time will be necessary to conduct the conversations there. The Minister does not intend to stay in Geneva any longer than required for establishing the necessary contacts.[17]

3) You may, however, when informing Göring with reference to the Minister, state that, as far as Geneva is concerned, Poland's policy is known for its resistance to pressure or yielding to concessions. On the other hand, information about the atmosphere prevailing in the world is naturally desirable in order to form a judgment on the situation.

*M. Łubieński*

[17] Finally Beck did not go to Geneva and the meeting with Göring did not take place.

# The Party Congress at Nuremberg
## September 7–12, 1938

ON THE EVENING of September 6 Ambassador Lipski proceeded with other members of the diplomatic corps to Nuremberg to attend the annual congress of the National Socialist Party. This provided him with an opportunity for a number of political conversations.

DOCUMENT 95  Ambassador Lipski's Conversations at Nuremberg, *September 7–12, 1938*

*Strictly Confidential*

### I. With Field Marshal Göring on September 9, 1938

1) The planned meeting with Minister Beck. It was agreed that on his way back from Geneva Minister Beck would be able to meet with Göring; if the date were September 20 or immediately thereafter, the meeting would take place at Rominten; if at a later date, in Berlin. In case Minister Beck did not go to Geneva, the Ambassador on his part suggested a meeting at Rominten, where Beck could arrive by car from Augustowo. Göring was very pleased with this suggestion.

2) Göring was concerned about press attacks on Minister Beck. It had come to his knowledge that some press organs allegedly started a campaign against the Minister's policy. From further deliberations it became clear that these rumors were instigated by Forster. The Ambassador gave mitigating explanations.

3) The Ambassador pointed to certain steps taken toward us by the Western Powers, in particular England, in connection with the international situation. Göring, in his last conversation with the Ambassador, recalled such overtures made toward Italy, Yugoslavia, and Poland. The Ambassador laid stress upon the fact that Poland's policy did not cede

to pressure and followed a set line. He added that we valued more highly a sincere cooperation with the Reich than passing advantages. It was obvious that some international elements were against good Polish-German relations. Arguments used in an attempt to sway public opinion in Poland were (*a*) the problem of Danzig; (*b*) the thesis that the Reich interposes ever new claims. *Ad a*), Göring remarked that he had summoned Forster and had admonished him that Danzig matters should not complicate Polish-German relations. *Ad b*), Göring is aware how difficult it is to persuade Polish opinion that the Reich has sincerely given up revisionist aspirations concerning Poland. In his opinion, the fact that during the last five years the Reich's policy has been scrupulously observed in respect to the Polish state should confirm the sincere intentions of Germany. He referred to pronouncements by leading elements of the Reich during this period in relation to Poland, all of which aimed at influencing German public opinion in a way positive for Polish-German relations.

4) *Czechoslovakia.* Göring declared that the Karlsbad points [1] request, among other things, dissolution by Czechoslovakia of the pact with Russia. Göring does not believe in the possibility of an agreement with Czechoslovakia. If the Czech government were to make an agreement, it would do so with the intention of breaking it. Even if Beneš were to accept its conditions, military elements would come out against it. From Göring's words it was clear that he is convinced that the necessity will arise to act by force. Göring shared the Ambassador's opinion that international armed conflict should be avoided. Göring thinks the problem should be placed on the League's agenda in order to define the aggressor. The Germans, though not members of the League, will be able to prove that they were not aggressors. Before a decision is taken by the League, action in the field might already be finished. In Göring's opinion, France is simply looking for an honorable way out. England also is not willing to go to war and is exerting really strong pressure on Prague.

5) The Ambassador drew attention to the fact that there are international elements striving to provoke a conflict among the European powers. The Second and Third International and the masonic lodges are

[1] See *DGFP*, Series D, Vol. II, No. 135.

among them. There ensued a longer discussion about masonic lodges, the Ambassador stressing the fact that French and British lodges remain in close contact. He also pointed to the fact that Beneš has considerable support from the lodges. Göring rather significantly questioned the connections of Jan Masaryk, the Czech envoy in London.

6) *Rumania.* The Ambassador raised the question of the Havas Agency communiqué about the alleged Rumanian-Soviet agreement for Russian transit through Rumania. He pointed to the *démenti* issued by Bucharest.[2] Göring questioned in detail the internal Rumanian situation, the King's role, his internal political plans, and, finally, the position of the new Rumanian envoy in Berlin, Djuvara.

7) *Russia.* Göring stressed that in the future the real Russian attack against Germany could not be directed through Rumania or the Baltic states but only via Poland. Göring remarked that in case of a Polish-Russian conflict the Reich would come to Poland's assistance. A discussion followed about the situation in Russia and the strength of Russian armed forces.

8) *Hungary.* Göring revealed a number of confidential bits of information from his conversations with Horthy (the first point, not mentioned here, was told to the Ambassador for his information under a word-of-honor plea for secrecy). Göring declared quite openly to the Hungarian side that under no circumstances would Germany act as intermediary in matters of interest to Hungary and Poland. The Hungarian government should settle these matters directly with Warsaw. Göring acted in this way in order to deprive Budapest of any illusions in this respect. Göring also pointed out to Horthy the necessity of granting broad autonomy to Slovakia. He did this in consequence of his last conversation with the Ambassador. Horthy was not too eloquent on this point. Göring was under the impression that, in spite of Hungarian statements that in case Czechoslovakia were attacked by another state no Hungarian government could maintain itself in power unless it decided to act, Hungary would probably go into action very late.

[2] On September 7 the official Rumanian agency Rador issued information denying the news that Rumania had agreed to the flight of Soviet planes over its territory. On September 18 the same agency issued a categorical denial of repeated rumors with regard to Rumania's consent for transit of Soviet troops through its territory.

9) Horthy allegedly told the Chancellor that it would take England ten years to forgive Hungary if it attacked Czechoslovakia today. Hitler, upset by such a naïve concept, replied that if this action took place in five years, when England would be armed to the teeth, it would be even less ready to forgive. Göring confirmed that territorial matters between Hungary and Poland are of no concern to Germany. The Germans are not prepared to pull chestnuts out of the fire for the Hungarians.

10) *Italy*. The Rome-Berlin axis is based upon the principle that neither of the states can allow the other to be defeated. Ideological solidarity is at stake here.

## II. With Minister of Foreign Affairs Ribbentrop at a Reception Given by Hess on September 7, 1938

Ribbentrop declared to the Ambassador:

1. Germany's position has never been so strong as it is now.

2. Ribbentrop has not yet examined the last proposals presented in writing by Beneš. He is studying them now.[3]

3. Chancellor Hitler would never again let another May 21, 1938, happen. May 21 was a provocation against the Reich. In case such a provocation were repeated, the Chancellor would react immediately.

## III. With Minister Ribbentrop on September 10, 1938

1) The Ambassador stated that on his way back from Geneva Minister Beck is expecting a personal meeting with Minister Ribbentrop. The Ambassador is not yet in a position to state if or when the Minister will go to Geneva. The Ambassador stressed that our [Polish] participations in the Council is also not yet resolved.

With regard to currently circulated rumors, the Ambassador remarked that our policy is not yielding to external pressure. Poland's policy is unanimous throughout the government, being a heritage of Marshal Piłsudski. The Ambassador pointed to certain proposals extended to Poland by the Western Powers, adding that sincere cooperation with the Reich means more to us than passing advantages. International propaganda is striving to undermine Polish-German relations, making use of the Sudetenland problem. It operates with two arguments: (*a*) the Danzig problem (a short historical outline of Polish-German conversations on Danzig and the Chancellor's declaration of

[3] *DGFP*, Series D, Vol. II, No. 440, pp. 714–19.

November 5, 1937); (*b*) instilling public opinion with the idea that the Reich is resorting to ever new claims.

The Ambassador mentioned that with the settlement of the Czechoslovak problem we would have to expect a much stronger campaign.

2) *Relation to Poland.* Herr von Ribbentrop emphasized the necessity of good Polish-German relations; this was his own conviction regarding the common interests linking the two states. His personal view was confirmed by the line adopted by the Chancellor. As long, therefore, as the Chancellor desired to maintain him in his present post, he would work positively for the development of Polish-German relations.

Granted this assumption, minor issues disturbing Polish-German relations must be settled in a friendly spirit.[4]

3) *Czechoslovakia.* Ribbentrop: We strive for a solution by agreement. Beneš, as yet, has not granted any adequate concession. Misgivings as to Beneš' frankness. Remark that the Chancellor would never allow the provocation of May 21 to recur again. In such circumstances the Chancellor would definitely act by force, ignoring international repercussions, since then Germany's honor would be at stake.

Ribbentrop called attention to the anomaly of the signing of the Franco-Czech agreement at a moment when Germany was weak. The agreement was to serve the Czechs as an instrument to exert pressure on the Germans. In Ribbentrop's opinion, Great Britain would not budge on the Sudetenland case. France would encounter unyielding resistance with regard to armed intervention. Germany is now stronger than ever. The Ambassador declared it to be most important that the problem be solved locally to avoid international conflict. Ribbentrop replied that evidently no government would lightheartedly jump into an international brawl. Ribbentrop questioned our position on the Czechoslovak problem. The Ambassador replied that we are interested in a certain region. He stressed the necessity of autonomy for Slovakia. He pointed to the pro-Russian policy permanently pursued by Czechoslovakia, displayed in the geographical composition of the Czechoslovak state at the Peace Conference. In the course of further deliberations on this issue, when the Hungarian question was raised the conversation had to be interrupted.

4) *Rumania.* The Ambassador raised the question of the Havas

[4] *Polish White Book,* No. 40.

communiqué about the alleged Rumanian-Soviet understanding with regard to the transit of troops. He pointed out that this rumor is false. He stressed that approximately on May 21 there were attempts on the part of the Soviets for an overflight of the Polish territory toward Czechoslovakia. We rendered them void. Ribbentrop showed interest in this information.

5) *Italy*. Ribbentrop laid stress on his statement that all he could say is that direct relations between Hitler and Mussolini are based upon far-reaching confidence.

### IV. With Minister Ribbentrop on September 12, 1938

During a military parade, Ribbentrop mentioned casually that he wanted to continue discussions with the Ambassador but had been prevented from doing so these last days. The Ambassador remarked that he was proceeding to Warsaw to contact Minister Beck and learn about his views on the situation, particularly with regard to the stand taken by the Western Powers and Russia. The Ambassador also pointed to the official British declaration published the previous day.[5]

Ribbentrop seemed not to attach special attention to this. The Ambassador observed that the passage on the exchange of opinion between the British and American governments made him think. They decided to continue their conversations immediately upon the Ambassador's return from Warsaw.

### V. Conversation with von Moltke on September 7, 1938 after Lunch in the Diplomat's Train

Moltke was visibly disturbed by the prospect of an international conflict. He suggested that rumors are current that from my discussions with Göring on August 24 last it was evident that I was optimistic concerning Great Britain's position. I corrected this statement, declaring that I did not express myself as to the possible stand of Great Britain. Talking frankly, Moltke asked what Poland's position would be in case of a conflict. In his opinion Poland would remain neutral. It would occupy the region of interest to it in Czechoslovakia only in case the conflict is localized for certain. Ambassador Lipski did not reply explicitly, hinting that the opinion of Ambassador Moltke rather follows the right trend. He stressed the necessity for a local settlement.

[5] *DGFP*, Series D, Vol. II, No. 458.

### VI. Conversation with Secretary of State Weizsäcker
### on September 11, 1938

The Secretary of State, visibly disturbed by the possibility of an international conflict, told the Ambassador, underlining his friendly and sincere approach, that if we are expecting the possibility of an outbreak of an international conflict, we should openly and without reserve confirm this to the authorities of the German government; for, bearing in mind their attitude, words uttered in a diplomatic form are not necessarily considered. The Ambassador referred to his conversations with Göring and Ribbentrop during which he insisted that an international conflict should be avoided. Weizsäcker said that he could not observe any reaction, and that stronger words should be used.

REMARK: I know that similar words were also spoken to the Italian and Belgian ambassadors here.

### VII. Conversation with von Moltke on September 12, 1938
### during a Lunch at the Grand Hotel

Ambassador Lipski advised Moltke that he would tell von Ribbentrop that he is going to Warsaw to get in touch with the government in connection with the international situation and the Nuremberg conversations.

### VIII. Conversation with von Moltke on September 13, 1938,
### in Berlin

Ambassador Lipski informed Moltke about his conversation with Minister von Ribbentrop on the preceding day. Ambassador Moltke said he is staying in Berlin, since the Minister of Foreign Affairs wants to continue his conversations with him. He asked for permanent contact with Ambassador Lipski through the counselor of the German Embassy in Warsaw, Scheliha. Ambassador Lipski expressed satisfaction with the passage of the Chancellor's speech dealing with Poland.[6] He added, and this was his own conviction, that he would consider it as most desirable, bearing in mind the international situation and the atmosphere prevailing in Poland, that a certain act should take place following the Chancel-

---

[6] In his speech at the Congress at Nuremberg on September 12 Hitler, speaking about Poland, said: "In Poland a great patriot and a great statesman was ready to make an accord with Germany; we immediately proceeded to action and completed an agreement which was of greater importance to the peace of Europe than all the chattering in the temple of the League of Nations at Geneva."

lor's speech, namely, a declaration about our mutual frontiers, something like that which was granted to Italy. Moltke showed understanding for such a concept.

### IX. Conversation with the British Ambassador
### on September 11, 1938

Ambassador Henderson remarked that, unfortunately, competent German elements do not understand the British position and do not take it seriously. They continually insist that Great Britain could not be interested in entering a conflict over the Sudetenland. Henderson remarked further that his government had already long ago considered the necessity of revising the treaty. He is only concerned that this revision be executed by peaceful means. The Ambassador told him that with such a revision Germany would obtain the Sudetenland; Poland, Teschen; Hungary, its part. (Henderson cited 700,000 Hungarians in Czechoslovakia.) The Czechs with Slovakia would, in his opinion, form a uniform and united state. Henderson sharply criticized the Czech government and Beneš, adding that chances for a conflict increase with the delay.

### X. Conversation with the Hungarian Envoy
### on September 11, 1938

He very confidentially disclosed that Horthy would shortly proceed to Rominten as a private guest of Göring. Ambassador Lipski called the attention of the Hungarian Envoy to the necessity of quick action on the part of the Hungarians in view of the rapid course of events. In addition, he stressed the necessity of considering the fact that the Czechoslovak problem would develop on the basis of plebiscites. In such an event, broad action should be considered. The Hungarian Envoy admitted that he is fully aware of this, and that a broad scope of autonomic rights should be promised beforehand.

# Conversations with Chamberlain
## at Berchtesgaden and Godesberg
### *September 15–26, 1938*

WE QUOTE from Lipski's personal papers:

From Nuremberg I proceeded to Warsaw with a short stop in Berlin.
In Warsaw I finally obtained precise instructions with regard to our requests in relation to Germany. They were to be embodied in three documents:

1) a Polish-German declaration similar to the Italian-German one;

2) an extension of the nonaggression declaration of January 26, 1934;

3) a precise definition in writing of the Chancellor's declaration on Danzig of November 5, 1937, safeguarding our economic interests by assuring free development of Polish trade in the Free City.

When I was taking the night train for Berlin on September 14, a clerk of our Ministry of Foreign Affairs who brought the diplomatic mail informed me that, according to broadcast information, Chamberlain was coming to Berchtesgaden the next day. The West had capitulated. It was too late to present our demands to Germany.

I raised these demands as early as September 16 in my conference with Göring. He did not refute them, but even added a few items, such as a possible exchange of population, the avoidance of friction in the minorities field, and the question of the superhighway to East Prussia. However, in a very characteristic way he added that the settlement of these matters should be postponed to a later period, after the settlement of the Czech crisis. Chamberlain's arrival changed the whole situation to the advantage of Germany. Göring was in high spirits, acknowledging Chamberlain's visit as a great success for Hitler. He started to give advice for the benefit of Poland and Hungary, how these two states should act in order not to jeopardize their interests in relation to Czechoslovakia when the Sudetenland question was settled.

Following Minister Beck's instructions, during the same conversation I presented our definite requests with regard to the plebiscite in Teschen as well as the common Polish-Hungarian request on a plebiscite in Slovakia.

Late in the evening of September 15, on Beck's instructions, Lipski telephoned State Secretary Weizsäcker at Berchtesgaden, informing him that, in case the Czech problem was settled by plebiscite, the Polish government would categorically request an adequate solution of the Teschen region and would under no circumstances retire its claim. This stand was fully agreed to by the Hungarians.[1]

DOCUMENT 96     Lipski to Beck

NO. N/52/31/38                     Berlin, September 16, 1938
                                   *Strictly Confidential*

I. Referring to my telegram of today's date, I report information received through the Auswärtiges Amt on the Hitler-Chamberlain conference,[2] this being more precise than the information wired after my conversation with Göring.

The conversation was sincere in tone and lasted for several hours. The Chancellor presented a demand for the immediate settlement of the Sudetenland question in one way or another, insisting openly on the annexation of the Sudetenland to the Reich. He made it clear that the situation calls for an immediate decision, and that in case of delay he would not hesitate to use force.

Chamberlain accepted this request of the Chancellor to seek a solution, reserving the decision to his cabinet. He took a plane today for London, where at 12 noon a session of the Council of the cabinet was to convene, followed by a consultation with the French government. A further meeting of Hitler with Chamberlain is planned probably for next Monday in the vicinity of Cologne. During this meeting the execution of the decision is to be discussed. The next stage of conferences is to deal with British-German subjects. Göring considers Chamberlain's coming

[1] For the German version, see *DGFP*, Series D, Vol. II, No. 508.
[2] The Hitler-Chamberlain conference at Berchtesgaden took place on September 15 (*ibid.*, No. 487, pp. 786–98.)

to Berchtesgaden as a great personal success for Hitler. As far as the plebiscite is concerned, Göring and his staff have misgivings as to whether it is at all possible. I could feel that the Field Marshal is still speculating on the possible occupation of the Sudetenland by German armed forces. He remarked casually that it would be well if we could be prepared for any eventuality.

II. Göring was alarmed by the possibility of a settlement of the Czechoslovak problem at present exclusively with regard to the Sudetenland, which would leave sources of further conflicts in this region. He therefore advises that Poland should categorically insist on a plebiscite in the region inhabited by Polish population, using all possible means of pressure, agitation, etc., as well as approaching the Western Powers in this respect. He is giving similar advice to the Hungarians. In his opinion Slovakia should place a request for a plebiscite supported by Poland and Hungary. He has some misgivings here as to whether Hungary is acting promptly enough with regard to autonomic concessions. He understands the necessity of a common Polish-Hungarian frontier, which —as he put it—would join in Slovakia. It was obvious that Göring was anxious to separate Slovakia from the rest of Czechoslovakia, in order thus to create a Czech state economically dependent on the Reich.

Following your instructions, I categorically communicated our stand with regard to the plebiscite in Teschen as well as our common demand with the Hungarians for a plebiscite in other parts of Slovakia.

III. Reflecting upon Chamberlain's decision to proceed to Berchtesgaden, Göring remarked that a change in the front had occurred in Paris, with London following suit.

As, in accordance with your instructions, I was to present our demands, I informed Göring in strict confidence that even at the last moment the British side had made some approaches to us that were not accepted.

I then passed to our problems.

1) Referring to Hitler's speech at Nuremberg, I presented the concept of a declaration on Polish-German relations similar to that exchanged by Hitler and Mussolini.[3] I am refraining from citing here the

[3] In his speech on May 7, 1938, at the Palazzo Venezia in Rome during a state visit to Italy, Hitler gave assurances on the stabilization of the present German-Italian frontier (Brenner Pass), the inviolability of which was an integral part of German-Italian friendship. (The text is in *Documents on International Affairs, 1938*, II, 32–34; see also *DGFP*, Series D, Vol. I, Nos. 759, 761, and 767.)

arguments used to this effect. I mention that Göring was quite positively disposed toward this idea.

2) I brought up the necessity of removing permanent frictions in the Danzig region through a definition in writing of the Chancellor's declaration dated November 5, 1937, and repeated to you on January 14, 1938. I stressed that, in my opinion, the definition should underline the necessity of a guarantee for Polish economic interests in the Free City through a free development of Poland's trade. I laid stress on the thesis that Danzig is a product not of the Treaty of Versailles but of history.

Göring also accepted this point positively, adding on his part that he does not expect any difficulties in a formulation which would reserve to Poland the freedom of trade. In his opinion the agreement should be based on two premises: Poland, as it was stated, would not intervene in the development of the German population in the Free City; and, on the other hand, Danzig would consider the interests and economic rights of Poland, which are of essential need to its own development. Göring remarked that, if it were not for Poland, the Reich would not be in a position to assure Danzig of its present commercial turnover, for at best East Prussia, with a port of its own at Królewiec [Königsberg], could serve as a hinterland for Danzig. In conclusion he added that immediately upon the settlement of the Czechoslovak problem we should get together, possibly with economic experts, to investigate Poland's economic problems in Danzig. He thinks a suitable solution could be reached without difficulty. Here I brought up customs matters as an example.

To recapitulate, I stated that the Polish government considers Polish-German relations as a long-range problem, that in order to conduct such a policy it is indispensable to create an atmosphere of confidence, that in my opinion this could be achieved by way of three things:

1) a declaration similar to the Italian-German one,

2) the removal of frictions from Danzig problems in the field of Poland's economic interests,

3) an extension of the declaration of January 26, 1934.

Göring on his part mentioned the necessity of avoiding dissent in minority cases, and I replied that, with these three conditions settled, things would improve on our side. Here Göring returned again to the possible exchange of minorities, that is, the removal of some of the landowners from Poland to Germany. The General Field Marshal also brought up the question of the superhighway to East Prussia.

IV. As to your possible meeting with Göring, in view of the fact that events are moving so rapidly, he suggested that in case of emergency such a meeting could take place somewhere near the border.

*Józef Lipski*

DOCUMENT 97   Lipski to Beck

September 17, 1938
*Code*

1) Yesterday Göring invited the Hungarian Envoy and exerted his influence on him for action regarding Hungary's claims.

2) In my conversation with the Italian Ambassador I raised the subject of our thesis, stressing the necessity of settling all minorities questions in Czechoslovakia in order to achieve a definite stabilization of relations in that region. The Ambassador showed full understanding, stressing that this conforms with Mussolini's stand.

*Lipski*

We quote from Lipski's personal papers:

On September 19 I was informed that Hitler desired to receive me the next afternoon at his residence in Berchtesgaden, and that for this purpose a plane would be placed at my disposal at Tempelhof airport. I was also informed, from other sources, that Hungary's prime minister, Imredy, and the Hungarian chief of the General Staff were invited to Berchtesgaden for the same day. I was therefore not quite sure whether a common German-Hungarian-Polish consultation would take place. Minister Beck, informed accordingly, succeeded in sending his instructions on September 20.

DOCUMENT 98 Beck to Lipski

Warsaw, September 19, 1938
*Strictly Confidential*

Please adopt the following directives in the conversation with the Chancellor:

1) The Polish government declares that by its stand it has paralyzed the possibility of Soviet intervention on a wider scope in the Czechoslovak problem. Pressure exerted by us on Bucharest achieved the desired result. Our current maneuvers in Volhynia were understood by Moscow as a warning.

2) Poland considers Soviet intervention in European affairs as intolerable.

3) We consider the Czechoslovak Republic to be an artificial creation convenient for certain doctrines and combinations, but one that does not take into account the concrete needs and sound claims of the states of Central Europe.

4) In the course of the last summer the Polish government four times rejected propositions to join international interventions in Czechoslovakia.

5) Poland's direct claims in the problem under discussion are restricted to the Teschen-Silesian region, that is, not far beyond the Teschen and Frystat districts plus access to the Bohumin railway station [Oderberg].

6) Bearing in mind our immediate proximity, we are interested in a general settlement of the Czechoslovak crisis. We consider favorably the idea of a common frontier with Hungary, since we are cognizant of the fact that the geographical scope of the Czechoslovak Republic was meant to serve as a bridgehead for Russia. In this problem we lack the definite decision of Hungary, whose role here is vital. From our point of view, Hungarian aspirations have more chances in Carpathian Ruthenia. Slovakia could only be considered within the frame of broad autonomy. We are not convinced that these problems are properly prepared by the Hungarians, and Poland could not possibly settle the matter for them.

7) According to recent information, the Western Powers might try to maintain the present concept of Czechoslovakia with partial concessions to Germany. On September 19 we protested such a solution.

We place our local claims categorically. We communicate confidentially that frontier control is reinforced. On September 21 we shall have considerable military forces in the southern part of Silesia. We formally declare that this grouping of troops is not directed against Germany.[4]

8) From the Polish side, the further course of events depends, in the first place, on the decision of the government, but also on the feelings of public opinion at large. In this field, especially for the future, a stabilization of Polish-German relations is essential. Attention is called here to the following problems:

a) The Danzig problem has a key role for the atmosphere. With this in mind and owing to the League of Nations' bankruptcy, a simple agreement stabilizing the situation in the Free City seems indispensable.

b) An explicit formula with regard to the frontiers, similar to the German-Italian one, might contribute to a paralysis of international intrigues trying to come between Poland and Germany.

c) Extension of the 1934 pact might be an additional factor for stabilization of the situation.

### REMARKS

I. The item relating to Hungary to be settled by you, depending on the conversation, in a dialogue or *à trois* with the Hungarian Prime Minister.

II. Please bear in mind that the exceptional importance of the situation calls for a bold approach to problems, far stronger than in normal negotiations.

III. If necessary, especially on the Chancellor's initiative, I am ready for personal contact with the Chancellor or Göring, in spite of possible technical or political difficulties.

IV. If in doubt, take matters *ad referendum*.

*Beck*

From Lipski's personal notes:

At Berchtesgaden audiences were arranged separately for the Hungarian ministers and for me. I agreed with Ribbentrop on a communiqué

---

[4] On September 20 a Polish Telegraph Agency communiqué announced that frontier control of Poland had been reinforced on the Czech frontier by special detachments of frontier guards. On September 22 news appeared about keeping in service certain units of the Polish Army's older lists and reservists called for maneuvers.

which only confirmed the fact that I had been received by Hitler. On the other hand, the communiqué relating to the conversation with the Hungarians brought up the *meritum* of the problem.

DOCUMENT 99    Lipski to Beck

September 20, 1938
*Strictly Confidential*

The Chancellor received me today in Obersalzberg in the presence of the Reich minister of foreign affairs, Ribbentrop, at 4 P.M. The conversation lasted for more than two hours.

The Chancellor had previously received the Hungarian Prime Minister and the Chief of the General Staff of Hungary.[5]

Audiences for the Polish and Hungarian sides were arranged separately. In like manner, the press communiqué relating to the reception for Prime Minister Imredy deals with the *meritum* of the problem, while the communiqué relating to my audience simply acknowledges the fact of the reception. I coordinated this with Minister of Foreign Affairs von Ribbentrop.

Chancellor Hitler opened the conversation with me with a statement that events had taken a different turn than he first expected. He then gave a historical outline of the Sudetenland problem, starting from his speech at the Reichstag this February. He laid special emphasis on the events of May 21 which compelled him to take a decision on May 28 to accelerate rearmaments and fortifications in the west. He then remarked that he was taken aback to a certain extent by Chamberlain's proposition to come to Berchtesgaden. It was of course impossible for him not to receive the British Prime Minister. He thought Chamberlain was coming to make a solemn declaration that Great Britain was ready to march. He would, of course, then reply that Germany was aware of such a possibility. The Chancellor declared to Chamberlain that the Sudetenland problem must be settled peacefully *or by war,* resulting in the return of the Sudetenland to Germany. As a result of this conversation Chamberlain, persuaded of the necessity of separating the Sudetenland,

[5] For a recapitulation of the conversation with the Hungarian ministers, see *DGFP,* Series D, Vol. II, No. 554.

returned to London. Up to now the Chancellor has had no further news about London's decisions. Neither has he definite information as yet about the date of the meeting which allegedly is to take place tomorrow. However, incoming news seems to indicate that the Chancellor's claims will be honored. Nevertheless, a version is circulating that the settlement of the Sudetenland problem will be executed not by self-determination but by a new delineation of frontiers. Allegedly where there is an 80 percent German majority, the territory would go to Germany without a plebiscite. The Chancellor declared that he prefers the plebiscite and is standing firm on this. He would of course insist on a plebiscite in order to secure votes for people who left the territory after 1918. The status of 1918 must be restored. Otherwise, it would mean acceptance of Czechization, which has been under way since 1918.

Occupying the Sudetenland by force would, in the Chancellor's opinion, be a fuller and more definite solution. However, the Chancellor declares that, in case his claims are recognized, then it would not be possible for him not to accept them before his people, even if the rest of the Czechoslovak problem remained unsolved. That is why the Chancellor wonders what could be done with the balance of the problem concerning Hungary and Poland. He therefore invited the Hungarian Prime Minister and me to confer on this problem.

In reply I declared that I would like to present in detail Poland's point of view. I did this following the guiding directive contained in points 1 to 7 inclusive of your instructions dated September 19. In view of the shortness of time, I just want to underline that when discussing the Teschen problem I twice stressed that the territory in question does not reach far beyond the districts of Teschen-Frystat *and access to the railway station of Bohumin* [Oderberg].

With regard to Hungarian demands, I particularly emphasized the question of Carpathian Ruthenia, calling attention to the strategic moment with regard to Russia, the spreading of Communist propaganda over this territory, etc. I had the impression that the Chancellor was particularly interested in this problem. This was even more apparent when I mentioned to him that the Polish-Rumanian frontier is comparatively narrow, and that through a common Polish-Hungarian frontier via Carpathian Ruthenia we would obtain a broader barrier against Russia.

I wish to add that I pointed out in respect to Carpathian Ruthenia that this territory, not claimed by Slovakia, was entrusted to Czechoslovakia only as a mandate. The very low level of population is strongly mixed; as a matter of fact, Hungary has its greatest interests there.

Defining our stand with regard to the region of Poland's direct interest (Teschen), I stated:

a) that we had approached London, Paris, Rome, and Berlin categorically requesting a plebiscite when this idea was brought up for the Sudetenland,

b) that we had approached the same Powers yesterday with regard to news spread about the alleged plan of territorial delimitations (I presented our declaration in writing to Ribbentrop),[6]

c) that Poland's position is especially strong in view of the assurance received from Prague, which was confirmed at that time by London and Paris, that our minorities in Czechoslovakia would enjoy the same status as the most privileged other minorities.

I concluded, when questioned by the Chancellor, that we would not retreat at this point from recourse to force if our interests were not recognized.

Analyzing further tactics to apply in settlement of the Czechoslovak problem as a whole, the Chancellor stated:

1) If his conditions are not accepted by Chamberlain, the situation is clear, and according to his warning he would use armed force to annex the Sudetenland to the Reich.

2) In case the Sudetenland condition is accepted and guarantees are claimed from him for the rest of the Czechoslovak territory, he would take the position that he might grant such a guarantee only in case a similar guarantee is given by Poland, Hungary, and Italy. (He considers the introduction of Italy important to counterbalance French and British guarantees.) He understands that neither Poland nor Hungary would issue such guarantees prior to the settlement of the problem of their minorities. Here I gave assurances on behalf of the Polish government.

3) For my confidential information, remarking that I could use it at my discretion, the Chancellor declared today that, in case a conflict would arise between Poland and Czechoslovakia over our interests in Teschen, Germany would be on our side. (I think that a similar declaration was made by the Chancellor to the Hungarian Prime Minister,

[6] For the text, see *ibid.*, No. 553.

though I was not told so.) The Chancellor suggests, in such an eventuality, that we undertake action only after the Germans occupy the
Sudeten Mountains, since then the whole operation would be shorter.

Further in the conversation the Chancellor very strongly stressed that
Poland is an outstanding factor safeguarding Europe against Russia.

From other long deliberations of the Chancellor the following results
were clear:

a) that he does not intend to go beyond the Sudetenland territory;
naturally with armed force he would go deeper, especially since, in my
opinion, he would then be under pressure from the military elements
who for strategic reasons push toward the subjugation of the whole of
ethnographic Czechoslovakia to Germany;

b) that besides a certain line of German interests we have a totally
free hand;

c) that he sees great difficulties in reaching a Rumanian-Hungarian
agreement (I think the Chancellor is under Horthy's influence, as I
reported to you verbally);

d) that the cost of the Sudetenland operation, including fortifications
and armaments, adds up to the sum of 18 billion RM;

e) that upon settlement of the Sudetenland question he would present
the problem of colonies;

f) that he has in mind an idea for settling the Jewish problem by way
of emigration to the colonies in accordance with an understanding with
Poland, Hungary, and possibly also Rumania (at which point I told him
that if he finds such a solution we will erect him a beautiful monument
in Warsaw).[7]

[7] Lest Lipski's words be misinterpreted, we give the following facts:
In 1937 there were about 3,350,000 Jews in Poland; most of them were concentrated in cities (Białystock, 43 percent Jewish; Stanisławów, 41.4 percent;
Warsaw, 30.1 percent) and small towns. The Jews living in rural areas made their
living as agricultural brokers. However, as agricultural cooperatives developed in
Poland, these middlemen were no longer needed and the Jews were deprived of
this means of livelihood; they were left destitute and with no means of support.
This had nothing to do with anti-Semitism; it was solely a natural economic development. The Jews in Poland, with their traditional clannishness, posed a
serious problem in the overpopulated Polish state. The Polish government felt
that a partial solution to this problem would be for them to emigrate, principally to Palestine.
The matter was considered so serious that Polish delegates to the League of
Nations, in October, 1936, insisted that some immediate solution would have to be
found, one possibility being the creation of a Jewish state in Palestine as a natural

Following your instructions, I also brought up Polish-German relations in the above conversation. I must mention that the moment was not especially well chosen, since the Chancellor was very much absorbed by his approaching talk with Chamberlain. I referred to the Danzig question, suggesting the possibility of a simple Polish-German agreement to stabilize the situation in the Free City. I cited a series of historical and economic arguments. In reply the Chancellor mentioned that we have the agreement of 1934. He also considers it desirable to take another step forward, instead of simply taking the position that force should be excluded in our relations, and to make a definite recognition of frontiers. He referred here to the concept of the superhighway connected with railways, which you are already familiar with. The width of such a belt would, in his words, reach about thirty meters. This would be a certain *novum*—a time when technical means would serve politics. He said he would not bring this up now, since it could be realized later on. Under these circumstances I did not discuss the matter any further.

At the close of the conversation I referred to your possible meeting with the Chancellor in the near future in case of necessity. The Chancellor accepted the suggestion with satisfaction, remarking that this might be desirable, especially after his conference with Chamberlain.

For his part, Ribbentrop asked me to find out if you would be ready to make a declaration regarding Polish demands to Czechoslovakia similar to that made by the Hungarian Prime Minister, in order that it might be used in the conversation with Chamberlain. Besides, Ribbentrop stated that the German press will give wide publicity to our action regarding minorities in Czechoslovakia.

The above report has been dictated by me before the departure of the courier after my return by plane from Berchtesgaden, so please forgive any possible shortcomings.

*Józef Lipski*

---

home for Jewish émigrés. The Polish government further stressed that additional territories for émigrés would have to be found to house the large number of Jews. Polish ambassadors discussed this matter with Paris, London, and Washington.

It should be noted that during this same time the Polish government was giving financial aid to the Zionist organization of Vladimir Zabotynski; also, with the approval of Minister Beck and Marshal Śmigły-Rydz, the Jewish Military Organization (Irgun Tsevai Leumi) was training several hundreds of its instructors at secret military courses in Poland. (See Pobóg-Malinowski, II, 614–29.)

DOCUMENT 100   Lipski to Beck

Telegram                                                September 22, 1938

The Hungarian Envoy asked me again yesterday about Rumania's stand in the possible Hungarian-Czech conflict.

The Rumanian Envoy, who is realistic about the situation, upon arriving at an understanding with the Yugoslav Envoy, telegraphed the King that a basic change in Czechoslovakia is to be expected. He pointed to the necessity of a prompt reorientation of Rumanian policy toward an understanding with Warsaw and Belgrade in order definitely to balance relations with Budapest, compensating Hungary on the Czechoslovakian side.

*Lipski*

Received: Warsaw, Rome, Budapest, Bucharest

On September 22 and 23 a conference of Chancellor Hitler with Chamberlain took place at Godesberg.[8]

Lipski notes in his personal papers:

Mr. S. Dembiński, the director of the Polish Telegraph Agency, represented the press on the Polish side.

On the second day of consultations Ribbentrop reported to me by telephone Hitler's rejection of a nonaggression pact and guarantee for Czechoslovakia. The Undersecretary [Woermann] handed the German memorandum which Chamberlain undertook to execute in Prague.[9] The Auswärtiges Amt expressed satisfaction over Warsaw's firm reply to the Soviet note. The Polish Ministry of Foreign Affairs asked for wide publicity by the German press regarding our reply.[10] Beck's instructions arrived with maps dealing with three variants of our claims in the Teschen region.

[8] See *DGFP*, Series D, Vol. II, Nos. 562, 572, 573, 574, and 583.
[9] For the text, see *ibid.*, No. 584, pp. 908–10.
[10] On September 23 Vladimir Potemkin, vice-commissar for foreign affairs in Moscow, handed to Polish Chargé d'Affaires Tadeusz Jankowski a note declaring that if the Polish government did not deny the news of a concentration of Polish troops on the Czech frontier, and if Polish troops crossed the frontier, the Soviet government would be compelled to denounce the Polish-Soviet pact of nonaggression. Upon telephone contact with Warsaw, Mr. Jankowski presented a note to Potemkin to the effect that the Polish government had the incontestable right, without rendering account, to undertake all measures which ap-

### DOCUMENT 101    Beck to Lipski

Warsaw, September 23, 1938

In view of the shortly expected possibility of the beginning of concrete conversations regarding our territorial claims on Teschen Silesia with the German government, I am enclosing herewith three variants of a map illustrating our above demands.[11]

*Variant A* represents the maximum of our territorial claims, covering the whole territory of Silesia proper beyond the river Olza, and *also Moravska Ostrava and Vitkovice.*

*Variant B* covers the same region, the southern part of Frydek district excluded.

*Variant C* is an alternative for Variant B (*Moravska Ostrava and Vitkovice excluded*); it represents the minimum of our claims.

More detailed instructions on this matter will be forwarded to you by telegram.

*Beck*

### DOCUMENT 102    Lipski to Beck

Refer to code of telegram of          Berlin, September 23, 1938
   September 22                                *Telegram by code*

I was informed in strict confidence that the minister of foreign affairs of Rumania, Comnen, at present in Geneva, undertook measures against the Hungarian action. He resents the excessive growth of Hungary and threatens that in the event of Hungarian aggression a *casus foederis* might take place. I think that he is under the influence of Geneva circles. To counteract this, I am approaching local authorities and competent

---

peared to it necessary for the security of Polish territory. The Polish government was aware of the possibility of the denunciation of the nonaggression pact. Orally Mr. Jankowski also added, in accordance with instructions, that the Polish government was all the more astonished over the Soviet step since the Polish government had taken no special measures on the Polish-Czechoslovak frontier. (*DGFP,* Series D, Vol. II, No. 582, No. 593, and, for text of notes, No. 621.)

[11] There are no maps in Lipski's papers.

foreigners with the thesis that the moment has come for a definite understanding between Rumania and Hungary that would give an outlet to the
Hungarians in Czechoslovakia. I am stressing that this is in conformity
with the opinion of the governments of Poland, Germany, and Italy.

*Lipski*

Received: Warsaw, Budapest, Bucharest, Rome

DOCUMENT 103   Lipski to Beck

Berlin, September 23, 1938
*Telegram by code*

The Italian Ambassador communicated to Ribbentrop the text of
Ciano's conversation with the British Ambassador.[12] Ciano stated that
satisfying Polish and Hungarian demands is imperative for the regulation of the Czechoslovak question. Asked about Italy's guarantee for
Czechoslovakia, Ciano replied that he cannot presently take a stand, and
that in any case such a guarantee would not be granted unless Polish
and Hungarian claims were satisfied.

*Lipski*

Received: Warsaw, Rome

DOCUMENT 104   Lipski to Beck

NO. N/1/171/38                          Berlin, September 24, 1938

Since the conference of the Chancellor with Chamberlain yesterday
lasted until 1:30 A.M., it was impossible for me, in spite of several
telephone calls, to obtain detailed information regarding its results.

This morning I received a communication from Godesberg that Ribbentrop and Secretary of State Weizsäcker will see Chamberlain off at
the airport and that the Secretary of State will probably return to Ber-

[12] See *DGFP*, Series D, Vol. II, No. 571.

lin in the evening. Von Ribbentrop will remain with the Chancellor's staff for several more days.

This morning I received the German memorandum sent to me by Undersecretary of State Woermann which, in accordance with the communiqué issued yesterday, is to be presented by Chamberlain to the Czech government. I am enclosing this memorandum herewith, remarking that the Auswärtiges Amt asked for strictly confidential handling of same.[13]

I also went this very morning to Undersecretary of State Woermann in order to obtain more details.

To my question as to why the British side did not in principle agree with the above memorandum, Woermann replied that it is his understanding that a difference of opinion occurred over the German claim to occupy by armed force a part of the Sudetenland (red line). It allegedly would be difficult for Chamberlain to accept this condition and impose it on public opinion. However, the Secretary of State remarked that as a matter of fact the British and German points of view did not differ greatly.

To my question whether a deadline is stated in the memorandum, Woermann replied that, since in point (1) of the memorandum it is stated that a part of the Sudetenland territory is to be occupied on October 1, the deadline is thus determined.

The memorandum refers to a map in several places. However, I was not able to secure one from the Secretary of State, who made the excuse that he did not have it yet, since it had been decided on in Godesberg.

I also raised the question of the general mobilization ordered by the Czechs,[14] stressing that yesterday was a day marked by international activities aimed at creating a specific atmosphere. Among these maneuvers I included also the Soviets' note to us. The Secretary of State expressed great appreciation for our firm reply, stressing that the German press published special commentaries on the Soviets' action and our reply. With regard to Czech mobilization, Woermann was not very much concerned about it, since the army had already been mobilized. The press also, although it attacked this order, is not particularly up in arms.

Questioned about other matters under discussion, especially during

[13] Missing from Lipski's papers. For the text, see *ibid.*, No. 584.
[14] Czech mobilization was proclaimed on September 23. The next day France called to arms some categories of reservists.

the last conversation of Hitler with Chamberlain, Herr Woermann was unable to give me any explanation. Neither did he have any details as to whether the problem of the Soviet-Czech agreement had been discussed. I asked him for prompt information with regard to principal motifs of the Hitler-Chamberlain conferences to be communicated to you either by me or by von Moltke.

*Józef Lipski*

DOCUMENT 105    Lipski to Beck

*Receptus* code No. 134 (GMP)          Berlin, September 26, 1938
                                            *Coded*

I executed your instructions with regard to Ribbentrop. At Godesberg a discussion *ad meritum* dealt exclusively with the Sudetenland question. The problem of a general solution was only touched upon casually. Our problems and those of the Hungarians were referred to indirectly in connection with the proposal of a nonaggression pact. The Chancellor brought it up by remarking that such an agreement would become an instrument in the hands of the Czechs against the aspirations of the Polish and Hungarian minorities. The Chancellor also rejected the proposal for a guarantee without Poland, Hungary, and Italy.

Ribbentrop, referring to our conversation at Berchtesgaden, confirmed this stand of the Chancellor most firmly. I consider this to be of importance in view of the rumors that the Czechs are returning to the concept of a nonaggression pact.

*Lipski*

DOCUMENT 106    Lipski to Beck

Berlin, September 26, 1938
*Secret Code*

Ribbentrop told me in strictest confidence that Chamberlain secretly assured the Chancellor at Godesberg that he is taking it upon himself to communicate the memorandum, but he cannot endorse it officially.

Today Wilson is coming to see the Chancellor on behalf of the Foreign Office. I was indirectly informed that Chamberlain's situation has become awkward. Ribbentrop assured me that, although the Chancellor is at present very much absorbed by the Sudetenland problem, he is standing firm on the Polish and Hungarian demands.

Ribbentrop suggested that, upon acceptance of the memorandum and the occupation of the Sudetenland planned for October 1, a closer definition of Polish and Hungarian demands should take place.

*Lipski*

DOCUMENT 107    Lipski to Beck

NO. N/1/172/38                                Berlin, September 26, 1938

I am taking the liberty of supplementing the two telegrams sent today after this morning's conversations with Secretary of State Weizsäcker and Minister of Foreign Affairs Ribbentrop with the following information:

I had difficulty in securing sufficient information about the real meaning of the conference at Godesberg, inasmuch as both Minister von Ribbentrop and Secretary of State Weizsäcker returned to Berlin only today.

Besides, the international press has been full of false rumors to misguide foreign observers.

Under these circumstances, the only reliable document resulting from this conference was the German memorandum communicated to the representatives of Poland, Hungary, and Italy here. I forwarded it with my letter of September 24, No. N/1/171/38.

May I also remind you that on the second day of the conference at Godesberg von Ribbentrop communicated to me at about 1 o'clock that the Chancellor had rejected the plan of a nonaggression pact and guarantee for Czechoslovakia, about which I immediately reported by wire.

A version confidentially circulated by the British side among representatives of the Polish press at Godesberg (Director Dembiński of the Polish Telegraph Agency) informed me that the crisis at Godesberg stemmed from the Chancellor's demand to settle simultaneously the whole complex of Czechoslovak problems, that is, Polish and Hungarian demands. Allegedly the tension was eased when the Chancellor, in his final nocturnal conversation with Chamberlain, withdrew this demand.

The Hungarian Envoy, who called on me this morning, also made the statement that the Chancellor yielded to British pressure in his last talk with Chamberlain, when the latter declared that he must leave Godesberg the next day. The Hungarian Envoy thinks that the Chancellor's decision was also influenced by pressure on the part of German military circles, who feared an international conflict. Top officials of the Auswärtiges Amt, who, as I have observed, always warn about the possible action of England and France, might have also used some pressure. The Hungarian Envoy also expressed anxiety over information in his possession that the Czech government, although it accepted the German memorandum for the time being, would return to the question of a nonaggression pact not for the whole territory of Czechoslovakia but for the newly delimited German-Czech sector, and that the Chancellor under British pressure might agree to this. I declared to the Hungarian Envoy that I consider this to be out of the question in view of the stand precisely defined to me by the Chancellor during our conversation at Berchtesgaden.

After this meeting with the Hungarian Envoy I had a conversation at the A.A., first with Weizsäcker[15] and afterward with von Ribbentrop.

From explanations given it develops that in factual conversations at Godesberg the Chancellor restricted himself to discussions on the Sudetenland problem only. In his opinion, discussing the whole complex of problems on his initiative would only complicate the matter. On the other hand, our problem and that of the Hungarians were indirectly brought up when the Chancellor rejected the plan of a nonaggression pact and a guarantee. Ribbentrop told me that the Chancellor refused the nonaggression pact, arguing that it would become an instrument in the hands of the Czechs against the aspirations of the Polish and Hungarian minorities. The guarantee was rejected by the Chancellor on the principle that he would have to make it dependent on whether it would also be granted by Poland, Hungary, and Italy. Ribbentrop added that the question of the guarantee was rather weakly proposed by the British

[15] For the German version of this conversation, see *DGFP,* Series D, Vol. II, No. 608.

government, since it was rather inconvenient from the traditional angle of British policy.

Weizsäcker made an interesting remark about the guarantee, stating that it would not surprise him if Beneš, giving up the idea of guarantees by other countries, would claim them only from France and England, and insist on this as a condition for acceptance of the German memorandum.

To my question concerning the real cause of the crisis at Godesberg, Ribbentrop replied that after the conversation at Berchtesgaden Chamberlain strove to find a more digestible form of the problem of the transfer of the Sudetenland territories to serve to the West. This would confirm the information I communicated to you after my conversation with Woermann, namely, that Germany's claim to occupation of the territories by armed force before October 1 evoked Chamberlain's serious reservations.

Nevertheless Ribbentrop, in strictest confidence, asked me to inform you that Chamberlain personally pledged to the Chancellor that he would take measures to push the memorandum through. Officially, of course, this could not be disclosed, and hence it was mentioned in the communiqué that the British Prime Minister would present the memorandum to the Czech government.

In Ribbentrop's reception drawing room, I met the ambassadors of Great Britain and Italy. The British Ambassador just had time to remark that he considers the situation to be critical. The Italian Ambassador, following news from Rome, expressed anxiety that Chamberlain's position is becoming awkward. I could imagine that Mussolini feared the British Prime Minister's position might be compromised. The Italian Ambassador told me that on Mussolini's recommendation he would call on Ribbentrop and ask him to influence Hitler not to aggravate the situation further by his speech today. He would propose that Hitler declare that he is ready to grant a guarantee upon reaching an understanding with Czechoslovakia's neighbors (Poland and Hungary) and Italy.

To my question whether the Chancellor in his speech today would take up the question of settling the whole Czechoslovak problem, Ribbentrop replied that as yet he had not received the text of the speech. He is still to confer with the Chancellor today.

More definitely from Weizsäcker's statements, and less explicitly from

Ribbentrop's declarations, it was clear that Hitler, for the time being, as long as the Sudetenland problem remains unsolved, has to concentrate on this question. Nevertheless, von Ribbentrop assured me that Hitler stands firm on the Polish and Hungarian demands.

Furthermore, Ribbentrop, in rather general terms, said he sees two possibilities. First, it is possible that the Czech government will accept the memorandum, in which case the territory will be peacefully occupied. In such an event, he suggested that it might be advisable to meet with us in order to discuss further proceedings in the Polish and Hungarian matter. I replied evasively, as we had mentioned in Berchtesgaden, that the possibility would exist for your meeting with the Chancellor. The second alternative von Ribbentrop considers is the possible necessity for Germany to march into Czechoslovakia. And here he asked whether in such an eventuality we would march as well. I replied that naturally I could not express myself on this matter, since the decision is up to the government. Quite personally I mentioned that, if our demands were not met, force might possibly be used in either case—whether in marching or settling the problem by peaceful occupation of the territory by Germany.

Von Ribbentrop remarked at the end of the conversation that it would be well, for operational reasons, to be in contact if necessary, to which I did not reply.

Von Ribbentrop remarked that he is at my disposal at any time, that he considers the closest contact as desirable, and that, in case something particularly important results from the conversation with Wilson, he will inform me immediately.

*Józef Lipski*

On the same day (September 26) Hitler delivered a speech at the Sport Palace—with a long section about Poland. (See *Polish White Book,* No. 42.)

# Munich and the Teschen Silesia Problem
### *September 27—October 21, 1938*

IN THE AFTERMATH of the Sudetenland issue, the Teschen Silesia problem was raised, particularly with regard to Bohumin (Oderberg).

On September 27 the British ambassador in Warsaw, Sir Howard William Kennard, communicated to Minister Arciszewski, acting vice-minister of foreign affairs, that he had seen a copy of the map attached to the German memorandum. On that map, Bohumin was located in the red zone to be occupied by the Germans immediately, and Moravska Ostrava and Frydek (Friedeck) in the green zone, to be subject to a plebiscite.[1]

Polish action to secure Bohumin was begun.

The same day Beck sent instructions to Lipski, written in the form of a private letter using the friendly term of second singular form. In his private papers, Lipski stresses that points 8, 9, and 10 of these instructions were not carried out by him.

Beck informed Ambassador von Moltke on the same day about Poland's stand with regard to Teschen Silesia (*DGFP,* Series D, Vol. II, No. 652).

### DOCUMENT 108   Beck to Lipski

Warsaw, September 27, 1938

Dear Ambassador:

In the rapid flow of events I am sending instructions in telegraphic style for your conversation and your own orientation.

1) Beneš, in his letter to the President, explicitly agrees that it is necessary to rectify our frontiers in order to improve relations between Poland and Czechoslovakia for the future. No closer definition of political conditions.

2) I received simultaneously a notice from the British and French

[1] See *DGFP,* Series D, Vol. II, map 1.

governments confirming our territorial *revindications légitimes* in Teschen Silesia.

3) Today a reply was dispatched by plane containing acknowledgment by the President that territorial problems were essentially the factor spoiling the good-neighborly relations between the two countries. Further action is referred by the President for agreement between the governments.

4) At the same time I recommended to Papée that he present a note demanding immediate agreement in the following matters:

a) acceptance of the principle of rectification on the basis of the desires of the population in connection with the Polish-Czech agreement of 1918–19;

b) a guarantee that this important decision of the governments is timely through formal occupation by Polish forces of the districts of Teschen and Frystat, since they have an incontestable Polish majority.

The request for immediate agreement is motivated by the grave situation, but it does not bear the character of an ultimatum with a time limit.

5) Today the French Military Attaché presented to us the map of German claims attached to the Chancellor's memorandum. In accordance with this map, the Bohumin region is marked in red, as being contained within the frame of the *Sofortprogram* occupation, while a considerable part of the territory east of the river Ostravica (see map "C") is included in the plebiscite region.

6) Under these conditions the problem should be solved promptly, in order to avoid political dissent or, even worse, a military clash between us and the Germans.

7) Within the limit presently considered by you as possible, please inform any one among the competent political leaders of the Reich about our point of view.

To define the general scope of our interests use map "C"; others are not valid. If necessary, show the map of our immediate claims forwarded today to Prague, which you will find enclosed. Do this in order to avoid friction and, in emergency, to find a prompt realistic compromise. In this occasion refer to your conversation with the Chancellor at Berchtesgaden.

8) Not insisting on indiscretion, express the expectation that we

would be informed about the start of any possible military action. We guarantee not to use this information to the detriment of the Reich's interests.

9) For your confidential information I add that we have at our disposal forces under arms capable of action. Relative to the development of the situation we could take prompt action following the outbreak of a German-Czech conflict.

10) Politically you can confirm that (*a*) our stand against the admittance of Soviet intervention is categorical and (*b*) we would not issue any more extensive guarantees to Czechoslovakia without Germany and Hungary.

*Beck*

DOCUMENT 109    Lipski to Beck

NO. N/1/182/38                          Berlin, September 27, 1938
                                         *Strictly Confidential*

I. Today I was summoned for a conversation at the Auswärtiges Amt by Weizsäcker at 7 P.M.; afterward, at the invitation of Ribbentrop, I conferred with him.

Weizsäcker informed me of the result of today's conversation of Sir Horace Wilson with the Chancellor, and he read the stenograph to me.[2] The Chancellor took the stand in this conversation that the German memorandum has to be accepted by the Czech government, and that he would not retreat from this stand. During the conversation Sir Horace Wilson—here I quote the stenograph—defined possible English action against Germany: "If Czechoslovakia refuses the German memorandum, no one knows where the ensuing conflict will end. If Germany attacks Czechoslovakia, France will fulfill her treaty obligations to Czechoslovakia. If this occurs and French forces were thereby to become actively engaged in hostilities with Germany—whether or not this would occur, he did not know—then Britain would feel herself obliged to support France." Herr von Weizsäcker explained that Wilson de-

[2] *Ibid.*, No. 634.

fined these words, remarking that he was quoting Chamberlain's ideas correctly.

I remarked to Weizsäcker that this formula is typical of British policy. Weizsäcker mentioned that in the course of the conversation Wilson pointed to the possibility of a British-German understanding on a number of questions. Of course, he also laid firm emphasis on the necessity of avoiding a calamity. He allegedly promised, at the end of the discussion, that he would act along these lines.

Herr von Ribbentrop, with whom I conversed later, is of the opinion that the British government will still exert firm pressure on Prague for acceptance of the memorandum. Questioned by me as to whether tomorrow's date at 2 P.M. is still in effect, the Secretary of State replied that he asked me for strict secrecy in order that this term not be precisely revealed. In consequence the time limit is elastic.

II. Furthermore, following your telegram, I informed the Minister of Foreign Affairs, as well as the Secretary of State, where we stand in our conversations with Prague. I stressed that we would not let ourselves be led into a trap and would request concrete settlements.[3]

III. Herr von Weizsäcker, who had a map of the General Staff before him, stressed that he would suggest that our military attaché establish a demarcation line with a competent expert of the General Staff, so as to prevent a collision between the two armies in case of a possible clash.[4]

I answered von Weizsäcker that in the first place it was important to establish with him the territory of our political interests in Czechoslovakia. As Herr Weizsäcker had no such map at the moment, I agreed that I would discuss this problem with him tomorrow in the morning hours. The problem of possible delimitation between military factors was postponed for the present.

IV. When my conversation with the Secretary of State passed to more general topics, we raised the question of France's and England's position. Von Weizsäcker told me that, unfortunately, the A.A. is not adequately informed about the position of France, for French Ambassador François-Poncet has not appeared at the Auswärtiges Amt for a fortnight, collecting his information from other sources, and Ambassador Welczek is absent from Paris. The Secretary of State, however, stated

[3] *Ibid.,* No. 639.
[4] *Ibid.,* Nos. 644 and 666.

that a considerable stiffening of French public opinion might be observed.

V. In a general exchange of opinion with von Ribbentrop he stressed that, as I already mentioned, the British side would still exert firm pressure on Prague. He thinks that the British side would do its utmost to avoid armed conflict and to settle the problem peacefully. He expects a local conflict. However, as he declared, he does not exclude the possibility of a general conflict, for which he is prepared. Referring to my previous conversations with him, I stressed how important the localization of the conflict is.

As far as Russia is concerned, von Ribbentrop's views are on the optimistic side.

To Herr Ribbentrop's question whether, in case the memorandum is executed by peaceful means, we would have recourse to military action, I replied that I was not in a position to forejudge the stand of my government.

Von Ribbentrop further raised the hypothesis that the Czechs would not accept the momorandum; then, as he put it, the Czechs would be destroyed. He lightly touched on the question whether in that case we would march. At this point I could deduce from Ribbentrop's words that in his opinion the Polish government, feeling that the eastern frontier was a great weight on its shoulders, would enter into action upon orienting itself whether the operation was a local flare-up or a world war. In case Germany occupies the whole of Czechoslovakia, von Ribbentrop considers it useful to establish in more detail the political and military interests. He asked me to draw your special attention to this point and obtain instructions on this.

VI. In conclusion, I am taking the liberty of stating that:

1. Further conversations on the German memorandum are useless, owing to the final decision of the Chancellor as declared to Wilson.

2. I would appreciate instructions agreed upon with the General Staff in view of the concrete proposition by the Secretary of State to create a demarcation line on our interests in the Teschen region.

3. Also, instructions as to Ribbentrop's motion, in case of military action and transgression by Germany of the line of its immediate interests in Czechoslovakia.

*Józef Lipski*

The following is Lipski's handwritten note relating to the report of September 27, 1938, on his conversation with Ribbentrop.

When I returned from the Auswärtiges Amt Ribbentrop called me on the telephone, inviting me at 10 P.M. to Kaiserhof for a conversation. Ribbentrop apologized for troubling me again on the same day, but he was in need of some explanations.

I dined together with Counselor of the Embassy Lubomirski and Colonel Szymański, the military attaché, in one of the restaurants near the Adlon (I do not remember its name), and I proceeded to Kaiserhof. I anticipated some very essential question in relation to the threatening conflict in the Sudetenland.

But Ribbentrop, returning to the conversation I had with him when he took office in March, 1938,[5] in a rather discreet manner asked me what our position would be to a suggestion to join the Anti-Comintern Pact.

A discussion ensued on this topic, while Ribbentrop made some evasive statement that he would like to have an idea about our stand with regard to conversations he was engaged in with the Japanese side. He underlined that collaboration with Japan was giving good results.

For my part I stressed our point of view, known already to Ribbentrop from our previous conversation. I pointed out that, having a common frontier with the Soviets, we did not want to bind ourselves by a pact against Russia. On the other hand, I laid stress on our negative attitude to Soviet attempts at marching through or overflight of our territory.

The conversation did not achieve concrete results, aside from a statement that on Ribbentrop's request I would inform Beck about his suggestion. Ribbentrop did not lay stress on urgency.

Bearing in mind that, as was disclosed later on, this was the vital moment of decision—war or peace over the Sudetenland—Ribbentrop, as I suppose, wanted discreetly to find out about our stand in case of a conflict; in the last days, both Moltke at Nuremberg and Ribbentrop at Berchtesgaden and again in a conversation on September 27 at the Auswärtiges Amt had asked if and under what circumstances Poland would act.

[5] See Document 83, p. 360.

On September 28 Ambassador Lipski received by special planes two instructions, both dated the same day, with regard to the delimitation of zones in Teschen Silesia.

### DOCUMENT 110    Beck to Lipski

Warsaw, September 28, 1938
*Strictly Confidential*

With regard to your conversations as to the delimitation of our and German interests in Teschen Silesia, we have worked out here the problem of Bohumin [Oderberg] with Marshal Śmigły-Rydz.

The Military Attaché received technical instructions and a clear map by the same courier. The railway problem, as I had already stressed to you before the meeting at Berchtesgaden, is of prime importance.

We have established with Marshal Śmigły that the first conversations based upon the military instructions will be conducted by you, while only afterward should the Military Attaché approach the General Staff (in accordance with this morning's instructions sent by earlier plane), with the exception of cases when immediate German operation would necessitate establishing immediate contact with the German command.

So the enclosed instructions for the Military Attaché are for the moment also instructions for the Ambassador. For lack of time, I do not repeat details separately.

I quote the latest information: in accordance with Krofta's statement, Prague will accept all our demands, but it is playing for delay in the usual Czech manner.

On the Soviet frontier, two days ago we had a series of demonstrations by larger Soviet detachments in the region of Minsk and in other smaller sectors, in addition to larger groups of planes close to our frontier. Yesterday and today all was peaceful. The character of the demonstrations was obviously political, sometimes taking rather grotesque forms. For the time being they are of no special importance from the military angle. Only a desire to call our attention to these demonstrations, which we are ignoring, is apparent.

However, please mention these demonstrations casually in Berlin.

*Beck*

DOCUMENT 111   Beck to Lipski

*Pro memoria* dictated by Minister Beck as instructions to Ambassador Lipski on September 28, 1938

In reply to your report of today and as a supplement to my instructions of yesterday, I communicate as follows:

1) Clarification of delimitation of German and Polish interests in Teschen Silesia is essentially a very important and urgent matter, since a clash of any sort might cause disastrous consequences.

2) The method chosen by you, namely, first political conversation and only as a result thereof an understanding between the General Staffs, is the only correct one. Marshal Śmigły-Rydz shares this conclusion and will issue instructions to the Military Attaché.

Under these circumstances it is necessary to compare in Berlin the original German map attached to the memorandum (we are naturally interested only in the northeastern sector) with our map "C" and the map attached to the note to Prague. Political conclusions can be drawn only from such a confrontation. Please telegraph or forward by rented plane the position taken by the Germans at such a confrontation.

3) With regard to the plebiscite in the zone between the western frontier of the Teschen and Frystat districts (map sent to the Czechs), it could be negotiated that this might be settled in the future in case the conflict is averted. Most urgent and drastically in need of explanation is the Bohumin region.

Most confidentially I communicate to you that if a rough-and-tumble German plan calls for the immediate occupation of this territory, possibly a slight compromise could be offered, bearing in mind, however, our interests in the railway tract to Bohumin.

I remind you that at present the railway line reaching this station on the Czech territory belongs to the Germans. I am citing this point for orientation, in case of action *in extremis;* for the present please clarify the problem.

DOCUMENT 112   Lipski to Beck

NO. N/1/183/38                              Berlin, September 28, 1938
                                            *Strictly Confidential*

This morning at 12:30 I was received by the Secretary of State whom, in accordance with our agreement of yesterday evening, I confronted with the map attached by the German government to the memorandum and with our map "C."

It appeared that the German red line reaches fairly deeply into the Bohumin region, while the line proposed by the Germans for the plebiscite oversteps into the region between our "frontier proposed" line more or less from Frydek to Silesian Ostrava, and in some places either oversteps or cuts back from the Teschen and Frystat districts.

In addition, Herr von Weizsäcker showed me a demarcation line established by the General Staff on which, as he put it, the German Army would stop in case of military action without overstepping it eastward. This line ran more or less alongside the above-traced line of the German plebiscite in the Frydek district, reaching to the north and joining the German red line to the east of Bohumin.

I declared to Weizsäcker that the German government in its demarcation overstepped the Polish region at two points: Bohumin and Frydek. I laid most pressure on the Bohumin problem, referring to the Chancellor's tacit consent at Berchtesgaden.[6]

The Secretary of State mentioned that he had to find out why this took place, and that he would confer with me again today.

For my part I remarked that in view of the situation the problem must be definitely settled today.

May I add that I showed to the Secretary of State a map attached to our note sent to Prague with our red line traced, stating that westward of the red line in the district of Frydek a plebiscite should be held, in accordance with our proposition to Prague.

At 6:30 P.M., together with Counselor Lubomirski, I had another consultation with Secretary of State Weizsäcker; Counselor Altenburg was also present. It was established as follows:

1) The German government withdraws its red line from the territory of Bohumin, transferring it to the line "frontier proposed" on map "C." In the sector west of Olza to Koblów, the German red line runs further

6 See Document 99, p. 409.

westward, leaving Moravska Ostrava for a plebiscite. Von Weizsäcker remarked that the withdrawal of the red line from the Bohumin region could be executed in connection with the anticipated alterations at the conference in Munich tomorrow.[7]

2) With regard to the overstepping of the German plebiscite line into the Frydek district, the Secretary of State presented the concept of a possible plebiscite for Germany, Czechoslovakia, or Poland. He implied that the German government had no territorial claims here, rather being concerned with the exchange of population to compensate for other territories. Besides, bearing in mind the change in the situation, in his opinion the question of the plebiscite territories will have to be reconsidered, so that any definition at present would be pointless.

In consequence we agreed as follows:

The German government will not settle the plebiscite in the district of Frydek prior to a consultation with us.

3) In view of the altered situation, the Secretary of State remarked that for the moment he does not deem it necessary to discuss the question of the German military demarcation line in the event of armed occupation. Here I observed that, in my opinion, the military demarcation line should follow the line of the Oder and Ostravica rivers. I laid some stress on the fact that in any case the Secretary of State should consider our "frontier proposed" line as the frontier of our region, adding that I was making this statement in the event of our military action.

The Secretary of State acknowledged my statement.

*Józef Lipski*

Map enclosed.[8]

DOCUMENT 113   Lipski to Beck

NO. N/1/184/38                                      Berlin, September 28, 1938
                                                     *Strictly Confidential*

Yesterday's situation resulted in increasing international tension. Herr von Ribbentrop summoned me for still another nocturnal conversation,

---

[7] The communiqué convoking the conference in Munich was issued on September 28.

[8] See *DGFP*, Series D, Vol. II, No. 666. The map is missing from Lipski's documents.

bringing up other topics (the Anti-Comintern Pact), on which I am reporting separately.[9] I simply mention that the matter under discussion is of no urgency, but is rather interesting as an indication of the attitude of the German government toward Russia.

The majority of diplomats here, not excluding the Italian Ambassador, who was in direct contact with Ciano and Mussolini, are of the opinion that we are quickening our pace in the march toward a European war. Comments were circulated that international circles are using the atmosphere observed in France and England for a showdown with competent Powers.

Today, right from this morning, a very strong diplomatic action could be observed here. The Chancellor first received the British Ambassador, who presented some plan considered as not acceptable.[10] Next, the French Ambassador called on the Chancellor, presenting a plan on behalf of the French government in more concrete form.[11] Finally, the Chancellor also received the Italian Ambassador acting in the name of Mussolini. Constant attempts were also made by President Roosevelt to reach Berlin directly.[12]

As a result of these endeavors, and after a direct telephone conversation between Mussolini and Hitler that allegedly cut the Gordian knot, a meeting is to take place tomorrow in Munich between Hitler, Mussolini, Chamberlain, and Daladier.

Under these circumstances, the general mobilization planned by the German government in case the memorandum is not accepted by the Czech government by Wednesday at two o'clock is to be postponed for twenty-four hours. The Secretary of State, however, told me that military orders are still being issued.

Next von Weizsäcker informed me that a certain willingness to compromise was noted on the part of France and Great Britain with regard to the peaceful occupation by German forces of a certain red line, and to the extension of international control over the remaining part of the territories destined for a plebiscite, as well as over some other territories. He added that delimitation of frontiers under the plebiscite is planned with the assistance of an international committee.

[9] This report is missing from Lipski's documents. Résumé in handwritten note (supra, p. 427).
[10] DGFP, Series D, Vol. II, No. 655.
[11] Ibid., Nos. 648 and 656.
[12] Ibid., No. 653.

The Secretary of State evaluated the situation as follows: a peaceful settlement is anticipated. Naturally, a possible failure to agree should still be considered.

I saw the Hungarian Envoy today, who had called on Göring to discuss Hungarian revindications. Göring will also attend the conference at Munich. The Hungarian Envoy hopes that Mussolini will very firmly support the Hungarian cause.

*Józef Lipski*

On September 29 a conference was held in Munich.[13] Lipski notes in his private papers:

Director Dembiński departed for Munich as a representative of the Polish Telegraph Agency. The Ministry of Foreign Affairs instructed me, while the conference was under way, to inform the Italian delegation about the alleged sabotage by Prague of the agreement with us on Teschen. This was accomplished by Dembiński.

### DOCUMENT 114   Lipski to Beck

NO. N/1/186/38                                           Berlin, September 30, 1938
*Strictly Confidential*

Referring to my telegram of today I confirm that von Ribbentrop telephoned me from Munich expressing his conviction that the Polish government would probably be satisfied with the way Polish interests were secured at yesterday's conference. He also acknowledged that the German government, in accordance with my agreement with the Chancellor at Berchtesgaden, made the granting of a guarantee to the future Czechoslovak state dependent upon the settlement of Polish and Hungarian problems. The Italian Ambassador confirmed to me today that Mussolini made a similar declaration.

I made it clear to Ribbentrop, while extending my congratulations to

[13] For the program, memoranda, and resolutions, see *ibid.*, Nos. 669, 670, 674, and 675.

him and the Chancellor, that the burden of the problem now weighs on us. Here Ribbentrop remarked that the formula regarding Polish and Hungarian interests accepted yesterday by the conference should be convenient for us since it deals with the whole Czechoslovak question.

I tried discreetly to sound von Ribbentrop out with regard to France's and England's guarantee for Czechoslovakia. Ribbentrop said that he does not know exactly what guarantee these two states gave to Czechoslovakia. This matter was dealt with between France, England, and Prague. Herr von Ribbentrop thinks that the declaration of England and France about the guarantee for Czechoslovakia, contained in an additional protocol, was executed by these states out of consideration for their public opinion and that of Czechoslovakia.

I was further informed by the Minister of Foreign Affairs that Prague had been notified of the agreement tonight, and that there can be no possible doubt as to its acceptance. Today at 5 P.M., as foreseen by the agreement, a committee will meet to discuss the evacuation.

I later saw the Italian Ambassador. He ascertained that Mussolini was practically leading the conference, presenting a concrete plan to settle the strife in a way acceptable to all parties.

The Polish-Hungarian question had naturally also been presented by Mussolini; he did so at the final nocturnal debate. Mussolini set a term of one month for these matters to be settled directly between Prague, Budapest, and Warsaw, while Chamberlain insisted on three months; a compromise proposition of two months suggested by Mussolini was not accepted.

However, the Italian Ambassador stressed the importance of the fact that the principle of direct negotiations between Warsaw and Prague had been maintained.

In answer to my question, the Italian Ambassador explained that Polish and Hungarian questions had not been dealt with *ad meritum* at all.

In accordance with your instructions transmitted to me by Director Łubieński, I immediately took steps to obtain first of all a map provided for *ad* point 4 of the agreement. I approached the German side and the Italian Ambassador on this. The Italian Ambassador gave me his map, and I had a copy of it made. The Secretary of State of the Auswärtiges Amt also sent a map on which the sectors for evacuation are marked. As the two maps agree, I am forwarding the German map. For the sake of order, I enclose the text of the agreement.

*Józef Lipski*

(add. to Document 114)
enclosures:
Map
Text[14]

DOCUMENT 115    Lipski to Beck

NO. 1/194/38                                    Berlin, October 1, 1938
                                                *Strictly Confidential*

Yesterday, September 30, in the evening hours, Undersecretary of State Woermann telephoned to ask whether it was true that the Polish government had sent an ultimatum to Prague. In reply I stated that up to then I knew only that the Polish government would make a serious decision that evening.[15]

This morning I was asked by Woermann to call him at the Auswärtiges Amt at 11:30 A.M. It was impossible for me to get in touch either with General Field Marshal Göring or with Herr von Ribbentrop prior to this meeting, since they were taking part in greeting the Chancellor upon his arrival in Berlin at 10:30 A.M.

Before I left for the Auswärtiges Amt, the British ambassador, Sir Nevile Henderson, called by phone, very upset by our ultimatum to Prague. He said that he had instructions to get in touch with the German government on this matter. He pointed to the "disastrous consequences military action against Czechoslovakia would entail for Poland during

---

[14] Both enclosures are missing from Lipski's documents.

[15] The decision to send an ultimatum was reached in Warsaw on September 30 in the afternoon, and the Polish Minister in Prague handed to Minister of Foreign Affairs Krofta the ultimatum note on the same day at 11:40 P.M. for a term of twelve hours, that is, until October 1 at noon. For the text see *Documents on British Foreign Policy, 1919–1939*, Third Series, Vol. III, Document No. 101. See *Journal*, pp. 342–43. See also Wojciechowski, *Stosunki polsko-niemieckie, 1933–1938*, pp. 484–85.

such a delicate international period." Poland would lose all sympathy in England and the United States. I tried to explain the situation to the Ambassador, advising him, as a sole remedy, that his government should influence Prague to accept our ultimatum.

Immediately afterward there was another telephone call; this one came from the Italian Ambassador who, although he did not threaten us with the wrath of the Italian people, was hurt and accused us of undermining Mussolini's work: the result of Munich, which had saved the peace. I explained that our ultimatum followed the lines of this conference, which left the problem of Teschen for direct settlement between Warsaw and Prague.

I then started for the Auswärtiges Amt. Undersecretary Woermann asked me to confirm the military demarcation line established by me with Secretary of State von Weizsäcker in the event of a Polish-Czechoslovak war. I confirmed that our demarcation line runs alongside the rivers Oder and Ostravica, and that the Polish General Staff, in accordance with my previous report, would keep to this line.

Herr Woermann did not wish to commit himself with regard to the political situation, remarking that Herr von Ribbentrop would receive me in a moment, after he got in touch with the Chancellor. He read to me Moltke's telegram on yesterday's conversation with you, when you asked if, in the event of an armed Czech-Polish conflict, we might count on the friendly attitude of the Reich government, as well as on a similar position by Germany in case of an armed conflict of Poland with the Soviets.[16]

Immediately afterward I was received by Herr von Ribbentrop, who informed me that the French, British, and Italian governments are exerting pressure on the German government to advise the Polish government to extend the term of the ultimatum. He was expecting a telephone call from Ciano at any moment. I set forth the situation to von Ribbentrop, concluding by stating that the ultimatum expired at 12 noon, that is, in a couple of minutes. Von Ribbentrop remarked that the Chancellor had told him that, if Poland waited for three months, not a single Pole would be left in Teschen Silesia. Although I could detect some embarrassment on his part, probably because of the Munich agreement with the Powers and the Hitler-Chamberlain declaration, von Ribbentrop tried to extricate himself from the Anglo-French-Italian pressure. Called on the tele-

16 For von Moltke's telegram, see *DGFP*, Series D, Vol. V, No. 54.

phone by Ciano, von Ribbentrop went to another room, returning to inform me that the Italian government, through its ambassador in Warsaw, this morning advised an extension of the ultimatum.

He then described the attitude of the Reich government as follows:

1) In the event of an armed Polish-Czech conflict, the German government would maintain a friendly attitude toward Poland.

2) In case of a Polish-Soviet conflict, the German government would take a far more than friendly attitude toward Poland, and he clearly hinted that the German government would come to Poland's assistance.

3) Von Ribbentrop would reply along these lines to the British, French, and Italian governments: that he hopes no armed conflict will occur between Poland and Czechoslovakia if Prague accepts Poland's claims. He would add that, bearing in mind the situation prevailing in Teschen Silesia, he cannot give advice to the Polish government.[17]

I was next invited to Field Marshal Göring's. Making the reservation that he was expressing his own opinion, he declared that the Reich government would give no advice to the Polish government in such a situation, being aware that Warsaw would not accept such advice, and that it would be right not to do so. He further stressed that in connection with military operations it might be important for our military authorities to know that the German pressure on Czechoslovakia could be much more effective upon the occupation of Sector IV, that is, on October 7. Finally—and he laid special stress on this—in case of a Soviet-Polish conflict, the Polish government could count on aid from the German government. It is absolutely out of the question that the Reich would not help Poland in its struggle with the Soviets.

Next, the conversation with Göring passed to general subjects, on which I am commenting separately in other reports.[18]

From Göring's attitude it was obvious that he is completely in agreement with the Polish government's point of view. In a conversation by telephone with me when the ultimatum was accepted, he characterized our step as "a very bold action performed in excellent style."

Ribbentrop also told me in the afternoon that the Chancellor today at lunchtime expressed to his entourage great appreciation for Poland's policy.

[17] For Ribbentrop's memorandum of his conversation with Lipski and Ciano, see *ibid.*, No. 55.

[18] These reports are missing form Lipski's documents, outside of a handwritten note dated October 1.

I must stress that our step was evaluated here as an expression of great strength and independent action, which represents the best guarantee of our good relations with the government of the Reich.

*József Lipski*

The following is Lipski's handwritten note of his conversation with Göring:

Göring joined in the conversations I had with Woermann and Ribbentrop on October 1 at the invitation of the Auswärtiges Amt on the ultimatum sent by the Polish government to Prague. In addition to his invitation by telephone, which already occurred after 12 noon (the term for the expiration of the ultimatum), I had a conversation with him at his residence in Berlin. I found him overjoyed by the result of the Munich conference, which he called a great success for Germany.

With his usual directness, he said that "now probably Poland also will draw consequences from the changed situation and change its alliance with France for an alliance with Germany." He was very well satisfied with his conversation with Daladier. Allegedly it would result in the French Prime Minister's striving to carry through elections to enable him to tighten French relations with Germany.

I maintained my reserve with regard to these revelations of Göring. With regard to our ultimatum to Prague on Teschen Silesia, Göring asked why we were asking for so little, and why we did not want to annex Moravska Ostrava to Poland, where obviously there was also some Polish population. I replied that our demand was restricted to Teschen Silesia, to which Göring insisted that, availing ourselves of the occasion, we should extend our claims.

On my return to the Embassy I received a telephone call from Göring. He asked, somewhat embarrassedly, that I not repeat his deliberations to Warsaw with regard to Moravska Ostrava. It was quite clear to me that he had probably been admonished by the Chancellor or by Ribbentrop that he should not display to the Polish side Germany's *désintéressement* with regard to Moravska Ostrava.[19]

[19] In this matter attention should be called to a memorandum by Secretary of State Weizsäcker dated October 4: "Field Marshal Göring told me today, with regard to the territory south of the southwestern corner of Silesia, that it must by all means become German. Should a dispute develop about it with the Poles, a deal could be made over Danzig. Otherwise it would be best to pass it to the Czechs." *DGFP*, Series D, Vol. V, No. 58.

DOCUMENT 116　Lipski to Beck

NO. N/1/198/38　　　　　　　　　　Berlin, October 4, 1938
　　　　　　　　　　　　　　　　　　*Strictly Confidential*

On October 3 Secretary of State Weizsäcker, in the course of a casual
conversation at the Auswärtiges Amt, told me that for the sake of order
he would like to compare our maps again.[20] For this purpose Counselor
Lubomirski met with Undersecretary of State Woermann in the evening
at the Auswärtiges Amt and confirmed that the German map copied
from ours on September 28 (see my report of 9/28, No. 1/183/38) is
in conformity with what was agreed between me and Weizsäcker on the
above date. Counselor Lubomirski was under the impression that
Woermann has had some difficulties with his authorities over the problem of the Bohumin region. Woermann mentioned casually the planned
Oder-Danube canal, which would possibly run across Polish territory.
However, he did not raise any other objections with regard to the established line.

This morning Secretary of State Weizsäcker called me by telephone,
remarking that probably Minister von Ribbentrop would like to see me
in connection with the intersection of lines in one spot on the delimitation of the territory.[21]

Herr Ribbentrop did not telephone during the day, but Undersecretary of State Woermann asked me to call on him at 6 P.M. He told me
that Herr Ribbentrop had a cold and could not receive me, and had
instructed him to declare as follows:

"The inclusion of Oderberg in the Polish zone is a new matter of fact.
Since, however, we will have to discuss the drawing of the frontiers, the
problem of Oderberg can then become the subject of debates."

I call attention to the fact that, in the first version of the declaration,
instead of the words "a new matter of fact" (*neue Tatsache*), Woermann said "a surprise" (*eine Überraschung*).

In a very outspoken manner I stated that I must categorically protest
that there could not possibly be any mention of any "surprise." On this
occasion I referred to your basic conversation on the problem of the
Polish region with Field Marshal Göring, to my conversation with the
Chancellor at Berchtesgaden, when I clearly discussed Oderberg, as well

[20] For the memorandum by Weizsäcker of his conversation, see *ibid.*, No. 57.
[21] *Ibid.*, No. 60.

as to a virtual and unequivocal agreement reached on this matter on September 28, on the basis of maps, with Secretary of State Weizsäcker.

Woermann, visibly embarrassed, replied that he had received his instructions, that the formula showed by itself the spirit of the forthcoming talks on these matters, and that besides this declaration no details were known to him.

For the sake of order I took literal notes of Woermann's declaration and told him sharply that I did not conceive how I could report such a declaration to my Minister. Woermann started to explain, very evasively, that in the conversation of September 28 Secretary of State Weizsäcker only discussed the line in the event of war. This, of course, is absolutely untrue. I corrected this statement, saying that, on the contrary, we were delimitating for a peaceful territorial occupation on the eve of the Munich conference. This put an end to the conversation.

Upon my return to the Embassy and a consultation with Counselor Lubomirski, we checked details, and I communicated to Woermann as follows:

I had studied the declaration as presented to me. I was not in a position either to accept it or to bring it to the knowledge of my government. I stated that I was unable to do so because the declaration is based upon untrue premises that the Oderberg matter was allegedly a *novum* for the government.

I asked Woermann to communicate this to Herr von Ribbentrop.

Woermann tried to explain that I could communicate any declaration to my government. Nevertheless, I replied firmly that I could not do it. The Secretary of State still observed that I might possibly communicate it to the Minister of Foreign Affairs. I replied that formally I was unable to do so.[22]

May I add to the above that, in my opinion, the Auswärtiges Amt possibly made inadvertent concessions on September 28 and is now under pressure from competent authorities. They are trying to make a narrow escape, creating a basis for future negotiations. I could not determine whether the German side is interested in a canal or access to Oderberg [Bohumin] by railway.

[22] For Woermann's version of the same matter, see *ibid.*, No. 61. See also Hitler's agreement to leave Bohumin on the Polish side (*ibid.*, No. 62), and the rejection by the Germans of a petition of this city (*ibid.*, No. 63).

In case von Moltke approaches you on this matter, I am taking the liberty of asking you to reject this declaration.

I think that under these circumstances it would be advisable to occupy the Bohumin region without delay.

*Józef Lipski*


DOCUMENT 117    Lipski to Beck [23]

NO. N/1/204/38                              Berlin, October 6, 1938
                                            (Personal)
                                            *Strictly Confidential*

This morning Ambassador von Moltke paid me a visit, remarking that he had received a telegram about my conversation with Undersecretary of State Woermann regarding Oderberg. Without further delay, and without discussing this matter with the Minister, he had immediately left for Berlin in order to get in touch with his authorities and, naturally, to remove the problem from the agenda. I explained the whole matter to von Moltke and why I had protested so vehemently to Undersecretary of State Woermann. Moltke fully shared my point of view.

He returned in the afternoon, stating quite confidentially that he finally realized how the matter stands. On the German side three points are essential:

1) the canal the German government is planning to build between the Oder and the Danube would have to run across the territory ceded to Poland by the Czech government;

2) the Berlin-Wrocław-Vienna railway line goes through Oderberg, crossing Polish and then Czech territory, necessitating the passing of six frontier stations;

3) the city of Oderberg itself has a majority of German population, and some objections have been raised in this connection.

Von Moltke agreed that all these matters should have been discussed peacefully in advance, and that undoubtedly the German side is to blame here. Nevertheless, the German side would like at present to iron

[23] For the Polish text, see *Sprawny Międzynarodowe* (Warsaw), 1958, No. 9, pp. 111–13.

out the situation and avoid hurting Poland. Moltke suggested that the Germans would like to adopt the following plan, bearing in mind, of course, that the Polish red line cannot be infringed upon:

1) With regard to the canal, the Germans would like to obtain assurances that the Polish government will agree in the future to its passage through Polish territory.

2) With regard to the railway, the German side would like to have its line on the Polish sector come up to the Czech frontier.

3) With regard to Oderberg, the German government would require some special minority guarantee.

Regardless of the result of his consultations, Moltke mentioned that he sees a solution in prompt negotiations on the problem with the Polish government upon his return to Warsaw. This might take place either tomorrow morning or the next day.

I promised von Moltke, upon his special request, that our conversation would be kept secret, as being strictly private.

Realizing it to be of importance that you should be warned about a possible *démarche* on this matter, I would like, for my part, to lay stress on the following:

With regard to the canal, which in any case would have to pass through the territory of other states, in my opinion such an assurance could be given—upon orienting ourselves which way the canal would run (von Moltke did not know this).

Regarding the railway problem, I think some agreement might be reached, especially since, as I was informed by Director Łubieński, a part of this railway has hitherto been in German hands.

Concerning the guarantee for minorities, I would be very careful not to go further than the provisions of the declaration of November 5, 1937.

I think that von Moltke will probably approach you with a concrete proposal for a compromise with regard to particular points, suggesting that negotiations be finalized in Warsaw as promptly as possible. Moltke understands the necessity of keeping the matter absolutely secret. If the news leaked out, it would appear to public opinion at large that there is frontier strife between Poland and Germany.[24]

[24] Upon his return to Warsaw, von Moltke had a conversation on this matter with Szembek on October 7 (*Journal*, p. 346, and *DGFP*, Series D, Vol. V, No. 66).

DOCUMENT 118   Lipski to Beck [25]

NO. N/1/207/38                                     Berlin, October 8, 1938
                                                   *Strictly Confidential*

In addition to my report of the 6th inst., No. N/1/204/38, I am taking
the liberty of informing you as follows:

On the 7th inst. I was invited by Secretary of State Weizsäcker to the
Auswärtiges Amt for a conversation. Weizsäcker referred to my conversation with Undersecretary of State Woermann on October 4. He mentioned that this conversation had been referred to the top authorities of
the Reich, who had justified my point of view ("Ihr Standpunkt ist von
den höchsten Stellen gewürdigt worden"). General Field Marshal Göring wanted to declare this to me personally but he was unfortunately
prevented from doing so. Von Ribbentrop is also bedridden with a cold.
That is why the Secretary of State communicated this to me.

Next, von Weizsäcker stated that he would like to inform me about
the instructions von Moltke received for his conversations in Warsaw.
Von Weizsäcker added that he would just give me an outline, since
details would be presented by von Moltke.

Specifically, the German government would like to present several
matters to us in a friendly way for settlement in connection with the take-
over of Teschen Silesia by Poland.

1) Of concern were communication problems in connection with the
line crossing Bohumin on the Annaberg-Oderberg-Vitkovice line; here
he added that this concerned certain property of the German railways.

2) In connection with the planned Oder-Danube canal, consent
should be given to the building of this canal through our territory in the
future.

3) The German side was concerned that the German minorities in
the territories occupied by Poland should not be treated worse than
hitherto. The Secretary of State mentioned that quite a number of claims
had been made with regard to Voivode Grażyński's action. He also
stated that the German side would like to have a consulate at Teschen.

The whole conversation was marked with the highest degree of courtesy on the part of Secretary of State Weizsäcker.

[25] For the Polish text, see *Sprawy Międzynarodowe* (Warsaw), 1958, No. 9,
pp. 113–14.

Further continuing our conversation, I asked the Secretary of State to authorize Counselor Altenburg to hand over the map of Sector V to Counselor Lubomirski. He promised to do so.

We touched casually on the Hungarian question, and Weizsäcker showed particular interest in the newly formed Slovakian government. He also expressed a desire to be kept informed about the recent conversations of Count Csáky with you in Warsaw.

I finally brought up the subject of Carpathian Ruthenia with the map in hand. At this point I referred to our discussion in detail with Chancellor Hitler at Berchtesgaden.[26]

*Józef Lipski*

DOCUMENT 119    Lipski to Beck

Telegram by Code No. 154                    Berlin, October 12, 1938
                                            Received: October 13, 9 A.M.
                                            *Secret*

During a conversation to which he invited me, the Secretary of State declared that in view of certain rumors in the Polish press [27] he wanted to warn me that the German government is not uninterested in Moravska Ostrava and Vitkovice. He communicated to me confidentially that the German government nevertheless would not call for a plebiscite in this region. However, it will place a reservation with the Commission [28] tomorrow; in case another party (read Poland) should be interested in Vitkovice and Moravska Ostrava, the German government would then request a plebiscite.

I declared conclusively that we do not claim Moravska Ostrava and Vitkovice, and that we would not go beyond the black line as communicated to the German government. I therefore confirmed that there is no difference of opinion between us.

Owing to my declaration, the Secretary of State considered the German government's reservation as purposeless and will not place it before the Commission tomorrow.

26 For the German version of this conversation, see *DGFP*, Series D, Vol. V, No. 65.
27 Von Moltke writes about this in his telegram of October 10. *Ibid.*, No. 68.
28 The International Commission for Executing the Terms of the Munich Agreement.

We acknowledged that consequently the region of Moravska Ostrava and Vitkovice would remain as a Czech territory between Poland and Germany.

Following instructions, I informed the Secretary of State about the direction of our negotiations with Prague with regard to the establishment of the Polish-Czech frontier in the region of Frydek.[29]

Received: Warsaw and Prague

On October 18 Beck went to Rumania for a conversation with King Carol, which took place at Galati on October 19. Before his departure, instructions were sent to a number of Polish ambassadors, Lipski among them; he was asked to try for a *neutralité bienveillante* with Germany with regard to transferring Carpathian Ruthenia to Hungary. Lipski was also to discuss all problems with Göring (Szembek, *Journal*, pp. 356–59).

On the 18th Lipski conferred with Weizsäcker on the problem of Carpathian Ruthenia. The report on this conversation is missing from Lipski's documents; for Weizsäcker's version, see *DGFP*, Series D, Vol. V, No. 75, pp. 96–98.[30]

Upon his return to Warsaw Beck sent instructions to Lipski on October 20 containing information about his conversation with the King.[31]

Lipski had a conversation with Göring on October 21, and on October 22 he repeated the same things to the director of the Political Department, Woermann (*DGFP*, Series D, Vol. V, No. 80; the report on the conversation with Woermann is missing from Lipski's documents).[32]

DOCUMENT 120     Beck to Lipski

Warsaw, October 20, 1938
*Strictly Confidential*

I communicate information and guiding lines for the conversation with Göring:

1) I had a conversation with King Carol yesterday which lasted for several hours, partly in the presence of Comnen, and partly alone. Prince Hohenzollern-Sigmaringen was also there.

---

[29] During those days Lipski was in Warsaw (see his conversation with Szembek on October 10 and that of Szembek with Beck on October 11, *Journal*, pp. 349–52). For the German version of Lipski's conversation with Weizsäcker, see *DGFP*, Series D, Vol. V, No. 69; also, on the same matter, Nos. 70, 71, and 74.

[30] See also von Moltke's report of October 19 (*DGFP*, Series D, Vol. V, Nos. 76 and 79).

[31] See Beck, *Final Report*, pp. 165–67.

[32] Regarding Carpathian Ruthenia, see also von Moltke's report of October 25, *DGFP*, Series D, Vol. V, No. 83, and Weizsäcker's information sent to Ribbentrop on October 22, *ibid.*, Series D, Vol. IV, No. 83.

I was under the impression that the King wanted to take advantage of the present situation to achieve a basic relaxation in his relations with Hungary. However, he has to cope with the feelings of many political circles in Rumania, and the main difficulty lies in Comnen's tendentious reporting to the King. Together with Prague, Comnen is pursuing his dream of a Czechoslovakia serving as a political corridor binding Rumania with the West. Comnen even goes so far as to weave fantastic plans for drilling tunnels for a new railway, once Hungary occupies the ethnographic territories which cut across the only railway artery hitherto. The King is not taking this seriously. One of the principal arguments suggested to the King against the Hungarian Carpatho-Ruthenian concept is the pressure allegedly exerted by the Reich against this concept. The "entourage of Marshal Göring" is even being quoted as a source of German policy on Ruthenia.

The King listened with satisfaction to my arguments contradicting Comnen's concepts. He is taking an interest in our *bons offices* between Rumania and Hungary, while he is very reticent about any allusions regarding frontier corrections to the advantage of Rumania in the eastern point of Ruthenia. He has scruples about his former allies—the Czechs. He, as well as Comnen, was deeply troubled by my remark that it is difficult to conceive how the Czechs can in the future be responsible for the control of Carpathian Ruthenia, and in consequence how they can guarantee that it would not become a settlement center for all kinds of destructive agitators among immigrant elements.

Please evaluate, on the basis of your own orientation, how far Göring should be informed about these details, besides the point of the alleged German policy which must be brought up.

2) Please utilize your talk with Field Marshal Göring to develop the following marginal argumentation:

Carpathian Ruthenia was invented during the Peace Conference to supply Russia with a bridge into Europe. Later, hopes were nourished, and are still timely, of creating on this territory a kind of springboard, some political cadre designed to exert influence on the real Ukraine at present situated within the frame of Soviet Russia. According to our opinion and our experience of 1918–20, as well as our present observation, this concept is proving to be sheer fiction. Neither Carpathian Ruthenians, nor the undoubtedly much more accomplished Galician Ruthenians, have any chance of controlling national movements in the real Ukraine. They are, and will always remain, a foreign element whom the local population will reject. The language, religion, and political concepts of these various Ruthenians of ours have very little in common with the real Ukraine; besides, in liberation movements, emigration, even of political groups—and particularly an artificially cultivated breed actually of alien origin—never represents a decisive factor. All this, taken together, is absolute fiction, and the Germans had an opportunity themselves to learn the value of all these pseudo-Ukrainians used for action on the sides of the Dnieper.

3) I report for your information that Prince Hohenzollern suggested to me at Galati the proposition that in case of an increase of difficulties in the Carpathian region we should foster the idea of calling a conference of representatives of Hungary, Czechoslovakia, Rumania, and Poland. The idea was that within the frame of such a consultation Rumania would join our thesis on the indispensable basic territorial revision of the former Czechoslovakia, thus bringing about a general relaxation in the whole region.

4) Please ask Göring, and if necessary also Ribbentrop, about the character of German mediation undertaken today between Prague and Budapest, communicating to Göring our readiness for contact and our agreement of opinion on the problems which you have already presented at the Auswärtiges Amt.

5) Our conversations with the Czechs as to the final delimitation are proceeding, while we have limited our claims to rather insignificant extensions of the occupied territory in Silesia, so that not only is there no question of crossing the Ostravica, but on its eastern bank we are prepared to give up Polish Ostrava and its mining region.

*Beck*


DOCUMENT 121   Lipski to Beck

Berlin, October 21, 1938
*Strictly Confidential*

In my conversation today at Karinhall with Field Marshal Göring, I utilized all the information and instructions received from you in the last days.

For lack of time before the plane leaves, I am not presenting extensive deliberations but am limiting myself to a short, broad outline of the conversation.

1) When I mentioned that Poland is trying to influence Budapest in order to attenuate Hungarian claims with regard to Slovakia, Göring said that German mediation was wrecked by the Hungarian claim to Koszyce [Kosice]. Göring thinks that this claim was quite unjustified from the ethnographical angle, as well as because of the importance of this point for Slovakia.

2) After I explained our point of view regarding Carpathian Ruthenia, which Göring noted carefully and today showed great personal understanding for, he asked me how this demand could be taken care of in practice. Seeking for a solution, we reached the common opinion that in a country 80 percent illiterate it is hardly possible to speak of self-determination. Göring agreed with my opinion that France and England are expressing their *désintéressement* in this matter.

In conclusion I stated that if we and Germany are in accord in this respect and the Italians, as I am informed, are also for it, then there is no objection to the settlement of the problem. Göring added here that naturally under these circumstances Hungary could occupy Ruthenia.

3) I discussed the results of your trip to Bucharest, criticizing Comnen's activity. Göring, for his part, holds an opinion similar to ours.

When I said that in the King's presence Comnen used the argument that Germany is opposing a common Polish-Hungarian frontier through the annexation of Ruthenia to Hungary, Göring exploded, declaring that he cannot conceive on what basis Comnen dares to make such a statement. Also, when I pointed out that Comnen still thinks in categories of the Little Entente, Göring declared that it was high time for the Little Entente to be formally buried, since in fact it does not exist any more.

During the conversation I tried to lay stress on the difference of opinion between the King and Comnen.

4) Asked about German mediation with regard to Hungarian demands, Göring replied that as far as Ruthenia was concerned the German government had taken on no obligations whatsoever. I stressed how important it was that the German side should do nothing in this matter.

Summing up the above conversation I state that I found Göring more understanding than on previous occasions on the subject of the settlement of the problem of Carpathian Ruthenia along the lines of our thesis. However, and I particularly stress this, he said that he does not know what conclusions might have been reached by the Chancellor in the last days, since he would not see him until next week. Therefore, Göring's revelations should not be taken as authoritative declarations of the German government.

It was rather interesting that Göring remarked that the Chancellor is facing very difficult problems with regard to Czechoslovakia as such, since Prague made very far-reaching attempts to come to an agreement with Germany, even to the extent of evoking certain suspicions in Berlin. Göring added that there are Czechs who approach him with propositions that Czechoslovakia be annexed into the German *organismus* autonomically. This might influence the Chancellor to make a prompt settlement of Hungarian revindication in order to deal with the Czechs on economic problems only afterward.

I shall try to see Ribbentrop as soon as possible; if necessary, I shall even go to Munich.

Yesterday I received very confidential information that Comnen gave orders to verify your declaration that Germany is not in the least interested in the matter of Ruthenia, to see whether it corresponds with reality, and that on this occasion all arguments against our common frontier with Hungary should be used.

I would ask you, for the sake of my friend, not to disclose this fact. I am doing all I can to undermine Comnen's activities.

*Józef Lipski*

Göring's notebook, in which he made very short notes on conversations conducted, was found after the war. In it he noted the above conversation he had with Lipski on October 21, 1938. The following note was published, somewhat abbreviated, by the *Daily Herald* (London) in the issue of July 11, 1945, after the paper had previously shown it to Ambassador Lipski, who at that time resided in London. Upon taking note of its contents, on July 6 Lipski sent his comments on the note to the editor; these appeared, with some deletions, in the *Daily Herald* on July 12.

The full text of the translation of Göring's note and the full text of Lipski's declaration are given below.

DOCUMENT 122     Göring's Note

LIPSKI                                         October 21

Information on Poland's intentions. Keep contact, avoid misunderstandings.

Problem Hungary-Slovakia: pressure on Hungary for giving way, but only toward Slovakia.

Problem Carpatho-Ukraine. Poland is interested, but not territorially. At Versailles, 1919, separation of Poland from Hungary was demanded. Ethnical mixture, in the south Hungarians down to the line Uzhorod-Munkacz.

Poland fears that a center of future troubles might develop there. The country tends toward Hungary. Should be a bridge toward the question of a Great Ukraine. But for the Great Ukraine this little territory does not mean anything. Different religions! Ruthenians are not Ukrainians. The Communist center for the Balkans against Poland was, and is, established there.

For Poland such a center for a hardening of Ukrainians is very alarming. Would lead to a stiffening of Ukrainian question in Poland.

Therefore Polish desire that this territory come to Hungary, so that it may be controlled.

Propaganda in the West that common frontier could be a danger for Germany. That would be absurd.

Information on Bucharest. The visit there took place on the King's initiative. The King's ideas. Understands interest to achieve better understanding with Hungary. Comnen exercises bad influence on policy. Completely taken in by Geneva. He alleges that Germany is opposed to solution of a common frontier. Beck denies it. Comnen is still a supporter of the idea of granting assistance to the Little Entente. If there was an agreement with us and Italy one might achieve a clear solution.

I protest against the treatment inflicted on the Germans on the Polish territories. Sending documents to Lipski. Stern warning sent to Warsaw to treat the Germans well.

DOCUMENT 123   Notes on Lipski's Conversation
with Göring on October 21, 1938

On identifying this particular conversation in my diary, I would like to submit the following remarks concerning the document at present in possession of the *Daily Herald*.

The conversation in question took place at Karinhall on the morning of October 21, 1938. I forwarded a detailed account to the Polish Foreign Office and luckily I am in possession of a copy of that report.

The prints which I have been given appear to be photographs of loose notes taken down in Göring's hand. The notes are a rough and incomplete summary of the points raised in our conversation; the arguments used by both Göring and myself are presented in some confusion and give no indication of the theme used by either party.

As regards the political background of the conversation, the following facts should be noted.

The Nazi leaders, intoxicated as they were at that time by their easy triumph at Munich, increased their activities in Eastern Europe. In connection with the Hungarian claims to Slovakia and Carpathian Ruthenia, Nazi activities concentrated mainly on the Ukrainian question; Vienna, which was then the headquarters of the Ukrainian terrorists (under the auspices of Himmler), became the center of this agitation in which every form of subversive intrigue and seditious propaganda was fully utilized. The Germans had two objects in bringing the Ukrainian problem to the fore. Firstly, they hoped by preaching the idea of separation of the Ukraine from Russia to injure the USSR; secondly, they thought that by making Carpathian Ruthenia a fictitious focus of Ukrainian nationalism and an unwelcome center of German propaganda on Poland's very doorstep they would be striking an indirect blow at Poland. Czechoslovakia, substantially weakened as a result of Munich, was consequently incapable of coping with German intrigues in so distant a region.

The aim of the Polish government was to stabilize conditions in Central Europe as far as possible. It strove to reduce Hungarian claims to Slovakia. As regards Carpathian Ruthenia, however, Poland favored its return to Hungary, to which country it had belonged before the Treaty of Trianon. Moreover, Polish diplomacy was striving to effect a rapprochement between Bucharest and Budapest.

A common frontier between Poland and Hungary would have formed a considerable obstacle to German ambitions in the east. Accordingly, they were resented in the Wilhelmstrasse.

Ribbentrop had retired in the period following Munich to Bavaria. There he made himself inaccessible to the diplomatic corps in Berlin. Information reached us, however, that he was busy contacting, among others, his Ukrainian agents and that the idea of a joint German-Italian ruling on the territories being disputed by Budapest and Prague was being formed. In the circumstances, I had to approach Göring in order to stress the Polish point of view.

The Soviet ambassador, Mr. Merekalov, was obviously interested in this question. It transpired, from conversations which I had with him at the time, that he was fully aware of the German aims. These events had considerable influence on the Soviet-Polish Declaration, signed in Moscow on November 26, 1938, reaffirming the will of both parties strictly to adhere to the agreements actually reached in the preceding years (for example, the nonaggression pact of 1932).[33]

J. Lipski
former Polish Ambassador in Germany

London, July 6, 1945

[33] See *Polish White Book,* Nos. 160 and 161.

# Ribbentrop Puts Forth Claims to Poland
## *October 24—December 15, 1938*

---

DOCUMENT 124   Note Concerning Ambassador Lipski's Conversation
with Reich Minister of Foreign Affairs von Ribbentrop
*at Berchtesgaden on October 24, 1938*

Polish Embassy in Berlin
*Strictly Confidential*

IN A CONVERSATION on October 24 over luncheon at the Grand Hotel in
Berchtesgaden, at which Herr Hewel was present, Herr von Ribbentrop
put forward to the Polish Ambassador a proposal for a basic settlement
of issues (*Gesamtlösung*) between Poland and Germany which, as he
expressed himself, would remove the causes of future strife. This included the reunion of Danzig with the Reich, while Poland would be
assured of retaining railway and economic facilities there. Poland would
agree to the building of an extraterritorial superhighway and railway line
across Pomerania. In exchange, von Ribbentrop mentioned the possibility of an extension of the Polish-German agreement by twenty-five
years and a guarantee of Polish-German frontiers. As a possible sphere
for future cooperation between the two countries, the German Foreign
Minister specified joint action in colonial matters, the emigration of
Jews from Poland, and a joint policy toward Russia on the basis of the
Anti-Comintern Pact. Herr von Ribbentrop asked the Ambassador to
communicate his suggestions to Minister Beck. He would like to discuss
these matters with him with the Ambassador's participation.

In his reply, Ambassador Lipski referred to the Chancellor's declaration on the Danzig question made to him on November 5, 1937,[1] and
repeated to Minister Beck in Berlin on January 14, 1938.[2]

[1] See Document 73, p. 303.
[2] See Document 77, p. 334.

The Ambassador also pointed to the importance of Danzig as a port for Poland, and repeated the Polish government's principle of noninterference in the internal life of the German population in the Free City, where complete self-government is established.

Finally, the Ambassador stated that he would like to warn von Ribbentrop that he could see no possibility of an agreement involving the reunion of the Free City with the Reich. He concluded by promising to communicate the substance of this conversation to Minister Beck.

After the conversation von Ribbentrop invited the Ambassador again to call on him and, mentioning the issue of the union of Carpathian Ruthenia with Hungary, put to him the question whether he was raising it with the German government as a Polish demand. He added that, if the Polish government agreed to the German concept regarding Danzig and the superhighway, the question of Carpathian Ruthenia could be solved in accordance with Poland's wishes on the matter. Ambassador Lipski answered that his only task was to inform the German government of Poland's attitude in regard to Hungary's demand in Carpathian Ruthenia, since Poland had already informed the Italian government.

The Conversation with Minister of Foreign Affairs von Ribbentrop
*at the Grand Hotel, Berchtesgaden, on October 24, 1938*

October 25, 1938
*Strictly Confidential*

Herr von Ribbentrop invited me for luncheon. The liaison officer between the Auswärtiges Amt and the Reich Chancellery, Herr Hewel, was also present.

I. In the first part of the conversation general issues were discussed, while von Ribbentrop deliberated at length on the international situation preceding the Munich Conference. He declared that he had been convinced all the time that a world war was out of the question. His arguments were based upon a calculation of power; he had been assured that, in case France mobilized, Italy would also mobilize, and if France attacked, Italy would attack France. From his calculations it ensued that in this conflict France would be isolated.

For my part, in the course of these deliberations I pointed to the action of international agencies which had been started on the very day of the Godesberg Conference with a protest lodged by Moscow against Poland.[3] I laid stress on our firm and determined stand on this matter.

## II. Hungary's Revindications

Herr von Ribbentrop exposed at length his personal objections to the Hungarian way of behavior. He recalled that during Horthy's visit the Chancellor quite frankly told the Regent that he had decided to act on the problem of the Sudetenland, and he advised the Hungarians to be ready for any eventuality. During this visit, to the utter surprise of the German government, Kanya showed Ribbentrop a communiqué from Bled,[4] which evidently made the worst possible impression in Berlin. The Hungarian side, during this visit, constantly warned against war entanglements, owing to the Anglo-French stand. It came to Ribbentrop's knowledge that upon their return to Budapest the rumor was spread there that he was conducting a madman's policy. Ribbentrop's resentment centered mainly on Kanya.

He further mentioned that on the eve of the Godesberg Conference the Chancellor invited Imredy to Berchtesgaden and gave him detailed information on the situation.[5] On Imredy's request, the Chancellor firmly supported Hungarian claims at the conference in Munich. Hungarians knew all about this, but not a single word of thanks followed, since they considered that German efforts were self-explanatory.

Next, von Ribbentrop discussed the problem of the German government's mediation. In the conversations with Darányi [6] at Berchtesgaden the Hungarian ethnographic line was discussed. It was established that Bratislava would remain outside the line and that Nitra would be subject to a plebiscite; Koszyce [Kosice] would remain within the Hungarian line, while Uzhorod and Munkacz [Munkacevo] would fall beyond the line (as far as I could understand, they were to be subject to a plebiscite).

Ribbentrop used his influence on Chvalkovský [7] to accept such a

---

[3] See p. 413, note 10.
[4] See p. 380, note 11.
[5] *DGFP*, Series D, Vol. II, No. 554.
[6] Kálmán Darányi, former prime minister (1936–38) and minister of agriculture in Hungary. See his conversation with Hitler and Ribbentrop of October 14 (*ibid.*, Series D, Vol. IV, Nos. 62, 63, and 65).
[7] František Chvalkovský, foreign minister of Czechoslovakia from October, 1938, to March 1939. See the Ribbentrop-Chvalkovský and the Hitler-Chvalkovský conversations, *ibid.*, Nos. 55 and 61.

Hungarian line and discussed it also with the Slovaks and representatives of Carpathian Ruthenia.[8]

The Slovaks were hurt by the Koszyce question; the representative of Carpathian Ruthenia was rather pleased that Uzhorod and Munkacz had been left outside the line of claims.

Ribbentrop emphasized here that he did not take any sides and was acting merely as a mediator.

When the results of these conversations were communicated to Budapest by Erdmannsdorf,[9] the Hungarian government bluntly rejected the proposal, in spite of Darányi's earlier approval. Under these circumstances the German government withdrew from mediation and washed its hands of the matter. The Italian side, informed about this, is allegedly also discouraged to some extent by the Hungarian methods.

Ribbentrop is of the opinion that, as matters stand, talks will continue for the time being between Budapest and Prague.

Asked about arbitration, he replied that at present he does not think arbitration could take place; besides, he raises the following objections:

1) Whether, with two other signatories of the Munich Agreement, arbitration with the participation of Germany and Italy would be possible.

2) In case of arbitration, its execution should be guaranteed. Here a military engagement would possibly be needed.

For my part, in accordance with my instructions, I only stated that, in case Germany and Italy agree on arbitration, Poland would join it also.

In my discussion with Ribbentrop I laid special detailed emphasis on our stand regarding the Polish-Hungarian frontier and Carpathian Ruthenia. I am not repeating my arguments here. I think that Ribbentrop was impressed by the Ukrainian argument contained in your instructions.[10] In conclusion he said that he would still reconsider this matter in the light of my deliberations. He asked whether we had territorial claims to Ruthenia; I replied that we did not, that we limited ourselves to support of Hungarian claims to that country.

Ribbentrop pointed here to difficulties created by Rumania's attitude, stressing the Reich's desire to maintain good relations with that country.

[8] *Ibid.*, Nos. 72 and 73.
[9] Otto von Erdmannsdorf, German minister in Hungary. See his report of October 20, 1938, *ibid.*, No. 75.
[10] Point 2 of Beck's instructions of October 20 (see Document 120, pp. 446–47).

He was also informed that Rumania does not insist on a territorial revision in Carpathian Ruthenia to its advantage.

I told him of certain details of your conversations at Galati, showing the contrast between the King's attitude and Comnen's policy.

### III. German-French Rapprochement

Ribbentrop mentioned that a desire for a rapprochement might be felt on this sector. He referred to the fact that the Chancellor spoke along these lines to Ambassador François-Poncet and that a certain document, similar to the Hitler-Chamberlain declaration, might be expected.[11] He also mentioned the twenty-five-year nonaggression pact. However, he added that all this is not for immediate action, and that an exchange of opinion with England and Italy must take first place. Here he made the reservation that this agreement should not be considered a sort of Four-Power Pact, since it would only be a bilateral German-French understanding.

### IV. General Policy

With regard to general policy, Ribbentrop dwelt on Germany's general endeavors to enter a phase of peaceful development. He pointed to the Chancellor's declaration that he has no further territorial claims.[12]

With regard to *colonial* problems, he remarked that this matter is becoming a reality, and that Germany will consistently strive to achieve its demands.

He laid special stress on the Japanese victory in China as a point detrimental to the British position.

### V. Military Matters

He mentioned in brief a new system of German fortifications in the west constructed in accordance with Todt's system, which, in his opinion, is superior to the construction of the Maginot Line. Allegedly trials on the Sudetenland line built on the French model showed that a heavy caliber German shell breaks through such fortifications.

[11] For the text, see *DGFP*, Series D, Vol. II, No. 676.

[12] In his speech at Saarbrücken on October 9, Hitler said: "As a strong state we are prepared at any time for a policy of understanding with our neighbors. We have no demands on them. All we want is peace."

### VI. Polish Matters

Ribbentrop stressed that in conversations with him the Chancellor kept returning to his idea of finding a solution to the Jewish problem through an organization for the purpose of emigration. We had an exhaustive talk on this subject. Ribbentrop interrogated me at length on the Jewish situation in Poland.

Speaking about our action with regard to Teschen, Ribbentrop remarked that the Chancellor repeated again and again to the circle of his collaborators his appreciation for our determined move, stating: "The Poles are tough guys. Piłsudski would be proud of them."

*Józef Lipski*

The problem of Ribbentrop's suggestion (*Gesamtlösung*) was referred to the Minister in my personal letter.

J.L.[13]

On October 31 instructions were prepared in Warsaw for Ambassador Lipski; however, he could not execute them until November 19. These instructions are published in the *Polish White Book*, No. 45 (pp. 48–50), but in paragraph 2 the following sentence is missing:

"On the other hand, our determined attitude in the period of final tensions, when Poland did not join in the international anti-German action on a large scale, was the best proof of the Polish government's loyal intentions." [14]

On November 2 arbitration took place in Vienna (the Vienna Award) between Hungary and Czechoslovakia in connection with the transferral to Hungary of Czechoslovak territory and the delimitation of new frontiers. Minister Ribbentrop and Minister Ciano served in the capacity of arbitrators.

[13] A copy of this letter is missing from Lipski's documents. After his conversation with Ribbentrop at Berchtesgaden, Lipski immediately proceeded to Warsaw to report on it to Beck. On October 29 he discussed this matter "d'une façon assez pessimiste" with Szembek (*Journal*, p. 366).

For the German version of this portion of the conversation, *see DGFP*, Series D, Vol. V, No. 81, pp. 104–7. In the *Polish White Book*, No. 44, this conversation is published in the form of Lipski's letter to Beck, and not as a note.

[14] H. Batowski is wrong in stating that "the translated text published in the *Polish White Book*, No. 45, is a full and exact translation of the Polish original." (Batowski, *Kryzys dyplomatyczny w Europie*, p. 147, note 36.)

DOCUMENT 125   Lipski to Beck

NO. N/1/223/38                                        November 9, 1938
                                                      *Strictly Confidential*

From my conversation with the Italian Ambassador I learned many
details concerning the Vienna Award. With the reservation that his report was confidential, he disclosed to me that, although in Rome Ciano
and Ribbentrop agreed to concede Uzhorod and Munkacz to Hungary,
the German side changed its mind on the eve of the arbitration, raising
objections against the Hungarian demands regarding these cities. The
German government used the argument that, since the countries of the
Berlin-Rome Axis were acting for the first time before international
public opinion in the role of arbitrators, any hint of bias should be
avoided. However, in Vienna Ciano categorically stood by the Rome
agreement to concede Uzhorod and Munkacz to Hungary. According to
Signor Attolico, nothing more could be obtained, particularly since the
Hungarians were in very bad form for negotiations. For instance, from
Carpathian Ruthenia not a single petition of the population for union
with Hungary had been forwarded to the arbitrators.

Answering my question, the Ambassador explained that, besides the
establishment of an ethnographic line, nothing had been settled in
Vienna, not even the possible guarantee for Czechoslovakia.

In Signor Attolico's opinion, upon its being separated from Uzhorod
and Munkacz, Ruthenia would face an acute problem in the future.
However, he thinks that in view of the tension accumulating at present
on this problem, especially on the part of the German government, a
public discussion of this matter, in the form of press polemics, such as is
taking place in Poland, would be harmful rather than useful for the
future realization of the common Polish-Hungarian frontier. For the
German government it is a matter of prestige, with Berlin engaged as
arbiter in Vienna.

As far as the guarantee for Czechoslovakia is concerned, Signor Attolico thinks that, if Berlin reached final agreement with Czechoslovakia
in particular fields and Prague would require a guarantee, the Reich
government would probably grant it. That is why the Ambassador would
prefer to press that the guarantee problem be postponed, rather than
settle for prompt action. In accordance with this information, under the

present changed circumstances the British government shows considerably less interest in the guarantee and is rather unwilling to grant it. This might be a sort of argument for Berlin.

When our conversation turned to Rumania, the Ambassador agreed with me that the Rumanian government, owing to Comnen's erroneous appraisal of the situation, has taken a negative stand toward the common Polish-Hungarian frontier. The Rumanians will not avail themselves of this occasion to improve their relations with Budapest with the help of Poland and Italy.

In the opinion of the Ambassador, it would be advisable to wait until after the visit of the Rumanian King to London. That visit is absorbing the monarch and his entourage to such an extent that any steps on the part of Rome and Warsaw in Bucharest should be undertaken only after this visit.

In connection with the above conversation and the [Polish] Ministry's telegram of the 7th inst. reporting on the alleged communication by the Reich government to the Hungarian government that it regards the Vienna Award as a final settlement of the Hungarian-Czechoslovakian frontier problem, and that it is interested that Czechoslovakia should remain within the frontiers established in Vienna, I would like to state that such a declaration is in conformity with official statements by the German authorities. May I recall here a fragment of Foreign Minister Ribbentrop's speech delivered on the 8th inst. at the banquet for the foreign press, which reads as follows:

"The arbitration decision which was pronounced by Italian Foreign Minister Count Ciano and myself, after the most thorough consideration and the most careful weighing of all interests involved, has now finally determined the frontier between Hungary and Czechoslovakia on the basis of ethnography."

This, in my opinion, does not actually preclude the possibility that the rest of Carpathian Ruthenia left outside Hungary could not be dealt with in the future. However, the approach to this problem from the propaganda angle should, in my opinion, be somewhat altered and cannot be based on the claim for a common Polish-Hungarian frontier, for this argument contradicts the arbitration based upon ethnographical ground. As far as this place [Berlin] is concerned, the problem could be more successfully promoted if it originated from the real internal development of the situation in Carpathian Ruthenia. As a matter of fact, I would not be surprised if, in spite of the present situation, the problem of Ruthenia, especially with the growing Ukrainian activity within the territory, would in the future return to haunt Bucharest and force the course of its tactics accordingly. Some outpourings made to me by Mr. George Bratianu would confirm such a point of view.

Finally, I would like to call your attention to the passage of von Ribbentrop's speech of the 8th inst. regarding the Reich's relations with Czechoslovakia, which reads as follows:

"If, following the final delineation of its frontier, the Czechoslovak government is ready to recognize fully the new reality and adopt a completely new orientation in its policy toward Germany, a reconciliation with this state, as well as a final settlement between the two nations, is possible."

From this declaration it might be deduced that the Reich's possible guarantee to Czechoslovakia would depend on a previous basic agreement of these states between themselves and the dissolution by Prague of the network of its present alliances.

*Józef Lipski*

On October 15 a decree of the Minister of the Interior, dated October 6 and issued jointly with the Minister of Foreign Affairs, was published in Poland in connection with the establishment abroad of a one-day control of Polish foreign passports.[15] This order went into effect on October 29 (the date for the control was later postponed until November 15).

Controlled passports received a pertinent annotation by Polish consulates. In cases in which circumstances might call for a revocation of citizenship, the consul could refuse the annotation, thus depriving the owner of a Polish passport of the possibility of crossing the Polish frontier.

In connection with the territory of Germany this problem could involve many thousands of Jews, formally Polish citizens, who, often having no connection with Poland whatsoever, could not obtain from the consuls the annotation indispensable for crossing the Polish frontier. Therefore, the Auswärtiges Amt strongly protested against this order, fearing that thousands of Jews who did not register in the period discussed would lose their right to return to Poland and would remain in Germany permanently. At the same time the A.A. informed the Polish government that the German authorities would start immediately to expel Jews from Germany.[16]

[15] *Dziennik Ustaw Rzeczpospolitej Polskiej*, 1938, No. 80, item 543.
[16] *DGFP*, Series D, Vol. V, No. 84. For Polish explanations, see *ibid.*, Nos. 88, 89, and 91; also *Journal*, pp. 363–65 and 374–75.

According to German calculations, by October 29, 17,000 Jews, citizens of Poland, were expelled from Germany and forced to cross the Polish frontier. Polish authorities threatened retaliations and the expulsion of the same number of Germans.

Under these circumstances Polish-German negotiations were started on November 2 in Berlin [17] with the participation of Lipski, who was later replaced by Counselor Lubomirski. This was a period of an extremely violent anti-Semitic drive in Germany, culminating in pogroms of Jews on November 8 and 9. These pogroms, inspired by governmental circles, were connected with the assassination in Paris of a German diplomat, Ernst vom Rath, by a young Polish Jew, Hershel Grynszpan, whose parents were expelled from Germany at that time.

Polish-German talks on this matter were concluded with a provisional agreement on January 24, 1939.[18] Jews expelled in October could return for the time being to Germany in order to liquidate their financial affairs.

DOCUMENT 126   Lipski to Beck

Berlin, November 12, 1938
(Personal)
*Strictly Confidential*

1. With reference to my handwritten letter of November 5, I am taking the liberty of communicating to you that until now my planned meeting with the foreign minister of the Reich, von Ribbentrop, has not taken place. I would like to recall that on the eve of the Vienna Award, on November 1, I announced at the secretariat of the Minister of Foreign Affairs my return from Warsaw, stating that I was at the disposal of Herr von Ribbentrop. I repeated the same thing to Secretary of State von Weizsäcker on November 3, as well as to Ambassador von Moltke. At the banquet for the foreign press on November 7, von Ribbentrop was present, but he left for Munich immediately after dinner to attend a celebration to be held there on November 8 and 9. I had no opportunity for an exchange of opinion, and the Minister only told me in passing that he would be back in Berlin from November 10 on. This was confirmed by his secretary, on his own initiative, with the explanation that owing to the many travels of the Minister lately it was impossible to fix a

[17] *DGFP*, Series D, Vol. V, Nos. 92, 95, and 107.
[18] *Ibid.*, No. 127.

meeting, but that the conversation could be arranged for November 11 or 12.

In the meantime, as I was informed, Herr von Ribbentrop, who returned just for a short while to the capital, left Berlin again, I believe, on November 10.

Of course, I do not deem it necessary that I press for this conversation, especially since Ribbentrop's initiative made to me at Berchtesgaden came from the German side. It also seems to me impossible to discuss the subjects raised at Berchtesgaden with any other official, unless I described in detail to von Ribbentrop the stand of the Polish government on this whole problem. Here I make the only exception for Herr von Moltke, who was the first to bring up the topic of Danzig in a conversation with me. As the ambassador accredited to us, he should have authoritative information on what limits beyond which we cannot go in this matter.

Considering the tactics applied by Herr von Ribbentrop, I must first of all mention that he is an unreachable minister for all diplomatic representatives accredited here. I was told yesterday by the American Ambassador that he has to leave for the United States to report to Roosevelt, and he has been vainly hunting for Ribbentrop for six weeks.

As far as our problem is concerned, I think that, following your interview, the position Chodacki [19] took toward Greiser, and certain explanations of Moltke, Ribbentrop must realize that our answer with regard to Danzig will not be a positive one. Possibly, in view of the unclear situation with regard to the Western states, he is not too anxious to start conversations with us, or possibly he would like to open them at a more convenient moment for the Reich government. The way in which both the Chancellor in his speeches and the local press here treated French-German relations for some time shows a desire to bring about a relaxation on that sector first of all.

Negotiations with Poland are possibly planned for a time following the finalization of an agreement with France.

It is rather characteristic that since the Munich Conference Polish-German relations have not improved but are considerably cooler.

All recent declarations of the Chancellor are openly unfriendly toward England; in spite of the fact that he is attacking the opposition, the

[19] Marian Chodacki, commissioner-general of the Polish government in Danzig from February, 1936, to September 1, 1939.

method he is using is nevertheless making it far from easy for Chamberlain to carry out his policy of rapprochement with the Reich.

I think that the recent anti-Jewish excesses on the whole territory of Germany, which reached hitherto unprecedented dimensions and could not be attributed to a mob impulse, since they were organized by Party organs, will further deepen the controversies existing between the Germany of the present era and the Anglo-Saxon world.

I am at a loss to judge whether these events will render difficult M. Daladier's policy of rapprochement with the Reich. Nevertheless, observing from this locality at a moment of a certain rapprochement between Paris and Berlin, any apparent improvement in the attitude of France toward Poland would be a very positive element for us in Berlin.

Information is reaching me from French industrial circles that their attitude toward Poland has considerably improved. These spheres call attention to the fact that at present, when Russian prestige has waned in Paris, it would be possible, through the use of material means, to influence the French press to write in a pro-Polish spirit, thus winning over wider circles of public opinion for us.

2. Our negotiations on Jewish matters, upon a definition of our common stand and to some extent a balancing of opinions, were arrested for lack of decision by competent German authorities. It is necessary to stress that the atmosphere created about the Jewish problem is weighing heavily on the German negotiators, including high-ranking officials who are simply anxious to save their own skins. I therefore think that a certain dose of patience is needed, all the more so since our decree and orders have remained in force.

I gave an order to the consulates that Jewish passports are very rarely to be stamped; beginning with November 15, when the *sursis* granted in Warsaw expires with regard to the revocation of citizenship, energetic action should be taken in the execution of this law.

Finally, I am taking the liberty of also calling your attention to the Ukrainian problem, and to its aspect now developing in the local territory.

Upon the occupation of Vienna, the local Ukrainian headquarters were transferred to the Reich. They consisted in the majority of groups of the Konowalec type, whose active character pushed them to the front line. A number of local organizations are dealing with Ukrainian matters, for instance, Ribbentrop's office, Rosenberg's office, certain offices of the Propaganda Ministry, and, last but not least, the German Intelligence Service. All these elements, as far as can be observed, at present lack a precise directive from the top as to the line to follow in such a complicated affair. But they are bursting with dynamism, and the groups most harmful to us, such as the Jaryj and Melnyk type, are taking advantage of this atmosphere. I conversed today with Professor Smal-Stocki, who is to report his observations to Director Kobylański.[20] For my part, I would only like to ask for your opinion whether, when the occasion presents itself, I should not take this matter up in more detail with high-ranking German officials, for instance with von Ribbentrop or Göring, in order to establish our point of view, for with some young, inexperienced leaders here the conviction is growing that the Ukrainian problem might be solved even without Poland, and the idea of penetration via Carpathian Ruthenia and Rumania is being inseminated. These, of course, are utopian ideas but, nevertheless, being presented by Ukrainian elements hostile to us, they might result in serious friction with Germany on the Ukrainian problem.

*Józef Lipski*

DOCUMENT 127  Lipski to Beck

Berlin, November 19, 1938
*Strictly Confidential*

In accordance with the conclusions contained in my letter to you dated November 12, I did not take any further steps to hasten my conversation with the Reich minister of foreign affairs, Herr von Ribbentrop.

On November 18 I was informed that Herr Ribbentrop would receive me at the Auswärtiges Amt on the 19th inst. at 12:30 P.M.

The conversation took the following course:

Herr von Ribbentrop opened the conversation by remarking that since our last meeting at Berchtesgaden on October 24 he has had no opportunity to see me because he was constantly traveling, and lately he

---

[20] Roman Smal-Stocki, professor of Warsaw University, secretary of the Ukrainian Institute in Poland. See his conversation with Szembek upon his return from Germany (*Journal,* pp. 376–78).

Tadeusz Kobylański, chief of the Eastern Division of the Polish Ministry of Foreign Affairs.

was absorbed in the problem of the assassination of the secretary of the Embassy in Paris, vom Rath.

I only mentioned that upon my return from Warsaw I called at the secretariat of the Minister, announcing that I was ready to meet him.

Next, in accordance with your instructions contained in your letter of October 31, I informed von Ribbentrop that I had acquainted you with his suggestion (*Anregung*) made at Berchtesgaden regarding a Polish-German agreement which would finally stabilize mutual relations between the two countries, and that you had requested me to communicate our attitude in answer.

To give greater weight to my arguments I availed myself of my written instructions, and exactly and emphatically communicated their contents to the Reich Minister of Foreign Affairs. Herr von Ribbentrop listened attentively to my exposition without discussing particular points.

I noticed that he was impressed by my statement that any tendency to incorporate the Free City into the Reich must inevitably lead to a conflict, not of a local character only, but one also jeopardizing Polish-German relations in their entirety. I concluded my exposition by quoting Marshal Piłsudski's opinion that the Danzig question would constitute a criterion for evaluating Germany's relations to Poland, adding a number of other explanations of a general nature.

In his reply Herr von Ribbentrop stated that the Reich desired to maintain the best possible relations with Poland, just as it did with Italy, and assured me that all his emphasis was in this direction. In a very friendly tone he stated that it was his desire to hold conversations with Poland, not in a diplomatic manner, but entirely as between friends, frankly and openly. He remarked that he had just conversed with the newly appointed French Ambassador, using diplomatic language.

Referring to the idea contained in your instructions, he stated that during the Czechoslovak crisis Polish-German relations stood the test to the advantage of both parties. Poland's determined attitude helped the Germans to achieve their demands while German action enabled Poland to recover Teschen Silesia. Here Herr von Ribbentrop was discursive, reverting to the history of the last crisis, and repeating a statement already known to me that in the political constellation of that time France was actually isolated and that he was all the time convinced that neither France nor England would move to the defense of Czechoslovakia. A certain *novum* was his explanation that a meeting of foreign ministers of the Reich and Italy had been planned, for the day the conference of Munich was later held, to be attended by Generals von Keitel and Pariani also, in order to establish common military action in case of an armed conflict of Germany with the Western Powers. Von Ribbentrop quoted this detail to me in order to stress that the Reich could absolutely count on Italy's military aid. The fact that the Italian and German General Staffs were to meet only on the day of Germany's mobilization would, in my opinion, point to the lack of a basic coordination for the event of war. Herr von Ribbentrop emphasized in his further deliberations Germany's military superiority at that time, remarking that at present the situation has become even more favorable for the Reich.

Reverting to Polish-German relations, von Ribbentrop emphasized that he would like to know that Germany conceived of relations with Poland on a very broad political plane, and that he had no intention of simply raising one question after another with Poland. He added that negotiations with Poland were of quite a different character from those with Mr. Beneš for Czechoslovakia. In the course of his argumentation he declared that for years you had been pursuing a definite and consistent course in Polish foreign affairs. I replied that, if the Reich conceived of its policy toward Poland on broad lines, then I had no fear as to our relations. Von Ribbentrop said that in any case he had more than once confirmed this in his conversations with me.

Von Ribbentrop then explained how the suggestion he had communicated to me at Berchtesgaden had arisen: taking as basis the Chancellor's conviction as to the necessity for maintaining the best of relations with Poland, which was a fundamental principle in Reich policy, he had been trying to find a solution which would completely stabilize the situation. He had talked only indefinitely (he used the word "vaguement") with the Chancellor on the subject, and on the basis that Danzig was a German city he had himself put forward his suggestions. (It was worthy of note that von Ribbentrop discreetly gave it to be understood that he was responsible for the initiative in this matter, leaving the Chancellor out of it.)

He returned again and again to his explanation that his sole desire was to achieve stabilized relations and that he had sought for a solution for this reason. He alluded to the interview you gave to the Hearst representative,[21] which he understood as the adoption of a negative

---

[21] Beck's interview given to Mr. Hillmar of the Hearst Press on October 29, 1938 (see *Polish White Book,* No. 46, p. 51).

attitude on the matter, and he revealed some disappointment that this had been done in a public statement. I said nothing to this. He also mentioned that he would gladly have a talk with you.

We discussed the Danzig question itself in general terms only. When he reverted to my statement that any tendency to incorporate Danzig into the Reich would lead to a conflict in Polish-German relations, I reaffirmed it most decisively. I added that the Danzig question was most irritating for our public opinion, the more so since we have made such great concessions to Danzig in respect of freedom of development for the German population and choice of their own form of government. I did not fail to mention the irritation caused by the activities of chauvinistic party elements, and specified Mr. Forster. With reference to our conception of the matter, I quoted Chancellor Hitler's words in his Reichstag speech on February 21, 1938. When speaking of Danzig, he said: "The Polish state respects national relations in that city, and that city and Germany respect the rights of Poland."

With regard to our suggestion of a Polish-German agreement guaranteeing the existence of the Free City, von Ribbentrop indicated that he could not express an opinion, and that he must study further and reflect still more on this whole problem in the light of my statement. Incidentally, he mentioned that apparently new irritation had arisen in Danzig in connection with postboxes, and asked me to raise the matter in Warsaw.

In the course of the conversation von Ribbentrop asked me what our attitude was with respect to the superhighway. I replied that my discussion in Warsaw had been primarily concerned with the Danzig question, so I could not give him any definite answer on this point. I simply expressed my personal belief that it might be possible to find a solution.

In its further course the conversation dealt with the Jewish problem; the Minister sharply criticized the attitude of the American government and President Roosevelt, pointing to the summoning of Ambassador von Dieckhoff to Washington.[22] He expressed his deep conviction that there would be anti-Semitic outbursts in America in the future, and that those now ruling the country would pay heavily for this. In his opinion the real power in the United States is lodged neither with the government nor the city but with the farmers. I availed myself of the discussion on this

[22] The American Ambassador in Berlin had been summoned to Washington and left Berlin on November 17.

subject to recall to the Minister that the Polish delegation in Warsaw for negotiations with the Reich on the Jewish problem is awaiting a reply from the German side in order to conclude the negotiations. The Minister promised to have this matter investigated.

Herr von Ribbentrop is leaving for Berchtesgaden in connection with the credentials to be presented to the Chancellor on Monday and Tuesday by a number of ambassadors and envoys, among others, the Belgian and French ambassadors.

Presentation of credentials at Berchtesgaden is explained by the fact that owing to the reconstruction of the Reich Chancellery in Berlin there are no adequate premises in the capital for these receptions.[23]

*Józef Lipski*

Immediately after his conversation with Ribbentrop, Lipski proceeded to Warsaw to report on it to Beck and Szembek.[24] The Danzig question came to the forefront. At that time Beck invited to Warsaw the high commissioner of the League of Nations in Danzig, Professor Burckhardt, in order to converse with him.[25] On November 22 Beck had a conversation with Ambassador von Moltke.[26] Lipski returned to Berlin with Beck's instructions to continue talks on the Danzig problem.

At that time, Poland conducted a series of exploratory conversations with Soviet Russia, with whom relations had deteriorated during the Munich period. A joint communiqué was published on November 26, stressing the durability of the contracted agreements between the two countries, including the nonaggression pact of 1932, and announcing an expansion of trade relations.[27]

In his report of December 3, Lipski informed Beck about his conversation with Ribbentrop.

[23] The *Polish White Book* published this report of Lipski with certain omissions (No. 46). For the German version, see *DGFP*, Series D, Vol. V, No. 101, pp. 127–29.

[24] For the Szembek-Lipski conversation on November 22, see *Journal*, pp. 379–80.

[25] For the conspectus, see *DGFP*, Series D, Vol. V, No. 102. See also Burckhardt, pp. 256–57.

[26] For Beck's note, see *Polish White Book*, No. 47; for Moltke's report, *DGFP*, Series D, Vol. V, No. 104, wherefrom, however, Danzig problems were omitted.

[27] *Polish White Book*, No. 160; see also the reports of Schulenburg, German ambassador to Moscow, to the A.A. of December 3, *DGFP*, Series D, Vol. V, No. 108, and von Moltke's reports of November 27, *ibid.*, No. 105.

DOCUMENT 128   Lipski to Beck

NO. N/1/243/38                              Berlin, December 3, 1938
                                            *Secret*

Following your instructions of November 25, No. P. I/MOR/386, with
regard to Danzig, on November 30 I asked to be received by the Foreign
Minister of the Reich. I had a conversation with him on Friday, December 2.

Unwilling to keep the discussion exclusively on the subject of Danzig
(I sent my report dated December 2, No. G/3/112/38,[28] on this subject), on this occasion I raised several other topics in the international
field. Since, in spite of the generally correct attitude taken by the German press, I could note a certain disorientation in local official circles
regarding the recently published Polish-Soviet communiqué, I availed
myself of this occasion to explain it to the Minister of Foreign Affairs of
the Reich, in accordance with your instructions telegraphed to me on
November 28. I deemed the occasion to be even more expedient, bearing in mind that von Ribbentrop, as the chief author of Anti-Comintern
agreements with Japan and Italy, might be a bit touchy about the communiqué, inasmuch as twice already since this spring he came out with
the suggestion that Poland should make up its mind to join this
agreement.

Upon stating that the Polish-Soviet communiqué has been repeatedly
misinterpreted and presented under a false aspect by the international
press, I added that I would like to make a few comments on it.

I recalled that tension entered Polish-Soviet relations in connection
with the Czechoslovak crisis, taking the form of military demonstrations, overflight of Polish territory by Soviet planes, our counteraction to
this, frontier incidents, etc. I added that this situation was obviously
aggravating and could not persist. The Polish-Soviet communiqué is
nothing but a reversion to the previous state of affairs, based upon the
nonaggression agreement. Also, normal trade transactions are under
way again in the economic field, as they were prior to the tension in
Polish-Soviet relations. Finally, some incidents are being liquidated.

Herr von Ribbentrop gave me to understand that he sees our position
in this matter. He simply expressed some regret that I had not informed

---

[28] This report is missing from Lipski's papers.

him in due time about it, since the communiqué came as a surprise and
he could not give adequate information to the Chancellor. He made a
slight allusion to the fact that, if only with regard to its three million
Jews as colporters of Communism, Poland should not be very much
interested in getting too close to Moscow. Here I pointed out that lately
Poland's internal situation shows a strong consolidation of national
forces and increasing executive power. I took some time to throw more
light on this point.

Herr von Ribbentrop here laid some extra pressure, as he had also
during this conversation with regard to another point, on the fact that
the Reich is very much interested that Poland should be as strong a
barrier as possible against Bolshevism.

From this subject he passed to the internal situation of France, remarking that in spite of Daladier's considerable victory the French situation cannot be regarded as stabilized. On the contrary, he still foresees
strong attacks from the left wing inspired by the Comintern. He added
that it has come to his knowledge that the Comintern has opened a new
central office. I agreed that Communist activity continues to act vigorously outside of Russia.

Next, I inquired about the results of conversations with the Rumanian
King.[29] Herr von Ribbentrop gave me the following explanation:

The Chancellor allegedly raised the question of Rumania's relations
with the Soviets. King Carol pointed to his anti-Soviet attitude; however,
he made the reservation that Rumania, as a country smaller than the
Reich and a neighbor of Russia, must act with more prudence in this
respect than Germany. Here the King referred to the Polish-Rumanian
alliance.

The necessity of closer economic ties between Germany and Rumania
was also discussed. I know that the King had special conversations with
General Field Marshal Göring on these problems in Leipzig. Therefore,
von Ribbentrop did not give me more extensive details on this matter.
To my question about the news which had appeared in the press about
the supposed plans to construct a pipeline for Rumanian oil, von Ribbentrop replied that he considers it a fantastic and unreal idea. However, he might still ask Göring about it. I think that, with regard to
German-Rumanian economic relations, I might get some more details on

[29] During a private visit of King Carol in Germany he had, in Ribbentrop's
presence, a conversation with Hitler on November 24 (*DGFP,* Series D, Vol. V,
No. 254), and on November 30 a conversation with Göring (*ibid.,* No. 257).

December 6, at the hunting party at Springe which Göring will attend.

Finally Herr von Ribbentrop told me that the assassination of Codreanu and his associates [30] made a most unfavorable impression in German circles. It is beyond conception how national leaders could be murdered in such a way. Von Ribbentrop let it be understood that German spheres are wondering whether this step was taken with King Carol's blessing.

On the occasion of the conversation about the visit of the Rumanian King, Herr von Ribbentrop brought up the question of Hungarian claims. He sharply criticized Mr. Kanya's tactics, while he laid special stress on the recent attempts to interpret falsely the German declaration to Rome. He remarked that two weeks after the Vienna Award, to which the parties agreed and which, even in Mussolini's opinion, gave 95 percent to the Hungarian side, Hungary suddenly, without consulting Germany, tried to campaign for the remaining 5 percent. Von Ribbentrop naturally criticized the Hungarians for their slowness in the past, and for being misinformed by Darányi at Berchtesgaden with regard to Munkacz and Uzhorod.[31]

He told me that, naturally, a negative attitude could be detected in the Rumanian King toward Hungarian demands, but the German side did not inform the King about the note sent by the German and Italian governments to Budapest, about which the Polish government had also been advised.[32]

From von Ribbentrop's words I could not detect any change in attitude regarding problems of Carpathian Ruthenia, which was to be expected after what General Field Marshal Göring told General Fabrycy. It was only characteristic that he underlined the fact that immediately after the arbitration Hungary wanted to take action on Carpathian Ruthenia.[33]

*Józef Lipski*

[30] Corneliu Codreanu, founder of the Legion of the Archangel Michael, and in 1931 of the Iron Guard, was assassinated on November 30, 1938, together with thirteen members of the Iron Guard.

[31] For the occupation by Hungary of territories of Carpathian Ruthenia on November 20, see *DGFP*, Series D, Vol. IV, Nos. 128, 129, 131, 132, 133, and 134. With reference to Darányi, see Document 124, pp. 455-56.

[32] *Ibid.*, No. 132.

[33] For Ribbentrop's version of this conversation, see *ibid.*, Series D, Vol. V, No. 106.

DOCUMENT 129 Lipski to Beck

NO. 1/246/38 Berlin, December 7, 1938
*Strictly Confidential*

Referring to my report of December 3, No. 1/244/38, I would like to communicate that tension developed in German-Rumanian relations in connection with the assassination of Codreanu and his associates. According to information from confidential sources, during King Carol's visit to Berchtesgaden the Chancellor allegedly remarked that in Germany, if a patriotic national leader like Codreanu were deprived of freedom for his activities, he would certainly be taken to a fortress and not to a prison. To this remark King Carol is said to have replied that the prison regimen of Codreanu was not too onerous. A few days later news came that Codreanu had been shot, and thereafter the Chancellor allegedly ordered Germans who were recipients of Rumanian decorations on the occasion of King Carol's visit to Germany not to wear these decorations.[34] Besides, the Chancellor adopted an utterly negative attitude toward Rumania since, in his opinion, Codreanu's assassination would have terrible repercussions on Rumania's internal situation and cohesion. This information explains why during our conversation on Friday, December 2, von Ribbentrop repeatedly asked himself whether the King was really informed about the fact that Codreanu had been shot. As other adherents of the Iron Guard movement were later also executed, no doubt remains that they must have been removed with the King's knowledge.

This might also explain why the German press, at first restrained and only repeating rumors which had appeared on this subject in other countries, including Poland, has taken a much sharper tone in the last few days. *Der Angriff* of December 6 brings a paraphrased assault on the King under the title: "The Story about the King and His Jewish Mistress." Against the background of the internal German situation it tries to explain that Codreanu's assassination was perpetrated on the instigation of international Jewry.

The Rumanian Envoy here was to intervene in connection with the *Angriff* article and the press campaign.[35]

[34] See *ibid.*, No. 261, footnote.
[35] See also the report of the German Legation at Bucharest of December 4 (*ibid.*, No. 260).

I think that the above events will weigh heavily on the personal relations of the King with Hitler and the leading elements of the Reich for some time. Nevertheless, it should not be forgotten that at present, after the solution of the Czechoslovak problem, competent German spheres are very much interested in Rumania as a result of the desire to control the Danube basin economically. Rumania, with its natural resources (grain, oil) and since it controls the Danube outlet into the Black Sea, has particular attraction for Germany. On the other hand, it borders on the Soviet Union, and specifically on the geographical line of Russia at which German expansion is aiming. That is why, in spite of a temporary tension, Germany will not cease in its endeavors to penetrate into Rumania. Collaboration would only be jeopardized by a deeper crisis in the internal Rumanian situation, which would possibly take place as a result of a struggle with the Iron Guard.

*Józef Lipski*

On December 8 Beck sent another set of instructions to Lipski in connection with his continued conversations with Ribbentrop. The text of these instructions is missing from Lipski's papers, as well as from the archives of the Ministry of Foreign Affairs in Warsaw; [36] however, in Szembek's *Journal*, under the date of December 7, there is a fairly accurate text for, as Szembek writes, Beck dictated it to him.[37]

"He [Beck] outlined his opinion on Ribbentrop and on the interior situation of Germany. He stated that the principles of the pact of 1934 had withstood the impact of recent events. However, today misunderstandings were occurring between us and the Germans; it would be necessary to clarify and dismiss them by direct contact between Beck and Ribbentrop. (Addressing me directly, Beck stressed that this seemed to him of even more importance because Ribbentrop had made some advancements to us, to which, as a matter of fact, we did not respond.) Lipski should invite Ribbentrop to come to Warsaw. This visit must not be just a courtesy visit. The question of Danzig would have to be approached, as well as the question of a declaration with regard to frontiers and the prolongation of the 1934 pact. Lipski would have to make a previous survey of all these problems with Ribbentrop. As far as Danzig was concerned, our *desiderata minima* would be that Hitler repeat his declaration according to which the question of the Free City could not constitute a cause for a conflict in Polish-German relations. Lipski could show some approbation for the highway, but unofficially, while chatting with

[36] Batowski, *Kryzys dyplomatyczny w Europie*, p. 152.
[37] *Journal*, p. 385.

Ribbentrop, stressing at the same time that this affair would be of no avail to the Danzig question. Lipski should not enter upon other subjects with the German minister that would otherwise become the object of conversation for the two ministers. The starting point of Lipski's conversation with Ribbentrop should be that none of our political activities were directed against the vital interests of Germany."

Lipski refused to execute these instructions, and Beck was annoyed by this.[38]

A few days later Lipski explained this matter to Szembek: [39]

"He [Lipski] explained to me why he thought it impossible to execute—in the way they were meant—the latest instructions of Beck. The questions that were being pushed to the front had recently been discussed many times between Lipski and the German government. Lipski was persuaded that Ribbentrop would come to Warsaw, but he judged that the ground should be prepared in advance. Hitler would like, so it seemed, to see Beck."

This attitude of Lipski prompted his being summoned to Warsaw in order to achieve an agreement on a *démarche* toward Ribbentrop. Lipski spent a few days in Warsaw and returned to Berlin on December 14 with new instructions for his conversation with Ribbentrop.

In November a new conflict arose between Danzig and Poland in connection with Poland's issuing of commemorative postage stamps on November 11 on the occasion of the twentieth anniversary of Poland's rebirth. In this series there was a 15-grosz stamp representing King Jagiełło and Queen Jadwiga, at whose feet two crossed swords were laid as symbols of Poland's victory over the Teutonic Knights at Tannenberg (Grunwald) in 1410. Also, a series of four stamps was issued bearing the inscriptions "Polish Post—Port of Danzig" and "Danzig in the XVI Century," illustrating the transaction of the sale of grain by Polish merchants to Danzig merchants.

The issuing of these stamps provoked a sharp protest by the Danzig Senate, presented to Marian Chodacki, the commissioner-general of the Polish Republic in Danzig. The Senate declared that the motifs on these stamps offended the feelings of the German population of Danzig.

The Commissioner-General made the reservation in his reply that he did not deem it necessary to discuss this matter, since it involved internal orders of the Polish authorities, who decided for themselves what motifs might be placed on Polish postage stamps.

In the Polish reply it was stressed that according to the reasoning contained in the Senate's protest it should be recognized as inadmissible to represent in art and literature any historical events, for each event from the history of a nation might be a recollection unpleasant for its neighbors or certain groups.

At the same time, the Polish answer expressed the conviction that the Danzig Senate probably would not be anxious to support such an opinion,

[38] *Ibid.,* p. 387.
[39] *Ibid.,* p. 389.

thus absolving the Commissioner-General from solving the riddle why the recollection of a battle fought by Poland over five hundred years ago with an organization of a religious-political character, against whom Danzig was fighting alongside Poland, should be especially offensive for the inhabitants of the Free City of Danzig.

The Commissioner-General further underlined that the introduction of special postage stamps with the inscription "Polish Post—Port of Danzig" indicated that the Polish Republic possessed its own postal service at the port of Danzig, which remained under joint administration—and this corresponded with the rights Poland was entitled to, as well as with reality.

It was also stressed that the principal theme for the stamps of Polish post in Danzig was drawn from a painting by Van der Block of 1608 which adorned the Chamber of the Danzig City Hall.

The Commissioner-General further stressed that this picture, representing the golden era of Danzig's economy when the Free City collaborated with the Republic of Poland, evidently did not hurt Danzig's feelings, since in the Chamber where it was hanging official receptions by the Senate were held. The Commissioner-General also stated that it was not in his power to change the fact that in the sixteenth century Danzig belonged to Poland.

Besides the protest of the Danzig Senate, Ribbentrop in his conversation with Lipski on November 19 declared his objections (see the text of Ribbentrop's version, *DGFP,* Series D, Vol. V, No. 101, p. 129). Taking this into consideration, and in order not to complicate relations with Danzig during the period of preparation for Ribbentrop's visit to Warsaw, the Polish government decided to withdraw the stamp with Jagiełło and Jadwiga with the two swords; instead, on March 2, 1939, another stamp was issued, which aroused great interest among philatelists, at the same price and with the same personages, but without the swords.[40]


DOCUMENT 130    Łubieński to Lipski


Telephonogram                                    Warsaw, December 10, 1938
To: Ambassador Lipski in Berlin          *Secret*
From: Director of the Minister's Cabinet, Michał Łubieński


Please hold up for the time being execution of instructions dated December 8. Instead please call on Minister Ribbentrop and declare to him:

  1) Inquire whether the message given by you to von Weizsäcker [41]

[40] *Ilustrowany Kurier Codzienny* (Cracow), December 11, 1938.

[41] The message referred to regarding the French-German declaration signed in Paris on December 6 during Ribbentrop's visit, had been presented by Lipski on December 5 to Woermann, not to Weizsäcker (*DGFP,* Series D, Vol. V, No. 109).

has been duly transmitted to Ribbentrop. Express surprise that the friendly position of the Polish press with regard to Herr Ribbentrop's trip and the Paris declaration has been ignored in German communiqués (as well as by the press).

2) You have been summoned to Warsaw, and in this connection you are asking if Minister von Ribbentrop would possibly like to communicate something to the Minister. Minister Beck of late referred repeatedly in his instructions to the lack of *einer direkten Aussprache* with Ribbentrop. The Ambassador would revert to this matter after his return from Warsaw.

3) If by chance von Ribbentrop questions you about the problem of the postage stamps, please state that the stamp with the picture of Jagiełło and Jadwiga with two swords of the Teutonic knights at their feet will be withdrawn from sale.

### DOCUMENT 131   Lipski to Beck

NO. N/52/46/38                        Berlin, December 15, 1938
                                      *Strictly Confidential*

I had a conversation with the minister of foreign affairs of the Reich, von Ribbentrop, today, and proceeded to execute the instructions you gave me verbally yesterday in Warsaw.

I opened the conversation by stating that you had summoned me to Warsaw to discuss the whole complex of problems pertaining to Polish-German relations. I referred to your extensive conversation with Ambassador von Moltke yesterday evening, which was already known to Ribbentrop.[42] I pointed to the fact that while Polish-German relations had stood firm during the Czechoslovak crisis as a weighty element of peace, nevertheless a number of misunderstandings had occurred since which resulted in bad feeling. This situation is driving us to the conclusion that an exchange of opinion between you and Minister von Ribbentrop would be desirable and useful.

Herr von Ribbentrop replied that he had already mentioned such a necessity at Berchtesgaden.

I responded that I was instructed by you to suggest a visit of von Ribbentrop to Warsaw.

[42] See *ibid.,* No. 113.

Herr von Ribbentrop declared that he would willingly consent to an exchange of visits and would come to Warsaw with pleasure. However, he would still like to discuss this matter with the Chancellor in more detail before the holidays, since he is expected in Berlin. (He added that he would also report then on all conversations hitherto held with us.) In principle he thanks you for your invitation.

Here it was possible for me to imply that in 1935 you paid an official visit, and that at that time a return visit had been planned, but it had never taken place. I also mentioned that you were in Germany several times unofficially.

Herr von Ribbentrop further stressed that, in his opinion, it would be desirable to have such visits preceded by suitable diplomatic preparations, and he thinks that you would share this opinion. He inquired in a general sense what subjects would be raised during this visit.

I cited as general topics the Danubian complex, that of the East and of the Baltic countries, referring to the precedent of similar visits in the past. I stressed that problems would be discussed in which the interests of the two states coincide, or could coincide.

On his own volition, von Ribbentrop mentioned problems of immediate Polish-German relations, asking about the superhighway.

I remarked that this problem had been referred to you and that it is being discussed in Warsaw, but that, naturally, this matter can only be dealt with within the frame of *der Gesamtlösung*.

With regard to Danzig, I referred to Chodacki's memorandum handed to Herr von Ribbentrop, pointing to the fact that local authorities there deliver speeches of the kind that perforce poison the atmosphere.

Defining further the course of the conversations, we established the following:

Herr von Ribbentrop expresses thanks for your invitation and will take up this matter with the Chancellor. Up to January 10, that is, until the Chancellor's reception for the diplomatic corps, he will be on leave; as a matter of fact, he already began his vacation but had to interrupt it. After January 10 he would like to bring up through diplomatic channels the subjects to be discussed with you in a concrete form. He indicated a desire for an exchange of opinion with me during this period as well.

Besides the above question of the visit, which ran through the whole conversation, we also discussed the following subjects:

1) I pointed out to Minister Ribbentrop that Ukrainian propaganda,

which makes use of Germany's name, is obviously detrimental to our relations. To illustrate this, I handed him a pamphlet by Jaryj written in German about the Ukraine, showing on the cover a Great Ukraine reaching up to Warsaw and Cracow. Besides, I remarked that in Warsaw we continually receive information from the territory of Slovakia about anti-Polish activity conducted there, which claims to be inspired by Germany.

Herr von Ribbentrop mentioned that he will have the problem investigated. When he deliberated on the Ukraine as an anti-Russian element, I replied that we have nothing against this, as long as such propaganda deals with territories situated outside the frontiers of the Republic.

Talking more generally about Russia, I recalled that Poland really is the state constituting a barricade against Communist, as well as imperialistic-panslavic, Russia.

2) For his part, von Ribbentrop laid special stress on the way the German minority is treated in Teschen. He remarked that this matter, which he has been personally investigating on the basis of reports and claims, has become detrimental for our relations. He urgently requested me to refer this problem to you, asking that the activities of the local authorities be investigated.

As far as I know, von Moltke approached our Ministry of Foreign Affairs on the same problem.[43] I think it would be advisable to investigate this matter more closely.

3) I expressed thanks that we were informed about the results of the Paris talks, while I pointed out our stand, which I had explained to Secretary of State Woermann on the eve of von Ribbentrop's departure for Paris.[44]

4) Stressing that we have navigational interests at Kłajpeda [Memel], in view of the fact that negotiations with Lithuania were under way, I inquired about this matter.

Von Ribbentrop answered rather noncommittally, remarking that France and England, as signatories of the convention,[45] had approached the Secretary of State on this matter. He was of the opinion that the signatories of the convention had had the opportunity, in the

[43] *Ibid.,* No. 113, last paragraph.
[44] *Ibid.,* No. 109.
[45] Reference is made to the convention concluded by the Great Powers with Lithuania on May 8, 1924, with regard to Kłajpeda territory under Lithuanian sovereignty.

course of many years, to care for the Kłajpeda population. However, they did nothing. From Ribbentrop's words it was clear that he is passing over this question. He further stressed that Kłajpeda is a German city. To my remark that I raised this question in connection with our trade interests, von Ribbentrop remarked that, in keeping with our good-neighbor policy, our economic interests would always be resolved satisfactorily.

At one phase of the conversation, when Ribbentrop was speaking of his positive attitude toward Polish problems, he gave way to some sort of regret that his intentions in the conversation at Berchtesgaden might possibly have been minsunderstood to some extent—hence our strong reaction to it.

Here I made a reply of a general character, saying that he could be assured that our leading authorities understand his intentions, while I pointed out that local authorities, for instance in Danzig, are jeopardizing an accord by their activities.

At the end of the conversation von Ribbentrop remarked that, if we are led by the principles drawn up by Marshal Piłsudski and Hitler in 1933, then we will undoubtedly reach agreement. However, he added that here it would be essential for the Polish side to understand certain principles of German policy.

As a result of this conversation, I have the following comments to make:

I assume that the Chancellor will accept the idea of Minister Ribbentrop's trip to Warsaw, perhaps will even suggest a meeting with you. I also think that the idea of diplomatic preparations would suit you too. Under these conditions, we have to be prepared for concrete conversations beginning January 10. Before this date it would be necessary to gain possession of material concerning Danzig, which I took the liberty of suggesting to you while I was in Warsaw. We should also state precisely our stand with regard to the superhighway (from press information and the planning of German superhighways disclosed recently, it would appear that a superhighway is intended for the narrowest northern sector, to unite Królewiec [Königsberg], Danzig, and Szczecin).

Besides, material should be collected concerning German-Ukrainian joint action detrimental to Polish interests, and possibly data on the anti-Polish activity of German diplomatic agents or others in Czechoslovakia and Lithuania.

In connection with my telegram of today regarding the statement made to Counselor Lubomirski by Reich Minister Frank, I am taking the liberty of suggesting that Frank should be informed even more fully than before with regard to the problems of Danzig and the Danubian complex, with a mention of the Ukrainian agitation. This matter seems to me particularly important since Minister Frank will undoubtedly report his conversations directly to the Chancellor. The orientation he achieves from his Warsaw conversations will constitute a serious factor for Hitler's decision, especially on the Danzig question, as well as on the Ukrainian problem in the light of our interests.[46]

*Józef Lipski*

[46] Frank was in Poland in the middle of December, 1938.

# Beck's Visit to Berchtesgaden and Ribbentrop's to Warsaw. Hitler's Speech at the Reichstag
## *January, 1939*

IN HIS REPORT of December 15, 1938, Lipski advanced the supposition that Hitler would suggest a meeting with Beck. In his conversation with Moltke on December 20, Beck brought up the possibility of a preliminary Polish-German discussion of problems prior to Ribbentrop's official visit to Warsaw.[1] As it was Beck's intention to spend the Christmas holidays at Monte Carlo, it would be possible for him to stop in Berlin on his way back. Hitler availed himself of this suggestion, and Beck's conversations with Hitler and Ribbentrop took place on January 5, 1939, at Berchtesgaden, and with Ribbentrop on January 6 in Munich.

These conversations added no new elements to the prevailing situation. The German side insisted again that Danzig must be reunited with the Reich, and that Poland should agree to an extraterritorial superhighway and railway line across Pomerania. However, Hitler exerted no special pressure in this matter, promising Poland access to the sea and assuring it that there would be no question of a *fait accompli* in Danzig. Ribbentrop was more aggressive regarding this problem, and received a stronger *repartie* from Beck, who said that for the first time he was pessimistic about Polish-German relations.[2]

Beck informed Polish representatives abroad about the substance of these talks by a telegram dated January 10.[3] The mitigating wording of the telegram contrasted with Beck's concern about the further development of Polish-German relations evident from his conversation with Ribbentrop. Immediately upon his return to Warsaw he considered it to be "my duty to warn the President of the Republic and Marshal Śmigły-Rydz of these alarming symptoms which could result in a war." [4]

[1] *DGFP*, Series D, Vol. V, No. 115.
[2] *Polish White Book*, Nos. 48 and 49; *DGFP*, Series D, Vol. V, Nos. 119 and 120; Beck, *Final Report*, pp. 171–72; *Journal*, pp. 404–8.
[3] For the German circular telegram to representatives about the conferences, see *DGFP*, Series D, Vol. V, No. 121.
[4] Beck, *Final Report*, p. 172. In Beck's book the date of this conversation is erroneously cited as January 4. Beck returned to Warsaw on January 7, after conversations with Hitler and Ribbentrop, and the conversation with the President could only have taken place on January 8 or 9.

DOCUMENT 132   Lipski to Beck

NO. N/1/11/39                              Berlin, January 23, 1939

I received strictly confidential information from the Hungarian Envoy regarding the stay of Count Csáky, foreign minister of Hungary,[5] in Berlin from January 16 through the 18th.

Csáky came at the invitation of the Germans. Some time ago, in his conversation with Envoy Sztójay, Ribbentrop suggested that German-Hungarian relations should be improved by a visit of Csáky to Berlin.

The Hungarian Envoy explained that of late a critical attitude toward Germany had increased considerably in Hungary, as manifested in many press articles. Count Bethlen's intervention in one of these articles hurt German feelings, and even top spheres took offense at it. These symptoms of opinion in Hungary compelled the Reich government to try to smooth out relations.

Count Csáky commented with satisfaction on his conversations in Germany. In the course of these conversations the German side went to great lengths to explain that, if Hungary's demands were not met, Hungary was to blame, not Germany. Stress was laid on the fact that Hungary did not go into action under the most favorable circumstances. It was mentioned that in its solutions the German government had to observe ethnographic principles, as agreed to at the Munich Conference.

Further, it was stressed that the military action which Hungary wanted to undertake at a certain moment against Carpathian Ruthenia was far too risky in view of the potentiality of a Czechoslovak war, the more so since at that time Germany had already released its recruited forces.

From further German deliberations it was clear that the Reich government does not regard the Czechoslovak situation as definitely settled. Allegedly Count Csáky had the impression that under the right conditions the Carpatho-Ruthenian problem could be reconsidered in the future. From the German side, it was mentioned that the Reich did not oppose the Polish-Hungarian frontier, and in general German spokesmen underlined the need for good relations between Poland and Hungary. They also insisted that the Reich desires to maintain as good relations as possible with Poland.

[5] For Minister Csáky's conversation with Hitler on January 16, see *DGFP*, Series D, Vol. V, No. 272; for his conversation with Ribbentrop, *ibid.*, No. 273.

The Chancellor allegedly denied rumors circulated by the foreign press about his alleged plans for the Great Ukraine. A seeming result from what was said by the German side was that in the future the Ukrainian problem at any rate could not be solved without Poland's participation.

The Hungarian envoy, Sztójay, whom I kept informed about the results of your conversations at Berchtesgaden, remarked that the German explanations to Count Csáky were in conformity with what has been said to us at Berchtesgaden.

As far as the guarantee for Czechoslovakia is concerned, Ribbentrop allegedly said to Csáky that Germany would not grant it unless a similar guarantee is granted by other states. To my question whether these "other states" meant the Powers participating in the Munich Agreement, or neighbors, Envoy Sztójay replied that Count Csáky understood this point to mean that the neighbors of Czechoslovakia were concerned.

By the way, I would like to add that the Hungarian Envoy, in view of his departure two days ago for Budapest, instructed his chargé d'affaires to communicate to me today that Secretary of State Weizsäcker, in his conversation with him with regard to guarantees, defined Germany's position thus: that the guarantee for Czechoslovakia would not be granted until Czechoslovakia is consolidated. There is therefore a certain deviation between Ribbentrop's statement and that of Weizsäcker.

According to explanations of Envoy Sztójay, Hungary's admission to the Anti-Comintern Pact would probably take the form of a declaration made by Count Csáky to the representatives of Italy, Germany, and Japan, with the formal signing of the agreement at a later date. This delay is due to difficulties in obtaining approval of the Japanese government with regard to the text, which has to be dispatched to Tokyo.

To my question as to the attitude of Hungary toward the League of Nations, I was told that the Hungarian government has decided to leave the Geneva institution. The date foreseen for the withdrawal is spring—April or May. The Envoy was at a loss to explain why this date had been chosen. From words of Mr. Ottlik, a Hungarian journalist accompanying Count Csáky, I could judge that the withdrawal from Geneva would take place at a suitable time.

Finally, Envoy Sztójay informed me that he thinks that German-Czech relations have considerably cooled off and that Chvalkovský would get a bad reception here, which subsequently proved to be true.

In brief, the Hungarians are of the opinion that the German Reich will for the time being conduct a policy of appeasement toward the Eastern states, while its attention will concentrate on events in Spain and the Mediterranean basin.

I must add that, prior to the above conversation with the Hungarian Envoy, Count Csáky informed me through Mr. Ottlik that he was pleased with his conversations here, particularly since the Germans had stressed that they are anxious that relations between Poland and Hungary should develop satisfactorily.

*Józef Lipski*

On January 25–27 Ribbentrop came to Warsaw on an official visit. Weizsäcker prepared a note for the visit dated January 23, informing Ribbentrop about the problems to be discussed in Warsaw.[6] In his conversations with Beck, Ribbentrop once more returned to the problem of Danzig and the superhighway, but Beck again categorically rejected the proposals. It was only agreed that, in case the League of Nations withdrew from Danzig, a joint Polish-German declaration would be issued for the maintenance of the *status quo* in the Free City until agreement was reached on this matter between Poland and Germany.[7]

A circular telegram sent by Beck to representatives abroad on January 31 again did not reveal the essence of a deeper conflict between Polish and German interests.

DOCUMENT 133   Lipski to Beck

NO. N/49/22/39                                    February 2, 1939
                                                          *Secret*

Prior to relating in a separate report the speech of Chancellor Hitler delivered at the session of the Reichstag on January 30 last, I would like to draw your attention to passages dealing directly or indirectly with Polish-German relations.

[6] *Ibid.*, No. 125.
[7] For the Polish version of this conversation, see *Polish White Book*, Nos. 50–56; also Beck, *Final Report*, pp. 173–74, and *Journal*, pp. 411–17. For the German version: *DGFP*, Series D, Vol. V, No. 126. See also Florian Miedziński, "Rozmowy Becka z Ribbentropem i Gafencu w sprawozdaniach warszawskiego meża zaufania senatu gdanskiego," *Przegląd Zachodni* (Poznań), 1965, No. 4, pp. 295–311 (document texts in German).

A direct passage about Poland reads as follows:

"We have just celebrated the fifth anniversary of the conclusion of our nonaggression pact with Poland. There can scarcely be any difference of opinion today among the true friends of peace as to the value of this agreement. One only needs to ask oneself what might have happened to Europe if this agreement, which brought such relief, had not been entered into five years ago. In signing it, the great Polish marshal and patriot rendered his people just as great a service as the leaders of the National Socialist state rendered the German people. During the troubled months of the past year the friendship between Germany and Poland has been one of the reassuring factors in the political life of Europe." [8]

Further passages of the Chancellor's speech deal with Hungary, Yugoslavia, and economic relations with Bulgaria, Greece, Rumania, and Turkey are touched upon in a single sentence.

This statement follows: "Germany is happy to possess today friendly frontiers in the west, south, and north," and then general reference is made to the attitude toward the western and northern states. Finally, he warns Czechoslovakia against returning to Beneš' ideas.

The above passage about frontiers is characteristic for its omission of eastern frontiers. Despite the fact that relations with Poland are especially dealt with, and that reference to the frontiers is interwoven among other questions, nevertheless some consistent tendency might be detected here. I wish to recall that in his speech of September 12, 1938, on the occasion of the closing of the Reichstag in Nuremberg, Hitler used this sentence:

"Germany has today on *all* sides completely friendly frontiers."

However, this was later changed by D.N.B. to "on *many* sides" [emphasis added in both cases by Lipski].

In contradiction to the statement that Germany forced concessions from other states (Austria, Czechoslovakia) by military pressure, the Chancellor declares that, in regions where the English and other Western Powers have nothing to expect, Germany restored to millions of its compatriots the right to self-determination, and he adds next:

". . . and I need not assure you, my representatives of the German Reichstag, that in the future also we will not put up with it when Western Powers simply try to intrude in certain matters concerning us only,

[8] *Polish White Book,* No. 57.

in order, through their intervention, to harm natural and rational solutions."

In my opinion, this statement is not void of meaning with regard to relations between Western and Eastern Europe.

Yesterday, at a reception of the Finance Minister, I congratulated von Ribbentrop on words of appreciation the Chancellor addressed to him in his speech. The Foreign Minister of the Reich did not conceal his satisfaction with regard to these words of the Chancellor, and said they were a surprise to him.

At the same time he stressed how pleasant his stay in Poland was. He added that efforts should be made to have Polish-German relations develop satisfactorily, and he made reference to his conversation with you in Warsaw, saying that he is counting on my help to find a solution in these matters. He recalled that the Chancellor treats these matters "von der hohen Werte" ["of high value"].

As this took place on a purely social level, there was no opportunity to expand the discussion.

I would like to add that von Ribbentrop and all the German officials who accompanied the Minister to Warsaw expressed their satisfaction over the reception they met with in Poland.

Minister Ribbentrop is leaving for a ten-day vacation; he is coming back for a few days, and then is leaving again for a week.

*Józef Lipski*

DOCUMENT 134   Lipski to Beck

NO. N/7/7/39                                         February 7, 1939
                                                      *Secret*

With reference to my report of the 2d inst., No. N/49/22/39, where I raised points dealing with Polish-German relations contained in the speech delivered by the Chancellor at the Reichstag on January 30 last, I am now taking the liberty of analyzing this speech more extensively.

Upon the reunion of Austria and Sudetenland with the Reich, and thus the achievement of the most essential demand of National Socialism—the union of all Germanic countries—the question arose as to what Hitler would attempt to do next.

Bearing in mind the fact that in connection with the Carpatho-Ruthenian problem the Ukrainian question began more intensely than before to absorb the minds of the so-called annexes of the local Ministry of Foreign Affairs (Ribbentrop's office, Rosenberg's office, certain sections of the Ministry of Propaganda, the Institute for Eastern Europe), it was commonly supposed that the Chancellor would start a wide-ranging eastern program. Others suggested that the year 1939 would be devoted to colonial problems.

Chancellor Hitler spent the last two months of 1938 at Berchtesgaden in order to arrive at a decision as to the basic line of his policy. Your conversation with the Chancellor at Berchtesgaden on January 6 [9] provided some orientation to the Polish government in this respect.

Hitler's Reichstag speech of January 30, 1939, defined the guiding lines for the Reich's foreign policy, as well as its internal affairs, for the near future.

In contrast to his speech delivered last year (on February 20, 1938), when the problem of Austria and the Sudetenland was quite unequivocally presented,[10] the Chancellor drafted only the principal goals of the Reich in the domain of foreign policy, without spelling out how and when he intends to realize his demands. This probably derives from the very problem of colonialism.

The Chancellor's speech is so extensive that a detailed analysis would take too much space in this report. I therefore limit myself to the most essential matters, omitting material already familiar from other speeches of the Chancellor.

First of all, attention is arrested by the calm, matter-of-fact tone of the speech and his restraint from aggressive accents against other states. This exterior garb of the speech has caused the foreign press to label it a peace speech. I think that this kind of reasoning needs some correction. Although this speech is calmer than usual, it nevertheless contains statements which leave no illusions as to the fact that Germany will realize its demands in a very decisive manner.

I. It is characteristic that Chancellor Hitler, as far as the sequence and direction of his aspirations is concerned, has followed consistently his basic program, namely, *the revision of the Versailles Treaty.*

[9] The date is in error; it should be January 5.
[10] See p. 340.

Pushing the sequence of claims to the forefront, he passed over in silence eastern problems, reserving them for a later date.

This is undoubtedly the first speech of the Chancellor in which he has taken such a deeply motivated stand on the problem of claims for the return of colonies. He based these claims neither on premises of justice nor on prestige, but on the economic needs of the German nation. The Chancellor supported his claims to the Western Powers for the return of the colonies by the argument that the Reich is bound either to export at any cost—which would consequently be detrimental to the interests of these states—or to recover its colonies. He declared that, because the victorious states of the Great War are reluctant to settle the colonial problem, only the first alternative is left to Germany. The Chancellor predicts that, in case the Powers undertake to hamper German export, the Reich will undertake "a desperate economic drive."

In connection with his colonial demands the Chancellor stresses the common interest uniting the Reich and Italy, saying:

"Germany understands that other nations want their share in the riches of the world, to which they are entitled by their numbers, courage, and value; a decision has been taken, in recognition of these rights, to act jointly (with Italy) for the sake of common interests."

In conclusion regarding the colonial point, it is worth mentioning that a tendency runs through Hitler's speech to support Italy in its Mediterranean action, undoubtedly expecting that this is the way to render colonial questions timely. On the other hand, as I mentioned before, the Chancellor is threatening England and France—in case the colonies are not recovered—with disorganization of their trade markets by means of increased export.

II. It is characteristic that the Chancellor did not mention Russian subjects at all; the words "Ukraine" and "Russia" were not uttered in the speech (outside of the usual invectives against Bolshevism). The Chancellor's statement that in *the north, west, and south the Reich possesses peaceful frontiers, with an omission of the eastern frontier,* should undoubtedly be understood as a sort of reservation about the Czechoslovak question (Hitler hopes that Czechoslovakia will not fall into Beneš' errors in politics) and the Danzig and Kłajpeda [Memel] questions.

The special traditional passage about *Poland,* about which I reported on February 2, No. N/49/22/39, confirms the desire to continue a policy based upon the 1934 agreement.

To other states of the *Danubian basin* the Chancellor refers in the sense of increased economic ties with them, while he has particularly warm words for Hungary, which joined the Anti-Comintern Pact, and also Yugoslavia.

With regard to the *Baltic and Northern states,* the Chancellor welcomes their intention to remain neutral, and thus escape obligations under Article 16 or the Pact of the League of Nations.

III. As far as Germany's relations with the *Western Powers* are concerned, attention is first of all arrested by the fact that the Chancellor did not mention a single word about the *French-German declaration* signed in Paris by Ribbentrop and Bonnet.

While German opinion at large was utterly different toward France than toward England a few months ago, when negotiations and the signing of the declaration were under way, at present the Chancellor in his speech repeatedly poses his demands to both states simultaneously, or tries to identify them in his criticism as democracies. So, for instance, he says:

"Germany has no territorial claims against England and France, outside of the return of German colonies."

He adds, however, that "this problem is not in the category of problems which would demand war solutions."

Throughout the whole speech runs a polemic with statesmen and pressmen of the so-called democratic states who are critical of the system and activities of the Reich. Nevertheless, even here a moderation more marked than usual may be observed. Even against America his polemic is more or less restricted to repulsing complaints directed against Germany, while a statement is made that Germany desires peace and friendship with America also. The supposition that the speech would contain an assault against Roosevelt was not realized.

IV. In the field of relations with foreign states, the most definite passage clearly relates to *Italy*. The Chancellor motivates the rapprochement of the two nations on the ideological premises of the Fascist and National Socialist systems, the common history of national rebirth in Italy and Germany, as well as a common action in the period of the Abyssinian war and the events of 1938.

A categorical declaration that the Reich would come to Italy's assistance in case it was drawn into war is contained in the following sentence:

"It might just serve the cause of peace that there is no doubt but that a war against Italy today, for whatever cause it might be unleashed, would call Germany to the side of its friend."

(It is characteristic that in the translation of this passage for the use of the French press, the German official press agency added to the word "war" the adjective "ideological," a word not to be found in the official German text.)

The passage about the Reich's determination to assist Italy constitutes a sort of answer to the declaration made by Mussolini some time ago with regard to the Czech conflict, which was later confirmed in the speech of Count Ciano.

V. German-*Japanese* relations are treated on the level of their anti-Bolshevist principles. However, the actual Anti-Comintern Pact is referred to rather loosely in the form of a hypothesis for the future:

"The Anti-Comintern Pact might one day perhaps become a crystallization point for a group of powers whose main goal would be no other than to ward off the threat to the peace and culture of the world from a satanic phenomenon."

Closing the analysis of the part of the speech pertaining to international relations, I wish to underline the Chancellor's words that he believes in a lasting peace. I think that these words should be understood thus: that the Chancellor supposedly believes it possible to achieve his demands by way of political and economic pressure, without having recourse to military action.

VI. In the field of internal politics, the following more important issues are worth noting:

1) The declaration that the reunion of Austria and the Sudetenland with the Reich constitutes the crowning of a thousand years' struggle to unite all German tribes into one state.

2) *Outlining National Socialist tasks* for the future, unlimited in time, and striving for the creation of "a true people's community." To bring about the situation that all the elements of the German community predestined to become leaders would have the possibility to come to the top, creating a new leading sphere. Here the Chancellor is getting rid of all class prejudice. I quote a characteristic passage:

"For in the mass-millions of a nation there are talents enough to occupy successfully all made-to-measure posts. This offers the best safe-guard for the state and for the community against revolutionary designs of individuals and destructive tendencies of the times. For danger ever threatens only from those overlooked, never just from the negative criti-cal groups or the malcontent. . . . The true revolutionists on a world pattern are in all times those who were misunderstood or who were not admitted to be leaders by nature by a presumptuous, sclerotic, secluded community layer."

Besides these statements of a general nature, the speech brings no new points in the field of internal reforms.

3) Justifying his anti-Jewish action, the Chancellor refers to the suffering sustained by the German nation during the period of the Treaty of Versailles until the liberation by National Socialism—the Jews being the main culprits causing this ordeal. He argues with the democracies which take pity on the Jews but are unwilling to help them by granting territory for Jewish emigration. He states that National Socialism will consistently follow its policy on this issue. Special attention should be given to the passage suggesting that European states otherwise having difficulties in agreeing might reach a common platform on the Jewish problem:

"It is quite possible that over this problem, sooner or later, a union will take place in Europe spontaneously among those nations that could not easily find a way to each other."

In connection with confidences I heard at one time from the Chancel-lor, it is not impossible that he is considering Poland here also, as well as other East European countries.

4) An extensive passage is devoted to the two religions: Catholic and Protestant.

In reply to attacks of the democracies that there is persecution of churches in Germany, the Chancellor states that:

a) no one has hitherto been persecuted in Germany because of his religious attitude;

b) large funds are contributed every year from the state budget, as well as by the provinces and communities, to both churches; the land and forest estates of the churches in Germany amount to 10 billion marks, with an income of 300 million per year;

c) not a single church has been closed and no pressure has been exerted on church rites;

d) in case the churches continue their complaints, the National Socialist state is ready, following the example of France, America, and other states, to *bring about a division between the church and the state.* Then follow attacks against clergymen for their political attitude or moral offenses.

With regard to the Protestant church, the Chancellor states that he strove to create one great state church in Germany out of the separated, dispersed churches. This attempt met with opposition on the part of the bishops and had to be abandoned.

The above deliberations of the Chancellor relating to the Catholic church do not deal with the basic difficulties which exist between the totalitarian National Socialist system and the church, for example, in the field of education of the youth, etc. The enumeration of governmental subsidies for the churches as well as the state of their property might contain a certain threat that, after the confiscation by the state of Jewish property, their turn will come.

5) The principal part of the speech relates to economic problems.

It should be stressed that such a pessimistic evaluation of the Reich's economic situation was heard for the first time from Hitler. In this respect the speech is very skillfully constructed, since economic problems are closely tied with the demands for a just division of the world's riches. So here also there is a scapegoat: the powers now in possession of German colonies.

With regard to the Reich's financial system, the Chancellor repeats statements previously contained in other speeches that wages, as well as prices and currency, should be maintained at a certain fixed level. In his system currency is based not on gold but on the increasing capacity of production. With regard to a different system applied by other states, the Chancellor is of this opinion:

"In other countries they take the wrong way. Production is prevented, national property is raised by an increase in wages, the purchasing value of money is thereby lowered, and depreciation of currency finally results."

The Chancellor agrees that the German system is in itself unpopular, remarking:

"I agree that the German way is in itself an unpopular one, since it means nothing else but that any rise of wages can forcibly derive only from an increase in production."

As guidance for the future the Chancellor recommends rationalization of industries and reinforcement of technical organization. The capital market should therefore be more open to technical development of enterprises and free from governmental burdens (loans).

This statement is similar to the exposition contained in the well-known letter of Hitler addressed to the new president of the Reichsbank, Funk, after Schacht's resignation (see report No. N/7/2/39, dated January 23, 1939).[11]

Next, the Chancellor predicts the reorganization of the Reichsbank in accordance with principles also expressed in the above letter.

The Chancellor's speech, which also stresses the necessity of reinforcing armaments, brings no precise answer to the question by what means, in the long run, the Reich intends to finance the *Arbeitsbeschaffung* and armaments. However, one thing is clear, that the Reichsbank will have to take over an even more considerable burden than hitherto in this respect.

The Chancellor's economic deliberations sound similar to Schacht's ideas on one essential issue. Schacht, as I often wrote, considered the autarchy system a *malum necessarium* but not a final goal. His intention was to bring about, in the final stage, normal relations in economic exchange between the Reich and the rest of the world, and to increase this turnover. The Chancellor is getting close to this truth when he poses as a guiding principle the necessity of exporting at any cost, which means nothing but an increase of the Reich's share in international trade.

If the Chancellor presents the return of the colonies as an alternative, it is worth recalling that Schacht was one of the most zealous adherents of the colonial thesis, being fully aware that this was the way for the Reich to get access to raw materials and food supplies that would guarantee its economic independence.

*Józef Lipski*

[11] This report is missing from Lipski's papers.

# Further Aggravation of Polish-German Relations
## *February—March, 1939*

ON JANUARY 29, 1939, an incident took place at a cafeteria in Danzig which caused further complications in Polish-Danzig relations. On that day a group of Polish students of the Danzig Polytechnic were at the Café Langfuhr, talking in Polish. German students present in the café started to shout: "It is forbidden to speak Polish here." One of the German students hit a Pole, and a general fight broke out.

Two weeks later the owner of the Café Langfuhr forwarded a letter to the Fellowship Society of Polish students, advising them that he did not wish Polish students to frequent his premises. The Poles ignored this letter and appeared at the café on February 12. German students placed a sign at the entrance with the inscription: "To dogs and Polish students entrance is forbidden! The poor dogs!" A new scuffle started among the students.[1]

This incident was the source of many riots between Polish and German students on the premises of the Polytechnic, where lectures were temporarily suspended in order to calm the youths.

News about these incidents in Danzig upset students in Polish universities, and anti-German demonstrations were staged in Poznań, Cracow, Lwów, and other cities.

In Warsaw, on February 25 a group of students demonstrated before the building of the German Embassy, a windowpane was broken by a rock, and anti-German slogans were shouted. On Beck's orders, the chief of protocol of the Polish Ministry of Foreign Affairs expressed words of regret to Ambassador Moltke.[2]

This incident was even more embarrassing and troublesome for the Germans, since it happened during the official visit to Warsaw of Minister Ciano. (Ciano was in Warsaw from February 25 to March 1.) Consequently, Ribbentrop reacted strongly in his conversation with Lipski on February 28.[3]

[1] *German White Book*, No. 195; see also *Ilustrowany Kurier Codzienny* (Cracow), February 20, 1939, where a picture is shown of a card with an inscription offensive to Poles.

[2] *German White Book*, No. 146; also *DGFP*, Series D, Vol. V, No. 137.

[3] *DGFP*, Series D, Vol. V, No. 131. The Polish version of this conversation is missing from Lipski's papers.

Lipski took up the question of the incidents in Danzig in his conversation with Hitler and Göring on March 2.

DOCUMENT 135    Lipski to Beck

NO. G/3/27/39                        March 2, 1939
*Strictly Confidential*

Yesterday at the Chancellor's reception for the diplomatic corps I had occasion for a casual exchange of opinion with Chancellor Hitler and also with Göring with regard to the recent student incidents in Poland caused by the situation in Danzig.

Immediately after the reception I sent you a short telegraphic account describing only the background of the two conversations, which I am now supplementing more extensively.

In my conversation with the Chancellor I followed the instructions contained in your telegram of the 1st inst.[4] I first mentioned the regrettable student demonstrations before the Embassy in Warsaw, stressing that they were being exploited by the elements of the opposition. The Chancellor did not make too much of these incidents.

I further pointed out that these incidents were provoked by the anti-Polish sign posted in Danzig and the ensuing beating of Polish students. I stated that public opinion in Poland is especially touchy about Danzig matters, and that this sensitivity has been on the upswing lately because German policy toward Danzig is not clear to Polish public opinion. I added that, naturally, this situation is being exploited by elements of the opposition.

The Chancellor replied that Danzig problems are ticklish. That is why he thinks that they should be determined by a solution which would totally remove all complications. In the course of his deliberations he stressed that as long as he, as a partner of Marshal Piłsudski in the Polish-German agreement, is in charge of the Reich's policies, there will be no conflict. In Poland, at the head of Polish foreign policy, stands Minister Beck, "a very clever and noble man." Nevertheless, in the future someone might take the Chancellor's place in Germany, just as some changes may occur in the political leadership in Poland. Therefore, it would be desirable to reach an agreement on this matter before

----

[4] Missing from Lipski's papers.

then. Such an agreement, though bilaterally painful, would remove forever all misunderstandings—as was done at the Brenner Pass. The Chancellor remarked that Germany's approval of the Corridor is not an easy decision. He added that there are more Germans in Pomerania than Poles in Danzig. He also mentioned that some time ago he was strongly attacked by the *Deutschnationale* for his policy toward Poland. Such an attack on him by Oldenburg-Januschau took place at Neudeck, while the late Field Marshal Hindenburg extended his support to him. If he had not removed the *Deutschnationale* from rule, he could not have reached an agreement with Poland. Naturally, Socialists and Communists did not take any interest in these matters.

The Chancellor also mentioned that it is quite natural that many elements desire to spoil Polish-German relations. He stressed that he understands that you also came upon elements who attack you for your policy toward Germany.

The Chancellor closed the conversation in a positive tone concerning our relations.

Next, I had a conversation with Göring. He remarked that the student demonstrations in Warsaw as such would not have meant much to him if they had not coincided with Minister Ciano's visit to Warsaw. As he learned from the Italian side, Ciano was greatly embarrassed to hear shouts for the Italians and against the other partner of the Axis.

He discreetly inquired whether it was true that some military elements took part in the demonstrations, which I denied. Göring replied that he also thought it to be impossible, since the demonstrations were conducted against the government and you.

For my part, I laid pressure on the necessity of promptly liquidating student incidents in Danzig by acceptance of a Polish proposal to settle the matter by way of a commission.

Göring said that he sent a special clerk to Danzig to investigate who the author of the offensive inscription against Poland was. If we are in possession of any information, he would be obliged if we would share it with him. I understood that he might suspect the possibility of a provocation against Polish-German relations.

For my part, I underlined the sensitivity and hurt feelings of Polish public opinion with regard to the situation in Danzig.

Göring showed understanding. He said that he personally is always trying to iron things out and check such incidents. Stressing that he spoke as a friend, he said that, in his opinion, these matters should be discussed on some occasion. He added that, as long as the Chancellor and he control the government, these matters can always be balanced (*ausbalancieren*). Following the trend of his ideas, he declared that it cannot be denied that Danzig is a German city, while it is a known fact that Poland needs the port of Danzig. If Poland, he went on, had not built Gdynia, this would be even more obvious. Nevertheless, even so Poland's interest is sufficiently evident.

Göring understands the great difficulties this problem is causing inside Poland. He added that it was a misfortune that Marshal Piłsudski died too early, for only a person like him could make a decision on such a problem. Göring closed this point by stating that he is hoping for the best, since we always did find a solution, even in difficult situations.

Göring also added that he is often approached by people from East Prussia and Silesia with many claims and complaints. However, he pays no attention to them. In order to illustrate how the Chancellor cares for our interests, he stressed that, when decision was taken regarding Bohumin, many local Germans tried to influence the Chancellor to re-unite that territory with Germany. However, the Chancellor took the position that Poland's interests had to be taken into consideration there.

Göring remarked that rumors spread by the Western press about alleged German plans for a Great Ukraine are sheer fiction. About Carpathian Ruthenia he said that this problem could still be resolved.

The above conversations of yesterday, which, as I already mentioned, were conducted rather casually in a loose exchange of opinion, made it clear that the Chancellor did not feel personally hurt by the Warsaw anti-German demonstrations, as I had first feared, since he might have suspected that they constituted a reply to his suggestions with regard to Danzig. On the other hand, these demonstrations must have shown both to the Chancellor and to Göring how very irritating the Danzig problems are for public opinion in Poland. From this angle, the demonstrations might even be of some use; under the condition, however, that they will not be repeated and will not result in consequences undesirable for this opinion.

It is rather characteristic that both the Chancellor and Göring laid pressure on the fact that as long as they are directing the Reich's policy there will be no conflict over the Danzig problem. It could be gathered from this that no drastic solution is planned, and that the Chancellor remains willing to come to an understanding with Poland on this issue.

My aim was to prove to the Chancellor and to Göring how very strongly our public opinion is reacting on these matters, so that no illusion would remain in this respect among top elements here.

Finally, I was under the impression that the Party elements in Danzig and those on our border undoubtedly exerted pressure on the political leadership to obtain concessions for the northeastern region of the Reich, which must feel to a certain extent overlooked and neglected after the reunion of Austria and the Sudetenland. This might also be felt as a reaction in the territory.

I would also like to add that Göring, who just underwent a rigorous reducing regimen (he lost over 45 lbs.), looks very tired and is leaving in a few days for four weeks in San Remo.

*Józef Lipski*

On March 15 the annexation of Czechoslovakia to the Reich took place, about which Moltke informed Beck officially on the same evening.[5] Poland recognized the newly proclaimed independence of Slovakia on that day and sent a chargé d'affaires to Bratislava. However, when Slovak Minister President Tiso made an agreement with Hitler on March 16, and Hitler extended a protectorate over Slovakia, the Polish Ministry of Foreign Affairs reacted with concern and sent instructions by telephone to Lipski on March 17.[6]

On March 15 the Czechs accepted the Hungarian ultimatum to give up Carpathian Ruthenia, and on that day Hungarian troops entered this territory. On March 16 they reached the Polish frontier.

DOCUMENT 136  Łubieński to Lipski

Telephonogram                                    March 17, 11:07 A.M.
                                                 *Secret*

Instructions for Ambassador Lipski for the conversation with Field Marshal Göring.

1) Yesterday evening Minister Arciszewski invited Ambassador von

[5] *DGFP,* Series D, Vol. VI, No. 4.
[6] See *ibid.,* Nos. 12 and 18. For the text of the German-Slovak treaty, see *ibid.,* No. 40.

Moltke and asked for a genuine interpretation of the Tiso-Hitler declaration.

2) The very fact of placing us in the face of ever new decisions without previous notification does not contribute to the creation of a good atmosphere in Polish-German relations.

3) Besides, please stress that you are talking without being instructed.

### DOCUMENT 137    Lipski to Beck

NO. 54                                         Berlin, March 17, 1939
                                      Received: March 17, 17:10 [5:10 P.M.]
                                               *Coded*

From my conversation with Göring, to whom I mentioned that I was speaking without being instructed, the following are the results:

I. German-Slovak negotiations in Vienna on the form of the *Schutzstaat* are being finalized.

II. The principles are, approximately, as follows: maintainance of Slovakian sovereignty, defense from external threats, common foreign policy, financial aid, probable customs and currency union.

III. I made clear our relation to Slovakia, which took us by surprise with this decision; bad impression in Poland.

Göring stated that the decision about the *Schutzstaat* is final; he said he will call the Chancellor's attention to Polish interests connected with this problem, so that, for instance, there would be no German garrisons in central and eastern Slovakia.

IV. I could feel in Göring a desire to maintain good relations with us; he referred on this occasion to his last conversations with the Chancellor. Nevertheless, he explained the failure to communicate with us (besides the unexpected, even for Germany, turn of events) by a certain dissatisfaction on the part of Hitler caused by the fact that the Warsaw demonstrations put him in an awkward position with Mussolini.

Details in my report today.[7]

In Lipski's papers there is a handwritten sheet of paper with very short remarks, from which the trend of the Ambassador's thoughts—in those crucial days after the annexation of Czechoslovakia by Hitler and the extension of the Reich's protectorate over Slovakia—may be pieced together.

[7] Report missing from Lipski's papers.

On March 19 Lipski proceeded to Warsaw to discuss matters of personal concern with leading factors in Poland. Prior to his departure he had two conversations with Robert Coulondre, French ambassador in Berlin. These conversations, as Lipski noted, dealt with the question of the Polish-French-British alliance. Coulondre's opinions, very pessimistic as to the possibility of checking Hitler's expansion, are contained in his long report to Paris dated March 19.[8] Coulondre presumed that Hitler's next blow would be directed eastward, toward Rumania and Poland, giving these states the alternative, as he had to Austria and Czechoslovakia, of a massacre of the population and destruction of cities or acceptance of German terms. Besides, Coulondre did not exclude the possibility that Hitler might first attack France and England, before they reached the level of the Reich in their armaments. Coulondre's comments were in favor of an increase, jointly with England, of the military potential of the two countries, especially in the air force, avoiding any publicizing of this armaments build-up.

Coulondre dispatched his report on the same day that he had the conversation with Lipski. It may be assumed that the Ambassador of allied France had informed the Ambassador of allied Poland about the pessimistic tenor of his report.

Lipski arrived in Warsaw with the intention of resigning from the post of ambassador in Berlin. He saw clearly that all his work of many years to establish peaceful relations between Poland and Germany had been ruined. He thought that his resignation might, as he writes in his note, help "to bring the country back to its senses."

The Ambassador's intention to resign sprang up some time earlier (such is the opinion of persons close to him). After his conversation with Ribbentrop at Berchtesgaden on October 24, 1938 (Document No. 124), Lipski understood that the policy he had been conducting was coming to an end; that neither written nor verbal promises and obligations of Hitler and Ribbentrop could be trusted; and that possibly it would serve the cause to change Polish ambassadors in Berlin.

Now, after Hitler's occupation of Prague, Lipski decided to present this matter formally to Beck.

On the morning of March 20, upon his arrival in Warsaw, Lipski was informed about disturbances in the capital and about "demonstrations against Beck, when words against me were also uttered." On the same day he had a conversation with Beck and Marshal Śmigły-Rydz, during which he presented his resignation and reported on his conversations with Coulondre. Both the Minister and the Marshal were upset by this information.[9]

Lipski's resignation was not accepted, and during the day he received a

[8] *Livre jaune,* No. 80, pp. 87–92.

[9] Three days after the conversation with Lipski, on March 23, Marshal Śmigły-Rydz issued special instructions to the western inspectors of the army (who in case of war would take command of the armies), defining the war tasks of their armies. *Polish Armed Forces in the Second World War,* Vol. I, Part 1: "September Campaign, 1939" (London, 1951), p. 271.

telephone message from Berlin that Ribbentrop was awaiting him for a conversation.

In Warsaw, Lipski encountered intentions of a Polish-British rapprochement. For some time already Beck had intended to go to London.[10] With regard to conversations with the British, Lipski made the reservation "for my part to keep the Polish-British rapprochement absolutely confidential until all security military measures between the three [Poland, England, and France] were achieved."

On the evening of March 20 Lipski departed for Berlin, where he had a conversation with Ribbentrop the next day. In this conversation Ribbentrop once more repeated the German propositions that Danzig be returned by Poland and an extraterritorial superhighway and railway line be constructed across Pomerania, and in exchange he guaranteed that Poland would keep Pomerania and its access to the sea.[11] He complained about Polish student excesses and talked about Polish-German minority negotiations, about which no joint communiqué had been agreed to.[12]

Lipski, for his part, stressed Poland's concern over Germany's solution of the Slovakia question, which definitely had an anti-Polish aspect.

Ribbentrop suggested that Beck should come to Berlin to discuss basic matters with him and Hitler, and advised Lipski to proceed in the next days to Warsaw to refer this offer to Beck.

On the following day, March 22, Lithuania was compelled to sign an agreement ceding Kłajpeda (Memel Territory) to the Reich.[13]

On that day Lipski arrived in Warsaw in a highly pessimistic mood.[14]

He wrote in his note: "My appraisal is that the situation is far more dangerous than Warsaw realizes." Waiting for Beck, he had a conversation in the hall with Beck's secretary, Starzeński, and "several other officials of the Polish Ministry of Foreign Affairs, who were of a different opinion."

Germany's position with regard to Danzig and the superhighway had been very bluntly defined by Ribbentrop in his plan of instructions for von Moltke dated March 23.[15] However, Hitler did not consent that it be sent to Warsaw.

---

[10] DGFP, Series D, Vol. V, Nos. 130 and 140.

[11] For the contents, see Polish White Book, No. 61, and DGFP, Series D, Vol. VI, No. 61.

[12] These negotiations were held in Berlin from February 27 to March 3. See DGFP, Series D, Vol. V, Nos. 128, 132, and 134.

[13] For the text of the agreement, see ibid., No. 405.

[14] See the Lipski-Szembek conversation of March 22, Journal, p. 433.

[15] DGFP, Series D, Vol. V, Nos. 73 and 88.

DOCUMENT 138   Memorandum on the Conference of Senior Officials
with the Polish Minister of Foreign Affairs
*on March 24, 1939*

*Secret*

Minister: The tension of the situation requires an investigation of the whole complex of problems. The situation is serious and it cannot be ignored. And it is serious because one of the elements hitherto timely for the definition of the state's situation, that is, Germany, has lost its calculability, with which it was endowed even amidst difficult problems.

Therefore a number of new elements have appeared in our politics and a number of new problems in the state.

As far as the basic line of action is concerned, a straight and clear line has been established with the top factors in the state. We defined with precision the limits of our direct interests, and beyond this line we conduct a normal policy and undertake action dealing with it as with normal current work. Below this line comes our Polish *non possumus*. This is clear: we will fight. Once the matter is put this way, chaos is overcome by a considerable share of calm, and thinking becomes orderly.

Where is the line? It is our territory, but not only that. The line also involves the nonacceptance by our state, regarding the drastic spot that Danzig has always been, of any unilateral suggestion to be imposed on us. And, regardless of what Danzig is worth as an object (in my opinion it may perhaps be worth quite a lot, but this is of no concern at the moment), under the present circumstances it has become a symbol. This means that, if we join that category of eastern states that allow rules to be dictated to them, then I do not know where the matter will end. That is why it is wiser to go forward to meet the enemy than to wait for him at home.

This enemy is a troublesome element, since it seems that he is losing the measure of thinking and acting. He might recover that measure once he encounters determined opposition, which hitherto he has not met with. The mighty have been humble to him, and the weak have capitulated in advance, even at the cost of honor. The Germans are marching all across Europe with nine divisions; with such strength Poland would not be overcome. Hitler and his associates know this, so that the question of a political contest with us will not be like the others.

I started with the extreme problem, in order to establish immediately an outlet for our thinking on this matter. On this basis we shall start international action. We have arrived at this difficult moment in our politics with all the trump cards in our hand. This does not speak badly for us.

I would like you, Gentlemen, to use your influence on your junior colleagues in order to bestow on our Ministry the bearing commensurate with these serious premises.[16]

Lipski attended this conference at which Beck defined the political line for Poland to follow. The next day Lipski received instructions within the frame of this policy and proceeded immediately to Berlin, requesting a meeting with Ribbentrop.

These instructions are contained in the *Polish White Book* (No. 62) with a number of basic omissions, and with the complete elimination of the last paragraph dealing with Russia. In Lipski's papers there is the full text, which reads as follows:

DOCUMENT 139     Beck's Instructions to Lipski

Warsaw, March 25, 1939
*Strictly Confidential*

With reference to the questions addressed to you on the 21st inst. by Herr von Ribbentrop relating to the complex of Polish-German relations, please communicate the following reply:

1) As in the past, so now, the Polish government attaches full importance to the maintenance of good-neighborly relations to the utmost extent with the German Reich.

The Polish government has given definite proof of this by the fact that in 1933 it was first to adopt a friendly attitude toward the Third Reich by opening conversations with a view to eliminating difficulties—conversations which led to the Polish-German declaration of January 26, 1934.

[16] Szembek quotes this memorandum in his *Journal* (pp. 434–35) but not *in extenso*.

It will be appropriate, at this moment, to remind the German Reich of the friendly attitude adopted by the Polish government toward the first National Socialist Senate of the Free City of Danzig.

During the five years following, in all its political activity in the international sphere, the Polish government always refused to take any part in action directed against the interests of the German Reich.

Finally, it is a known fact that in 1938 the firm attitude of the Polish government, marked with understanding for national German revindications, contributed in a great measure to the avoidance of the catastrophe of war.

2) In regard to questions on which agreement has hitherto always been achieved, but concerning which the German Reich has recently put forward new proposals, namely, on the question of transit between the Reich and East Prussia and on the question of regulating the future of the Free City of Danzig, the Polish government considers that:

a) It has no interest in hindering the German government's free communication with the Eastern Province of the Reich. For this reason also, despite many changes which have occurred in recent years by comparison with the previous state of affairs (for instance, the payment of transfers), the Polish government not only has not placed any difficulties in the way of privileged rail transit but has arranged the financial side of this transit in accordance with German interests. This being its attitude, the Polish government is quite willing to study together with the German government the possibility of further simplification and more facilities in rail and road transit between Germany and East Prussia, so that German citizens shall not encounter unnecessary difficulties while using these communications. To this end technical experts could set to work to draw up plans which would by degrees render possible an improvement also in the technical aspect of these communications. All facilities granted on Polish territory could only exist, however, within the limits of Polish sovereignty, and therefore extraterritorial status for ways of communication could not be considered. With this exception, the Polish government's intentions are in the direction of the most liberal treatment of the German *desiderata*.

The solution of the problem, however, depends upon the attitude the German government adopts in regard to my suggestions in the following point.

b) So far as the status of the Free City of Danzig is concerned, the Polish government recalls that it has for a long time now made references to the necessity for a settlement of this issue by way of an understanding between Warsaw and Berlin, this because it would correspond to the essence of the problem, and all the more because the League of Nations is losing the possibility of fulfilling the obligations it has undertaken in the matter.

From previous conversations it is clear that there is no difference of opinion as to the basic approach to the problem, that is, that the Polish government in no way hinders the free national life of the Free City of Danzig, while the German government has declared its respect for Polish rights and interests in the spheres of economy, communications, merchant marine, and the Polish population on the territory of the Free City. As the entire problem is contained in these two points, the Polish government considers it would be possible to find a solution based on a joint Polish-German guarantee to the Free City of Danzig. Such a guarantee would need to meet the aspirations of the German population on the one hand, and to safeguard Polish interests on the other, which interests for that matter are synonymous with the interests of the population of the Free City, considering that the City's well-being has, for centuries, been based upon Polish maritime trade.

The problem of the superhighway is primarily of a technical nature. In the opinion of the Polish government it should be studied by technical experts. On the question of the Free City of Danzig it would be advisable first to have a discussion of political principles between the government of the German Reich and the Polish government so as to ensure that in this organism, in the Chancellor's words employed in February last year, the national conditions of the Free City on the one hand, and the rights and interests of Poland on the other, would be respected.[17] To ensure a stabilization of conditions in our part of Europe, the Polish government considers it desirable to carry on conversations on all these questions as quickly as possible, so as to find a basis for a lasting consolidation of good-neighborly relations between Poland and Germany.

I request you to add orally, and with some emphasis, that Marshal Piłsudski explicitly stressed to me that the method of handling the Polish-

[17] See *Polish White Book*, No. 37.

Danzig problem would be a touchstone of Polish-German relations. I ask you to add that you would be grateful if this opinion were brought to the Chancellor's notice.

You can present your statement, *in extenso* or recapitulated in the form of a memorandum, to the Reich Foreign Minister. On this occasion please add that, if there is a question of my possible meeting with the Reich Chancellor, I always regard this contact as a factor of immeasurable importance, not only to relations between our countries, but to general European policy. Yet I would add that in the present difficult situation I think it indispensable that such conversations should be prepared for by a previous elucidation of the above-mentioned questions, at least in outline form. For, in the atmosphere existing today, personal contacts which yielded no positive results might prove to be a retrogressive step in relations between our states. That my government would desire to avoid.

Please add at the same time that we must now devote great attention to our mutual relations. For owing to Germany's latest steps in regard to both Slovakia and Lithuania, of which the Polish government was not informed even at the last moment, although they concerned territories situated right on the frontiers of the Polish Republic, the general atmosphere demands clarification, and the methods of progress utilized by both governments must be chosen with particular caution.

In case the conversation turns to the subject of relations with Soviet Russia, please, recalling my conversation with von Ribbentrop in Warsaw and my explanation given to the Chancellor at Berchtesgaden, confirm that we always considered Russia's access to European politics a dangerous thing. Also please stress that we consider blocking the penetration of Communism into Poland one of the supreme tasks of our state.

*Beck*

Lipski executed the instructions of March 25 on the next day when he was received by Ribbentrop. The Polish Ambassador handed the Minister of Foreign Affairs a memorandum containing the main points of the instructions. Once more Ribbentrop stressed that a basis for conversations with Poland might be his conditions presented in the conversation of March 21.

He considered Polish military measures carried out at that time as a strange answer to his proposal for a final settlement of Polish-German relations.[18] The conversation gave no positive results. Ribbentrop stubbornly insisted on Danzig's incorporation into the Reich and on an extraterritorial superhighway in exchange for a twenty-five-year nonaggression agreement and a guarantee of the frontier with Germany. The Polish side was for a settlement of the Danzig question between Germany and Poland, without basically changing the status of the Free City, and was ready to further facilitate transit through Pomerania, maintaining Poland's sovereignty on that territory.[19]

On March 27 anti-German demonstrations took place at Bydgoszcz. Ribbentrop availed himself of this occasion to summon Lipski and deliver a strong protest. Stressing that, to the "generous proposal which Germany had made to Poland," Poland had replied evasively, the Reich Foreign Minister considered that relations between the two states "were therefore deteriorating sharply." [20]

[18] On March 25 Admiral Canaris, head of the Intelligence Department, telephoned the Auswärtiges Amt about Polish mobilization orders as follows: "1) Some 4,000 Polish troops are concentrated at Gdynia. 2) The troops of a garrison previously stationed in the southern part of the Corridor have been transferred to the immediate vicinity of the Danzig frontier. 3) Poland has mobilized three age-groups. All these measures concern only the northern part of Poland; in the other districts of the country there is nothing to report militarily. General Keitel does not believe in any aggressive intentions on the part of the Poles." *DGFP*, Series D, Vol. V, No. 90.

[19] See *Polish White Book*, Nos. 63 and 64, and *DGFP*, Series D, Vol. II, No. 101, with enclosed text of Polish memorandum.

[20] The report on this conversation is missing from Lipski's papers. For the German version, see *DGFP*, Series D, Vol. II, Nos. 108, 118, and 126. See also *Journal*, pp. 437–38, for Szembek's conversation with Moltke on March 24.

# Hitler's Hesitation as to the Direction of Attack [1]
## January—March, 1939

IN MY ARTICLES I called attention to a series of facts denoting certain hesitations by Hitler—from Munich until the spring of 1939—as to the sequence of future political and strategic moves of the Third Reich. My suppositions were confirmed by the declarations of Hitler himself, as well as by the general assumptions of his policy in relation to England, France, and, at that period also, Poland. The book of German Ambassador von Hassell contains a number of details in confirmation of my thesis. As far as the relations with Poland are concerned, German policy shows in its moves two seemingly contradictory tendencies. One of them is a drive for territorial revision with regard to Danzig and Pomerania; the other, a desire to gain Poland's partnership in a coalition formed under the leadership of Germany. Ribbentrop's proposals of October 24, 1938, the so-called *Gesamtlösung,* take both of these tendencies under consideration. Requests for Danzig's reunion with the Reich and for an extraterritorial superhighway and railway line across Pomerania represent no less than a reduced program of territorial claims, while an offer to Poland that it join in the Anti-Comintern Pact and in collaboration on colonial and emigration matters is in keeping with the broad aspirations of Hitlerite policy.

Upon the rejection by Poland, on November 19, 1938, of the claim to Danzig, the German side apparently made some gesture of withdrawal. A few days later Moltke (on November 22) told Beck that Ribbentrop was considering Polish-German relations on the level of high policy, and that Poland's reply of November 19 made him better realize that is was impossible for Poland to give up the Free City.

The German Ambassador gave assurances that he was always warn-

---

[1] Printed in *Bellona* (London), 1950, No. 1, under the general title "New Contributions Concerning the Outbreak of the Polish-German War in 1939."

ing his government not to have illusions concerning this problem. Such illusions persisted within Party circles, especially in Forster, the gauleiter of Danzig, who was always inciting Hitler's entourage.

The German government outwardly pretended that no changes had occurred in its relations with Poland. During Ribbentrop's visit to Paris on December 6, 1938, in connection with the signing of the French-German nonaggression pact, Georges Bonnet declared that France had two agreements: one with Poland and another with Soviet Russia, the free action of which was formally provided for in the document prepared for signing.[2] To which Ribbentrop replied: "I know them both. I know about your pact with Russia, supervised by the League of Nations, and your alliance with Poland. These points do not constrain us. As a matter of fact, we ourselves have the best relations with the Poles, with whom we are also bound by an agreement."

In spite of the signing of this pact between France and Germany, the atmosphere in French-British circles was very tense with concern. This is confirmed by M. Georges Bonnet's description of the conference held by him and Daladier with Chamberlain and Halifax at the Quai d'Orsay on November 20 with regard to the mutual defense of the two countries.

"The dialogue between the French and British ministers is a good illustration of our mutual concern. We were far from believing that the Munich Agreement canceled the danger of war in the east. And what is more, we even asked each other who would first receive the German blow in the west—England or France? Mr. Chamberlain did not share the opinion of M. Daladier, who thought that France—owing to its geographical position—would be attacked first in case of a conflict. Mr. Chamberlain thought, owing to the present attitude taken by Germany, it was more probable that strife would erupt between England and Germany, and then England would suffer the first blow. Experts should investigate the problem of possible aggression against England by Germany and the means of assistance on the part of France."[3]

On January 5, 1939, Beck was to meet with Hitler at Berchtesgaden. Secretary of State Weizsäcker prepared material for the conversation. He handed it to Ribbentrop on January 2, 1939,[4] with the following conclusions:

[2] Bonnet, *Fin d'une Europe*, p. 38.
[3] *Ibid.*, p. 55.
[4] *DGFP*, Series D, Vol. V, No. 119 (footnote).

a) Poland should do more for our minorities.

b) Poland should at present remain satisfied with small economic advantages, in case Kłajpeda [Memel] shortly becomes German.

c) It will probably become evident from the conversations whether it is still too early to determine Poland's attitude toward other points of our eastern policy. Beck should understand how very weak his position is and that we await the moment when he becomes more conciliatory.

From this opinion it is clear that the Auswärtiges Amt did not urge a prompt Polish-German solution in accordance with Ribbentrop's proposals of October 24, 1938. Weizsäcker confessed at the Nuremberg trial that, since Poland lost sympathy in the West upon its occupation of Teschen Silesia, he counted on a further deterioration of its relations with France and England, and in consequence on more concessions on its part.

A report from the Berchtesgaden conference was distributed to German posts by a circular telegram dated January 10, 1939. It was signed by Weizsäcker, who undoubtedly must have confirmed the text with Ribbentrop, who was present at the Hitler-Beck conversation. The text of the telegram is as follows: [5]

"The visit of Foreign Minister Beck, which was motivated by a Polish desire to discuss the new situation, took place in a friendly atmosphere. It was noted on both sides that the agreement of January, 1934, had provided its worth and continued to form the basis of German-Polish relations.

"More particularly the question of Danzig was discussed, but did not reach a practical stage. The Führer reassured Beck with respect to the alleged danger of *faits accomplis* being engineered in Danzig, and confirmed Poland's need for access to the sea. The question of Memel was touched upon briefly. The Führer also dissipated Polish misgivings regarding Germany's Ukraine policy. No agreements of any kind were reached. Beck repeated the familiar Polish explanation of the origin of the Polish-Soviet declaration, which became necessary on account of numerous border incidents.

"The Reich Foreign Minister accepted in principle Beck's invitation to Warsaw extended at the end of last year. The date is still open."

From these instructions it is evident that, in spite of the fact that no agreement had been reached on the Danzig problem along the line of

[5] *Ibid.,* No. 121.

German claims, the German government continued to avoid open conflict with Poland.

Upon his return to Warsaw Beck, as he told me himself, warned the President of the Republic and Marshal Śmigły-Rydz that the situation on the Danzig problem was becoming serious.[6] Polish diplomacy intensified its activity in Paris and London.

As yet we have no access to the full German documentation with regard to Ribbentrop's visit to Warsaw (January 25–27, 1939). We only know that on January 13 Ribbentrop issued an order to Forster to desist from new steps in Danzig until his return from Warsaw.[7]

Among the measures planned for the near future were:

a) introduction of the official Hitlerite salute in Danzig,

b) introduction of the German flag,

c) formation of an S.S. *Totenkopf* detachment.

In the same instructions for the Gauleiter of Danzig, it was also mentioned that upon his return from Warsaw Ribbentrop would have a consultation with him, and at that time a decision would be made as to whether these measures would have to be introduced, or whether they would become unessential in view of a general understanding with Poland.

A series of articles appeared in Germany written by P. Kleist, a member of the Polish Desk at Ribbentrop's office.[8] Kleist accompanied the Reich Foreign Minister to Warsaw in January, 1939. The main aim of this visit was, in his opinion, to obtain from the Polish government basic consent for collaboration with Germany against the Soviet Union. Ribbentrop's conversations with the President of the Republic and Marshal Śmigły-Rydz yielded no results. As Kleist put it, "The Poles always skillfully avoided this subject."

Late on the afternoon of January 26 Ribbentrop held a conversation with Beck at the Brühl Palace on principles of the whole complex of Polish-German problems. In accordance with Beck's desire, I agreed with Ambassador von Moltke that we would leave the foreign ministers to converse alone, in order to facilitate a freer exchange of opinion. The conversation lasted for more than two hours. High-ranking officials gathered in the German Embassy had to wait a long time before they could take their places at the dinner table.

[6] See p. 482.
[7] *DGFP*, Series D, Vol. V, No. 122.
[8] *Die Zeit*, October, 1949, I: "Die Reise nach Warschau."

In this basic conversation Beck once more stressed Poland's negative stand with respect to Danzig's reunion with the Reich. Passing to the other problem no less urgent for Hitler, he cut himself off unequivocally from Poland's participation in the Anti-Comintern Pact.

Ribbentrop's mission therefore, proved to be a failure. Kleist called it "the collapse of an attempt on the part of Germany to overcome the problem of Danzig and the Corridor by way of an anti-Soviet solution in conjunction with Poland." Kleist presumably had in mind compensations for Poland at the expense of Soviet Russia in exchange for Danzig and the Corridor.

With growing distrust in the West as to the results of the Munich policy, Polish credit was on the rise. London received at that time disturbing news from Germany. Bonnet writes that according to information received on January 29 at the Quai d'Orsay by the British ambassador in Paris, Hitler, influenced by Ribbentrop and Himmler, was turning over in his mind the idea of striking against the Western Powers as an inaugural operation, with a later assault in the east. This information originated from high-ranking Germans whose sincerity was beyond any doubt. Other similar news was received from foreigners, hitherto Germanophiles, who were in contact with leading German personalities.

"As yet, there was no reason to suppose that Hitler had declared himself for some definite plan. Information in our possession pointed to the fact that he could:

"1) Encourage Italy to support its claims by force and, taking advantage of his obligations toward Italy, enter into war.

"2) Attack Holland. By becoming master of Holland and its coastline, Germany would try to dictate its conditions to Great Britain, at the same time paralyzing France. In the meantime, it could draw Poland, and possibly also other states, to its side by luring them with promises of colonial compensation.

"3) Put colonial claims in the form of an ultimatum.

"4) Attack England by air and, upon this surprise assault, undertake land and sea operations against the Western Powers.

"We received information from high-ranking Germans according to whom such a surprise attack was being prepared." [9]

At that time President Roosevelt communicated to the Dutch envoy information according to which the President had been advised "from

[9] Bonnet, *Fin d'une Europe*, pp. 126–27.

three reliable sources that Germany was allegedly determined to turn against the West, in all probability at a moment when Italy officially placed its territorial claims." [10]

In connection with Ciano's trip to Warsaw (February 23), the French government feared that the Polish government might collaborate on colonial problems. Activities of the Maritime and Colonial League (Liga Morska i Kolonialna) were disturbing for Paris, as was clear from Noël's report. On the request of the French government, Beck made a declaration that he would not support Ciano's colonial plans and, as Noël put it, he kept his word.[11]

Such was the picture of the situation prior to Hitler's occupation of Prague.

Public opinion in Poland was seriously disturbed by incidents involving students in Danzig. Hostile demonstrations against the German Embassy in Warsaw during Ciano's visit gave vent to these feelings. The irritating problem of Carpathian Ruthenia, as well as anti-Polish action of German agents in Slovakia, further inflamed the atmosphere.

Camouflaging the growing conflict with Poland during this period in the field of international relations became a characteristic feature of German tactics. Berlin still hoped to achieve its aim by direct conversations with Warsaw under more convenient political circumstances (after the occupation of Prague).

Germany did not want to drop the Polish card, which was of basic value to the Reich in Hitler's vast plans in the west and east.

Polish diplomacy, on its part, did everything in its power to avoid a conflict with Germany, and therefore remained outwardly discreet. After November, 1938, it tried to balance relations with Soviet Russia that had deteriorated owing to events in Czechoslovakia. Primarily, Polish diplomacy sought stronger support in the West. The restraint displayed by the Polish government in informing the Western Powers about the growing Polish-German tension might also be explained by fear that Poland's international position would be weakened in the eyes of the West.

[10] Ibid.
[11] Ibid., p. 129.

# Further Hesitation of Hitler [1]
## *March, 1939*

THE PERIOD of the occupation of Austria and the Sudetenland, which was so thoroughly investigated during the Nuremberg trial, did not provide much new material concerning direct Polish-German relations. Documents brought before the International Military Tribunal dealt, in the first place, with German activities which confirmed the aggressive attempts of the leaders of the Third Reich in relation to Austria and Czechoslovakia.

Sir Hartley Shawcross,[2] British prosecutor, in discussing German preparations for aggression against Poland, cited two documents [TC-76 and GB-31] stressing the connection between Germany's action against Czechoslovakia and Poland. One of these documents contains instructions of the Auswärtiges Amt regarding tactics to be used in the problem of Czechoslovakia in order to avoid conflict with the Western Powers and not evoke an undesirable reaction on the part of Poland. This document, destined for Ribbentrop, is dated August 26, 1938.

In opening remarks it is stated "that the most pressing problem of German policy, the Czech problem, might easily but does not have to lead to a conflict with the Entente. Neither France nor England is looking for trouble regarding Czechoslovakia. Both would perhaps leave Czechoslovakia to itself if it should, without direct foreign interference and through internal signs of disintegration due to its own faults, suffer the fate it deserves." Warning against the use of force to settle the Czech problem, the Auswärtiges Amt advised promoting the catchword popular in London circles: "autonomy for the Sudetenland." This kind of

[1] Printed in *Sprawy Międzynarodowe* (London), 1947, Nos. 2–3.

[2] There is a mistake in name here. This part of the indictment was read not by Shawcross but by Colonel Griffith-Jones on the thirteenth day of the Nuremberg trial, December 5, 1945 (*The Trial of German Major War Criminals*, Part II, p. 133).

method seemed desirable to the Foreign Affairs Ministry also in connection with relations with Poland, for encroachment of frontiers by Germany in the southeast would forcibly cause a reaction among Poles owing to frontier questions existing in the north and northeast. It is further stated in the document:

"The fact is that, after the liquidation of the Czech question, it will generally be assumed that Poland will be the next in turn. But the later this assumption penetrates international politics as a firm factor, the better. In this sense, however, it is important for the time being to carry on the German policy under the well-known and proved slogans of 'the right to autonomy' and 'racial unity.' Anything else might be interpreted as pure imperialism on our part and create the resistance to our plan by the Entente at an earlier date and more energetically than our forces could stand up to."

Shawcross also quoted General Jodl regarding the strategic importance of occupying Czechoslovakia for the future war with Poland. Jodl assumed that "the bloodless solution of the Czech conflict in the autumn of 1938 and the spring of 1939 and the annexation of Slovakia rounded off the territory of Greater Germany in such a way that it then became possible to consider the Polish problem on the basis of more or less favorable strategic premises." [3]

It could therefore be assumed that Hitler had been determined in advance to inflict armed aggression on Poland, upon capturing Czechoslovakia, and that events took exactly the course provided for them in his original plans and expectations. Was it so in fact?

In order to reply to this question, it would be necessary to investigate, from the material now made available, not only the development of Polish-German relations from Munich until the spring of 1939, but also the attitude of the Reich government toward France and Great Britain, as well as to establish the circumstances under which Nazi policy in relation to Russia underwent a change in May, 1939, or perhaps already in the middle of April.

The closer we come to the date of the outbreak of the war, the fuller and more abundant in detail becomes the Nuremberg documentation. In the last days of August, 1939, the course of events is fixed nearly from hour to hour.

[3] Speech of Colonel Taylor (not Shawcross) on the twenty-seventh day of the trial (January 4, 1946) quoting from Jodl's paper of 1943 (Doc. L-172, USA-34).

Let us first listen to Hitler himself, the person most responsible for the course of events. In his speech delivered to commanders of German armed forces, on August 22, 1939, when he disclosed his final decision to attack Poland within the next few days, Hitler used these words to motivate his decision:

"It was clear to me that a conflict with Poland had to come sooner or later. I had already made this decision in spring, but I thought that I would first turn against the West in a few years, and only afterward against the East. But the sequence could not be fixed. One cannot close one's eyes before a threatening situation. I wanted to establish an acceptable relationship with Poland in order to fight first against the West. But this plan, which was agreeable to me, could not be executed since essential points had changed. It became clear to me that Poland would attack us in case of a conflict with the West." [4]

At a conference with commanders of the armed forces on November 23, 1939, that is, already after war operations against Poland, Hitler confirmed his previous statements. Here are his words:

"One year later, Austria came; this step also was considered doubtful. It brought about a considerable reinforcement of the Reich. The next step was Bohemia, Moravia, and Poland. This step also was not possible to accomplish in one campaign. . . . It was not possible to reach the goal in one effort. It was clear to me from the first moment that I could not be satisfied with the Sudeten-German territory. That was only a partial solution. The decision to march into Bohemia was made. Then followed the erection of the Protectorate and with that the basis for the action against Poland was laid, but I was not quite clear at that time whether I should start first against the East and then the West or vice versa. Moltke often made the same calculations in his time. Under pressure the decision came to fight with Poland first." [5]

Hitler's attitude toward France left no doubt from the moment he started to build up the National Socialist Party. In *Mein Kampf* he called France the eternal enemy of Germany. He consistently strove to weaken France's position in Europe from the time he came to power. However, outwardly his action toward that country was camouflaged by a pretended desire for an agreement on the basis of Germany's renunciation of its territorial claims. In the first years of his rule, Hitler achieved

[4] *Trial of the Major War Criminals,* Vol. XXVI, No. PS-798.
[5] *Ibid.,* No. PS-789.

his greatest success at the expense of direct French interests, owing to France's internal weakness which compelled it to abandon its independent policy. Among his victories were the reunion of the Saar with Germany and the remilitarization of the Rhineland. In November, 1937, Hitler was absolutely aware of France's dependence on Great Britain. This became even clearer to him after Munich. He then started to act toward loosening relations between Paris and London. The German-French declaration of December 6, 1938, signed by Ribbentrop and Bonnet, was, for the German side, aimed at neutralizing British influence.

In contrast with his early anti-French arguments, Hitler declared himself in *Mein Kampf* for an agreement with Great Britain. He condemned Wilhelm II for bringing about a war between the German and Anglo-Saxon races. His emissaries traveled to England prior to 1933. They did not succeed, judging by the failure of Rosenberg's mission. Ideological programs and ideas of anti-Bolshevik crusades did not find a fertile soil in the British community. Hitler, however, was obstinate. The choice of Ribbentrop for the office of delegate extraordinary for disarmament matters had been decided on because of his allegedly widespread relations in the Anglo-Saxon world, about which that weird ambassador of the new regime was so eager to boast. In spite of some initial successes, primarily the conclusion of a sea pact between Great Britain and the Reich in 1935, the later mission of Ribbentrop as ambassador to London ended in utter failure. The anti-Comintern plans with which he approached the English, with the idea of thus gaining a free hand for the Reich in the East, failed completely. From an advocate of a rapprochement with Great Britain, he then became its most dogged adversary. Plenty of proof might be found to this effect in the Nuremberg documents.

In a personal, strictly confidential memorandum sent from London on January 2, 1938, to the Chancellor of the Reich,[6] describing the complex of German-British relations, Ribbentrop reached the following conclusions:

1) England is late with its armaments and therefore wants to gain time.

2) England believes that in the competition with Germany time is playing into its hands. It is counting on exploiting its larger economic

[6] *DGFP*, Series D, Vol. I, No. 93.

potential in the field of armaments, as well as on extending its treaties, for example, with the United States.

3) Halifax's visit should be regarded solely as a desire to investigate the situation and as a camouflage. English Germanophiles also are only playing the roles they have been assigned to perform.

4) England and its Prime Minister do not see in the visit of Halifax any possibility of creating the basis for an understanding with Germany. They have only as much confidence in National Socialist Germany as the Germans have in England. That is why they fear that some day they might be forced to accept solutions not agreeable to them. In order to cope with this, England is preparing militarily and politically—in case of emergency—for a war with Germany.

And here are Ribbentrop's final conclusions:

1) Outwardly, further agreement with England to safeguard the interests of Germany's friends.

2) In utter secrecy, creation, with unflinching persistence, of a coalition against England, namely, by tightening the friendship with Italy and Japan, as well as by winning over all nations whose interests are linked directly or indirectly with German interests. To establish close and confidential collaboration between the diplomacies of these three Great Powers in order to achieve the goal sought.

Not even a whole month elapsed from the time this memorandum was written before Joachim von Ribbentrop became foreign minister of the Reich. It is therefore easy to guess how Hitler reacted to the advice of his London emissary.

The Chamberlain-Hitler agreement at Munich brought no change in the situation. It conformed with Ribbentrop's recommendations in keeping up the appearances of an agreement with Great Britain. Hitler's speech delivered at Saarbrücken came as an unpleasant surprise to English Munich-adherents. At the same time information reached the British government from German opposition circles about military and particularly air plans of Germany directed against England.

Against the background of this general situation my conversation with von Ribbentrop took place at Berchtesgaden on October 24, 1938.[7]

Ribbentrop presented a concept of a large-scale Polish-German

[7] See Document 124, p. 453.

agreement, calling it "eine sekulaere Loesung" ["a solution for centuries"]. In exchange for Danzig's reunion with the Reich and the extraterritorial superhighway and railway line across the Pomeranian Corridor, the German government would disclaim further aspirations to the Polish western provinces and would extend the nonaggression declaration by a further twenty-five years. But this was not the end of the German proposal. Ribbentrop suggested that Poland should join the Anti-Comintern Pact and that there should be Polish-German collaboration on colonial problems. This would be equivalent to Poland's joining a coalition formed under Hitler's leadership.

Theoretically speaking, Hitler could have abstained from burdening his proposals that Poland enter within the orbit of German politics with the highly irritating problems of Danzig and the superhighway. He might have expected that, if Poland were joined with Germany, it would have later surrendered to the will of Germany's dictator on territorial questions. Or did Hitler still, after so many rejected attempts, have some hope of persuading Poland to renounce its relations with the West and its independent position between Germany and Russia? Were the return of Danzig and the superhighway just to be a tribute, which Hitler was in the habit of claiming in advance in exchange for the so-called friendship offered by the Third Reich to its future satellites? Hitler must have had, of course, to consider local pressure from the Reich's eastern provinces. After the Saar and the Rhineland, after Austria and the Sudetenland, the German eastern provinces must have felt neglected. Gauleiters who kept promising for years that a great day would come in Danzig just could not wait to see it come. The Prussian Junker caste, whose influence reached as far as the Reich Chancellery, did not tire in its agitation for the reunion of the Corridor with Germany. In Hitler's concept, the demand for the return of Danzig and the possession by Germany of an extraterritorial superhighway represented a minimum program of German claims, since it was possible to execute this program under convenient international circumstances without an armed conflict with Poland. Hitler and his immediate entourage believed this to be possible, in spite of unequivocal warnings on the part of Polish diplomacy. General Keitel's order issued on November 24, 1938,[8] that is, just five days after my conversation with Ribbentrop, when on behalf of Minister Beck I gave a reply to the proposal of October 24, stating that any

[8] *Trial of the Major War Criminals,* Vol. XXXIV, No. C-137.

attempt to incorporate the Free City into the Reich would evoke a Polish-German conflict, confirmed this belief. Keitel's order anticipated the occupation of Danzig by surprise attack. However, it contained a clear reservation that this operation should not mean a war with Poland. The occupation of the Free City was to take place at a politically convenient moment, under the appearance of a revolt in the city. Another interesting detail contained in the order was a message that German forces in East Prussia, destined for the occupation of Danzig, should not be simultaneously engaged in the move on Kłajpeda [Memel], in order that, if necessary, these two operations could take place at the same time. It is worth recalling that, when in March, 1939, Hitler occupied Kłajpeda, the Polish command—counting on the possible synchronization of the two operations—took steps for a military cover of the Free City of Danzig.

The Nuremberg files contain quite a lot of material dealing with German activities in relation to Slovakia and Carpathian Ruthenia for the period of the March crisis after Munich. There is not so much material to enlighten us with regard to German moves against Poland.

The published memoirs of former German Ambassador von Hassell, who was executed on Hitler's orders after the July, 1944, attempt, correct this shortcoming to a certain extent. Among other things, Hassell reports on a conversation held with Weizsäcker on December 16, 1938. The Secretary of State, who talked very openly with his colleague and friend, defined the policy of Ribbentrop and Hitler as one definitely leading to war. He also pointed to some hesitation among the top authorities of the Reich whether to turn immediately against England, safeguarding Poland's neutrality to this end, or to move eastward to liquidate the Polish and Ukrainian problems and occupy Kłajpeda. Hassell gives no explanation as to what Weizsäcker had in mind when he spoke of the liquidation of Polish and Ukrainian questions.

Under the date of January 26, 1939, von Hassell noted in his memoirs, following further information from Weizsäcker, that there was a peaceful atmosphere also with regard to the East, where at most they would like to start something with Poland (on that day Ribbentrop was in Warsaw). At the same time, in Weizsäcker's opinion, Hitler's program anticipated a total occupation of Czechoslovakia.

Ribbentrop's conversations with Beck in Warsaw produced no results. The Reich Minister met with firm resistance regarding the incorporation of Danzig into Germany. He also once more had the occasion to learn from his conversation with Minister Beck about Poland's negative attitude toward joining anti-Comintern agreements. Upon his return to Berlin Ribbentrop, as appears from Hassell's report, influenced Hitler to liquidate the Czechs in the first instance, leaving Danzig and the Corridor question to be settled later. Hassell, who notes this detail as a result of information received from von Nostitz, a German diplomat who at that time was assigned to the Auswärtiges Amt, adds his own commentary that if the Corridor question were placed ahead of the Czech problem there was a chance to arrive at a solution agreeable to German demands. Hassell justifies this assumption by the fact that only after Prague was occupied did the resultant deep shock strike international public opinion, causing a change in the Powers' attitude toward Hitlerite Germany. According to further information from von Nostitz, Ribbentrop, owing to his tactical mistake and his erroneous appraisal of the reaction in England, for a few weeks fell into disfavor with Hitler.

Ribbentrop undoubtedly thought that, owing to the occupation of Prague and the extension of the German protectorate over Slovakia, a militarily threatened Poland would be readier for concessions. That is why on March 21, immediately upon the termination of the Czech operation, he renewed his claims against Poland.

Hitler's attitude toward Poland during these critical days of March is disclosed by a note on the conversation held by the commander in chief of the Land Army, General Brauchitsch, with the Reich Chancellor [9] on March 25, 1939. This very important document, to which not enough attention was paid during the Nuremberg trial, is of particular value in taking stock of the situation at that time.

I quote verbatim paragraphs dealing with Poland:

"*Danzig problem.* L. [Lipski] is returning from Warsaw on Sunday, March 26; his mission there was to inquire whether Poland was ready to make an arrangement about Danzig. The Führer left Berlin on the evening of March 25 and does not wish to be here when L. returns. For the present R. [Ribbentrop] is to conduct the negotiations. The Führer *does not* wish to solve the Danzig question by force, however. He does not wish to drive Poland into the arms of Britain by this means.

"A possible military occupation of Danzig could be contemplated *only* if L. gave an indication that the Polish government could not justify

[9] *DGFP,* Series D, Vol. VI, No. 99 (emphasis appears in the official text).

voluntary cession of Danzig to its own people and that a *fait accompli* would make a solution easier for it."

When making such a supposition, Hitler possibly thought about some instances from the negotiations with Czechoslovakia. However, they could not possibly be applied in Poland's case.

*"The problem of Poland.* For the present the Führer does not intend to solve the Polish question. However, it should now be worked upon. A solution in the near future would have to be based on especially favorable political preconditions. In such a case Poland would have to be so beaten down that, during the next few decades, it need not be taken into account as a political factor. In a solution of this kind the Führer envisages an advanced frontier, extending from the eastern border of East Prussia to the eastern tip of Silesia. The questions of evacuation and resettlement still remain open. The Führer does *not* wish to enter the Ukraine. Possibly a Ukrainian state might be established. But these questions too still remain open."

Further directives in the note dealt with problems of Slovakia and the Protectorate.

It transpires from this document that Hitler feared that Poland might bind itself with England. He still made the solution of the Polish problem dependent on favorable international circumstances. Nevertheless, his future plans concerning Poland, together with the question of the future frontier, were clearly drafted in his mind.

On March 31, 1939, Chamberlain made a declaration in the House of Commons granting a guarantee to Poland in case its independence were threatened.

Three days later, on April 3, 1939, Keitel signed the first order dealing with preparations for war with Poland (code: "Operation White").[10] We see on the order in Hitler's handwriting a postscript that military preparations were to be finished by September 1, 1939.

The London conversations of Minister Beck were followed with utmost attention by the German government. News about the text of the Polish-English communiqué of April 6, stating that England and Poland united themselves with a bilateral guarantee, evoked a reaction of utmost dissatisfaction in Berlin. The German government evaluated this step as Poland's entry into the orbit of British politics. A conversation I had on that day with Weizsäcker left no illusions in this respect.

[10] *Ibid.,* Nos. 149 and 185.

Gisevius, author of the well-known book *Bis zum bitterem Ende,* and one of the leading witnesses at the Nuremberg trial, writes of Hitler's reaction when he learned about England's guarantee for Poland.

Gisevius' chief, the famous Admiral Canaris, head of the German Intelligence Service, returned one day from the Reich Chancellery, shocked by the state in which he found Hitler. Bad news had come from London. The British had decided to grant a guarantee to Poland. Canaris confirmed this news to Hitler, adding on his part that any further step to the east would bring about an armed conflict.

At this Hitler flared up with rage. Infuriated, he ran across the room, hammering with his fists against a marble table and spewing forth a tirade of the worst curses. His eyes glaring malevolently, he hissed a venomous threat: "I shall prepare a diabolic beverage for them."

Gisevius was of the opinion that this was the first hint of a pact with Stalin.

# Breach by Hitler of the
# Nonaggression Declaration of 1934
## March—July, 1939

THE OCCUPATION of Prague by Germany and the liquidation of the Czechoslovak state met with the determined reaction of British political circles. On
March 21, Sir Howard Kennard, ambassador of Great Britain in Warsaw,
presented to the assistant vice-minister, Mirosław Arciszewski, a memorandum regarding the declaration by four states—Great Britain, France, the
USSR, and Poland—announcing immediate consultations as to steps to be
taken in order jointly to counteract any action threatening the political
independence of any of the European states.[1]

In answer, Beck proposed to Halifax a bilateral Polish-British declaration
in the same spirit instead of a multilateral declaration.[2] On March 30 Ambassador Kennard advised Beck that Chamberlain intended to make a declaration in the House of Commons to the following effect:

"In the event of any action which clearly threatened Polish independence,
and which the Polish government accordingly considered it vital to resist
with their national forces, His Majesty's government would feel themselves
bound at once to lend the Polish government all support in their power."

Beck acknowledged this statement, and Chamberlain delivered his speech
in the House of Commons.[3]

In order to discuss these matters, Beck proceeded to London on April 2.
However, counting on a possible German reaction, especially in Danzig, he
held a conference on April 1, prior to his departure, with senior officials of
the Polish Ministry of Foreign Affairs and with General Wacław Stachiewicz,
chief of the General Staff.

[1] *Polish White Book*, No. 65.
[2] *Ibid.*, No. 66.
[3] *Ibid.*, Nos. 68 and 69.

DOCUMENT 140   Director of the Minister's Cabinet

April 1, 1939

Conference in Minister Beck's office on the Danzig problem.

Present: Messrs. General Stachiewicz, Vice-Minister Szembek, Minister Arciszewski, M. Łubieński, T. Kobylański.

Minister Beck does not think that we face an immediate decisive conflict over Danzig. However, we must be prepared for that eventuality and be in possession of emergency means which represent a compromise between military action and diplomacy.

The Minister envisages the following possibilities of a conflict:

I. Direct German military intervention in the form of trespassing of troops or landing of detachments. In that case our immediate counteraction follows in accordance with principles established by the General Staff. Entry of the fleet alone, without landing of detachments, would be dealt with as a diplomatic incident. In case of illegal entry of the German fleet into the Danzig harbor, our navy will not salute it in this port.

II. An internal Danzig putsch, that is, a case where initiative remains in the hands of the Senate or the Danzig Party.

Version A. Political declaration for reunion with the Reich. In the first stage only a diplomatic incident is created. On our side a protest is lodged in Danzig and in Berlin. Note to the German government should be formulated as follows: the Polish government supposes it to be only a sally of the local authorities; the German government should recognize that this cannot be tolerated by the Polish government. If the German government does not take this declaration under consideration, we shall consider this a violation of Polish rights and interests. Recognition by the Reich results in a Polish-German incident and our reaction as *ad* p. I (hypothetically).

Version B. Attack on Polish state organs in Danzig takes place, active reaction follows as *ad* p. I, but in proportion to the extent of the attack.

In case of an incident, railway orders are issued (Chief of the General Staff):

I. If the incident is confined to the Danzig territory only, transit communication at the sector of all transit lines across the Danzig territory is closed;

II. if Germany participates in the incident, all privileged transit is closed;

III. active reaction follows and mobilization orders are issued; a complete halt in communications.

General principles:

1) We are interested in maintaining the incident, as long as possible, within a local frame. Transfer of the quarrel to the level of Poland-Germany should not occur on our initiative but on the Reich's.

2) In case of a German ultimatum, answer that we cannot take it into consideration. In general do not get involved in any discussion as to yes or no. Act only on the basis of the Danzig or German *Uebergriff*.

3) In any case, the Minister is interrupting his trip and is returning to Warsaw.

In the evening hours of April 2, Beck, passing through Berlin, conversed with Lipski in the Nord Express. In a short note the Ambassador wrote that he called Beck's attention to the fact that, according to Attolico, the Italian ambassador in Berlin, a reguarantee on the Polish side would be considered by the German government as the end of its conversations with Poland. Lipski, therefore, suggested that the reguarantee should be linked with the Polish-French alliance, which was connected with the French-British alliance.

Lipski advised that nothing be done which might be interpreted as contradictory to the declaration of January 26, 1934. Beck replied that Director Jó-zef Potocki was carrying with him documents relating to Lipski's negotiations regarding the 1934 declaration, and that they would do their best to avoid controversy in London. Verbal instructions for Lipski read as follows:

1) Any Polish-British agreement will be bilateral, defensive, and in the character of a reguarantee,

2) Poland will not join the anti-German bloc.

Lipski also stressed the "fairly great tension in Berlin" and remarked that he preferred to converse with Weizsäcker rather than with Ribbentrop, who rendered the situation more acute.

On April 3 Lipski sent the following telegram to Beck:

DOCUMENT 141   Lipski to Beck in London

April 4, 1939

The local inspired press information contains very clearly a tendency to represent British action as trying to encircle Germany. Reference is made to the Chancellor's speech [4] predicting counteraction in anticipation of the attempt at encirclement. Insinuations addressed to Poland are beginning to appear openly.

I therefore think it would be desirable for Polish-German relations still to lay special stress outwardly in London on our attitude toward Germany, based upon the 1934 agreement.

Dirksen is absent from London. I suggest that perhaps the German Chargé d'Affaires and the Italian Ambassador could be received and our position explained to them, the more so since I feel a certain anxiety here from the Italian side that the rapprochement with England might complicate relations with Germany.

*Lipski*

A joint Polish-British communiqué about the necessity of contracting a bilateral pact of mutual aid in order jointly to counteract any action in case the independence of the two states was threatened was published in London on April 6, 1939. Poland took on the obligation to aid Great Britain in case of aggression.[5]

On the same day, even prior to the publication of the communiqué, Secretary of State Weizsäcker summoned Lipski to declare to him that German proposals in relation to Poland were no longer valid, since Poland's reaction to them had taken the form of military orders. On the basis of press information in respect to Beck's conversations in London, Weizsäcker was at a loss to understand how they could be in conformity with the spirit of the 1934 declaration.

Lipski, for his part, strongly criticized German policy in the last weeks, which acted by surprise against Poland, and stressed the necessity of reinforcing Poland's security.

Contents of the Lipski-Weizsäcker conversation were published in the *Polish White Book*, No. 70, but with a couple of omissions. After the first paragraph, the following sentence of Lipski was omitted: "I further stressed that we are not aiming for any association with Russia." At the end two sentences were omitted: "We did not go deeper into the matter, especially since this was only a first general exchange of opinion after a longer interruption of more than three weeks in my personal contacts with the Auswärtiges Amt. Herr Weizsäcker finally stressed that the German government is maintaining absolute calm, and he said that he regrets that our relations have taken such a course."

[4] Hitler's speech of April 1 at Wilhelmshaven on the occasion of the launching of the battle cruiser *Tirpitz*.
[5] *Polish White Book*, No. 71.

Weizsäcker's account of this conversation is different; he insists that a sharply toned statement was made to the Polish Ambassador.[6] During the Nuremberg trial, Weizsäcker finally conceded that the text of the *White Book* was rather more reliable.[7]

This was one of Lipski's last conversations with Weizsäcker. With Ribbentrop Lipski had one more conversation, on August 31, 1939, at 6:30 P.M.— ten hours before Germany attacked Poland.

After May, 1939, the number of Lipski's reports to the Ministry diminishes. He is more and more isolated from the A.A. and he visits Warsaw more frequently. The counselor of the Embassy, Prince Stefan Lubomirski, in the character of a chargé d'affaires, filled in for him in Berlin.

On April 8 Beck, in bad health, was returning from London via Berlin to Warsaw. In the morning at the station in Berlin he was greeted by Dornberg, chief of the A.A. protocol. Lipski writes in his personal notes that Beck was not yet ready and had to dress in a great rush. "He did not look well, and I was chagrined to see him exchange a few sentences with Dornberg in a hoarse voice." Lipski, together with the military attaché, Colonel Szymański, accompanied Beck by train to Frankfurt-an-der-Oder. In his conversation with Beck, Lipski called attention to the fact that demonstrations on the Polish side in honor of Beck's return should not take the form of an anti-German agitation. Beck issued orders that calm should be observed. Lipski further communicated to the Minister that the atmosphere in Berlin was becoming more tense from day to day and that the results of the London conversations further contributed to the deterioration of Polish-German relations. The whole German press overflowed with invective regarding the policy of encirclement applied by Great Britain and Poland to Germany. Lipski related to Beck his conversation with Weizsäcker of April 6, stressing his unwillingness to confer with Ribbentrop. To Beck's question about Göring's role, Lipski answered that he thought Göring's prestige had gone down. There were rumors that Göring was against the occupation of Prague. It was a fact, however, that Ribbentrop's influence on the Chancellor had become stronger. Hitler believed Ribbentrop in his evaluation of British policy, that is, that England would not go to war. Here Beck remarked that this concept was absolutely false and dangerous.

In conclusion, Lipski stressed that war was coming, but not immediately.

Colonel Szymański gave a pessimistic analysis of the situation.[8] He described it as dangerous, using the German term "Aufmarschbereitschaft— Richtung nach Osten" ("Preparation for marching up—direction toward the east"). The German *Ordre de Bataille* provided for the use of 60–70 divisions in 48 hours, and German drill-mobilization made it possible to place this force on Polish frontiers. However, Beck thought this opinion to be too

<hr>

[6] *DGFP*, Series D, Vol. VI, No. 169. See also the characteristic instructions for Moltke of April 5, *ibid.*, No. 159.

[7] "Trials of War Criminals," mimeographed transcript, pp. 7839–40.

[8] Szymański, pp. 128–31.

pessimistic; he explained to Lipski the character of the agreement with
England and thought that an understanding on Danzig might still be reached
on the conditions stated by Poland.

Lipski and Szymański took leave of Beck in Frankfurt and returned to
Berlin by plane.

Between April 18 and April 20 Gafencu, the foreign minister of Rumania,
paid a visit to Berlin and had a conversation first with Ribbentrop and then
with Hitler. Lipski noted in his papers that he had occasion to talk with
Gafencu after his meeting with Hitler. The Chancellor used very strong
words against Poland.[9]

On April 28 Hitler delivered a major address at the Reichstag in which he
deliberated on the complex of international relations. With regard to Poland
he disclosed for the first time German proposals for a settlement of the
Danzig question, the extraterritorial superhighway and the railway line
through Pomerania, as well as the twenty-five-year pact of nonaggression.
Poland had rejected this generous offer, had mobilized its army, and by the
agreement with England had infringed on the declaration of nonaggression
of 1934, which, under the circumstances, should be considered void.[10]

On the same day (April 28), immediately before Hitler's speech at noon
in the Reichstag, the German chargé d'affaires in Warsaw, Krümmer,
handed Vice-Minister Szembek a memorandum dated April 27 containing a
reiteration of all the charges against Poland from the Chancellor's speech.[11]

DOCUMENT 142   Lipski to Beck

NO. N/52/30/39                                        Berlin, April 29, 1939
                                                              *Secret*

I am evaluating as follows Chancellor Hitler's speech delivered at the
Reichstag on April 28, which had been anxiously awaited by German
and international opinion:

1) Chancellor Hitler followed the trend of diplomatic, rather than
military, action.

2) The chief aim of this action is to weaken or else loosen the united
front which was formed (between the Powers of the East and the West)
after the occupation of Bohemia, the extension of the *Schutz* over Slovakia, and the take-over of Kłajpeda [Memel].

[9] *DGFP*, Series D, Vol. VI, No. 234.
[10] For the text of Hitler's speech relating to Poland, see *Polish White Book*,
No. 75.
[11] For the text, see *ibid.*, No. 76, and *DGFP*, Series D, Vol. VI, Nos. 276
and 274. See also *Journal*, pp. 449–50.

3) While the polemic with England and the breach of the naval agreement constitute two of the principal features of the speech, it nevertheless resulted in direct pressure being brought to bear on Poland.

The fact that the Chancellor decided on tactics designed to loosen the front created to counteract German aggression indicates that the method adopted by the Powers of granting mutual support to each other in case of aggression proved to be effective. Its future success, in my opinion, depends on the partners' consistent willingness to keep their previously adopted positions.

Here I would like to mention that in my conversation today with the French Ambassador [12] we came to identical conclusions, and he assured me very definitely, on the basis of his constant contact with Prime Minister Daladier, that the French government would keep firmly to its adopted line. At the same time he urged that efforts be made to see that London, owing to Chamberlain's inclination for negotiations, does not stray from the adopted path. The Ambassador stated that the principle that Poland alone has the right to define the limits of its concessions to Germany should be respected.

Analyzing yesterday's speech of the Chancellor in a general review, I would like to call attention to the following details:

I. *The reply to Roosevelt,* which was to be the pivot of the speech, is dealt with on the level of skillful propaganda polemics, while essential political aspects relate to other fields.[13]

II. Most striking is the paragraph concerning German-*English* relations. It is conciliatory, reiterating Hitler's old concept of maintaining the best of relations with the British Empire. It might be possible to read between the lines an idea with regard to a partition of the world between England and the Reich. This had already been told to me by Minister Gafencu after he met with Hitler. At the same time, Hitler attacks England for the policy of encirclement and on this basis revokes the naval agreement.

Beyond any doubt, action undertaken by Great Britain against German aggression and the decision of Parliament to introduce conscription [14] are the reasons for the change of tone toward Great Britain. This

[12] *Livre jaune,* No. 115.

[13] See Roosevelt's telegram to Hitler of April 15 (*DGFP,* Series D, Vol. VI, No. 200).

[14] On April 26, Chamberlain informed the House of Commons that Great Britain intended to present a bill for compulsory military service.

tone, compared with invective cast by the German press and local statesmen against England, is most striking.

III. Although Hitler is sticking to his previous attitude toward *France,* namely, that upon settlement of the Saar problem territorial questions have been resolved, nevertheless there is a slight warning to France that renunciation of Alsace-Lorraine cannot be taken for granted, but that it stems from the desire to surrender national demands to higher international interests.

IV. Arguments justifying the occupation of Bohemia are clearly lacking in logic. The argument that the Czech element insinuated itself within the German tribe to create an enclave is groundless from the historical point of view. All this portion of the speech, barren of real arguments, is the weakest part.

V. The paragraph about a possible *guarantee for Rumania's frontiers* (about which I reported in my telegram) [15] is not contained in the speech. Instead, Hitler used an unguarded expression uttered by the Rumanian King to him at Berchtesgaden that Rumania should be entitled to a direct corridor through Carpathian Ruthenia and Slovakia toward the Reich. He used it to deny his aggressive intentions toward that country.

VI. Lengthy deliberations about *Lithuania* might not be explained solely by the question of uniting Kłajpeda with the Reich. Here tendencies should be considered for economic occupation of this country, as well as of the *Baltic states.*

VII. Through the speech runs a clear note that *Western Powers* should keep away from *Central and Eastern Europe.* The Chancellor explains that he could envisage their financial collaboration. Nevertheless, he adds that financial aid, as in the Czech instance, would result in military action of the Eastern states against the Reich.

VIII. A characteristic statement in confirmation of my earlier observations that the Chancellor felt that *without the Munich Agreement* a more favorable *solution of the Czechoslovak* problem could have been achieved by the Reich.

The statement that the Chamberlain-Hitler consultative agreement dealt exclusively with German-British relations, and that the Munich Agreement has nothing to do with Czech and Moravian problems, as well as that the appeal for arbitration made by the Hungarians and

[15] Missing from Lipski's papers.

Czechs on the matter of frontiers for Slovakia excluded the other two partners of Munich, might only be evaluated in the light of documents. Prime Minister Chamberlain himself will be the most competent interpreter of whether the Chancellor is right or wrong in his deliberations.

IX. In his speech the Chancellor returns repeatedly to the idea of *Lebensraum*. Explaining the annexation of Austria and Bohemia to the Reich, he states that within the frame of the present Great Reich there is not a single territory which had not long ago belonged to the Reich, had not been connected with it, or had not been under its sovereignty.

X. While there is a traditional paragraph about friendship *with Italy*, and praise for *General Franco* as the conqueror of Bolshevism, *Japan* is mentioned only by a single word, which undoubtedly results from the negative attitude Japan took with regard to efforts to change the Anti-Comintern Pact into a military alliance directed against England and France. Here I might mention in passing that, contrary to its previously employed practice, the German press for the first time printed information about Chinese successes in their offensive against Japan.

XI. The Chancellor made a characteristic statement that war would end in the destruction of European culture by *Bolshevism*.

XII. The portion devoted to Poland this time is particularly extensive; it maintains a rather realistic tone and is devoid of a clearly aggressive note. It is, however, bent to conform to the German thesis.

In other parts of the speech Poland is only mentioned in connection with the Teschen Silesia problem and Carpathian Ruthenia, as striving for a common frontier with Hungary.

In the main paragraph about Poland the following points are worth noting:

1) Reference by the Chancellor to the provision of the 1934 declaration which reads as follows:

"Each of the two governments, therefore, lays it down that the international obligations undertaken by it toward a third party do not hinder the peaceful development of their mutual relations, do not conflict with the present Declaration, and are not affected by this Declaration,"
and reference to the fact that in practice the provision had only been granted to Poland.

This statement is inaccurate, inasmuch as in 1934, as well as now, the German government was bound by the Treaty of Rapallo and the Berlin agreement with the Soviets. The fact that the negotiators in the 1934 declaration mentioned the hitherto accepted international obligations in relation to third parties is self-explanatory, since they could only make declarations in respect to contracted agreements. Besides, and this we have to bear in mind, these agreements were not disclosed to the parties, and it was only considered that these agreements were not in contradiction with the declaration.

The Chancellor speaks on this occasion about the Polish-French alliance but does not mention the Polish-Rumanian alliance, which, as a matter of fact, refers to Soviet Russia. However, he also fails to mention obligations under Article 16 of the Covenant of the League of Nations. I pass over here the legal argumentation to ascertain the conformity of the 1934 declaration with the Polish-British pact.

2) With regard to *Danzig,* I draw attention to the fact that the following is mentioned:

"The Danzig problem must at the latest, with the gradual extinction of this disastrous institution [the League of Nations], be discussed at any rate."

This might explain why the Chancellor opened a discussion on the subject of Danzig. At the same time this is also a loophole to postpone the settlement of the problem.

3) The statement that the Corridor and the superhighway through the Corridor have no military importance; their meaning is only of a psychological and economic nature.

4) At point 1 of the German offer, mention that Danzig returns "as a free state" to the Reich, which was not spelled out in conversations by the German side, while in the German note is only mentioned "return of Danzig to the Reich."

5) At point 2 of the offer, underlining that Germany had to obtain a *superhighway* and *railway line* for its use across the Corridor, of the same *extraterritorial* character as the Corridor is for Poland. The editing is not clear; it may be designed for a German audience, to show that the problem of the Corridor would thus also be settled.

6) At point 1 of the German concessions, it is said that all *economic rights in Danzig* would be granted to Poland. This would mean that this concerns also the customs union.

Note here that mention is also made of "the safeguarding of Poland's economic interests in Danzig" and of the "far-reaching settlements of the remaining problems for Poland in the field of economy and communication with the reunion of Danzig with the Reich."

7) The Chancellor states that he offered us a *twenty-five-year pact of nonaggression.*

In my report on my conversation with Ribbentrop of March 21, I only find an offer as to the guarantee of our frontiers. The question of the extension of the nonaggression pact had been brought up in previous conferences by the German side. I fail to remember whether von Ribbentrop, talking about the guarantee on March 21, also referred to the possibility of extending the pact. If so, he did it only very casually.

8) Also in connection with *Slovakia,* von Ribbentrop in the conversation of March 21 only mentioned that it would be possible to discuss it.

The Chancellor, however, speaks about guaranteeing the independence of the Slovakian state by Germany, Poland, and Hungary, which in practice would mean withdrawal of Germany's unilateral position in that country.

The note states Germany's readiness to consider also Poland's interests when securing Slovakia's independence.

9) Both paragraphs regarding our answer as to Danzig and the superhighway are inaccurate and minimize our counteroffer. Here we have to keep to my note handed to Ribbentrop on March 26.

10) The final statement of the Chancellor in the paragraph regarding Poland, of basic importance, is worded quite inexplicably, for an explanation is required to clarify the meaning of "readiness for a new agreement with Poland under the condition that such a *solution would be based on a quite clear obligation equally binding for both parties."*

*Józef Lipski*

In Warsaw Lipski for a second time handed Beck his resignation from the post of ambassador to Berlin,[16] this time in writing. In his opinion, after Hitler's renunciation of the nonaggression declaration of 1934, which had been the major achievement of Lipski's efforts, his further stay in Berlin was purposeless. Beck agreed with Lipski's argumentation; he conferred about the resignation with President Mościcki, but finally for the time being did not accept it. In any case, he considered the possibility of recalling Lipski from

[16] *Journal*, p. 451; see also the conversations between Szembek and Lipski (*ibid.*, p. 456), and between Szembek and Beck (*ibid.*, pp. 465 and 478).

Berlin and delegating him to the Embassy in the Vatican (a post which was filled by Kazimierz Papée, previously envoy in Prague), and replacing him in Berlin with Vice-Minister Szembek.

Beck's speech at the Diet on May 5 [17] came as an answer to the German speech and memorandum. Beck stressed in it that the 1934 declaration had been an event of great importance, bringing positive values into the lives of Poland, Germany, and Europe. Therefore, the breach of it by Hitler was not a meaningless act. Danzig was of enormous importance for Poland as an outlet to the Baltic, and Poland would not let itself be cut off from the Baltic. Poland was ready to make further transit concessions through the Pomeranian Corridor. However, Beck did not see any reason "to restrict our sovereignty on our own territory." Poland was ready to conduct further negotiations with the Reich in order to maintain peace, as the Chancellor mentioned, but under the condition that the Reich maintain its "peaceful intentions" and "peaceful methods of procedure." Beck closed his speech with the statement that "peace, like almost everything in this world, has its price, high but definable. We in Poland do not recognize the conception of peace at any price! There is only one thing in the life of men, nations, and states which is beyond price, and that is honor."

On that day the Polish chargé d'affaires in Berlin, Lubomirski, presented to Secretary Weizsäcker a memorandum dated May 5 containing the Polish answer to the German memorandum of April 28.[18] In principle it followed the same line as Beck's speech.

DOCUMENT 143    Lipski to Beck

NO. N/52/175/39                                           May 24, 1939
                                                              *Secret*

In respect to the political-military alliance [19] contracted on May 22, 1939, between the Reich and Italy, and with reference to my report of May 22, No. N/52/159/39,[20] I am taking the liberty of communicating as follows:

The government here bestowed on the act of the signing of the alliance an exceptionally festive and demonstrative character for internal and foreign propaganda purposes. The Chancellor of the Reich person-

[17] *Polish White Book*, No. 77.

[18] For the text, see *DGFP*, Series D, Vol. VI, No. 334, or *Polish White Book*, No. 78; see also *DGFP*, Series D, Vol. VI, No. 335.

[19] Pact of Friendship and Alliance between Germany and Italy (Pact of Steel); for the text, see *DGFP*, Series D, Vol. VI, No. 426.

[20] Missing from Lipski's papers.

ally attended the signing ceremony. An exchange of telegrams followed between the King of Italy and the Chancellor. Both foreign ministers were recipients of highest-ranking decorations (von Ribbentrop received the Annunciata). The Reich government prepared a most pompous reception for Ciano. The two foreign ministers broadcast speeches which were afterward repeated to representatives of the press (texts were enclosed with my report No. N/52/159/39 of May 22).

So much about the exterior frame of this historic act, as it is called by the German press.

Analyzing the document itself, first of all it strikes one by its considerable deviation from the type of the hitherto-contracted alliances between the states. It does not, in my opinion, deserve the title of either an offensive or a defensive alliance. It represents a *sui generis* international instrument based upon a common ideology of Germany and Italy. I should say that it is an understanding aimed at coordinating the dynamics of Fascism and Hitlerism, and at creating a common flow of their activities in order militarily to bind Hitlerite Germany with Fascist Italy.

Within a number of circles, both on the German and on the Italian side, the achievement of such an extensive alliance between the two countries evokes anxieties and forebodings. On the German side, the slogan "the strong man is most powerful alone" is popular, and where memories of alliances with the Austro-Hungarian Monarchy, Italy, and Rumania evoke bitter echoes from the period of the world war, elements of former diplomacy and the army in particular have misgivings about such strong links binding the policies of the Reich with Italian policy. Critical voices may be heard in those spheres even today. Nevertheless, close ties with Italy, at a moment when the Reich is faced with the British action of so-called encirclement, are regarded by decisive factors and the Party as a far-reaching success. And they are trying to make the best of it abroad.

With regard to the Italian side, I shall restrict myself to communicating the information I received from Envoy Gawroński. He has contacts with Italian military figures who came to Berlin on the occasion of signing the alliance. In accordance with this information, even General Pariani [21] himself is seriously prejudiced against the signing of a military pact. His anxieties are shared by other army men as well. With the Italians, this attitude might be considered the mentality of the weaker

[21] General Alberto Pariani, Italian chief of the General Staff of the Army.

fearing the stronger, as well as consideration for the unfavorable position of Italy in case of a world war, into which they would be plunged, for example, in the east, by German policy.

The Italian side lays special pressure—when commenting on the agreement—on the fact that the Italian government, through consultations, has the possibility of influencing the German government and of checking its actions.

Ambassador Attolico, with whom I conferred today, interprets Article I of the alliance [22] thus: that consultation, as it is stated *expressis verbis* in this article, concerns not only *common interests* but also *problems dealing with the complex of the European situation,* and as such it must bring about agreement in order to make the alliance valid. To my question as to the concept of "warlike complications" contained in Article III,[23] Signor Attolico explained that this sentence was used because it was more explicit than the previously employed concept of aggression, which is always a subjective one.

With regard to Article VI,[24] the Italian Ambassador only remarked that it is expressed in a general form and concerns friendly countries and those which in the future would like to approach the Axis.

I think that annexes to the agreement might exist which were not given publicity.[25] I received indirectly from the Italians information that there are three annexes, namely, to Article VI, for military collaboration, and allegedly—and this sounds incredible—even a division of interests after the possible war. Many Italians who arrived here commented on the alliance in a very inconsistent way. They even went so far as to state that in the first place the alliance is an act directed against the West, and especially against France, which would be the first to receive

[22] Art. I. The High Contracting Parties will remain in continuous contact with each other in order to reach an understanding on all questions affecting their common interests or the general European situation.

[23] Art. III. If, contrary to the wishes and hopes of the High Contracting Parties it should happen that one of them became involved in warlike complications with another Power or Powers, the other High Contracting Party would immediately come to its assistance as an ally and support it with all its military forces on land, at sea, and in the air.

[24] Art. VI. The two High Contracting Parties are aware of the significance that attaches to their common relations with Powers friendly to them. They are resolved to maintain these relations in the future also and together to shape them in accordance with the common interests which form the bonds between them and these Powers.

[25] There was one secret additional protocol consisting of two paragraphs. *DGFP,* Series D, Vol. VI, pp. 563–64.

the blow. The Italian Ambassador, however, tried to comment on the situation to the effect that there is now a possibility of a vast international understanding which would even comprise disarmament. He did not fail to observe that the main obstacle at present is the Danzig problem.

Also the German press, as I mentioned before, declares that the Western Powers must now make a decision whether they are willing to try for a just peace, acting jointly with the Axis.

*Józef Lipski*

## DOCUMENT 144    Lipski to Beck

NO. N/52/214/39             Berlin, June 5, 1939
                                   *Strictly Confidential*

Within the last few days I had a long conversation with French Ambassador Coulondre. I report on the more important points:

1) M. Coulondre first of all stated that not only he, but also the British Ambassador, gave the German government to understand unequivocally that in case of German aggression against Danzig their two governments would immediately take a position on the side of Poland. This statement has reached the knowledge of top elements of the Reich.

2) The French Ambassador thinks that the completion of agreements with Russia by England and France would have a decisive impact on the Reich, in restraining it from any aggressive moves. He is informed that General Keitel's and General Brauchitsch's opinion is that, with Russia's entry into the antiaggression front, the chances for the Reich to win the war would be nil. However, without Russia, both of these generals think that the Reich has a chance to win the war.

M. Coulondre, who knows conditions in Russia, is well aware that Russia's entry into the pacts would be less important from the military angle than from the psychological point of view.

I would like to stress that I share M. Coulondre's opinion that Russia's entry into an agreement with England and France would have a decisive meaning in restraining the Reich from aggressive steps.

*Józef Lipski*

The following handwritten note is among Lipski's papers under the date of June 27, 1939:

I gave a farewell dinner party for Ambassador Labougle, who had been transferred to Santiago, and his wife. It was attended by ambassadors and a few envoys. From the German side, only a few unofficial guests attended.

During my whole stay in Berlin I had the most cordial relations with M. and Mme Labougle. He was quite an expert on Germany, having served as secretary of the Argentinian Legation during the last war.

The premises of the Argentinian Legation belonged to Frau von Stamm, who had considerable estates in Argentina. A few years prior to the outbreak of the war, Frau von Stamm donated her palace to Argentina. The interior of the building was in the most outrageous bad taste— a vestige of the worst era.

Among the last Germans I met before the war broke out were the von Stamms (she was Baroness Wolff), the von Tries, and Frau von Rechthofen, who spoke in panic about the threat of war.

The bulk of society, with relations deteriorating, steered clear of our Embassy.

From the Party, Lutze [26] and his wife behaved properly up to the end. Among the socialites, the worst behaved was Frau von Dirksen's clan. Her son kept himself far removed. Besides, his behavior toward his Polish business partner was simply scandalous.

DOCUMENT 145    Lipski to Beck

NO. N/52/266                                     Berlin, June 28, 1939
                                                  Strictly Confidential

I am taking the liberty of communicating the following observations and information from the local territory:

1) The ambassador of Argentina, Labougle, who, after many years spent in Berlin, will be transferred to Santiago de Chile, had an audience with Hitler at Berchtesgaden a few days ago.

Labougle informed me yesterday that in the course of the conversation the Chancellor also brought up Polish problems.

[26] Victor Lutze, chief of the S.A.

As usual, Hitler's deliberations were lengthy and not very clear. The Ambassador had the impression that the Chancellor expects, as it were, some initiative on our part toward Germany in connection with problems which have caused tension between the two states (Danzig, the superhighway). Besides, the Chancellor presented Poland as the aggressive side, referring to Poland's claim to East Prussia, etc. He even had knowledge of such details as the speech delivered by a certain Polish general who, according to the German press, promoted the reunion of Opole-Silesia and East Prussia with Poland.[27] According to the Ambassador's relation, in his conversation with him Hitler did not consider Poland and England as the No. 1 foes but directed the brunt of his attack against President Roosevelt. As could be noted, the Chancellor was obviously hurt by the fact that Roosevelt ignored his speech of April 28. He also blamed the United States for opposing economic negotiations between the Reich and the states of South America.

The Chancellor's reaction to the Ambassador's suggestion that it is indispensable to restore confidence in international relations was positive.

When Mr. Labougle and I analyzed the Chancellor's deliberations more closely, he remarked that he is not in a position to conceive clearly how the Chancellor envisages the further development of events and what his goal seems to be. The tone of his words was rather appeasing.

The fact that Hitler was especially aggressive toward the United States might easily be explained if we bear in mind that he was talking with a representative of South America.

In connection with the fact that Hitler presented Poland as a state with aggressive intentions toward the German Reich, I would like to refer to my previous reports. I called attention in these reports to the fact that the German side is very eager to catch even the slightest hints from the speeches of unions and Polish organizations and political parties which advocate reunion of East Prussia and Opole-Silesia with Poland, for this provides the Germans with an excellent weapon for interior action which strives to unite the German community in the face of the encirclement policy conducted under the leadership of England. That is why the argument of our aggressive tendencies is being exploited by German propaganda abroad also, especially for Anglo-Saxon states. Even today, the latest resolutions of the National Party, claiming East Prussia and the Oder frontier, are printed by the *Völkischer Beobachter*

[27] *DGFP*, Series D, VI, 819.

with the annotation that British opinion has not been informed about these Polish tendencies.

2) I am receiving information from various sources about differences of opinion to be detected among eminent leading local personalities with regard to the international situation.

However, in my opinion no special attention should be paid to these possible discords, for as long as Hitler is in command he decides all basic problems of the state.

Nevertheless, it is worth while noting some symptoms of personal animosity or of rapprochement among certain persons on the basis of kindred ideas. In Goebbels' offices some kind of rivalry exists in the field of foreign propaganda.

I know that Ribbentrop is not satisfied with Goebbels' last speeches. He even expressed his feelings in the presence of several members of the diplomatic corps.

I heard, however, from a reliable source that Goebbels got his instructions directly from the Chancellor, evidently behind the Foreign Minister's back, whose feelings thus were hurt.

Göring, as he allegedly disclosed to one of the diplomats, has ceased to act in international politics. He stands now on the margin of these affairs, unless they directly concern his competence (the four-year plan, the air force).

Nevertheless, symptoms exist that this certain eclipse of his is only temporary. I heard that of late such personalities as Lutze, chief of the S.A., Himmler, and military personages such as General von Brauchitsch are gravitating toward him.

3) Recently a number of rumors reached me that the German side is preparing certain moves concerning Polish-German relations for August.

Such information was communicated by the Consulate General at Leipzig in its report of June 23, No. N/3/a/55/39.

The French Ambassador also has some information pointing to certain preparations for August. M. Coulondre suggests in this connection that German tactics with regard to Danzig might strive to create on the territory of the Free City a military force, camouflaged for the time being, out of elements immigrating from the Reich. Then would come the proclamation of reunion with the Reich in such a way as to shift over to Poland—in the eyes of public opinion—the responsibility for possible reaction to such a step taken by Danzig.

On this occasion he suggested that it might perhaps be advisable for the governments of Poland, France, and England to get together in advance, and to warn the German government that a violation of the statute of the Free City is subject to the Polish-French-British guarantee.

I am taking the liberty, while reporting on the above suggestions of M. Coulondre, of calling your attention to the fact that on our part a restriction of this sort has already been lodged with the government of the Reich. It was contained in your declaration to Ambassador von Moltke on March 29, 1939.[28] I do not know whether the governments of France and England are aware of this. I think it could possibly serve as a basis for action of these governments in Berlin.

*Józef Lipski*

### DOCUMENT 146   Lipski to Beck

NO. N/297/II/151/39

Berlin, July 27, 1939
*Strictly Confidential*
*Urgent*

Re: Tactics of German authorities
    relation to Polish minorities

Referring to previous reports on the same subject, and particularly to report No. N/303/23 of July 11,[29] I would like to give you a general picture of the situation in which the Polish minorities find themselves in Germany, in connection with tactics recently applied by the German authorities.

### *I. Press Action Rendered Impossible*

In spite of the difficult and ever-worsening situation of the Polish minorities due to numerous acts of oppression and terror at present, this minority has ever-fewer possibilities of presenting its case in the press. This has been achieved by German police authorities in the following way:

1) Secret state police, in spite of the fact that preventive censorship does not exist in Germany, requested the editors of three daily Polish

[28] *Ibid.,* No. 118.
[29] Missing from Lipski's papers.

papers in Germany, namely, the editors of *Nowiny, Naród,* and *Gazeta Olsztyńska* (two remaining papers, *Dziennik Berliński* and *Głos Pogranicza,* are printed jointly with those mentioned above, as reprints), to present to police headquarters for approval the first-edition copy of each issue of these dailies. Upon presentation of the copy for approval, the editors are obliged to continue the printing of the issue (allegedly in order to avoid delays in publication), but they can distribute the papers only after the police grant their approval. Thus, in case the distribution of the paper is prohibited, the editors' offices are not only exposed to losses on the already printed issues but, owing to the lateness of the date, they cannot repeat the issues.

Prohibition of distribution has already been ordered several times in the case of each of the above-mentioned daily papers. Usually they confiscate the whole issue, without stating a reason or citing the questioned articles. Thus the editors are even unable to repeat the issue with the omission of certain articles, while for propaganda reasons the effect of white censorship patches would serve the cause well.

The editor of *Naród* was even refused the right to print in following editions a notice about the confiscation; other editors cannot disclose the reasons for the confiscation of the paper.

Although the Gestapo does not disclose the reasons for the confiscation, nevertheless from the hitherto fairly numerous cases it can be observed that:

a) For *Naród* those issues are confiscated with any mention of terror against Polish nationalism, of unfavorable acts of authorities, or of protests lodged by the Union of Poles. The Gestapo explicitly requested the editor of *Naród* not to insert notices about the oppression of Poles.

b) For the *Gazeta Olsztyńska* issues are confiscated which contain news subject to Gestapo restrictions.

c) Confiscations of *Nowiny,* according to the editor, are made in the following way: the Gestapo confiscates issues containing news which evokes the Gestapo's disapproval. Besides, the Gestapo withholds permission for distribution until it is informed that a corresponding issue of *Kattowitzer Zeitung* was not confiscated. If it was confiscated, *Nowiny* is confiscated regardless of its contents.

As a result, in a part of the Polish press, among others, in *Dziennik Berliński,* the reader does not find either notices about oppression of the Polish population or white patches, and cannot orient himself as to the real condition of the Polish minority. As the press in Poland and the Western press drew their information on the fate of Poles in Germany from the Polish press in Germany, mainly from *Dziennik Berliński,* news about oppression of the Polish population in Germany disappeared from the press in Poland and from the press in the West. In contrast to this, news about oppression of the German population in Poland is multiplying in the Western press. This is not devoid of a certain political meaning.

A further fact should also be noted: in recent days the editors of *Nowiny* and *Głos Pogranicza* were notified by the paper producers' union that the union is not interested in supplying paper for the dailies of the Polish press and is discontinuing the supply. As there is an allocation of paper to the daily newspapers in the Reich, and there are no other sources from which to acquire paper, and as the editors of the journals in question evaluate that their stock of paper will last for two weeks, we have to envisage the possibility of the suspension of publication of these papers.

## II. Freezing of Organization Life

In the last week the Gestapo in Westphalia has been conducting intensified action against Polish organizational life, on which report No. N/197/II/147, dated July 18, completed by telegram,[30] was sent by the Embassy.

According to news recently received, the fourteen persons arrested in the first days have all been released after interrogation, while there is no further information about a number of other people arrested in the following days of interrogation.

Without going into the details here of the many house searches, police interrogations, and prohibitions to hold meetings, even in private apartments, I am concentrating only on the essential things.

1) All persons interrogated and examined were prohibited to communicate to anyone the fact and the contents of the political interrogation.

2) All these people were forbidden to leave their permanent addresses and communicate with their organizations.

Thus, the Westphalian District of Unions of Poles is even deprived of legal means of informing its headquarters about what happened, and

---

[30] Missing from Lipski's papers.

conversely the headquarters of the Union of Poles cannot legally obtain any information concerning the District, which renders any kind of intervention impossible.

It is also worth mentioning that, after the Gestapo released the offices of the Westphalian District of the Union of Poles, clerks were allowed to remain on the premises of the office but were prohibited from communicating with other organization centers.

In case the method adopted by the Gestapo in Westphalia is extended to other regions, a total paralysis and freezing of organizational activities of the Union of Poles will take place. The perfidy of the method consists in the fact that the organization remains in existence, and no action is apparently taken either against the organization or its members, but the organization is dead.

### III. Threat to the Existence of Schools

School authorities conducted detailed investigations of three schools in Warmia and six in the borderland, exposing in all cases a number of shortcomings of a constructional and hygienic nature. As a result of the survey, all investigated schools plus eleven schools in the borderland, or twenty schools in all, are threatened with being closed. At the same time, instructions were issued to publicize this in the press. As far as we can judge, German authorities thus want to enforce the reopening of three German schools allegedly closed recently in Poland (at Gniezno, Międzychód, and Wolsztyn). During the survey, the German commission explicitly declared that the threat of closing Polish schools corresponds to the closing of German schools.

Let us stress here that for the closing of three German schools the reaction was to threaten the closing of twenty Polish schools, that is, 40 percent of the number of Polish schools in Germany.

From the above remarks it is evident that the situation exists where the total liquidation of Polish organizational life in Germany might take place without any propaganda effect to our advantage, while in contrast to this each attempt to reduce the German state of possessions in Poland meets with unfavorable comments in the Western press.

Under these circumstances, I am taking the liberty of formulating certain general motions with regard to informing public opinion on the one hand, and on the other hand in respect to the very *meritum* of the minority problems.

## *I. Informing Public Opinion*

In view of certain information about the German attack on the minority sector, expected relatively soon, it seems to me that there arises the necessity of building an information apparatus that would enable us not just to fill the lack which lately occurred in informing Western opinion about the actual situation of Polish minorities but also to refute the possible offensive of German propaganda. The following points can be delineated here:

1) The Ministry is always informed about any hostile acts against Polish nationals through detailed statements of all events forwarded periodically to Section E. II.[31]

2) Bearing in mind the confidential character of this material, as well as consequences which might threaten the interested organizations and persons belonging to the minority at the hands of the German authorities in case this material is published, not all of it may be printed in the press. However, some of this material could be published in the local press in Poland as well as in the Western press, under the condition that press releases are given in the following form: "We learn from refugees recently arrived from German territory that . . ." Obviously, only in this manner could facts generally known and obvious to anyone in the given locality appear in print, such, for instance, as the breaking of windowpanes, assaults, attacks on schools, liquidation of associations or meetings, extradition, arrests, expropriations, demonstrations, etc., while more confidential information could not be used.

3) It would seem advisable to exploit with precision in the local press in Poland and the West all information still appearing in the Polish press in Germany, especially in *Nowiny* and *Gazeta Olsztyńska*.

4) For lack of more profuse and printable material of a concrete nature, even now the preparation of a series of basic articles from various fields of life of Polish minorities in Germany should begin, with the aim of using them at the proper moment. I am taking the liberty of suggesting that synthetically prepared material recently supplied by particular consulates to Section E. II of the Ministry might be of considerable assistance.

5) I recently approached Editor K. Smogorzewski with regard to several such general articles, in order to dispatch them to our embassies

[31] Section of Poles Abroad of the Consular Department of the Ministry of Foreign Affairs.

in London and Paris. They would be published (without the signature of the author) in the Western press.

6) It would also serve a purpose, in my opinion, to hold off insertion in the Polish press of any notices about action taken by the Administration, or any other acts unfavorable for German minorities in Poland if they do not directly concern cases of acts against the state, for such comments are being reprinted by the German and foreign press. Obviously, it would also be advisable to reduce press comments about the ill-treatment of German minorities in Poland in the press of that minority.

## II. Tactics on the Minority Sector

Abstaining from forming concrete conclusions in this field because of the variety of aspects of the matter as such, as well as a lack of precise information as to the whole complex and details of action conducted in relation to German minorities in Poland by the Ministry of the Interior (the only information is what I find daily in the German press), I would just like to state clearly the necessity of a basic definition of our tactics in the field of minorities as early as possible, for the basic question arises whether, in the face of new acts of oppression by the German side in relation to the Polish population and the impossibility of establishing whether they occur on German initiative or as a reaction to the treatment of German minorities in Poland, we have further to tolerate German organizational life, or to resort to fighting more energetically against this minority, using the same methods which are at the disposal of the German side. However, in the event of applying repressions we should bear in mind the standards resulting from the strict numerical ratio between the two minorities. So, for instance, for each Polish school closed in Germany, to liquidate eight German schools in Poland (the numerical ratio of the number of schools, 50:400) and define in detail methods of action. It is difficult, of course, to say now whether the choice of such a method would result in the final liquidation of organizational life of both minorities, or rather whether it would restrain the German side from further oppressing the Polish minority.

*Józef Lipski*

# The Polish-German Crisis [1]
## March—April, 1939

ON MARCH 29, 1939, President of the Senate Greiser and Dr. Boettcher [2] called on Weizsäcker to obtain information of Polish-German conversations with regard to Danzig. They were informed of the course of discussions held on March 21 and 26, 1939, between the Reich Foreign Minister and the Ambassador of Poland in Berlin. [3]

Greiser came out with a question as to what the further action of Danzig toward Poland should be, to which the Secretary of State cautiously replied that, while the situation should not be made easy for the Polish government, on the other hand Poland should not be provoked. Weizsäcker was of the opinion that it might be possible to push Poland onto the track of a policy which would weaken it internally (*Zermürbungspolitik*). This might render the Polish government more conciliatory when settling a number of German demands, one of which was Danzig. Danzig should continue to apply the same tactics as during the previous weeks and months.

To Greiser's question as to how he should behave toward the high commissioner of the League of Nations, Burckhardt, Weizsäcker thought that Burckhardt's return to Danzig was for the time being undesirable, since it might be feared that the Polish Commissioner-General would abuse Burckhardt's authority for the interests of Poland and of the Committee of Three. Weizsäcker also dissuaded Greiser from appearing before the Committee of Three in London if an invitation were extended to him.

[1] Printed in *Bellona* (London), 1950, No. 1, under the general title "New Premises on the Outbreak of the Polish-German War in 1939."

[2] Victor Boettcher, Staatsrat, Director of the Department of Foreign Affairs of the Danzig Senate. For the memorandum of von Weizsäcker, see *DGFP*, Series D, Vol. VI, No. 124.

[3] *Ibid.*, Nos. 61 and 101, and *Polish White Book*, Nos. 61 and 63.

On the same day (March 29, 1939), the Hungarian Envoy in Berlin, referring to his last audience with Hitler, questioned Weizsäcker about the result of Polish-German conversations with regard to Danzig.[4] He hinted that Hungary's foreign minister, Csáky, would be ready to use his influence in Warsaw to bring about a compromise with Germany. Weizsäcker rejected this idea as futile. During the discussion Weizsäcker commented on his point of view, explaining that since his Austrian days Hitler had remained prejudiced against all that was Hungarian, and especially against the Hungarian upper classes; therefore it was out of the question that Count Csáky could serve as mediator.[5]

A few days later, on April 5, after England's guarantee for Poland and while Beck was still in London, Weizsäcker sent instructions for Moltke in Warsaw.[6] I quote them in extenso, since they are a key to the further tactics of Germany:

"Lipski will probably be received here again before Easter. At this interview he will be told the following with reference to his last conversation with the Foreign Minister.

"Our offer to Poland will not be repeated. The Polish government had apparently not fully understood the significance of this offer. We could not help that. The future would show whether Poland had been well advised. The counterproposal put forward by Lipski had, as was known, already been rejected by the Foreign Minister as a basis for negotiations.

"End of the statement to Lipski.

"Please do not enter into any further material discussions on the German offer and the Polish counteroffer. We must prevent Poland from throwing the ball back to us and then maneuvering us into the position of appearing to have let a Polish offer go unheeded. Other principal missions have likewise been instructed not to enter into serious discussions on the Polish question but rather to evade the subject calmly and not to give any indication of further German intentions."

These instructions were written two days after Hitler signed German military dispositions against Poland on April 3, 1939.[7] In the light of

[4] DGFP, Series D, Vol. VI, No. 123.
[5] Depositions made by Weizsäcker on June 8, 1948.
[6] DGFP, Series D, Vol. VI, No. 159.
[7] The directive of April 3, 1939, was signed by Keitel. Enclosure II contained "Operation White" directed against Poland (ibid., No. 149). Hitler signed a final directive dealing with operations against Poland and the occupation of Danzig on April 11 (ibid., No. 185).

these instructions, it becomes clear to us why Moltke evaded seeing Beck upon his return from London and left Warsaw for a long time.

On the next day, April 6, 1939, on Weizsäcker's invitation, I had a conversation with him.[8] This conversation was overshadowed by the British-Polish guarantee. During the Nuremberg trial it was established that at that very moment the German propaganda thesis of the "blank check" allegedly issued by Great Britain to Poland was born.

According to Weizsäcker's depositions, Ribbentrop kept hoping to the end that Great Britain would not execute its guarantee toward Poland. Hitler shared his Minister's expectation. In this connection, it is worth while to recall telegraphic instructions Lord Halifax sent to Ambassador Henderson in Berlin on May 13, 1939, which were inserted into the documents of the trial. The contents of this telegram, a copy of which was forwarded for the attention of the British ambassador in Rome, fell into the hands of the Italians, who happened to know the English code. At that time Mussolini was anxious to hold Hitler back from war action. He therefore instructed Count Ciano to communicate the text of the telegram to the German ambassador in Rome, Herr von Mackensen. The instructions, in very firm terms, acknowledged to the full extent the obligations of the government of Great Britain toward Poland in case of war, confirming that the guarantee also covered Danzig.[9]

The Polish-German declaration of January 26, 1934, put an end for a number of years to German open propaganda in France and England against the western frontiers of Poland. This created a rather awkward situation for the Auswärtiges Amt when in the spring of 1939 the revisionist campaign had to be launched again. It was necessary to brush up long-forgotten French and English utterances which had been gathering dust in the files. In the instructions of May 10, 1939, to German embassies in Paris and London, Weizsäcker recommended compiling declarations of eminent French and British personalities who at one time had made statements against resolutions of the Versailles Treaty with regard to Danzig and the Corridor.[10] Such statements, commented the instructions, might be found in the archives of the Locarno period as well as in the aftermath of Locarno.

[8] *Polish White Book*, No. 70 (also *DGFP*, Series D, Vol. VI, No. 169).
[9] *DGFP*, Series D, Vol. VI, No. 377.
[10] "Trials of War Criminals," mimeographed transcript, No. N.G. 2019 (Lipski's papers, File 22).

In his instructions dated July 4, 1939, addressed to a number of embassies and legations, Weizsäcker informed about the situation in Poland to be used in conversations.[11] The purpose of these instructions was to show that two contradictory tendencies—chauvinist and moderate—were in conflict in Poland. The chauvinist group was composed of various private societies, party organizations, clerks of local administration, and primarily of the military element. This group instigated anti-German demonstrations, dreaming of annexing East Prussia and waging a battle for Berlin. Minister Beck was numbered among the moderate group—"for we had reason to believe that Minister Beck, though without a definite program, was yet seeking a settlement with Germany."

A memorandum of July 4, 1939, about the stay of the Ministry counselor, Altenburg, in Danzig, is a good illustration of German propaganda methods with regard to the Free City.[12]

A number of other documents originating from the Auswärtiges Amt deal with the technicalities of preparation of the diplomatic side in case of war. Most of them are signed by Weizsäcker or Woermann.

Among the latter's files, under the date of August 26, 1939, there is his report on a conversation with the Polish Ambassador, who lodged a protest with regard to serious frontier incidents (two Polish notes), as well as concerning the break in telephone communication of the Polish Embassy in Berlin with Poland, and of the Polish Embassy with Polish consulates on the territory of the Reich.[13]

The intensity of German incidents on August 25, 1939, was connected with Hitler's originally fixed date of August 26, 1939, at dawn for the attack on Poland.

[11] *Ibid.*, No. N.G. 2323; see also *DGFP,* Series D, Vol. VI, No. 592, note 7.
[12] "Trials of War Criminals," mimeographed transcript, No. N.G. 2025.
[13] *DGFP,* Series D, Vol. VII, No. 331.

# Final Endeavors
## *August, 1939*

AMBASSADOR LIPSKI gave a detailed relation (see pages 574–610) of events of the last month prior to the outbreak of the war. We are limiting ourselves here to the exposition of documents pertaining to this period that have been preserved in Lipski's papers. They do not cover this period fully. During that tragic month, the tempo of work at the Polish Embassy in Berlin and at the Ministry of Foreign Affairs in Warsaw was so feverish that quite a number of documents might easily have been mislaid both in Berlin and in Warsaw. Nevertheless, the documents presented below, together with Lipski's description referred to above, give a full and correct illustration of the tension in Polish-German relations on the eve of war, as seen from the post of the Polish Ambassador in Berlin.

The following is Lipski's handwritten note, dated August 9, 1939.

On August 8, I was in Warsaw for conversations with Minister Beck. I was received on the same day by Marshal Śmigły-Rydz, who inquired about the situation in Germany.

My statements took the following trend:

1) German armaments and preparations for war are in full swing.

2) It is difficult to have an exact orientation at present as to the precise German plan. From the German point of view, upon defeating Poland, Germany would come upon the USSR in the east while it was at war with the Allies in the west. Under these circumstances the war with Poland would not bring them a solution—element of a local contest.

3) We should be prepared for any eventuality.

I then left with Beck for Nałęczów, where I spent a day and a night. One of the American correspondents called on Beck while I was there. On the evening of August 9 we were informed about Weizsäcker's declaration handed, in my absence, to Lubomirski.[1]

---

[1] The declaration dealt with the problem of Polish customs inspectors in Danzig. Weizsäcker termed the Polish demands an "ultimatum," remarking that, with the Polish side threatening reprisals, Polish-German relations would suffer. For the text of the declaration, see *DGFP*, Series D, Vol. VII, No. 5.

Beck got the report and said: "Now it begins." He decided to return to Warsaw in the early morning hours.

At the Ministry of Foreign Affairs I met Arciszewski, with whom I made an appointment for lunch. Beck went to Śmigły-Rydz.

At lunch Arciszewski confided to me his anxiety that Beck might answer too sharply. I was quite in accord with this opinion and we agreed that we would try to use our influence in rendering the form of the declaration less adamant, so it would outwardly show the furthest-reaching good will on our part with regard to Danzig, where we met with sabotage and the undermining of our rights. We exposed our point of view to Beck. However, he obstinately kept to his own concept and decided that Arciszewski would present the declaration in accordance with the text edited by him.

DOCUMENT 147   Lubomirski to the Ministry of Foreign Affairs

Berlin, August 10, 1939
*Secret*

On August 8 the British ambassador, Henderson, invited me for a talk. He opened the conversation by expressing his concern over the development of the situation in Danzig. From his approach to this question I got the impression that conversations he had had of late with Secretary of State Weizsäcker, as well as with other Germans, were not without an impact on his judgment. It seemed to me that he accepted German information with a certain dose of faith; I was confirmed in this impression by a certain detail: namely, when I communicated to him a detailed genesis of our last note addressed to the Danzig Senate, Henderson took from his desk the manuscript of a report he had apparently prepared according to these conversations, and he made some alterations in it.

Henderson next developed his point of view as follows:

From information in his possession, he knows that Chancellor Hitler has not yet taken any decision on how to settle the problem of Danzig. He might use force to achieve a solution, or proceed by peaceful means. Radical German elements, among whom Forster and Zarsky [2] should be

[2] Wilhelm Zarsky, editor of *Der Danziger Vorposten.*

numbered, who right now are in Berchtesgaden for consultation with the Chancellor, are pushing the Chancellor to act on impulse. They represent the matter in such a way as to make it appear that Poland has aggressive tendencies toward Danzig. Under such circumstances, it would be wise to abstain from any action which would provide grist for the radicals' mill, and possibly accelerate Hitler's decision, for Henderson thinks that everything possible should be done to make the crisis last until late into the autumn, or even until spring, when the situation will be quite different. In following this idea, Henderson reached the conclusion that it might be desirable to establish a certain diplomatic contact, purely informative, between the Polish Ambassador in Berlin and Secretary of State von Weizsäcker. At present Weizsäcker is replacing Ribbentrop. Experience shows that contact with Ribbentrop is not very essential, for Ribbentrop relates to the Chancellor his conversations with diplomatic representatives from memory only, and not too precisely. On the other hand, Weizsäcker is an experienced official, and each conversation with him, in the form of an exact note, is being forwarded to the Chancellor. Here Henderson made the reservation that it is not his intention to advise concrete talks with Weizsäcker about Danzig. He only thinks that through normal diplomatic contact the question could be clarified and thus the tendentious versions presented to Hitler by his entourage could be counteracted. As an example of tendentious informing of the Chancellor by his collaborators, Henderson cited an incident which took place after the occupation of Prague. Upon his arrival in Prague, the Chancellor expressed his wish to pay a hospital visit to injured members of the German minority about whom the German press had reported at length. The Chancellor's entourage faced quite a problem, since such victims did not exist at all. Finally, Hitler received a delegation of "wounded Germans" whose heads were bandaged *ad hoc.*

To my remark that the German side shows evident ill-will by provoking difficulties in Danzig, obviously striving to increase tension by creating incidents and by conducting a falsification campaign in the press, which accuses the Polish side of aggressive tendencies while it strives for conquests, Henderson remarked that German behavior toward England is far from correct also, but in his opinion the duty of a diplomatic representative is to maintain contact with official factors of the government of the state to which he is accredited. That is why, if the situation does not deteriorate basically, he intends to accept, even this year, an invitation to take part in the Congress of the Party at Nuremberg. He explained the German activity which strives to intensify tension by saying that the Chancellor possibly figures that with strong tension it will be easier for him to settle problems.

*St. Lubomirski.*

DOCUMENT 148   Invitation to Ambassador Lipski
to Attend a Hunting Party

Chief-Hunting-Master Scherping              Berlin, August 11, 1939

H. Excellency
Mr. Ambassador Lipski

Berlin, W. 35
Kurfürstenstrasse 135

Your Excellency,

On behalf of General Field Marshal Göring, hunting master of the Reich, I take the liberty of inviting Your Excellency for hunting in the state forests.

As I perceive from my list, Your Excellency has already killed red deer, elk, and chamois in the German preserves, but no muffle-ram; I would like to suggest to Your Excellency hunting this year for muffle-ram.

The best time to hunt a muffle-ram is October or November, since the ram is in full hair then. Of course, it can also be killed at an earlier date merely as a trophy.

If Your Excellency would wish for a good stag to deerstalk at rutting season, I would take the liberty to ask for a reply, and then I would immediately send information with regard to preserve and time to Your Excellency.

With the assurance of my deepest respect and with *Weidmannsheil* [a hunter's greeting], I am, Your Excellency, very sincerely

*Scherping*

## DOCUMENT 149 Lipski to Beck

NO. W/52/440                                        Berlin, August 15, 1939

Yesterday I had a visit from the British Ambassador, who came to share with me his opinions on the political situation.

He remarked first of all that the declaration of the German government of August 9 with regard to Danzig [3] and the reply of the Polish government dated August 10 [4] had resulted in a considerable deterioration in the situation. The Chancellor felt particularly hurt by the last paragraph of the Polish declaration. When Ciano raised the Danzig problem in Salzburg,[5] the German side presented to him the exchange of the declarations in question, stressing that the honor of Germany, as well as that of the Axis, was at stake. Thus the Italian side had to abandon its moderator's mission in the case of Danzig.

Besides, the argument of Germany's honor made its appearance in the columns of the German press after the conference of Salzburg.

Repeating this version—probably heard from the German side— Ambassador Henderson told me that he is awaiting further explanations on the results of Italian-German conversations from his colleague in Rome.

I may add that I did not fail to clarify to Henderson the very essence of the German declaration and to explain more precisely our reply.

In his further deliberations the British Ambassador gave way to his concern that, if the hitherto absolutely negative line of policy toward Germany is maintained, we will be entangled in a war in a short time. In his opinion, Hitler would not knuckle down even if faced by a coalition reinforced by Russia. Since March the parties have not been on speaking terms, while the situation is becoming ever more complicated and the conflict is deepening.

London, the Ambassador told me, took the stand that we should abstain from any conversations with the Reich. Besides, the internal situation in England is such that Chamberlain could do nothing for peace at present, and neither could Mussolini. The Ambassador thinks

[3] *DGFP*, Series D, Vol. VII, No. 5.
[4] *Polish White Book*, No. 86.
[5] Ciano conversed with Ribbentrop in Salzburg on August 11, and with Hitler in Obersalzberg on August 12 and 13 (*DGFP*, Series D, Vol. VII, Nos. 43 and 47; see also Editor's Note, p. 35).

that, as matters stand now, only France or Poland could take a step toward Germany to save peace.

Sir Nevile thinks that there is just time until the Congress in Nuremberg; then, if Hitler takes a position in his speech, it will be too late.

To quote a characteristic feature of Henderson's deliberations, here is what he said: if after seven months of war it will be necessary to strive for peace, it is better to find a peaceful solution now.

Henderson has the idea, for example, that Poland should declare to the German side that it considers it essential to calm the minds on the German and Polish side first, which would make it possible to demobilize troops in Poland and Germany, and only afterward (without spelling out the time limits) to open conversations to find a solution for Danzig.

In Henderson's opinion, such a declaration would strengthen considerably Poland's position. In accordance with his words, German government circles reduce the Polish-German strife to Danzig only, stressing that Hitler has already given up the Corridor question. Besides, the French Ambassador confirmed to me that Welczek recently made a similar statement to Bonnet.

I cited to the two ambassadors totally contradictory reports from the German press, with recent aspirations even for Silesia. Finally Henderson repeated what he previously said to Counselor Lubomirski: that Secretary of State Weizsäcker told him that he has no contact whatsoever with me.

I replied to the Ambassador that in this case it is the German side that is making demands. I am always at the disposal of the German government, if it has anything to communicate to me, while on my part the line of the Polish government is strictly defined.

Recapitulating, I may observe that I noticed that the British Ambassador was visibly upset by the prospect of an armed conflict. I am sure that he will act in London to find some solution to the situation.

For my part I told him that what is causing most concern in international relations is the complete lack of confidence in Hitler's government, as a result of the bitter experiences of the past. I added that, in my opinion, persuasion is hardly a weapon to be used with Germany.

Besides, of course, I expressed my best intentions to do everything possible to avoid the catastrophe of war.

Although Henderson did not say so, from what he said to Lubomirski it was clear that he is anxious first of all to secure more time.

Coulondre, who was quite calm and composed, told me yesterday more or less the same things.

*Józef Lipski*

DOCUMENT 150   Lipski to Beck

NO. N/52/449/39                                    Berlin, August 17, 1939

Today, in the afternoon hours, I had the visit first of the British Ambassador and then of the French Ambassador.

The two ambassadors informed me about conversations they had on August 15 with Secretary of State von Weizsäcker.[6]

Sir Nevile Henderson read to me a long report on his conversation forwarded to Lord Halifax,[7] of which I shall try to give a general outline.

Herr von Weizsäcker, who, as the Ambassador thinks, is working to prevent war, stated that while in his last conversation with the British Ambassador on August 4 he evaluated the situation rather calmly, considering it to be better than it had been at the same time last year as far as peace was concerned, it has since become very serious. Weizsäcker blames this

1) on the Polish ultimatum to Danzig regarding customs inspectors;

2) on the declaration of the Polish government dated August 10 in reply to the German declaration of August 9 (allegedly, especially the last passage of our reply caused a sharp reaction from the Chancellor); and, finally,

3) on the alleged growing violence perpetrated against the German population in Poland. According to the Secretary of State's words, the situation, beyond any measure, is reaching crisis proportions.

The British Ambassador replied to these statements by (1) pointing to the illegal militarization of Danzig, (2) stressing that the Polish government, in the last passage of its declaration dated August 10, only stated that it would consider as an act of aggression any possible intervention of the German government to the detriment of *rights and interests of Poland under the treaty,* and (3) stating that the Polish

[6] *Ibid.,* Nos. 64 and 66.
[7] *British Blue Book,* No. 48.

Ambassador, for his part, had informed him of persecutions of Polish minorities in Germany.

Herr von Weizsäcker further stated that Poland is conducting a suicidal policy, that Russian assistance for Poland in case of war would be of minor value, and that in case of a conflict Germany would enter into an agreement with Russia to the detriment of Poland. Von Weizsäcker observed that he cannot conceive how England can guarantee the irresponsible action of Poland, and expressed the opinion that such a guarantee would not be valid in case Poland caused the conflict.

Sir Nevile observed that Poland is conducting a prudent policy and that each of its steps of a basic character is agreed upon with the British government.

Weizsäcker interrupted, saying that the ultimatum for the Free City of Danzig regarding customs inspectors, as well as the reply to the German declaration of August 9, had not been agreed upon with the British side.

Sir Nevile firmly stated that England would come to Poland's assistance in case of German aggression. With regard to the British guarantee for Poland on the matter of Danzig, he referred to Lord Halifax's declaration.

Further statements of the Ambassador on the British guarantee for Poland, repeated in the course of this long conversation, were quite explicit and followed the line of our policy.

At a certain point of the report the Ambassador mentioned that he felt that Weizsäcker was making very light of the specific gravity of British military action.

Talking about the prevailing impasse, Weizsäcker remarked that under the present circumstances any step by the German side in order to reduce tension with Poland has become impossible. The Secretary of State also stated that Minister Beck's speech of May rendered difficult the resumption of conversations. Namely, it stated that such conversations could only proceed upon the principles defined in this speech, thus creating a prestige obstacle for Germany.

In conclusion I note that von Weizsäcker was trying to present us as an irresponsible partner; he added that there are only a few men in Poland who have a reasonable concept of the situation, but their position is of no importance.

Henderson got the impression from this conversation that a total impasse now prevails in Polish-German relations, and if the situation continues it will threaten to end in an armed conflict. He fears that, if events are allowed to take their course, then either at Tannenberg or at Nuremberg [8] the Chancellor might go so far that conflict will be inevitable. Henderson's thesis is that the Chancellor is misinformed by his entourage; they do not inform him about Polish arguments, but rather stir him up. That is why Henderson returned to his previous idea of my meeting with Göring and telling him things he might bring to the knowledge of the Chancellor. I recall that in his previous conversation with me (report No. N/52/440/39 dated August 15) Henderson proposed a formula in which the two partners should return to the *status quo* on Danzig of March, and do their best to appease public opinion in both countries. Only then could conversations be started. I did not conceal from Henderson that with the present German approach such propositions could hardly achieve a positive result. I cited news from the German press, which for the past two days has categorically urged the reunion of Danzig and even of the Corridor with the Reich. Henderson thinks that this is rather an answer to our claims to East Prussia. Looking for a way to avoid war, he thinks that the invitation to the stag hunt in the autumn sent to him by Göring through Scherping, as well as to me, could serve as an occasion to meet the General Field Marshal.

Next I had a visit from French Ambassador Coulondre. Referring to his conversation with Weizsäcker, he called special attention to the fact that the Secretary of State posed the same question to Henderson and to him: namely, would France come to the assistance of Poland in case Poland provoked military action by Germany? [9]

M. Coulondre told me that, reading Weizsäcker's camouflaged thoughts, he declared in an absolutely emphatic way, leaving no room for the slightest doubt, that France would always stand at Poland's side. He stressed that in March French public opinion felt threatened at the very heart of freedom. As a result, the alliance with Poland had been reinforced. M. Coulondre placed this alliance on the level of the *indissoluble common security of France and Poland.*

M. Coulondre was under the impression that this categorical declaration of his had not been understood by Weizsäcker but—since the Secretary of State was striving to hamper whatever unpredictable step might be contemplated by the top German factors—he accepted the declara-

[8] Celebrations at Tannenberg were to take place on August 27, but were called off earlier. The annual congress of the National Socialist Party was to be held at Nuremberg on September 2–11, but did not take place because of the war.

[9] *Livre jaune,* No. 194.

tion rather as an argument to be presented to those authorities. Today M. Coulondre already had certain confirmation that his declaration had been circulated further. M. Coulondre is of the opinion, which I share wholeheartedly, that only a determined stand taken by England, France, and Poland can save the peace. Only this can stop Hitler's risky policy. He fears just such reticence as in 1914 paved the way for the outbreak of the war. Even today, in certain German circles the supposition prevails that England would soften in the last moment. The French Ambassador does not believe this; nevertheless, he thinks that such rumors should be denied by the British side.

In connection with this, I remark that I told Henderson that such opinions were repeated to me. They resulted from misinterpretation of certain British probing of the German position. I was referring here to news supplied by an informant of Consul General Chiczewski with regard to this subject (Chiczewski's report No. 3/N/a/62/39 of August 12, 1939).[10]

Henderson was positive here, stating that he never met with a shadow of a doubt on the part of competent German factors as to England's determination to fulfill its obligations toward its allies.

Returning to Coulondre's conversation with the Secretary of State, I stress that Weizsäcker shared the Ambassador's opinion that the war would only turn to the advantage of Trotsky, as Coulondre put it.[11]

I am taking the liberty of recalling to you that last year during the Czech crisis Weizsäcker was one of the German diplomats who did everything possible to avoid war. I therefore do not doubt that he is now following the same line. According to Coulondre's information, Ambassador Welczek in Paris and Count Schulenburg in Moscow also strongly recommend prudence to the German government.

Finally, Coulondre evaluates the result of the conference at Salzburg thus: that Ciano did not yet take on any obligation, leaving the final word to Mussolini and a possibility to act further for peace. Ambassador Attolico left Salzburg for Rome and has not yet returned to Berlin.

*Józef Lipski*

[10] Missing from Lipski's papers.

[11] Weizsäcker finished his memorandum of the conference with Coulondre in these words: "In conclusion the ambassador assured me of his willingness to cooperate in any way in preserving peace. A European war would end with the defeat of all, even present-day Russia, and the victor would not be Stalin, but Trotsky" (*DGFP*, Series D, Vol. VII, No. 64, p. 71).

DOCUMENT 151   Lipski to Beck

NO. N/52/450/39                                       August 18, 1939
                                                *Strictly Confidential*

I would like to take up in a more concrete way a number of problems in connection with my last reports:

1) I would like to know whether you consider it desirable in principle that I should try to meet Göring.

I am enclosing a copy of an invitation I received for stag hunting in the autumn,[12] which might make it easier for me to renew, even at present, my contact with Göring. In case you consider such a conversation to be desirable, I would like to have, under the present circumstances, definite instructions as to the subjects I should take up.

For my part, I think that reference could be made in a general way to intentions wrongly attributed to Poland and to mendacious propaganda. Poland's consistent policy should be underlined, with a slight hint to Russia, stressing that we are going to fight if aggression takes place. And inquire in whose interest this European war would be waged.

Such a conversation with Göring, if it could take place at all, would rather be aimed at presenting to Hitler, through Göring, our determined, but not aggressive, standpoint.

2) At present, the worst tension in Polish-German relations appears on the sector of minorities. This tide is clearly reaching a crescendo. Bearing in mind that this sector, from the international angle, is particularly inconvenient for us, in addition because of other minority problems in Poland besides the German, I am trying to do my best to supply documentary proof about the persecutions of our minorities in Germany. Special files, containing more than 600 incidents, were recently handed to the British and French embassies. Nevertheless, even in a man so devoted to us as Coulondre, I can detect anxiety. He fears that our minorities measures may cause a Polish-German conflict, judging that sector to be particularly exposed.

Observing these matters from Berlin, as well as from the Polish territory, I came to the conclusion that coordination is indispensable between our Ministry of Foreign Affairs and the activities of our local administration.

3) I am taking the liberty of suggesting that it might be desirable,

[12] See Document 148, p. 556.

even prior to Tannenberg and Nuremberg, to issue some official declaration explaining that the loyal German minority has nothing to fear and can live peacefully in Poland, developing its own culture, while anti-Polish incidents and organizations created for diversion will be persecuted with absolute determination. I think that such a declaration could be issued by the Prime Minister or the Minister of the Interior to a representative of the German minorities in Poland—one most digestible for us.

4) Yesterday invitations for Nuremberg arrived. The time limit for reply is fixed at August 26.

You would therefore oblige me by sending me a decision in connection with my reports No. N/52/442/39 of August 15 and No. N/52 443/39 of August 16.[13]

*Józef Lipski*

### DOCUMENT 152    Beck to Lipski

August 19, 1939
*Coded*

I think it advisable to accept Göring's invitation. Please telegraph exact date of stag hunt. Possibly come first to Warsaw to discuss instructions for conversations.[14]

*Beck*

### DOCUMENT 153    Lipski to Beck

NO. N/52/464/39                    Berlin, August 21, 1939
*Strictly Confidential*

Our Consulate General in Prague has for some time been receiving information that Germany is considering possible changes in the formal legal structure in the territory of the Protectorate to the benefit of the Czechs. The report of our Consul General in Prague, No. 52/C/15 of

---

13 Missing from Lipski's papers.
14 For the Lipski-Göring conversation, see pp. 590–92.

August 16, a copy of which is enclosed herewith, brings some recent news.[15] In my opinion, this matter should have most careful attention.

The above information, if accepted as reliable, would show that tendencies of the German side to take a milder course toward the Czechs, including changes in the structure of the Protectorate, might, in my opinion, aim to (1) win over the Czechs with the war approaching (I recall that similar steps of a tactical nature were often taken toward the Polish population in the region of Poznań when Prussia, and later on the Reich, had to face an international crisis) or (2) serve as a springboard for action toward the Western world which the Chancellor would take during the Congress of "Peace" at Nuremberg.

The first alternative is a purely tactical local maneuver that would have no broader political meaning.

However, the second hypothesis, camouflaging some deeper German attempts, could become a threat to our interests.

If, as a matter of fact, the Chancellor decided at present to make even a fake exit from the Protectorate, after a military, political, and economic subjugation of the Czechs, he could present it as an intention to return to the Munich policy, thus restoring the ethnographical principle obliterated by the occupation of Prague. The Chancellor could do this by offering this cheap concession to the West in order to add more weight to the Danzig demand on the ethnic level.

*Józef Lipski*

The following is Lipski's handwritten note of August 20, 1939.

On the afternoon of August 20 [16] I took a plane for Warsaw to discuss with Beck my oncoming meeting with Göring. I prepared a letter for Göring in Berlin, signed it, and left it in the hands of the Embassy staff to await orders from Warsaw. In the letter I referred to the invitation sent in Göring's name for a hunting party in the autumn, and I mentioned that I would like to extend personally my thanks for it. I left the date *in blanco*. In my conversation with Beck I received no margin for negotiations, only general instructions to ask Göring whether it was worth while for our two states to enter into a conflict, and to repeat to him our basic political principles.

[15] This report has been omitted.
[16] Error in date; it should be August 21.

In the evening, after dinner, General Stachiewicz joined us.[17] In the course of the conversation he asked whether we should expect a German attack against Poland on all fronts simultaneously. I confirmed this absolutely unequivocally. Beck praised the antiaircraft defense of the capital, which allegedly numbered a hundred heavy artillery guns. In general, as usual, he appeared well satisfied with our military power.

In the morning I awoke (I stayed at the Brühl Hotel) to the news of Ribbentrop's trip to Moscow. This was a terrible moment for me. The two adversaries shook hands against us.

In the morning I met Beck, who was disturbed. I gave orders by telephone to Berlin to send the letter to Göring immediately, dating it August 20,[18] and I left by plane for Berlin at noon.

My greatest concern was that in the face of the German-Soviet pact the West might weaken and start to withdraw the support it had hitherto shown to us.

German opinion at large accepted the pact with joy, as proof that there would be no war.

However, in the Party itself, particularly among Party doctrinaires, symptoms of sharp criticism could be noted.

The enthusiasm of the masses soon evaporated in the face of the growing danger of war in spite of the German-Soviet pact.

On August 23 a nonaggression pact was signed between Germany and the Soviet Union.[19] On August 26 the Soviet ambassador in Warsaw, Nicolas Sharonov, called on Minister Beck, about which Beck informed the Polish Embassy in Moscow (and other posts) by telegram as follows:

DOCUMENT 154    Beck to Grzybowski

Warsaw, August 26, 1939
(Telegram No. 240)

Yesterday's visit of Sharonov under the pretext of a second-rate frontier incident was supposedly aimed to show that in spite of the Soviet-German pact relations between Moscow and Warsaw remain unchanged.

*Beck*

[17] General Wacław Stachiewicz, chief of the General Staff.
[18] The date should be August 21.
[19] For the text, see *DGFP*, Series D, Vol. VII, Nos. 228 and 229.

DOCUMENT 155   Beck to Raczyński

Polish Embassy, London                                    August 28, 1939
                                                          *Secret Code*

The British Ambassador consulted me about the answer to Hitler.[20]

I agreed to inform the German government that Poland is ready for negotiations, and asked for a definition of what the British government means by the concept of "international guarantee." Please treat the whole matter of consultation as strictly confidential.

*Beck*


DOCUMENT 156   Szembek to Representatives Abroad

                                                Warsaw, August 29, 1939
                                                (Telegram No. 263)

Within the past few days the representative of Germany at Bucharest declared to Rumanian political factors, showing the relative instructions from Berlin, that German-Soviet conversations on a nonaggression pact had been going on for the past two and one-half months, and that all details of the pact were established in advance.

Please, Mr. Ambassador, exploit the above fact in the light of Voroshilov's declaration that only the negative attitude of Poland toward staff conversations of the Soviet's with England and France caused the agreement with Germany.

*Szembek*


DOCUMENT 157   Declaration of Minister Szembek [21]
                to the Allied Ambassadors

                                                Warsaw, August 29, 1939

Please declare to Allied ambassadors:

1) The concentration of German forces on the Polish frontier is growing continuously.

[20] See *British Blue Book*, Nos. 72 and 74.
[21] See *Journal*, p. 497.

2) German forces entering Slovakia constitute a further threat to the Polish state.

3) Frontier incidents and aggressive action of the Reich on the territory of the Free City leave no doubt as to the aggressive intentions of the Reich.

4) The Polish government received from most reliable sources, including the government of Great Britain, explicit warnings about the planned attack on Poland by surprise in the next few days.

5) Under these circumstances the President of the Republic, on a motion of the government, proclaimed general mobilization.

6) General mobilization is but a completion of the previously issued military directives, which called to arms three fourths of the Polish Army.

7) Introduction of a state of war is not intended. Dispositions usually supplementing mobilization will be limited to a minimum.

8) The Polish policy remains unchanged.


DOCUMENT 158    Beck to Representatives Abroad

Warsaw, August 30, 1939
(Telegram No. 269)

The mobilization order which we postponed yesterday so as not to hamper action in Berlin was executed today. Please stress that, in spite of its official name, this mobilization is, as a matter of fact, a disposition on a smaller scope than the preparedness for war of units previously called to arms. In accordance with mobilization techniques, publication by posters will be utilized.

*Beck*

The last days of August were a continuum of tension and feverish work for the Polish Embassy in Berlin. This is evident, among other things, from a note, quoted below, of the first secretary of the Embassy, Mr. Henryk Malhomme, from his conversation with Ambassador Henderson.

With regard to a sentence of the Ambassador included in this note expressing his wish that his words be repeated to Malhomme's compatriots, it should be remembered that in August, 1939, Ambassador Henderson was hopelessly ill with cancer, a fact of which he was aware. After the outbreak of the war he retired from all other work and devoted himself completely to his book *Failure of a Mission: Berlin, 1937–1939.* The manuscript was ready in December, 1939, and the first edition appeared in London (Hodder & Stoughton) in April, 1940. Another book of his, a collection of short personal reminiscences, *Water under the Bridges,* was written in seclusion in the last months of his life.

Ambassador Henderson died on December 30, 1942.

*Excerpts from Notes of Mr. Henryk Malhomme,*
*First Secretary of the Polish Embassy in Berlin*

I spent most of the night of August 30 to August 31 working in the offices of the Embassy.

That night Ambassador Lipski had a long conversation with the British ambassador, Sir Nevile Henderson, and he returned to the Embassy only at 4 A.M.

After a short exchange of opinions with the Ambassador, we retired to have some rest. For the past few days I, as well as the majority of the officials, had moved to the Embassy to facilitate our work. We had bedrooms assigned there.

That night I did not sleep for long, for already at 7 A.M. I was summoned by the Ambassador.

I received instructions to proceed immediately to the British Ambassador, who had expressed the desire, in the course of his telephone conversation with Ambassador Lipski, that one of the Embassy staff should call on him without delay.

The choice fell on me.

I presented myself at the British Embassy at 8 A.M. I found the same strain of work there. It was obvious that the members of the Embassy had just left the offices.

Immediately upon my arrival I was led to the Ambassador's study.

I found Sir Nevile absolutely changed; he looked at least ten years older. He looked worn out, and the strain of several nights spent behind his desk was evident.

He greeted me with the words: "Malhomme, I do not like war" ("Malhomme, je n'aime pas la guerre"), and repeated them several times. It was clear that he was wondering how to start the conversation.

I replied that I did not like war either, but that unfortunately the decision was in the hands of a single man who was, so it seemed striding toward it consistently.

After a longer moment of silence, Sir Nevile told me that he was glad that Ambassador Lipski had delegated me, since he had known me for a long time, ever since the Belgrade days. What he was going to say was rather in the nature of a personal confidence, and therefore it would be easier for him to talk with someone he knew well.

He then explained to me that he had done his utmost to stop the war, and that until the last moment he would work to maintain peace; however, at present he had lost almost all hope that the conflict could be settled by peaceful means, if only for the reasons just mentioned by me.

Of late he had been under the impression that the Poles did not understand him and regarded him as a sympathizer of Germany unfriendly toward Poland. As a matter of fact, this was not so. He had many true friends in Poland; he knew Poland well because of his passion for hunting, and he had grown fond of the country and its people.

In case of war Poland would undoubtedly be destroyed and would lose its independence. For a long time Great Britain and France would not be able to come to its assistance. Probably after long years the war would be won by Great Britain, and Poland would recover its independence, but losses sustained by it would be irreparable.

These, and no other, were the motives of his endeavors to settle the Polish-German conflict by peaceful means.

He now considered that his mission had come to an end, and he would like me, when the war was over, to repeat his motives to my compatriots.

I thanked him for his confidence and we parted with a long handshake.

When I left the Embassy I met the former ambassador of the Reich in Rome, von Hassell, on the Unter den Linden.

I was absolutely taken aback when he approached me and, in spite of the tension in Polish-German relations, greeted me with exceptional warmth, even manifesting cordiality. He told me that he was going to the Auswärtiges Amt to, as he put it, save the peace. Of course, he was acting primarily in Germany's interest, but if he succeeded, he would also render a great service to all mankind. He thought that Poland would have to make some concessions which, however, would be much better for it than the results of a war. Taking leave of him, I stressed that we were also doing everything possible to settle the conflict, the sources of which were not in our country but in his.

DOCUMENT 159   Lipski to the Ministry of Foreign Affairs

NO. GMS/5165                          Berlin, August 31, 1939
                                      Received: August 31, 1939, 10:55 A.M.
                                      Cipher-Code, incoming No. 243

According to Henderson's information, the German terms prepared for
a fully empowered Polish plenipotentiary:

I. A demobilized Danzig returns to Germany.

II. Gdynia remains with Poland.

III. Within a year a plebiscite in the Corridor, the southern bound-
ary of which to run from Marienburg [22] through Grudziądz, Bydgoszcz,
Schonlanke [Trzcianka]. Plebiscite on the basis of population of 1919.
Decision by absolute majority.

IV. Commission for the plebiscite: England, Italy, France, and
Russia.

*Lipski*

DOCUMENT 160   Lipski to the Ministry of Foreign Affairs

NO. 242                               Berlin, August 31, 1939
                                      Received: August 31, 1939, 11:45 A.M.
                                      *Secret*

Coulondre has told me that Henderson's informative giving the impression that the Germans were prepared to wait only until 12 comes from
Ribbentrop's circles. Coulondre thinks that we, for our part, might tell
the German government after 12, in keeping with our reply to Roosevelt
and the British government, that the Ambassador in Berlin is always at
the disposal of the German government. This would be a gesture for
peace.

Of course the German government might use such a step for propaganda purposes, saying that we are giving in.

*Lipski*

[22] This is a mistake; it should be Marienwerder.

### DOCUMENT 161    Beck to Lipski

Telephonogram to the Polish                    Warsaw, August 31, 1939
Ambassador in Berlin

With reference to your reports, please request an interview with the
Minister of Foreign Affairs or the Secretary of State, and inform him as
follows:

Last night the Polish government was informed by the British government of an exchange of views with the Reich government as to the
possibility of direct understanding [23] between the Polish and the German governments.

The Polish government is favorably considering the British government's suggestion and will make them a formal reply on the subject in
the next few hours at the latest.

End of declaration for the Ministry of Foreign Affairs. Next passage
for the Ambassador's information.

Please do not engage in any concrete discussions, and if the Germans
put forward any concrete demands, say you are not authorized to accept
or discuss them and will have to ask your government for further
instructions.

### DOCUMENT 162    Lipski to the Ministry of Foreign Affairs

NO. 239                                     Berlin, August 31, 1939 [24]
                                            Received: August 31, 2 P.M.

For the Minister

Lubomirski arriving tomorrow noon by plane. Please receive him
immediately.

*Lipski*

[23] The Ambassador was also informed that the word "understanding" was
meant in the sense "communicating with each other" and should therefore be
translated as *Verständigung* and not as *Vereinbarung*. The Ministry also instructed the Ambassador that, as he had already requested an interview in the
Auswärtiges Amt (in accordance with previous instructions), he was not to
insist on being received at once.
[24] The date should be August 30.

DOCUMENT 163   Lipski to the Ministry of Foreign Affairs

NO. GMS 5185                Berlin, August 31, 1939
NO. 244                     Received: August 31, 1939, 2:45 P.M.
                            *Cipher telephonogram, incoming*
                            *Secret*

The British Ambassador sent to me, accompanied by the Counselor of
the Embassy, a Swede, Dahlerus, who is a friend of Göring and who is
acting as a mediator between England and Germany. Dahlerus confirmed that Göring, in opposition to the extremists who wanted to annex
to Germany the whole Prussian territory, limited his claims to Danzig
and the Corridor, as per coded telegram No. 243. I shall telephone
conditions by press cipher as strictly confidential.[25] . . . with the British
Counselor separately. Of course, I did not discuss with D.

I regard *démarche* D. as a further symptom of pressure on us, which
took especially drastic form today. I react calmly, very firmly.

*Lipski*

These are the last telegrams sent by Ambassador Lipski to Warsaw.

In the *Polish White Book,* No. 147, pp. 141–52, there is a final report of
Lipski covering his whole activity in Berlin from September, 1933, to August, 1939.

[25] A few words are illegible here.

# The Last Month before the Outbreak of the War [1]
## August, 1939

---

### Hitler Resolves upon War against Poland

IN THE EARLY HOURS of April 8, 1939, Minister Beck was traveling through Berlin on his return journey from London. With the military attaché, Colonel Szymański, I met him at the Zoo Station and traveled with him as far as Frankfurt-an-der-Oder. First of all we reviewed the political situation. Then Colonel Szymański gave an account of the military position, stressing its gravity in connection with the information received that the dispositions of the Reichswehr were concentrating upon an operation directed to the east. Colonel Szymański's military considerations reckoned with the possibility of an early German initiative, which actually took place later. Nevertheless, the outlines of his account turned out to be accurate. It appears from Reichswehr documents now in Allied hands that—from April 3 on—preparations for "Operation White" (code name for the war against Poland) were advancing at great speed.

On April 11 Hitler issued further orders, containing detailed instructions for "Operation White" (Appendix II) aiming at the occupation of Danzig (Appendix III) and the organization and exercise of power in East Prussia in case of a warlike conflict (Appendix IV). [2]

On May 10 Hitler signed the order on the "uniform preparation for war by the armed forces," which in its Part VI contained instructions for economic warfare. [3]

Already in these first orders the basic political outlines of the war against Poland appeared. The principal object was to localize the war with Poland. The German supreme authorities considered this possible,

[1] Printed in *Sprawy Międzynarodowe* (London), 1947, No. 4, under the title *Stosunki polsko-niemieckie w świetle aktów norymberskich.*
[2] *DGFP,* Series D, Vol. VI, No. 185.
[3] *Trial of the Major War Criminals,* XXXIV, 402–8.

in view of the inner weakness of France, which might prevent England from entering the war.

The directives of April 11 assumed the entry of German troops into Slovak territory in order to attack the southern flank of Poland as well as rapidly to occupy Pomerania and to cut off Poland from its ports in the Baltic. Economic directives prescribed the occupation of industrial plants in Poland without damaging them, especially in Upper Silesia and Teschen Silesia. The whole operation should be mounted in such a manner that the attack could be launched before general mobilization had been proclaimed.

The discussion in detail of these directives of the Reichswehr against Poland is outside the scope of this article. Moreover, the subject is more a matter for military examination. It is a most unusual case that after a war we should be able to know exactly what were the enemy's plans, on the basis of statements of members of the High Command and authentic General Staff documents. The documentation in our possession makes it possible to reconstruct the German strategic plan against Poland and the subsequent stages through which it passed. Hitler considered himself to be not only a statesman but also a strategist. We know from the Nuremberg documents that he surprised his entourage, including many outstanding specialists in military art, by the great scope of his strategic conceptions, by his profound knowledge of the subject, including the most trifling details, and above all by his remarkable memory. In discussions he outstripped his generals and discarded their schemes, replacing them by his own conceptions, which proved to be right, especially in the first period of the war.

The indisputable superiority of Hitler over his associates increased his inborn vanity and megalomania, which chiefly accounted for his defeat, particularly since he lacked the main elements of science and true insight into international politics.

Hitler's speeches addressed to his most trusted associates should be considered the true expression of German policy, since he was a paramount factor in the Third Reich, in domestic affairs as well as in foreign policy. As regards the aggression against Poland, the Nuremberg Tribunal considered the exposition addressed by Hitler on May 23 to a meeting of his commanders in chief as inculpating him most.[4]

The minutes of this meeting were taken by Lieutenant Colonel

[4] *DGFP*, Series D, Vol. VI, No. 433.

Schmundt, Hitler's aide-de-camp. The conference was attended by Göring, Räder, Brauchitsch, Keitel, Milch, Halder, Bodenschatz, Schnievindt, and others of lower rank. Hitler opened his address with a general
survey of Germany's position. He reached the same conclusions as on
November 5, 1937 (in spite of the fact that Austria and Czechoslovakia
had since been annexed), that Germany needed vital space (*Lebensraum*) to solve its economic problems; this could not be achieved
without "incursions into alien territories." In the way of ascension to
power Germany met the resistance of Great Britain, which considered
all new claims as disturbing the balance of power. England was consequently the driving force against Germany. No longer believing in the
possibility of peaceful settlement with Great Britain, Hitler reached the
conclusion that it was necessary to be prepared for a conflict, which
would be a life-and-death struggle. As the first stage of this war, Hitler
planned an attack against Poland. One can follow the course of his
reasoning from short minutes made by Schmundt:

"The Pole is not a fresh enemy. Poland will always be on the side of
our adversaries. In spite of treaties of friendship, Poland has always
been bent on exploiting every opportunity against us. It is not Danzig
that is at stake. For us it is a matter of expanding our living space in the
east and making food supplies secure and also solving the problem of
the Baltic states." And further on: "The problem 'Poland' cannot be
dissociated from the showdown with the West. . . . Poland sees danger in
the German victory over the West and will try to deprive us of victory."
Then follows his definition of Polish-Russian relations in the light of
German interests: "Poland's internal solidarity against Bolshevism is
doubtful. Therefore Poland is also a doubtful barrier against Russia."
Here is manifest Hitler's discontent with the refusal by Poland of many
of his anti-Russian proposals. In the concluding part of his address Hitler
stated that the attack against Poland must be launched at the first
occasion. But at the same time the conflict with Poland should not drag
Germany into war with Great Britain and France; the main and nearest
objective of German policy would be to isolate Poland.

Most striking is the change of tone toward Soviet Russia. There are
no more aggressive accents and threats. The judgment becomes more
objective: "Economic relations with Russia are only possible if and
when political relations have improved. In press comments a cautious
trend is becoming apparent. It is not ruled out that Russia might disin-

terest herself in the destruction of Poland. If Russia continues to agitate against us, relations with Japan may become closer."

Further military orders of Hitler and his generals in June, July, and August, 1939, only carried out the general directives established at this conference in May.

### Danzig as the Trump Card in the German Game

August, 1939, began with an outbreak of new Nazi provocations in Danzig. Some Polish customs inspectors on the frontier between the Free City and East Prussia were informed on August 4 by the local Danzig authorities that after 7 A.M. on August 6 they would be prevented from carrying out their duties. In view of such drastic violation of fundamental Polish rights, the Polish government, which displayed great patience and forbearance in face of the remilitarization of the Free City carried out by the Hitlerite organization, was compelled to react abruptly. The note delivered that very day by the Polish Commissioner-General to the President of the Senate, presuming that the orders issued by minor officials must be due either to a misunderstanding or to a wrong interpretation of the respective instructions, left an open door for retreat to the authorities of the Free City. Nevertheless, the note asked that the orders be canceled within a prescribed time, namely, by August 6 at 6 P.M.; informed the Senate that the Polish customs officials would be instructed to serve in uniform and armed; and in the last instance announced that any further interference with the discharge of the customs control would call forth reprisals.[5] The President of the Senate on the following day immediately gave reassuring oral explanations, and only three days later—namely, on August 7—evidently after getting into touch with Berlin, sent a reply to the Polish note in which it was denied that any alleged orders directed against Polish customs inspectors had been issued and took exception to the attitude adopted in the matter by the Polish government.[6] For a short while it was believed in political circles that the customs conflict was, if only for the time being, wound up owing to the peremptory, but at the same time moderate, line adopted by Poland, supported by the Western Powers, who were supplied by Warsaw with full information on the course of events. In this particularly tense situation the Polish press showed as a rule more

[5] *Polish White Book*, Nos. 82 and 83; *DGFP*, Series D, Vol. VI, Nos. 773 and 774.
[6] *Polish White Book*, No. 84; *DGFP*, Series D, Vol. VI, No. 780.

discretion and forbearance than the press in the West, where much too optimistic conclusions were drawn from an alleged withdrawal by the Danzig Senate.

As a matter of fact, as early as August 9, during my short stay in Poland, where I had to report to the Foreign Minister and Marshal Śmigły-Rydz on the development of the situation in Berlin, news reached Warsaw in the late hours of a statement made that day by Secretary of State Weizsäcker to Polish Chargé d'Affaires Lubomirski in connection with the last incident in Danzig.[7] In its statement the German government took a strong view of the contents of the Polish note to the Senate on August 4, declaring that another Polish ultimatum or threat of reprisals would lead to aggravation of Polish-German relations.

The German step raised a question of principle, since the government of the Reich was interfering in relations between Poland and Danzig in a moment of increasing tension, when an action against the Danzig statute and Polish rights and interests in Danzig was initiated by an order from Berlin and closely followed directives from there. Minister Beck, in a conversation with me, took the view that the German move meant the opening of a final stage in the contest with Poland. After consultation with Marshal Śmigły-Rydz he instructed the assistant of the Undersecretary of State, Arciszewski, to inform the German Chargé d'Affaires in Warsaw of the text of the Polish government's reply contesting the German right to interfere in relations between Poland and Danzig and warning that the Polish government would consider any future intervention by the German government to the detriment of Polish rights in the Free City as an act of aggression.[8] The last reservation was a simple repetition of a formal statement made by Minister Beck to Ambassador Moltke on March 28, 1939,[9] in reply to Ribbentrop's declaration that "Polish aggression against the Free City of Danzig would be regarded by the Reich government as aggression against Germany itself." Ribben-

[7] *Polish White Book*, No. 85 and *DGFP*, Series D, Vol. VII, No. 5. In his report of August 9, Polish Chargé d'Affaires Lubomirski, citing Weizsäcker's statement in German, adds: "Secretary of State von Weizsäcker again underlined the verbal character of this declaration. Outside of this, he refrained from any personal remarks or comments, mentioning that he had only the above to declare."

[8] For Mr. Archiszewski's statement to Herr Von Wuhlisch, see *Polish White Book*, No. 86, and *DGFP*, Series D, Vol. VI, No. 10.

[9] *Polish White Book*, No. 64.

trop then used this expression in a conversation with me when sharply criticizing military measures taken by Poland during the occupation of Memel by Hitler, when there was a danger of a simultaneous German invasion of Danzig.[10]

After my return to Berlin, Counselor Lubomirski informed me of a conversation in the British Embassy on August 8, at Sir Nevile Henderson's request. . . .[11]

A few days later, on August 14, I had a long talk with the French ambassador, Coulondre, to whom I was bound by an old friendship and who was my precious support in those exhausting days. Coulondre, while not sparing any effort to preserve peace, was of the opinion that in no case should the mistakes made in the solution of the Czechoslovak problem be repeated, for the sake of France's security.

Coulondre's position was not an easy one, with a personality so wavering as M. Georges Bonnet, then French foreign minister. Being well acquainted with the German mentality, the French Ambassador was aware of the impossibility of preventing Hitler from starting a war. In his view the only efficient manner of repressing the Nazi impulses was to maintain a compact allied front, if possible extended to Russia. Being afraid that Hitler might have had some illusions about the French attitude in the event of German aggression against Poland, Coulondre never ceased to stress to the Germans that France would take up arms in the case of aggression, and would give immediate assistance to its ally. As may be presumed from the very weak protection left by the Germans on the western front during the September campaign, Hitler did not believe in the offensive spirit of the French Army and its High Command. According to Keitel's evidence, in September, 1939, there were on the western front, including reserves in the Rhineland and behind the West Wall, roughly twenty German divisions, only five of which were first class.

As I had been constantly in touch with the British and French ambassadors I had the opportunity of following the maneuvers of the Germans to throw upon Poland the responsibility for the ever-increasing tension in the political situation. Secretary of State Weizsäcker, who during the occupation of Prague had scrupulously avoided any contacts with foreign diplomats, now appeared as a conciliating factor, trying to find

[10] *Ibid.*, No. 63.
[11] See Document 147, pp. 554–56.

some outlet from a difficult situation and to preserve peace. In this way he made use of some credit which he had with foreign diplomats, in order to disparage Poland in their eyes as a reckless factor in international politics. In this way the German Foreign Office played the role detailed to it by Hitler, within his general political-strategic scheme. At the head of this Office, by the way, was Ribbentrop, who was entirely devoted to Hitler and was a most fanatical protagonist of the use of force in international politics. One of the most essential tasks of the Polish Embassy in Berlin was to counteract this German propaganda by the rectification of false news spread by German broadcasting stations and the press. As the main object of German attacks was concentrated on minority problems, the Embassy passed to the representatives of the Western Powers all details of the persecution of the Polish population in Germany. In mid-August the French and British embassies received a list of 600 instances of gross offenses against the Polish minority, the whole structure of which, as well as its cultural and economic institutions, was being destroyed extremely ruthlessly.

The disappointing visit of Ciano to Salzburg served to launch new accusations against Poland. On August 14 Sir Nevile Henderson told me that the Germans were spreading rumors, according to which Hitler, deeply hurt by the last passage of the Polish government's statement on Danzig, had declared to Ciano that German honor was involved from now on, and consequently also Axis honor.[12] This made it impossible for the Italian Foreign Minister to use his influence to stop the warlike impulses of the Dictator of the Reich. Henderson was not yet in possession of the report of his colleague in Rome on the Ciano-Hitler meeting. Nevertheless, as the German press after the Salzburg conference availed itself of the arguments of German honor, the Ambassador drew very pessimistic conclusions. Being fully aware of the military unpreparedness of Great Britain and its Allies, and not trusting Russia, Henderson made every effort to gain time at least. He regretted that Polish and German diplomacy had not discussed fundamental problems since the spring, confining themselves to delivering mutual protests and complaints.

Were there any bases for such talks in view of the described general German attitude? The Polish government voiced the Polish opinion, rejecting all claims to the incorporation of Danzig into the Reich and to extraterritorial corridors across the Corridor, stating in its reply of

[12] See Document 149, p. 557.

March 26, 1939, the extent of possible concessions.[13] The German government did not then accept the compromise proposed by Poland, and more and more peremptorily insisted on acceptance of the demands affecting the independence of Poland. In this state of affairs Poland received the English guarantee. From that time on the German government declined any conversations with the Polish government. Moltke, invited by Beck after his return to Poland, did not call at the Polish Foreign Office, and left Warsaw for a long time.

On April 28, 1939, Hitler denounced the nonaggression pact with Poland, to which Beck answered in a speech delivered in the Polish Diet on May 5.

Henderson did not sufficiently explore the true reasons for the Polish-German conflict, which was bound up with the general European situation, and was closely connected with the main aims of Hitler's policy and his wide plans for conquest. The British Ambassador was under the illusion that a catastrophe might be avoided by talks and arguments. Having for many years closely watched the development of the situation in the Third Reich, and being well acquainted with Hitler's mentality, I had no such hopes in this respect. Hitler used to make decisions and carry them out, basing himself on his own directives and taking into account only the real strength of the adversary. As I believed at that time, Hitler might have been inclined to believe then that by conflict with Poland he might incur too great a risk, and that its outcome would not profit him, if he were to face an unfriendly Russia in the east after the occupation of Poland. For this reason there were still some hopes of preserving peace, in spite of German military preparations and increasing tension, so long as the German-Soviet pact was not signed.

### Differences between the Axis Partners at the Time of the Outbreak of the War

What was the course of events in the first half of August, 1939, in the light of the Nuremberg documents? The memoirs of Ciano and the German records of the Salzburg conversations supply a fair amount of documentation divulging the true designs of Hitler and his tactics at that period.

In spite of assurances given more than once by Ribbentrop to the Italian Ambassador in Berlin that the Reich government would not go to

13 *Polish White Book,* No. 63.

extremes in its claims against Poland, Mussolini did not trust his ally. Disturbed by the development of German-Polish relations in the first half of August, he sent Foreign Minister Ciano to Germany for an exchange of views with Hitler and Ribbentrop. Having arrived in Salzburg on August 11, 1939, Ciano went to Fuschl, Ribbentrop's residence, where he held his first conversation with him. He related it as follows: "While we were waiting to be seated at the dinner table, Ribbentrop informed me of the decision that the storm must break, as he would have talked with me of a minor, ordinary administrative measure. 'Well, Ribbentrop,' I asked, 'what do you want? The Corridor or Danzig?' 'Not that any more,' he said, gazing at me with his cold expressionless eyes, 'we want war!' "

At the Nuremberg trial, on April 1, 1946, Ribbentrop denied having said this: "I told Count Ciano that Hitler was resolved to settle the Polish problem by any means; Hitler ordered me to tell Ciano this. It is simply preposterous to affirm that I said 'we want war,' for one does not say such things even to one's best and most faithful ally—certainly not to Count Ciano." Had he confessed to having made such an announcement Ribbentrop would have condemned himself for a crime against peace.

We have an account of the subsequent conversation held on August 12, 1939, at Obersalzburg between Ciano and Hitler, at which Ribbentrop also took part. It was made by Minister Plenipotentiary Schmidt, chief German interpreter, who attended all important conferences. It appears from this bulky document that the discussion was concerned with an essential question—the time of the outbreak of the war.

When Hitler put forward the reasons for the immediate outbreak of hostilities, Ciano offered stubborn resistance, trying to win two or three years' delay. In connection with this point they argued about the possibility of localizing the conflict. Hitler replied that "he personally was absolutely convinced that the Western democracies would, in the last resort, recoil from unleashing a general war."

Trying to convince his Italian ally that in view of the present strategic position the risks of war with the Western Powers were considerably less, owing to the present military superiority of the Axis, than they would be in a few years, Hitler stated that the destruction of the Polish war potential could only be beneficial to the Axis. Since the Poles had clearly shown that in a conflict they would side with the enemies of

Germany and Italy, a quick liquidation of Poland at the present moment could only be of advantage for the unavoidable conflict with the Western democracies. Should a hostile Poland remain on the German eastern frontier it would tie up not only eleven East Prussian divisions but even more German units in Pomerania and Silesia. By an earlier liquidation of Poland this necessity would be eliminated. Generally speaking, the best thing would be for the pseudo-neutrals to be eliminated one after the other, concluded Hitler, indicating Yugoslavia and other Balkan states, unreliable from the Axis point of view. A further reason brought forward by Hitler with the purpose of reassuring Ciano as regards France was his statement that after a quick defeat of Poland the Germans would have 100 divisions available on the western front, which would compel France to withdraw its armies from all fronts, including units stationed on the Italian Frontier.

Hitler gave his opinion of the Polish war potential and the internal situation as follows: "The quality of the Polish Army was extremely uneven. Alongside a few crack divisions there was a host of units of inferior quality. Poland's antitank and antiaircraft defenses were very weak. At present France and England could send it no supplies. But, if Poland were given economic assistance by the West over a fairly long period, it could secure these arms, and Germany's superiority would thereby be diminished. Over and against the fanatics in Warsaw and Cracow there was a rural population in other districts which was quite indifferent. Furthermore, the comparison of the population of the Polish state should be taken into account: of the 34 million inhabitants there were 1½ million Germans, some 4 million Jews, and approximately 9 million Ukrainians, so that considerably less than the total population were actual Poles, and, as he had already said, even the fighting qualities of the Poles could not be considered uniform. In these circumstances, Poland would be defeated by Germany in a very short time."

Hitler adapted his argument on Danzig to his Italian interlocutor, comparing Danzig, "the Nuremberg of the North," to Italian Trieste. He stressed that the east, the northeast, and the Baltic states were within the German sphere of interest, comparing the importance of this area for Germany with the Mediterranean, which undoubtedly constituted the Italian sphere of interest.

The reasons put forward by Ciano for postponing the conflict were of no avail: he referred to the Duce's idea for an international conference, but Hitler maintained a negative attitude. Eventually he proposed the issue of a declaration which would lead to a gradual withdrawal of support by the Western Powers from Poland, which in turn would eventually force Poland to accept the German claims. Hitler's answer was that he had no time to lose in settling the Polish problem. After autumn had set in, military operations in Eastern Europe would be more difficult. From September to May, Poland was a great marsh and entirely unsuited to any kind of military operations. In fact, Poland could occupy Danzig in October, and was probably ready to do so, when Germany would be unable to do anything about it, since the use of artillery against Danzig and the destruction of the town were out of the question.

After Hitler's statement Ciano asked bluntly how soon the Danzig question must be settled. Hitler replied, "By the end of August," repeating his well-known accounts of offers most advantageous to Poland, which were alleged to have been refused as the result of British intervention. He gave warning that he was prepared to use the occasion of the next Polish provocation—an ultimatum, some brutal ill-treatment of Germans, an attempt to starve out Danzig, or something of the kind —for the invasion of Poland within forty-eight hours and the final settlement of the problem in such a way. In his opinion it would greatly improve the Axis position, as would the liquidation of Yugoslavia by Italy.

Hitler concluded that such action against Poland must be expected at any moment.

In the last passage of Schmidt's minutes it is said that the conversation was interrupted for a short time because Hitler received telegrams from Moscow and Tokyo.

When the conversation was resumed Ciano was told that the Soviet government agreed to the dispatch of a German envoy to Moscow for political negotiations.

### German Camouflage Goes On

From mid-August the tension between Germany and Poland increased from day to day. The war of nerves was at its peak. The Hitlerite propaganda machinery, which had stood the test during the occupation of Austria and Czechoslovakia, was working with great skill and precision. Its weakness consisted in such methods of propaganda as spreading false rumors and simply inventing some facts, which were used not for the first time and were consequently well known to foreign observers.

The action of camouflage recommended by Hitler at the meeting with his commanders in chief on May 23 [14] was systematically carried out. Nevertheless, the intensive military preparations and troop movements did not escape the attention of Polish and Allied observers. The concentration of German divisions against Poland was ascertained with great precision. The military attaché at the Polish Embassy in Berlin, Colonel Szymański, maintained a day by day contact with his French and British colleagues, as did the three Allied ambassadors among themselves.

The Tannenberg celebration fixed for August 27, at which Hitler was to make a speech, and which was to have been attended by the military attachés invited on this occasion, was part of the German camouflage measures, serving among other things to cover mobilization action in East Prussia. On August 17, 1939, the heads of diplomatic missions received, as in previous years, invitations to the annual Party Congress at Nuremberg, for the first half of September. It was asked that answers to these invitations be given before August 26, 1939, the date previously appointed by Hitler for the invasion of Poland. But what was most unexpected was an invitation sent to me in mid-August by Oberjäger-meister Scherping, on behalf of Göring, to a hunt in the Prussian game preserves.[15] From May on I had had no close contact with Göring. This move on his part was a puzzle to me, but I soon heard that the British Ambassador had received a similar invitation.

On August 17 I was informed in detail by Ambassadors Henderson and Coulondre of their conversations with Weizsäcker, held on August 15. . . .[16] At the end of this long and sometimes tumultuous exchange of views with the British Ambassador, Weizsäcker let it be understood unequivocally that Germany reckoned on an understanding with Russia to the detriment of Poland. After Moscow's approval of the start of political conversations, transmitted to Hitler on August 12,[17] Weizsäcker was in a position to play this trump card with the representative of Great Britain.

[14] *DGFP*, Series D, Vol. VI, No. 433.
[15] See Document 148, p. 556.
[16] See Document 150, pp. 559–62. See also *DGFP*, Series D, Vol. VII, Nos. 64 and 66.
[17] See *DGFP*, Series D, Vol. VII, No. 43, pp. 48–49, and No. 50.

*Last Visit to Warsaw*

The events subsequent to August 21, 1939, were fully disclosed in the Nuremberg trial. It would take many volumes to comment on all evidence brought to light by this trial. The Tribunal aimed firmly to establish the guilt of crimes against peace caused by launching a war of aggression accompanied by violation of international agreements. The defendants strove to portray in the most favorable light their part in the events which occurred in the last days of August. To this effect they supplied the Tribunal with vast evidence and called many witnesses for the defense, among them the famous Dahlerus. The arguments put forward by the defense, aiming sometimes even at charging Polish diplomatic representatives in connection with German proposals summed up in sixteen points, were much like the tactics of the German Foreign Office on the eve of the war. Nevertheless, in this case the official German documents which were in Allied possession spoke for themselves, refuting the statements of the defendants and putting witnesses in a most awkward position.

The events which occurred on August 25, 1939, and also the sixteen points of the German demands which raised wide discussion and numerous comments in the press are of particular importance for the history of German-Polish relations.

In the afternoon of August 21 I flew to Warsaw for one day. I had some urgent business which had to be transacted orally.

To my suggestion to accept the invitation sent to me on behalf of Göring and to write to him proposing a meeting, Beck answered in the affirmative,[18] asking me to come to Warsaw for a few hours to receive detailed instructions.

German military preparations were going to such lengths and tension was increasing to such a degree that one had to reckon with the outbreak of war at any moment. Orders to the Embassy and to the consular posts in Germany in the event of war had already been issued for some time, and were gradually put into force. Final decisions had still to be given on some particular points, among them the question of evacuating part of the staff and their dependents, as well as taking over the protection of Polish interests in Germany, in the case of war, by a neutral state.

18 See Document 152, p. 564.

Other matters to be discussed referred to problems closely connected with our relations with the Western Powers, in view of German attempts to discredit Poland in their eyes. I always advised the most prudent treatment of minority problems and the coordination of all moves by the home authorities with the directives of the Foreign Office. For years hostile propaganda had been exploiting the minority problems, and that had left some traces. Even in circles friendly to us opinions were expressed that Poland might be represented in an unfavorable light in connection with minority incidents. The problem became still more delicate through the fact that the Hitlerite Reich, in the last months before the outbreak of the war, quite openly used the German minority in Poland for diversionist and propaganda purposes.

I was received by Minister Beck at Brühl Palace in the evening hours. I received general directions for my conversation with Göring. The purpose of this conversation was to be the rectification of false accusations against Poland, stressing the consistent Polish policy toward Germany within the general framework of the nonaggression pact of 1934, emphasizing our fortitude regarding defense against aggression, and in the last instance putting the question: Whose ends would a European war serve? The main idea of the meeting with Göring should be an attempt to exercise some influence on Hitler through him, following Henderson's advice to some extent, who always asserted that Hitler was misinformed by his entourage and men like Ribbentrop. Before the conversation with the Foreign Minister was brought to an end, General Stachiewicz, chief of the General Staff, called. Minister Beck asked me to call on him again the following day in the morning before I flew back to Berlin. For a while we three exchanged among ourselves our views on the political and military situation. Beck, reviewing different assumptions, took into account the possibility of German aggression confined to Danzig and the cutting off of Pomerania. In view of the extent of German preparations I did not agree with this opinion. The Danzig problem, which had been an object of constant worry and preoccupation to the Foreign Minister since spring, had become the outpost of an undisguised struggle led by Hitlerite Germany against Poland. By putting this problem forward and with it absorbing Polish and international public opinion, Germany was trying to obscure the true picture of the situation. This circumstance also had its consequences in influencing some Polish military moves. I replied to a question put by General Stachiewicz, stating peremptorily that we must reckon with a German attack along the whole front, including the Slovak sector.

In the early hours of the following day Warsaw was informed by a communiqué published in Berlin during the night that Ribbentrop was soon to fly to Moscow for negotiations over a nonaggression pact. This news profoundly upset Polish public opinion, aware of the political situation. I gave the order by telephone to the Embassy in Berlin to send my letter to Göring, dated August 21 and signed by me before my departure. I found Beck in the Foreign Office, profoundly worried, although he maintained an apparent calm. Our interview was short. I was in haste to get to the airport.

In view of the big diplomatic success scored by Hitler, considerably strengthening the German strategic position, I was very much disturbed as to what might be the repercussions in the West from the new German agreement. Beck expressed the opinion that Great Britain would keep its pledges to Poland.

Being aware that there were no more chances to preserve peace, I left Warsaw with great anxiety.

### Hitler's Speech to the Commanders in Chief

In the files of the "Oberkommando der Wehrmacht" at Flensburg the Allied authorities found copies of the two speeches addressed at Berchtesgaden on August 22, 1939, to the German commanders in chief.[19] The purpose of the meeting was, according to Hitler's own words, to inform the commanders of his decision to begin war operations in the next few days, and in connection with this "to strengthen their confidence."

That day Hitler was in high spirits, feeling that he had reached the peak of his successes.

From the picture of the situation given by him it clearly appeared that the situation was so favorable for Germany that it would be more advisable to start the war at once instead of waiting two or three years more. His own personality was a very important factor which influenced his decision. "No one will ever again," said Hitler, "have the confidence of the whole German people as I have. There will probably never again be a man with more authority than I possess. My existence is therefore a

[19] *DGFP*, Series D, Vol. VII, No. 192.

factor of great value. But I can be eliminated at any time by a criminal or a lunatic."

On the enemy's side, in Hitler's opinion, there were no outstanding personalities. He also stressed as particularly favorable factors for Germany the fact that the Duce and Franco were in power. Economic reasons were summed up by Hitler in the following words: "It is easy for us to make decisions. We have nothing to lose, we have everything to gain. Because of our restrictions, our economic situation is such that we can only hold out for a few more years. Göring can confirm this. We have no other choice, we must act." His further arguments pointed out the rivalry between France and England in the Mediterranean, the increasing tension in the Near East, the uneasy position of the British Empire, the weakness of France, the internal decomposition of Yugoslavia, the position of Rumania threatened by Hungary and Bulgaria, and the lack of an outstanding personality in Turkey after the death of Kemal Pasha. Hitler confessed that the creation of a Greater Germany was a big political achievement, but open to question on the military side since it was gained by a bluff on the part of the political leaders. It must now be tested in war. He stressed that his Polish policy was contrary to popular feeling in Germany. From the difficulties met by Poland in obtaining a loan from England for rearmament, Hitler drew the conclusion that England did not really want to support Poland. It did not want to risk eight million pounds in Poland, although it had put half a billion into China.

The enemy hoped—said Hitler—that Russia would become our enemy after the conquest of Poland. The enemy did not reckon with my great capacity to take decisions. The publication of the nonggression pact with Russia was a bombshell. The consequences cannot be overlooked. The effect on Poland will be tremendous. "Now Poland is in the position in which I wanted her."

In his second speech there were the following most significant announcements:

"The destruction of Poland has priority. The aim is to eliminate active forces, not to reach a definite line. Even if war breaks out in the West, the destruction of Poland remains the priority. A quick decision is in view because of the season. I shall give a propagandist reason for starting the war—no matter whether it is plausible or not. The victor will not be asked afterward whether he told the truth or not. When starting and waging a war, it is not right that matters, but victory. . . . New German frontier delimination according to sound principles, and possibly a protectorate as a buffer state."

Expressing his conviction that Germany would be equal to the task, Hitler concluded that the start would probably be ordered for Saturday morning (August 26, 1939).

### The Last Meeting with Göring

On August 23, 1939, the British government took an initiative to save peace. On that day Sir Nevile Henderson conveyed to Hitler a personal letter from Chamberlain in which the British government—in spite of the announcement of the German-Soviet agreement—while confirming its pledges to Poland, expressed its readiness to discuss with the Reich government all questions arising between Germany and England, if only a proper atmosphere of confidence could be created, and finally called for direct negotiations between Germany and Poland on minority questions.[20] The first news of a negative outcome of the conversations between Henderson and Hitler was told to me on the night of the same day by the Belgian ambassador, Davignon, at the house of the Rumanian envoy, Crutzescu, where I also met Prince Ghica, former Rumanian foreign minister, who was passing through Berlin. All present were profoundly depressed.

The following day I had a telephone call from Göring's office. Referring to my personal letter, the aide-de-camp asked me whether I would like to meet the Field Marshal. To my reply that I was ready to call on him at any time, the aide-de-camp gave me a significant answer, asking me to call the same day at 5 P.M., "since later on it might be too late." The meeting took place at Göring's Berlin residence and lasted one hour. Göring made the reservation that the conversation was a private one. He started by saying that the policy of maintaining good relations with Poland, for which we had both cooperated for so many years, had foundered and he was examining the reasons for that turn of events. Then followed a long exchange of views, each of us mutually advancing his arguments. Göring complained among other things of our distrust of Germany and of Hitler's pledges, which he always observed on the Polish side. In his opinion the distrust greatly contributed to rendering

[20] *Ibid.*, No. 200; see also *British Blue Book*, Nos. 56, 57, 58, and 59.

impossible cooperation between the two states. He tried to convince me that Hitler was sincere when he declared that he dismissed the Corridor problem. That sounded rather cynical in the light of the frantic German campaign for the revision of Poland's western frontier. As regards Danzig, Göring admitted that the decision had been taken to annex this city to Germany. When I referred to the formal pledges made on many occasions before me by the Chancellor to respect the statute of the Free City and Polish rights in Danzig, Göring replied that Poland should have no illusions on this point, in view of the action led by the National Socialists in the Free City. Even in Danzig questions "we have had our tussles, but things between us would never have got so far ("wir hätten uns gerauft, aber es wäre nicht so weit zwischen uns gekommen") without British intervention. We would never have been placed in such a position as we are at present." "What does Mr. Beck expect?" Göring kept repeating. Even in the case of England's intervention that country was quite unable to give Poland efficient assistance.

Alluding to the German-Soviet agreement, I pointed out that Poland had followed a consistent policy toward both Germany and Russia in agreement with the nonaggression pacts with these countries, refusing to side with one of them against the other. Göring did not deny this. I put to him then the question whether the German-Soviet agreement would not in its consequences turn against the Reich, provoking war in Europe, which must profit only the Soviets. Göring looked down and did not answer. After a while he admitted that German foreign policy had made a *volte-face* of 100 degrees, but that was Great Britain's fault. One must keep in mind that Germany had to choose between Great Britain and Russia. The pact with Russia would have far-reaching consequences. "From now on we have to agree on all our moves toward Poland with Soviet Russia." The last words of Göring remained deeply impressed in my mind.

Referring to my continuous efforts for fourteen years to normalize Polish-German relations and establish a possible cooperation between the two countries, I said that I remained at this crucial moment in Berlin (Moltke left Warsaw in July) in order that I might be at the Chancellor's disposal if he wanted to ease the tension with Poland. Göring assured me that he would inform the Chancellor accordingly.

It appeared from the conversation with Göring and from his behavior that he considered the war with Poland to be a foregone conclu-

AUGUST, 1939

sion. He expressed regrets that he should, on the Führer's order, fight in the opposite camp to me, and he took leave of me with a theatrical gesture.

## Events of August 25, 1939

In the last days before the outbreak of the war there were rumors in Berlin of the alleged hesitations of Hitler as regards starting the war. Much evidence points to the fact that the attack against Poland was originally ordered for August 26 and then postponed.

From August 23 reports were coming in of incidents provoked by German groups along the Polish frontier. These incidents assumed vast proportions on August 25, and on the following day the tension was still increasing.[21] At this time an incident occurred which threw light on the German plans. On the night of August 25 to 26 a German detachment, starting from Slovak territory and stealing through woods, attacked the railway station at Mosty and the railway tunnel in the Jablonka Pass. In the morning it was destroyed by a Polish detachment of the 21st Mountain Division.[22] The German lieutenant who commanded the detachment confessed that he had carried out this task in connection with the outbreak of the war. The Germans withdrew immediately from this incident. The commander of the 7th German Infantry Division expressed his regrets to General Kustroń for an incident caused by "an irresponsible man." This fact could not be fully used by Polish propaganda, since there was so much news of incidents multiplying from hour to hour.

When on August 26 I lodged a protest against the violation of the Polish frontier with Undersecretary of State Woermann,[23] the Embassy obtained news circuitously that on August 25 in the late afternoon the Polish Consulate at Marienwerder [Kwidzyń] was occupied by the police and Consul [Edward] Czyżewski interned with all his staff. This step by the German authorities must have been connected with the general measures which had been taken in the event of war on the territory of East Prussia, which was under special watch.[24] In reply to an intervention by the Polish Embassy, the German Foreign Office was unable to

[21] See *Polish White Book*, No. 116.
[22] Gisevius, in his book *Bis zum bitteren Ende*, states wrongly that this German detachment maintained the Jablonka Pass for a whole week until the war broke out.
[23] *DGFP*, Series D, Vol. VI, Nos. 330, 331, and 335.
[24] *Ibid.*, No. 336.

state any valid reason which might have explained this step of the local authorities in East Prussia. Owing to our intervention, Consul Czyżewski, with all his staff, left a few days later for Lithuania via Königsberg. They thus had the chance to escape the fate of their colleagues from other consular posts in East Prussia, some of whom died in German prisons during the war, such as the consul in Allenstein [Olsztyn], Bohdan Jałowiecki; the attaché to the consulate in Königsberg, Witold Winiarski; and the clerk of the same consulate, Emil Schuller.[25]

Our assumption that the date of August 26, 1939, was originally chosen for the outbreak of the war was confirmed in the Nuremberg trial, and the course of events of that day was set up with full precision on the ground of the evidence given by the defendants and documents produced before the Tribunal. Hitler's main idea was to localize the conflict with Poland. He believed that he could achieve this by his agreement with Russia; he anticipated a government crisis in England and in France under the shock of the news of the German-Russian agreement; and he was sure that he would compel Poland to surrender. The position taken by the British government and conveyed to him by Henderson on August 23, as well as the declarations of the British ministers in the House of Commons and the House of Lords (August 24), had shaken his confidence that the Western Powers would not come to Poland's assistance.[26] This may explain the approach by Hitler to Great Britain with a comprehensive offer, as well as his conciliatory gesture toward France. Between the conversations held on August 25, first with Henderson at 1:30 P.M., then with Coulondre at 5:30 P.M., Hitler issued an order at 2 P.M. to start the attack against Poland at dawn the following day.[27]

At the same time conversations were held between Rome and Berlin, as disclosed in Ciano's memoirs. In the night from August 24 to August 25, Ribbentrop advised Ciano by telephone that the situation had become critical on account of Polish "provocation." The following day,

[25] Consul Bohdan Jałowiecki was imprisoned in Königsberg and in concentration camps Hohenbruch and Działdowo, where he died in February, 1941. Witold Winiarski, imprisoned in Königsberg, died in concentration camp Działdowo in August, 1941. Emil Schuller committed suicide in prison in Königsberg in May, 1941. In Lipski's papers (File 31), there is a list of 51 Polish foreign service employees arrested by the Germans, 27 of whom were executed or died in concentration camps.

[26] *British Blue Book*, Nos. 56 and 64.

[27] *DGFP*, Series D, Vol. VI, No. 265 and Editor's Note on p. 302, as well as *Livre jaune*, No. 242.

before noon, Ciano called twice on Mussolini, who was perplexed whether he should stay outside the conflict or declare his allegiance to Hitler. At 2 P.M. Hitler sent a communication to Mussolini, through Mackensen, that he would start an armed intervention, asking for an "Italian understanding." The Italians availed themselves of this last passage. Mussolini's answer was conveyed to Hitler through Attolico at 3 P.M. The Italian ally refused to take part in the war, alleging that Italy was not ready for the time being, and that it could not intervene unless supplied "with the military supplies and the raw materials." [28] Shortly afterward even worse news reached Berlin, namely, that on the same afternoon a treaty of alliance between Poland and England had been signed.[29]

Under interrogation Ribbentrop said the following about the steps he had taken when this news was communicated to him: "When I heard this news from Press quarters, subsequently confirmed by the Reich Chancellery, I went at once to the Führer and, hearing that military steps had been taken against Poland, I asked him to withdraw and stop the advance. Hitler hesitated for a moment and then agreed with me. He gave orders to his military adjutant—I think that Marshal Keitel called at the same time—to convene the generals and stop the military measures which had already been started. Hitler told me on that occasions that he had received two items of bad news that day and assumed that news of the attitude adopted by Italy must have reached London immediately, which accounted for the final signing of the treaty of alliance." [30]

Keitel also made a statement on this subject: "I was surprised by an urgent call from Hitler to the Reich Chancellery. He told me to 'stop everything at once, and to call Brauchitsch. I need time for negotiations.' I telephoned to the Commander in Chief of the Army and transmitted to him the order, and he was called to Hitler." [31]

Göring supplemented Ribbentrop's and Keitel's statements by saying: "On the day when England gave its formal guarantee to Poland, that was on August 25, 1939, the Führer called me on the telephone and told me that he had stopped the planned invasion of Poland. I asked him

[28] *DGFP*, Series D, Vol. VI, Nos. 266 and 271.
[29] For the text of the Anglo-Polish Agreement of Mutual Assistance, see *Polish White Book*, No. 91. For the secret protocol, see Jędrzejewicz, *Poland in the British Parliament, 1939–1945*, I, 191, and III, 513–17.
[30] *Trial of the Major War Criminals*, 94th day of the trial, March 29, 1946.
[31] *Ibid.*, 99th day, April 4, 1946.

whether this was just temporary or for good. He said, 'No, I will have to see whether we can eliminate British intervention.' " [32]

## The Affairs of the Sixteen Points

After August 25 the Nazi leaders redoubled their efforts to neutralize Great Britain, and in this way France also, in the conflict with Poland. The principal roles were clearly shared out. Hitler took the direction of the whole action. Ribbentrop, as foreign minister, carried out his orders in conversations held with the British government through Henderson. Finally, Göring—with the knowledge and consent but allegedly behind the back of Ribbentrop—in great secrecy initiated unofficial steps with London, using Dahlerus as his trusted confidant.

The history of the exertions of Dahlerus, a Swedish industrialist, who in this tragic period meddled in negotiations for peace with utterly irrelevant proposals, being completely in the dark as regards German designs, as he confessed at Nuremberg, was widely discussed during the trial. Even before the trial started and he was himself cited as a witness by Göring, Dahlerus had published a book in Swedish in which he related his adventures in detail.[33] We learn about Dahlerus' past life from these memoirs, written in the form of a report and imbued with an exaggerated feeling of the historic importance of his mission and displaying his gullibility. He was thoroughly acquainted with Germany and England, having stayed as an industrialist in both countries for a long time. He came into contact with Göring in 1934 over personal matters: Göring helped him in the settlement of the financial affairs of Dahlerus' future wife, a German by birth, and in return Dahlerus took care of Göring's stepson, who was staying in Sweden. After 1935 they both met a few times each year, which gave Dahlerus the opportunity of making the acquaintance of the rulers of the Third Reich. From close observation Dahlerus reached the conclusion that, while Hitler and his protégé Ribbentrop were aiming at war for territorial conquests, Göring inclined toward peaceful settlement, as tested during the Sudetenland crisis in 1938.

Dahlerus was extremely worried that the breach between Germany and England was widening because of the lack of understanding among the Nazi rulers, including Göring, of British policy and of the firm

[32] *Ibid.*, 87th day, March 21, 1946.
[33] Dahlerus, *The Last Attempt*. See also *The Times Literary Supplement* (London), May 25, 1946, for the article "An Interloper in Diplomacy."

decision of the British nation to resist all further German aggression. When the tension between Germany and Great Britain was increasing in the summer of 1939, it occurred to him that it would be useful if Göring could get into direct touch with prominent representatives of the British nation for a free exchange of views, outside the well-worn ruts of diplomacy. For this purpose, on June 24, 1939, he left Sweden for London, where over dinner at the Constitutional Club he met leading men from the industrial, financial, and commercial worlds, and held a discussion with them on the subject of British-German relations. At the request of the Britons who attended the conference a summary of the discussion was made, consisting of a few paragraphs.

The conclusions of the British participants were that the British nation had reached the limit of its patience and would not put up with any further conquests. The British nation, nevertheless, wished to live in peace with the German nation and did not see any valid reason for an armed conflict, the more so as the Germans could gain much more by agreements than by war. The British party stressed the pledges to Poland, also as regards Danzig. It was clearly pointed out that the occupation of Danzig would mean war with Poland and that Great Britain would automatically be involved in war with Germany.

Pursuant to this meeting, Dahlerus arrived in Berlin on July 5 and on the following day was received by Göring, to whom he produced the conclusions of the London conversation, suggesting a meeting between German and British statesmen. As Göring persisted in saying that the English guarantee to Poland was a bluff, Dahlerus proposed to summon to Berlin three persons who had attended the conference at the Constitutional Club and who were staying at that time in Copenhagen. They were to confirm the opinion expressed by Dahlerus to Göring. With Göring's approval three Englishmen, among them Spencer, reached the Reich capital on July 7; they confirmed what had been discussed in London, met a German general, detailed to show them the Air Ministry, and after a tour of the city left Berlin the following day. On July 8 Dahlerus was told that Hitler had accepted the idea of an interview of the British group with Göring, provided that strict secrecy was preserved. In this way they met on August 7, 1939, at Sonke Nissen Koog, a place in northern Schleswig. Before that, on July 20, Dahlerus was received by Lord Halifax, who was interested in the idea of the meeting, but emphasized that the British government would not take part in the conference. For this reason there were no members either of the government or of Parliament among the Britons who attended the conference. Dahlerus did not disclose in his memoirs the names of those who were present, whose number was seven, except for Spencer.

On the German side the meeting was attended by Göring, with General Bodenschatz and other high officials. According to Dahlerus' recital of the meeting, which lasted some hours (Göring stayed at Sonke Nissen Koog from 10 A.M. to 6 P.M.), it was confined to the presentation by both parties of their points of view in a friendly atmosphere and with mutual recriminations. Göring, who was more and more cheerful and outspoken, alluded once to the fact that Germany had abstained from criticizing the Soviet Union for some months past, and to the Rapallo pact as still being valid. When the British representatives pointed out the recurring German method of putting on the agenda the minority problem, as an introduction to the incorporation of certain areas into Germany, Göring assured them "upon his word as a statesman and an officer" that Germany's demand for Danzig and the Pomeranian Corridor did not aim at the encirclement of Poland, and that Germany would not raise any further territorial claims after the settlement of the Danzig problem. The meeting was closed with the adoption of a recommendation of both governments to convene an official conference, attended by delegates with full powers. Dahlerus writes that the meeting became more and more cordial and was closed by mutual toasts, and that its outcome gave hope for a peaceful settlement of outstanding difficult problems.

The next day the British representatives raised a proposal before Dahlerus to extend the conference of the two powers to France and Italy also, which meant that Poland as well as the Soviets would have been excluded. Dahlerus went after Göring to the island of Sylt to obtain his agreement. Göring, who seemed to be satisfied with the outcome of the meeting, expressed the opinion "that the conference of the four powers would be agreed to by the German government, provided it was well prepared."

Returning to Sweden full of good hope, Dahlerus told his English friends three days later that Germany agreed to a secret meeting of the four powers, and that Sweden would be the most agreeable meeting place for them. Dahlerus felt elated as his dreams took shape. New chances for saving the peace were secured, but he omits to state that it

could be done only at the price of a new Polish Munich. He urged the
Swedish minister of state to suggest that Sweden accept its responsibili-
ties and not refuse its hospitality should it be requested to grant it by the
British and German governments.

"And now," further writes Dahlerus, "an episode occurred, inexplicable to me, pregnant with consequences." The negotiations came to
a complete stop. A dilettante diplomatist was unable to understand
that.

On August 23 Göring summoned Dahlerus from Stockholm by telephone to come at once to Berlin. The zealous Dahlerus was at Karinhall
the next day. Göring delivered a long speech in which he told Dahlerus
that the German political and military position had greatly improved
owing to the treaty with Russia. Assuring him that Germany sincerely
desired an understanding with Great Britain, Göring asked Dahlerus to
go immediately to London and declare to the British government on his,
Göring's, behalf that he was ready to risk all his authority in order to
achieve this end. Distrusting the German Foreign Office—which must
have meant that he placed no reliance on Ribbentrop—he was trying his
own channels to make contact with London.

On August 25 at 1:30 P.M. Dahlerus landed at Croydon, at the
moment when Hitler was seeing Henderson, and less than an hour before he ordered the attack against Poland. As Dahlerus confessed afterward, he knew nothing about that.

Stating the reasons for which he had taken upon himself this mission
to London, Göring explained at Nuremberg as follows: "During all
these negotiations it was not a question, as far as I was concerned, of
isolating Poland and keeping England out of the matter, but rather it
was a question, since the problem of the Corridor and Danzig had come
up, of solving it peacefully as far as possible along the lines of the
Munich solution." [34] Göring was fully aware that the acceptance of
German territorial claims would deliver Poland lock, stock, and barrel
to Germany, canceling all its alliances with the Western Powers. Moreover, from August 23, 1939, Germany was bound to Soviet Russia by a
secret protocol which stipulated the delimitation of the spheres of interest between these powers along the Narew, Vistula, and San in the case
of any territorial and political changes in the areas belonging to the

[34] *Trial of the Major War Criminals,* Testimony of Göring on the 85th day of
the trial, March 19, 1946.

Polish state.[35] Infringement of the territorial status of Poland would automatically bring into force the German-Soviet agreement, which meant the partition of Poland between Germany and Russia. Göring believed that it would be possible to settle the Polish problem by cunning and artful devices without risking war with the coalition.

The French ambassador in Berlin rightly assessed the German aims, drawing the attention of his government, in a telegram of August 26, to the necessity not to commit two essential mistakes when negotiating with Germany: the first would be if the international guarantee for Poland were stipulated without the necessary precision. M. Coulondre warned against the second mistake in the following words: "The second stumbling block would be to lend oneself to intrigues aimed at dissociating the Allies. No pressure of the sort to demoralize Poland could be exerted. Danzig is merely the point of least resistance at which the Reich tries to break into Poland. M. Lipski said to me last night: 'What the Germans want is to place their hands on Poland and one day to have the Polish Army at their disposal.' Negotiations, and this is a preliminary condition, can only start if all threat of force is discarded." [36]

An official stage of the German-British negotiations was reopened by a conversation between Hitler and Henderson on August 25. Then followed Henderson's flight to London on the 26th, his return to Berlin on the 28th, and a conversation with Hitler the same day at 10:30 P.M. In these negotiations the British government took a favorable stand toward the question of reaching an agreement with the Reich if the differences between Germany and Poland were settled peacefully.

At the same time Dahlerus was carrying on his job. On August 25 he called on Halifax who, in view of the news from Berlin that official negotiations had been reopened, thanked him for his further services for the time being. Nevertheless, when Göring warned him on the telephone at night that the war might break out at any moment under the shock of the signing of the Anglo-Polish Treaty of Mutual Assistance, Dahlerus saw Halifax again the morning of the next day, obtained from him a personal letter to Göring, and flew to Berlin. The same night he met Göring and then was received by Hitler. After a long monologue and a hysterical violent outburst, Hitler asked Dahlerus to return immediately

[35] For the text of the Treaty of Nonaggression between Germany and the USSR and the Secret Additional Protocol, see *DGFP*, Series D, Vol. VI, Nos. 228 and 229.

[36] *Livre jaune,* No. 248.

to England, conveying through him orally his proposals to the British government, summed up in six points which differed considerably from the note handed over through Henderson. In return for friendship offered to England, Hitler wished to secure its assistance in obtaining Danzig and the Corridor—Poland to retain Gdynia and to be given a free port in Danzig. He demanded adequate guarantees for the German minority in Poland, but at the same time agreed to guarantee Poland's future frontiers.[37]

On August 27 Dahlerus was received at Downing Street by Chamberlain and Halifax in the presence of Cadogan and Horace Wilson. The British negotiators were in a rather awkward position, being confronted by two reports on the German demands, one officially conveyed by Henderson, and the other unofficially transmitted by Dahlerus. Their position could not fail to increase the English distrust of Hitler and his government. When the meeting was over, Cadogan explained to Dahlerus the British stand toward Hitler's proposals and said that the British government recommended direct German-Polish negotiations and asked for the participation of Germany, Russia, France, Italy, and Great Britain in the international guarantees for Poland.

Returning to Berlin on August 27 at 11 P.M., Dahlerus informed Göring of the results of his endeavors in London. After seeing Hitler, Göring decided that the situation was taking a favorable turn.

At this crucial moment for Poland the bonds of alliance to the Western Powers put on its shoulders a heavy and responsible duty to follow a line of conduct imbued with the maximum good will in spite of hostile German maneuvers.

To the appeal addressed to Poland and Germany by the Belgian King on behalf of the Oslo group, as well as by President Roosevelt, the President of Poland replied in the affirmative, agreeing to direct negotiations between the two powers concerned, respectively to the application of conciliation procedures and the participation of an impartial and disinterested factor.[38]

---

[37] Hitler's six points in his talk with Dahlerus were to cover the following: (1) An agreement or alliance of Germany with England. (2) England must help Germany in the annexation of Danzig and the Corridor. (3) Germany would guarantee the western frontier of Poland. (4) There must be an agreement on the matter of German colonies. (5) The treatment of German minorities would be guaranteed. (6) The Germans would agree to fight for the British Empire anywhere it might be attacked. (Testimony of Dahlerus in Nuremberg on the 85th day of the trial, March 19, 1946.)

[38] *Polish White Book*, Nos. 87, 88, 89, and 90.

On August 28, after a consultation between the British Ambassador in Warsaw and Mr. Beck on the answer to be given to the German note of August 25, the British government was authorized to convey to Berlin the news that Poland was ready for conversations.[39]

In connection with this decision of the Polish government, a meeting took place on August 29 in the afternoon, at Mr. Beck's house, attended by a small number of higher officials of the Polish Foreign Office. The object was to choose the Polish delegate and the place where the talks should be held. During the meeting Mr. Beck spoke on the telephone with President Mościcki and Marshal Śmigły-Rydz in order to reach a common agreement on these two matters. The opinion prevailed that it would not be advisable for Mr. Beck himself to go to Berlin, or to another place, in view of the precedents set by Schuschnigg and Hacha. As regards the place for the conference, it was recommended to hold it either in a town near the frontier or in a railway coach close to the Polish-German frontier, in order to avoid the use by the Germans of their ill-famed means of pressure. During the discussion of the names for the Polish emissary several names were put forward, among others that of Mr. Anthony Roman, minister of trade and industry, former Polish envoy in Stockholm, who on some occasions had led the negotiations with Danzig. Eventually Beck gave his preference to the Polish Ambassador in Berlin, an official diplomatic representative to Germany, as the most suitable man for reopening and carrying out the negotiations.[40]

At almost the same time, a few days before this meeting at the Polish Foreign Office, I obtained from a good German source a confidential piece of news—transmitted to me by Dr. Wnorowski, press attaché at the Embassy for many years—which appeared to me to be vitally important and which I immediately conveyed to Warsaw. The Auswärtiges Amt was allegedly preparing a draft of German claims to Poland, but the whole document must be drafted in such a way as to create the appearance of a conciliatory spirit on the German side and yet be quite unacceptable to Poland on its merits. The purpose of the document was to provoke a rupture between Poland and the Western countries.

On the evening of August 28 Henderson transmitted to the Chancellor the answer of the British government, which, among other things, recommended a peaceful settlement of the Polish-German dispute by

[39] *British Blue Book,* Nos. 72 and 74.
[40] According to the notes made by Mr. Paweł Starzeński, secretary to Mr. Beck.

way of direct discussions with safeguards for Poland's essential interests, and stressed the necessity of granting international guarantees to Poland by the five Great Powers. The note also said that His Majesty's government "has already received a definite assurance from the Polish government that it is ready to negotiate on that basis." In the exchange of views which followed between Hitler and Henderson the Chancellor raised his price, asking not only for the return of Danzig and the whole Corridor but also for the rectification of the frontier in Upper Silesia to the advantage of the Germans.

When Henderson was received at the Reich Chancellery the next day at 7:15 P.M., Hitler handed him the German reply.[41] While fully maintaining German demands for the return of Danzig and the Corridor and the safeguarding of the German minorities in Poland, the note declared that Germany was prepared to enter into discussion with Poland if the Polish emissary arrived by Wednesday, August 30, 1939. This condition sounded like an ultimatum and was considered as such by the Allied governments. It provoked a sharp reply from the British Ambassador, and an extremely vivid discussion with Hitler followed. Moreover, the German note contained reservations, the meaning of which is today quite obvious in the light of the claims of the secret Soviet-German protocol, namely, that "in the event of a territorial rearrangement in Poland, the German government could no longer give a guarantee without the USSR." There was also a paragraph which said that the German government would immediately draw up proposals for a solution acceptable to itself and would, if possible, place these at the disposal of the British government before the arrival of the Polish negotiator.

After his return from the Reich Chancellery, Henderson told me of the text of the German note, and we had a long conversation on the situation arising from it.

In order to ascertain the opinions prevailing that evening in the Reich Chancellery it is worth while to refer to the evidence given by General Bodenschatz, Göring's trusted man and his liaison officer with the Reich Chancellery. During the interrogation Bodenschatz stated unequivocally that Hitler wanted war with Poland. He said then that he was present at the Reich Chancellery that evening when Hitler handed Henderson his conditions with the demands for the return of Danzig and the Corridor,

[41] *DGFP*, Series D, Vol. VI, No. 421, and *British Blue Book*, Nos. 78, 79, and 80. See also Henderson, pp. 262–68.

and stressed that after all the discussions between the Chancellor and the British Ambassador he was under the impression that Hitler did not at all wish Poland to accept his conditions. At the hearing Bodenschatz was more cautious in his statement, in which he said the following:

"I was not present at the conference. If I said that, I did not express myself correctly. I was not at the conference that the Führer had with Henderson, but I was standing in the antechamber with the other adjutants, and in the hall one could hear the various groups, some saying one thing, some another. From their talks I gathered the conditions which Henderson received for the Poles in the evening—that the deadline for answering these questions, which was noon of the next day, was so short that one could conclude that there was some intention behind it." [42]

Bodenschatz's account, while not quite accurate in details, speaks for itself, since during conclusive discussions at the Chancellery all those present in the antechamber were usually the highest and most initiated members of the party.

When cross-examining Ribbentrop, Sir David Maxwell Fyfe put a straightforward question:

"Q. Now did you really expect after the treatment of von Schuschnigg, of Tiso, of Hacha, that the Poles would be willing to send a fly into the spider's parlor?

"A. We certainly counted on it and hoped for it. I think that a hint from the British government would have sufficed to bring that Ambassador to Berlin.

"Q. And what you hoped was to put the Poles in this dilemma, that either the terms would stand as a—to use Hitler's phrase—propagandist cause for the war, or else you would be able, by putting pressure on the Polish plenipotentiary, to do exactly what you had done before with Schuschnigg and Tiso and Hacha, and get a surrender from the Poles." [43]

The evening of August 29 was really a crucial moment. Göring was fully aware of that and, being extremely worried by the critical turn caused by the outcome of the conversation between Henderson and Hitler, summoned Dahlerus that very night and set him moving. He requested him to go at once to London and confidentially say there that

[42] *Trial of the Major War Criminals*, testimony of Bodenschatz on the 77th day of the trial, March 8, 1946.
[43] *Ibid.*, 96th day of the trial, April 1, 1946.

Hitler was preparing a magnanimous offer to Poland (*grosszügiges Angebot*), that he had decided to deliver to Poland on August 30 a note offering such lenient terms that Poland would be able to accept them and England would recommend acceptance. The previous day Hitler had been busy with this draft, and for this reason the last disagreement with Henderson was most regrettable. Besides the annexation of Danzig by the Reich, Hitler's proposals would ask for a plebiscite in the Corridor on the lines of the one held in the Saar. Special lines of communication would be granted to the state which was the loser in the plebiscite.

Dahlerus, as a good tradesman, wanted to know the kind of goods he had to deal with. Göring replied that the matter was still under consideration, but tore out a page from the atlas and drew a line for the plebiscite area, reaching as far as Lodz.[44]

The indefatigable Dahlerus was in the plane by 5 A.M. and landed at Heston at 9 o'clock. He carried out Göring's commission before Chamberlain and Halifax in the presence of Cadogan, and did not fail to repeat the story concocted by Göring for British ears about the shooting by Polish soldiers of eight German refugees trying to cross the Warta. This story had "utterly shocked" Hitler.

On this occasion Dahlerus got the impression that the patience of the British government was at the breaking point and that it was becoming more and more suspicious of Göring's maneuvers and initiatives. Trying to discard these suspicions, he telephoned from Cadogan's office to Göring and obtained the information that the German document was ready and contained more favorable terms for Poland than those told to Dahlerus at night.

When all again met, Chamberlain declared that he had to summon another cabinet meeting in order to review the situation, after which new instructions would be forwarded to Henderson. Then Dahlerus had a separate talk with Cadogan, who produced an idea that the discussions between Poland and Germany should be held not in Berlin but rather in a neutral country. Dahlerus telephoned again to Göring, who became angry, saying that it was "nonsense," for the conversations must be held in Berlin where the Chancellor was. At 11 P.M. Dahlerus landed at Tempelhof airport.

[44] *Ibid.*, 85th day of the trial, March 19, 1946. During the trial Göring explained that the line he had drawn had delimited the area with a German population.

On August 30 the atmosphere in Berlin was tense, and this atmosphere was felt also in the diplomatic corps. Many heads of diplomatic missions called on me that day. In the evening Coulondre called also, as usual self-possessed and calm. He communicated to me the news obtained from most confidential quarters that the attack on Poland originally planned for August 26 had subsequently been postponed, that Hitler was hesitating as regards war operations, and that he had had a nervous breakdown in recent days. This information showed also that in certain high German military quarters the opposition to risking war with France and Great Britain was increasing. This opposition was coming to a head. It was therefore most important to gain time. I then discussed with Coulondre how to proceed in connection with the German demand for a Polish emissary to be sent to Berlin. Together we reached the conclusion that the best solution would be my announcement to the German government that I, in my capacity as ambassador, was ready at any time to enter into contact with them. It would be a further proof of our good will, and would at the same time give a possibility of reopening negotiations. Any trust in Hitler and his entourage was already out of the question, and extreme caution was recommended in order to avoid the well-known Nazi methods of blackmail and pressure.[45]

Warsaw was informed in detail of the official conversations between London and Berlin through the British ambassador, Kennard, who took the advice of the Polish government and agreed on the procedure with them. I obtained my information from Henderson, contacts with whom were rather casual and did not give the whole picture of the exchange of views between Warsaw and London. My contact with the Foreign Office in Warsaw was made more and more difficult by the German authorities. Telephone conversations were often interrupted. The dispatch of telegrams met with obstacles. The wireless station of the Embassy was the only means left for communication with the head office. In view of these circumstances I asked Counselor Lubomirski to go to Warsaw in the early hours, and it was arranged that he would go by road to Poznań, then by plane to Warsaw, and would return as soon as possible.[46] It had great weight with me that Lubomirski might give Beck the latest news, sound his opinions, and obtain his authorization for the

[45] See *Livre jaune*, No. 296.
[46] See Lubomirski, "Ostatnia misja z Berlina," *Wiadomości* (London), 1943, No. 182.

establishment of contact with the Reich government. When I was going to rest in the late hours, Henderson telephoned me, at 2 A.M., asking me to come over. I found him highly excited after a violent discussion with Ribbentrop. The account of this discussion is well known from official British publications and from Henderson's book.[47] It is known that, after presenting the reply of his government to the British note of August 29, Ribbentrop read out in German at top speed the German proposals for the Polish emissary, consisting of sixteen articles. When asked by Henderson for the text, Ribbentrop refused, stating that these proposals no longer existed because the Polish representative had not arrived in Berlin within the prescribed time. Explaining his behavior toward the British Ambassador, Ribbentrop stated as follows:

"I should like to state here once more under oath that the Führer had expressly forbidden me to let these proposals out of my hands. He told me that I might communicate only the substance of them, if I thought it advisable, to the British Ambassador." [48]

Dahlerus informed Göring of the incident with Ribbentrop the same night. Then Göring authorized him to convey by telephone the text of the sixteen points to the counselor of the British Embassy, Forbes [Sir George Ogilvie-Forbes]. At Nuremberg Göring stated the following: "To do this was, as I have already said, actually an enormous risk, since the Führer had forbidden that this information should be made public at present."

The purpose of this document was manifest. It was not to constitute a basis for normal negotiations with Poland but was to serve as a trump card in the perfidious game of Hitler. The draft was undoubtedly the result of thorough researches by the best experts of the Auswärtiges Amt. By no means could it have been dictated by Hitler. A well-informed student of Polish-German relations could immediately discover the hidden poison dart concealed in the highly polished, glib words of the document, which, should it be put into execution, would strangle Poland with iron claws. If we examine, for instance, the principles on which the plebiscite in Pomerania, presented as Hitler's magnanimous offer, was to be arranged, we find they were drafted in such a way that the outcome was considered as a foregone conclusion.

[47] *British Blue Book,* No. 92; Henderson, pp. 269–71; and *DGFP,* Series D, Vol. VI, Nos. 461 and 458 (Hitler's sixteen proposals).

[48] *Trial of the Major War Criminals,* testimony of Ribbentrop on the 94th day of the trial, March 29, 1946.

Today it is obvious that Hitler did not take into account any plebiscite at all. But his prudent advisers took their precautions to provide for all contingencies. The Polish forces, police, and administrators should leave the plebiscite area in Pomerania, leaving all power in the hands of a commission composed of representatives of France, Great Britain, Italy, and Russia. The poll would take place only a year later. In such a way, during this whole time Poland, whose vital problem of access to the sea was at stake, would have to live in a state of anxious uncertainty, while Nazi propaganda could be freely carried out under the protective wings of its two allies, Soviet Russia and Italy. The right to vote should belong to the Poles as well as Germans born in the plebiscite area before January 1, 1918, or who lived there before that date. Germans who left Pomerania after 1918 were entitled to come back and take part in the poll. Consequently, all Polish inhabitants settled in Pomerania after the Versailles Treaty, as well as all the Polish generation born on this territory after January 1, 1918, would have to stay as passive witnesses of a tragic plebiscite.

On the memorable night of August 30, Henderson was unable to memorize the text of all these sixteen articles, and even more to understand the far-reaching consequences of this portentous document. In our conversation he was able only to reproduce to me some provisions concerning the plebiscite. Nevertheless the offer, as such, impressed him as being "on the whole not too unreasonable." For this reason he urged me to approach Ribbentrop, still on the same night, with the request to convey to me the terms with reference to his conversation with the British Ambassador.

I considered that to approach Ribbentrop in such circumstances would have meant asking him to deliver me an ultimatum, which in view of the well-known attitude of Hitler and Ribbentrop would be understood as our surrender and appropriate use made of the step. Since Ribbentrop was really so eager to reach an understanding with Poland by negotiations, it was completely inexplicable that he should refuse to hand to Henderson the text of the sixteen articles. I put forward an argument to the British Ambassador that I could not act in such an important matter without the knowledge of my government, and promised him to get in touch with Warsaw immediately. I did this as soon as I returned to the Embassy, sending the appropriate telegrams.[49] I suc-

[49] See Document 159, p. 571.

ceeded in informing Lubomirski before his departure for Warsaw of my conversation with Henderson.

In the early hours Henderson telephoned me that he had received information according to which the German government would be disposed to wait only until 12 o'clock. He asked for an answer from Warsaw and wished to see me once more. Being unable to leave the Embassy premises, since I was waiting for instructions, I sent to Henderson the first secretary of the Embassy, Malhomme, whom Henderson knew from Belgrade. . . .[50]

From the early hours the Embassy was seized by feverish activity. My colleagues of the diplomatic corps called without previous warning. Coulondre called also and told me that Henderson's information about 12 o'clock came from Ribbentrop's entourage. The Italian Ambassador, a consummate diplomat and a friend of mine, terrified by the prospect of war and its consequences for Italy as the Axis partner, exercised the heaviest pressure on me that morning. He was seconded by the Hungarian envoy. Other heads of missions, with the Papal Nuncio, kept inquiring about the development of the situation. In this flood of calls the British Ambassador, having previously warned me on the telephone, sent to me the counselor of the Embassy, Sir George Ogilvie-Forbes, accompanied by an individual unknown to me, who introduced himself as a friend of Göring and *homme de confiance* of the British government. He was Dahlerus. I saw him then for the first time, and I had no knowledge whatever of the role of go-between he had played with Berlin and London. In the conversation that followed Dahlerus stated that Göring was opposing the extremists of the Party who wanted to annex to Germany the whole part of Poland taken by Prussia after the partition of Poland, and made a proposal limited to Danzig and the Corridor.

To my astonishment Dahlerus began to read aloud from a handwritten page those famous sixteen articles which had raised such a storm. Pretending that there was no time to lose, Dahlerus urged me to go immediately to Göring, accept his terms and sign them, and then the whole problem would be settled and we would be able to shoot stags together. In order to stop this ghastly business I told him that I could not understand what the matter was about, and asked Dahlerus to dictate the contents of the note to my secretary, Miss Gimzicka.

When I was left alone with Forbes I told him of my dissatisfaction

[50] See p. 569.

with his bringing to me an unknown individual who put forward proposals infringing the territorial integrity of the Polish state. I warned him
against the discussion of Poland's territorial problems, as it would bring
about moral breakdown and military collapse in Poland. I insisted that
the only course to be followed was the maintaining of a united front by
England, France, and Poland, and I added that Poland would defend
itself in any case.

Dahlerus handed me the typewritten text, and our conversation came
to an end.

My meeting with Dahlerus, described in his book, had been an item
vividly discussed at the Nuremberg trial. The defense made use of a
passage from Dahlerus' account, according to which I was alleged to
have said to Forbes, when we were left alone, that I was not interested
in German proposals, since I was convinced that riots would break out
in the event of war and the victorious Polish Army would march into
Berlin.

Sir David Maxwell Fyfe, when cross-examining Dahlerus, put to him
the following questions, undoubtedly basing himself on Forbes's account
of the conversation with me:

"And did not Sir George Ogilvie-Forbes tell you that Lipski made his
opinion quite clear, that the German offer was a breach of Polish sovereignty, and in his view Poland and France and England must stand firm
and show a united front, and that Poland, if left alone, would fight and
die alone?" Dahlerus' answer was "Yes." [51]

The same day Beck summed up the Polish attitude to Lubomirski,
who had just arrived in Warsaw to carry out his mission. The Foreign
Minister informed him that pursuant to the conversation with the British
Ambassador he had sent instructions to Berlin, ordering the Polish Ambassador to establish immediate contact with the German Foreign Minister and the Secretary of State respectively.[52] Beck added also that the
Polish government consented to enter into discussions with the Reich
under the condition that both parties would be on an equal footing and
that Poland would not be faced with *faits accomplis* before the discussions ended. The instructions from Warsaw reached me at 12:40 P.M. I
immediately asked for an interview with Ribbentrop, but it did not take
place until 6:30 P.M.

[51] *Trial of the Major War Criminals*, cross-examination of Dahlerus by Maxwell Fyfe, 85th day of the trial, March 19, 1946.
[52] *Polish White Book*, No. 110, and Document 161, p. 572.

In his book Hassell writes that he was entertained at lunch by Ambassador Moltke that day and was told by the latter that Ribbentrop was reluctant to receive the Polish Ambassador. At 3 P.M. Weizsäcker telephoned me, asking in which capacity I wished to be received by the Foreign Minister. I answered that I was asking for an interview in my capacity as Ambassador in order to remit a communication from my government.[53]

When I was driving to the Auswärtiges Amt in the Wilhelmstrasse for the last time, a big crowd filled the road. A cordon of S.S. was keeping order. In the hall downstairs and along the staircase members of the S.S. in uniform were posted. Before I reached the first floor I was photographed several times. Nobody was waiting in the familiar oblong reception room with portraits from Bismarck's time; this room was between the study of the Foreign Minister and that of the Secretary of State on duty. Involuntarily I glanced at the desk, Empire style, on which six years before I had signed the declaration of nonaggression with Neurath.

Shortly afterward the door opened and for the last time I had occasion to speak with Ribbentrop. I handed him the communication of the Polish government, which ran as follows:

"Last night the Polish government was informed by the British government of an exchange of views with the Reich government as to the possibility of direct negotiations between the Polish and German governments. The Polish government is favorably considering the British government's suggestion and will make a formal reply on the subject within the next few hours."

The interview was short. Ribbentrop's manner was icy.[54]

At 9 P.M. the sixteen proposals were broadcast by Berlin Radio Station, with the addition that they had been rejected by Poland. It is known that these proposals had never been communicated to the Polish government. They were simply a "propagandist reason" for starting the war, in accordance with Hitler's announcement at the meeting of his commanders in chief on August 22.

[53] *Polish White Book*, No. 111, and *DGFP*, Series D, Vol. VI, No. 475.
[54] *Polish White Book*, No. 112, and *DGFP*, Series D, Vol. VI, No. 476.

# Last German Moves in Danzig before the War [1]
## August, 1939

AT THE END of May, 1939, the high commissioner of the League of Nations, Burckhardt, was in Berlin, where he met first with Ribbentrop and then with Weizsäcker (the note from this last interview is dated June 1).[2]

Burckhardt intended, although rather reluctantly, to spend the summer months in Danzig, hoping that his very presence there might have some effect contributing to calm excited minds. He kept hoping that no new steps would be taken in the Free City during this period which would force him to take decisions which could afterward be interpreted as anti-German. From Burckhardt's statements that followed it was evident that he tried to use his influence in Berlin in order to alleviate tension with Poland. He mentioned that he had a conversation in Warsaw with Beck, who hoped that it might be possible to reopen Polish-German conversations on a broader level and in a more peaceful atmosphere. Burckhardt further confirmed that from his interview with Lord Halifax, as well as with other British officials, he got the impression that England would keep its obligations in relation to Poland in case of a conflict. However, he added that, according to information obtained from the British Ambassador in Warsaw, a special commission formed at the suggestion of the British side was touring the western provinces—on behalf of the Polish Ministry of the Interior—to supervise the correct treatment of German minorities problems.

When referring to these matters, it seems that the High Commissioner acted with Beck's knowledge. As a matter of fact, Beck made such peaceful advances through the good offices of several other persons.[3]

---

[1] Printed in *Bellona* (London), 1950, No. 1, under the general title "New Premises on the Outbreak of the Polish-German War in 1939."

[2] *DGFP,* Series D, Vol. VI, No. 464; see also Burckhardt, pp. 317–19.

[3] See Gafencu, *The Last Days of Europe,* and Peter Kleist, "Hammer, Sickel und Hakenkreutz," *Die Zeit* (Hamburg), October 13, 1949.

In defiance of binding agreements, as of spring, 1939, Germany began to form military detachments on the territory of Danzig, at first clandestinely, and later on more and more openly. By July the militarization of the Free City already had become quite obvious. At that time General Keitel approached the Auswärtiges Amt for its opinion on the performance of artillery drill exercises in Danzig, in the course of which twelve light guns and four heavy caliber guns, hitherto hidden in the city, would be brought out into the open. In his letter dated July 14, Weizsäcker suggests the postponement of such a demonstration until Poland committed some new tactical error.[4]

The German fleet command was also ready for demonstrations in Danzig. Vice-Admiral Schnievindt urged the Auswärtiges Amt on July 14 for a reply concerning the visit of war-cruisers planned for the end of the month.[5] The problem was of such scope that it could not be decided without Hitler's agreement. Weizsäcker refers to it in his opinion dated July 19.[6] Evasively and with caution, Weizsäcker adds this significant sentence: "For we must always bear in mind that a solution of the Danzig question might occur by force of arms, and that we must put the blame for this on the Poles, while the dispatch of this naval unit to Danzig would be interpreted internationally as a prelude to the generally awaited German-Polish conflict."

In the first days of August a Polish-Danzig conflict broke out with regard to customs inspectors. This matter was to drag on until the end of August, when the frontier between Danzig and East Prussia was formally opened.

In the middle of August Undersecretary of State Keppler delegated to Danzig his trusted collaborator, a National Socialist by conviction, a certain Veesenmayer. (He was to play an important role later in the Balkans and in Hungary.) Vessenmayer confessed at the trial that he had never before been in Danzig, and even at the last moment asked that he not be entrusted with this mission. However, as a National Socialist he had to obey, "so it was always his luck that he was always sent where a fire was to break out."

In Danzig the consul general, Grolman, quarreled with Forster, and the Auswärtiges Amt was left without information. It was necessary to

[4] *DGFP*, Series D, Vol. VI, No. 670.
[5] *Ibid.*, No. 687, footnote.
[6] *Ibid.*, No. 687.

find a liaison between that office and the very ambitious and well-protected Gauleiter, who was accustomed to making policy on his own. So the choice fell on Veesenmayer.

In spite of ever-deepening tension in relations in the Free City and open violation by the Danzig authorities of Polish right for control of customs, the Polish government, in order to show its good will, expressed agreement to undertake conversations for the reduction of the number of customs inspectors. These conversations were started by Commissioner-General Chodacki with President of the Senate Greiser on August 18. Next Maksymowicz, chief director of the Customs Board in Warsaw, came to Danzig, in his capacity of professional negotiator.

A note signed by Weizsäcker, dated August 19, shows the conclusion of Veesenmayer's report as to what methods, recommended by the Gauleiter [7] should be used in negotiations with Poland. Forster declared that pressure should be exerted on Poland to the utmost limits. From the conversation with Chodacki it resulted that Poland was ready to withdraw twelve inspectors within the period of eight to fourteen days. Conversations between experts were to start on August 21. Forster was of the opinion that the immediate withdrawal of fifty customs officials should be requested. In case the Poles gave in again, further requests were to be made to render the negotiations impossible. Veesenmayer asked for instructions. Weizsäcker gave the following answer: "I agree with your views on the conduct of negotiations on the customs officials controversy. Negotiations must, however, be conducted in such a way, and pressure on Poland in other respects must be so applied, that the responsibility for the breakdown of the negotiations and for all consequences falls on Poland." [8]

On August 22 Veesenmayer sent Weizsäcker a detailed plan of action set in five points: [9]

"1) A final breakdown after long negotiations on the question of customs officials. Blame on the side of the Poles.

"2) Then comes the complete removal of all Polish customs officials and the abolition of the customs frontier with East Prussia.

"3) There follows reaction one way or the other on the part of the Poles.

[7] *DGFP*, Series D, Vol. VII, No. 119.
[8] *Ibid.*, No. 139.
[9] *Ibid.*, No. 176.

"4) Thereupon the arrest of numerous Poles in Danzig territory and the clearing of numerous Polish arms dumps; the discovery of these arms dumps is assured.

"5) If this does not produce sufficient action by the Poles in reply, then finally the Westerplatte is to be attacked."

Veesenmayer was not yet informed as to the decision on this matter during Forster's conference at Berchtesgaden.

According to a later report of Veesenmayer dated August 24, points 1, 2, 3, and 5 of the above plan were approved by Hitler.[10]

The Polish desk officer at the A.A. [Bergman] received a report by telephone on August 23 from Grolman, the consul general in Danzig. It reads as follows: [11]

"1) At noon today the Danzig Senate will pass a resolution to offer Gauleiter Forster the post of head of state of the Free City of Danzig. Greiser then will have the post of head of the Danzig government.

"2) In Danzig-Polish negotiations the Danzig representative will demand the immediate withdrawal of fifty Polish customs inspectors. We expect the Poles to refuse this demand. A statement is then to be made about 6 P.M. saying that the negotiations have broken down through the fault of the Poles.

"3) The *Schleswig-Holstein* will come to Danzig instead of the cruiser *Königsberg,* perhaps even tomorrow. The reason for this is that this ship is armed with 28 cm. guns with which it could reach the Hel peninsula from its berth [near the Westerplatte].

"4) Last week berths were already prepared in Danzig harbor for several more warships.

"5) A British steamship berthed in the port of Danzig, which was scheduled to stay three days longer in Danzig to take on cargo, has today received orders from Britain to sail immediately."

No comment is needed on these documents.

[10] *Ibid.,* No. 244.
[11] For the full text, see *ibid.,* No. 197.

# Slovakia on the Eve of the Polish-German War [1]
## August, 1939

---

IN SPITE of bonds of genuine friendship between the Polish and Slovakian population, as well as of racial kinship of languages and the common Catholic faith of the two nations, fate would have it that, during the crisis of March and at the outbreak of the war, Slovakia became a trump card and an instrument in Hitler's hands in his action against Poland.

Some errors of Polish policy, such as minor frontier alterations (which were, besides, of no special importance for the interests of the Polish state), carried out late in the autumn of 1938, provoked public opinion in Slovakia, paving the way for German operations. This, however, had no decisive impact on Slovakia's attitude toward Poland, which at that time was the object of various conflicting influences. The disproportion of strength between the Third Reich and Poland, which could not effectively oppose German plotting on the territory of Slovakia in the aftermath of Munich, determined the outcome.

When on March 13, 1939, Hitler coerced Tiso to separate Slovakia forthwith from the Czech state, the Third Reich established a protectorate over that country.[2]

An agreement defining the mutual relations of the two states [3] was signed on March 23, 1939, by the German and Slovakian governments. Under this agreement Germany was entitled to station garrisons in Western Slovakia up to the line of the Little Carpathians, the White Carpathians, and the Jawornik Mountains. The agreement also provided for the organization of Slovakian armed forces, modeled on the German Army, and obliged Slovakia to conduct its foreign policy in close understanding with the German government.

[1] Printed in *Bellona* (London), 1950, No. 1, under the general title "New Premises on the Outbreak of the Polish-German War in 1939."

[2] *DGFP*, Series D, Vol. VI, No. 10.

[3] *Ibid.*, No. 40.

In relation to Poland this agreement in practice was nothing but the creation out of Slovakia of a base for the concentration of German armed forces, which would facilitate an attack from the south. Resolutions of the agreement were applied in practice on the eve of the war.

At the moment when Hitler decided to start war operations against Poland (Ribbentrop was in Moscow at that time), Woermann sent telegraphed instructions to the German envoy at Bratislava on August 23, 1939,[4] ordering him to communicate forthwith their contents to the Slovakian government. These instructions were a blatant confirmation that the marching of Polish troops into Slovakia was to be expected at any moment. In order to protect Slovakia from a surprise attack, the Reich government requested the Slovakian government immediately to express its agreement to the following:

a) In order to protect the northern part of the country, the command of the Slovakian Army should immediately be taken over by the commander in chief of the German Army.

b) The chief commander of the German air force should have access to the Spiz [Zipser]-Neudorf Airport, and, if necessary, should be able to issue general orders to stop all planes from leaving Slovakia.

In exchange for this the German government was ready to

a) defend the Slovakian frontier against Hungary,

b) return to Slovakia, in case of war with Poland, territories ceded to Poland in 1938,

c) give a guarantee that in case of a Polish-German war Slovakian forces would not be used outside of their country.

On August 26, 1939, the Slovakian envoy in Berlin, Černak, called on Woermann. He expressed satisfaction over the promise of the return to Slovakia of the territory ceded to Poland in 1938 in case of a Polish-German war. The Envoy also asked whether the German government would be ready to return to Slovakia the territory allotted to Poland in 1920. Woermann replied that in this matter he would have to consult before making a decision. In his opinion Slovakia's request would meet with approval.[5]

On August 29, 1939, Černak reiterated his request to Woermann regarding the territory lost in 1920.[6] Woermann confirmed the friendly

---

[4] *DGFP*, Series D, Vol. VII, No. 214.
[5] "Trials of War Criminals," mimeographed transcript, No. N.G. 2774.
[6] *DGFP*, Series D, Vol. VII, No. 468.

attitude of the Germans to this problem, but he could not make a binding decision on his own. Černak then asked whether declarations regarding the territory of 1938 would remain binding also in case the German-Polish conflict were settled peacefully. To this Woermann gave a negative reply. The Slovakian Envoy asked on behalf of his government for an extension of the German promise in case of a peaceful settlement.

Finally, Woermann expressed thanks for the friendly attitude toward Germany taken in the last days by the Slovakian government, and particularly for the proclamation of Prime Minister Tiso.

In his conversation with the Slovakian Envoy on August 31, 1939, Weizsäcker accepted with satisfaction the request for the return to Slovakia of the 1938 territory in case of a peaceful settlement of the conflict with Poland, as well as of the 1920 territory in case of war. Weizsäcker remarked that he was not in a position to grant a formal agreement in the two matters for lack of time, owing to the tense international situation.[7]

[7] *Ibid.*, No. 488.

# Remarks on the Trial against German Diplomacy
## at Nuremberg
### *1948–1949*

LIPSKI gave two lectures in London about the second Nuremberg trial of 1948–49, one, on June 26, 1949, at the Polish Institute of Research on International Affairs, and the second on June 13, 1951, at the Polish School of Political Sciences. The texts of these lectures are included in Lipski's papers.

As some of the same problems were referred to by the lecturer (although in different form) in both lectures, and as some parts of them were printed in *Bellona*,[1] in this section the main texts of the two lectures are connected into a single entity.

Lipski's affidavit on Weizsäcker's case, referred to by him in his lectures, is given *in extenso* in the following section.

## Introduction

In the aftermath of the war years, and upon the termination of the Nuremberg trial, memoirs of German politicians, army men, and diplomats began to appear. Among the diplomats who recently published their memoirs are: Herbert von Dirksen, former ambassador in Moscow, Tokyo, and London (until the outbreak of the war); Erich Kordt, for long years secretary to Ribbentrop, a brother of Theo Kordt, known for his depositions at Nuremberg and counselor of the Embassy in London; Paul Schmidt, interpreter of the Auswärtiges Amt in Weimar times and under Hitler; and primarily Ernst von Weizsäcker, former secretary of state at the Wilhelmstrasse from the spring of 1938 to 1943, and later ambassador at the Vatican. In this category of memoirs should also be included the reminiscences of Peter Kleist, who before the war was a clerk in Ribbentrop's office with special assignment to eastern problems.

The reading of these books clearly shows the goal they are striving to

---

[1] See "The Polish-German Crisis," p. 549; "Last German Moves in Danzig before the War," p. 611; "Slovakia on the Eve of the Polish-German War, p. 615.

achieve. The authors' concern is not only to whitewash themselves of the accusation that when collaborating with Hitler's regime they were blind executors of the Third Reich's aggressive policy. They have something more in mind. These memoirs are to serve as propaganda tools for the German population, as well as for public opinion at large. In each of these books a declaration is repeated that it was not Germany, at least not Germany alone, which was guilty of the calamities that befell Europe in the last thirty years.

Weizsäcker, who, owing to his position, has the most to say, clearly shifts responsibility to the Western Powers and their smaller East European allies. He accuses them of not giving sufficient assistance to the democratic Weimar Republic, of being too long in opposition to Germany's equality of rights. This was the cause for the growth of German nationalism, which later on burst out into Hitlerism.

Another propaganda trick is to underline the importance of the actually rather doubtful movement of German resistance, which allegedly already strove to overthrow the Nazi regime in the prewar years. On this subject men from the Canaris Intelligence Service and agents of the Gisevius type are writing extensively. The post-mortem memoirs of Ambassador Ulrich von Hassell also contain many details on this subject.

Weizsäcker complains that the resistance movement was not properly understood in the West and that attempts to overthrow Hitler during the Sudetenland crisis were thwarted by Chamberlain's visit to Berchtesgaden. The former Secretary of State further claims that during the war the principle of unconditional surrender, resolved at the Roosevelt-Churchill conference in January, 1943, clipped the wings of the German resistance.

Besides these general theses there are also to be found in these memoirs arguments brought against Poland. Among others, there is the statement that the British guarantee granted to Poland in the spring of 1939 was to some extent "a blank check." This British *démarche* supposedly stiffened Poland's stand, rendering its understanding with Berlin impossible. The German memoir writers accuse Poland, since it was in possession of a British cover, of indulging in anti-German demonstrations connected with violence against German minorities, thus provoking Hitler.

German diplomats also refer to the idea of German revisionism in the east. Von Dirksen's claims to this effect are the furthest reaching. He claims not only the Corridor for Germany but also Upper Silesia and a part of the Poznań region. It is worth recalling that, at the time of the Weimar Republic, von Dirksen was for a number of years chief of the Eastern Department of the A.A., to which Polish problems belonged.

Erich Kordt says that in October, 1939, in a memorandum worked out by him which was to serve as a basis for peace negotiations with the West and which was confirmed by a group of German generals belonging to the anti-Hitler opposition, he set, as one of the conditions, the reunion of East Prussia with the Reich and the return of the Polish part of Upper Silesia. This solution, in Kordt's opinion, was to secure for the Reich an overwhelming influence over a rump Poland, as well as over Czechoslovakia, whose frontiers with the Reich remained within the frame of the Munich agreements.

### The Auswärtiges Amt and Poland

Prior to discussing the trial itself against top officials of the Auswärtiges Amt, I would like to make a few comments with regard to the role played by this office in relation to Poland in the interwar period.

German diplomacy, with which we had to deal before 1939, had been trained in the Bismarck tradition. The "Iron Chancellor," founder of a united Germany under the Prussian dynasty of the Hohenzollerns, was a model statesman in the eyes of the average clerk of the foreign service. He was someone who, owing to farsighted and skillful diplomacy, supported by concrete power, was able to contribute important gains to his fatherland through victorious warfare. And by a prudent policy of alliance and reinsurance he succeeded in maintaining his conquests. Bismarck's ideas on Polish problems were well known. He regarded the rise of the Polish state as a threat to Prussia. He used the definition that Poland would become an advance guard of France to the east of Germany. In the Berlin Prussian camarilla this opinion was deeply rooted.

If after World War I critical voices were raised in Germany regarding the foreign policy of prewar Germany, these reservations were directed at the period of the reign of William II, after Bismarck's removal from office. Widespread rumors circulated about the mysterious role of Baron Holstein, an éminence grise of that epoch. Almost continuously secluded in his study at the Wilhelmstrasse, he struck terror not just in his own office but also among top governing spheres of the state. His influence on the course of events was of utmost importance, although it was detrimental to German's policy. Criticism concerned the loss of Russian reinsurance (*Rückversicherungsvertrag*), the impulsive action of William II which caused unnecessary friction and inflammation, expecially in relation to England. Blame was also laid on the weak and inefficient political leadership which succumbed to great pressure from military circles and was driven into a war unfortunate for the future of Germany.

The downfall of the monarchy and the introduction of the republican system did not result in basic changes in the clerical staff of the German Foreign Affairs Office. Only a few nonprofessional diplomats, chiefly from the so-called *November-Socialisten,* were admitted to this resort. These were men who joined Social Democracy at the outbreak of the November, 1918, revolution, some of them just for a short time. To these exceptions belonged Ulrich Rauscher, later envoy of Germany in Warsaw. He played a positive role in Polish-German relations during the great economic liquidation negotiations conducted between the two states in the years 1927–30.

The Auswärtiges Amt, and particularly its Eastern Department (*Ost Abteilung*), was a forge of anti-Polish policy, conducted by German governments in the aftermath of the Treaty of Versailles. Within its walls the definition was born of Poland as a season-state (*Saisonstaat*). German diplomacy, in connection with the Reichswehr, created a basis for the agreement with Soviet Russia at Rapallo, which was, under different conditions, a sort of return of Germany to the policy of Bismarck. The Auswärtiges Amt kept to a stand of revision of frontiers with Poland. In the midst of the most complicated Polish-German relations, whole tactics were directed from the revisionistic angle. If at special periods when, for the sake of higher interests, the German government was compelled to agree to some concessions on a larger scale in relation to Poland, as, for example, at the liquidation agreement of October, 1929, connected with the introduction of the Young Plan, the most stubborn resistance was usually encountered on the part of the bureaucrats at the Wilhelmstrasse.

The signing of the Polish-German nonaggression declaration of January 26, 1934, when Hitler was already in power, was pepper in the eye of that office. In negotiations on this agreement, officials of the Eastern Department of the A.A. did not participate; conversations went on at the highest level with Hitler, Minister of Foreign Affairs von Neurath, and the confidential legal counselor, Gaus.

Under Hitler, the prestige of the Auswärtiges Amt declined. A number of facts contributed to this decline.

Decisions of principle in international affairs were taken by Hitler alone, who personally received ambassadors and representatives of foreign governments on matters of special import. In the long run, as his power grew and the regime became more self-confident, the myth of professional diplomacy slowly sank in the horizon, giving way to dilettantish high-spirited improvisation.

High-ranking Party dignitaries began to enter the domain of the Ministry of Foreign Affairs.

Alfred Rosenberg, the Party ideologist, created an office of his own, "Aussem-politisches Amt," which made direct contacts abroad. Göring's ambitions also reached into the international field. He performed many missions on behalf of the Chancellor. He went to Italy, to Yugoslavia, to Hungary. As of the spring of 1935, he was plenipotentiary for Polish-German relations.

Propaganda Minister Goebbels had his extensive press apparatus and exerted considerable impact on the formation of relations between the Reich and particular states. Finally, Ribbentrop, after he became the delegate for disarmament, opened an office in Berlin which was in a way a miniature of the Auswärtiges Amt. This office had its delegates in various capitals, and they informed their chief behind the backs of official German representatives. The office's special field was anti-Comintern problems. When Ribbentrop became ambassador in London, this cell continued its activities.

There were two ministers of foreign affairs in the time of Hitler, Neurath and Ribbentrop. The first was a professional diplomat of the old school, with great experience gained in long years of service abroad and at headquarters. He had no great personal ambitions. Called to the government of von Papen in 1932, he remained under Hitler until February, 1938. Hitler had confidence in him. Neurath tried generally to impose a soothing influence on the dynamic trend of Nazi policy. However, he was not a fighter, in the best meaning of that word. He shielded his office, as best he could, from internal disintegration, but was helpless in the face of Party initiatives that intruded into the field of international politics. Weizsäcker, who for several months in 1933 performed the functions of chief of personnel of the Auswärtiges Amt, writes that at that very period the first "house cleaning" was undertaken at the office.

Prince Waldeck acted on behalf of the Party, whose ranks he had joined. Such "house cleanings" afterward occurred from time to time when National Socialists such as Wilhelm Keppler or Ernst Bohle took over high-ranking posts of undersecretaries of state for special commitments.

A chief personality and official manager of the office was the secretary of state. In Weimar times, when foreign ministers were usually recruited from representatives of political parties, the position of a professional secretary of state was a very responsible one, and his voice had weight on international decisions. In the first years of Hitler's regime this post was held by von Bülow, a nephew of the former Chancellor, who in his time had achieved fame for introducing in the Prussian Chambers the anti-Polish resolution for expropriation (1908). Upon Bülow's death, a short interregnum prevailed caused by difficulties in having a candidate approved by the Party. Finally, von Neurath succeeded in introducing his son-in-law, Hans von Mackensen, son of the famous field marshal of World War I, whose name carried weight in Party spheres.

Changes made by Hitler in February, 1938, in the top military brass after the famous affair of Blomberg's marriage extended also to the Auswärtiges Amt. To the removed Neurath, to dry his tears, was offered the direction of the so-called Council of State, which in practice had no voice or power. Then came the era of Ribbentrop, who, in the light today of German documents, depositions, and memoirs of his close collaborators as well as reports of foreign diplomats, played an outrightly sinister role as confidential adviser to Hitler. He bears the major responsibility for the outbreak of the war. A few months after his nomination, Ribbentrop nominated Weizsäcker secretary of state. Weizsäcker became the leading personality in the trial against German diplomacy at Nuremberg.

## The Trial

For the prosecution of major German war criminals, Great Britain, the United States, Soviet Russia, and France contracted an agreement on August 8, 1945, creating adequate legal bases for future trials. Three categories of crimes were established by this agreement: crimes against peace; war crimes; and crimes against mankind.

The greatest *novum* in international law is the determination of the idea of a crime against peace. The definition reads as follows:

". . . planning, preparation, initiation or waging of a war of aggression, or a war in violation of international treaties, agreements or assurances, or participation in a common plan or conspiracy for the accomplishment of any of the foregoing."

After the termination of the main trial at Nuremberg, on November 15, 1947, a bill of indictment was placed with the Secretariat General of American War Tribunals at Nuremberg against a number of diplomats and high-ranking German personalities, twenty-one persons in all, for crimes against peace, crimes against mankind, and war crimes.

On December 19, 1947, the case was transferred to the Fourth Military American Tribunal at Nuremberg, and proceedings were opened on January 7, 1948. The sentence was published on April 11, 1949. The dimension of the trial may be judged by the fact that the files of court proceedings cover 28,085 pages of print; 9,067 documents were attached to the files, making a total of 39,000 pages. Justification of the sentence is written in 800 pages, not counting the *votum separatum* deposited by Judge W. Powers.

Among the personalities who found themselves on the defendants' bench, the group of German diplomats were at the forefront. As a matter of fact, this was a trial against the Auswärtiges Amt of the Third Reich. Persons in this trial who arouse the most interest on our part are Secretary of State Ernst von Weizsäcker and Undersecretary of State Ernst Woermann. Other diplomats on the defendants' bench were Steengracht von Moyland, Weizsäcker's successor in the post of secretary of state after 1943; Karl Ritter, for long years chief of the Economic Department at the A.A., former ambassador in Rio de Janeiro, who during the war served as liaison for the office with the German commander in chief; and, finally, Otto von Erdmannsdorf, envoy to Budapest, later assistant chief of the Political Department at the A.A. Besides these professional diplomats, names of persons appeared in the trial to whom special missions were entrusted by the Wilhelmstrasse, owing to their Party membership. Among these are Wilhelm Keppler, Ernst Bohle, and Edmund Veesenmayer, known for his diplomatic activities in Danzig on the eve of the outbreak of the war and for his later military action in the Balkans. The remaining defendants who were included in the trial of the diplomats were selected rather at random. That is why this trial was called the "omnibus" trial. Besides former Finance Minister of the Reich Schwerin von Krosigk and Food Minister

Walter Darré, there were to be found two secretaries of state at the Reich Chancellery, Otto Meissner and Hans Lammers, as well as Director of the Reichsbank Puhl, Director of the Dresdener Bank Rosche, Göring's deputy in the four-year plan, Koerner, Chief of the S.S. Intelligence Department Walter Schellenburg, Chief of the Reich's Press Otto Dietrich, and others. Only Erdmannsdorf and Meissner were released. The latter was a faithful servant of all regimes, performing functions in the civil chancellery under Ebert, Hindenburg, and Hitler. All those remaining were sentenced by the Tribunal to prison from four to twenty-five years.

### Character of the Sentence

The sentence contains some important points of a broad political meaning. As the trial was pending before an American Tribunal, Soviet problems were brought out in fuller relief than during the main Nuremberg trial. The political situation of Germany had also changed to its advantage, and the defense took full advantage of this, presenting much bolder theses.

1) The defense used the principle of *Tu quoque* ("and you too"), claiming that the co-culprit of a crime cannot pass judgment on the same case. The presentation of this thesis, confirmed by Soviet Russia's partnership in the aggression against Poland, aimed to undermine the legal foundations upon which the Nuremberg sentences were based. The Tribunal took a negative stand on the point of view of the defense in this matter, declaring as follows: [2]

". . . the defendants have offered testimony and supported it by official documents which tend to establish that the Union of Soviet Socialist Republics entered into a treaty with Germany in August 1939, which contains secret clauses whereby not only did Russia consent to Hitler's invasion of Poland, but at least tacitly agreed to send its own armed forces against that nation, and by it could demand and obtain its share of the loot, and was given a free hand to swallow the little Baltic States with whom it had then existing nonaggression treaties. The defense asserts that Russia, being itself an aggressor and an accomplice to Hitler's aggression, was a party and an accomplice to at least one of

[2] *Trials of War Criminals before the Nuremberg Military Tribunals under Control Council Law No. 10*, XIV, 322.

the aggressions charged in this indictment, namely, that against Poland, and therefore was legally inhibited from signing the London Charter and enacting Central Council Law No. 10, and consequently both the Charter and the Law are invalid, and no prosecution can be maintained under them.

"The justifications, if any, which the Soviet Union may claim to have had for its actions in this respect were not represented to this Tribunal. But if we assume *arguendo,* that Russia's action was wholly untenable and its guilt as deep as that of the Third Reich, nevertheless, this cannot in law avail the defendants or lessen the guilt of those of the Third Reich who were themselves responsible."

2) The court dealt with the arguments of the defense that in view of the fact that Germany had an unjust peace treaty imposed on it and had to take recourse to force to free itself of the resolutions of the treaty its acts in consequence could not be regarded as aggression. The court took the stand that a moment always comes when the prevailing *status quo,* regardless of the conditions under which it came into existence, should be regarded as lasting, at least as regards the change of such status by violence and aggression.

The court's argument was a reference to Hitler's declaration with respect to territorial clauses regarding Austria, Czechoslovakia, and Poland, as well as to nonaggression pacts concluded by Germany with those states. These pacts and declarations created, in the opinion of the court, that very state of relaxation and permanence of the prevailing situation. The court stated as its motives that those declarations were made without compulsion and that the pacts were contracted freely.

3) A politically important statement on motives of the sentence refers to Hitler's agreement with Stalin:

"He [Hitler] did not dare to make the attack in the face of the British and French guarantees to Poland until he had secured his eastern boundaries from possible attack by Russia. This he did by means of the German-Soviet Treaty of August 23, 1939. There he not only protected himself; but apparently by giving the Soviets a free hand in the Baltic States and in Bessarabia and by agreeing to share the loot in Poland, he gained a partner. As long as the Polish State existed, it is sheer nonsense to talk about Hitler's fear that the Soviets might attack. Whatever may have been the attitude of Poland toward Germany, there can be no question that had the Russians attacked the Reich, Poland and the Baltic States for their own preservation would have been thrown to the side of Germany, and the suspicion which Poland felt toward Russia would have made a Polish-Russian alliance wholly unlikely. If a Russian offensive took place in the north, it could only go through Poland, and if it took place in the south, Hungary and Rumania were bound to stand alongside the German forces." [3]

4) During the trial Weizsäcker sharply criticized Poland's prewar foreign policy. His main arguments dealt with the British guarantee issued to Poland, as he put it, a "blank check" in treating the German minorities in Poland and in Poland's relation to the Free City of Danzig. In addition, his criticism was aimed at Poland's stand durng the Munich period and its action toward Lithuania in March, 1938.

Under these circumstances the American prosecutor approached me officially, requesting me to present my deposition with regard to the points attacked by Weizsäcker.

The points referred to by the prosecutor in his letter were dealt with in the extensive statement deposed by me under oath at the American Embassy in London on September 23, 1948. This deposition contains four principal chapters:

a) an outline of Polish-German relations from Hitler's coming to power to March, 1939;

b) the problem of the British guarantee for Poland and a refutation of the German thesis about a "blank check";

c) rectification of German statements with regard to alleged persecution of German minorities in Poland;

d) a true picture of the Polish-Danzig strife with regard to customs inspectors.

Forwarding the Final Prosecution Brief to me on November 18, 1948, the prosecutor remarked: "Your testimony has been invaluable in bringing the affairs of German foreign policy into the true historical and legal perspective." In his motions the prosecutor availed himself of the material contained in my deposition, quoting literally part of the passage dealing with the British guarantee for Poland (refutation of the German thesis about a "blank check") and the passage rectifying the false statement about the persecution of Germans in Poland.

[3] *Ibid.*, p. 355.

*More Important Documents Concerning Polish-German Relations*
*Disclosed at the Trial*

During the trial against Weizsäcker, as well as at the main Nuremberg trial, the prosecution presented a number of documents from archives of the German Auswärtiges Amt. Some of them, although not so sensational as Hitler's directive or the dispositions of the German headquarters, have their meaning for the history of diplomacy. They throw some light on the activities of the Auswärtiges Amt, and particularly on that of the Secretary of State and his immediate collaborators; they reveal the form through which German diplomacy tried to camouflage the most drastic dispositions of the Hitlerite leaders of the Third Reich's foreign policy. Weizsäcker, who at the trial condemned Hitler's policies and vented his bile on Ribbentrop, who was the object of hatred of German professional diplomats, deprecated authorship of certain notes which he had personally handed to foreign representatives. For instance, Weizsäcker confessed on June 16, 1948, that the declaration on Danzig presented by him on August 9, 1939,[4] to Polish Chargé d'Affaires *ad interim* Lubomirski, as recommended by the Reich government, did not originate from him but was written by Hitler's order and forwarded to him for delivery without alterations. As a matter of fact, Weizsäcker agreed that this declaration was unfortunate, while he did not abstain from criticizing the final paragraph of the Polish government's reply, referring to remarks contained in Noël's book on this subject.[5]

In the files was found a circular telegram to German representatives abroad (a copy to the Embassy in Warsaw) signed by Weizsäcker, referring to the exchange of notes of August 9 and 10, 1939, between Berlin and Warsaw. The telegram, dated August 14,[6] reads:

"You are requested not to initiate any conversation in your capital on the German and Polish statements. If you are questioned about it, the Foreign Minister asks you to say that the Polish communication is a further proof of the megalomania and the warmongering policy of the Polish rulers. If Poland chooses to run amok now it will have to bear the responsibility and the consequences. We cannot understand how any Powers could still be prepared to further such an insane policy or even to encourage it, thereby making themselves jointly responsible."

[4] *DGFP*, Series D, Vol. VII, No. 5.
[5] Noël, pp. 397–98.
[6] *DGFP*, Series D, Vol. VII, No. 57.

Weizsäcker insisted that Ribbentrop and not he had written these instructions. He stated that on purpose he often did not alter the very individual style of Ribbentrop, thus signaling to the recipients at the posts from whom the instructions originated. To illustrate his depositions, Weizsäcker quoted the fact that at the time Ribbentrop recommended that he communicate to the officials of the Auswärtiges Amt that they should use most categorical language, adding that if any of them indulged in defeatist remarks they would be shot in their own offices. At the conference of directors of the ministry Weizsäcker repeated this declaration literally, to which someone present asked jokingly: "In whose office? Weizsäcker's or Ribbentrop's?"

When during the trial reports were shown to Weizsäcker from his conversations with foreign representatives, from which it was obvious that he was wholeheartedly defending Hitler's official policy, he tried to explain that diplomatic language, for people of Ribbentrop's type, was beyond comprehension. That is why he was obliged to elaborate these reports to fit the level of the readers.

My conversation with Weizsäcker of April 6, 1939, dealing with the British guarantee for Poland was included in the *German White Book* published during the war.[7] In the German version of this conversation the tone allegedly used by the Secretary of State when addressing me was presented in a version considerably at variance with the truth. At that time he probably wanted to display to Ribbentrop his smart dealings with the Polish Ambassador, unaware that the time would come for him to face a tribunal. When asked at the proceedings about this conversation, Weizsäcker had no choice but to make reference to the *Polish White Book*,[8] where our exchange of opinion is stated in conformity with the truth.

With great skill, displaying himself to be an agile diplomat, Weizsäcker was able to answer the questions, presenting more and more arguments when efforts were made to drive him to the wall in connection with documents bearing his signature. He was far from questioning the guilt of Hitler and Ribbentrop for starting the war with Poland; on the contrary, he accused them both of aggressive intentions. He based his defense on proving that he personally, though harnessed in the Reich's diplomatic machine, was against aggression and, in secret from the Nazi

[7] *German White Book*, No. 212, p. 242, or *DGFP*, Series D, Vol. VI, No. 169.
[8] *Polish White Book*, No. 70.

top echelon, was acting to save the peace. Until July, 1939, he still did not see any immediate threat of war. When he found out that Hitler was decided on aggression, he began to act, particularly toward London and Rome. His explanation of his methods of action is often lost in diplomatic finesse. Allegedly what he strove to achieve was that French and British diplomacy should restrain Warsaw, hinting to the Poles that they would obtain no assistance from the West if they persisted in provoking (*sic*) Hitler. On the other hand, he wanted British and French diplomacy to make Hitler understand categorically that in case of aggression against Poland both Powers would fulfill their obligations toward that state. Weizsäcker tries to present his conversations in the last months before the war with the ambassador of France and particularly the ambassador of Great Britain from that angle. Weizsäcker also referred to his attempts to stop Hitler's aggression by means of the mediation of Mussolini. His contacts with Attolico, the Italian ambassador in Berlin, constitute a large chapter in his trial. His further argument was that he wanted to gain time in order, as he put it, to get through the critical month of August.

Weizsäcker did not conceal at the trial that his opinion with regard to the contents and form of the British guarantee for Poland was critical. He stated that in any case the guarantee should not have been issued in such form and publicly. His statements with regard to the German-Soviet pact were, in my opinion, of most interest. He confessed that he regarded the agreement of Hitler with Stalin as "catastrophic for peace," since Hitler was persuaded that with this pact in his grasp he could attack Poland without any risk. Weizsäcker referred to steps undertaken by him in order to warn London about the threat of an agreement with Russia (confidential mission of Erich Kordt to England in June, 1939, and later conversations with Henderson). This, however, did not stop him from participating in diplomatic action for a rapprochement with Moscow and counteraction against an understanding of the Western Powers with Soviet Russia.

### Analysis of Documents

*1. Polish-Danzig Problems.* We find in the files three documents relating to Polish-Danzig problems dating prior to January, 1939.

The first document is a memorandum of October 15, 1936, signed by Weizsäcker,[9] at that time political director. It deals with conversations to be undertaken between the Senate of the Free City and the Polish government. The first five points of the instructions deal with general considerations; point 6 contains motions.

Here is a recapitulation: It is agreed that the Danzig problem cannot be separated from the Reich's general foreign policy, owing to the fact that relaxation or tension in Polish-German relations depends on how the problem of Danzig is developing. Consequently, the Senate must collaborate closely with the Auswärtiges Amt. Weizsäcker explains this point by the necessity of holding Forster tightly in check, for his exuberant activity might be dangerous in relations with Poland, which at that time were developing rather satisfactorily.

The second point states that Danzig policy should be aimed at the return of the Free City to the Reich. This is not possible under present circumstances, unless by a *coup d'état*. A *coup d'état* is not to be considered at present, since this would actualize the hitherto unsolved question of the Corridor. Weizsäcker's commentary on this point (deposed at the trial on June 9, 1948) reads as follows:

"The later incorporation of Danzig as the final aim was not only justified because without a plebiscite Danzig had been taken away from Germany and was almost completely German, but also in a political sense this aim was justified because there was not one problem during the year beginning with 1920 with which the League of Nations had to make so constant and so useless an effort as the Danzig problem. A complete clarification of the Danzig question was essential for any practical European peace policy. I remind you that the Danzig problem at that time was somewhat similar to the Trieste problem, and I do not think that I am the only one who holds that opinion because the British foreign minister, Lord Halifax, one year after I wrote that memorandum, that is in 1937, stated publicly that changes in the European order would have to come sooner or later and that one of these changes for him was Danzig, while another one was Austria, and so on and so forth."

The memorandum further points out that subordination of Danzig to the League of Nations would be inconvenient; it refers to the necessity of replacing Lester and considers the possibility of transferring part of the League's powers to Poland and nominating a Pole as high commis-

[9] "Trials of War Criminals," mimeographed transcript, No. N.G.-1998 (Lipski's papers, File 22).

sioner of the League. However, he arrives at the conclusion that this would be undesirable. Under the prevailing good Polish-German relations this would relax the situation, while if those relations deteriorated the Polish hand could weigh on Danzig, especially since the high commissioner was authorized to call on Polish forces to restore order in the Free City.

In point 5 the question of the high commisioner's right to intervene in the Free City's internal affairs in accordance with the statute is discussed. A motion follows that an attempt should be made to soften the actual situation.

Then motions follow, expressed in seeking a successor to Lester, jointly with Poland, and restoring order in the internal situation of Danzig so as to give Poland the opportunity to declare at the next session of the League of Nations that an appeasement has been accomplished. In conversations with Poland no concessions should be allowed which in the future might render difficult the return of Danzig to the Reich. And finally, contact with the Auswärtiges Amt should be maintained during negotiations with Poland.

The next two documents, one of February 8, 1937,[10] and the other undated,[11] relate to candidates for the post of high commissioner in Danzig. Weizsäcker gives priority to Burckhardt; second comes Rothmund; and third, Reimers. Weizsäcker instructs Greiser what tactics should be applied to deal with the Polish side. Burckhardt should not be pushed before his candidacy is presented. In the second document, Greiser reports that Poland's commissioner suggested Reimers, to which he protested. Then the Polish side suggested Burckhardt; Greiser declared that this candidacy seems to be possible, but he reserved his answer. Now Greiser would give his formal consent for Burckhardt.

It should be recalled that Weizsäcker and Burckhardt were acquainted since 1920 and maintained close contact. Burckhardt's name appears in the document of July 15, 1938, signed by Schliep, in charge of the Polish Desk at the A.A.[12] It refers to an invitation to be sent to Burckhardt for the Nuremberg Congress.

Owing to attacks by the Swiss left-wing press, Burckhardt would prefer (according to a report of the German consul general in Danzig) to avoid this invitation. The A.A. shared this opinion.

[10] *Ibid.,* NG-5403.
[11] *Ibid.,* NG-5402.
[12] *Ibid.,* NG-5404.

2. *Beck's Visit to Berchtesgaden and Ribbentrop's to Warsaw.* On January 5, 1939, Beck was to meet with Hitler at Berchtesgaden. Weizsäcker prepared material for the conversation. Presenting it to Ribbentrop on January 2,[13] he made the following motions:

a) Poland should do more for the German minority.

b) Poland should now be satisfied with small economic profits in case Kłajpeda [Memel] shortly became German.

c) It would probably ensue from the conversation that it was still too early to establish Poland's stand toward other points of Germany's eastern policy. Beck should understand how weak his position was and that Germany was waiting for a moment when he would be more flexible.

From this note it could be gathered that the A.A. did not at that time exert pressure for a quick solution of Polish-German problems as suggested by Ribbentrop on October 24, 1938.

The basic line of German policy at that time is confirmed by a circular telegram sent by Weizsäcker on January 10, 1939,[14] to representatives abroad, evidently on the instructions of Ribbentrop, who took part in the conference together with Hitler:

"For information and guidance in your conversations:

"The visit of Foreign Minister Beck, which was motivated by a Polish desire to discuss the new situation, took place in a friendly atmosphere. It was noted on both sides that the agreement of January, 1934, had proved its worth and continued to form the basis of German-Polish relations.

"More particularly, the question of Danzig was discussed, but a practical stage was not reached. The Führer reassured Beck with respect to the alleged danger of *faits accomplis* being engineered in Danzig, and confirmed Poland's need for access to the sea. The question of Memel was touched upon briefly. The Führer also dissipated Polish misgivings regarding Germany's Ukraine policy. No agreements of any kind were reached. Beck repeated the familiar Polish explanation of the origin of the Polish-Soviet declaration, which had become necessary on account of numerous border incidents.

"The Reich Foreign Minister accepted in principle Beck's invitation to Warsaw extended at the end of last year. The date is still open."

After Beck's visit to Hitler, Ribbentrop and Gauleiter Forster deter-

[13] *DGFP,* Series D, Vol. V, No. 119, note 3.
[14] *Ibid.,* No. 121.

mined their tactics on the territory of Danzig. In a note dated January 13, 1939, and signed by Hewel,[15] it is stated that no new steps should be taken on the territory of Danzig prior to Ribbentrop's return from Warsaw. The measures contemplated were, in part:

    a) official adoption of the German salute,

    b) adoption of the German flag,

    c) formation of a Death's Head (*Totenkopf*) unit of the S.S. in Danzig.

Upon Ribbentrop's return from Warsaw, it would be decided whether these measures should be applied or whether they would become dispensable in view of a "global" settlement of the question with Poland.

On the eve of Ribbentrop's departure for Warsaw, on January 24, 1939, I had a conversation with Weizsäcker. It was preceded, on my recommendation, by an exposition, by our press attaché, Wnorowski, to Herr Kleist of Ribbentrop's office. This was an intervention by the Polish side in a number of matters which, rather characteristically, coincided in the last days. The exposition concerned a map published by the *Völkischer Beobachter* on January 24, 1939, showing Danzig reunited with the Reich, and news from Kaunas, in the same issue of the paper, in which a request for the return of Wilno to Lithuania was printed. It also dealt with the withdrawal, by the order of the Auswärtiges Amt, of a communiqué about reaching a temporary Polish-German agreement regarding the expulsion of Polish Jews from Germany, as well as postponement of the signing of this agreement.

Documents from January, 1939, although they give a very superficial illustration of the attitude of German governmental factors, nevertheless represent valuable premises for the history of their period. We know today from other sources that at that time Hitler was hesitating about the future direction of attack—west or east.

Documents show that the Auswärtiges Amt, estimating that the Polish card in the West was losing its value, judged that it might be possible to force Poland into concessions on the question of Danzig. The A.A waited, however, for a more suitable moment. This is confirmed by Weizsäcker, who at the trial on June 9, 1948, deposed as follows:

"The Polish position during these years was by no means strengthened. I have already mentioned that in international politics Poland had been considered, after Munich, a so-called hyena; it had been weakened

[15] *Ibid.*, No. 122.

to such a point that, according to my own conviction, if one could only apply a certain amount of patience, the necessary compromise between Warsaw and Berlin would have been achieved without any special intervention."

Here the question arises whether such an opinion did not change the sequence: first Czechoslovakia and afterward Danzig. However, it is significant that Weizsäcker took an active part in preparations for the occupation of Prague, and that he was convicted for that very reason.

Another characteristic feature is a certain convergence in German and Polish tactics to keep secret the growing strife between the two states. Germany continued to count on reaching its goal by way of direct conversations with Warsaw. It also tried to keep the Polish card, in view of its broad schemes in Europe. Polish diplomacy strove to avoid conflict with Germany. However, it started to seek reinsurance in the West, trying simultaneously to balance its relations with Soviet Russia. It would not serve Poland's interests to show its cards too early, since this might weaken Poland's position abroad, rendering its rapprochement with the West more complicated.

# Affidavit of Ambassador Lipski in the Case of von Weizsäcker during the Nuremberg Trials
## 1948–1949

ON AUGUST 2, 1948, William H. W. Caming, chief prosecutor in the trial of twenty-one Germans in Nuremberg, wrote to Lipski, who was at that time residing in London, inviting him to the trial at Nuremberg in order to testify in the case of the accused former secretary of state, Baron von Weizsäcker. In the event that Lipski could not appear in person, he was asked to present a written affidavit.

In his letter, enclosing the pertinent documents from Weizsäcker's hearings,[1] Mr. Caming wrote:

"The defendant Weizsacker has not denied that he faithfully executed the orders of the late von Ribbentrop. His defense pursues two lines of reasoning. Firstly, although participating in the German diplomatic mobilization for aggression against Poland, he secretly committed himself to every possible effort to maintain the peace through contacts with British Ambassador Henderson and Italian Ambassador Attolico. (Upon cross-examination, this defense was substantially destroyed.) Secondly, he contended that the greater proportion of the guilt for the provocation of the German-Polish conflict fell upon Poland. He emphasized that the Polish government willfully permitted the persecution of German ethnic minorities in Poland proper, which activities reached a crescendo in violence in August, 1939. Further, he contended that the British guarantees in March and April, 1939, presented the Polish government with a "blank check," permitting it to maintain an unbridled policy of intimidation and lawlessness against Germany and Danzig. Thirdly, he contended that the Polish authorities provoked the Danzig customs dispute in August, 1939, and their actions further contributed to the deterioration of conditions in Danzig. He described the Polish governmental leaders as jackals and hyenas who slyly attempted to secure territories and rights for themselves at the expense of their neighbors."

Lipski chose the form of presenting an affidavit in writing and sent it to the Chief Prosecutor at Nuremberg on September 23, 1948.

On April 11, 1949, sentence was passed on Weizsäcker, confining him to prison for seven years for his part in the occupation of Czechoslovakia in

[1] Lipski's papers, File 24.

March, 1939, and the transportation of Jews for annihilation from Slovakia and France. By the decision of the high commissioner, John J. McCloy, of January 31, 1951, the sentence was commuted to time served.

Lipski's affidavit reads as follows:

60 Pelham Court
London, SW 3

In the statement which I am submitting below I was able to refer to my diplomatic dispatches from Berlin, many of which were published in the *White Book* issued by the Ministry of Foreign Affairs of the Republic of Poland (concerning Polish-German and Polish-Soviet relations, 1933 to 1939). Moreover, a number of these reports was put before the International Military Tribunal of Nuremberg at the trial of the Major War Criminals, sentenced for their participation in the planning, preparation, initiation, and waging of a war of aggression against Poland.

I had been in charge of German problems at the Ministry of Foreign Affairs in Warsaw between 1925 and the autumn of 1933, first as chief of the German Section and subsequently as head of the Western Department there. Between 1925 and 1930 I took part in numerous negotiations with the German government, and myself concluded a series of agreements, the most important of which was the Liquidation Treaty of October 31, 1929, connected with recommendations of the Young Plan. The Polish-German Trade Agreement, on which I had been working for many years, signed in Warsaw on March 17, 1930, was to have complemented this Liquidation Treaty; it was never ratified by the Reichstag on account of opposition from Prussian agrarian circles against the importation of agricultural produce from Poland.

I was, moreover, in touch with German diplomacy in international conferences at Locarno (October, 1925), The Hague (July, 1929, and January, 1930), and Lausanne (July, 1932). In September, 1933, I was appointed Polish minister to Berlin, and ambassador in October, 1934. I held the latter post until the outbreak of war in 1939.

At the time of Hitler's accession to power, in January, 1933, Polish-German relations had reached a critical stage owing to the Nazis' anti-Polish agitation. In order to ease the tension which had then developed, a meeting was arranged through Polish initiative on May 2, 1933, between my predecessor in Berlin, Mr. Wysocki, and Hitler, as a result of which "the Chancellor laid stress on the firm intention of the German government to maintain its attitude and its actions strictly within the limits of the existing treaties" (communiqué issued on May 3 by the Wolff Agency on the interview between Chancellor Hitler and Mr. Wysocki).

A further step toward the improvement of relations was the Polish-German declaration of nonaggression, which was negotiated and signed by myself on January 26, 1934.

In the said declaration, concluded for a period of ten years, both sides agreed to abstain from the use of force for the purpose of reaching a decision in possible disputes. This pact became the basis for mutual relations between the two countries in the years which followed.

The value which the Germans at that time attached to their relations with Poland can be seen from numerous subsequent statements: for example, Hitler's speeches to the Reichstag on May 21, 1935, March 7, 1936, January 30, 1937, and February 20, 1938, of which the following words might be quoted:

"It fills us, in the fifth year following the first great foreign political agreement of the Reich, with sincere gratification to be able to establish that in our relationship to the state with which we had perhaps the greatest differences, not only has there been a *détente,* but in the course of these years a constant improvement in relations has taken place."

Moreover, also in Hitler's Sport Palace speech of September 26, 1938, and even in the Reichstag speech of January 30, 1939 ("We have just celebrated the fifth anniversary of the conclusion of our nonaggression pact with Poland. There can scarcely be any difference of opinion today among the true friends of peace with regard to the value of this agreement . . .").

The beginning of a crisis in German-Polish relations that revealed its full gravity at the end of March, 1939, might be traced back to the late autumn of 1938 when, after having occupied Austria and the Sudetenland, the Nazi government came to its decision for further territorial aggrandizement at Poland's expense. However, even earlier, the Bohumin (Oderberg) incident had already given grounds for dispute between Berlin and Warsaw.

Bohumin had belonged to the former Cieszyn Principality, mainly inhabited by a Polish population, and had constitued, ever since 1920 when this territory was occupied during the Polish-Bolshevik war by the Czechs, a bone of contention between Poland and Czechoslovakia. When, in the summer of 1938, the problem of Czechoslovakia's national minorities was raised in the light of the Czech-German dispute over the Sudetenland, the Polish government received an assurance from France, as well as from the Czechoslovak government, that the Polish ethnic minorities in the Cieszyn province would be granted the same privileges as any other minority.

Thus, on the eve of the Munich Conference, when it had become evident that the Sudetenland would be ceded to Germany, the Polish government instructed me to endeavor to fix with the German government a demarcation line on the map which would leave the Cieszyn District outside the German claims.

This step became essential owing to information received on September 27, 1938, by the Ministry of Foreign Affairs in Warsaw from the British Ambassador that at the Godesberg Conference the strategically vital Bohumin junction (one of the most important railroad junctions in Central Europe) had been included in the German claims and that the so-called Red Line which delimited these claims entered well into the Cieszyn area.

I then clearly agreed with Herr von Weizsäcker (at a conference on September 28, 1938, in the presence of Counselor Altenburg and Counselor of the Polish Embassy Lubomirski) that Bohumin was to be left outside the German demarcation line. Nevertheless, on October 4 the Auswärtiges Amt endeavored to revoke the agreement which we had reached on September 28. This met with a protest from the Polish side. Moreoever, at that period there coincided some alarming activities of organized Nazi bands in the Bohumin district.

Therefore, the Defendant's (Herr von Weizsäcker's) statements regarding the Cieszyn matter seem misconstrued, to say the least, coming from so highly graded a representative of the Auswärtiges Amt of that time.

At a talk I had at Ribbentrop's invitation at Berchtesgaden on October 24, 1938, the Reich Foreign Minister raised for the first time the demand to incorporate Danzig into Germany. This was contrary to the attitude hitherto shown by the German government, as proved by numerous statements made in the highest quarters.

The understanding between Germany and Poland as far as Danzig was concerned was based, ever since 1934, on the principle of noninterference on the part of Poland into the life of the German population of the Free City, with due reciprocal consideration on the part of the Danzig anuthorities to Polish rights and interests, the statute of the Free City, and the Polish population.

Official statements which confirmed this state of affairs were made to me personally, among others by Hitler on November 5, 1937, reiterated by him before Minister Beck in Berlin on January 14, 1938, finally in a public utterance in his speech to the Reichstag on February 20, 1938, in the following words:

"The Polish state respects the national conditions in this state and both the city of Danzig and Germany respect Polish rights. And so the way to a friendly understanding has been successfully paved, an understanding which, starting from Danzig, has today succeeded, in spite of attempts by certain mischief-makers, in finally taking the poison out of the relations between Germany and Poland and transforming them into a sincere, friendly cooperation."

The demands for the return of Danzig to Germany and the creation of an extraterritorial highway and railroad through Polish Pomerania were accompanied, among others, by proposals for Poland's accession to the Anti-Comintern Pact. Ribbentrop had already earlier, that is, in March and September of that year (1938), made similar suggestions in his talks with me; these had, however, always been turned down by the Polish government.

In reality, the so-called *Gesamtlösung* which Ribbentrop had proposed merely boiled down to the wish to open the question of the Corridor and the surrender of Danzig to Germany. This was tantamount to severing Poland's access to the sea. The joining of the Anti-Comintern Pact by Poland would automatically have forced it to give up its treaty of alliance with France, put it at loggerheads with Russia, and ultimately drawn Poland into the orbit of the Nazi policy of conquest.

Ribbentrop's action, thus understood by the Polish Minister of Foreign Affairs, resulted in a reassertion by the mutual Polish-Soviet declaration of November 26, 1938, that "the relations between the Polish Republic and the Union of Soviet Socialist Republics are and will continue to be based to the fullest extent on all the existing agreements, including the Polish-Soviet Pact of nonaggression dated July 25, 1932."

The demands put forward by Ribbentrop on October 24 came up again in the talks between Hitler and Beck at Berchtesgaden on January 5, as well as during Ribbentrop's trip to Warsaw on January 25-27,

1939. This period was characterized by a growing tension in Polish-German relations, the smoldering flame being strongly fanned by anti-Polish agitation in Danzig and the highly disturbing movements of German agents working on the Ukrainian and Slovakian questions, of which movements the Polish government was well aware.

That the Polish government's fears regarding Danzig were well conceived has now been proved by the publication at the Nuremberg trial of General Keitel's instructions of November 24, 1938, which referred to the occupation of Danzig at a politically opportune moment by means of an internal putsch.

The German methods at that time might well be illustrated by document N.G. 2771 of January 13, 1939, signed by the liaison officer between the Auswärtiges Amt and the Reich Chancellery, Hewel. This document recommends a delay in the issue of certain new instructions for Danzig, among others the official introduction of the German salute, introduction of the German flag, the formation of the Death's Head units of the S.S., etc., until the time when the results of Ribbentrop's trip to Warsaw were known.

The crisis in Polish-German relations reached a crucial stage in the later part of March when, in equal surprise to both the Polish Government and Polish public opinion, Hitler occupied Prague, German military formations entered Slovakia, a protectorate over that country was established, and Lithuania was forced to give up Memel.

Poland felt itself threatened both from the north and from the south. A feeling of anxiety invaded the whole Eastern European atmosphere.

With regard to Lithuania, I would like to make it clear, in connection with the Defendant's (Herr von Weizsäcker's) allegations as to Polish policy, that a considerable rapprochement between Lithuanians and Poles had been achieved since Poland's drastic step of the preceding March (1938) to bring about the establishment of normal diplomatic relations with that country.

Poland's attitude at that moment (March, 1938) was dictated exclusively by considerations of security and was devoid of any other aims.

It was in these circumstances that, on March 21, 1939, Ribbentrop reiterated his demands to me, laying strong emphasis on the urgency of the matter. When I reported the course of this talk in my dispatch to Warsaw, I expressed my view on the situation in the following words:

"Herr von Ribbentrop's suggestion of a conversation (Beck-Hitler) and his emphasis on its urgency are a proof that Germany has resolved to carry out its eastern program quickly, and so desires to have Poland's attitude quickly defined."

In spite of the most unfavorable circumstances for negotiations, the Polish government did not shrink from further discussions. At my next meeting with Ribbentrop, on March 26, I handed my government's counterproposals for a solution of the Danzig problem in the bounds of a bilateral Polish-German agreement and suggesting the creation of a Polish-German commission in order to provide the best possible facilities for communications between the Reich and East Prussia. Ribbentrop, however, presented his case in such a manner that the German demands were to be accepted as a whole, refusing to commit himself in any way whatsoever as to the merits of the Polish counteroffer, regarding which, in consequence, complete silence was deliberately imposed by the German government.

Such a form of negotiation was a departure from both the letter and the spirit of the Polish-German declaration of January 26, 1934.

Ribbentrop, on March 26, and Weizsäcker, on April 6, 1939, gave me ample expression of their indignation regarding the Polish military measures which were taken as a result of the March incidents. With regard to these measures, I should like to point out that the Polish orders had strictly local meaning and were of a purely defensive character, being moreover entirely justified in view of the large-scale German military moves in the vicinity of Poland's borders; alarm was also felt over the demonstrations held near the Polish Baltic coastline in connection with Hitler's triumphant visit to Memel. There was a feeling of deep concern in the Polish government with regard to the danger of a surprise occupation of Danzig. It can now be seen from Keitel's order dated November 24, 1938, that these fears were not without substance.

With reference to Herr von Weizsäcker's statement concerning Poland's attitude in the last months before the outbreak of the war:

I

On the question of the British guarantee to Poland and the effect which that guarantee had on Polish-German relations, I would like to say the following:

The British guarantee, given as it was in the face of a threat from

Hitler to the security of Eastern Europe, was aimed at deferring him from further conquests; by then it was generally realized that his next move would most likely affect Poland, now strategically weakened by the occupation of Prague and the placing of the Slovakian wedge in the reach of the German military system. Conceived as a weapon of peace, it was by no means contrary to the Polish-German declaration of non-aggression dated January 26, 1934. Furthermore, this declaration was based on the Paris Pact of August 17, 1928, which stipulated a general renunciation of war as an instrument of national policy; both Germany and Poland were cosignatories of this pact.

On his way through Berlin to London in the beginning of April, 1939, the Polish Minister of Foreign Affairs told me that in its further relationship to Germany the Polish government was determined to adhere to the principles of the 1934 declaration. I confirmed that to Secretary of State von Weizsäcker on April 6. Mr. Beck saw no reason why, after the Polish-British guarantee, Polish-German relations should not return to their previous satisfactory state, provided, of course, that the German government had a sincere intention of respecting mutual interests in accordance with the 1934 declaration. It was for this reason that, immediately after his return from London to Warsaw, Mr. Beck invited German Ambassador von Moltke in order to give him an adequate version of the results of his London visit and thus to resume a firmer exchange of views between Warsaw and Berlin. However, the German Ambassador declined to face Mr. Beck, and left Warsaw ostentatiously. He only returned to his post after Hitler had broken off unilaterally the declaration of nonaggression with Poland and the naval pact with Great Britain. Herr von Moltke never again approached Mr. Beck but kept aside, in complete reserve.

The Polish-British guarantee evoked sharp resentment in German government circles, as became evident to me at my next conversation, on April 6, with Secretary of State von Weizsäcker. He then adopted a highly critical attitude with regard to the Polish-British agreement and put to doubt the explanations which I offered.

As I had supposed at the time, the British guarantee came as a shock to Hitler and upset his calculations. Hitler's intentions with regard to Poland have now been made clear by document No. R. 100 concerning his conversation with General Brauchitsch of March 25, 1939; I quote the relevant clause:

*"Problem Poland.* For the time being, the Führer does not intend to solve the Polish question. However, it should now be worked on. A solution in the near future would have to be based on specially favorable political conditions. In that case Poland shall be knocked down so completely that it need not be taken into account as a political factor for the next decades. The Führer has in mind such a solution, a border line advanced from the eastern border of East Prussia to the eastern tip of Upper Silesia."

After the Polish-British guarantee, the Germans altered their tactics. Purposely avoiding all further talks with the Polish government, their endeavors were centered on putting Poland into bad odor. Their aim became to achieve Poland's isolation. Thus the German propaganda machine was put to work and one of its products was the slogan of the "blank check" given by the British government to Poland.

I should like to make it clear that the whole idea of a "blank check" was pure invention. In reality it was quite the other way round. The British-Polish guarantee imposed on Poland the duty to coordinate its actions with both the British and the French governments in matters which might have evoked friction with the Germans. The Polish government took care to observe this provision as strictly as possible and was extremely cautious in all its actions, as can well be seen from the diplomatic dispatches of the British and French ambassadors then accredited to Warsaw.

From information which I kept on receiving in the last months preceding the outbreak of war from my colleagues in the Berlin diplomatic corps, especially from the French and British ambassadors, I knew that Secretary of State von Weizsäcker had been swamping them with arguments purporting Polish responsibility for the growing tension. I was forced to endeavor to rectify the deluge of false news about the situation in Poland which was being given to foreigners and distributed to the radio and press; this brought about critical comment from the Auswärtiges Amt with regard to the Polish Embassy's activities.

## II

With regard to the defendant von Weizsäcker's statements as to the situation of the German minorities in Poland, I would like to state that, first of all, the question of the German minorities in Poland as well as of the Polish minorities in Germany was governed by the following provisions:

a) by the treaty between the principal Allied Powers and Poland, signed at Versailles on June 28, 1919;

b) by the Polish-German convention regarding Upper Silesia, of June 15, 1922;

c) by the appropriate clauses of the Polish Constitution and by the German Constitution of Weimar.

With the accession to power of National Socialism in Germany and after the German exit from the League of Nations, the problem of minorities underwent a deep change.

On the one hand, the Nazi totalitarian system, having taken up the theories of racism, brought out a new legislation in the exclusive favor of Germanic interests (*Deutschtum*) which automatically curtailed the development and life of the Polish minorities. On the other hand, the Third Reich endeavored to subordinate, for the furtherance of its own aims, all the German minorities in other countries (that is, in Poland) and use them as a tool for its policy of expansion.

To substantiate the above statement, it is enough to recollect the succession of events in the Sudetenland in the autumn of 1938, on the details of which full light was thrown at the Nuremberg trial.

As to Herr von Weizsäcker's statement regarding the alleged abuse suffered by the German minority in Poland in the period preceding the German aggression, I wish to state that the Polish government was well aware, thanks to the Czech precedent, of the Nazi methods of using the minorities as an implement of political action and diversion. It was for that reason, when the Germans embarked upon a war of nerves against Poland, using Danzig and the minorities problem as a background, that the Polish government gave express warning to the administrative authorities to take the greatest care in dealing with infringements on the part of German minorities and to take action only with regard to instances of sabotage or open provocation. The Polish Prime Minister was in constant touch with the voivodes (provincial governors) and had regular conferences with them in the presence of representatives of the Ministry of Foreign Affairs. A senior official of the Ministry of Foreign Affairs was on tour in the summer of 1939 through the western provinces of Poland, in order personally to verify the strict execution of the government's orders.

In order to substantiate what has been said above, I would like to quote some reports of the French and British ambassadors in Warsaw

for the period directly preceding the outbreak of the war, as published in
the *Livre jaune français, Documents Diplomatiques, 1938–1939* (Im-
primerie Nationale, Paris, 1939), and in the *Documents Concerning
German-Polish Relations* (H.M. Stationery Office, London, 1939):

*No. 102.* A report from April 17, 1939, in which the French Ambassador defines the German war of nerves against Poland in the following
manner:

"The German tactics toward the Poles seem very clear: The Reich
propaganda machine is doing its best to disturb them, play on their
nerves, tire them by the multiplicity and persistence of false news, criti-
cisms, and more or less veiled threats, endeavoring either to evoke a
change of opinion among the Polish people or to weaken the moral
resistance of this potential adversary."

The Ambassador points out the instructions given to correspondents
of the German press in Poland to overpublicize even the smallest incidents, and mentions the rumor spread by German agents in Silesia that
the German Army was to enter on April 24; the report ends with an
assertion that the Polish authorities and population "are showing remarkable calm."

*No. 107.* The French Ambassador stated on April 29, 1939:

"Contrary to German allegations, the Polish population has displayed
great calm up till now and the functioning of the authorities is bent on
utmost moderation. This fact has been ascertained by all foreign observers. . . . Furthermore, the most serious incidents noted recently in
the Reich press were due to German provocations."

Some examples of these provocations follow.

*No. 142.* June 22, 1939. The French Ambassador reiterates that for
three months Poland has been kept in a state of tension. He states:

"At the beginning of that period, it was possible to doubt whether,
under these circumstances, Polish public opinion could long endure in
its calm, without losing some degree of its determination. The trial has
turned out entirely in the Poles' favor."

*No. 52.* August 24, 1939. A detailed report of the British Ambassador rectifying false statements regarding alleged abuses committed
against the German minorities:

"While I am of course not in a position to check all the allegations
made by the German press of minority persecutions here, I am satisfied from enquiries I have made that the campaign is a gross distortion

and exaggeration of facts. Accusations of beating with chains, throwing on barbed wire, being forced to shout insults against Herr Hitler in chorus, etc., are merely silly, but many individual cases specified have been disproved."

There follow several examples of ungrounded statements of German propaganda.

*No. 55.* August 27, 1939. Wire from the British Ambassador:

"So far as I can judge, German allegations of mass ill-treatment of German minority by Polish authorities are gross exaggerations if not complete falsifications.

"2. There is no sign of any loss of control of situation by Polish civil authorities. Warsaw—and, so far as I can ascertain, the rest of Poland —is completely calm.

"3. Such allegations are reminiscent of Nazi propaganda methods regarding Czechoslovakia last year.

"4. In any case, it is purely and simply deliberate German provocation in accordance with fixed policy that has since March exacerbated feeling between the two nationalities. I suppose this has been done with the object of (*a*) creating war spirit in Germany, (*b*) impressing public opinion abroad, (*c*) provoking either defeatism or apparent aggression in Poland.

"5. It has signally failed to achieve either of the two latter objectives.

*No. 276.* August 28, 1939. The French Ambassador writes:

"The ill-treatment, murders, etc., of which the Poles are being accused by Chancellor Hitler are pure slander. The denials given by the Polish authorities cannot be doubted. It is impossible for Germans to have been killed in the vicinity of Danzig or Bielsko without some information about it. It should be stressed besides that the Germans have failed to provide a single precise fact, a single name, or a single date."

*No. 281.* August 28, 1939. The French Ambassador, while refuting invented statements of the German press, gives the following explanation:

". . . the instances of pillage by bands of insurgents in Silesia are a product of invention in every detail. Captain Blacha, their alleged leader, has been dead for two years."

In the mutual declarations made on November 5, 1937, by the Polish and German governments regarding the principles governing the treatment of the minorities, it was stated that "the above principles can in no way affect the duty of the minorities to give complete loyalty to the state to which they belong."

This rule was strictly adhered to by Polish minority organizations in Germany, whose activities were limited to cultural, benevolent, and economic matters. It was hardly so with the German minority in Poland, gathered together in Nazi organizations and governed by Party discipline and directives from the Reich. In the war of nerves against Poland, it became an implement of disruption by the spreading of false rumors and provocative action. On the outbreak of the war, the German minority entered on preplanned subversive operations, thus becoming an advance guard of Hitler's Army. This was revealed at the time of the campaign in Poland and was confirmed by documents seized by Polish military authorities. (See Appendix I.)[2]

To complete the picture of the minorities problem, I refer to a memorandum of the Polish Embassy in Berlin dated August 26, 1939, which described the situation of the Polish minority in Germany on the eve of the outbreak of the war. (See Appendix II.)[3]

I might add that in the middle of August, 1939, the Polish Embassy in Berlin handed to the French and British embassies a list of over 600 cases of persecutions of the Polish minority in Germany within recent months. These included arrests, deportations, religious persecutions, measures against schools and the press, compulsory removal from the frontier zones, and the destruction of property.

Such incidents became more and more widespread and grew in violence as the date of the German aggression approached.

## III

With reference to defendant von Weizsäcker's statement regarding the conflict over the customs inspectors in Danzig, August, 1939:

The Free City of Danzig, under the care of the League of Nations represented by the high commissioner, was, in accordance with its statute and constitution, a demilitarized area.

In the spring of 1939, contrary to the existing legal status, military

[2] Instructions to be brought to the notice of troops engaged against Poland, Polish Ministry of Information. *The German Fifth Column in Poland*, pp. 149–52.
[3] *Polish White Book*, No. 93.

units began to be formed on the territory of the Free City—clandestinely at first, more boldly and openly as time progressed. Old, disused barracks were being prepared to accommodate troops. Young men, organized under S.S. and S.A. colors, received military training in Danzig by instructions (army officers) posted from the Reich, or were sent for that purpose to Germany. Growing numbers of "tourists" were arriving in Danzig from adjacent East Prussia. From May, 1939, the militarization was getting more and more noticeable. By now, closed formations of troops were beginning to parade openly in the streets, unarmed at first, later carrying small arms. In July, 1939, the military unit formed on Danzig free territory under the name of the *Freikorps* under the command of General Eberhard, who came from Germany for this purpose, had grown to the strength of one division.

In spite of such blatant provocation, to the accompaniment of inflammatory speeches by Party members and dignitaries visiting the Free City from the Reich, the Polish government did not allow itself to lose temper.

The Free City of Danzig formed part of the Polish customs area in accordance with the provisions of the Treaty of Versailles and of the Paris Convention of July, 1920. Subsequent executive agreements, in particular the Polish-Danzig agreement of October 24, 1921, made detailed arrangements as to the application of Polish customs regulations and control through Polish inspectors.

Until the spring of 1939, cooperation between Polish and Danzig customs executives on the whole progressed on reasonable and appropriate terms. Friction inevitably arose when, together with the militarization of the Free City, the smuggling of arms and ammunition from East Prussia began. At that time, a violent press campaign against the control exercized by Polish customs inspectors was unleashed, both in Danzig and inside the Reich. A series of incidents was provoked with the aid of Nazi bands, the most noteworthy of which was the coup against the customs office in Kalthof on May 20, 1939.

The Danzig Senate simultaneously endeavored, in its letter of June 3, 1939, to the Polish Commissioner-General, to curtail the inspectors' scope of competence to that of mere document control. In its subsequent letter of July 29, 1939, the Senate went even further by stating that it did not consider itself any longer under obligation to adhere to the agreements regarding the Polish inspectors. This was rejected by the

Polish Commissioner-General in his letter of August 3, which simultaneously expressed his readiness to discuss the matter as a whole.

In accordance with the Senate's letter of July 29, the chief of Danzig customs, in a letter dated August 4, 1939, informed the chief Polish customs inspector that the Danzig customs offices would no longer recognize the Polish inspectors posted on duty in the frontier zone sectors. On the same day, the superintendents of four Danzig customs posts on the East Prussian frontier verbally informed the Polish inspectors on duty that as of 7 A.M. on August 6 they would no longer be admitted to work.

The timing of this step and the general sequence of events, with the Senate's letter of July 29, 1939, and the Danzig customs directorate's letter of August 4, 1939, made it clear that an attempt to breach the customs barrier between the Free City and the Reich was being made.

This time, the Polish government felt compelled to oppose the threatened violation of one of its most vital rights in the Free City; hence the note from the Commissioner-General to the Danzig Senate dated August 4, 1939.

The President of the Senate on the following day gave oral reassuring explanations, and only three days later, namely, on August 7—evidently after getting in touch with Berlin—sent a written reply to the Polish note. This note, while denying the order issued on August 4, endeavored to charge the Polish authorities for the tension which had arisen.

Nevertheless, for a short time it was believed in political circles that the customs conflict was, if only for the time being, wound up owing to the peremptory but at the same time moderate line adopted by Poland. The Polish press showed discretion and forbearance in order not to complicate matters.

However, on August 9, 1939, the German government intervened in the direct relations between the Free City and Poland, when Secretary of State von Weizsäcker made the known statement to the Polish Chargé d'Affaires in Berlin on August 9. Herr von Weizsäcker refused to enter into any discussion on the subject with the Polish Chargé d'Affaires.

In these circumstances, the Polish government had no other way than to state that it could see no legal basis that could be held as justifying any interventions in the relations between Poland and the Free City and made a strong reservation against possible attempts on the part of the German government to infringe on the agreed Polish rights in Danzig.

In its endeavors, nevertheless, to find a way to a compromise, the Polish government started conversations with the Free City authorities as of August 16 (Chodacki-Greiser). For that reason, the director of the Central Customs Office, Mr. Maksymowicz, was especially delegated from Warsaw to Danzig. In spite of the fact that the unceasing contraband war matériel from Germany to Danzig hardly warranted a cut in the force of customs inspectors there, Mr. Maksymowicz received instructions to make substantial concessions in that respect, as a good-will gesture. The discussions gave no results since Polish concessions only evoked further demands on Danzig's part.

I was told at that time that the Auswärtiges Amt was endeavoring to charge Poland with the responsibility for the events in Danzig. This was also confirmed to me by Sir Nevile Henderson on August 27 when he told me of his conversation with Herr von Weizsäcker two days before.

That Danzig served merely as a trump card in the German game against Poland can be seen from Hitler's sentence at a conference on May 23, 1939:

"Danzig is not the subject of the dispute at all. It is a question of extending our living space."

September 23, 1948

*J. Lipski*

# Select Bibliography

## I. Official Documents

Czechoslovak Sources and Documents, No. 2. *Struggle for Freedom*. New York, 1943.

Degras, Jane, ed. *Soviet Documents on Foreign Policy, 1917–1941*. 3 vols. London, 1951–53.

*Documents on International Affairs, 1939–1946*. Ed. by A. J. Toynbee. Vol. I: March–September, 1939. London, 1951.

France. Ministère des Affaires Étrangères. *Documents diplomatiques, 1938–1939: Pièces relatives aux événements et aux négotiations qui ont précédé l'ouverture des hostilités entre Allemagne d'une part, la Pologne, la Grande-Bretagne et la France d'autre part*. (*Livre jaune français*.) Paris, 1939.

—— *Documents diplomatiques français, 1932–1939*. 2me série (1936–1939), Tome I, II. Paris, 1964.

Germany. Auswärtiges Amt. *Documents and Materials Relating to the Eve of the Second World War*. Vol I: November, 1937–1938. Vol. II: Dirksen papers, 1938–1939. Moscow, 1948.

—— *Documents Concerning the Last Phase of the German-Polish Crisis*. Berlin–New York, 1939.

—— *Documents on German Foreign Policy, 1918–1945*. Series C: 1933–1937, Vols. I–V. Series D: 1937–1945, Vols. I–II, IV–VII. Washington, 1949–62.

—— *Documents on the Events Preceding the Outbreak of the War*. New York, 1940.

—— *Documents on the Origin of the War*. Berlin, 1939.

—— *Dokumente zur Vorgeschichte des Krieges*. (*Weissbuch*, No. 2.) Berlin, 1939.

—— *The German White Paper: Full Text of the Polish Documents Issued by the Berlin Foreign Office*. New York, 1940.

—— *Nazi-Soviet Relations, 1939–1941: Documents*. Dept. of State Publication 3023. Washington, 1948.

—— *Negotiations for the Solution of the Sudeten German Question*. (*White Book*, 1938, No. 1.) 1938.

—— *Polish Acts of Atrocity Against the German Minority in Poland*. Berlin–New York, 1940.

—— *Polish Documents Relative to the Origin of the War*. 1st series, No. 3. Berlin, 1940.

—— *Weissbuch der deutschen Regierung: Urkunden zur letzten Phase der deutsch-polnischen Krise.* Basel, 1940.

—— *Zweites Weissbuch der deutschen Regierung: Dokumente über die Entwickelung der deutsch-polnischen Beziehungen und die Ereignisse von 1933 bis zur Gegenwart.* Basel, 1940.

Great Britain. Foreign Office. *Correspondence Showing the Course of Certain Diplomatic Discussions Directed Towards Securing an European Settlement, June 1934 to March 1936.* Parliament, Papers by Command, Cmd. 5143. London, 1936.

—— *Documents Concerning German-Polish Relations and the Outbreak of Hostilities Between Great Britain and Germany on Sept. 3, 1939. (British Blue Book.)* London, 1939.

—— *Documents on British Foreign Policy, 1919–1939.* 2d series, Vol. I. 3d series, Vols. I, VII. London, 1949–54.

*Nazi Conspiracy and Aggression.* 8 vols. and suppls. A–B. Washington, 1946–48.

Poland. Ministerstwo Spraw Zagranicznych. *Official Documents Concerning Polish-German and Polish-Soviet Relations, 1933–1939. (Polish White Book.)* London, 1940.

—— *Polskie Siły Zbrojne. Komisja Historyczna. Polskie Siły Zbrojne w drugiej Wojnie Światowej.* Vol. I: *Kampania wrześniowa 1939;* part 1: Polityczne i wojskowe położenie Polski przed wojną. London, 1951.

—— *"Przeglad Informacyjny Polska a Zagranica."* Warsaw, Ministry of Foreign Affairs. Secret. Mimeographed. Years 1933–39.

*Sbornik dokumentow o wnieszniej politikie SSSR.* Vols. I-III. Moscow, 1944.

*Survey of International Affairs.* Ed. by A. J. Toynbee. 1935, Vol. I. 1938, Vols. II–III. 1939, Vol. I. London, 1936–52.

*The Trial of German Major War Criminals: Proceedings of the International Military Tribunal Setting at Nuremberg, Germany, 20th Nov. 1945 to 1st Oct. 1946.* London, 1946–50.

*Trial of the Major War Criminals: Nuremberg, 14 Nov. 1945–1 Oct. 1946.* 42 vols. Nuremberg, 1947–49.

"Trials of War Criminals." Mimeographed transcript of trials of war criminals before the Nuremberg Military Tribunals.

*Trials of War Criminals before the Nuernberg Military Tribunals under Control Council Law No. 10, Nuernberg, Oct. 1947–April 1949.* Vols. XII–XXIV, *Case 11: U.S. vs. Von Weizsäcker ("Ministries case").* Washington, 1951–52.

United States. Department of State. *Foreign Relations of the United States: Diplomatic Papers.* 1938, Vol. I. 1939, Vol. I. Washington, 1955–56.

—— *Peace and War: U.S. Foreign Policy, 1931–1941.* Washington, 1943.

## II. *Other Sources*

Batowski, Henryk. "August 31st, 1939 in Berlin," *Polish Western Affairs* (Poznań), Vol. IV, No. 1 (1963).

—— *Kryzys dyplomatyczny w Europie, jesień 1938–wiosna 1939.* Warsaw, 1962.

—— "O dyplomacji niemieckiej, 1919–1945," in Paul Schmidt, *Statysta na dyplomatycznej scenie* (Polish translation), pp. 563–626. Cracow, 1965.

—— *Ostatni tydzień pokoju.* Poznań, 1964.

—— "Rumuńska podróż Becka w październiku 1938 r.," *Kwartalnik Historyczny* (Warsaw), No. 2 (1958), pp. 423–37.

Beck, Józef. *Dernier rapport: Politique polonaise, 1926–1939.* Neuchâtel, 1951.

—— *Final Report.* New York, 1957.

—— *Przemówienia, deklaracje, wywiady, 1931–1937.* Warsaw, 1938.

—— *Przemówienia, deklaracje, wywiady, 1931–1939.* 2d ed. Warsaw, 1939.

Benedykt, Stefan. "Zajazd O.R.P. 'Wicher' na Gdańsk," *Wiadomości* (London), No. 108 (1948).

Bonnet, G. E. *Défense de la paix.* Vol. I: *De Washington au quai d'Orsay.* Vol. II: *Fin d'une Europe: De Munich à la guerre.* Geneva, 1946–48.

Breyer, Richard. *Das Deutsche Reich und Polen, 1932–1937: Aussenpolitik und Volksgruppenfragen.* Würzburg, 1955.

Bullock, A. L. C. *Hitler, a Study in Tyranny.* New York, 1952.

Burckhardt, C. J. *Ma mission à Danzig.* Paris, 1961.

Cerruti, Elisabeth. *Memoirs.* London, 1952.

Chudek, Józef. "Polska wobec wrześniowego kryzysu czechosłowackiego 1938 r.," *Sprawy Międzynarodowe* (Warsaw), No. 4 (1958), pp. 72–79.

—— "Rozmowy Beck-Göring z 23 lutego 1938," *Sprawy Międzynarodowe* (Warsaw), No. 5 (1960), pp. 53–57.

—— "Sprawa Bogumina w dokumentach polskich," *Sprawy Międzynarodowe* (Warsaw), No. 9 (1958), pp. 108–14.

Ciano, Galeazzo. *Ciano's Diplomatic Papers.* London, 1948.

Cienciala, Anna. "The Significance of the Declaration of Nonaggression of January 26, 1934, in Polish-German and International Relations: A Reappraisal," *East European Quarterly,* No. 1 (1967).

Coulondre, Robert. *De Staline à Hitler: Souvenirs de deux ambassades, 1936–1939.* Paris, 1950.

Craig, G. A., and Felix Gilbert. *The Diplomats: 1919–1939,* Princeton, N.J., 1953.

Cyprian, Tadeusz, and Jerzy Sawicki. *Agresja na Polskę w świetle dokumentów.* 2 vols. Warsaw, 1946.

—— *Sprawy polskie w procesie norymberskim.* Poznań, 1956.

Czarnecki, Bogdan. *Fall Weiss: Z genezy hitlerowskiej agresji przeciw Polsce.* Warsaw, 1960.

—— "Gdy Niemcy chciały z Polską pokoju: Z genezy polsko-niemieckiego układu z 26 stycznia 1934 r.," *Sprawy Międzynarodowe* (Warsaw), No. 12 (1958), pp. 69–82.

—— "Od 'Monachium' do kryzysu kwietniowego 1939 r.: Z historii niemieckich przygotowań do agresji," *Sprawy Międzynarodowe* (Warsaw), No. 10–11 (1958), pp. 55–69.

Dahlerus, J. B. E. *The Last Attempt.* London, 1947.

Dębicki, Roman. *Foreign Policy of Poland, 1919–1939, from the Rebirth of the Polish Republic to World War II.* New York, 1962.

Dirksen, Herbert von. *Moskau, Tokio, London: Erinnerungen und Betrachtungen zu 20 Jahren deutschen Aussenpolitik, 1919–1939.* Stuttgart, 1949.

Dodd, Martha. *My Years in Germany.* London, 1939.

Dodd, W. E. *Ambassador Dodd's Diary, 1933–1938.* London, 1941.

Dopierała, Bogdan. *Gdańska polityka Józefa Becka.* Poznań, 1967.

Flandin, P. E. *Politique française, 1919–1940.* Paris, 1947.

François-Poncet, André. *Souvenir d'une ambassade à Berlin, septembre 1931–octobre 1938.* Paris, 1946.

Gafencu, Grigore. *The Last Days of Europe.* London, 1947.

Gamelin, M. G. *Servir.* Vol. II: *Le prologue du drame (1930–août 1939).* Paris, 1946.

Gąsiorowski, Z. J. "The German-Polish Non-aggression Pact of 1934," *Journal of Central European Affairs,* XV, No. 1 (1955), 3–29.

—— "Stresemann and Poland before Locarno," *Journal of Central European Affairs,* XVIII, No. 1 (1958), 25–47.

Gawroński, Jan. *Moja misja w Wiedniu 1932–1938.* Warsaw, 1965.

Gelbert, Ludwik. "Anulowanie przez III Rzeszę polsko-niemieckiej deklaracji z 26 stycznia 1934 r.," *Sprawy Międzynarodowe* (Warsaw), No. 6 (87) (1959), pp. 78–94.

*The German Fifth Column in Poland.* London, 1940.

Gisevius, H. B. *Bis zum bitteren Ende.* Zurich, 1954.

Hassell, Ulrich. *Vom anderen Deutschland: Aus den nachgelassenen Tagebüchern, 1938–1944.* Vienna, 1948.

Henderson, Nevile. *Failure of a Mission: Berlin, 1937–39.* London, 1940.

Hilger, Gustav, and A. G. Meyer. *The Incompatible Allies: A Memoir History of German-Soviet Relations, 1918–1941.* New York, 1953.

Hitler, Adolf. *Mein Kampf.* London, 1939.

—— *The Speeches of Adolf Hitler, April 1922–August 1939.* Ed. by N. H. Baynes. 2 vols. London–New York, 1942.

—— *Table Talk, 1941–1944.* London, 1953.

Horthy, Nicolas. *Memoirs.* New York, 1957.

Jędrzejewicz, Wacław. "Dziewiętnaście decydujących bitew świata," *Bellona* (London), No. 3–4 (1963), pp. 216–23.

—— "The Polish Plan for a 'Preventive War' Against Germany in 1933," *The Polish Review* (New York), XI, No. 1 (1966), 62–91.

Jędrzejewicz, Wacław, ed. *Poland in the British Parliament, 1939–1945.* Vol. I: March, 1939–August, 1941. New York, 1946.

Jurkiewicz, Jarosław. *Pakt wschodni: Z historii stosunków międzynarodowych w latach 1934–1935.* Warsaw, 1963.

—— "Polska wobec planów paktu wschodniego w latach 1934–1935," *Sprawy Międzynarodowe* (Warsaw), No. 3 (84) (1959), pp. 18–51.

—— "Węgry a Polska w okresie kryzysu czechosłowackiego 1938 r. (nieopublikowane dokumenty)," *Sprawy Międzynarodowe* (Warsaw), No. 7–8 (1958), pp. 69–73.

—— "Wizyta Prezydenta Rauschinga w Warszawie w grudniu 1933," *Najnowsze dzieje Polski, materiały i studia z okresu 1914–1939* (Warsaw), III (1960), 163–82.

Keyserling, R. W. *Unfinished History.* London, 1948.

Kleist, Peter. *Zwischen Hitler und Stalin, 1939–1945: Aufzeichnungen.* Bonn, 1950.

Komarnicki, Tytus. *Piłsudski a polityka wielkich mocarstw zachodnich.* London, 1952.

—— *Rebirth of the Polish Republic: A Study in the Diplomatic History of Europe, 1914–1920.* London, 1957.

Korbel, Josef. *Poland Between East and West: Soviet and German Diplomacy Toward Poland, 1919–1933.* Princeton, N.J., 1963.

Kordt, Erich. *Nicht aus den Akten: Die Wilhelmstrasse im Frieden und Krieg; Erlebnisse, Begegnungen und Eindrücke, 1928–1945.* Stuttgart, 1950.

—— *Wahn und Wirklichkeit: Die Aussenpolitik des Dritten Reiches; Versuch einer Darstellung.* 2d ed. Stuttgart, 1948.

Kozeński, Jerzy. *Czechosłowacja w polskiej polityce zagranicznej w latach 1932–1938.* Poznań, 1964.

Kozłowski, Eugeniusz. "Stosunki polsko-niemieckie przed II Wojną Światową: Dokumenty z Archiwum Generalnego Inspektora Sił Zbrojnych," *Najnowsze dzieje Polski, materiały i studia z okresu 1914–1939* (Warsaw), III (1960), 195–261.

Krasuski, Jerzy. *Stosunki polsko-niemieckie, 1919–1925.* Poznań, 1962.

—— *Stosunki polsko-niemieckie, 1926–1932.* Poznań, 1964.

Kremer, Jan. "Remilitaryzacja Niemiec w roku 1935," *Sprawy Międzynarodowe* (Warsaw), No. 2 (119) (1962), pp. 56–64.

Kuźminski, Tadeusz. *Polska, Francja, Niemcy, 1933–1935: Z dziejów sojuszu polsko-francuskiego.* Warsaw, 1963.

Laeuen, Harald. *Polnisches Zwischenspiel: Eine Episode der Ostpolitik.* Berlin, 1940.

Lapter, Karol. *Pakt Piłsudski-Hitler: Polsko-niemiecka deklaracja o niestosowaniu przemocy z 26 stycznia 1934 roku.* Warsaw, 1962.

Laroche, J. A. *La Pologne de Piłsudski: Souvenirs d'une ambassade, 1926–1935.* Paris, 1953.

Lipski, Józef. "Nowe przyczynki dotyczące wybuchu wojny polsko-niemieckiej w 1939 r.," *Bellona* (London), No. 1 (1950), pp. 16–40.

—— "Przyczynki do polsko-niemieckiej deklaracji o nieagresji," *Bellona* (London), No. 1–2 (1951), pp. 18–37; No. 3, pp. 3–21.

—— "Rzut oka na zagadnienie granic polsko-niemieckich," *Bellona* (London), No. 2 (1947), pp. 3–11.

—— "Stosunki polsko-niemieckie przed wybuchem wojny w świetle aktów norymberskich," *Sprawy Międzynarodowe* (London), No. 2–3 (1947), pp. 11–26; No. 4, pp. 24–51.

—— "Uwagi o polityce i strategii," *Bellona* (London), No. 4 (1946), pp. 3–13.

Lipski, Józef, E. Raczyński, and S. Stroński. *Trzy podróże gen. Sikorskiego do Ameryki.* London, Gen. Sikorski Historical Institute, 1949.

Łossowski, Piotr. "Stosunki polsko-niemieckie w latach 1933–1939 a klęska wrześniowa," *Wojskowy Przegląd Historyczny,* No. 1 (1963), pp. 132–62; No. 1 (1964), pp. 189–226.

Louis Ferdinand, Prince of Prussia. *The Rebel Prince: Memoirs.* Chicago, 1953.

Łubieński, Michał. "Ostatnie negocjacje w sprawie Gdańska," *Dziennik Polski i Dziennik Żołnierza* (London), Dec. 3, 1953.

Lubomirski, Stefan. "Fałszowanie prawdy historycznej przez przemilczenie faktów," *Dziennik Polski i Dziennik Żołnierza* (London), Nov. 26, 1957.

—— "Ostatnia misja z Berlina," *Wiadomości* (London), No. 182 (1943).

Lukacs, J. A. *The Great Powers and Eastern Europe.* New York, 1953.

Łukasiewicz, Juliusz. "Pamiętniki." Unpublished manuscript in the Józef Piłsudski Institute of America, New York, N.Y.

—— "Sprawa czechosłowacka w 1938 r. na tle stosunków polsko-francuskich," *Sprawy Międzynarodowe* (London), No. 6–7 (1948), pp. 27–56.

Macartney, C. A. *October Fifteenth: A History of Modern Hungary, 1929–1945.* 2 vols. Edinburgh, 1957.

Mackiewicz, Stanisław. *Colonel Beck and His Policy.* London, 1944.

—— *O jedenastej, powiada autor, sztuka jest skończona: Polityka Józefa Becka.* London, 1942.

Meissner, Otto. *Staatssekretär unter Ebert, Hindenburg, Hitler: Der Schicksalsweg des deutschen Volkes von 1918–1945, wie ich ihn erlebte.* Hamburg, 1950.

Miedziński, Bogusław. "Droga do Moskwy," *Kultura* (Paris), No. 188 (1963), pp. 74–86.

—— "Pakty Wilanowskie," *Kultura* (Paris), No. 189–90 (1963), pp. 113–32.

Morgenstern, T. "Wejście O.R.P. 'Wicher' do Gdańska w 1932 r.," *Bellona* (London), No. 1 (1953), pp. 44–48.

Namier, L. B. *Diplomatic Prelude, 1938–1939.* London, 1948.

—— *Europe in Decay: A Study in Disintegration, 1936–1940.* London, 1950.

—— *In the Nazi Era.* London, 1952.

Noël, Léon. *L'aggression allemande contre la Pologne.* Paris, 1946.

Pajewski, Janusz. *Problem polsko-niemiecki w Traktacie Wersalskim: Praca zbiorowa.* Poznań, 1963.

Paul-Boncour, Joseph. *Entre deux guerres: Souvenirs sur la III<sup>e</sup> République.* 3 vols. Paris, 1945–46.

Petresco-Comnène, N. M. *Preludi del grande dramma.* Rome, 1947.

Pobóg-Malinowski, Władysław. *Najnowsza historia polityczna Polski, 1864–1945.* 3 vols. London, 1956–61.

Raczyński, Eduard. *In Allied London.* London, 1962.

Rauschning, Hermann. *Gespräche mit Hitler.* Zurich, 1940.

Roos, Hans. *Geschichte der polnischen Nation, 1916–1960: Von der Staatsgrundung im ersten Weltkrieg bis zur Gegenwart.* Stuttgart, 1961.

—— *A History of Modern Poland from the Foundation of the State in the First World War to the Present Day.* London, 1966.

—— *Polen und Europa: Studien zur polnischen Aussenpolitik, 1931–1939.* Tübingen, 1957.

Rose, Adam. *La politique polonaise entre les deux guerres.* Neuchâtel, 1944.

Schmidt, Paul. *Statist auf diplomatischer Bühne, 1923–45: Erlebnisse des Chefdolmetschers im Auswärtigen Amt mit den Staatsmännern Europas.* Bonn, 1949.

Schuman, F. L. *Europe on the Eve: The Crises of Diplomacy, 1933–1939.* New York, 1939.

Seton-Watson, R. W. *From Munich to Danzig.* London, 1939.

Shirer, W. L. *The Rise and Fall of the Third Reich: A History of Nazi Germany.* New York, 1960.

Smogorzewski, K. M. *Czy dziejowy zwrot w stosunkach polsko-niemieckich?* Poznań, 1934.

—— *Poland's Access to the Sea.* London, 1934.

Sokulski, H. "Wojna celna Rzeszy przeciwko Polsce w latach 1925–1934," *Sprawy Międzynarodowe* (Warsaw), No. 9 (1955), pp. 39–40.

Sontag, R. J. "The Last Month of Peace, 1939," *Foreign Affairs,* April, 1957, pp. 507–24.

Stanisławska, Stefania. *Polska a Monachium.* Warsaw, 1967.

—— "Umowa Göring-Beck z 23 lutego 1936 r.," *Najnowsze dzieje Polski, materiały i studia z okresu 1914–1939* (Warsaw), III (1960), 183–93.

—— *Wielka i mała polityka Józefa Becka, marzec–maj 1938.* Warsaw, 1962.

Starzeński, Paweł. "Marzec 1939," *Wiadomości* (London), No. 323 (1952).

—— "Powrót do Warszawy," *Wiadomości* (London), No. 329 (1952).

—— "Umowa z Anglią," *Wiadomości* (London), No. 326 (1952).

Stroński, Stanisław. "Polska i Niemcy, 1937–1938: Czechosłowacja i z Karpat nad Bałtyk," *Wiadomości* (London), No. 405 (1954).

Szembek, Jan. *Diariusz i teki Jana Szembeka, 1935–1945.* Vol. I, 1935. Vol. II, 1936. Ed. by Tytus Komarnicki. London, 1964–65.

—— *Journal, 1933–1939.* Paris, 1952.

Szymański, Antoni. "Fragmenty niemieckich przygotowań wojennych w ostatnim przedwojennym półroczu 1939 r.," *Bellona* (London), No. 3 (1954), pp. 4–11.

—— *Zły sąsiad: Niemcy 1932–1939 w oświetleniu polskiego attaché wojskowego w Berlinie.* London, 1959.

Taylor, Telford. *Sword and Swastika: Generals and Nazis in the Third Reich.* New York, 1952.

Trocka, Halina. *Gdańsk a hitlerowski "Drang nach Osten."* Danzig, 1965.

Turlejska, Maria. *Rok przed klęską, 1 wrzesień 1938–1 wrzesień 1939.* 2d ed. Warsaw, 1962.

Wandycz, P. S. *France and Her Eastern Allies, 1919–1925: French-Czechoslovak-Polish Relations from the Paris Peace Conference to Locarno.* Minneapolis, 1962.

Weizsäcker, E. H. *Erinnerungen.* Munich, 1950.

Wheeler-Bennett, J. W. *Munich: Prologue to Tragedy.* New York, 1948.

—— *The Nemesis of Power: The German Army in Politics, 1918–1945.* New York, 1954.

Wiskemann, Elizabeth. *The Rome-Berlin Axis: A History of the Relations Between Hitler and Mussolini.* London, 1949.

Wojciechowski, Marian. "Polska i Niemcy na przełomie lat 1932–1933," *Roczniki historyczne* (Poznań), XXIX (1963), 152–75.

—— *Stosunki polsko-niemieckie, 1933–1938.* Poznań, 1965.

Wolski, Aleksander. "Pakt polsko-niemiecki z 1934 r.," *Sprawy Międzynarodowe* (Warsaw), No. 6 (26) (1953), pp. 64–77.

Wysocki, Alfred. "Początek dramatu," *Tygodnik Powszechny* (Cracow), No. 7 (525), Feb. 15, 1959.

Zaleski, August. *Przemowy i deklaracje.* Warsaw, 1929.

Zay, Jean. *Souvenirs et Solitude.* Paris, 1946.

# Index

Abyssinia, 208, 222, 223–24, 235, 240–43, 244n, 247, 253, 337, 490; League of Nations sanctions on Italy, 251

Adamkiewicz, Włodzimierz, legal counselor of the Polish Foreign Ministry, 14, 20

*Admiral Scheer* (battleship), 257

Alsace-Lorraine, 178, 388

Altenburg, Günther, head of the Political Division of the A.A., 430, 444, 552

*Angriff, Der,* 473-74

*Anschluss,* 60–63 *passim,* 81, 85–86, 321, 324, 240–46 *passim,* 349–51, 352, 363, 366; *see also* Austria; Czechoslovakia

Anti-Comintern Pact (1936–37), 313–17, 320, 518, 533; Poland and, 427, 453, 509, 520, 522, 640; Hungary and, 484

Antonescu, Victor, Rumanian foreign minister, 272, 273, 285

Antonov-Ovsieyenko, Vladimir A., Soviet minister to Poland, 86–87; and Piłsudski, 86–87

Arciszewski, Mirosław, Polish minister to Rumania, *1932–38,* 347, 422, 499, 525, 526, 578

Arciszewski, Tomasz, leader of the Polish Socialist Party, 382n, 554

Armaments and rearmament, 2, 35, 162, 165, 167, 168, 173, 177, 182, 205–6, 276, 338, 494, 518

Army, German: introduction of conscription, 176, 252; changes on top level, 339–40, 343; Hitler as supreme commander, 339, 343, 575–77; Keitel's Danzig attack order, 521, 523, 550–51, 612, 641; plans for westward movement, 529–30, 550–51, 567–68 (*see also* "Operation White" *under* Germany, relations with Poland)

Aschmann, head of the Press Department of the A.A., 227n

Association of Poles, 296

Attolico, Bernardo, Italian ambassador to Germany, 415, 562, 581–82, 594; and Lipski, 251–52, 366, 436, 459–60, 527, 538, 608

Austria, 146, 208, 268–69, 316, 491; *Anschluss,* 60 ff., 81, 85–86, 321, 324, 340–46 *passim,* 349–51, 352, 363, 366; German military occupation of, 350–51, 517, 520, 533, 576, 584
—— relations with: Germany, 31, 43, 85, 108, 145, 151–52, 169–70, 186, 191, 285, 311, 318, 321–28 *passim,* 331–32, 336, 341 ff. (*see also* Anschluss); Poland, 323, 328, 333, 350, 351; Czechoslovakia, 345, 346

Auswärtiges Amt: and Poland, 620–23

Avenol, Joseph L., secretary-general of the League of Nations, *1933–40,* 61, 63

Babiński, Wacław, Polish minister to the Netherlands, *1931–39,* 67

Baczyński, Włodzimierz, director of financial turnover of the Polish Ministry of Finance, 225

Balbo, General Italo, 61; governor general of Libya, *1933–40,* 377, 379

Baldwin, Stanley: Conservative member of the British Parliament, 62, 158; prime minister, *1935–37,* 206, 240n

Baltic states, 146, 184, 220–21, 224, 246–47, 307, 490, 576, 583; proposed Polish-Soviet pact, 131–34, 147

Balugdžic, Živojin, Yugoslav minister to Germany, 34

Bandera, Stefan, Ukrainian nationalist, 142n

Barthou, Louis: French war minister, 4; foreign affairs minister, *1934,* 143, 157, 159–60

Bassewitz, Count, German chief of protocol, 76, 98

Lipski, Józef: biography, xi–xviii, 637;
in Polish Legation at Paris, 5, 7; head
of German Section of Polish Foreign
Ministry, 9, 637; chief of Western
Division of Polish Foreign Ministry,
*1933–34*, 12, 14, 16–19, 25, 52–54,
63, 87, 637; Polish minister and ambassador to Germany, *1934–39*, 90;
credentials meeting with von Hindenburg, 94; Piłsudski's briefing of, 94–
98; resignation offers, 501–2, 535–36;
lectures on Nuremberg trials, 623–35;
affidavit on Secretary of State Weizsäcker at Nuremberg, 636–51
—— and: Hindenburg, 37, 130; von
Neurath, 98–101, 108–11, 130, 132–
34, 148–50, 153–54, 171–76, 179–83,
192–97, 225–26, 232–36, 260, 289–
92, 296–99; Hitler, 99, 101, 124–26,
154–56, 161, 163–65, 183–87, 203–6,
241–47, 279, 303–5, 309, 344, 405,
408–11, 417; Goebbels, 112–15; Gaus,
115–17, 118–24; Potocki, 151–53,
527; von Bülow, 157, 216, 218–20;
von Moltke, 182–83, 293–95, 351,
398–400, 436, 441–42, 463, 499;
Göring, 188–92, 197–99, 200–2, 212–
15, 217, 226–27, 252, 260–62, 270,
298n, 306–7, 321, 322, 353–54, 356–
57, 370–73, 377–78, 382–87, 390,
393–405 *passim*, 437, 438–39, 445,
447–49, 451–53, 497–99, 500–1, 556,
563, 590–92; Schacht, 209–12, 248–
49; Attolico, 251–52, 366, 436, 459–
60, 527, 538, 608; Dieckhoff, 264–65;
Śmigły-Rydz, 306, 368, 501, 553, 578;
von Ribbentrop, 316–17, 354–55,
357–60, 396–98, 412, 417, 425–28,
431–32, 436–37, 453–58, 465–69,
470–72, 477–80, 487, 502, 507–8,
519–20, 535, 610, 639–40, 641–42;
Weizsäcker, 363, 393, 418, 424–25,
430–31, 432, 442–45, 462, 528–29,
551, 555, 610, 629, 634, 642; Łubieński, 380–82, 387–89, 442; Horthy,
380, 388–89; Henderson, 400, 435–
36, 557–61 *passim*, 569, 580, 602,
607–8; Coulondre, 501, 539, 542–43,
559, 561–62, 571, 579, 599, 605, 608;
Beck, during crisis, 527, 529–30, 553,
565–66, 574, 578, 586, 643; Dahlerus,
608–9
—— communications from: to Wysocki, 25–33, 34–35, 41–43, 67; to

Beck, 100–3, 108–20, 124–29, 131–
34, 144–50, 153–57, 159–215, 218–
22, 227–36, 238–48, 259–62, 272–78,
289–98, 303–7, 341–44, 356–66, 368–
79, 390–91, 402–5, 408–13, 414–21,
424–26, 430–49, 459–74, 477–81,
483–99, 500, 527–28, 530–48, 557–
65; to Dębicki, 104–8, 129–30; to
Szembek, 121–22, 222, 270–72; to
Ministry of Foreign Affairs, 122–24,
225–27, 262–66, 298–300, 350, 571,
572, 573; to Potocki, 151–53; to
Łubieński, 387–89
—— communications to: from Wysocki, 33–34, 39–41; from Dębicki,
104–8, 129–30; from Beck, 301–2,
406–7, 414, 422–24, 428–29, 504–7,
564, 572; from Łubieński, 380–82,
391–92, 476–77, 499–500
Lisiewicz, Adam, Polish consul general
in Munich, *1931–39*, 136
Lithuania, 132, 143, 158, 224, 244, 256,
315, 479n; relations with Poland,
352–55, 641; relations with Soviet
Union, 353; relations with Germany,
480, 502, 507, 532, 641 (*see also*
Kłajpeda)
Little Entente, 63, 65, 144, 146, 187,
188, 195, 380, 382, 448
Litvinov, Maxim M., people's commissar for foreign affairs of the Soviet
Union, *1930–39*, 75, 133, 134, 143;
and von Neurath, 144, 146–47
Lloyd George, David, British prime
minister, *1916–22*, 5
Löbe, Paul, president of the Reichstag,
*1925–32*, 45
Locarno Conference and Treaties
(1925), 1, 2n, 8, 9–11, 13, 16, 110,
115–17, 120 ff., 167, 551
London Committee of Nonintervention,
292
London Conference (1936), 252
Lozorajtis, Stasys, Lithuanian foreign
minister, *1934–38*, 224
Lübbe, Marinus van der, 50
Łubieński, Count Michał, director of
the cabinet of the Polish foreign minister, *1935–39*, 434, 526; and Lipski,
380–82, 387–89, 442; communications to Lipski, 380–82, 391–92, 476–
77, 499–500
Lubomirski, Prince Stefan, counselor at
the Polish Embassy in Germany,